Professional Microsoft® SQL Server Programming

Professional
Microsoft® SQL Server® 2008 Programming

Professional
Microsoft® SQL Server® 2008 Programming

Rob Vieira

WILEY

Wiley Publishing, Inc.

Professional Microsoft® SQL Server® 2008 Programming

Published by
Wiley Publishing, Inc.
10475 Crosspoint Boulevard
Indianapolis, IN 46256
www.wiley.com

Copyright © 2009 by Wiley Publishing, Inc., Indianapolis, Indiana

Published simultaneously in Canada

ISBN: 978-0-470-25702-9

Manufactured in the United States of America

10 9 8 7 6 5 4 3 2 1

Library of Congress Cataloging-in-Publication Data

Vieira, Robert.
  Professional Microsoft SQL server 2008 programming / Rob Vieira.
       p. cm.
  Includes index.
  ISBN 978-0-470-25702-9 (paper/website)
1. SQL server. 2.   Client/server computing. 3.   Database management. I.   Title.
  QA76.9.C55V535 2009
  005.75'85–dc22

                                        2009010578

*This book is dedicated with all my heart to **Ashley**, **Addy**, and **Anna**. It's hard to believe that Ashley was still in elementary school when I wrote my first book (she'll graduate from college later this year) and didn't have to share this dedication with other kids (heck, she isn't much of a kid anymore — eeek!). Then there's Addy, who literally dreads me writing, yet continues to put up with me "disappearing" into my home office during the lengthy period of time I work on a book. Finally, there's Anna, who came in the middle of this round of writing, and didn't have any real history on what to expect from my writing disappearances.*

*A dedication of this book would most certainly not be complete without a particularly special thank you to **Deb**, who has leveraged my efforts in this and my recent Beginning title to redefine for me what the terms "love" and "support" mean.*

As I've said for many releases now, I wish Wrox would let me print a picture of the women in my life on the cover of this book rather than my ugly mug — I'm certain that you, the reader, would appreciate it too!

About the Author

Experiencing his first infection with computing fever in 1978, **Rob Vieira** knew right away that this was something "really cool." In 1980 he began immersing himself into the computing world more fully — splitting time between building and repairing computer kits, and programming in BASIC as well as Z80 and 6502 assembly. In 1983, he began studies for a degree in Computer Information Systems, but found the professional mainframe environment too rigid for his tastes and dropped out in 1985 to pursue other interests. Later that year, he caught the "PC bug" and began the long road of programming in database languages from dBase to SQL Server. Rob completed a degree in business administration in 1990 and since has typically worked in roles that allow him to combine his unique knowledge of business and computing. Beyond his bachelor's degree, he has been certified as a Certified Management Accountant (CMA); Microsoft Certified as a Solutions Developer (MCSD), Trainer (MCT), and Database Administrator (MCDBA); and even had a brief stint certified as an Emergency Medical Technician (EMT).

Rob is currently the Database Team Lead for Stockamp, a Huron Consulting Group practice. He has published six books on SQL Server development

He resides in Vancouver, Washington, where he does his best to take care of "his girls," and even takes his best shot at letting Deb take care of him some too.

Credits

Executive Editor
Bob Elliott

Development Editor
Sydney Jones
Adaobi Obi Tulton

Technical Editor
John Mueller

Production Editor
Daniel Scribner

Copy Editor
Kim Cofer

Editorial Manager
Mary Beth Wakefield

Production Manager
Tim Tate

Vice President and Executive Group Publisher
Richard Swadley

Vice President and Executive Publisher
Barry Pruett

Associate Publisher
Jim Minatel

Project Coordinator, Cover
Lynsey Stanford

Proofreader
Publication Services, Inc.

Indexer
Robert Swanson

Acknowledgments

Nearly a decade has gone by since I finished my first book on SQL Server, and the list of those deserving some credit continues to grow.

As always, I'll start with **my kids**. They are the ones who most sacrifice time when a new release comes along and I spend so much time writing.

Deb — This was the first time she had to deal with one of my writing cycles, and she couldn't have done anything more to make me feel more supported. Deb has helped me redefine the meaning of the word support. She is my rock.

You — the readers. You continue to write me mail and tell me how I helped you out in some way. That continues to be the number one reason I find the strength to write another book. The continued support of my *Professional* series titles has been amazing. We struck a chord — I'm glad. Here's to hoping we help make your SQL Server experience a little less frustrating and a lot more successful.

As always, I want to pay special thanks to several people past and present. Some of these are at the old Wrox Press, but they remain so much of who I am as a writer that I need to continue to remember them. Others are new players for me, but have added their own stamp to the mix — sometimes just by showing a little patience:

Kate Hall — Who, although she was probably ready to kill me by the end of each of my first two books, somehow guided me through the edit process to build a better book each time. I have long since fallen out of touch with Kate, but she will always be the most special to me as someone who really helped shape my writing career. I will likely always hold this first "professional" dedication spot for her. Wherever you are Kate, I hope you are doing splendidly.

Sydney Jones — Normally, when you add someone new to a list like this, they seem to wind up at the bottom — that didn't seem quite right for Syd. Syd first appeared to me as one of a cast of seemingly thousands (it was less than that, but it seemed like a constantly changing set of people), but has evolved into one of the constants in my last few titles. Syd has done a great job of finding some balance between upholding the notion of "Wiley standards" versus allowing my books to be *my* books. It's beyond time that she got her due — here is at least a little bit of it.

Adaobi Obi Tulton — Four books now — who'd a thunk it? Adaobi is something of the "figure out where everything is" person of the book. She has a way of displaying a kind of "peace" in most things I've seen her do — I need to learn that.

Dominic Shakeshaft — Who got me writing in the first place (then again, given some nights filled with writing instead of sleep lately, maybe it's not thanks I owe him). I've had the pleasure of re-establishing contact with Dominic recently, and it's great to see him doing well.

Catherine Alexander — Who played Kate's more than able-bodied sidekick for my first title and was central to round two. Catherine was much like Kate in the sense she had a significant influence on the

Acknowledgments

shape and success of my first two titles. I've also recently managed to be in touch with "Cath" again, and am glad she also seems to be doing well.

John Mueller — Who continues to have the dubious job of finding my mistakes. I've done tech editing myself, and it's not the easiest job to notice the little details that were missed or are, in some fashion, wrong. It's even harder to read someone else's writing style and pick the right times to say, "You might want to approach this differently" and the right times to let it be. John did a terrific job on both counts.

John faced an especially trying time during the latter stages of this book's development, and did an amazing job of holding it all together. I wish he and his wife Rebecca great fortunes and good health in the year ahead.

Richard Waymire — Who has been such a pillar of the SQL Server community for oh so long. Richard is one of the true "nice guys" who isn't just nice — he just plain "gets it" when it comes to SQL Server. Richard has provided the answer to many a question over the years.

This book has been in development for so long and touched enough people that I'm sure I've missed one or two — if you're among those missed, please accept my humblest apologies and my assurance that your help was appreciated.

Contents

Contents

Contents

Contents

Contents

Contents

Contents

Contents

Contents

Contents

Contents

Introduction

And so we begin anew. While the wait for SQL Server 2005 took a ghastly five years, Microsoft has blessed us (and, no, I'm not being sarcastic!) with SQL Server 2008 in just three short years.

It probably shouldn't be surprising to me that SQL Server 2008 comes up short in terms of marquee features — the flash and glitz stuff. Yet, what I am surprised by is just how many "little things" have made it into this release. While there are some key feature areas (Policy Based Management, for example) that Microsoft can hang their marketing hat on, the most striking new features in SQL Server 2008 are far more subtle in nature.

SQL Server 2008 is jam-packed with a host of seemingly small, but extremely useful smaller additions such as:

❑   New, very useful data types (discrete date and time data types as well as support for geospatial data and hierarchical data representation)

❑   The new MERGE command (combining the options of INSERT, UPDATE, and DELETE all into one statement, this is sometimes referred to as an UPSERT in other products)

❑   A revamping of Reporting Services to allow for far more elegant reports

❑   Tracking and availability of "missing" index information (noticing at time of optimization that a non-existent index would have been useful had it been there)

And these are just for starters.

For those of you that have read the 2005 versions of my books, the change toward the separation of beginning and professional level content continues. The real "beginning" level discussion is now almost completely moved into its own book (*Beginning SQL Server 2008 Programming*). There are some topics that I consider borderline in terms of whether they are a beginner, intermediate, or professional level topic that I have continued to provide some degree of coverage on, but, with this edition, most all genuinely beginner content exists solely in the *Beginning* title (a new appendix has been added at the end of the book to give extremely short syntax listings and a few examples, but what was hundreds of pages is now in the tens of pages).

There is, however, good news that has continued to free up even more space, and this has allowed the *Professional* title to return to more broad coverage of a wider range of topics. This allows me to get closer to the original goal I had for the *Professional* book: to give you enough grounding in most of the product that, even if you couldn't write at an expert level in each area, you would understand SQL Server as a whole and build a better system, knowing what's involved in the many areas where SQL Server offers functionality, and being prepared to go get even more information if need be.

Other than that, this book maintains most of the style it has always had. We cover most of the add-on services, as well as advanced programming constructs (such as .NET assemblies) and some of the supporting object models (which allow for management of your SQL Server and its various engines).

Version Issues

This book is written for SQL Server 2008. It does, however, maintain roots going back a few versions and keeps a sharp eye out for backward compatibility issues with SQL Server 2005 and even SQL Server 2000. Prior versions are old enough now where little to no time is spent on them except in passing (in short, few remain that have even seen SQL Server 6.5 and SQL Server 7.0 was just shy of a decade old at release of SQL Server 2008).

Who This Book Is For

This book assumes that you have some existing experience with SQL Server and are at an intermediate to advanced level. Furthermore, the orientation of the book is highly developer focused.

Aside from a quick reference-oriented appendix, very little coverage is given to beginner level topics. It is assumed you already have experience with data manipulation language (DML) statements, and know the basics of all the mainstream SQL Server objects (views, stored procedures, user defined functions and, to a much lesser extent, triggers). If you feel you are ready for more advanced topics, but also feel that brushing up on the basics can't hurt, I highly encourage you to check out *Beginning SQL Server 2008 Programming*, as the two books are now much more designed to work as a pair with some, but relatively limited, overlap.

What This Book Covers

This book is about SQL Server. More specifically, it is oriented around developing on SQL Server. Most of the concepts are agnostic to what client language you use, though the examples that leverage a client language generally do so in C#. (A few are shown in more than one language.)

For those of you migrating from earlier versions of SQL Server, some of the "gotchas" that inevitably exist any time a product has versions are discussed to the extent that they seem to be a genuinely relevant issue.

How This Book Is Structured

As is the case for all my books, this book takes something of a lassez faire writing style. We roam around a bit within a relatively loose structure. Each chapter begins with an explanation of the things to be covered in that chapter, and then we go through those items. Within each topic covered, some background is provided, and then we work through an example if appropriate. Examples are generally created to be short, and yet still quickly get at several of the concepts you need for whatever topic is being covered at the time.

In terms of "what to cover next," there is a logical progression. We review tools and data types early on (since there are changes there), but move on very fast to topics that assume you are already comfortable with the product.

To make reasonable use of this book, you will need administrative access to a computer that is capable of running SQL Server 2008. While I highly recommend using the Developer Edition, the vast majority of samples and advice applies to virtually all editions of SQL Server. I do, however, recommend staying with a full version of SQL Server rather than using the Express Edition.

Conventions

To help you get the most from the text and keep track of what's happening, we've used a number of conventions throughout the book.

> **Boxes like this one hold important, not-to-be forgotten information that is directly relevant to the surrounding text.**

Notes, tips, hints, tricks, and asides to the current discussion are offset and placed in italics like this.

As for styles in the text:

❑ We *highlight* new terms and important words when we introduce them.

❑ We show keyboard strokes like this: Ctrl+A.

❑ We show file names, URLs, and code within the text like so: `persistence.properties`.

❑ We present code in two different ways:

```
We use a monofont type with no highlighting for most code examples.
We use gray highlighting to emphasize code that's particularly important in the
present context.
```

Source Code

As you work through the examples in this book, you may choose either to type in all the code manually or to use the source code files that accompany the book. All of the source code used in this book is available for download at `http://www.wrox.com`. Once at the site, simply locate the book's title (either by using the Search box or by using one of the title lists) and click the Download Code link on the book's detail page to obtain all the source code for the book.

Because many books have similar titles, you may find it easiest to search by ISBN; this book's ISBN is 978-0-470-25702-9.

Once you download the code, just decompress it with your favorite compression tool. Alternatively, you can go to the main Wrox code download page at `http://www.wrox.com/dynamic/books/download.aspx` to see the code available for this book and all other Wrox books.

Errata

We make every effort to ensure that there are no errors in the text or in the code. However, no one is perfect, and mistakes do occur. If you find an error in one of our books, like a spelling mistake or faulty piece of code, we would be very grateful for your feedback. By sending in errata you may save another reader hours of frustration and at the same time you will be helping us provide even higher quality information.

To find the errata page for this book, go to `http://www.wrox.com` and locate the title using the Search box or one of the title lists. Then, on the book details page, click the Book Errata link. On this page you can view all errata that has been submitted for this book and posted by Wrox editors. A complete book list including links to each book's errata is also available at `www.wrox.com/misc-pages/booklist.shtml`.

If you don't spot "your" error on the Book Errata page, go to `www.wrox.com/contact/techsupport .shtml` and complete the form there to send us the error you have found. We'll check the information and, if appropriate, post a message to the book's errata page and fix the problem in subsequent editions of the book.

p2p.wrox.com

For author and peer discussion, join the P2P forums at `p2p.wrox.com`. The forums are a Web-based system for you to post messages relating to Wrox books and related technologies and interact with other readers and technology users. The forums offer a subscription feature to e-mail you topics of interest of your choosing when new posts are made to the forums. Wrox authors, editors, other industry experts, and your fellow readers are present on these forums.

At `http://p2p.wrox.com` you will find a number of different forums that will help you not only as you read this book, but also as you develop your own applications. To join the forums, just follow these steps:

1. Go to `p2p.wrox.com` and click the Register link.
2. Read the terms of use and click Agree.
3. Complete the required information to join as well as any optional information you wish to provide and click Submit.
4. You will receive an e-mail with information describing how to verify your account and complete the joining process.

You can read messages in the forums without joining P2P but in order to post your own messages, you must join.

Once you join, you can post new messages and respond to messages other users post. You can read messages at any time on the Web. If you would like to have new messages from a particular forum e-mailed to you, click the Subscribe to this Forum icon by the forum name in the forum listing.

For more information about how to use the Wrox P2P, be sure to read the P2P FAQs for answers to questions about how the forum software works as well as many common questions specific to P2P and Wrox books. To read the FAQs, click the FAQ link on any P2P page.

www.professionalsql.com

Limited support for the book and occasional blog entries can also be found at http://www.professionalsql.com. While formal support requests should be sent through the p2p.wrox.com website, professionalsql.com provides a mirror of the key downloads as well as occasional commentary from the author on the general state of the development world. You can contact me at robv@professionalsql.com; my sole requests for questions or contacts are:

❑   Please don't send me the questions from your take home mid-term or other school quizzes/tests (and yes, people really have done that).

❑   Focus questions to those not readily answered from general sources (Google, the p2p.wrox.com website, the many popular SQL Server websites, or a simple Books Online query).

❑   Understand that, while I try, I cannot always respond to every request for help, advice, or other questions.

❑   Recognize that the exposure of my e-mail address in this book represents a certain degree of trust in you, the reader, that you will not abuse that openness.

I am always happy to hear about people's SQL experiences, so please feel free to drop me a line and brag about the wonderful things you've managed to do with SQL Server.

Being Objective: Re-Examining Objects in SQL Server

If you're someone who's read my Professional level titles before, you'll find we're continuing the path we started in *Professional SQL Server 2005 Programming* and have the "Professional" become a little bit more "Pro" in level. That said, I still want to touch on all the basic objects and also address some things like new data types and additional objects that are new with SQL Server 2008.

So, What Exactly Do We Have Here?

Seems like sort of a silly question doesn't it? If you're here reading this title, you obviously know we have a database, but what makes up a database? It is my hope that, by now (meaning by the time you're ready for a professional level title), you've come to realize that a *Relational Database Management System (RDBMS)* is actually much more than data. Today's advanced RDBMSs not only store your data, they also manage that data for you, restricting what kind of data can go into the system, and also facilitating getting data out of the system. If all you want is to tuck the data away somewhere safe, you can use just about any data storage system. RDBMSs allow you to go beyond the storage of the data into the realm of defining what that data should look like — this has never been more true than with SQL Server 2008. Improved support for hierarchies means that you can store hierarchical data in a far more native way, and still access it very efficiently. The new Policy Based Management feature allows you to control many elements of how your data is administrated using a rules-driven approach. SQL Server also provides services that help automate how your data interacts with data from other systems through such powerful features as the SQL Server Agent, Integration Services, Notification Services, the increasingly popular Reporting Services, and more.

This chapter provides an overview to the core objects used in SQL Server. Much of what is discussed in this chapter may be old news for you at this stage of your database learning, so this is the only point in the book where we will call them out in broad terms of how they relate to each other. I will assume that you are already somewhat familiar with most of the objects discussed here, but the goal is to fill in any holes and fully prepare you for the more advanced discussions to come.

In this chapter, we will take a high-level look into:

- ❑ Database objects
- ❑ Data types (including some that are new with SQL Server 2008!)
- ❑ Other database concepts that ensure data integrity

An Overview of Database Objects

An RDBMS such as SQL Server contains many *objects*. Object purists out there may quibble with whether Microsoft's choice of what to call an object (and what not to) actually meets the normal definition of an object, but, for SQL Server's purposes, the list of some of the more important database objects can be said to contain such things as:

The database itself	Indexes
The transaction log	CLR assemblies
Tables	Reports
Filegroups	Full-text catalogs
Diagrams	User-defined data types
Views	Roles
Stored procedures	Users
User-defined functions	Encryption Keys

This is far from being a comprehensive list, and is in no particular order, but it does give you some of a feel for the breadth of objects that your SQL Server can manage.

The Database Object

The database is effectively the highest-level object that you can refer to within a given SQL Server. (Technically speaking, the server itself can be considered to be an object, but not from any real "programming" perspective, so we're not going there.) Most, but not all, other objects in a SQL Server are children of the database object.

If you are familiar with old versions of SQL Server you may now be saying, "What? What happened to logins? What happened to Remote Servers and SQL Agent tasks?" SQL Server has several other objects (as listed previously) that exist in support of the database. With the exception of linked servers, and perhaps Integration Services packages, these are primarily the domain of the database administrator and as such, you generally don't give them significant thought during the design and programming processes. (They are programmable via something called the SQL Management Objects [SMO], but that is far too special a case to concern you with here. We will look at SMO more fully in Chapter 26.)

A database is typically a group that includes at least a set of table objects and, more often than not, other objects, such as stored procedures and views that pertain to the data stored in the database's tables.

When you first load SQL Server, you will start with four system databases:

❑ master

❑ model

❑ msdb

❑ tempdb

All of these need to be installed for your server to run properly. (Indeed, for some of them, it won't run at all without them.) From there, things vary depending on which installation choices you made. Examples of some of the databases you may also see include the following:

❑ AdventureWorks or AdventureWorks2008 (the sample databases downloadable from `codeplex.com`)

❑ AdventureWorksLT or AdventureWorksLT2008 (a "lite" version of the main sample database)

❑ AdventureWorksDW or AdventureWorksDW2008 (sample for use with Analysis Services)

In addition to the primary examples supported by Microsoft, you may, when searching the Web or using other tutorials, find reference to a couple of older samples:

❑ pubs

❑ Northwind

The master Database

Every SQL Server, regardless of version or custom modifications, has the master database. This database holds a special set of tables (system tables) that keeps track of the system as a whole. For example, when you create a new database on the server, an entry is placed in the sysdatabases table in the master database (though, if you're interested in data from sysdatabases, you should only access it via the sys.databases metadata view). All extended and system stored procedures, regardless of which database they are intended for use with, are stored in this database. Obviously, since almost everything that describes your server is stored in here, this database is critical to your system and cannot be deleted.

The system tables, including those found in the master database, can, in a pinch, be extremely useful. That said, their direct use is diminishing in importance as Microsoft continues to give more and more other options for getting at system level information.

> I used to be a significant user of system tables; that is no longer the case.

> Microsoft has recommended against using the system tables since prior to version 7.0 (1998 or so?). They make absolutely no guarantees about compatibility in the master database between versions — indeed, they virtually guarantee that they will

change. The worst offense comes when performing updates on objects in the master database. Trust me when I tell you that altering these tables in any way is asking for a SQL Server that no longer functions. (I've saved a system doing this, and I've killed a system doing this; I don't like 50/50 odds with the life of my server . . . .).

Microsoft has created several alternatives (for example, system functions, system stored procedures, `information_schema` views, and a wide array of system metadata functions) for retrieving much of the information that is stored in the system tables. These alternatives are what you should be using.

The model Database

The model database is aptly named, in the sense that it's the model on which a copy can be based. The model database forms a template for any new database that you create. This means that you can, if you wish, alter the model database if you want to change what standard, newly created databases look like. For example, you could add a set of audit tables that you include in every database you build. You could also include a few user groups that would be cloned into every new database that was created on the system. Note that since this database serves as the template for any other database, it's a required database and must be left on the system; you cannot delete it.

There are several things to keep in mind when altering the model database. First, any database you create has to be at least as large as the model database. That means that if you alter the model database to be 100MB in size, you can't create a database smaller than 100MB. There are several other similar pitfalls. As such, for 90 percent of installations, I strongly recommend leaving this one alone.

The msdb Database

msdb is where the SQL Agent process stores any system tasks. If you schedule backups to run on a database nightly, there is an entry in msdb. Schedule a stored procedure for one-time execution, and yes, it has an entry in msdb. Other major subsystems in SQL Server make similar use of msdb. SQL Server Integration Services (SSIS) packages and Policy Based Management definitions are examples of other processes that make use of msdb.

The tempdb Database

tempdb is one of the key working areas for your server. Whenever you issue a complex or large query that SQL Server needs to build interim tables to solve, it does so in tempdb. Whenever you create a temporary table of your own, it is created in tempdb, even though you think you're creating it in the current database. Whenever there is a need for data to be stored temporarily, it's probably stored in tempdb.

tempdb is very different from any other database in that not only are the objects within it temporary, but the database itself is temporary. It has the distinction of being the only database in your system that is completely rebuilt from scratch every time you start your SQL Server.

> Technically speaking, you can actually create objects yourself in tempdb — I strongly recommend against this practice. You can create temporary objects from within any database you have access to in your system — it will be stored in tempdb. Creating objects directly in tempdb gains you nothing but adds the confusion of referring to things across databases. This is another of those "Don't go there!" kind of things.

> tempdb is dropped and rebuilt from scratch each time you restart your SQL Server.

AdventureWorks/AdventureWorks2008

SQL Server included samples long before these came along. The old samples had their shortcomings though. For example, they contained a few poor design practices. (I'll hold off the argument of whether the AdventureWorks databases have the same issue or not. Let's just say that AdventureWorks was, among other things, an attempt to address this problem.) In addition, they were simplistic and focused on demonstrating certain database concepts rather than on SQL Server as a product or even databases as a whole.

From the earliest stages of development of Yukon (the internal code name for what we look back on today as SQL Server 2005) Microsoft knew they wanted a far more robust sample database that would act as a sample for as much of the product as possible. AdventureWorks is the outcome of that effort. As much as you will hear me complain about its overly complex nature for the beginning user, it is a masterpiece in that it shows it *all* off. Okay, so it's not really *everything*, but it is a fairly complete sample, with more realistic volumes of data, complex structures, and sections that show samples for the vast majority of product features. In this sense, it's truly terrific. AdventureWorks2008 is the natural evolution of the original AdventureWorks database in the sense that it alters and extends the model to make use of features that are new with SQL Server 2008.

I use AdventureWorks2008 as the core sample database for this book.

AdventureWorksLT/AdventureWorksLT2008

The LT in this stands for lite. This is just an extremely small subset of the full AdventureWorks database. The idea is to provide a simpler sample set for easier training of basic concepts and simple training. While I've not been privy to the exact reasoning behind this new sample set, my suspicion was that it is an effort to try and kill the older Northwind and Pubs sample sets, which have been preferred by many trainers over the newer AdventureWorks set, as the AdventureWorks database is often far too complex and cumbersome for early training. However, I've recently heard that there are plans for some updating and additional development to the Northwind sample, so perhaps they aren't ready to totally kill that one off after all.

AdventureWorksDW/AdventureWorksDW2008

This is the Analysis Services sample. (The DW stands for data warehouse, which is the type of database over which most Analysis Services projects will be built.) Perhaps the greatest thing about it is that Microsoft had the foresight to tie the transaction database sample with the analysis sample, providing a whole set of samples that show the two of them working together.

We will utilize this database extensively when reviewing OLAP concepts and taking a look at Analysis Services. Take a look at the differences between the two databases. They are meant to serve the same fictional company, but they have different purposes; learn from this.

The Transaction Log

If you're far enough along in your SQL Server learning to be reading this title, then I would think you would have at least a basic familiarity with the log. That said, it is among the most misunderstood objects in SQL Server. Although the data is read from the database, any changes you make don't initially go to the database itself. Instead, they are written serially to the *transaction log*. At some later point in time, the database is issued a *checkpoint* — it is at that point in time that all the changes in the log are propagated to the actual database file.

The database is in a random access arrangement, but the log is serial in nature. While the random nature of the database file allows for speedy access, the serial nature of the log allows things to be tracked in the proper order. The log accumulates changes that are deemed as having been committed, and the server writes the changes to the physical database file(s) at a later time.

We'll take a much closer look at how things are logged in Chapter 11, but for now, remember that the log is the first place on disk that the data goes, and it's propagated to the actual database at a later time. You need both the database file and the transaction log to have a functional database.

The Most Basic Database Object: Table

Databases are made up of many things, but none are more central to the make-up of a database than tables. A table is made up of what is called *domain* data (columns) and *entity* data (rows). The actual data for a database is stored in tables. Each table definition contains the *metadata* (descriptive information about data) that describes the nature of the data the table is to contain. Each column has its own set of rules about what can be stored in that column. A violation of the rules of any one column can cause the system to reject an inserted row or an update to an existing row, or prevent the deletion of a row.

A table can have additional objects associated with it — these objects exist only within the construct of a particular table (or, in somewhat rare cases, a view). Let's take a look at each of these.

Indexes

An *index* is an object that exists only within the framework of a particular table or view. An index works much like the index does in the back of an encyclopedia; there is some sort of lookup (or "key") value that is sorted in a particular way, and, once you have that, you are provided another key with which you can look up the actual information you are after.

An index provides us ways of speeding the lookup of our information. Indexes fall into two categories:

- ❑ **Clustered** — You can have only one of these per table. If an index is clustered, it means that the table on which the clustered index is based is physically sorted according to that index. If you were indexing an encyclopedia, the clustered index would be the page numbers; the information in the encyclopedia is stored in the order of the page numbers.

❑   **Non-clustered** — You can have many of these for every table. This is more along the lines of what you probably think of when you hear the word *index*. This kind of index points to some other value that will let you find the data. For our encyclopedia, this would be the keyword index at the back of the book.

Note that views that have indexes — or *indexed views* — must have at least one clustered index before they can have any non-clustered indexes.

Triggers

A *trigger* is an object that generally exists only within the framework of a table. Triggers are pieces of logical code that are automatically executed when certain things, such as inserts, updates, or deletes, happen to your table. Triggers can be used for a great variety of things but are mainly used for either copying data as it is entered or checking the update to make sure that it meets some criteria.

A special kind of trigger — called a before trigger — can be associated with a view. We will take a more in-depth look at these in Chapter 12.

Constraints

A *constraint* is yet another object that exists only within the confines of a table. Constraints are much like they sound; they confine the data in your table to meet certain conditions. Constraints, in a way, compete with triggers as possible solutions to data integrity issues. They are not, however, the same thing; each has its own distinct advantages.

Unlike triggers and indexes, constraints can *only* be associated with tables (no views).

Schemas

Schemas provide an intermediate namespace between your database and the other objects it contains. The default schema in any database is dbo (which stands for database owner). Every user has a default schema, and SQL Server will search for objects within that user's default schema automatically. If, however, the object is within a namespace that is not the default for that user, then the object must be referred with two parts in the form of `<schema name>.<object name>`.

> Schemas replace the concept of "owner" that was used in prior versions of SQL Server. While Microsoft now seems to be featuring their use (the idea is that you'll be able to refer to a group of tables by the schema they are in rather than listing them all), I remain dubious at best. In short, I believe they create far more problems than they solve, and I generally recommend against their use (I have made my exceptions, but they are very situational).

Filegroups

By default, all your tables and everything else about your database (except the log) are stored in a single file. That file is a member of what's called the *primary filegroup*. However, you are not stuck with this arrangement.

SQL Server allows you to define a little over 32,000 *secondary files*. (If you need more than that, perhaps it isn't SQL Server that has the problem.) These secondary files can be added to the primary filegroup or created as part of one or more *secondary filegroups*. While there is only one primary filegroup (and it is actually called "Primary"), you can have up to 255 secondary filegroups. A secondary filegroup is created as an option to a CREATE DATABASE or ALTER DATABASE command.

The concept of a filegroup is there primarily to allow you to manage your physical storage of data in a somewhat segmented fashion. You can backup just the files in a given filegroup (rather than the entire database). You can use individual files to spread data across multiple physical storage devices (which may provide more I/O bandwidth).

Diagrams

A database diagram is a visual representation of the database design, including the various tables, the column names in each table, and the relationships between tables. In your travels as a developer, you may have heard of an *entity-relationship* diagram — or ERD. In an ERD the database is divided into two parts: entities (such as supplier and product) and relations (such as supplies and purchases).

> *The database design tools included in SQL Server 2008 remain a bit sparse. Indeed, the diagramming methodology the tools use doesn't adhere to any of the accepted standards in ER diagramming.*
>
> *Still, these diagramming tools really do provide all the "necessary" things; they are at least something of a start.*

Figure 1-1 is a diagram that shows some of the various tables in the AdventureWorks database. The diagram also (though it may be a bit subtle since this is new to you) describes many other properties about the database. Notice the tiny icons for keys and the infinity sign. These depict the nature of the relationship between two tables.

Views

A view is something of a virtual table. A view, for the most part, is used just like a table, except that it doesn't contain any data of its own. Instead, a view is merely a preplanned mapping and representation of the data stored in tables. The plan is stored in the database in the form of a query. This query calls for data from some, but not necessarily all, columns to be retrieved from one or more tables. The data retrieved may or may not (depending on the view definition) have to meet special criteria in order to be shown as data in that view. For most views, this serves two major purposes: security and ease of use. With views you can control what the users see, so if there is a section of a table that should be accessed by only a few users (for example, salary details), you can create a view that includes only those columns to which everyone is allowed access. In addition, the view can be tailored so that the user doesn't have to search through any unneeded information.

In addition to these most basic uses for view, we also have the ability to create what is called an *indexed view*. This is the same as any other view, except that we can now create an index against the view. This results in a few performance impacts (some positive, one negative):

❑   Views that reference multiple tables generally perform *much* faster with an indexed view because the join between the tables is preconstructed.

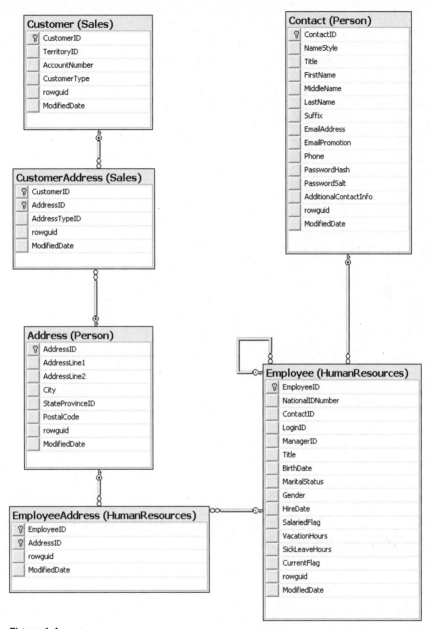

Figure 1-1

❏   Aggregations performed in the view are precalculated and stored as part of the index; again, this means that the aggregation is performed one time (when the row is inserted or updated), and then can be read directly from the index information.

❏   Inserts and deletes have higher overhead because the index on the view has to be updated immediately; updates also have higher overhead if the key column of the index is affected by the update.

We will look more deeply into these performance issues as well as other special uses for views in Chapter 8.

> *It is important to note that, while the code to create an indexed view will work in all editions, the query optimizer will only consider an indexed view when used in the Enterprise Edition of the product.*

Stored Procedures

Stored procedures (or *sprocs*) are historically the bread and butter of programmatic functionality in SQL Server. Stored procedures are generally an ordered series of Transact-SQL (the language used to query Microsoft SQL Server) statements bundled up into a single logical unit. They allow for variables and parameters as well as selection and looping constructs. Sprocs offer several advantages over just sending individual statements to the server in the sense that they:

- ❑ Are referred to using short names, rather than a long string of text; as such, less network traffic is required in order to run the code within the sproc.

- ❑ Are pre-optimized and precompiled, saving a small amount of time each time the sproc is run.

- ❑ Encapsulate a process, usually for security reasons or just to hide the complexity of the database.

- ❑ Can be called from other sprocs, making them reusable in a somewhat limited sense.

In addition, you can utilize any .NET language to create assemblies and add program constructs beyond those native to T-SQL to your stored procedures.

User-Defined Functions

User-defined functions (or *UDFs*) have a tremendous number of similarities to sprocs, except that they:

- ❑ Can return a value of most SQL Server data types. Excluded return types include text, ntext, image, cursor, and timestamp. Note that you *can* return varchar(max) and varbinary(max) values.

- ❑ Can't have "side effects." Basically, they can't do anything that reaches outside the scope of the function, such as changing tables, sending e-mails, or making system or database parameter changes.

UDFs are similar to the functions that you would use in a standard programming language such as VB.NET or C++. You can pass more than one variable in, and get a value out. SQL Server's UDFs vary from the functions found in many procedural languages, however, in that *all* variables passed into the function are passed in by value. If you're familiar with passing in variables By Ref in VB, or passing in pointers in C++, sorry, there is no equivalent here. There is, however, some good news in that you can return a special data type called a table. We'll examine the impact of this in Chapter 10.

Users and Roles

These two go hand in hand. *Users* are pretty much the equivalent of logins. In short, this object represents an identifier for someone to log in to the SQL Server. Anyone logging in to SQL Server has to map (directly or indirectly depending on the security model in use) to a user. Users, in turn, belong to one or more *roles*. Rights to perform certain actions in SQL Server can then be granted directly to a user or to a role to which one or more users belong.

Rules

Rules and constraints provide restriction information about what can go into a table. If an updated or inserted record violates a rule, then that insertion or update will be rejected. In addition, a rule can be used to define a restriction on a *user-defined data type*. Unlike rules, constraints aren't really objects unto themselves but rather pieces of metadata describing a particular table.

> **While Microsoft has not stated a particular version for doing so, they continue to warn that rules will be removed in a future release. Rules should be considered for backward compatibility only and should be avoided in new development. You should also begin phasing out any you already have in use in your database.**

Defaults

There are two types of defaults. There is the default that is an object unto itself and the default that is not really an object, but rather metadata describing a particular column in a table (in much the same way that we have rules, which are objects, and constraints, which are not objects but metadata). They both serve the same purpose. If, when inserting a record, you don't provide the value of a column and that column has a default defined, a value will be inserted automatically as defined in the default.

> **Much like rules, the form of default that is its own object should be treated as a legacy object and avoided in new development and actively removed from existing code. Use of default constraints is, however, still very valid.**

User-Defined Data Types

User-defined data types are extensions to the system-defined data types. The possibilities here are almost endless, but you must keep backward compatibility in mind. Although SQL Server 2000 and earlier had the idea of user-defined data types, they were really limited to different filtering of existing data types. Since SQL Server 2005, we have the ability to bind .NET assemblies to our own data types, meaning we can have a data type that stores (within reason) about anything we can store in a .NET object.

Careful with this! The data type that you're working with is pretty fundamental to your data and its storage. Although being able to define your own thing is very cool, recognize that it will almost certainly come with a large performance and most likely a security cost. Consider it carefully, be sure it's something you genuinely need, and then, as with everything like this, TEST, TEST, TEST!!!

Full-Text Catalogs

Full-text catalogs are mappings of data that speed the search for specific blocks of text within columns that have full-text searching enabled. Although these objects are joined at the hip to the tables and columns that they map, they are separate objects and are as such, not necessarily updated (the default is for automatic updating, but you can change it to manual update) when changes happen in the database.

SQL Server Data Types

This is an area of relatively significant change over the last release or two. SQL Server 2005 began the change in blob related data types (`text` and `ntext` became `varchar(max)` and `nvarchar(max)`, and image became `varbinary(max)`). Now SQL Server 2008 adds several new time and date related data types as well as a special data type for handling hierarchical data.

Note that since this book is intended for developers and that no developer could survive for 60 seconds without an understanding of data types, I'm going to assume that you already know how data types work and just need to know the particulars of SQL Server data types.

SQL Server 2008 has the intrinsic data types shown in the following table:

Data Type Name	Class	Size in Bytes	Nature of the Data
Bit	Integer	1	The size is somewhat misleading. The first `bit` data type in a table takes up 1 byte; the next seven make use of the same byte. Allowing nulls causes an additional byte to be used.
Bigint	Integer	8	This just deals with the fact that we use larger and larger numbers on a more frequent basis. This one allows you to use whole numbers from -2^{63} to $2^{63}-1$. That's plus or minus about 92 quintrillion.
Int	Integer	4	Whole numbers from –2,147,483,648 to 2,147,483,647.
SmallInt	Integer	2	Whole numbers from –32,768 to 32,767.
TinyInt	Integer	1	Whole numbers from 0 to 255.
Decimal or Numeric	Decimal/ Numeric	Varies	Fixed precision and scale from $-10^{38}-1$ to $10^{38}-1$. The two names are synonymous.
Money	Money	8	Monetary units from -2^{63} to 2^{63} plus precision to four decimal places. Note that this could be any monetary unit, not just dollars.
SmallMoney	Money	4	Monetary units from –214,748.3648 to +214,748.3647.
Float (also a synonym for ANSI Real)	Approximate Numerics	Varies	Accepts an argument (for example, `Float(20)`) that determines size and precision. Note that the argument is in bits, not bytes. Ranges from –1.79E + 308 to 1.79E + 308.

Data Type Name	Class	Size in Bytes	Nature of the Data
DateTime	Date/Time	8	Date and time data from January 1, 1753, to December 31, 9999, with an accuracy of three-hundredths of a second.
DateTime2	Date/Time	Varies (6-8)	Updated incarnation of the more venerable DateTime data type. Supports larger date ranges and large time fraction precision (up to 100 nanoseconds). Like DateTime, it is not time zone aware, but, does align with the .NET DateTime data type.
SmallDateTime	Date/Time	4	Date and time data from January 1, 1900, to June 6, 2079, with an accuracy of one minute.
DateTimeOffset	Date/Time	Varies (8-10)	Similar to the DateTime data type, but also expects an offset designation of −14:00 to +14:00 offset from UTC time. Time is stored internally as UTC time, and any comparisons, sorts, and indexing will be based on that unified time zone.
Date	Date/Time	3	Stores only Date data from January 1, 0001, to December 31, 9999 as defined by the Gregorian calendar. Assumes the ANSI standard date format (YYYY-MM-DD), but will implicitly convert from several other formats.
Time	Date/Time	Varies (3-5)	Stores only Time data in user-selectable precisions as granular as 100 nanoseconds (which is the default).
Cursor	Special Numeric	1	Pointer to a cursor. While the pointer takes up only a byte, keep in mind that the result set that makes up the actual cursor also takes up memory — exactly how much will vary depending on the result set.
Timestamp/ rowversion	Special Numeric (binary)	8	Special value that is unique within a given database. Value is set by the database itself automatically every time the record is either inserted or updated — even though the timestamp column wasn't referred to by the UPDATE statement (you're actually not allowed to update the timestamp field directly).

Continued

Data Type Name	Class	Size in Bytes	Nature of the Data
UniqueIdentifier	Special Numeric (binary)	16	Special Globally Unique Identifier (GUID). Is guaranteed to be unique across space and time.
Char	Character	Varies	Fixed-length character data. Values shorter than the set length are padded with spaces to the set length. Data is non-Unicode. Maximum specified length is 8,000 characters.
VarChar	Character	Varies	Variable-length character data. Values are not padded with spaces. Data is non-Unicode. Maximum specified length is 8,000 characters, but you can use the "max" keyword to indicate it as essentially a very large character field (up to 2^31 bytes of data).
Text	Character	Varies	Legacy support as of SQL Server 2005 — use varchar(max) instead!
NChar	Unicode	Varies	Fixed-length Unicode character data. Values shorter than the set length are padded with spaces. Maximum specified length is 4,000 characters.
NVarChar	Unicode	Varies	Variable-length Unicode character data. Values are not padded. Maximum specified length is 4,000 characters, but you can use the "max" keyword to indicate it as essentially a very large character field (up to 2^31 bytes of data).
Ntext	Unicode	Varies	Like the Text data type, this is legacy support only — in this case, use nvarchar(max). Variable-length Unicode character data.
Binary	Binary	Varies	Fixed-length binary data with a maximum length of 8,000 bytes.
VarBinary	Binary	Varies	Variable-length binary data with a maximum specified length of 8,000 bytes, but you can use the "max" keyword to indicate it as essentially a LOB field (up to 2^31 bytes of data).
Image	Binary	Varies	Legacy support only as of SQL Server 2005. Use varbinary(max) instead!

Data Type Name	Class	Size in Bytes	Nature of the Data
Table	Other	Special	This is primarily for use in working with result sets — typically passing one out of a User-defined Function or as a parameter for Stored Procedures. Not usable as a data type within a table definition (you can't nest tables).
HierarchyID	Other	Special	Special data type that maintains hierarchy positioning information. Provides special functionality specific to hierarchy needs. Comparisons of depth, parent/child relationships, and indexing are allowed. Exact size varies with the number of and average depth of nodes in the hierarchy.
Sql_variant	Other	Special	This is loosely related to the Variant in VB and C++. Essentially, it is a container that allows you to hold most other SQL Server data types in it. That means you can use this when one column or function needs to be able to deal with multiple data types. Unlike VB, using this data type forces you to *explicitly* cast it in order to convert it to a more specific data type.
XML	Character	Varies	Defines a character field as being for XML data. Provides for the validation of data against an XML Schema as well as the use of special XML-oriented functions.

Note that compatibility with .NET data types is even stronger than it was before. For example, the new date and time cross neatly into the .NET world, and the new datetime2 data type also crosses to .NET more cleanly than the previous datetime data type does.

> Unfortunately, SQL Server continues to have no concept of unsigned numeric data types. If you need to allow for larger numbers than the signed data type allows, consider using a larger signed data type. If you need to prevent the use of negative numbers, consider using a CHECK constraint that restricts valid data to greater than or equal to zero.

In general, SQL Server data types work much as you would expect given experience in most other modern programming languages. Adding numbers yields a sum, but adding strings concatenates them. When you mix the usage or assignment of variables or fields of different data types, a number of types convert implicitly (or automatically). Most other types can be converted explicitly. (You say specifically what type you want to convert to.) A few can't be converted between at all. Figure 1-2 contains a chart that shows the various possible conversions.

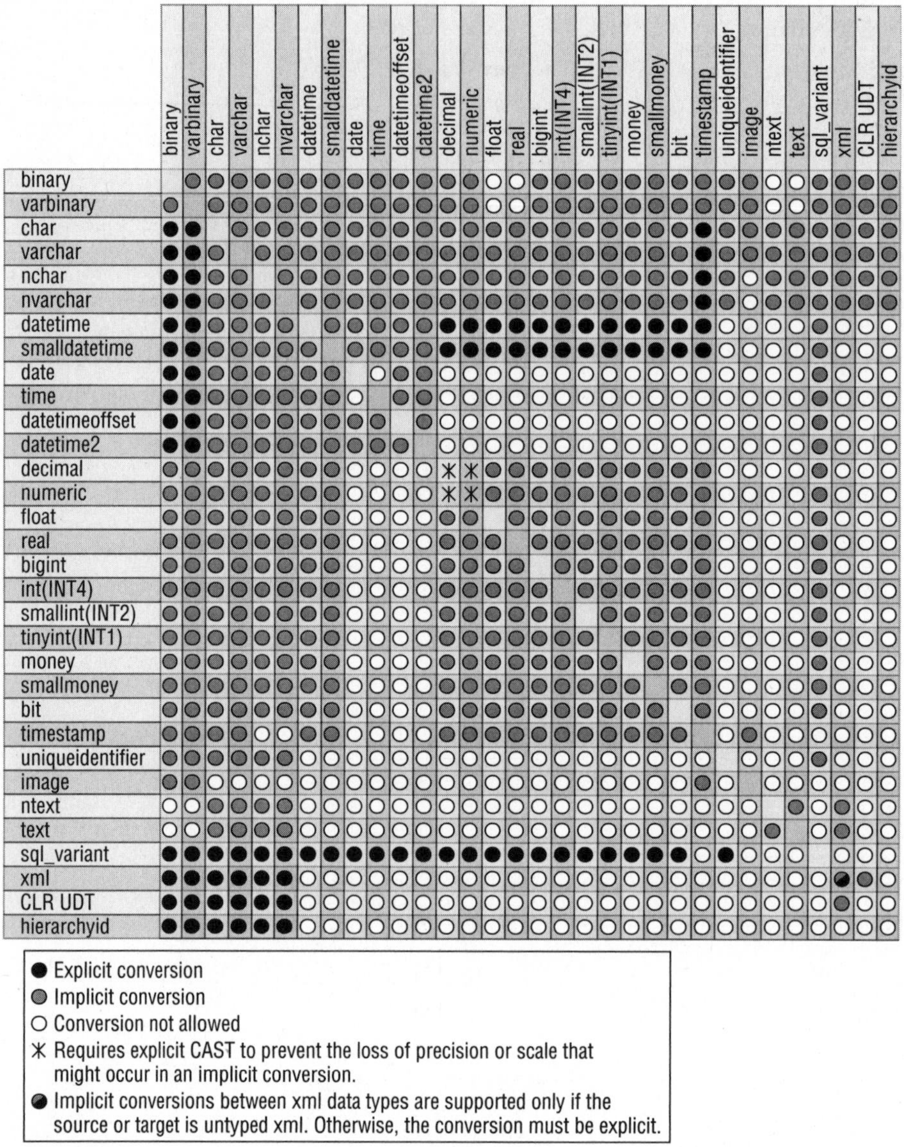

Figure 1-2 — SQL Server data type conversion chart. The chart lists the following data types along both the rows and columns: binary, varbinary, char, varchar, nchar, nvarchar, datetime, smalldatetime, date, time, datetimeoffset, datetime2, decimal, numeric, float, real, bigint, int(INT4), smallint(INT2), tinyint(INT1), money, smallmoney, bit, timestamp, uniqueidentifier, image, ntext, text, sql_variant, xml, CLR UDT, hierarchyid.

Legend:

- ● Explicit conversion
- ◕ Implicit conversion
- ○ Conversion not allowed
- ✳ Requires explicit CAST to prevent the loss of precision or scale that might occur in an implicit conversion.
- ◑ Implicit conversions between xml data types are supported only if the source or target is untyped xml. Otherwise, the conversion must be explicit.

Figure 1-2

In short, data types in SQL Server perform much the same function that they do in other programming environments. They help prevent programming bugs by ensuring that the data supplied is of the same nature that the data is supposed to be (remember 1/1/1980 means something different as a date than as a number) and ensures that the kind of operation performed is what you expect.

NULL Data

What if you have a row that doesn't have any data for a particular column — that is, what if you simply don't know the value? For example, let's say that we have a record that is trying to store the company performance information for a given year. Now, imagine that one of the fields is a percentage growth over the prior year, but you don't have records for the year before the first record in your database. You might be tempted to just enter a zero in the PercentGrowth column. Would that provide the right information though? People who didn't know better might think that meant you had zero percent growth, when the fact is that you simply don't know the value for that year.

Values that are indeterminate are said to be NULL. It seems that every time I teach a class in programming, at least one student asks me to define the value of NULL. Well, that's a tough one, because, by definition, a NULL value means that you don't know what the value is. It could be 1; it could be 347; it could be –294 for all we know. In short, it means *undefined* or perhaps *not applicable*.

SQL Server Identifiers for Objects

Now you've heard all sorts of things about objects in SQL Server. But let's take a closer look at naming objects in SQL Server.

What Gets Named?

Basically, everything has a name in SQL Server. Here's a partial list:

Stored procedures	Tables	Columns
Views	Rules	Constraints
Defaults	Indexes	Filegroups
Triggers	Databases	Servers
User-defined functions	Logins	Roles
Full-text catalogs	Files	User-defined types
Schemas		

And the list goes on. Most things I can think of except rows (which aren't really objects) have a name. The trick is to make every name both useful and practical.

Rules for Naming

The rules for naming in SQL Server are fairly relaxed, allowing things like embedded spaces and even keywords in names. Like most freedoms, however, it's easy to make some bad choices and get yourself into trouble.

Here are the main rules:

❑ The name of your object must start with any letter as defined by the specification for Unicode 3.2. This includes the letters most westerners are used to — A–Z and a–z. Whether "A" is different from "a" depends on the way your server is configured, but either makes for a valid beginning to an object name. After that first letter, you're pretty much free to run wild; almost any character will do.

❑ The name can be up to 128 characters for normal objects and 116 for temporary objects.

❑ Any names that are the same as SQL Server keywords or contain embedded spaces must be enclosed in double quotes (" ") or square brackets ([ ]). Which words are considered keywords varies, depending on the compatibility level to which you have set your database.

Note that double quotes are acceptable as a delimiter for column names only if you have set QUOTED_IDENTIFIER *on. Using square brackets ([and]) eliminates the chance that your users will have the wrong setting but is not as platform independent as double quotes are. I do, however, recommend against having* QUOTED IDENTIFIER *on due to issues it can create with indexed views.*

These rules are generally referred to as the rules for identifiers and are in force for any objects you name in SQL Server. Additional rules may exist for specific object types.

> **I can't stress enough the importance of avoiding the use of SQL Server keywords or embedded spaces in names. Although both are technically legal as long as you qualify them, naming things this way will cause you no end of grief.**

Summary

Database data has *type*, just as most other programming environments do. Most things that you do in SQL Server are going to have at least some consideration of type. While very little has changed in terms of basic objects available in SQL Server 2008, several new data types have been added. Be sure and review these new types (in the date and time arena as well as hierarchical data support). Review the types that are available, and think about how these types map to the data types in any programming environment with which you are familiar.

Consider the many objects available to you in SQL Server 2008. While you should be pretty familiar with tables and the basics of views and scripting prior to using this book (if not, you may want to take a look at *Beginning SQL Server 2008 Programming*), my hope is that you also realize that tossing together a few tables and a stored procedure or two seldom makes a real database. The things that make today's RDBMSs great are the extra things — the objects that enable you to place functionality and business rules that are associated with the data right into the database with the data.

2
Tool Time

If you are already familiar with the SQL Server Management Studio (which would imply you are moving from a SQL Server 2005 environment or have already been working with SQL Server 2008), then this is a chapter (probably the last) you can probably get away with only skimming for new stuff. If you decide to skim, you may want to slow down going through some of the more seldom used tools such as the Configuration Manager and the discussion of Net-Libraries (usually just referred to as NetLibs). Again, if you're new to all of this, I would suggest swallowing your pride and starting with the *Beginning SQL Server 2008 Programming* title — it covers the basics in far more detail. For this book, our purpose in covering the stuff in the first few chapters is really more about providing a reference than anything else, with an additional smattering of new stuff.

With that in mind, it's time to move on to the toolset. If you are skipping forward in versions from SQL Server 2000 or earlier, then this is where you'll want to pay particular attention. Back in SQL Server 2005, the toolset changed — *a lot*. SQL Server 2008 adds some new nodes within the SQL Server 2005 tools and moves around a few more.

For old fogies such as me, the new tools are a rather nasty shock to the system. For people new to SQL Server, I would say that the team has largely met a 2005 design goal to greatly simplify the tools. In general, there are far fewer places to look for things, and most of the toolset is grouped far more logically.

The tools we will look at in this chapter are:

- ❑   SQL Server Books Online
- ❑   The SQL Server Configuration Manager
- ❑   SQL Server Management Studio
- ❑   SQL Server Business Intelligence Development Studio
- ❑   SQL Server Integration Services (SSIS): including the Import/Export Wizard

❏   Reporting Services

❏   The Bulk Copy Program (bcp)

❏   Profiler

❏   sqlcmd

Books Online

Is *Books Online* a tool? I think so. Let's face it: It doesn't matter how many times you read this or any other book on SQL Server; you're not going to remember everything you'll ever need to know about SQL Server. SQL Server is one of my mainstay products, and I still can't remember it all. Books Online is simply one of the most important tools you're going to find in SQL Server.

> *Here's a simple piece of advice: Don't even try to remember it all. Remember that what you've seen is possible. Remember what is an integral foundation to what you're doing. Remember what you work with every day. Then remember to build a good reference library (starting with this book) for the rest.*

Everything works pretty much as one would expect here, so I'm not going to go into the details of how to operate a help system. Suffice it to say that SQL Server Books Online is a great quick reference that follows you to whatever machine you're working on at the time. Books Online also has the added benefit of often having information that is more up to date than the printed documentation.

> Technically speaking, it's quite possible that not every system you move to will have the Books Online (BOL) installed. This is because you can manually de-select BOL at the time of installation. Even in tight space situations, however, I strongly recommend that you always install the BOL. It really doesn't take up all that much space when you consider cost per megabyte these days, and it can save you a fortune in time by having that quick reference available wherever you are running SQL Server. (On my machine, Books Online takes up 100MB of space.)

The SQL Server Configuration Manager

Administrators who configure computers for database access are the main users of this tool, but it is still important for us to understand what this tool is about.

The SQL Server Configuration Manager is really an effort to combine some settings that were, in past versions of SQL Server, spread across multiple tools into one spot. The items managed in the Configuration Manager fall into two areas:

❏   Service Management

❏   Network Configuration

Service Management

Let's cut to the chase — the services available for management here include:

❑ **Integration Services** — This powers the Integration Services functionality set.

❑ **Analysis Services** — This powers the Analysis Services engine.

❑ **Full-Text Filter Daemon** — Again, just what it sounds like — powers the Full-Text Search Engine.

❑ **Reporting Services** — The underlying engine for Report Services.

❑ **SQL Server Agent** — The main engine behind anything in SQL Server that is scheduled. Utilizing this service, you can schedule jobs to run on a variety of different schedules. These jobs can have multiple tasks assigned to them and can even branch into doing different tasks depending on the outcome of some previous task. Examples of things run by the SQL Server Agent include backups as well as routine import and export tasks.

❑ **SQL Server** — The core database engine that works on data storage, queries, and system configuration for SQL Server.

❑ **SQL Server Browser** — Supports advertising your server so those browsing your local network can identify your system has SQL Server installed.

Network Configuration

A fair percentage of the time, connectivity issues are the result of client network configuration or how that configuration matches with that of the server.

SQL Server provides several of what are referred to as *Net-Libraries* (network libraries), or *NetLibs*. NetLibs serve as something of an insulator between your client application and the network protocol that is to be used — they serve the same function at the server end, too. The NetLibs supplied with SQL Server 2008 include:

❑ Named Pipes

❑ TCP/IP (the default)

❑ Shared Memory

❑ VIA (a proprietary virtual adaptor generally used for server-to-server communication based on special hardware)

The same NetLib must be available on both the client and server computers so that they can communicate with each other via the network protocol. Choosing a client NetLib that is not also supported on the server will result in your connection attempt failing (with a Specified SQL Server Not Found error).

Regardless of the data access method and kind of driver used (SQL Native Client, ODBC, OLE DB, or DB-Lib), it will always be the driver that talks to the NetLib. The process works as shown in Figure 2-1. The steps in order are:

1. The client app talks to the driver (SQL Native Client, ODBC, OLE DB, or DB-Lib).

2. The driver calls the client NetLib.

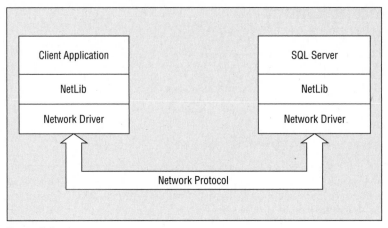

Figure 2-1

3. This NetLib calls the appropriate network protocol and transmits the data to a server NetLib.

4. The server NetLib then passes the requests from the client to the SQL Server.

Replies from SQL Server to the client follow the same sequence, only in reverse.

> In case you're familiar with TCP/IP, the default port that the IP NetLib will listen on is 1433. This can be reconfigured to use another port (and sometimes is for security reasons), but you'll need to make sure that your client systems know what port to talk to your server on. In general, I'm not a fan of changing this as I believe that most hackers scanning for a SQL Server port are going to scan wide enough to find it no matter what port it's on. That said, it's still a practice many believe is the right way to do things, so consider your installation choice carefully.

The Protocols

Let's start off with that "What are the available choices?" question. We can see what our server *could* be listening for by starting the SQL Server Computer Manager and expanding the Protocols for MSSQLSERVER tree under SQL Server Network Configuration, as shown in Figure 2-2.

Note that Figure 2-2 shows the Configuration Manager as it appears on a 64-bit system. The 32-bit nodes do not appear on a 32-bit installation, as they are the default nodes.

> By default, only Shared Memory will be enabled. Older versions of the product had different NetLibs enabled by default depending on the version of SQL Server and the O/S.

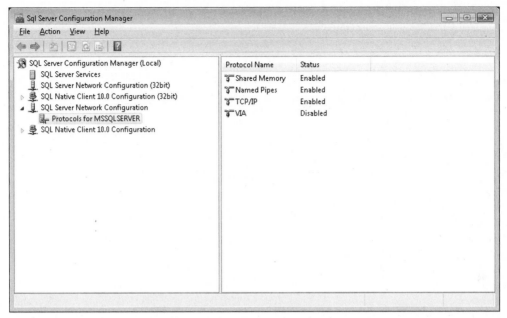

Figure 2-2

> You will need to enable at least one other NetLib if you want to be able to remotely contact your SQL Server (say, from a Web server or from different clients on your network).

Keep in mind that, in order for your client to gain a connection to the server, the server has to be listening for the protocol with which the client is trying to communicate and on the same port. Therefore, if we were in a Named Pipes environment, we might need to add a new library. To do that, we would go back to the Protocols tree, right-click the Named Pipes protocol, and choose Enable (indeed, I've enabled all NetLibs except VIA in Figure 2-2).

At this point, you might be tempted to say, "Hey, why don't I just enable every NetLib? Then I won't have to worry about it." This situation is like anything you add onto your server — more overhead. In this case, it would both slow down your server (not terribly, but every little bit counts) and expose you to unnecessary openings in your security (why leave an extra door open if nobody is supposed to be using that door?).

Okay, now let's take a look at what we can support and why we would want to choose a particular protocol.

Named Pipes

Named Pipes can be very useful in situations where either TCP/IP is not available or there is no Domain Name Service (DNS) server to allow the naming of servers under TCP/IP. Use of Named Pipes is decreasing, and, to make a long story short, I like it that way. The short rendition of why is that you're going to have TCP/IP active anyway, so why add another protocol to the mix (especially since it opens another way that hackers could potentially infiltrate your system).

> Technically speaking, you can connect to a SQL Server running TCP/IP by using its IP address in the place of the name. This will work all the time as long as you have a route from the client to the server — even if there is no DNS service (if it has the IP address, then it doesn't need the name).

TCP/IP

TCP/IP has become something of the de facto standard networking protocol. It is also the only option if you want to connect directly to your SQL Server via the Internet (which, of course, uses IP only).

Don't confuse the need to have your database server available to a Web server with the need to have your database server directly accessible to the Internet. You can have a Web server that is exposed to the Internet but that also has access to a database server that is not directly exposed to the Internet (the only way for an Internet connection to see the data server is through the Web server).

Connecting your data server directly to the Internet is a security hazard in a big way. If you insist on doing it (and there can be valid reasons for doing so), then pay particular attention to security precautions.

Shared Memory

Shared Memory removes the need for interprocess marshaling (which is a way of packaging information before transferring it across process boundaries) between the client and the server if they are running on the same box. The client has direct access to the same memory-mapped file where the server is storing data. This removes a substantial amount of overhead and is *very* fast. It is useful only when accessing the server locally (say, from a Web server installed on the same server as the database), but it can be quite a boon performance-wise.

VIA

VIA stands for *Virtual Interface Adapter*, and the specific implementation will vary from vendor to vendor. In general, it is usually a network kind of interface but is usually a very high-performance, dedicated connection between two systems. Part of that high performance comes from specialized, dedicated hardware that knows that it has a dedicated connection and therefore doesn't have to deal with normal network addressing issues.

On to the Client

Once we know what our server is offering, we can go and configure the client. Most of the time, the defaults are going to work just fine. In the Computer Manager, expand the Client Network Configuration tree and select the Client Protocols node, as shown in Figure 2-3.

Beginning with SQL Server 2000, Microsoft added the ability for the client to start with one protocol, and then, if that didn't work, move on to another. In Figure 2-3, we are first using Shared Memory, then trying TCP/IP, and finally going to Named Pipes if TCP/IP doesn't work as defined by the "Order" column. Unless you change the default (changing the priority by using the up and down arrows), Shared Memory is the NetLib that will be used first for connections to any server not listed in the Aliases list (the next node under Client Network Configuration), followed by TCP/IP, and so on.

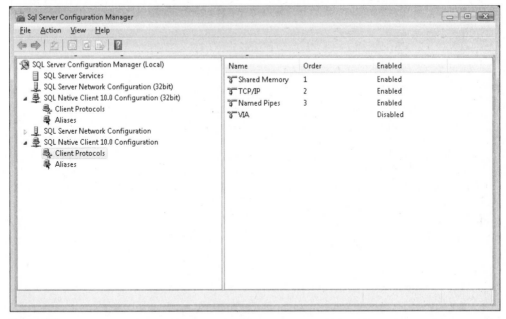

Figure 2-3

Note that your dialog may look slightly different than Figure 2-3 if you are running a 32-bit installation instead of the 64-bit I have pictured. In 64-bit environments, you can configure 64-bit separately from 32-bit to adjust to the different types of applications.

> **If you have TCP/IP support on your network, leave your server configured to use it. IP has less overhead and just plain runs faster — there is no reason not to use it unless your network doesn't support it. It's worth noting, however, that for local servers (where the server is on the same physical system as the client), the Shared Memory NetLib will be quicker, as you do not need to go across the network to view your local SQL server.**

The Aliases list is a listing of all the servers where you have defined a specific NetLib to be used when contacting that particular server. This means that you can contact one server using IP and another using Named Pipes — whatever you need to get to that particular server. In this case, shown in Figure 2-4, we've configured our client to use the Named Pipes NetLib for requests from the server named HOBBES, and to use whatever we've set up as our default for contact with any other SQL Server.

Again, remember that the Client Network Configuration setting on the network machine must either have a default protocol that matches one supported by the server or have an entry in the Aliases list to specifically choose a NetLib supported by that server.

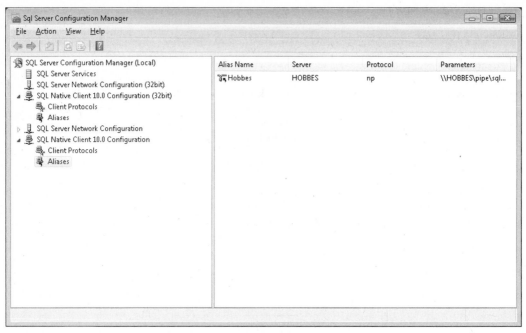

Figure 2-4

The SQL Server Management Studio

The *SQL Server Management Studio* is pretty much home base when administering a SQL Server. It provides a variety of functionality for managing your server using a relatively easy-to-use graphical user interface. Management Studio was first introduced in SQL Server 2005 and has received only minor changes in SQL Server 2008. Patterned loosely after the Developer Studio IDE environment, it combines a myriad of functionality that used to be in separate tools.

For the purposes of this book, we're not going to cover everything that the Management Studio has to offer, but let's make a quick rundown of the things you can do:

❑   Create, edit, and delete databases and database objects

❑   Manage scheduled tasks such as backups and the execution of SSIS package runs

❑   Display current activity, such as who is logged on, what objects are locked, which client they are running, and even more advanced performance information

❑   Manage security, including such items as roles, logins, and remote and linked servers

❑   Initiate and manage the Database Mail Service

❑   Manage configuration settings for the server

❑   Create and manage both publishing and subscribing databases for replication

We will be seeing a great deal of Management Studio throughout this book, so let's take a closer look at some of its key functions.

Getting Started

When you first start Management Studio, you'll receive a connection dialog that will ask for basic connection information (which SQL Server service, server name, authentication type, and depending on the authentication type, maybe a username and password).

Again, since we're assuming that you have prior knowledge of SQL Server (if you don't, you may want to check out the *Beginning SQL Server 2008 Programming* book first), we're not going to dwell much on basic connections. That said, there are a couple that are handled a bit differently than they were in older versions of SQL Server (2000 or older), so let's look at those in depth.

Server Type

This relates to which of the various sub-systems of SQL Server you are logging in to (the normal database server, Analysis Services, Report Server, or Integration Services). Since these different types of "servers" can share the same name, pay attention to this to make sure you're logging in to what you think you're logging in to.

SQL Server

As you might guess, this is the SQL Server into which you're asking to be logged.

> **SQL Server allows multiple "instances" of SQL Server to run at one time. These are just separate loads into memory of the SQL Server engine running independently from each other.**

Note that the default instance of your server will have the same name as your machine on the network. There are ways to change the server name after the time of installation, but they are problematic at best, and deadly to your server at worst. Additional instances of SQL Server will be named the same as the default (KIERKEGAARD or HOBBES in many of the examples in this book), followed by a dollar sign, then the instance name — for example, ARISTOTLE$POMPEII.

If you select local — you can also use a single period to mean the same thing — then your system will connect to the SQL Server on the same computer as you are trying to connect from and will use the Shared Memory NetLib regardless of what NetLib you have selected for contacting other servers. This is a bad news/good news story. The bad news is that you give up a little bit of control (SQL Server will always use Shared Memory to connect — you can't choose anything else). The good news is that you don't have to remember what server you're on, and you get a high-performance option for work on the same machine. If you use your local PC's actual server name, then your communications will still go through the network stack and incur the overhead associated with that just as if you were communicating with another system, regardless of the fact that it is on the same machine (which can be good if you're trying to accurately simulate a remote system).

Authentication Type

You can choose between *Windows Authentication* (formerly NT authentication) and Mixed Authentication. No matter how you configure your server, Windows Authentication will always be available. Logins using usernames and passwords that are local to SQL Server (not part of a larger Windows network) are acceptable to the system only if you have specifically turned Mixed Authentication on.

Windows Authentication

Windows Authentication is just as it sounds. You have users and groups defined in Windows 2000 or later. Those Windows users are mapped into SQL Server "Logins" in their Windows user profile. When they attempt to log in to SQL Server, they are validated through the Windows domain and mapped to "roles" according to the Login. These roles identify what the user is allowed to do.

The best part of this model is that you have only one password (if you change it in the Windows domain, then it's changed for your SQL Server logins, too); you pretty much don't have to fill in anything to log in (it just takes the login information from how you're currently logged in to the Windows network). Additionally, the administrator has to administer users in only one place. The downside is that mapping out this process can get complex and, to administer the Windows user side of things, it requires that you be a domain administrator.

Mixed Authentication

The security does not care at all about what the user's rights to the network are, but rather what you have explicitly set up in SQL Server. The authentication process does not take into account the current network login at all — instead, the user provides a SQL Server–specific login and password.

This can be nice, since the administrator for a given SQL Server does not need to be a domain administrator (or even have a username on your network for that matter) in order to give rights to users on the SQL Server. The process also tends to be somewhat simpler than it is under Windows Authentication. Finally, it means that one user can have multiple logins that give different rights to different things.

Query Editor

This part of the Management Studio has some minor changes for SQL Server 2008 and takes the place of a separate tool in SQL Server 2005 and earlier that was called *Query Analyzer*. It is your tool for interactive sessions with a given SQL Server. It is where you can execute statements using *Transact-SQL* (*T-SQL* — I lovingly pronounce it "Tee-Squeal," but it's supposed to be "Tee-Sequel"). T-SQL is the native language of SQL Server. It is a dialect of Structured Query Language (SQL).

Over the last few years, I've gotten more used to this tool replacing Query Analyzer, but also find it to be somewhat cluttered due to the number of things you do with the one tool. That said, for those without the expectations of the past, Microsoft hopes it will actually prove to be more intuitive for you to use it within the larger Management Studio, too.

Since the Query Editor window is where we will spend a fair amount of time in this book, let's take a quick look at this tool and get familiar with how to use it. If you're familiar with SQL Server 2005, you may want to skip ahead to sections on the new SQLCMD mode.

> **The Query Editor window continues to have the character length limitation in results that existed under Query Analyzer. By default, Query Editor Window will return a maximum of 256 characters for any one column under text, results to file, or SQLCMD mode. You can change this in the Tools➤Options➤Query Results➤SQL Server settings to a maximum of 8092, but any longer than that, and your data (say from blob columns) will always be truncated.**

Getting Started

Open a new Query Editor window by clicking the New Query button toward the top left of Management Studio or choosing File≻New≻New Query With Current Connection from the File menu. When the Query Editor Window is up, we'll get menus that largely match what we had in Query Analyzer back when that was a separate tool. We'll look at the specifics, but let's get our simple query out of the way.

Let's start with:

```
SELECT * FROM INFORMATION_SCHEMA.TABLES;
```

Much as was true in SQL Server 2000's Query Analyzer, statement keywords should appear in blue; unidentifiable items, such as column and table names (these vary with every table in every database on every server), are in black; and statement arguments and connectors are in red. You'll find most icons along the toolbar to be pretty similar. For example, the check mark icon on the toolbar quickly parses the query for you without the need to actually attempt to run the statement — just as it did in Query Analyzer.

Now click the Execute button in the toolbar (with the red exclamation point next to it). The Query Editor Window changes a bit, as shown in Figure 2-5.

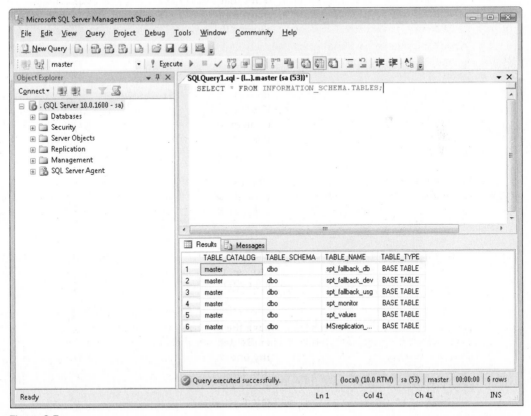

Figure 2-5

Figure 2-6

Just as it was in the old Query Analyzer, the main window is divided into two panes. The top is your original query text; the bottom contains the results.

Now, let's change a setting or two and see how what we get varies. Take a look at the toolbar above the Query Editor Window, and check out the set of three icons, shown in Figure 2-6.

These control the way you receive output. In order, they are Results to Text, Results to Grid, and Results to File. The same choices can also be made from the Query menu under the Results To sub-menu.

Results in Text

The Results in Text option takes all the output from your query and puts it into one page of text results. The page can be of virtually infinite length (limited by the available memory in your system).

I use this output method in several different scenarios:

❑ When I'm getting only one result set and the results have only fairly narrow columns

❑ When I want to be able to easily save my results in a single text file

❑ When I'm going to have multiple result sets, but the results are expected to be small, and I want to be able to see more than one result set on the same page without dealing with multiple scroll bars

Note that this and the Results to File option are areas where the Query Editor window may, as I mentioned earlier in the chapter, wind up truncating longer character columns. By default, it will truncate character data that is longer than 256 characters. You can change your settings to increase this to as high as 8192 characters, but that is the maximum you can show other than in the grid mode.

Results in Grid

This one divides up the columns and rows into a grid arrangement. Specific things that this option gives us that the Results in Text doesn't include:

❑ You can resize the column by hovering your mouse pointer on the right border of the column header and then clicking and dragging the column border to its new size. Double-clicking the right border will result in the auto-fit for the column.

❑ If you select several cells, and then cut and paste them into another grid (say, Microsoft Excel or the Calc application if you use Open Office), they will be treated as individual cells (under the Results in Text option, the cut data would have been pasted all into one cell).

❑ You can select just one or two columns of multiple rows (under Results in Text, if you select several rows all of the inner rows have every column selected — you can only select in the middle of the row for the first and last row selected).

I use this option for almost everything, since I find that I usually want one of the benefits I just listed.

Results to File

Think of this one as largely the same as Results to Text, but instead of to screen, it routes the output directly to a file. I use this one to generate files I intend to parse using some utility or that I want to easily e-mail.

SQLCMD Mode

SQLCMD mode is new with SQL Server 2008, and changes the behavior of the Query Editor Window to more closely match that of the SQLCMD utility. The idea is to allow you to run batch files, queries, and scripts designed for command-line use through the interactive window for debugging or other purposes. By default, the Query Editor Window does not honor SQLCMD-specific commands; using SQLCMD mode activates these commands.

Show Execution Plan

Every time you run a query, SQL Server parses your query into its component parts and then sends it to the *Query Optimizer*. The Query Optimizer is the part of SQL Server that figures out what is the best way to run your query to balance fast results with minimum impact on other users. When you use the Show Estimated Execution Plan option, you receive a graphical representation and additional information on how SQL Server plans to run your query. Similarly, you can turn on the Include Actual Execution Plan option. Most of the time, this will be the same as the estimated execution plan, but it's possible you'll see differences here for changes that the optimizer decided to make while it was running the query and for changes in the actual cost of running the query versus what the optimizer *thought* was going to happen.

Let's see what a query plan looked like in our simple query. Click the Include Actual Execution Plan option, and re-execute the query, as shown in Figure 2-7.

Note that you actually have to click the Execution Plan tab for it to come up, and that your query results are still displayed in whichever way you had selected. The Show Estimated Execution Plan option will give you the same output as an Include Actual Execution Plan with two exceptions:

❑ You get the plan immediately rather than after your query executes.

❑ While what you see is the actual "plan" for the query, all the cost information is estimated, and the query is not actually run. Under Show Query Plan, the query was physically executed, and the cost information you get is actual rather than estimated.

The DB Combo Box

Finally, let's take a look at the *DB combo box*. In short, this is where you select the default database that you want your queries to run against for the current window. Initially, the Query Editor Window will start with whatever the default database is for the user that's logged in (for the sa user, that is the master database unless someone has changed it on your system). You can then change it to any other database that the current login has permission to access.

The Object Explorer

This useful little tool allows us to navigate the database, look up object names, and even perform actions such as scripting and looking at the underlying data.

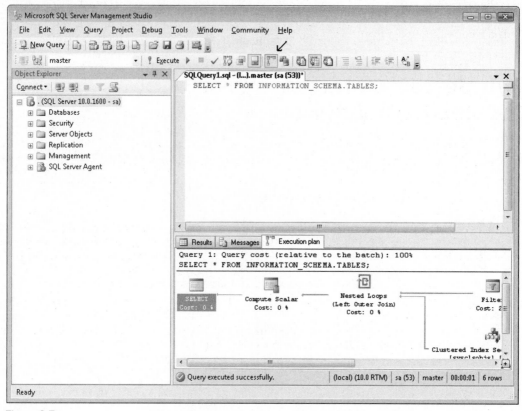

Figure 2-7

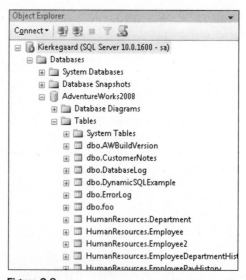

Figure 2-8

In the example in Figure 2-8, I've expanded the database node all the way down to the listing of tables in the AdventureWorks2008 database. You can drill down even further to see individual columns (including data type and similar properties) of the tables — a very handy tool for browsing your database.

SQL Server Business Intelligence Development Studio

The SQL Server Business Intelligence Development Studio — sometimes referred to simply as BIDS — is just an incredibly long-winded name for what amounts to a special version of Visual Studio. Indeed, what this tool looks like when it comes up will vary depending on whether you have Visual Studio 2008 installed on your system or not. If you do, it will mix an array of Visual Studio menus in with your SQL Server Analysis Services and Integration Services related menus and templates.

Business Intelligence Development Studio was new back in SQL Server 2005, replacing the Analysis and Integration Services tools that were there in SQL Server 2000. What exists now is far more of a true development environment than the relatively narrow cube builder or DTS designer that we had in SQL Server 2000.

From Business Intelligence Development Studio, we can design Integration Services packages (we'll touch on these next), design reports for Reporting Services, and, of course, work directly with Analysis Services projects. We will be looking at the various services that Business Intelligence Development Studio supports in separate chapters later in this book.

SQL Server Integration Services (SSIS)

Your friend and mine — that's what *SSIS* (formerly known as Data Transformation Services — or DTS) is. With SSIS, a tremendous amount of the coding (usually in some client-side language) that had to be done to perform complex data extracts or imports becomes relatively easy. SSIS allows you to take data from any data source that has an OLE DB or .NET data provider and pump it into a SQL Server table or other data destination.

While transferring our data, we can also apply what are referred to as *transformations* to that data. Transformations essentially alter the data according to some logical rule(s). The alteration can be as simple as changing a column name, or as complex as an analysis of the integrity of the data and application of rules to change it if necessary. To think about how this is applied, consider the problem of taking data from a field that allows nulls and moving it to a table that does not allow nulls. With SSIS, you can automatically change out any null values to some other value you choose during the transfer process (for a number, that might be zero, or, for a character, it might be something like "unknown"). We will explore SSIS in Chapter 16.

Reporting Services

Reporting Services was first introduced as a Web release after SQL Server 2000 and became part of the core product with SQL Server 2005. It has again received a major makeover in SQL Server 2008, adding new scalability features and several new design elements. Reporting Services provides both a framework and an engine for generating reports. For SQL Server 2005 and earlier, it works in conjunction with the built-in Windows Web server to produce reports in a Web environment. With SQL Server 2008, Reporting Services includes its own Web server, so it can avoid the need to configure a full Internet Information Services (IIS) installation.

The reports are defined using an XML-based definition language called Report Definition Language (or RDL). The Business Intelligence Development Studio provides a set of templates for generating both simple and complex reports. The reports are written to an RDL file, which is processed on demand by the Reporting Services engine. We will look more fully into Reporting Services in Chapter 14.

Bulk Copy Program (bcp)

If SSIS is, as I've often called it, "your friend and mine," then the Bulk Copy Program, or bcp, would be that old friend that we may not see that much any more, but we really appreciate when we do see them.

Bcp is a command-line program, and its sole purpose in life is to move formatted data in and out of SQL Server en masse. It was around long before what has now become SSIS was thought of, and while SSIS is replacing bcp for most import/export activity, bcp still has a certain appeal to people who like command-line utilities. In addition, you'll find an awful lot of SQL Server installations out there that still depend on bcp to move data around fast. We discuss bcp fully in Chapter 15.

SQL Server Profiler

I can't tell you how many times this one has saved my bacon by telling me what was going on with my server when nothing else would. It's not something a developer (or even a DBA for that matter) will tend to use every day, but it's extremely powerful and can be your salvation when you're sure nothing can save you.

SQL Server Profiler is, in short, a real-time tracing tool. Whereas the Performance Monitor is all about tracking what's happening at the macro level — system configuration stuff — the Profiler is concerned with tracking specifics. This is both a blessing and a curse. The Profiler can, depending on how you configure your trace, give you the specific syntax of every statement executed on your server. Now, imagine that you are doing performance tuning on a system with 1,000 users. I'm sure you can imagine the reams of paper that would be used to print out the statements executed by so many people in just a minute or two. Fortunately, the Profiler has a vast array of filters to help you narrow things down and track more specific problems — for example: long-running queries or the exact syntax of a query being run within a stored procedure (which is nice when your procedure has conditional statements that cause it to run different things under different circumstances). We will touch on SQL Server Profiler somewhat in Chapter 22.

sqlcmd

You won't see *sqlcmd* in your SQL Server program group. Indeed, it's amazing how many people don't even know that this utility (or its older brothers — osql and isql) is around; that's because it's a console rather than a Windows program.

There are occasionally items that you want to script into a larger command-line process. sqlcmd gives you that capability. sqlcmd can be very handy — particularly if you make use of files that contain the scripts you want to run under sqlcmd. Keep in mind, however, that there are usually tools that can do what you're after from sqlcmd much more effectively, and with a user interface that is more consistent with the other things you're doing with your SQL Server.

In addition to command-line operation, sqlcmd supports some special commands that are more inline with other command-line utilities. For example, !!DIR gives a directory listing.

> *Once again, for history and being able to understand if people you talk SQL Server with use a different lingo, sqlcmd is yet another new name for this tool of many names. Originally, it was referred to as isql. In SQL Server 2000 and 7.0, it was known as osql.*

We will explore the basics of sqlcmd together with the Bulk Copy Program (bcp) in Chapter 15.

Summary

Most of the tools that you've been exposed to here are not ones you'll use every day. Indeed, for the average developer, only the SQL Server Management Studio will get daily use. Nevertheless, it is important to have some idea of the role that each one can play. Each has something significant to offer you. We will see each of these tools again in our journey through this book.

Note that there are some other utilities available that don't have shortcuts on your Start menu (connectivity tools, server diagnostics, and maintenance utilities), which are mostly admin-related.

3

Asking a Better Question: Advanced Queries

Before I get rambling along with the topics of this chapter, let me warn those of you that are already pretty familiar with the many features of SQL Server that this is an area of significant change! SQL Server now has support for keywords such as INTERSECT and EXCEPT. There is the ability to merge the results of one statement as part of the action for another statement using the new MERGE command. We also need to take a look at recursive query support. In short, don't change that dial . . . .

The topic of advanced queries requires some tough decisions for me each time I write a book. For example, what exactly is "advanced"? In the past I've debated such things as whether to do advanced queries before or after cursors. This time around I briefly considered that question again, but also found myself asking how much overlap I wanted to have with topics I also cover in my Beginning title. Then there are other questions, such as do I want to have an advanced discussion of indexing first? How about the XML discussion? You see, it's something of a chicken and egg thing (which came first?). You don't need to know anything about cursors to make use of the topics covered in this chapter, but, for example, we'll be discussing some benefits of different query methods that avoid cursors — and it really helps to understand the benefits if you know what you're trying to avoid. There are similar issues when I consider integrating relational vs. XML-based data, or want to discuss how a different query strategy affects the Query Optimizer's indexing choices.

> Several of the topics in this chapter represent, to me, significant marks of the difference between a "beginner" and "professional" when it comes to SQL Server programming. While they are certainly not the only thing that marks when you are a true "pro," developers that can move from "Yeah, I know those exist and use one or two of them" to using them to make unsolvable queries solvable are true gold. I write on some of these subjects for beginners to let them know they are there and give them a taste of what they can do. I write and expand on them for professionals because full understanding of these concepts is critical to high-level success with SQL Server (or almost any major DBMS for that matter).

In this chapter, we're going to be looking at our queries differently than you may have looked at them before. We'll examine ways to ask what amounts to multiple questions in just one query — essentially, looking at ways of taking what seems like multiple queries and placing them into something that will execute as a complete unit. We'll take a look at some relatively new features (some new to 2008, and some that came in 2005) that can give us even more options than we ever had before. With all this in mind, we'll also take a look at query performance, and what we can do to get the most out of our queries. Writing top-notch queries isn't just about trickiness or being able to make them complex — it's making them perform.

Among the topics we'll be covering in this chapter are:

- ❑ A quick review of subqueries
- ❑ Correlated subqueries
- ❑ Derived tables
- ❑ Making use of the EXISTS operator
- ❑ Utilizing INERSECT and EXCEPT operators
- ❑ Common Table Expressions (CTEs)
- ❑ Utilizing recursive queries
- ❑ The MERGE command
- ❑ Using external calls to perform complex actions
- ❑ Optimizing query performance

We'll see how by using subqueries we can make the seemingly impossible completely possible, and how an odd tweak here and there can make a big difference in our query performance.

A Quick Review of Subqueries

A *subquery* is a normal T-SQL query that is nested inside another query — using parentheses — created when you have a SELECT statement that serves as the basis for either part of the data or the condition in another query.

Subqueries are generally used to fill one of several needs:

- ❑ Break a query up into a series of logical steps
- ❑ Provide a listing to be the target of a WHERE clause together with [IN|EXISTS|ANY|ALL]
- ❑ Provide a lookup driven by each individual record in a parent query

Some subqueries are very easy to think of and build, but some are extremely complex — it usually depends on the complexity of the relationship between the inner (the sub) and outer (the top) query.

It's also worth noting that most subqueries (but definitely not all) can also be written using a join. In places where you can use a join instead, the join is usually the preferable choice.

Building a Nested Subquery

A *nested subquery* is one that goes in only *one* direction — returning either a single value for use in the outer query, or perhaps a list of values to be used with the IN operator. In the loosest sense, your query syntax is going to look something like one of these two syntax templates:

```
SELECT <SELECT list>
FROM <SomeTable>
WHERE <SomeColumn> = (
        SELECT <single column>
        FROM <SomeTable>
        WHERE <condition that results in only one row returned>)
```

Or:

```
SELECT <SELECT list>
FROM <SomeTable>
WHERE <SomeColumn> IN (
        SELECT <single column>
        FROM <SomeTable>
        [WHERE <condition>)]
```

Obviously, the exact syntax will vary. Not for just substituting the select list and exact table names, but also because you may have a multi-table join in either the inner or outer queries — or both.

Nested Queries Using Single Value SELECT Statements

Let's get down to the nitty-gritty with a fast example. Let's say, for example, that we wanted to know the ProductIDs of every item sold on the first day any product was purchased from the system. If you already know the first day that an order was placed in the system, then it's no problem; but what if you don't already know? We can easily obtain the date of first sale within a nested subquery, and then utilize it in an outer query all in one statement:

```
USE AdventureWorks2008;

SELECT DISTINCT soh.OrderDate, sod.ProductID
FROM Sales.SalesOrderHeader soh
JOIN Sales.SalesOrderDetail sod
  ON soh.SalesOrderID = sod.SalesOrderID
WHERE soh.OrderDate =
    (SELECT MIN(OrderDate) FROM Sales.SalesOrderHeader);
```

Which gets us 47 rows back:

```
OrderDate               ProductID
----------------------- -----------
2001-07-01 00:00:00.000 707
2001-07-01 00:00:00.000 708
2001-07-01 00:00:00.000 709
...
...
2001-07-01 00:00:00.000 776
```

```
2001-07-01 00:00:00.000 777
2001-07-01 00:00:00.000 778

(47 row(s) affected)
```

It's just that quick and easy. The inner query (SELECT MIN...) retrieves a single value for use in the outer query. Since we're using an equals sign, the inner query absolutely must return only one column from one single row, or we will get a runtime error.

Nested Queries Using Subqueries That Return Multiple Values

Perhaps the most common of all subqueries that are implemented are those that retrieve some form of domain list and use it as a criterion for a query. What we want is a list of all the employees that have applied for another job within the company. We keep our applicants listed in a table called HumanResources.JobCandidate, so what we need is a list of EmployeeIDs (actually referred to as BusinessEntityID in the table) that have a record in the job candidate table. The actual list of all employees is, of course, in our HumanResources.Employee table. We will also have to use our Person.Person table to get things like the employee's name.

We might write something like this:

```
USE AdventureWorks2008;

SELECT e.BusinessEntityID, FirstName, LastName
FROM HumanResources.Employee e
JOIN Person.Person pp
  ON e.BusinessEntityID = pp.BusinessEntityID
WHERE e.BusinessEntityID IN
  (SELECT DISTINCT BusinessEntityID FROM HumanResources.JobCandidate);
```

This gets us back just two rows:

```
BusinessEntityID FirstName              LastName
---------------------------------------- ---------------------------
212              Peng                    Wu
274              Stephen                 Jiang

(2 row(s) affected)
```

Queries of this type almost always fall into the category of one that can be done using an inner join rather than a nested SELECT. For example, we could get the same results as the preceding subquery by running this simple join:

```
USE AdventureWorks2008;

SELECT e.BusinessEntityID, FirstName, LastName
FROM HumanResources.Employee e
JOIN Person.Person pp
  ON e.BusinessEntityID = pp.BusinessEntityID
```

```
JOIN HumanResources.JobCandidate jc
  ON e.BusinessEntityID = jc.BusinessEntityID;
```

For performance reasons, you want to use the join method as your default solution if you don't have a specific reason for using the nested SELECT — we'll discuss this more before the chapter is done.

Using a Nested SELECT to Find Orphaned Records

This type of nested SELECT is nearly identical to the previous example, except that we add the NOT operator. The difference this makes when you are converting to join syntax is that you are equating to an outer join rather than an inner join.

This is for the scenario where you want to see what's left out. In many cases, this might be something like order details that don't have a parent record in the header table (this can't happen in the AdventureWorks2008 database thanks to your foreign key constraint, but there are databases out there where this kind of thing happens). For our example, we'll change the scenario around to ask which employees have *not* applied for a different job in the company. See that "not" in there and you know just what to do — add the NOT to our query (but beware a special case issue here that we have to deal with):

```
USE AdventureWorks2008

SELECT e.BusinessEntityID, FirstName, LastName
FROM HumanResources.Employee e
JOIN Person.Person pp
  ON e.BusinessEntityID = pp.BusinessEntityID

WHERE e.BusinessEntityID NOT IN
  (SELECT DISTINCT BusinessEntityID
   FROM HumanResources.JobCandidate
   WHERE BusinessEntityID IS NOT NULL);
```

Run this, and, of course, you get a large result set (every employee but the two we saw in the previous example).

> As always, beware tests against sets that might contain a NULL value. Comparisons against NULL always result in NULL. In the preceding case, the JobCandidate table has rows where the BusinessEntityID is null. If I had allowed NULL to come back in my subquery, then every row in the outer query would have evaluated false when compared to NOT IN — I would get an empty list back (I recommend experimenting with it to make sure you understand the distinction).

The ANY, SOME, and ALL Operators

OK, so in every book I've written until now, I've always spent a page covering these. I guess I could do it again and pad the number of pages I have written, but each time I read it, I get more annoyed by it, so I've decided to be more succinct.

In addition to the IN operator, SQL Server also supports the ANY, SOME, and ALL operators. In short, they are *junk*. As near as I can tell, their primary purpose is to suck up a page of text in a book and waste perhaps 10 minutes you could have spent learning something useful. The functionality of each can be replicated by using more common operators (such as >=, <=, <>, !>, and so on) in the proper way, and will, in literally every example I've ever seen, come out more readable that way.

In short, know these are there, but don't waste your time on them beyond that. They offer nothing new.

Correlated Subqueries

Two words for you on this section: Pay attention! This is another one of those little areas that, if you truly "get it," can really set you apart from the crowd. By "get it" I don't just mean that you understand how it works but also that you understand how important it can be.

Correlated subqueries are one of those things that make the impossible possible. What's more, they often turn several lines of code into one, and often create a corresponding increase in performance. The problem with them is that they require a substantially different style of thought than you're probably used to. Correlated subqueries are probably the single easiest concept in SQL to learn, understand, and then promptly forget because it simply goes against the grain of how you think. If you're one of the few who choose to remember it as an option, then you will be one of the few who figure out that hard to figure out problem. You'll also be someone with a far more complete toolset when it comes to squeezing every ounce of performance out of your queries.

How Correlated Subqueries Work

What makes correlated subqueries different from the nested subqueries we've been looking at is that the information travels in *two* directions rather than one. In a nested subquery, the inner query is only processed once, and that information is passed out for the outer query, which will also execute just once — essentially providing the same value or list that you would have provided if you had typed it in yourself.

With correlated subqueries, however, the inner query runs on information provided by the outer query, and vice versa. That may seem a bit confusing (that chicken or the egg thing again), but it works in a three-step process:

1. The outer query obtains a record and passes it into the inner query.
2. The inner query executes based on the passed in value(s).
3. The inner query then passes the values from its results back out to the outer query, which uses them to finish its processing.

Correlated Subqueries in the WHERE Clause

I realize that this is probably a bit confusing, so take a look at it in an example.

Let's look again at the query where we wanted to know what orders happened on the first date that an order was placed in the system. However, this time we want to add a new twist: We want to know the OrderID(s) and OrderDate of the first order in the system for each customer. That is, we want to know the first day that a customer placed an order and the IDs of those orders. Let's look at it piece by piece.

First, we want the `OrderDate`, `OrderID`, and `CustomerID` for each of our results. All of that information can be found in the `SalesOrderHeader` table, so we know that our query is going to be based, at least in part, on that table.

Next, we need to know what the first date in the system was for each customer. That's where the tricky part comes in. When we did this with a nested subquery, we were looking only for the first date in the entire file — now we need a value that's by individual customer. This wouldn't be that big a deal if we were to do it in two separate queries — we could just create a temporary table, and then join back to it, but building two completely separate result sets, more often than not, has a negative impact on performance.

Sometimes using this two-query approach is simply the only way to get things done without using a cursor — this is not one of those times.

Okay, so if we want this to run in a single query, we need to find a way to look up each individual. We can do this by making use of an inner query that performs a lookup based on the current `CustomerID` in the outer query. We will then need to return a value back out to the outer query, so it can match things up based on the earliest order date.

It looks like this:

```
SELECT o1.CustomerID, o1.SalesOrderID, o1.OrderDate
FROM Sales.SalesOrderHeader o1
WHERE o1.OrderDate = (SELECT MIN(o2.OrderDate)
                      FROM Sales.SalesOrderHeader o2
                      WHERE o2.CustomerID = o1.CustomerID)
ORDER BY CustomerID;
```

With this, we get back the 19,134 rows. There are a few key things to notice in this query:

❑   We see only one row(s) affected line — giving us a good clue that only one query plan had to be executed (with separate queries, there would have been two).

❑   The outer query (in this example) looks pretty much just like a nested subquery. The inner query, however, has an explicit reference to the outer query (notice the use of the "o1" alias).

❑   Aliases are used in both queries — even though it looks like the outer query shouldn't need one — that's because they are required whenever you explicitly refer to a column from the other query (inside refers to a column on the outside or vice versa).

> The latter point of needing aliases is a big area of confusion. The fact is that sometimes you need them, and sometimes you don't. While I don't tend to use them at all in the types of nested subqueries that you looked at in the early part of this chapter, I alias everything when dealing with correlated subqueries.

> The hard-and-fast "rule" is that you must alias any table (and its related columns) that's going to be referred to by the other query. The problem is that this can quickly become very confusing. The way to be on the safe side is to alias everything — that way you're positive of which table in which query you're getting your information from.

We see that `19134 row(s) affected` only once. That's because it affected 19,134 rows only one time. Just by observation, we can guess that this version probably runs faster than the two-query version, and, in reality, it does. Again, we'll look into this a bit more shortly.

In this particular query, the outer query references the inner query only in the `WHERE` clause — it could also have requested data from the inner query to include in the select list.

Normally, it's up to us whether we want to make use of an alias or not, but, with correlated subqueries, they are usually required. This particular query is a really great one for showing why because the inner and outer queries are based on the same table. Since both queries are getting information from each other, without aliasing, how would they know which instance of the table data that you were interested in?

Correlated Subqueries in the SELECT List

Subqueries can also be used to provide a different kind of answer in your selection results. This kind of situation is often found where the information you're after is fundamentally different from the rest of the data in your query (for example, you want an aggregation on one field, but you don't want all the baggage from that to affect the other fields returned).

To test this, let's just run a somewhat modified version of the query we used in the last section. What we're going to say we're after here is just the name of the customer and the first date on which they ordered something.

This one creates a somewhat more significant change than is probably apparent at first. We're now asking for the customer's name, which means that we have to bring the `Customer` and `Person` tables into play. In addition, we no longer need to build any kind of condition in — we're asking for all customers (no restrictions), we just want to know when their first order date was.

The query actually winds up being a bit simpler than the last one, and it looks like this:

```
SELECT pp.FirstName, pp.LastName,
    (SELECT MIN(OrderDate)
         FROM Sales.SalesOrderHeader o
         WHERE o.CustomerID = c.CustomerID)
         AS "Order Date"
FROM Person.Person pp
JOIN Sales.Customer c
  ON pp.BusinessEntityID = c.PersonID;
```

This gets us data that looks something like this:

```
FirstName            LastName                 Order Date
-------------------  -----------------------  -----------------------
Catherine            Abel                     2003-09-01 00:00:00.000
Kim                  Abercrombie              2001-09-01 00:00:00.000
Humberto             Acevedo                  2001-09-01 00:00:00.000

...
...
...
Krystal              Zimmerman                2004-01-29 00:00:00.000
```

```
Tiffany          Zimmerman          2003-01-26 00:00:00.000
Jake             Zukowski           2001-09-02 00:00:00.000

(19119 row(s) affected)
```

Notice that the dates vary by customer — the Order Date provided is the first date that particular customer has ordered.

Derived Tables

Sometimes you need to work with the results of a query, but you need to work with the results of that query in a way that doesn't really lend itself to the kinds of subqueries that I've discussed up to this point. An example is where, for each row in a given table, you may have multiple results in the subquery, but you're looking for a more complex action than your IN operator provides. Essentially, what I'm talking about here are situations where you wish you could use a JOIN operator on your subquery.

It's at times like these that you turn to a somewhat lesser known construct in SQL — a *derived table*. A derived table (sometimes called in "inline view") is made up of the columns and rows of a result set from a query (heck, they have columns, rows, data types, and so on, just like normal tables, so why not use them as such?).

Imagine for a moment that you want to get a list of customers that ordered a particular product — say, a minipump. No problem! Your query might look something like this:

```
SELECT pp.FirstName, pp.LastName
  FROM Person.Person AS pp
  JOIN Sales.Customer sc
    ON sc.PersonID = pp.BusinessEntityID
  JOIN Sales.SalesOrderHeader AS soh
    ON sc.CustomerID = soh.CustomerID
  JOIN Sales.SalesOrderDetail AS sod
    ON soh.SalesOrderID = sod.SalesOrderID
  JOIN Production.Product AS p
    ON sod.ProductID = p.ProductID
  WHERE p.Name = 'Minipump'
```

Okay, so that was easy. Now I'm going to throw you a twist — now say I want to know all the customers that ordered not only a minipump, but also the AWC Logo Cap. Notice that I said they have to have ordered both — now you have a problem. Your first inclination might be to write something like:

```
WHERE p.Name = 'Minipump' AND p.Name = 'AWC Logo Cap'
```

But that's not going to work at all — each row is for a single product, so how can it have both minipump and AWC Logo Cap as the name at the same time? Nope — that's not going to get it at all (indeed, while it will run, you'll never get any rows back at all).

What we really need here is to join the results of a query to find buyers of minipumps with the results of a query to find buyers of AWC Logo Caps. How do we join results though? Well, as you might expect given the title of this section, through the use of derived tables.

To create our derived table, we need two things:

- ❏ To enclose our query that generates the result set in parentheses
- ❏ To alias the results of the query

So, the syntax looks something like this:

```
SELECT <select list>
FROM (<query that returns a regular result set>) AS <alias name>
JOIN <some other base or derived table>
```

So let's take this now and apply it to our requirements. Again, what we want is the names of all the persons that have ordered both a minipump and AWC Logo Cap. So, our query should look something like this:

```
SELECT DISTINCT pp.FirstName, pp.LastName
    FROM Person.Person AS pp
    JOIN (SELECT sc.PersonID
        FROM Sales.Customer sc
        JOIN Sales.SalesOrderHeader AS soh
          ON sc.CustomerID = soh.CustomerID
        JOIN Sales.SalesOrderDetail AS sod
          ON soh.SalesOrderID = sod.SalesOrderID
        JOIN Production.Product AS p
          ON sod.ProductID = p.ProductID
        WHERE p.Name = 'Minipump') pumps
      ON pp.BusinessEntityID = pumps.PersonID
    JOIN (SELECT sc.PersonID
        FROM Sales.Customer sc
        JOIN Sales.SalesOrderHeader AS soh
          ON sc.CustomerID = soh.CustomerID
        JOIN Sales.SalesOrderDetail AS sod
          ON soh.SalesOrderID = sod.SalesOrderID
        JOIN Production.Product AS p
          ON sod.ProductID = p.ProductID
        WHERE p.Name = 'AWC Logo Cap') caps
      ON pp.BusinessEntityID = caps.PersonID;
```

As it happens, it seems that the combination of minipumps and caps is very popular — we get 83 rows:

```
FirstName                                         LastName
------------------------------------------------- ----------------------------
Aidan                                             Delaney
Alexander                                         Deborde
Amy                                               Alberts
. . .
. . .
. . .
Valerie                                           Hendricks
Yale                                              Li
Yuping                                            Tian

(83 row(s) affected)
```

If you want to check things out on this, just run the queries for the two derived tables separately and compare the results.

For this particular query, I needed to use the DISTINCT *keyword. If I didn't, then I would have potentially received multiple rows for each customer.*

As you can see, we were able to take a seemingly impossible query and make it both possible and even reasonably well performing.

Keep in mind that derived tables aren't the solutions for everything. For example, if the result set is going to be fairly large and you're going to have lots of joined records, then you may want to look at using a temporary table and building an index on it (derived tables have no indexes). Every situation is different, but now you have one more tool in your arsenal.

The EXISTS Operator

I call EXISTS an operator, but Books Online calls it a keyword. That's probably because it defies description in some senses. It's both an operator much like the IN keyword is, but it also looks at things just a bit differently.

When you use EXISTS, you don't really return data — instead, you return a simple TRUE/FALSE regarding the existence of data that meets the criteria established in the query that the EXISTS statement is operating against.

Let's go right to an example, so you can see how this gets applied. For this example, we're going to reuse one of our nested selects examples from earlier — we want a list of employees that have applied for another position within the company at some point:

```
SELECT e.BusinessEntityID, FirstName, LastName
FROM HumanResources.Employee e
JOIN Person.Person pp
  ON e.BusinessEntityID = pp.BusinessEntityID
```

```
WHERE EXISTS
  (SELECT BusinessEntityID
   FROM HumanResources.JobCandidate jc
   WHERE e.BusinessEntityID = jc.BusinessEntityID);
```

This gets us what amounts to the same two records that we had under the more standard nested query:

```
EmployeeID  FirstName                                  LastName
----------- ------------------------------------------ --------------------
212         Peng                                       Wu
274         Stephen                                    Jiang

(2 row(s) affected)
```

As we saw when we examined the nested query version, we could have easily done this same thing with a join:

```
SELECT e.BusinessEntityID, FirstName, LastName
FROM HumanResources.Employee e
```

```
JOIN Person.Person pp
  ON e.BusinessEntityID = pp.BusinessEntityID
JOIN HumanResources.JobCandidate jc
  ON e.BusinessEntityID = jc.BusinessEntityID;
```

This join-based syntax, for example, would have yielded exactly the same results (subject to possible sort differences). So why, then, would we need this new syntax? Performance — plain and simple.

When you use the EXISTS keyword, SQL Server doesn't have to perform a full row-by-row join. Instead, it can look through the records until it finds the first match and stop right there. As soon as there is a single match, the EXISTS is true, so there is no need to go further. The performance difference here is even more marked than it is with the inner join. SQL Server just applies a little reverse logic versus the straight EXISTS statement. In the case of the NOT we're now using, SQL can still stop looking as soon as it finds one matching record — the only difference is that it knows to return FALSE for that lookup rather than TRUE. Performance wise, everything else about the query is the same.

Using EXISTS in Other Ways

If you work around SQL creation scripts much, you will see an oddity preceding many CREATE statements. It will look something like this:

```
IF EXISTS (SELECT * FROM sysobjects WHERE id =
object_id(N'[Sales].[SalesOrderHeader]') AND OBJECTPROPERTY(id, N'IsUserTable') = 1)
DROP TABLE [Sales].[ SalesOrderHeader]
GO

CREATE TABLE [Sales].[ SalesOrderHeader] (
  ...
  ...
```

You may see variants on the theme — that is, they may use sys.objects, sys.databases, or the INFORMATION_SCHEMA views — but the concept is still the same: They are testing to see whether an object exists before performing a CREATE. Sometimes they may just skip the CREATE if the table already exists, and sometimes they may drop it (as I did in the preceding example). The idea is pretty simple though — they want to skip a potential error condition (the CREATE would error out and blow up your script if the table already existed).

Just as a simple example, we'll build a little script to create a database object. We'll also keep the statement to a minimum since we're interested in the EXISTS rather than the CREATE command:

```
USE master

GO

IF NOT EXISTS (SELECT 'True' FROM sys.databases WHERE name = 'DBCreateTest')
BEGIN
    CREATE DATABASE DBCreateTest
END
ELSE
BEGIN
    PRINT 'Database already exists. Skipping CREATE DATABASE Statement'
```

```
END
GO
```

The first time you run this, there won't be any database called DBCreateTest (unless by sheer coincidence that you created something called that before you got to this point), so the database will be created.

Now run the script a second time, and you'll see a change:

```
Database already exists. Skipping CREATE DATABASE Statement
```

So, without much fanfare or fuss, we've added a rather small script in that will make things much more usable for the installers of your product. That may be an end user who bought your off-the-shelf product, or it may be you — in which case it's even better that it's fully scripted.

The long and the short of it is that EXISTS is a very handy keyword indeed. It can make some queries run much faster, and it can also simplify some queries and scripts.

A word of caution here — this is another one of those places where it's easy to get trapped in "traditional thinking." While EXISTS blows other options away in a large percentage of queries where EXISTS is a valid construct, that's not always the case — just remember that rules are sometimes made to be broken.

The INTERSECT and EXCEPT Operators

INTERSECT and EXCEPT are special keywords that operate against two result sets much as UNION does. They are relatively new to SQL Server, but have been around in other RDBMS packages for many years.

So, what do they do? Well, INTERSECT and EXCEPT give us additional options in what to show when looking at the combination of separate result sets. Figure 3-1 shows what data is included depending on which result set combination operator you utilize. To summarize, it works something like this:

❏   **UNION** — Rows are included from both result sets, but duplicates are eliminated (just one instance of any overlapping rows).

❏   **UNION ALL** — *All* rows are included from both result sets, regardless of whether they are duplicate or not.

❏   **EXCEPT** — Only those rows that are on the left side of the EXCEPT keyword and do not exist in the right-hand result set are included. Basically, this says "show me any rows that exist in A, but do *not* exist in B."

❏   **INTERSECT** — Only rows that exist in *both* result sets are included. INTERSECT operates much like an inner join, except that it operates on the notion of rows that would be duplicated between result sets rather than a specific join column.

Now, everyone who has read any of my previous books knows that I am keen on examples, and I'm going to provide some here, but I'll point out from the beginning that these statements are fairly easily simulated using the EXISTS operator, so we'll examine both, but let's take a quick look at the syntax for each first.

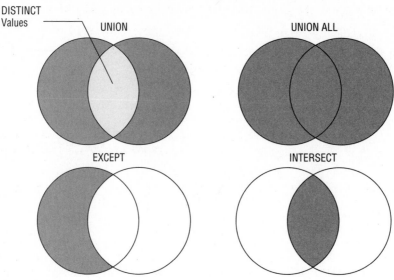

Figure 3-1

EXCEPT

The EXCEPT operator provides all data from the left set that does not exist in the right set. The syntax is relatively straightforward, and works almost just like a UNION:

```
<table or tabular result>
EXCEPT
<table or tabular result with same number of columns and type as top query>
```

If you were paying attention when we reviewed EXISTS and NOT EXISTS, you can probably translate this to its NOT EXISTS equivalent, which would logically look something like this:

```
<base query >
WHERE NOT EXISTS
   (SELECT 1
    FROM <table or result with same number of columns and type as top query>
    WHERE <base query first column> = <comparison table first column> [, ...])
```

We'll see this in an example in the section following the INTERSECT syntax.

INTERSECT

The INTERSECT operator provides all data that matches on both sides of the INTERSECT. As with EXCEPT, the syntax is straightforward and works similar to a UNION:

```
<table or tabular result>
INTERSECT
<table or tabular result with same number of columns and type as top query>
```

Again, you can translate this to an EXISTS (this time without the NOT), which would logically look something like this:

```
<base query >
WHERE NOT EXISTS
  (SELECT 1
    FROM <table or result with same number of columns and type as top query>
    WHERE <base query first column> = <comparison table first column> [, ...])
```

Now that we've seen the syntax for both EXCEPT and INTERSECT, let's move on to a set of examples that show them both in action and compare them to the versions based on the EXISTS operator.

Comparing *EXCEPT* and *INTERSECT* with Their *EXISTS* and *NOT EXISTS* Equivalents

As I indicated when discussing the basic concepts of EXCEPT and INTERSECT, both can, in terms of end result, be replicated via appropriate use of the EXISTS or NOT EXISTS operators. Let's run an example of each form, along with a simple UNION so we can see how similar the syntax is. We'll start by populating some small test data tables, then take a look at the UNION, then move on to the EXCEPT and INTERSECT operators with their EXISTS equivalents.

```
SET NOCOUNT ON;   -- Eliminate the row counts after each query to save space

-- Create our test tables and populate them with a few relevant rows
CREATE TABLE UnionTest1
(
    idcol    int        IDENTITY,
    col2     char(3),
);

CREATE TABLE UnionTest2
(
    idcol    int        IDENTITY,
    col4     char(3),
);

INSERT INTO UnionTest1
VALUES
    ('AAA'),
    ('BBB'),
    ('CCC');

INSERT INTO UnionTest2
VALUES
    ('CCC'),
    ('DDD'),
    ('EEE');

PRINT 'Source and content of both tables:';
PRINT '';

SELECT 1 AS SourceTable, col2 AS Value
```

```
        FROM UnionTest1

        UNION ALL

        SELECT 2, col4
        FROM UnionTest2;


        PRINT 'Results with classic UNION';
        SELECT col2
        FROM UnionTest1

        UNION

        SELECT col4
        FROM UnionTest2;

        PRINT 'Results with EXCEPT';
        PRINT '------------------------';

        SELECT col2
        FROM UnionTest1

        EXCEPT

        SELECT col4
        FROM UnionTest2;

        PRINT 'Equivilent of EXCEPT but using NOT EXISTS';
        PRINT '-------------------------';

        SELECT col2
        FROM UnionTest1 ut1
        WHERE NOT EXISTS
           (SELECT col4 FROM UnionTest2 WHERE col4 = ut1.col2);

        PRINT 'Results with INTERSECT';
        PRINT '------------------------';

        SELECT col2
        FROM UnionTest1
        INTERSECT
        SELECT col4
        FROM UnionTest2;

        PRINT 'Equivilent of INTERSECT but using EXISTS';
        PRINT '------------------------';

        SELECT col2
        FROM UnionTest1 ut1
        WHERE EXISTS
           (SELECT col4 FROM UnionTest2 WHERE col4 = ut1.col2);

        -- Clean up after ourselves
        DROP TABLE UnionTest1;
```

```
DROP TABLE UnionTest2;

SET NOCOUNT OFF; -- Don't forget to turn this back to the default!
```

Let's walk through the results of this a bit at a time — focusing on the points specific to EXCEPT and INTERSECT as well as their EXISTS-related equivalents.

First, let's check out the results of the EXCEPT operator and its related NOT EXISTS version:

```
Results with EXCEPT
-------------------------
col2
----
AAA
BBB


Equivalent of EXCEPT but using NOT EXISTS
-------------------------
col2
----
AAA
BBB
```

As you can see, the results were the same. It is, however, worth noting that the query plans were different. For example, on my system, the cost (you can find more on this in the chapter on Performance Tuning) of the EXCEPT was more than twice that of the NOT EXISTS approach. If you're in a performance sensitive environment, you may want to test out both methods on a realistic set of data for your application, and see what you wind up with.

> We'll see this same theme of the EXISTS version performing better than the EXCEPT/INTERSECT equivalent as we look at INTERSECT. As of this writing, every example I've seen personally or on the web yields a plan that is either more efficient with the EXISTS approach, or is identical; never have I seen the EXCEPT/INTERSECT approach perform better.
>
> Does this mean you shouldn't use EXCEPT and INTERSECT? Well, perhaps, but I don't believe things are quite that easy to decide. For example, in your development community, which reads more easily? Which is easier to understand? If the performance you're seeing is slower, but insignificantly so or "close enough," then you may be interested in using EXCEPT and INTERSECT because they make the desired result much more exact to someone who is reviewing the code later. EXISTS and NOT EXISTS are not that hard, but they have many more possible uses, so are slightly less intuitive; the right choice is often a matter of opinion.

Now let's move on to the INTERSECT results:

```
Results with INTERSECT
-------------------------
col2
----
CCC


Equivalent of INTERSECT but using EXISTS
```

```
--------------------------
col2
----
CCC
```

The results were, again, a match; we are able to replicate the functionality of the INTERSECT by using the EXISTS operator.

*Much like with EXCEPT, the EXISTS performs much better (about 30% of the cost of the EXCEPT. The result will vary somewhat depending on the amount of data you're looking at. As I will so often say, "your mileage may vary," by which I mean, make sure you've tested the impact in **your** environment.*

> In general, the **EXISTS** approach will perform at least as well as the **EXCEPT/ INTERSECT** approach. The latter is, however, somewhat more readable. Take your specific situation into account when choosing between the two.

Common Table Expressions (CTEs)

Common Table Expressions (CTE) were first introduced back in SQL Server 2005. They provide a means to refer to a temporary result set by name, and thus utilize it as a table (albeit both temporary and virtual in nature). Perhaps the coolest thing about them is that you define them before actually using them, so you can avoid separate physical steps storing and re-referencing the table (as you would do with a temporary table — or even a table variable). This can have very favorable performance impacts since SQL Server can plan the work between the CTE and the queries that utilize it as part of one logical operation rather than as a series of separate activities. In their simplest form, CTEs are similar to views created on the fly, but a CTE can also enable other things that you can't really do with a view (for example, see the following section on recursive queries).

The basic syntax for a CTE utilizes the WITH keyword followed by a name and definition:

```
WITH <CTE name> [ ( <column name> [,...n] ) ]
AS
( <query returning tabular data> )
<statement that will make use of the CTE>
```

After the CTE is defined, you can refer to it by name just as if it were a table.

Note that while a CTE can nest, and a CTE can refer to a parent CTE, you cannot have completely independent CTEs at the same time, nor can you reference forward in your nested CTEs. Indeed, whatever statement is going to use the CTE must immediately follow the CTE declaration.

So, as an example of CTE use, we could replace part of our earlier derived table with a CTE reference:

```
USE AdventureWorks2008;

WITH pumps (BusinessEntityID)
AS
```

```
(
    SELECT sc.PersonID AS BusinessEntityID
    FROM Sales.Customer sc
    JOIN Sales.SalesOrderHeader AS soh
        ON sc.CustomerID = soh.CustomerID
    JOIN Sales.SalesOrderDetail AS sod
        ON soh.SalesOrderID = sod.SalesOrderID
    JOIN Production.Product AS p
        ON sod.ProductID = p.ProductID
    WHERE p.Name = 'Minipump'
)

SELECT DISTINCT pp.FirstName, pp.LastName
    FROM Person.Person AS pp
    JOIN pumps
      ON pp.BusinessEntityID = pumps.BusinessEntityID

        JOIN (  SELECT sc.PersonID AS BusinessEntityID
                FROM Sales.Customer sc
                JOIN Sales.SalesOrderHeader AS soh
                    ON sc.CustomerID = soh.CustomerID
                JOIN Sales.SalesOrderDetail AS sod
                    ON soh.SalesOrderID = sod.SalesOrderID
                JOIN Production.Product AS p
                    ON sod.ProductID = p.ProductID
                WHERE p.Name = 'AWC Logo Cap') caps
            ON pp.BusinessEntityID = caps.BusinessEntityID;
```

Notice that I was able to cut the first derived table out entirely and replace it with the CTE reference. I cannot, however, also replace the caps derived table, as I can only make one CTE reference at a time. I can replace pumps, or I can replace caps, but not both.

It's worth noting that certain constructs cannot be used within a CTE. These include:

- ❑   COMPUTER and COMPUTE BY
- ❑   ORDER BY
- ❑   INTO
- ❑   The FOR XML, FOR BROWSE, and OPTION query clauses

CTEs may seem a bit worthless at first given all these restrictions, but they show their power as we begin to work with recursive queries (which are effectively impossible without CTEs). Having said that, let's move right into looking at those .... .

Recursive Queries

Historically, one of the more tricky things to deal with in a relational system has been hierarchical data. Microsoft has done much in the last two releases to ease the pain in this area. One of the pieces of functionality that is very powerful is the notion of a recursive query. A query or piece of code is considered to be recursive when it calls itself either directly or indirectly. We have long had the ability to have recursive stored procedures and functions, but the notion of a recursive query didn't become available until SQL Server 2005.

Prior to the native hierarchical data type that is new with this release (we'll examine the new HierarchyID data type extensively in Chapter 7), most hierarchical data was stored in what is called a unary relationship — that is, a table that has a relationship where both the parent and the child columns are in the same table. A need for recursion is best seen in such unary relationships where the hierarchical data represented is "ragged" in structure. That is, the depth of each branch of the tree may vary, so you need to recurse until you find the bottom of the hierarchical structure — however deep that may be. Recursive queries make that possible.

Recursive queries are made possible by using a properly constructed CTE. A recursive CTE needs to have at least two major parts: a foundation or "anchor" member, and a recursive member. The anchor member establishes the foundation to which the rest of the query data can be added. The recursive member handles the repetitive calls and provides the recursion check.

As an example, let's look at a very typical ragged hierarchy — employee reporting chains. To take a look at this, we'll create a version of the AdventureWorks2008 Employees table where the reporting structure is represented in the older schema style (the 2008 version of AdventureWorks uses the newer HierarchyID data type). We'll generate this using data from the existing Employees table, so our data will easily match that used elsewhere in the AdventureWorks2008 database.

```
CREATE TABLE HumanResources.Employee2
(

    BusinessEntityID   int             NOT NULL PRIMARY KEY,
    ManagerID          int             NULL,
    JobTitle           nvarchar(50)    NULL
);

INSERT INTO HumanResources.Employee2
SELECT hre.BusinessEntityID,
       (SELECT BusinessEntityID
        FROM HumanResources.Employee hre2
        WHERE hre.OrganizationNode.GetAncestor(1) = hre2.OrganizationNode
       ) AS ManagerID,
       JobTitle
FROM HumanResources.Employee hre;
```

This should get 290 rows into a new table called HumanResources.Employee2, which we'll use for the remainder of our CTE examples.

So, now that we have your typical mix where a few employees (your basic "C" level staff) report to the CEO, and then managers report to those executives, supervisors report to the managers, and so on, we're ready to begin. The exact depth of the managerial chain varies by individual department and group. We can use a recursive query to crawl that chain for us.

First, we need to build the root — or "anchor" — of the hierarchy. In this case, that would obviously be the CEO (no one is higher than he is!), but the way we'll format it is to grab any record where the employee has no one that they report to:

```
-- Establish the "Anchor Member"
-- This essentially defines the top node of the
-- recursion hierarchy
  SELECT hre.ManagerID,
         hre.BusinessEntityID,
         hre.JobTitle,
         hredh.DepartmentID,
         0 AS Level
  FROM HumanResources.Employee2 AS hre
  JOIN HumanResources.EmployeeDepartmentHistory AS hredh
    ON hre.BusinessEntityID = hredh.BusinessEntityID
   AND hredh.EndDate IS NULL  -- Current employees only!
  WHERE hre.ManagerID IS NULL;
```

Now, we need to add to that all the various employees that report to this root node, and then recurse down the tree until we get to the bottom. We'll UNION these results to those we just got for the root:

```
UNION ALL
-- Define the piece that actually recurses
  SELECT hre.ManagerID,
         hre.BusinessEntityID,
         hre.JobTitle,
         hredh.DepartmentID,
         r.Level + 1
  FROM HumanResources.Employee2 AS hre
  JOIN HumanResources.EmployeeDepartmentHistory AS hredh
    ON hre.BusinessEntityID = hredh.BusinessEntityID
   AND hredh.EndDate IS NULL  -- Current employees only!
  JOIN Reports AS r
    ON hre.ManagerID = r.BusinessEntityID
```

Now, let's put that all together, and then create a statement to make use of our CTE. I can add a WHERE clause to the calling statement, so I can filter my data down to just the groups, departments, or positions I want the reporting information on — for example:

```
USE AdventureWorks2008;
GO


-- Establish the CTE foundation for the recursion
WITH Reports (ManagerID, BusinessEntityID, JobTitle, DepartmentID, Level)
AS
(

-- Establish the "Anchor Member"
-- This essentially defines the top node of the
-- recursion hierarchy
  SELECT hre.ManagerID,
         hre.BusinessEntityID,
         hre.JobTitle,
         hredh.DepartmentID,
```

```
         0 AS Level
   FROM HumanResources.Employee2 AS hre
   JOIN HumanResources.EmployeeDepartmentHistory AS hredh
     ON hre.BusinessEntityID = hredh.BusinessEntityID
    AND hredh.EndDate IS NULL   -- Current employees only!
   WHERE hre.ManagerID IS NULL
   UNION ALL
-- Define the piece that actually recurses
   SELECT hre.ManagerID,
          hre.BusinessEntityID,
          hre.JobTitle,
          hredh.DepartmentID,
          r.Level + 1
   FROM HumanResources.Employee2 AS hre
   JOIN HumanResources.EmployeeDepartmentHistory AS hredh
     ON hre.BusinessEntityID = hredh.BusinessEntityID
    AND hredh.EndDate IS NULL   -- Current employees only!
   JOIN Reports AS r
     ON hre.ManagerID = r.BusinessEntityID
)

-- Code to get it all started.
SELECT ManagerID, BusinessEntityID, JobTitle, Level
FROM Reports r
JOIN HumanResources.Department AS dp
  ON r.DepartmentID = dp.DepartmentID
WHERE dp.GroupName LIKE '%Admin%'
ORDER BY Level, ManagerID, JobTitle;
GO
```

Note that the CTE is not controlling what group names are returned; instead, that is being driven from the calling query. The WHERE clause is, however, merged into the plan prior to execution and therefore the query will be optimized differently depending on the specific makeup of the calling query.

Let's take a look at the results:

```
ManagerID   BusinessEntityID JobTitle                             Level
---------   ---------------- ------------------------------------ -----------
NULL        1                Chief Executive Officer              0
1           234              Chief Financial Officer              1
1           263              Information Services Manager          1
25          227              Facilities Manager                   2
...
...
264         266              Network Administrator                3
228         229              Janitor                              4
228         230              Janitor                              4
228         231              Janitor                              4
228         232              Janitor                              4

(35 row(s) affected)
```

"What is the level?" you may ask. It is something that I've inserted arbitrarily here to give you a feel for the depth each row has relative to the overall hierarchy. We could just as easily have left it out.

The key thing to understand here is that recursive queries are now not only possible, but also relatively easy. The trick is to understand your root node and how to build off of that anchor.

MERGE

In previous versions of SQL Server, when you heard the word "merge" you generally thought of merge replication. With SQL Server 2008, however, we have a whole new way of thinking about the word merge and, more importantly, of thinking about DML statements.

With MERGE, we have the prospect of combining multiple DML action statements (INSERT, UPDATE, DELETE) into one overall action, improving performance (they can share many of the same physical operations) and simplifying transactions. MERGE makes use of a special USING clause that winds up working somewhat like a CTE. The result set in the USING clause can then be used to conditionally apply your INSERT, UPDATE, and DELETE statements. The basic syntax looks something like this:

```
MERGE <target table> [AS <alias>]
USING
(
   <source query>
)
WHEN {[NOT] MATCHED | <expression> THEN
   <action statement>
[<additional WHEN clauses>, [...n]]
```

Let's use the example of receiving a shipment for inventory. We'll assume that we're keeping a special rollup table of our sales for reporting purposes. We want to run a query daily that will add any new sales to our monthly rollup. On the first night of the month, this is pretty much a no brainer, as, since there are no other rollup records for the month, any sales for the day are just rolled up and inserted. On the second day, however, we have a different scenario: We need to rollup and insert new records as we did the first day, but we need to just update existing records (for products that have already sold that month).

Let's take a look at how MERGE can manage both actions in one overall step. Before we get going on this, however, we need to create our rollup table:

```
USE AdventureWorks2008;

CREATE TABLE Sales.MonthlyRollup
(
   Year       smallint    NOT NULL,
   Month      tinyint     NOT NULL,
   ProductID int         NOT NULL
     FOREIGN KEY
       REFERENCES Production.Product(ProductID),
   QtySold    int         NOT NULL,
   CONSTRAINT PKYearMonthProductID
     PRIMARY KEY
       (Year, Month, ProductID)
);
```

This is a pretty simple example of a monthly rollup table — making it very easy to get sales totals by product for a given year and month. To make use of this, however, we need to regularly populate it with rolled up values from our detail table. To do this, we'll use MERGE.

First, we need to start by establishing a result set that will figure out what rows we need to be sourcing data for our rollup from. For purposes of this example, we'll focus on August of 2003, and start with our query for the first day of the month:

```
SELECT soh.OrderDate, sod.ProductID, SUM(sod.OrderQty) AS QtySold
FROM Sales.SalesOrderHeader soh
JOIN Sales.SalesOrderDetail sod
  ON soh.SalesOrderID = sod.SalesOrderID
WHERE soh.OrderDate >= '2003-08-01'
  AND soh.OrderDate < '2003-08-02'
GROUP BY soh.OrderDate, sod.ProductID;
```

This gets us the total sales, by ProductID, for every date in our range (our range just happens to be limited to one day).

There is a bit of a trap built into how we've done this up to this point. I've set the GROUP BY to use the OrderDate, but OrderDate is a datetime data type as opposed to a date data type. If our order were to start coming in with actual times on them, it would mess with our assumption that all orders will group nicely into one date. If this were a production environment, we would want to cast the OrderDate to a date data type or use DATEPART to ensure that the grouping was by day rather than by time.

With this, we're ready to build our merge:

```
MERGE Sales.MonthlyRollup AS smr
USING
(

    SELECT soh.OrderDate, sod.ProductID, SUM(sod.OrderQty) AS QtySold
    FROM Sales.SalesOrderHeader soh
    JOIN Sales.SalesOrderDetail sod
      ON soh.SalesOrderID = sod.SalesOrderID
    WHERE soh.OrderDate >= '2003-08-01' AND soh.OrderDate < '2003-08-02'
    GROUP BY soh.OrderDate, sod.ProductID

) AS s
ON (s.ProductID = smr.ProductID)
WHEN MATCHED THEN
    UPDATE SET smr.QtySold = smr.QtySold + s.QtySold
WHEN NOT MATCHED THEN
    INSERT (Year, Month, ProductID, QtySold)
    VALUES (DATEPART(yy, s.OrderDate),
            DATEPART(m, s.OrderDate),
            s.ProductID,
            s.QtySold);
```

> Note that the semicolon is required at the end of the MERGE statement. While the semicolon remains optional on most SQL statements for backward compatibility reasons, you'll find it working its way into more and more statements as a required delimiter of the end of the statement; this is particularly true for multipart statements such as MERGE.

When you run this, you should get 192 rows affected assuming you haven't been altering the data in AdventureWorks2008. Now, since our Sales.MonthlyRollup table was empty, there wouldn't have been any matches, so all rows were inserted. We can verify that by querying our Sales.MonthlyRollup table:

```
SELECT *
FROM Sales.MonthlyRollup;
```

This gets us back the expected 192 rows:

```
Year    Month ProductID    QtySold
------  ----- ----------- -----------
2003    8     707         242
2003    8     708         281
2003    8     711         302
...
...
2003    8     997         43
2003    8     998         138
2003    8     999         103

(192 row(s) affected)
```

Every row that was in the basic SELECT that powered our MERGE wound up being inserted into our table. Let's move on, however, to the 2nd day of the month:

```
MERGE Sales.MonthlyRollup AS smr
USING
(
  SELECT soh.OrderDate, sod.ProductID, SUM(sod.OrderQty) AS QtySold
  FROM Sales.SalesOrderHeader soh
  JOIN Sales.SalesOrderDetail sod
    ON soh.SalesOrderID = sod.SalesOrderID

  WHERE soh.OrderDate >= '2003-08-02' AND soh.OrderDate < '2003-08-03'

  GROUP BY soh.OrderDate, sod.ProductID
) AS s
ON (s.ProductID = smr.ProductID)
WHEN MATCHED THEN
  UPDATE SET smr.QtySold = smr.QtySold + s.QtySold
WHEN NOT MATCHED THEN
  INSERT (Year, Month, ProductID, QtySold)
```

```
VALUES (DATEPART(yy, s.OrderDate),
        DATEPART(m, s.OrderDate),
        s.ProductID,
        s.QtySold);
```

We update the date we're running this for (simulating running it on the 2nd day of the month), and running it should get us 38 rows:

```
(38 row(s) affected)
```

But something is different this time; we already had rows in the table that our new batch of sales may have matched up with. We know we affected 38 rows, but *how* did we affect them. Re-run the SELECT on our table:

```
SELECT *
FROM Sales.MonthlyRollup
```

And instead of 230 rows (the 192 plus the 38), we only get 194 rows. Indeed, 36 of our 38 rows were repeat sales, and were therefore treated as updates rather than insertions. Two rows (ProductIDs 882 and 928) were sales of product that had not been previously sold in that month, and thus needed to be inserted as new rows — one pass over the data, but the equivalent of two statements ran.

We could perform similar actions that decide to delete rows based on matched or not matched conditions.

Using External Calls to Perform Complex Actions

We have always had the need, on occasion, to get information that is sourced outside of SQL Server. For the vast, vast majority of installations, actually getting that information from within SQL Server was out of reach. Instead, there was typically a client or middle tier component that sorted out what was needed from SQL Server and what was needed from the external source.

In many ways, this was just fine — after all, having your database server hung up waiting on an external call seems risky at best, and deadly at worst. Who knows how long before that call is going to return (if ever?). The risk of hung processes within your database server winds up being fairly high.

Now, I said for the *majority* of installations, and that implies that a few got around it — and they did. There were a few different methods available.

First, there was the idea of an extended stored procedure. These are DLLs that you can create in C using special SQL Server libraries. They run in process with SQL Server and can be (assuming you have a smart DLL writer) very fast, save for one problem — an external call. That means that we are beholden to the external process we are calling to return to us in a timely fashion. The additional issue was one of general safety. Since you're running in process to SQL Server, if your DLL crashes, then SQL Server is going to crash (if you're distributing software, I'm sure you can guess at how your customer would react if your product was taking down their SQL Server installation). Last, but not least, very few had the knack for figuring out how to get these written.

Another solution was added to SQL Server in the OLE/COM era. The sp_CreateOAMethod family of stored procedures allowed you to instantiate a COM object and make calls to it. These passed data back and forth using variants, and were always run out of process. They were safer, but they were clumsy at best and painfully slow.

With the advent of .NET and SQL Server becoming CLR language aware, we live in a new world. You can write your scripts using any .NET language, and can instantiate the objects you need to get the job done. You can create user-defined functions to call external processes — such as cross-communicating with some other online system that you cannot directly link to. Imagine, for a moment, allowing SQL Server to apply information gleaned from a Web service and merge that data in the end query? Heady stuff.

The possibilities are endless; however, you need to keep your head about this. External calls are still external calls! Any time you rely on something external to your system, you are at the mercy of that external system. Be very, very careful with such calls.

> **External calls should be considered to be an extreme measure. You are taking risks in terms of security (what is the risk of someone spoofing your external source?) and also taking an extreme performance risk. Tread lightly in this area.**

Performance Considerations

We've already touched on some of the macro-level "what's the best thing to do" stuff as we've gone through the chapter, but, like most things in life, it's not as easy as all that. What I want to do here is provide something of a quick reference for performance issues for your queries. I'll try to steer you toward the right kind of query for the right kind of situation.

Yes, it's time again folks for one of my now famous soapbox diatribes. At issue this time is the concept of blanket use of blanket rules.

What I'm going to be talking about in this section is the way that things usually work. The word usually is extremely operative here. There are very few rules in SQL that will be true 100 percent of the time. In a world full of exceptions, SQL has to be at the pinnacle of that — exceptions are a dime a dozen when you try and describe the performance world in SQL Server.

In short, you need to gauge just how important the performance of a given query is. If performance is critical, then don't take these rules too seriously — instead, use them as a starting point, and then TEST, TEST, TEST!!!

JOINs vs. Subqueries vs. ?

Deciding between joins and subqueries (and for that matter, other options) is that area I mentioned earlier in the chapter that I had a heated debate with a coworker over. And, as you might expect when two people have such conviction in their point of view, both of us were correct up to a point (and it follows, wrong up to a point).

The long-standing, traditional viewpoint about subqueries has always been that you are much better off to use joins instead if you can. This is absolutely correct — sometimes. In reality, it depends on a large number of factors. The following is a table that discusses some of the issues that the performance balance will depend on, and which side of the equation they favor.

Situation	Favors
The value returned from a subquery is going to be the same for every row in the outer query.	Prequery. Declaring a variable and then selecting the needed value into that variable will allow the would-be subquery to be executed just once rather than once for every record in the outer table. The Optimizer in SQL Server is actually pretty smart about this and will do the prequery for you if it detects the scenario, but do not rely on it. If you know this is the scenario, perform your own prequery just to be sure.
Both tables are relatively small (say 10,000 records or less).	Subqueries. I don't know the exact reasons, but I've run several tests on this, and it held up pretty much every time. I suspect that the issue is the lower overhead of a lookup vs. a join when all the lookup data fits on just a data page or two. The Optimizer continues to get smarter about this with every release, so you may find some scenarios where the two options return exactly the same query plan.
The match, after considering all criteria, is going to return only one value.	Subqueries. Again, there is much less overhead in going and finding just one record and substituting it than in having to join the entire table.
The match, after considering all criteria, is going to return only a relatively few values, and there is no index on the lookup column.	Subqueries. A single lookup or even a few lookups will usually take less overhead than a hash join.
The lookup table is relatively small, but the base table is large.	Nested subqueries if applicable; joins vs. a correlated subquery. With subqueries the lookup will happen only once and has relatively low overhead. With correlated subqueries, however, you will be cycling the lookup many times — in this case, the join would be a better choice in most cases.
Correlated subquery vs. join	Join. Internally, a correlated subquery is going to create a nested loop situation. This can create quite a bit of overhead. It is substantially faster than cursors in most instances, but slower than other options that might be available.
Derived tables vs. whatever	Derived tables typically carry a fair amount of overhead, so proceed with caution. The thing to remember is that they are run (derived if you will) once, and then they are in memory, so, most of the overhead is in the initial creation and the lack of indexes in larger result sets. They can be fast or slow — it just depends. Think before coding on these.
EXISTS vs. whatever	EXISTS. It does not have to deal with multiple lookups for the same match — once it finds one match for that particular row, it is free to move onto the next lookup — this can seriously cut down on overhead.

Situation	Favors
Use of a CTE	A CTE is merged into the query plan of the calling query. In general, this means that a basic CTE will have no significant effect on the end performance.
MERGE vs. Multiple Statements	MERGE allows for the separate action statements to be accomplished in the same pass over the data and utilizing the same locks where applicable. The result will generally be improved performance. Keep in mind, however, that, for many users, it may make for code that is more difficult to read.

These are just the highlights. The possibilities of different mixes and additional situations are positively endless.

> I can't stress enough how important it is, when in doubt — heck, even when you're not in doubt but performance is everything — to make reasonable tests of competing solutions to the problem. By reasonable, I mean that your tests should cover most of the typical scenarios that you users will execute the code in. In addition, your tests should be conducted against a database and load that is somewhat equivalent to what you expect to see in production. Most of the time the blanket rules will be fine, but not always. By performing reasonable tests, you can be certain you've made the right choice.

Summary

The query basics you've learned in your experience with SQL up to this point will cover perhaps 80 percent or more of the query situations that you run into, but it's that other 20 percent that can kill you. Sometimes the issue is whether you can even find a query that will give you the answers you need. Sometimes it's that you have a particular query or sproc that has unacceptable performance. Whatever the case, you'll run across plenty of situations where simple queries and joins just won't fit the bill. You need something more, and, hopefully, the options covered in this chapter have given you a little more of an arsenal to deal with those tough situations.

4

XML Integration

Extensible Markup Language (XML) — looking back at its history is something of a funny thing to me. Part of its strength lies in its simplicity, so it would seem like it wouldn't change much. Indeed, the basic rules of it haven't changed at all — but all the things surrounding XML (such as how to access data stored in XML) have gone through many changes. Likewise, the way that SQL Server supports XML has seen some fairly big changes from the time it was first introduced.

So, to continue my "it's a funny thing" observation, I realized some time back that I used to refer to XML support as being an "extra" — what a truly silly thing for me to say. Yeah, yeah, yeah — I always tempered that "extra" comment with the notion that it's only because XML support isn't really required to have a working SQL Server, but I've come to realize in today's world that it isn't much of a working SQL Server without support for XML. It is with this in mind, and looking back at how integral XML integration has become to the product, that I've moved my coverage of XML much further forward in the book versus where I had it in prior editions (where it was more of an afterthought).

XML has, over the decade or so that it has grown into widespread use, become a fundamental consideration in the vast majority of data designs. Sure, there are many well thought out and well designed systems out there that do not use so much as one line of XML code, but there are very, very few that haven't had at least a moment of "should we use XML?" consideration in them. XML is used in websites, for data exchange, and for simple storage of things such as hierarchies — if you aren't at least considering XML in your data applications, then you probably aren't giving your data applications full consideration.

So, with all that said, in this chapter we'll look at:

- ❑ The XML data type
- ❑ XML schema collections
- ❑ Methods of representing your relational data as XML

❑ Methods of querying data that we have stored natively in XML (XQuery, Microsoft's XDL language (a variant on XQuery), and other methods)

Some of these are actually embedded within each other, so let's get to taking a look so we can see how they mix.

> This chapter assumes that you have an existing knowledge of at least basic XML rules and constructs. If you do not have that foundation knowledge, I strongly recommend picking up a copy of the latest edition of a good XML book such as *Beginning XML* (also available from Wrox) or another XML-specific book before getting too far into this chapter. Keep in mind though, that other chapters may occasionally reference material introduced in this chapter.

The XML Data Type

The XML data type was first introduced in SQL Server 2005. It was a watershed moment in the history of mixing relational and XML data. With the xml data type, SQL Server takes data that is in XML format and recognizes it as truly being XML data. In previous versions, there were an increasing number of ways to address XML data, but all of it was done from the foundation of basic character data. The XML data type recognizes XML as XML and that opens up a host of new possibilities from indexing to data validation.

The number of different things going on here is massive. Among the various things that we need to talk about when discussing the XML data type include:

❑ **Schema collections** — A core concept of XML is the notion of allowing XML to be associated with schema documents. XML schemas define the rules that allow us to determine whether our XML is "valid" (that is, does it meet the rules that this particular kind of XML document is supposed to do). XML schema collections in SQL Server are a way of storing schemas and allowing SQL Server to know that is what they are — validation documents. You can associate instances of XML data (column data or variables, for example) with XML schemas, and SQL Server will apply the schema to each instance of that XML to determine whether it is valid XML or not.

❑ **Enforcing constraints** — Relational data systems have always had the notion of requiring a column to meet certain criteria before we'll let it into our table, but what about XML? XML allows for multiple pieces of discrete data to be stored within just one column — how do we validate those individual pieces of data? The XML data type understands XML, and, while direct definition of constraints is not allowed, we can utilize wrapper functions (in the form of stored procedures or triggers) to define constraints for specific nodes within our XML.

❑ **XML data type methods** — When referring to a column or variable that is typed XML, you can utilize several methods that are intrinsic to that data type. For example, you can test for the existence of a certain node or attribute, execute XDL (a Microsoft-defined extension to XQuery that allows for data modification), or query the value of a specific node or attribute.

Let's get more specific.

Defining a Column as Being of XML Type

We've already seen the most basic definition of an XML column. For example, if we examined the most basic definition of the `Production.ProductModel` table in the AdventureWorks2008 database, it would look something like this:

```
CREATE TABLE  Production.ProductModel (
  ProductModelID      int         IDENTITY(1,1)      NOT NULL,
  Name                dbo.Name                       NOT NULL,
  CatalogDescription  xml                            NULL,
  Instructions        xml                            NULL,
  rowguid             uniqueidentifier  ROWGUIDCOL   NOT NULL,
  ModifiedDate        datetime  NOT NULL,
 CONSTRAINT  PK_ProductModel_ProductModelID  PRIMARY KEY CLUSTERED
(
   ProductModelID  ASC
);
```

So, let's ask ourselves what we have here in terms of our two XML columns:

1. We have defined them as XML, so we will have our XML data type methods available to us (more on those coming up soon).

2. We have allowed nulls, but could have just as easily chosen NOT NULL as a constraint. Note, however, that the NOT NULL would be enforced on whether the row had any data for that column, not whether that data was valid.

3. Our XML is considered "non-typed XML." That is, since we have not associated any schema with it, SQL Server doesn't really know anything about how this XML is supposed to behave to be considered "valid."

The first of these is implied in any column that is defined with the data type XML rather than just plain text. We will see much more about this in our next XML data type section.

The second goes with any data type in SQL Server — we can specify whether we allow NULL data or not for that column.

So, the real meat in terms changes we can make at definition time has to do with whether we specify our XML column as being typed or non-typed XML. The non-typed definition we used in the preceding example means that SQL Server knows very little about any XML stored in the column and, therefore, can do little to police its validity. If we set the column up as being typed XML, then we are providing much more definition about what is considered "valid" for any XML that goes in our column.

The AdventureWorks2008 database already has schema collections that match the validation we want to place on our two XML columns, so let's look at how we would change our CREATE statement to adjust to typed XML:

```
CREATE TABLE  Production.ProductModel (
  ProductModelID     int        IDENTITY(1,1) NOT NULL,
  Name               dbo.Name                 NOT NULL,
```

```
    CatalogDescription  xml
        (CONTENT  Production . ProductDescriptionSchemaCollection ) NULL,
    Instructions         xml
        (CONTENT  Production . ManuInstructionsSchemaCollection ) NULL,
    rowguid               uniqueidentifier  ROWGUIDCOL  NOT NULL,

  ModifiedDate          datetime  NOT NULL,
 CONSTRAINT  PK_ProductModel_ProductModelID  PRIMARY KEY CLUSTERED
(
    ProductModelID  ASC
);
```

This represents the way it is defined in the actual AdventureWorks2008 sample. In order to insert a record into the `Production.ProductModel` table, you must either leave the `CatalogDescription` and `Instructions` fields blank or supply XML that is valid when tested against their respective schemas.

XML Schema Collections

XML schema collections are really nothing more than named persistence of one or more schema documents into the database. The name amounts to a handle to your set of schemas. By referring to that collection, you are indicating that the XML typed column or variable must be valid when matched against all of the schemas in that collection.

We can view existing schema collections. To do this, we utilize the built-in `XML_SCHEMA_NAMESPACE()` function. The syntax looks like this:

```
XML_SCHEMA_NAMESPACE( <SQL Server schema> , <xml schema collection> , [<namespace>] )
```

This is just a little confusing, so let's touch on these parameters just a bit:

Parameter	Description
SQL Server schema	This is your relational database schema (not to be confused with the XML schema). For example, for the table `Production.ProductModel`, `Production` is the relational schema. For `Sales.SalesOrderHeader`, `Sales` is the relational schema.
xml schema collection	The name used when the XML schema collection was created. In our create table example previously, we referred to the `ProductDescriptionSchemaCollection` and `ManuInstructionsSchemaCollection` XML schema collections.
namespace	Optional name for a specific namespace within the XML schema collection. Remember that XML schema collections can contain multiple schema documents — this would return anything that fell within the specified namespace.

So, to use this for the `Production.ManuInstructionsSchemaCollection` schema collection, we would make a query like this:

```
SELECT XML_SCHEMA_NAMESPACE('Production','ManuInstructionsSchemaCollection')
```

This spews forth a ton of unformatted XML:

```
<xsd:schema xmlns:xsd="http://www.w3.org/2001/XMLSchema"
xmlns:t="http://schemas.microsoft.com/sqlserver/2004/07/adventure-
works/ProductModelManuInstructions"
targetNamespace="http://schemas.microsoft.com/sqlserver/2004/07/adventure-
works/ProductModelManuInstructions"
elementFormDefault="qualified"><xsd:element name="root"><xsd:complexType
mixed="true"><xsd:complexContent mixed="true"><xsd:restriction
base="xsd:anyType"><xsd:sequence><xsd:element name="Location"
maxOccurs="unbounded"><xsd:complexType mixed="true"><xsd:complexContent
mixed="true"><xsd:restriction base="xsd:anyType"><xsd:sequence><xsd:element
name="step" type="t:StepType" maxOccurs="unbounded"
/></xsd:sequence><xsd:attribute name="LocationID" type="xsd:integer"
use="required" /><xsd:attribute name="SetupHours" type="xsd:decimal"
/><xsd:attribute name="MachineHours" type="xsd:decimal" /><xsd:attribute
 name="LaborHours" type="xsd:decimal" /><xsd:attribute name="LotSize"
type="xsd:decimal"
/></xsd:restriction></xsd:complexContent></xsd:complexType></xsd:element></xsd
:sequence></xsd:restriction></xsd:complexContent></xsd:complexType></xsd:eleme
nt><xsd:complexType name="StepType" mixed="true"><xsd:complexContent
mixed="true"><xsd:restriction base="xsd:anyType"><xsd:choice minOccurs="0"
maxOccurs="unbounded"><xsd:element name="tool" type="xsd:string"
/><xsd:element name="material" type="xsd:string" /><xsd:element
name="blueprint" type="xsd:string" /><xsd:element name="specs"
type="xsd:string" /><xsd:element name="diag" type="xsd:string"
/></xsd:choice></xsd:restriction></xsd:complexContent></xsd:complexType></xsd:
schema>
```

SQL Server strips out any whitespace between tags, so if you create a schema collection with all sorts of pretty indentations for readability, SQL Server will remove them for the sake of efficient storage.

> **Note that the default number of characters returned for text results in Management Studio is only 256 characters. If you're using text view, you will want to go Tools➤Options➤Query Results➤SQL Server➤Results to Text and change the maximum number of characters displayed.**

Creating, Altering, and Dropping XML Schema Collections

The CREATE, ALTER, and DROP notions for XML schema collections work in a manner that is *mostly* consistent with how other such statements have worked thus far in SQL Server. We'll run through them here, but pay particular attention to the ALTER statement, as it is the one that has a few quirks versus other ALTER statements we've worked with.

CREATE XML SCHEMA COLLECTION

Again, the CREATE is your typical CREATE <object type> <object name> syntax that we've seen throughout the book, and uses the AS keyword we've seen with stored procedures, views, and other less structured objects:

```
CREATE XML SCHEMA COLLECTION [<SQL Server schema>.] <collection name>
    AS { <schema text> | <variable containing the schema text> }
```

So if, for example, we wanted to create an XML schema collection that is similar to the Production.ManuInstructionsSchemaCollection collection in AdventureWorks2008, we might execute something like the following:

```
CREATE XML SCHEMA COLLECTION ProductDescriptionSchemaCollectionSummaryRequired
AS
    '<xsd:schema
targetNamespace="http://schemas.microsoft.com/sqlserver/2004/07/adventure-
works/ProductModelWarrAndMain"
        xmlns="http://schemas.microsoft.com/sqlserver/2004/07/adventure-
works/ProductModelWarrAndMain"
        elementFormDefault="qualified"
        xmlns:xsd="http://www.w3.org/2001/XMLSchema" >
        <xsd:element name="Warranty"  >
            <xsd:complexType>
                <xsd:sequence>
                    <xsd:element name="WarrantyPeriod" type="xsd:string"  />
                    <xsd:element name="Description" type="xsd:string"  />
                </xsd:sequence>
            </xsd:complexType>
        </xsd:element>
    </xsd:schema>
    <xs:schema
targetNamespace="http://schemas.microsoft.com/sqlserver/2004/07/adventure-
works/ProductModelDescription"
        xmlns="http://schemas.microsoft.com/sqlserver/2004/07/adventure-
works/ProductModelDescription"
        elementFormDefault="qualified"
        xmlns:mstns="http://tempuri.org/XMLSchema.xsd"
        xmlns:xs="http://www.w3.org/2001/XMLSchema"
        xmlns:wm="http://schemas.microsoft.com/sqlserver/2004/07/adventure-
works/ProductModelWarrAndMain" >
        <xs:import
 namespace="http://schemas.microsoft.com/sqlserver/2004/07/adventure-
works/ProductModelWarrAndMain" />
        <xs:element name="ProductDescription" type="ProductDescription" />
            <xs:complexType name="ProductDescription">
                <xs:sequence>
                    <xs:element name="Summary" type="Summary" minOccurs="1" />
                </xs:sequence>
                <xs:attribute name="ProductModelID" type="xs:string" />
                <xs:attribute name="ProductModelName" type="xs:string" />
            </xs:complexType>
            <xs:complexType name="Summary" mixed="true" >
                <xs:sequence>
```

```
                    <xs:any processContents="skip"
namespace="http://www.w3.org/1999/xhtml" minOccurs="0" maxOccurs="unbounded"
/>
                  </xs:sequence>
            </xs:complexType>
      </xs:schema>'
```

> Note that the URL portion of the namespace declaration must be entered on a single line. They are shown here word wrapped onto multiple lines because there is a limit to how many characters we can show per line in print. Make sure you include the entire URL on a single line.

This one happens to be just like the `Production.ManuInstructionsSchemaCollection` schema collection, but I've altered the schema to require the summary element rather than having it optional. Since the basic structure is the same, I utilized the same namespaces.

ALTER XML SCHEMA COLLECTION

This one is just slightly different from other ALTER statements in the sense that it is limited to just adding new pieces to the collection. The syntax looks like this:

```
ALTER XML SCHEMA COLLECTION [<SQL Server schema>.] <collection name>
    ADD { <schema text> | <variable containing the schema text> }
```

I would not be at all surprised if the functionality of this is boosted a bit in a later service pack, but, in the meantime, let me stress again that this is a tool for adding to your schema collection rather than changing or removing what's there.

DROP XML SCHEMA COLLECTION

This is one of those classic "does what it says" things and works just like any other DROP:

```
DROP XML SCHEMA COLLECTION  [<SQL Server schema>.] <collection name>
```

So, to get rid of our `ProductDescriptionSchemaCollectionSummaryRequired` schema collection we created earlier, we could execute:

```
DROP XML SCHEMA COLLECTION ProductDescriptionSchemaCollectionSummaryRequired;
```

And it's gone.

XML Data Type Methods

The XML data type carries several intrinsic methods with it. These methods are unique to the XML data type, and no other data type has anything that is at all similar. The syntax within these methods varies a bit because they are based on different, but mostly industry-standard, XML access methods. The basic syntax for calling the method is standardized though:

```
<instance of xml data type>.<method>
```

There are a total of five methods available:

- ❑ **.query** — An implementation of the industry-standard XQuery language. This allows you to access your XML by running XQuery-formatted queries. XQuery allows for the prospect that you may be returning multiple pieces of data rather than a discrete value.

- ❑ **.value** — This one allows you to access a discrete value within a specific element or attribute.

- ❑ **.modify** — This is Microsoft's own extension to XQuery. Whereas XQuery is limited to requesting data (no modification language), the modify method extends XQuery to allow for data modification.

- ❑ **.nodes** — Used to break up XML data into individual, more relational-style rows.

- ❑ **.exist** — Much like the IF EXISTS clause we use extensively in standard SQL, the exist() XML data type method tests to see whether a specific kind of data exists. In the case of exist(), the test is to see whether a particular node or attribute has an entry in the instance of XML you're testing.

.query (SQL Server's Implementation of XQuery)

.query is an implementation of the industry standard XQuery language. The result works much like a SQL query, except that the results are for matching XML data nodes rather than relational rows and columns.

.query requires a parameter that is a valid XQuery to be run against your instance of XML data. For example, if we wanted the steps out of the product documentation for ProductID 66, we could run the following:

```
SELECT ProductModelID, Instructions.query('declare namespace
 PI="http://schemas.microsoft.com/sqlserver/2004/07/adventure-
works/ProductModelManuInstructions";
    /PI:root/PI:Location/PI:step') AS Steps
FROM Production.ProductModel
WHERE ProductModelID = 66;
```

Note that the URL portion of the namespace declaration must be entered on a single line. They are shown here word wrapped onto multiple lines because there is a limit to how many characters we can show per line in print. Make sure you include the entire URL on a single line.

The result is rather verbose, so I've truncated the right side of it, but you can see that we've trimmed things down such that we're getting only those nodes at the step level or lower in the XML hierarchy.

```
ProductModelID Steps
-------------- -------------------------------------------------
66             <PI:step xmlns:PI="http://schemas.microsoft.com/sqlser...
                   Put the <PI:material>Seat post Lug (Product N...
               </PI:step><PI:step xmlns:PI="http://schemas.micro...
                   Insert the <PI:material>Pinch Bolt (Product N...
               </PI:step><PI:step xmlns:PI="http://schemas.micro...
                   Attach the <PI:material>LL Seat (Product Numb...
               </PI:step><PI:step xmlns:PI="http://schemas.micro...
```

```
                    Inspect per specification <PI:specs>FI-620</P...
            </PI:step>
```

```
(1 row(s) affected)
```

It's also worth pointing out that all the XML still came in one column in one row per data row in the database.

> It bears repeating that .query cannot modify data — it is a read-only operation.

Notice, by the way, my need to declare the namespace in this. Since a namespace is declared as part of the referenced schema collection, you can see how it really expands and virtually destroys the readability of our query. We can fix that by using the WITH XMLNAMESPACES() declaration:

```
WITH XMLNAMESPACES ('http://schemas.microsoft.com/sqlserver/2004/07/adventure-
works/ProductModelManuInstructions' AS PI)

SELECT ProductModelID, Instructions.query('/PI:root/PI:Location/PI:step') AS Steps

FROM Production.ProductModel
WHERE ProductModelID = 66;
```

Note that the URL portion of the namespace declaration must be entered on a single line. They are shown here word wrapped onto multiple lines because there is a limit to how many characters we can show per line in print. Make sure you include the entire URL on a single line.

This gives you a somewhat more readable query, but yields the same result set.

.value

The .value method is all about querying out discrete data. It uses an XPath syntax to locate a specific node and extract a scalar value. The syntax looks like this:

```
<instance of xml data type>.value (<XPath location>, <non-xml SQL Server Type>)
```

The trick here is making certain that the XPath specified really will return a discrete value.

If, for example, we wanted to know the value of the LaborHours attribute in the first Location element for ProductModelID 66, we might write something like:

```
WITH XMLNAMESPACES ('http://schemas.microsoft.com/sqlserver/2004/07/adventure-
works/ProductModelManuInstructions' AS PI)

SELECT ProductModelID,
    Instructions.value('(/PI:root/PI:Location/@LaborHours)[1]',
                        'decimal (5,2)') AS Location
FROM Production.ProductModel
WHERE ProductModelID = 66
```

Note that the URL portion of the namespace declaration must be entered on a single line. They are shown here word wrapped onto multiple lines because there is a limit to how many characters we can show per line in print. Make sure you include the entire URL on a single line.

Check the results:

```
ProductModelID Location
-------------- ---------------------------------------
66             1.50

(1 row(s) affected)
```

Note that SQL Server has extracted just the specified attribute value (in this case, the `LaborHours` attribute of the `Location` node) as a discrete piece of data. The data type of the returned values must be castable into a non-XML type in SQL Server, and must return a scalar value — that is, you cannot have multiple rows.

.modify

Ah, here things get just a little interesting.

XQuery, left in its standard W3C form, is a read-only kind of thing — that is, it is great for selecting out data but offers no equivalents to INSERT, UPDATE, or DELETE. Bummer deal! Well, Microsoft is apparently having none of that and has done its own extension to XQuery to provide data manipulation for XQuery. This extension to XQuery is called XML Data Manipulation Language, or XML DML. XML DML adds three new commands to XQuery:

❑   insert

❑   delete

❑   replace value of

> **Note that these commands, like all XML keywords, are case sensitive.**

Each of these does what it implies, with `replace value of` taking the place of SQL's UPDATE statement.

If, for example, we wanted to increase the original 1.5 labor hours in our `.value` example, we might write something like:

```
WITH XMLNAMESPACES ('http://schemas.microsoft.com/sqlserver/2004/07/adventure-
works/ProductModelManuInstructions' AS PI)

UPDATE Production.ProductModel
SET Instructions.modify('replace value of
(/PI:root/PI:Location/@LaborHours)[1] with 1.75')
WHERE ProductModelID = 66;
```

Note that the URL portion of the namespace declaration must be entered on a single line. They are shown here word wrapped onto multiple lines because there is a limit to how many characters we can show per line in print. Make sure you include the entire URL on a single line.

Now if we re-run our `.value` command:

```
WITH XMLNAMESPACES ('http://schemas.microsoft.com/sqlserver/2004/07/adventure-
works/ProductModelManuInstructions' AS PI)

SELECT ProductModelID, Instructions.value('(/PI:root/PI:Location/@LaborHours)[1]',
'decimal (5,2)') AS Location
FROM Production.ProductModel
WHERE ProductModelID = 66
```

Note that the URL portion of the namespace declaration must be entered on a single line. They are shown here word wrapped onto multiple lines because there is a limit to how many characters we can show per line in print. Make sure you include the entire URL on a single line.

We get a new value:

```
ProductModelID Location
-------------- ---------------------------------------
66             1.75

(1 row(s) affected)
```

Note the way that this is essentially an UPDATE within an UPDATE. We are modifying the SQL Server row, so we must use an UPDATE statement to tell SQL Server that our row of relational data (which just happens to have XML within it) is to be updated. We must also use the replace value of *keyword to specify the XML portion of the update.*

.nodes

`.nodes` is used to take blocks of XML and separate what would have been, were it stored in a relational form, multiple rows of data. Taking one XML document and breaking it into individual parts in this way is referred to as *shredding* the document.

What we are doing with `.nodes` is essentially breaking the instances of XML data into their own table (with as many rows as there are instances of data meeting that XQuery criteria). As you might expect, this means we need to treat `.nodes` results as a table rather than a column. The primary difference between `.nodes` and a typical table is that we must *cross apply* our `.nodes` results back to the specific table that we are sourcing our XML data from. So, `.nodes` really involves more syntax than just `.nodes` — think of it somewhat like a join, but using the special CROSS APPLY keyword in the place of the JOIN and `.nodes` instead of the ON clause. It looks like this:

```
SELECT <column list>
FROM <source table>
CROSS APPLY <column name>.nodes(<XQuery>) AS <table alias for your .nodes results>
```

This is fairly confusing stuff, so let's look back at our `.value` example earlier. We see a query that looked for a specific entry and, therefore, got back exactly one result:

```
WITH XMLNAMESPACES ('http://schemas.microsoft.com/sqlserver/2004/07/adventure-
works/ProductModelManuInstructions' AS PI)
```

```
SELECT ProductModelID,
    Instructions.value('(/PI:root/PI:Location/@LaborHours)[1]',
                        'decimal (5,2)') AS Location
FROM Production.ProductModel
WHERE ProductModelID = 66;
```

Note that the URL portion of the namespace declaration must be entered on a single line. They are shown here word wrapped onto multiple lines because there is a limit to how many characters we can show per line in print. Make sure you include the entire URL on a single line.

`.value` expects a scalar result, so we needed to make certain our XQuery would return just that single value per individual row of XML. `.nodes` tells SQL Server to use XQuery to map to a specific location and treat each entry found in that XQuery to be an individual row instead.

Let's modify our `.value` example to return all `LocationID`s and their respective labor hours. We want to be able to perform queries against the data in our XML as though it were relational data, so we need to break up our `LocationID` and `LaborHours` information into columns just as if they were in a relational table.

```
WITH XMLNAMESPACES ('http://schemas.microsoft.com/sqlserver/2004/07/adventure-
works/ProductModelManuInstructions' AS PI)

SELECT pm.ProductModelID,
    pmi.Location.value('./@LocationID', 'int') AS LocationID,
    pmi.Location.value('./@LaborHours', 'decimal(5,2)') AS LaborHours
FROM Production.ProductModel pm
CROSS APPLY pm.Instructions.nodes('/PI:root/PI:Location') AS pmi(Location);
```

Note that the URL portion of the namespace declaration must be entered on a single line. They are shown here word wrapped onto multiple lines because there is a limit to how many characters we can show per line in print. Make sure you include the entire URL on a single line.

Notice that through the use of our `.nodes` method, we are essentially turning one table (`ProductModel`) into two tables (the source table and the `.nodes` results from the `Instructions` column within the `ProductModel` table). Take a look at the results:

```
ProductModelID LocationID  LaborHours
-------------- ----------- ----------------------------------------
7              10          2.50
7              20          1.75
7              30          1.00
7              45          0.50
7              50          3.00
7              60          4.00
10             10          2.00
10             20          1.50
10             30          1.00
10             4           1.50
10             50          3.00
10             60          4.00
43             50          3.00
44             50          3.00
47             10          1.00
```

```
47          20          1.00
47          50          3.50
48          10          1.00
48          20          1.00
48          50          3.50
53          50          0.50
66          50          1.75
67          50          1.00

(23 row(s) affected)
```

As you can see, we are getting back multiple rows for many of what was originally a single row in the `ProductModel` table. For example, `ProductModelID` 7 had six different instances of the `Location` element, so we received six rows instead of just the single row that existed in the `ProductModel` table.

While this is, perhaps, the most complex of the various XML data type methods, the power that it gives to transform XML data for relational use is virtually limitless.

.exist

`.exist` works something like the `EXISTS` statement in SQL. It accepts an expression (in this case, an XQuery expression rather than a SQL expression) and will return a Boolean indication of whether the expression was true or not. (`NULL` is also a possible outcome.)

If, in our `.modify` example, we had wanted to show rows that contain steps that had spec elements, we could use `.exist`:

```
WITH XMLNAMESPACES ('http://schemas.microsoft.com/sqlserver/2004/07/adventure-
works/ProductModelManuInstructions' AS PI)

SELECT ProductModelID, Instructions
FROM Production.ProductModel
WHERE Instructions.exist('/PI:root/PI:Location/PI:step/PI:specs') = 1
```

Pay particular attention to the point at which the test condition is being applied!

For example, the code would show us rows where at least one step had a spec element in it — it does not necessarily require that every step has the spec element. If we wanted every element to be tested, we would either need to pull the elements out as individual rows (using .nodes) or place the test condition in the XQuery.

Note that the URL portion of the namespace declaration must be entered on a single line. They are shown here word wrapped onto multiple lines because there is a limit to how many characters we can show per line in print. Make sure you include the entire URL on a single line.

Enforcing Constraints beyond the Schema Collection

By the time you got to this book, you should have already become somewhat familiar with the basics of constraints in a relational database. Well, if our relational database needs constraints, it follows that our XML data does. Indeed, we've already implemented much of that idea through the use of schema collections. But what if we want to enforce requirements that go beyond the base schema?

Retrieving Relational Data in XML Format

This is an area that SQL Server already had largely figured out prior to the 2005 release. We had a couple of different options, and we had still more options within those options — between them all, things have been pretty flexible for quite some time. Let's take a look.

The FOR XML Clause

This clause is at the root of most of the different integration models available. With the exception of XML mapping schemas (fairly advanced, but we'll touch on them briefly later in the chapter) and the use of XPath, FOR XML will serve as the way of telling SQL Server that it's XML that you want back, not the more typical result set. It is essentially just an option added onto the end of the existing T-SQL SELECT statement.

Let's look at the SELECT statement syntax:

```
SELECT <column list>
[FROM <source table(s)>]
[WHERE <restrictive condition>]
[GROUP BY <column name or expression using a column in the SELECT list>
[HAVING <restrictive condition based on the GROUP BY results>]
[ORDER BY <I>]
[FOR XML {RAW|AUTO|EXPLICIT|PATH}
    [, XMLDATA][, ELEMENTS][, BINARY base64]]
[OPTION (<query hint>, [, ...n])]
```

Most of this should seem pretty trivial by now — after all, this is a *Professional* level title — but it's time to focus in on that FOR XML line.

FOR XML provides four different initial options for how you want your XML formatted in the results:

❑ **RAW** — This sends each row of data in your result set back as a single data element, with the element name of "row" and with each column listed as an attribute of the row element. Even if you join multiple tables, RAW outputs the results with the same number of elements as you would have rows in a standard SQL query.

❑ **AUTO** — This option labels each element with either the table name or table name alias that the data is sourced from. If there is data output from more than one table in the query, the data from each table is split into separate, nested elements. If AUTO is used, then an additional option, ELEMENTS, is also supported if you would like column data presented as elements rather than as attributes.

❑ **EXPLICIT** — This one is certainly the most complex to format your query with, but the end result is that you have a high degree of control of what the XML looks like finally. With this option, you define something of a hierarchy to the data that's being returned, and then format your query such that each piece of data belongs to a specific hierarchy level (and gets assigned a tag accordingly) as desired. This choice has largely been supplanted by the PATH option and is here for backward compatibility.

❑ **PATH** — This was added in SQL Server 2005 to try to provide the level of flexibility of EXPLICIT in a more usable format — this is generally going to be what you want to use when you need a high degree of control of the format of the output.

Note that none of these options provide the required root element. If you want the XML document to be considered to be "well formed," then you will need to wrap the results with a proper opening and closing tag for your root element. While this is in some ways a hassle, it is also a benefit — it means that you can build more complex XML by stringing multiple XML queries together and wrapping the different results into one XML file.

In addition to the major formatting options, there are other optional parameters that further modify the output that SQL Server provides in an XML query:

❑ **XMLDATA** — This tells SQL Server that you would like to apply an XML schema onto the front of the results. The schema will define the structure (including data types) and rules of the XML data that follows.

❑ **ELEMENTS** — This option is available only when you are using the AUTO formatting option. It tells SQL Server that you want the columns in your data returned as nested elements rather than as attributes.

❑ **BINARY BASE64** — This tells SQL Server to encode any binary columns (binary, varbinary, image) in base64 format. This option is implied (SQL Server will use it even if you don't state it) if you are also using the AUTO option. It is not implied but is currently the only effective option for EXPLICIT and RAW queries — eventually, the plan is to have these two options automatically provide a URL link to the binary data (unless you say to do the base64 encoding), but this is not yet implemented.

❑ **TYPE** — Tells SQL Server to return the results reporting the XML data type instead of the default Unicode character type.

❑ **ROOT** — This option will have SQL Server add the root node for you so you don't have to. You can either supply a name for your root or use the default (root).

Let's explore all these options in a little more detail.

RAW

This is something of the "no fuss, no muss" option. The idea here is to just get it done — no fanfare, no special formatting at all — just the absolute minimum to translate a row of relational data into an element of XML data. The element is named "row" (creative, huh?), and each column in the select list is added as an attribute using whatever name the column would have appeared with if you had been running a more traditional SELECT statement.

One downside to the way attributes are named is that you need to make certain that every column has a name. Normally, SQL Server will just show no column heading if you perform an aggregation or other calculated column and don't provide an alias — when doing XML queries, everything MUST have a name, so don't forget to alias calculated columns.

So, let's start things out with something relatively simple. Imagine that our manager has asked us to provide a query that lists a few customers' orders — say CustomerIDs 1 and 2. After cruising through just the first five or so chapters of the book, you would probably say "No Problem!" and supply something like this:

```
SELECT sc.CustomerID,
    pp.LastName,
```

```
    pp.FirstName,
    soh.SalesOrderID,
    soh.OrderDate
FROM Person.Person pp
JOIN Sales.Customer sc
  ON pp.BusinessEntityID = sc.PersonID
JOIN Sales.SalesOrderHeader soh
  ON sc.CustomerID = soh.CustomerID
WHERE sc.CustomerID = 29484 OR sc.CustomerID = 29485;
```

So, you go hand your boss the results:

```
29484   Achong          Gustavo         44132       2001-09-01 00:00:00.000
29484   Achong          Gustavo         45579       2002-03-01 00:00:00.000
...
...
29485   Abel            Catherine       65157       2004-03-01 00:00:00.000
29485   Abel            Catherine       71782       2004-06-01 00:00:00.000
```

Easy, right? Well, now the boss comes back and says, "Great — now I'll just have Billy Bob write something to turn this into XML — too bad that will probably take a day or two." This is your cue to step in and say, "Oh, why didn't you say so?" and simply add three key words:

```
SELECT sc.CustomerID,
    pp.LastName,
    pp.FirstName,
    soh.SalesOrderID,
    soh.OrderDate
FROM Person.Person pp
JOIN Sales.Customer sc
  ON pp.BusinessEntityID = sc.PersonID
JOIN Sales.SalesOrderHeader soh
  ON sc.CustomerID = soh.CustomerID
WHERE sc.CustomerID = 29484 OR sc.CustomerID = 29485
```

```
FOR XML RAW;
```

You have just made the boss very happy. The output is a one-to-one match versus what we would have seen in the result set had we run just a standard SQL query:

```
<row CustomerID="1" LastName="Achong" FirstName="Gustavo" SalesOrderID="44132"
  OrderDate="2001-09-01T00:00:00"/>
<row CustomerID="1" LastName="Achong" FirstName="Gustavo" SalesOrderID="45579"
  OrderDate="2002-03-01T00:00:00"/>
<row CustomerID="1" LastName="Achong" FirstName="Gustavo" SalesOrderID="46389"
  OrderDate="2002-06-01T00:00:00"/>
<row CustomerID="1" LastName="Achong" FirstName="Gustavo" SalesOrderID="47454"
  OrderDate="2002-09-01T00:00:00"/>
<row CustomerID="1" LastName="Achong" FirstName="Gustavo" SalesOrderID="48395"
  OrderDate="2002-12-01T00:00:00"/>
<row CustomerID="1" LastName="Achong" FirstName="Gustavo" SalesOrderID="49495"
  OrderDate="2003-03-01T00:00:00"/>
<row CustomerID="1" LastName="Achong" FirstName="Gustavo" SalesOrderID="50756"
```

```
      OrderDate="2003-06-01T00:00:00"/>
  <row CustomerID="2" LastName="Abel" FirstName="Catherine" SalesOrderID="53459"
      OrderDate="2003-09-01T00:00:00"/>
  <row CustomerID="2" LastName="Abel" FirstName="Catherine" SalesOrderID="58907"
      OrderDate="2003-12-01T00:00:00"/>
  <row CustomerID="2" LastName="Abel" FirstName="Catherine" SalesOrderID="65157"
      OrderDate="2004-03-01T00:00:00"/>
  <row CustomerID="2" LastName="Abel" FirstName="Catherine" SalesOrderID="71782"
      OrderDate="2004-06-01T00:00:00"/>
```

Let me just issue a reminder that Management Studio will truncate any column where the length exceeds the number set in the Tools➤Options menu in the Query Results Results to Text node (maximum is 8192). This issue exists in the results window (grid or text, though grid will allow larger numbers if the data is XML) and if you output directly to a file. This is an issue with the tool — not SQL Server itself. If you use another method to retrieve results (ADO.NET for example), you shouldn't encounter an issue with this.

> *Also, be aware that I added carriage returns in the preceding results for clarity's sake — SQL Server just runs all the elements together to make them more compact.*

We have one element in XML for each row of data our query produced. All column information, regardless of what table was the source of the data, is represented as an attribute of the row element. The downside of this is that we haven't represented the true hierarchical nature of our data — orders are placed only by customers. The upside, however, is that the XML Document Object Model (DOM) — if that's the model you're using — is going to be much less deep and, hence, will have a slightly smaller footprint in memory and perform better, depending on what you're doing.

AUTO

AUTO takes a somewhat different approach to our data than RAW does. AUTO tries to format things a little better for you — naming elements based on the table (or the table alias if you use one). In addition, AUTO recognizes the notion that our data probably has some underlying hierarchical notion to it that is supposed to be represented in the XML.

Let's go back to our customer orders example from the last section. This time, we'll make use of the AUTO option, so we can see the difference versus the rather plain output we got with RAW.

```
SELECT sc.CustomerID,
    pp.LastName,
    pp.FirstName,
    soh.SalesOrderID,
    soh.OrderDate
FROM Person.Person pp
JOIN Sales.Customer sc
    ON pp.BusinessEntityID = sc.PersonID
JOIN Sales.SalesOrderHeader soh
    ON sc.CustomerID = soh.CustomerID
WHERE sc.CustomerID = 29484 OR sc.CustomerID = 29485
```

The first apparent difference is that the element name has changed to be the name or alias of the table that is the source of the data — you'll want to consider this when choosing the aliases for your tables in a

FOR XML AUTO query. Perhaps an even more significant difference appears when we look at the XML more thoroughly. I have again cleaned up the output a bit for clarity:

```
<sc CustomerID="29484">
  <pp LastName="Achong" FirstName="Gustavo">
    <soh SalesOrderID="44132" OrderDate="2001-09-01T00:00:00"/>
    <soh SalesOrderID="45579" OrderDate="2002-03-01T00:00:00"/>
    <soh SalesOrderID="46389" OrderDate="2002-06-01T00:00:00"/>
    <soh SalesOrderID="47454" OrderDate="2002-09-01T00:00:00"/>
    <soh SalesOrderID="48395" OrderDate="2002-12-01T00:00:00"/>
    <soh SalesOrderID="49495" OrderDate="2003-03-01T00:00:00"/>
    <soh SalesOrderID="50756" OrderDate="2003-06-01T00:00:00"/>
  </pp>
</sc>
<sc CustomerID="29485">
  <pp LastName="Abel" FirstName="Catherine">
    <soh SalesOrderID="53459" OrderDate="2003-09-01T00:00:00"/>
    <soh SalesOrderID="58907" OrderDate="2003-12-01T00:00:00"/>
    <soh SalesOrderID="65157" OrderDate="2004-03-01T00:00:00"/>
    <soh SalesOrderID="71782" OrderDate="2004-06-01T00:00:00"/>
  </pp>
</sc>
```

Data that is sourced from our second table (as determined by the SELECT list) is nested inside the data sourced from the first table. In this case, our soh elements are nested inside our pp elements, which are in turn nested inside of our c elements. If a column from the SalesOrderHeader table were listed first in our select list, then Person and Customer would both be nested inside SalesOrderHeader.

> *Pay attention to this business of the ordering of your SELECT list! Think about the primary question your XML query is meant to answer. Arrange your SELECT list such that the style that it produces is fitting for the goal of your XML. Sure, you could always style it into the different form — but why do that if SQL Server could have just produced it for you that way in the first place?*

The downside to using AUTO is that the resulting XML data model ends up being slightly more complex. The upside is that the data is more explicitly broken up into a hierarchical model. This makes life easier when the elements are more significant breaking points — such as when you have a doubly sorted report (for example, SalesOrderHeader rows sorted within Contact rows).

EXPLICIT

The word *explicit* is an interesting choice for this option — it loosely describes the kind of language you're likely to use while trying to create your query. The EXPLICIT option takes much more effort to prepare, but it also rewards that effort with very fine granularity of control over what's an element and what's an attribute, as well as what elements are nested in what other elements.

> *Much of what you can do with EXPLICIT can now be replicated using PATH. EXPLICIT does, however, give you a very fine and, as the keyword name implies, explicit level of control about your output. In general, I would point you at PATH and tell you to look at EXPLICIT when PATH doesn't seem to be meeting your needs.*

EXPLICIT enables you to define each level of the hierarchy and how each level is going to look. To define the hierarchy, you create what is internally called the universal table. The universal table is, in many respects, just like any other result set you might produce in SQL Server. It is usually produced by making use of UNION statements to piece it together one level at a time, but you could, for example, build much of the data in a UDF and then make a SELECT against that to produce the final XML. The big difference between the universal table and a more traditional result set is that you must provide sufficient metadata right within your result set such that SQL Server can then transform that result set into an XML document in the schema you desire.

What do I mean by sufficient metadata? Well, to give you an idea of just how complex this can be, let's look at a real universal table — one used by a code example we'll examine a little later in the section:

Tag	Parent	sc!1! CustomerID	pp!2! LastName	pp!2! FirstName	soh!3! SalesOrderID	soh!3! OrderDate
1	NULL	29484	NULL	NULL	NULL	NULL
2	1	29484	Achong	Gustavo	NULL	NULL
3	2	29484	Achong	Gustavo	44132	9/1/2001
3	2	29484	Achong	Gustavo	45579	3/1/2002
3	2	29484	Achong	Gustavo	46389	6/1/2002
3	2	29484	Achong	Gustavo	47454	9/1/2002
3	2	29484	Achong	Gustavo	48395	12/1/2002
3	2	29484	Achong	Gustavo	49495	3/1/2003
3	2	29484	Achong	Gustavo	50756	6/1/2003
1	NULL	29485	NULL	NULL	NULL	NULL
2	1	29485	Abel	Catherine	NULL	NULL
3	2	29485	Abel	Catherine	53459	9/1/2003
3	2	29485	Abel	Catherine	58907	12/1/2003
3	2	29485	Abel	Catherine	65157	3/1/2004
3	2	29485	Abel	Catherine	71782	6/1/2004

This is what the universal table we would need to build would look like in order to make our EXPLICIT return exactly the same results that we received with our AUTO query in the last example.

Your first inclination might be to say, "Hey, if this is just producing the same thing as AUTO, why use it?" Well, this particular example happens to be producible using AUTO — I'm using this one on purpose to illustrate some functional differences compared to something you've already seen. We will, however, see later in this section that EXPLICIT will allow us to do the formatting extras that aren't possible with AUTO or RAW (but are with PATH) — so please bear with me on this one.

You should note several things about this result set:

❑   It has two special metadata columns — *Tag* and *Parent* — added to it that do not, otherwise, relate to the data (they didn't come from table columns).

❑   The actual column names are adhering to a special format (which happens to supply additional metadata).

❑   The data has been ordered based on the hierarchy.

Each of these items is critical to our end result, so, before we start working a complete example, let's look at what we need to know to build it.

Tag and Parent

XML is naturally hierarchical in nature (elements are contained with other elements, which essentially creates a parent-child relationship). `Tag` and `Parent` are columns that define the relationship of each row to the element hierarchy. Each row is assigned to a certain tag level (which will later have an element name assigned to it) — that level, as you might expect, goes in the `Tag` column. `Parent` then supplies reference information that indicates what the next highest level in the hierarchy is. When you do this, SQL Server knows at what level this row needs to be nested or assigned as an attribute (what it's going to be — element or attribute — will be figured out based on the column name — but we'll get to that in our next section). If `Parent` is `NULL`, then SQL Server knows that this row must be a top-level element or an attribute of that element.

So, if we had data that looked like this:

Tag	Parent
1	NULL
2	1

then the first row would be related to a top-level element (an attribute of the outer element or the element itself), and the second would be related to an element that was nested inside the top-level element (its `Parent` value of 1 matches with the `Tag` value of the first).

Column Naming

Frankly, this was the most confusing part of all when I first started looking at EXPLICIT. While `Tag` and `Parent` have nice neat demarcation points (they are each their own column), the name takes several pieces of metadata and crams them together as one thing — the only way to tell where one stops and the next begins is by separating them by an exclamation mark (!).

The naming format looks like this:

```
<element name>!<tag>![<attribute
name>][!{element|hide|ID|IDREF|IDREFS|xml|xmltext|cdata}]
```

The element name is, of course, just that — what you want to be the name of the element in the XML. For any given tag level, once you define a column with one name, any other column with that same tag must have the same name as the previous column(s) with that tag number. So, if you have a column already defined as [MyElement!2!MyCol], then another column could be named [MyElement!2!MyOtherCol], but [SomeOtherName!2!MyOtherCol] could not be.

The tag relates the column to rows with a matching tag number. When SQL Server looks at the universal table, it reads the tag number and then analyzes the columns with the same tag number. So, when SQL Server sees the row:

Tag	Parent	c!1! ContactID	c!1! LastName	c!1! FirstName	soh!2! SalesOrderID	soh!2! OrderDate
1	NULL	1	Achong	Gustavo	NULL	NULL

it can look at the tag number, see that it is 1, and know that it should process `sc!1!ContactID`, `c!1!LastName`, and `c!1!FirstName`, but that it doesn't have to process `pp!2!LastName` or `soh!3!SalesOrderID`, for example. Likewise it can look at the tag number in the next row, see that it is 2, and know that it should process `sc!1!ContactID`, `pp!2!LastName`, and `pp!2!FirstName`, but that it doesn't have to process `soh!3!SalesOrderID`.

That takes us to the attribute name, which is where things start getting more complex (hey, we still have one more to go after this!). If you do not specify a directive (which comes next), then the attribute is required and is the name of the XML attribute that this column will supply a value for. The attribute will be in the XML as part of the element specified in the column name.

If you do specify a directive, then the attribute falls into three different camps:

❑ **It's prohibited** — That is, you must leave the attribute blank (you do still use a bang (!) to mark its place though). This is the case if you use a CDATA directive.

❑ **It's optional** — That is, you can supply the attribute but don't have to. What happens in this case varies depending on the directive that you've chosen.

❑ **It's still required** — This is true for the `elements` and `xml` directives. In this case, the name of the attribute will become the name of a totally new element that will be created as a result of the `elements` or `xml` directive.

So, now that we have enough of the naming down to meet the minimum requirements for a query, let's go ahead and look at an example of what kind of query produces what kind of results.

We will start with the query to produce the same basic data that we used in our RAW and AUTO examples. You will notice that EXPLICIT has a much bigger impact on the code than we saw when we went with RAW and AUTO. With both RAW and AUTO, we added the FOR XML clause at the end, and we were largely done. With EXPLICIT, we will quickly see that we need to entirely rethink the way our query comes together.

It looks like this (yuck):

```
USE AdventureWorks2008

SELECT 1                   as Tag,
       NULL                as Parent,
       sc.CustomerID       as [sc!1!CustomerID],
       NULL                as [pp!2!LastName],
       NULL                as [pp!2!FirstName],
       NULL                as [soh!3!SalesOrderID],
       NULL                as [soh!3!OrderDate]
```

```
FROM Person.Person pp
JOIN Sales.Customer sc
  ON pp.BusinessEntityID = sc.PersonID
WHERE sc.CustomerID = 29484 OR sc.CustomerID = 29485

UNION

SELECT 2,
       1,
       sc.CustomerID            as [sc!1!CustomerID],
       pp.LastName              as [pp!2!LastName],
       pp.FirstName             as [pp!2!FirstName],
       NULL                     as [soh!3!SalesOrderID],
       NULL                     as [soh!3!OrderDate]
FROM Person.Person pp
JOIN Sales.Customer sc
  ON pp.BusinessEntityID = sc.PersonID
JOIN Sales.SalesOrderHeader soh
  ON sc.CustomerID = soh.CustomerID
WHERE sc.CustomerID = 29484 OR sc.CustomerID = 29485

UNION ALL

SELECT 3,
       2,
       sc.CustomerID            as [sc!1!CustomerID],
       pp.LastName              as [pp!2!LastName],
       pp.FirstName             as [pp!2!FirstName],
       soh.SalesOrderID,
       soh.OrderDate
FROM Person.Person pp
JOIN Sales.Customer sc
  ON pp.BusinessEntityID = sc.PersonID
JOIN Sales.SalesOrderHeader soh
  ON sc.CustomerID = soh.CustomerID
WHERE sc.CustomerID = 29484 OR sc.CustomerID = 29485

ORDER BY [sc!1!CustomerID], [pp!2!LastName], [pp!2!FirstName], [soh!3!SalesOrderID]
FOR XML EXPLICIT
```

> Notice that we use the **FOR XML** clause only once — after the last query in the **UNION**.

I reiterate — yuck! But, ugly as it is, with just a few changes, I could change my XML into forms that AUTO wouldn't give me.

As a fairly simple illustration, let's make a couple of small alterations to our requirements for this query. What if we decided that we wanted the LastName information to be an attribute of the soh rather than (or, as it happens, in addition to) the pp element? With AUTO, we would need some trickery in order to get this (for every row, we would need to look up the Customer again using a correlated subquery — AUTO won't let you use the same value in two places). If you had multiple lookups, your code could get very complex — indeed, you might not be able to get what you're after at all. With EXPLICIT, this is all relatively easy (at least, by EXPLICIT's definition of easy).

To do this with EXPLICIT, we just need to reference the LastName in our SELECT list again, but associate the new instance of it with soh instead of c:

```
USE AdventureWorks2008

SELECT 1                       as Tag,
       NULL                    as Parent,
       sc.CustomerID           as [sc!1!CustomerID],
       NULL                    as [pp!2!LastName],
       NULL                    as [pp!2!FirstName],
       NULL                    as [soh!3!SalesOrderID],

       NULL                    as [soh!3!OrderDate],
       NULL                    as [soh!3!LastName]

FROM Person.Person pp
JOIN Sales.Customer sc
  ON pp.BusinessEntityID = sc.PersonID
WHERE sc.CustomerID = 29484 OR sc.CustomerID = 29485

UNION

SELECT 2,
       1,
       sc.CustomerID           as [sc!1!CustomerID],
       pp.LastName             as [pp!2!LastName],
       pp.FirstName            as [pp!2!FirstName],
       NULL                    as [soh!3!SalesOrderID],

       NULL                    as [soh!3!OrderDate],
       NULL                    as [soh!3!LastName]

FROM Person.Person pp
JOIN Sales.Customer sc
  ON pp.BusinessEntityID = sc.PersonID
JOIN Sales.SalesOrderHeader soh
  ON sc.CustomerID = soh.CustomerID
WHERE sc.CustomerID = 29484 OR sc.CustomerID = 29485

UNION ALL

SELECT 3,
       2,
       sc.CustomerID           as [sc!1!CustomerID],
       pp.LastName             as [pp!2!LastName],
       pp.FirstName            as [soh!2!FirstName],
       soh.SalesOrderID,

       soh.OrderDate,
       pp.LastName

FROM Person.Person pp
JOIN Sales.Customer sc
  ON pp.BusinessEntityID = sc.PersonID
JOIN Sales.SalesOrderHeader soh
  ON sc.CustomerID = soh.CustomerID
```

```
WHERE sc.CustomerID = 29484 OR sc.CustomerID = 29485

ORDER BY [sc!1!CustomerID], [pp!2!LastName], [pp!2!FirstName], [soh!3!SalesOrderID]
FOR XML EXPLICIT
```

Execute this, and you get pretty much the same results as before, only this time you received the additional attribute you were looking for in your soh element:

```
<sc CustomerID="29484">
  <pp LastName="Achong" FirstName="Gustavo">
    <soh SalesOrderID="44132" OrderDate="2001-09-01T0:00:00"
LastName="Achong"/>
    <soh SalesOrderID="45579" OrderDate="2002-03-01T0:00:00"
LastName="Achong"/>
    <soh SalesOrderID="46389" OrderDate="2002-06-01T0:00:00"
LastName="Achong"/>
    <soh SalesOrderID="47454" OrderDate="2002-09-01T0:00:00"
LastName="Achong"/>
    <soh SalesOrderID="48395" OrderDate="2002-12-01T0:00:00"
LastName="Achong"/>
    <soh SalesOrderID="49495" OrderDate="2003-03-01T0:00:00"
LastName="Achong"/>
    <soh SalesOrderID="50756" OrderDate="2003-06-01T0:00:00"
LastName="Achong"/>
  </pp>
</sc>
<sc CustomerID="29485">
  <pp LastName="Abel" FirstName="Catherine">
    <soh SalesOrderID="53459" OrderDate="2003-09-01T0:00:00"
LastName="Abel"/>
    <soh SalesOrderID="58907" OrderDate="2003-12-01T0:00:00"
LastName="Abel"/>
    <soh SalesOrderID="65157" OrderDate="2004-03-01T0:00:00"
LastName="Abel"/>
    <soh SalesOrderID="71782" OrderDate="2004-06-01T0:00:00"
LastName="Abel"/>
  </pp>
</sc>
```

This example is really just for starters. You can utilize directives to achieve far more flexibility — shaping and controlling both your data and your schema output (if you use the XMLDATA option).

Directives are a real pain to understand. Once you do understand them, they aren't all that bad to deal with, though they can still be confusing at times (some of them work pretty counterintuitively and behave differently in different situations). My personal opinion (and the members of the dev team I know are going to shoot me for saying this) is that someone at Microsoft had a really bad day and decided to make something that would inflict as much pain as he/she was feeling but would be so cool that people wouldn't be able to help but use it.

All together, there are eight possible directives you can use. Some can be used in the same level of the hierarchy — others are mutually exclusive within a given hierarchy level.

The purpose behind directives is to allow you to tweak your results. Without directives, the EXPLICIT option would have little or no value (AUTO would take care of most real things that you can do with

EXPLICIT if you don't use directives, even though, as I indicated earlier, you sometimes have to get a little tricky). So, with this in mind, let's look at what directives are available.

element

This is probably the easiest of all the directives to understand. All it does is indicate that you want the column in question to be added as an element rather than an attribute. The element will be added as a child to the current tag. For example, let's say that our manager from the previous examples has indicated that he or she needs the OrderDate to be represented as its own element. This can be accomplished as easily as adding the element directive to the end of our OrderDate field:

```
SELECT 1                      as Tag,
       NULL                   as Parent,
       sc.CustomerID          as [sc!1!CustomerID],
       NULL                   as [pp!2!LastName],
       NULL                   as [pp!2!FirstName],
       NULL                   as [soh!3!SalesOrderID],

       NULL                   as [soh!3!OrderDate!element]

FROM Person.Person pp
JOIN Sales.Customer sc
  ON pp.BusinessEntityID = sc.PersonID
WHERE sc.CustomerID = 29484 OR sc.CustomerID = 29485

UNION

SELECT 2,
       1,
       sc.CustomerID          as [sc!1!CustomerID],
       pp.LastName            as [pp!2!LastName],
       pp.FirstName           as [pp!2!FirstName],
       NULL,
       NULL
FROM Person.Person pp
JOIN Sales.Customer sc
  ON pp.BusinessEntityID = sc.PersonID
JOIN Sales.SalesOrderHeader soh
  ON sc.CustomerID = soh.CustomerID
WHERE sc.CustomerID = 29484 OR sc.CustomerID = 29485

UNION ALL

SELECT 3,
       2,
       sc.CustomerID          as [sc!1!CustomerID],
       pp.LastName            as [pp!2!LastName],
       pp.FirstName           as [pp!2!FirstName],
       soh.SalesOrderID,
       soh.OrderDate
FROM Person.Person pp
JOIN Sales.Customer sc
  ON pp.BusinessEntityID = sc.PersonID
JOIN Sales.SalesOrderHeader soh
```

```
       ON sc.CustomerID = soh.CustomerID
   WHERE sc.CustomerID = 29484 OR sc.CustomerID = 29485

   ORDER BY [sc!1!CustomerID], [pp!2!LastName], [pp!2!FirstName], [soh!3!SalesOrderID]
   FOR XML EXPLICIT
```

Suddenly, we have an extra element instead of an attribute:

```
<sc CustomerID="29484">
  <pp LastName="Achong" FirstName="Gustavo">
    <soh SalesOrderID="44132">
      <OrderDate>2001-09-01T00:00:00</OrderDate>
    </soh>
    <soh SalesOrderID="45579">
      <OrderDate>2002-03-01T00:00:00</OrderDate>
    </soh>
    <soh SalesOrderID="46389">
      <OrderDate>2002-06-01T00:00:00</OrderDate>
    </soh>
    <soh SalesOrderID="47454">
      <OrderDate>2002-09-01T00:00:00</OrderDate>
    </soh>
    <soh SalesOrderID="48395">
      <OrderDate>2002-12-01T00:00:00</OrderDate>
    </soh>
    <soh SalesOrderID="49495">
      <OrderDate>2003-03-01T00:00:00</OrderDate>
    </soh>
    <soh SalesOrderID="50756">
      <OrderDate>2003-06-01T00:00:00</OrderDate>
    </soh>
  </pp>
</sc>
<sc CustomerID="29485">
  <pp LastName="Abel" FirstName="Catherine">
    <soh SalesOrderID="53459">
      <OrderDate>2003-09-01T00:00:00</OrderDate>
    </soh>
    <soh SalesOrderID="58907">
      <OrderDate>2003-12-01T00:00:00</OrderDate>
    </soh>
    <soh SalesOrderID="65157">
      <OrderDate>2004-03-01T00:00:00</OrderDate>
    </soh>
    <soh SalesOrderID="71782">
      <OrderDate>2004-06-01T00:00:00</OrderDate>
    </soh>
  </pp>
</sc>
```

xml

This directive is essentially just like the `element` directive. It causes the column in question to be generated as an element rather than an attribute. The differences between the `xml` and `element` directives will be seen only if you have special characters that require encoding — for example, the = sign is reserved in XML. If you need to represent an =, then you need to encode it (for =, it would be encoded as &eq). With the `element` directive, the content of the element is automatically encoded. With `xml`, the content is passed straight into the resulting XML without encoding. If you use the `xml` directive, no other item at this level (the number) can have a directive other than `hide`.

hide

Hide is another simple one that does exactly what it says it does — hides the results of that column.

Why in the world would you want to do that? Well, sometimes we include columns for reasons other than output. For example, in a normal query, we can perform an ORDER BY based on columns that do not appear in the SELECT list. For UNION queries, however, we can't do that — we have to specify a column in the SELECT list because it's the one thing that unites all the queries that we are performing the UNION on.

Let's use a little example of tracking some product sales. We'll say that we want a list of all of our products as well as the SalesOrderIDs of the orders they shipped on and the date that they shipped. We only want the ProductID, but we want the ProductID to be sorted such that any given product is near similar products — that means we need to sort based on the ProductSubcategoryID, but we do not want the ProductSubcategoryID to be included in the end results.

We can start out by building the query without the directive — that way we can see that our sort is working:

```
SELECT 1                          as Tag,
       NULL                       as Parent,
       p.ProductID                as [Product!1!ProductID],
       p.ProductSubcategoryID     as [Product!1!ProductSubcategoryID],
       NULL                       as [Order!2!OrderID],
       NULL                       as [Order!2!OrderDate]
FROM Production.Product p
JOIN Sales.SalesOrderDetail AS sod
    ON p.ProductID = sod.ProductID
JOIN Sales.SalesOrderHeader AS soh
    ON sod.SalesOrderID = soh.SalesOrderID
WHERE soh.OrderDate BETWEEN '2003-03-27' AND '2003-03-27'

UNION ALL

SELECT 2,
       1,
       p.ProductID,
       p.ProductSubcategoryID,
       soh.SalesOrderID,
       soh.OrderDate
FROM Production.Product AS p
JOIN Sales.SalesOrderDetail AS sod
    ON p.ProductID = sod.ProductID
JOIN Sales.SalesOrderHeader AS soh
    ON sod.SalesOrderID = soh.SalesOrderID
WHERE soh.OrderDate BETWEEN '2003-03-27' AND '2003-03-27'
ORDER BY [Product!1!ProductSubcategoryID],[Product!1!ProductID],
```

```
[Order!2!OrderID]
FOR XML EXPLICIT
```

Be sure to check out the way we dealt with the OrderDate *on this one. Even though I needed to fetch that information out of the* SalesOrderHeader *table, it was easy (since we're using* EXPLICIT *anyway) to combine that information with the* SalesOrderID *from the* SalesOrderDetail *table. As it happens, I could have also just grabbed the* SalesOrderID *from the* SalesOrderHeader *table, too, but sometimes you need to mix data from multiple tables in one element, and this query is yet another demonstration of how we can do just that.*

We can see from the results that we are indeed getting the sort we expected:

```
<Product ProductID="779" ProductSubcategoryID="1">
    <Order OrderID="49775" OrderDate="2003-03-27T00:00:00"/>
</Product>
<Product ProductID="782" ProductSubcategoryID="1">
    <Order OrderID="49774" OrderDate="2003-03-27T00:00:00"/>
</Product>
<Product ProductID="764" ProductSubcategoryID="2">
    <Order OrderID="49776" OrderDate="2003-03-27T00:00:00"/>
</Product><
Product ProductID="766" ProductSubcategoryID="2">
    <Order OrderID="49777" OrderDate="2003-03-27T00:00:00"/>
</Product>
```

Now we'll add our `hide` directive and get rid of the category information:

```
SELECT 1                          as Tag,
       NULL                       as Parent,
       p.ProductID                as [Product!1!ProductID],

       p.ProductSubcategoryID     as [Product!1!ProductSubcategoryID!hide],

       NULL                       as [Order!2!OrderID],
       NULL                       as [Order!2!OrderDate]
FROM Production.Product p
JOIN Sales.SalesOrderDetail AS sod
    ON p.ProductID = sod.ProductID
JOIN Sales.SalesOrderHeader AS soh
    ON sod.SalesOrderID = soh.SalesOrderID
WHERE soh.OrderDate BETWEEN '2003-03-27' AND '2003-03-27'

UNION ALL

SELECT 2,
       1,
       p.ProductID,
       p.ProductSubcategoryID,
       soh.SalesOrderID,
       soh.OrderDate
FROM Production.Product AS p
JOIN Sales.SalesOrderDetail AS sod
    ON p.ProductID = sod.ProductID
```

```
    JOIN Sales.SalesOrderHeader AS soh
        ON sod.SalesOrderID = soh.SalesOrderID
    WHERE soh.OrderDate BETWEEN '2003-03-27' AND '2003-03-27'
```

```
    ORDER BY [Product!1!ProductSubcategoryID!hide],[Product!1!ProductID],
        [Order!2!OrderID]
```

```
    FOR XML EXPLICIT
```

And we get the same results; only this time, our `Category` information is indeed hidden:

```
    <Product ProductID="779">
        <Order OrderID="49775" OrderDate="2003-03-27T00:00:00"/>
    </Product>
    <Product ProductID="782">
        <Order OrderID="49774" OrderDate="2003-03-27T00:00:00"/>
    </Product>
    <Product ProductID="764">
        <Order OrderID="49776" OrderDate="2003-03-27T00:00:00"/>
    </Product>
    <Product ProductID="766">
        <Order OrderID="49777" OrderDate="2003-03-27T00:00:00"/>
    </Product>
```

id, idref, and idrefs

None of these three has any affect whatsoever unless you also make use of the XMLDATA option (it goes after the EXPLICIT in the FOR clause) or validate against some other schema that has the appropriate declarations. This makes perfect sense when you think about what they do — they add things to the schema to enforce behavior, but, without a schema, what do you modify?

You see, XML has the concept of an id. An id in XML works much the same as a primary key does in relational data — it designates a unique identifier for that element name in your XML document. For any element name, there can be no more than one attribute specified in the id. What attribute is to serve as the id is defined in the schema for the XML. Once you have one element with a given value for your id attribute, no other element with the same element name is allowed to have the same attribute.

> **Unlike primary keys in SQL, you cannot have multiple attributes make up your id in XML (there is no concept of a composite key).**

Since XML has a concept that is similar to a primary key, it probably comes as no surprise that XML also has a concept that is similar to a foreign key — that's where idref and idrefs come in. Both are used to create a reference from an attribute in one element to an id attribute in another element.

What does this do for us? Well, if we didn't have these, there would only be one way to create a relationship between two elements — nest them. By giving a certain element an id and then making reference to it from an attribute declared as being an idref or idrefs attribute, we gain the ability to link the two elements, regardless of their position in the document.

This should bring on the question, "OK — so why are there two of them?" The answer is implied in their names: idref provides for a single value that must match an existing element's id value. idrefs provides a multivalued, whitespace-separated list — again, the values must *each* match an existing element's id value. The result is that you use idref if you are trying to establish a one-to-many relationship (there will only be one of each id value but potentially many elements with that value in an attribute of idref). Use idrefs when you are trying to establish a many-to-many relationship (each element with an idrefs can refer to many ids, and those values can be referred to by many ids).

To illustrate this one, we'll go with a slight modification of our last query. We'll start with the idref directive:

```
SELECT 1                         as Tag,
       NULL                      as Parent,

       p.ProductID               as [Product!1!ProductID!ID],

       p.ProductSubcategoryID    as [Product!1!ProductSubCategoryID!hide],
       NULL                      as [Order!2!OrderID],

       NULL                      as [Order!2!ProductID!idref],

       NULL                      as [Order!2!OrderDate]
FROM Production.Product AS p
JOIN Sales.SalesOrderDetail AS sod
    ON p.ProductID = sod.ProductID
JOIN Sales.SalesOrderHeader AS soh
    ON sod.SalesOrderID = soh.SalesOrderID
WHERE soh.OrderDate BETWEEN '2003-03-27' AND '2003-03-27'

UNION ALL

SELECT  2,
        1,
        p.ProductID,
        p.ProductSubcategoryID,
        sod.SalesOrderID,
        sod.ProductID,
        soh.OrderDate
FROM Production.Product AS p
JOIN Sales.SalesOrderDetail AS sod
    ON p.ProductID = sod.ProductID
JOIN Sales.SalesOrderHeader AS soh
    ON sod.SalesOrderID = soh.SalesOrderID
WHERE soh.OrderDate BETWEEN '2003-03-27' AND '2003-03-27'

ORDER BY [Product!1!ProductSubCategoryID!hide],[Product!1!ProductID!ID],
      [Order!2!OrderID]
FOR XML EXPLICIT, XMLDATA
```

When we look at the results, there are really just two pieces that we are interested in — the schema and our product element:

```
<Schema name="Schema1" xmlns="urn:schemas-microsoft-com:xml-data"
        xmlns:dt="urn:schemas-microsoft-com:datatypes">
    <ElementType name="Product" content="mixed" model="open">
        <AttributeType name="ProductID" dt:type="id"/>
        <attribute type="ProductID"/>
```

```
        </ElementType>
        <ElementType name="Order" content="mixed" model="open">
            <AttributeType name="OrderID" dt:type="i4"/>
            <AttributeType name="ProductID" dt:type="idref"/>
            <AttributeType name="OrderDate" dt:type="dateTime"/>
            <attribute type="OrderID"/>
            <attribute type="ProductID"/>
            <attribute type="OrderDate"/>
        </ElementType>
    </Schema>
```

In the schema, you can see some fairly specific type information. Our `Product` is declared as a type of element, and you can also see that `ProductID` has been declared as being the `id` for this element type. Likewise, we have an `Order` element with the `ProductID` declared as an `idref`.

The next piece that we're interested in is a `Product` element:

```
<Product xmlns="x-schema:#Schema1" ProductID="779">
    <Order OrderID="49775" ProductID="779" OrderDate="2003-03-27T00:00:00"/>
</Product>
```

In this case, notice that SQL Server has referenced our inline schema in the `Product` element. This declares that the `Product` element and everything within it must comply with our schema — thus ensuring that our `id` and `idrefs` will be enforced.

When we try to use the `idrefs` directive, we have to get a little trickier. SQL Server requires that the query that we use to build our `idrefs` list be separate from the query that builds the elements with the `ids`. This means we must add another query to our `UNION` to supply the `idrefs` (the list of possible `ids` has to be known before we can build the `idrefs` list — but the actual `ids` will come after the `id` list). The query to generate the `idrefs` must immediately precede the query that generates the `ids`. This makes the query look pretty convoluted:

```
SELECT 1                        as Tag,
        NULL                    as Parent,
        p.ProductID             as [Product!1!ProductID],
        NULL                    as [Product!1!OrderList!idrefs],
        NULL                    as [Order!2!OrderID!id],
        NULL                    as [Order!2!OrderDate]
FROM Production.Product p
JOIN Sales.SalesOrderDetail AS sod
    ON p.ProductID = sod.ProductID
JOIN Sales.SalesOrderHeader AS soh
    ON sod.SalesOrderID = soh.SalesOrderID
WHERE soh.OrderDate BETWEEN '2003-03-27' AND '2003-03-31'

UNION ALL

SELECT 1,
        NULL,
        p.ProductID,
        soh.SalesOrderID,
        NULL,
```

```
            NULL
FROM Production.Product AS p
JOIN Sales.SalesOrderDetail AS sod
    ON p.ProductID = sod.ProductID
JOIN Sales.SalesOrderHeader AS soh
    ON sod.SalesOrderID = soh.SalesOrderID
WHERE soh.OrderDate BETWEEN '2003-03-27' AND '2003-03-31'

UNION ALL

SELECT 2,
        1,
        p.ProductID,
        soh.SalesOrderID,
        soh.SalesOrderID,
        soh.OrderDate
FROM Production.Product AS p
JOIN Sales.SalesOrderDetail AS sod
    ON p.ProductID = sod.ProductID
JOIN Sales.SalesOrderHeader AS soh
    ON sod.SalesOrderID = soh.SalesOrderID
WHERE soh.OrderDate BETWEEN '2003-03-27' AND '2003-03-31'
ORDER BY [Product!1!ProductID], [Order!2!OrderID!id],
 [Product!1!OrderList!idrefs]
FOR XML EXPLICIT, XMLDATA
```

Note that I've expanded the date range a bit to make sure that there are multiple product IDs for a given range so you see the proper many-to-many relationship.

The schema winds up looking an awful lot like the one we got for `idref`:

```
<Schema name="Schema4" xmlns="urn:schemas-microsoft-com:xml-data"
        xmlns:dt="urn:schemas-microsoft-com:datatypes">
    <ElementType name="Product" content="mixed" model="open">
        <AttributeType name="ProductID" dt:type="i4"/>
        <AttributeType name="OrderList" dt:type="idrefs"/>
        <attribute type="ProductID"/>
        <attribute type="OrderList"/>
    </ElementType>
    <ElementType name="Order" content="mixed" model="open">
        <AttributeType name="OrderID" dt:type="id"/>
        <AttributeType name="OrderDate" dt:type="dateTime"/>
        <attribute type="OrderID"/>
        <attribute type="OrderDate"/>
    </ElementType>
</Schema>
```

But the elements couldn't be much more different:

```
<Product xmlns="x-schema:#Schema4" ProductID="763" OrderList="49790 49797">
    <Order OrderID="49790" OrderDate="2003-03-28T00:00:00"/>
    <Order OrderID="49797" OrderDate="2003-03-29T00:00:00"/>
</Product>
```

Using id, idref, and idrefs is very complex. Still, they allow you to make your output strongly typed. For most situations, this level of control and the hassles that go with it simply aren't necessary but, when they are, these three can be lifesavers.

xmltext

xmltext expects the content of the column to be XML and attempts to insert it as an integral part of the XML document you are creating.

While, on the surface, that may sound simple enough (Okay, so they're inserting some text in the middle — big deal!), the rules of where, when, and how it inserts the data are a little strange:

❑ As long as the XML you're trying to insert is well formed, the root element will be stripped out — but the attributes of that element will be retained and applied depending on the following few rules.

❑ If you did not specify an attribute name when using the xmltext directive, then the retained attributes from the stripped element will be added to the element that contains the xmltext directive. The names of the retained attributes will be used in the combined element. If any attribute names from the retained attribute data conflict with other attribute information in the combined element, then the conflicting attribute is left out from the retained data.

❑ Any elements nested inside the stripped element will become nested elements of the combined element.

❑ If an attribute name is provided with the xmldata directive, then the retained data is placed in an element of the supplied name. The new element becomes a child of the element that made the directive.

❑ If any of the resulting XML is not well formed, there is no defined behavior. Basically, the behavior will depend on how the end result looks, but I would figure that you're going to get an error (I haven't seen an instance where you can refer to data that is not well formed and escape without an error).

cdata

The term cdata is a holdover from DTDs and SGML. (SGML is an old markup language, used in the graphics industry that is the ancestor of both HTML and XML. DTDs are type definition documents that outline rules that your SGML [and later, HTML and XML] documents had to live up to.) Basically, cdata stands for character data. XML acknowledges a cdata section as something of a no man's land — it completely and in all ways ignores whatever is included inside a properly marked cdata section. Since there is no validation on the data in a cdata section, no encoding of the data is necessary. You would use cdata anytime you need your data completely untouched (you can't have encoding altering the data) or, frankly, when you want to move the data but have no idea what the data is (so you can't know if it's going to cause you problems or not).

For this one, we'll just take a simple example — the AdventureWorks2008 Production.Document table. This table has a field that has an nvarchar(max) data type. The contents are basically unknown. A query to generate the notes on employees into XML might look something like this:

```
SELECT 1                      as Tag,
       NULL                   as Parent,
```

```
        DocumentNode            as [Document!1!DocumentNode],
        DocumentSummary         as [Document!1!!cdata]
FROM Production.Document Document
WHERE DocumentSummary IS NOT NULL
ORDER BY [Document!1!DocumentNode]
FOR XML EXPLICIT
```

The output is pretty straightforward:

```
<Document DocumentNode="/1/2/">
  <![CDATA[It is important that you maintain your bicycle and keep it in good
repair. Detailed repair and service guidelines are provided along with
instructions for adjusting the tightness of the suspension fork.

]]>
</Document>
<Document DocumentNode="/2/2/">
  <![CDATA[Guidelines and recommendations for lubricating the required
components of your Adventure Works Cycles bicycle. Component lubrication is
vital to ensuring a smooth and safe ride and should be part of your standard
maintenance routine. Details instructions are provided for each bicycle
component requiring regular lubrication including the frequency at which oil
or grease should be applied.
]]>
</Document>
<Document DocumentNode="/3/2/">
  <![CDATA[Reflectors are vital safety components of your bicycle. Always
ensure your front and back reflectors are clean and in good repair. Detailed
instructions and illustrations are included should you need to replace the
front reflector or front reflector bracket of your Adventure Works Cycles
bicycle.

]]>
</Document>
<Document DocumentNode="/3/3/">
  <![CDATA[Detailed instructions for replacing pedals with Adventure Works
Cycles replacement pedals.  Instructions are applicable to all Adventure Works
Cycles bicycle models and replacement pedals. Use only Adventure Works Cycles
parts when replacing worn or broken components.
]]>
</Document>
<Document DocumentNode="/3/4/">
  <![CDATA[Worn or damaged seats can be easily replaced following these simple
instructions.  Instructions are applicable to these  Adventure Works Cycles
models: Mountain 100 through Mountain 500. Use only Adventure Works Cycles
parts when replacing worn or broken components.

]]>
</Document>
```

Basically, this was a pretty easy one.

PATH

Now let's switch gears just a little bit and get down to a more "real" XML approach to getting data.

While EXPLICIT has not been deprecated as yet, make no mistake — PATH is really *meant* to be a better way of doing what EXPLICIT originally was the only way of doing. PATH makes a lot of sense in a lot of ways, and it is how I recommend that you do complex XML output in most cases.

> *This is a more complex recommendation than it might seem. The Microsoft party line on this is that PATH is easier. Well, PATH is easier is many ways, but, as we're going to see, it has its own set of "except for this, and except for that, and except for this other thing" that can twist your brain into knots trying to understand exactly what to do. In short, in some cases, EXPLICIT is actually easier if you don't know XPath. The thing is, if you're dealing with XML, then XPath should be on your learn list anyway, so, if you're going to know it, you should find the XPath-based approach more usable.*
>
> *Note, however, that if you need backward compatibility to SQL Server 2000, then you're going to need to stick with EXPLICIT.*

In its most straightforward sense, the PATH option isn't that bad at all. So, let's start by getting our feet wet by focusing in on just the basics of using PATH. From there, we'll get a bit more complex and show off some of what PATH has to offer.

PATH 101

With PATH, you have a model that molds an existing standard to get at your data — XPath. XPath has an accepted standard, and provides a way of pointing at specific points in your XML schema. For PATH, we're just utilizing a lot of the same rules and ideas in order to say how data should be treated in a native XML sort of way.

How PATH treats the data you refer to depends on a number of rules, including whether the column is named or unnamed (like EXPLICIT, the alias is the name if you use an alias). If the column does have a name, then a number of additional rules are applied as appropriate.

Let's look at some of the possibilities.

Unnamed Columns

Data from a column that is not named will be treated as raw text within the row's element. To demonstrate this, let's take a modified version of the example we used for XML RAW. What we're doing here is listing the two customers we're interested in and the number of orders they have placed:

```
SELECT sc.CustomerID,
  COUNT(soh.SalesOrderID)
FROM Person.Person pp
JOIN Sales.Customer sc
  ON pp.BusinessEntityID = sc.PersonID
JOIN Sales.SalesOrderHeader soh
  ON sc.CustomerID = soh.CustomerID
WHERE sc.CustomerID = 29484 OR sc.CustomerID = 29485
GROUP BY sc.CustomerID
FOR XML PATH;
```

Check the output from this:

```
<row><CustomerID>29484</CustomerID>7</row>
<row><CustomerID>29485</CustomerID>4</row>
```

What it created is a row element for each row in the query — much as you had with RAW — but notice the difference in how it treated our column data.

Since the `CustomerID` column was named, it was placed in its own element (we'll explore this more in the next section) — notice, however, the number 7 in the results. This is just loose embedded text for the row element — it isn't even associated directly with the `CustomerID` since it is outside the `CustomerID` element.

Remember that the exact counts (7s in this case) that come back may vary on your system depending on how much you have been playing with the data. The key thing is to see how the counts are not associated with the `CustomerID` but are instead just raw text associated with the row.

My personal slant on this is that the number of situations where loose text at the level of the top element is a valid way of doing things is pretty limited. The rules do say you can do it, but I believe it makes for data that is not very clear. Still, this is how it works — use it as it seems to fit the needs of your particular system.

Named Columns

This is where things get considerably more complex rather quickly. In its most simple form, named columns are just as easy as unnamed were — indeed, we saw one of them in our previous example. If a column is a simple named column using PATH, then it is merely added as an additional element to the row:

```
<row><CustomerID>29484</CustomerID>7</row>
```

Our `CustomerID` column was a simple named column.

We can, however, add special characters into our column name to indicate that we want special behaviors for this column. Let's look at a few of the most important.

@

No, that's not a typo — the @ symbol is really the heading to this section. If we add an @ sign to our column name, then SQL Server will treat that column as an attribute of the previous column. Let's move the `CustomerID` to be an attribute of the top element for the row:

```
SELECT sc.CustomerID AS '@CustomerID',
    COUNT(soh.SalesOrderID)
FROM Person.Person pp
JOIN Sales.Customer sc
  ON pp.BusinessEntityID = sc.PersonID
JOIN Sales.SalesOrderHeader soh
  ON sc.CustomerID = soh.CustomerID
WHERE sc.CustomerID = 29484 OR sc.CustomerID = 29485
GROUP BY sc.CustomerID
FOR XML PATH;
```

Yields:

```
<row CustomerID="29484">7</row>
<row CustomerID="29485">4</row>
```

Notice that our order count remained a text element of the row — only the column that we identified as an attribute moved in. We could take this to the next step by naming our count and prefixing it to make it an attribute also:

```
SELECT sc.CustomerID AS '@CustomerID',
   COUNT(soh.SalesOrderID) AS '@OrderCount'
FROM Person.Person pp
JOIN Sales.Customer sc
  ON pp.BusinessEntityID = sc.PersonID
JOIN Sales.SalesOrderHeader soh
  ON sc.CustomerID = soh.CustomerID
WHERE sc.CustomerID = 29484 OR sc.CustomerID = 29485
GROUP BY sc.CustomerID
FOR XML PATH;
```

With this, we no longer have our loose text for the element:

```
<row CustomerID="29484" OrderCount="7"/>
<row CustomerID="29485" OrderCount="4"/>
```

Also notice that SQL Server was smart enough to realize that everything was contained in attributes — with no lower-level elements or simple text, it chose to make it a self-closing tag (see the / at the end of the element).

So, why did I indicate that this stuff was tricky? Well, there are a lot of different "it only works if ... " kind of rules here. To demonstrate this, let's make a simple modification to our original query. This one seems like it should work, but SQL Server will throw a hissy fit if you try to run it:

```
SELECT sc.CustomerID,
   COUNT(soh.SalesOrderID) AS '@OrderCount'
FROM Person.Person pp
JOIN Sales.Customer sc
  ON pp.BusinessEntityID = sc.PersonID
JOIN Sales.SalesOrderHeader soh
  ON sc.CustomerID = soh.CustomerID
WHERE sc.CustomerID = 29484 OR sc.CustomerID = 29485
GROUP BY sc.CustomerID
FOR XML PATH;
```

What I've done here is to go back to CustomerID as its own element. What, at first glance, you would expect to happen is to get a CustomerID element with OrderCount as an attribute, but it doesn't quite work that way:

```
Msg 6852, Level 16, State 1, Line 1
Attribute-centric column '@OrderCount' must not come after a non-attribute-centric
sibling in XML hierarchy in FOR XML PATH.
```

The short rendition of the answer to "What's wrong?" is that it doesn't really know what it's supposed to be an attribute of — is it an attribute of the row, or an attribute of the CustomerID?

/

Yes, a forward slash. Much like @, this special character indicates special things you want done. Essentially, you use it to define something of a path — a hierarchy that relates an element to those things that belong to it. It can exist anywhere in the column name except the first character. To demonstrate this, we're going to utilize our last (failed) example and build into what we were looking for when we got the error.

First, we need to alter the OrderID to have information on what element it belongs to:

```
SELECT sc.CustomerID,

  COUNT(soh.SalesOrderID) AS 'CustomerID/OrderCount'

FROM Person.Person pp
JOIN Sales.Customer sc
  ON pp.BusinessEntityID = sc.PersonID
JOIN Sales.SalesOrderHeader soh
  ON sc.CustomerID = soh.CustomerID
WHERE sc.CustomerID = 29484 OR sc.CustomerID = 29485
GROUP BY sc.CustomerID
FOR XML PATH;
```

By adding the / and then placing CustomerID before the slash, we are telling SQL Server that OrderCount is below CustomerID in a hierarchy. Now, there are many ways XML hierarchy can be structured, so let's see what SQL Server does with this:

```
<row><CustomerID>29484<OrderCount>7</OrderCount></CustomerID></row>
<row><CustomerID>29485<OrderCount>4</OrderCount></CustomerID></row>
```

Now, if you recall, we wanted to make OrderCount an attribute of CustomerID, so, while we have OrderCount below CustomerID in the hierarchy, it's still not quite in the place we wanted it. To do that, we can combine / and @, but we need to fully define all the hierarchy. Now, since I suspect this is a bit confusing, let's take it in two steps — first, the way we might be tempted to do it, but that will yield a similar error to the earlier example:

```
SELECT sc.CustomerID,

  COUNT(soh.SalesOrderID) AS 'CustomerID/@OrderCount'

FROM Person.Person pp
JOIN Sales.Customer sc
  ON pp.BusinessEntityID = sc.PersonID
JOIN Sales.SalesOrderHeader soh
  ON sc.CustomerID = soh.CustomerID
WHERE sc.CustomerID = 29484 OR sc.CustomerID = 29485
GROUP BY sc.CustomerID
FOR XML PATH;
```

Error time:

```
Msg 6852, Level 16, State 1, Line 1
Attribute-centric column 'CustomerID/@OrderCount' must not come after a non-
attribute-centric sibling in XML hierarchy in FOR XML PATH.
```

To fix this, we need to understand a bit about how things are constructed when building the XML tags. The key is that the tags are essentially built in the order you list them. So, if you want to add attributes to an element, you need to keep in mind that they are part of the element tag — that means you need to define any attributes before you define any other content of that element (subelements or raw text).

In our case, we are putting the CustomerID as raw text, but the OrderCount as an attribute (okay, backward from what would be likely in real life, but hang with me here). This means we are telling SQL Server things backward. By the time it sees the OrderCount information, it is already done with attributes for CustomerID and can't go back.

So, to fix things, we simply need to tell it about the attributes before we tell it about any more elements or raw text:

```
SELECT COUNT(soh.SalesOrderID) AS 'CustomerID/@OrderCount',
   sc.CustomerID

FROM Person.Person pp
JOIN Sales.Customer sc
   ON pp.BusinessEntityID = sc.PersonID
JOIN Sales.SalesOrderHeader soh
   ON sc.CustomerID = soh.CustomerID
WHERE sc.CustomerID = 29484 OR sc.CustomerID = 29485
GROUP BY sc.CustomerID
FOR XML PATH;
```

This probably seems counterintuitive, but, again, think of the order things are being written in. The attributes are written first and then, and only then, can we write the lower-level information for the CustomerID element. Run it, and you'll see we get what we were after:

```
<row><CustomerID OrderCount="7">29484</CustomerID></row>
<row><CustomerID OrderCount="4">29485</CustomerID></row>
```

The OrderCount has now been moved into the attribute position, just as we desired, and the actual CustomerID is still raw text embedded in the element.

Follow the logic of the ordering of what you ask for a bit, because it works for most everything. So, if we wanted CustomerID to also be an attribute rather than raw text, but wanted it to be after OrderCount, we could do that — we just need to make sure that it comes after the OrderCount definition.

But Wait, There's More . . .

As I said earlier, XPath has its own complexity and is a book's worth to itself, but I don't want to leave you with just what I said in the preceding sections and say that's all there is.

@ and / will give you a great deal of flexibility in building the XML output just the way you want it, and probably meet the need well for most simple applications. If, however, you need something more, then there is still more out there waiting for you. For example, you can:

❑   "Wildcard" data such that it's all run together as text data without being treated as separate columns

❑ Embed native XML data from XML data type columns

❑ Use XPath node tests — these are special XPath directives that change the behavior of your data

❑ Use the `data()` directive to allow multiple values to be run together as one data point in the XML

❑ Utilize namespaces

OPENXML

We've spent pages and pages dealing with how to turn our relational data into XML. It seems reasonably intuitive then that SQL Server must also allow you to open a string of XML and represent it in the tabular format that is expected in SQL.

`OPENXML` is a rowset function that opens your string much as other rowset functions (such as `OPENQUERY` and `OPENROWSET`) work. This means that you can join to an XML document, or even use it as the source of input data by using an `INSERT..SELECT` or a `SELECT INTO`. The major difference is that it requires you to use a couple of system stored procedures to prepare your document and clear the memory after you're done using it.

To set up your document, you use `sp_xml_preparedocument`. This moves the string into memory and pre-parses it for optimal query performance. The XML document will stay in memory until you explicitly say to remove it or you terminate the connection that `sp_xml_preparedocument` was called on.

> *Let me digress a moment and say that I'm not at all a fan of letting a system clean up for you. If you instantiate something, then you should proactively clean it up when you're done (if only I could teach my youngest child this when she pulls out her toys!).*

> *Much like Visual Basic, C#, and most other languages are supposed to clean up your objects when they go out of scope for you, SQL Server is supposed to clean up your prepared documents. Please do not take the lazy approach of relying on this — clean up after yourself! By explicitly deallocating it (using `sp_xml_removedocument`), you are making certain the clean up happens, clearing it from memory slightly sooner, and also making it very clear in your code that you're done with it.*

The syntax is pretty simple:

```
sp_xml_preparedocument @hdoc = <integer variable> OUTPUT,
[, @xmltext = <xml>]
[, @xpath_namespaces = <url to a namespace>]
```

> **Note that, if you are going to provide a namespace URL, you need to wrap it in the `<` and `>` symbols at both ends (for example, `<root xmlns:sql ="run: schemas-microsoft-com:xml-sql>`).**

The parameters of this sproc are fairly self-describing:

❑ **@hdoc** — If you've ever programmed to the Windows API (and to tons of other things, but this is a common one), then you've seen the "h" before — it's Hungarian notation for a handle. A handle is effectively a pointer to a block of memory where something (could be about anything) resides. In our case, this is the handle to the XML document that we've asked SQL Server to parse and hold onto for us. This is an output variable — the variable you reference here will, after the sproc returns, contain the handle to your XML. Be sure to store it away, as you will need it when you make use of OPENXML.

❑ **@xmltext** — Is what it says it is — the actual XML that you want to parse and work with.

❑ **@xpath_namespaces** — Any namespace reference(s) your XML needs to operate correctly.

After calling this sproc and saving the handle to your document, you're ready to make use of OPENXML. The syntax for it is slightly more complex:

```
OPENXML(<handle>,
    <XPath to base node>
    [, <mapping flags>])
[WITH (<schema Declaration>|<table Name>)]
```

We have pretty much already discussed the handle — this is going to be an integer value that you received as an output parameter for your sp_xml_preparedocument call.

When you make your call to OPENXML, you must supply the XPath to a node that will serve as a starting point for all your queries. The schema declaration can refer to all parts of the XML document by navigating relative to the base node you set here.

Next up are the mapping flags. These assist us in deciding whether we want to favor elements or attributes in our OPENXML results. The options are:

Byte Value	Description
0	Same as 1 except that you can't combine it with 2 or 8 (2 + 0 is still 2). This is the default.
1	Unless combined with 2 (described next), only attributes will be used. If there is no attribute with the name specified, then a **NULL** is returned. This can also be added to either 2 or 8 (or both) to combine behavior, but this option takes precedence over option 2. If XPath finds both an attribute and an element with the same name, the attribute wins.
2	Unless combined with 1 (described previously), only elements will be used. If there is no element with the name specified, then a **NULL** is returned. This can also be added to either 1 or 8 (or both) to combine behavior. If combined with 1, then the attribute will be mapped if it exists. If no attribute exists, then the element will be used. If no element exists, then a **NULL** is returned.
8	Can be combined with 1 or 2 (described previously). Consumed data should not be copied to the overflow property **@mp:xmltext** (you would have to use the metaproperty schema item to retrieve this). If you're not going to use the metaproperties — and most of the time you won't be — I recommend this option. It cuts a small (okay, *very* small) amount of overhead out of the operation.

Finally comes the schema or table. If you're defining a schema and are not familiar with XPath, this part can be a bit tricky. Fortunately, this particular XPath use isn't very complex and should become second nature fairly quickly (it works a lot like directories do in Windows, only with a lot more power).

The schema can vary somewhat in the way you declare it. The definition is declared as:

```
WITH (
    <column name> <data type> [{<column XPath>|<metaproperty>}]
    [,<column name> <data type> [{<column XPath>|<metaproperty>}]
```

❑ The column name is just that — the name of the attribute or element you are retrieving. This will also serve as the name you refer to when you build your SELECT list, perform JOINs, and the like.

❑ The data type is any valid SQL Server data type. Since XML can have data types that are not equivalents of those in SQL Server, an automatic coercion will take place if necessary, but this is usually predictable.

❑ The column XPath is the XPath pattern (relative to the node you established as the starting point for your OPENXML function) that gets you to the node you want for your column — whether an element or attribute gets used is dependent on the flags parameter as described above. If this is left off, then SQL Server assumes you want the current node as defined as the starting point for your OPENXML statement.

❑ Metaproperties are a set of special variables that you can refer to in your OPENXML queries. They describe various aspects of whatever part of the XML DOM you're interested in. To use them, just enclose them in single quotes and put them in the place of the column XPath. Available metaproperties include:

   ❑ @mp:id — Don't confuse this with the XML id that we looked at with EXPLICIT. While this property serves a similar function, it is a unique identifier (within the scope of the document) of the DOM node. The difference is that this value is system generated — as such, you can be sure it is there. It is guaranteed to refer to the same XML node as long as the document remains in memory. If the id is zero, it is the root node (its @mp:parentid property, as referred to next, will be NULL).

   ❑ @mp:parentid — This is the same as the preceding, only for the parent.

   ❑ @mp:localname — Provides the non-fully qualified name of the node. It is used with a prefix and namespace URI (Uniform Resource Identifier — you'll usually see it starting with URN) to name element or attribute nodes.

   ❑ @mp:parentlocalname — This is the same as the preceding, only for the parent.

   ❑ @mp:namespaceuri — Provides the namespace URI of the current element. If the value of this attribute is NULL, no namespace is present.

   ❑ @mp:parentnamespacerui — This is the same as the preceding, only for the parent.

   ❑ @mp:prefix: Stores the namespace prefix of the current element name.

   ❑ @mp:parentprefix — This is the same as the preceding, only for the parent.

   ❑ @mp:prev — Stores the mp:id of the previous sibling relative to a node. Using this, you can tell something about the ordering of the elements at the current level of the hierarchy. For example, if the value of @mp:prev is NULL, then you are at the first node for this level of the tree.

   ❑ @mp:xmltext — This metaproperty is used for processing purposes, and contains the actual XML for the current element.

Of course, you can always save yourself a ton of work by bypassing all these parameters. You get to do this if you have a table that directly relates (names and data types) to the XPath starting point that you've specified in your XML. If you do have such a table, you can just name it and SQL Server will make the translation for you!

Okay, that's a lot to handle, but we're not quite finished yet. You see, when you're all done with your XML, you need to call sp_xml_removedocument to clean up the memory where your XML document was stored. Thankfully, the syntax is incredibly easy:

```
sp_xml_removedocument [hdoc = ]<handle of XML doc>
```

Again, I can't stress enough how important it is to get in the habit of always cleaning up after yourself. I know that, in saying that, I probably sound like your mother. Well, like your mother, SQL Server will clean up after you some, but, like your mother, you can't count on SQL Server to clean up after you every time. SQL Server will clean things up when you terminate the connection, but what if you are using connection pooling? Some connections may never go away if your system is under load. It's an easy sproc to implement, so do it — every time!

Okay, I'm sure you've been waiting for me to get to how you really make use of this — so now it's time for the all-important example.

Imagine that you are merging with another company and need to import some of their data into your system. For this example, we'll say that we're working on importing a few shipping providers that they have and our company doesn't. A sample of what our script might look like to import these from an XML document might be:

```
USE AdventureWorks2008;

DECLARE @idoc      int ;
DECLARE @xmldoc    nvarchar(4000);

-- define the XML document
SET @xmldoc = '
<ROOT>
<Shipper CompanyName="Billy Bob&apos;s Pretty Good Shipping" Base="4.50"
Rate="1.05"/>
<Shipper CompanyName="Fred&apos;s Freight" Base="3.95" Rate="1.29"/>
</ROOT>
';

PRINT @xmldoc;
--Load and parse the XML document in memory
EXEC sp_xml_preparedocument @idoc OUTPUT, @xmldoc;

--List out what our shippers table looks like before the insert
SELECT * FROM Purchasing.ShipMethod;

--See our XML data in a tabular format

SELECT * FROM OPENXML (@idoc, '/ROOT/Shipper', 0) WITH (
    CompanyName        nvarchar(40),
    Base               decimal(5,2),
```

```
        Rate              decimal(5,2)) ;

    --Perform and insert based on that data
    INSERT INTO Purchasing.ShipMethod
    (Name, ShipBase, ShipRate)
    SELECT * FROM OPENXML (@idoc, '/ROOT/Shipper', 0) WITH (
        CompanyName       nvarchar(40),
        Base              decimal(5,2),
        Rate              decimal(5,2));

    --Now look at the Shippers table after our insert
    SELECT * FROM Purchasing.ShipMethod;

    --Now clear the XML document from memory
    EXEC sp_xml_removedocument @idoc;
```

The final result set from this looks just like what we wanted. (Note that I've snipped off the final two columns for brevity.)

```
ShipMethodID Name                                       ShipBase      ShipRate
------------ ------------------------------------------ ------------- ---------
1            XRQ - TRUCK GROUND                         3.95          0.99
2            ZY - EXPRESS                               9.95          1.99
3            OVERSEAS - DELUXE                          29.95         2.99
4            OVERNIGHT J-FAST                           21.95         1.29
5            CARGO TRANSPORT 5                          8.99          1.49
6            Billy Bob's Pretty Good Shipping           4.50          1.05
7            Fred's Freight                             3.95          1.29
```

It isn't pretty, but it works — XML turned into relational data.

A Quick Heads Up Regarding XML Indexes

We're going to defer discussion of XML indexes until we discuss some of the other indexing constructs in SQL Server, but I wanted to take a moment and make sure that you realized that indexes can be built over XML data. We will discuss them more fully in Chapter 7, but, for now, I want to make sure that you are taking XML indexes into consideration in your design efforts and performance expectations.

A Brief Word on Hierarchical Data

XML is naturally hierarchical. The concept of a root and then branching levels of elements and attributes pretty much says everything; one is higher in lineage than another. While XML has been index capable since SQL Server 2005, there is nothing inherent in the XML data type that allows for the handling of XML in a truly hierarchical fashion.

Beginning with SQL Server 2008, we have a new data type that is explicitly created for the purpose of dealing with hierarchical data — the HierarchyID data type. I want to make sure that you're aware of this new data type as a tool for keeping track of hierarchical data in a relational format. This has significant implications in terms of when you might want to store data in XML versus a more traditional data format.

We will defer full discussion of `HierarchyID` and other hierarchy design issues until Chapter 7 but keep the correlation in mind. You may well find that you want to store information on how deep your XML data is within the tree hierarchy to facilitate fast response to hierarchy questions.

Summary

The size of the XML portion of SQL Server has grown considerably since its original introduction as a "Web release" prior to SQL Server 2000, and it continues to grow. XML is one of the most important technologies to hit the industry in the last 20 or more years. It provides a flexible, very transportable way of describing data, and SQL Server now has more and more ways of meeting your XML needs.

In this chapter, we've taken a look at how to get relational data into XML format, and how to get XML data into a relational structure. We've also seen how SQL Server can supply Web service data directly using XML-based methods.

5

Daring to Design

And so I come to another one of those things where I have to ponder how much to assume you already know. "To normalize, or not to normalize — THAT is the question!" Okay, the real question is one of whether or not you already understand the most basic tenets of relational database design yet. Since you come to this book with a degree of experience already, I'm going to take an approach that assumes you've heard of it, know it's important, and even grasp the basics of it. I'm going to assume you need the information filled in for you rather than that you are starting from scratch.

With the exception of perhaps three or four chapters, this book has an *Online Transaction Processing*, or *OLTP*, flare to the examples. Don't get me wrong; I will point out, from time to time, some of the differences between OLTP and its more analysis-oriented cousin *Online Analytical Processing* (*OLAP*). My point is that you will, in most of the examples, be seeing a table design that is optimized for the most common kind of database — OLTP. Thus, the table examples will typically have a database layout that is, for the most part, *normalized* to what is called the third normal form.

What is "normal form"? We'll start off by taking a very short look at that and then will move quickly onto more advanced concepts. For the moment though, just say that it means your data has been broken out into a logical, nonrepetitive format that can easily be reassembled into the whole. In addition to normalization (which is the process of putting your database into normal form), we'll also be examining the characteristics of OLTP and OLAP databases. And, as if we didn't have enough to do between those two topics, we'll also be looking at many examples of how the constraints we've already seen are implemented in the overall solution.

Normalization 201

If you've read Beginning SQL Server 2008 Programming, *then you can probably safely skip this section and move on to the more advanced concepts.*

I want to start off by saying that there are six normal forms (plus or minus one or two depending on which academician you listen to). We'll leave several of those to the academicians though. Those in the real world usually deal with only three normal forms. Indeed, a fully normalized database is one that is generally considered to be one that is normalized to the third normal form.

> *The concept of normalization has to be one of most over-referenced yet misunderstood concepts in programming. Everyone thinks they understand it, and many do in at least its academic form. Unfortunately, it also tends to be one of those things that many database designers wear like a cross — it is somehow their symbol that they are "real" database architects. What it really is, however, is a symbol that they know what the normal forms are — and that's all. Normalization is really just one piece of a larger database design picture. Sometimes you need to normalize your data — then again, sometimes you need to deliberately de-normalize your data. Even within the normalization process, there are often many ways to achieve what is technically a normalized database.*

> *My point is that normalization is a theory, and that's all it is. Once you choose whether or not to implement a normalized strategy, what you have is a database — hopefully the best one you could possibly design. Don't get stuck on what the books (including this one) say you're supposed to do — do what's right for the situation that you're in. As the author of this book, all I can do is relate concepts to you — I can't implement them for you, and neither can any other author (at least not with the written word). You need to pick and choose between these concepts in order to achieve the best fit and the best solution.*

By this point in your database development background, I would expect that you already understand how to create a primary key and some of the reasons for using one in our tables — if we want to be able to act on just one row, then we need to be able to uniquely identify that row. The concepts of normalization are highly dependent on issues surrounding the definition of the primary key and what columns are dependent on it. One phrase you might hear frequently in normalization is:

> *The key, the whole key, and nothing but the key.*

The somewhat fun addition to this is:

> *The key, the whole key, and nothing but the key, so help me Codd!*

This is a super-brief summarization of what normalization is about out to the third normal form (for those who don't know, Codd is considered the father of relational design). When you can say that all your columns are dependent only on the whole key and nothing more or less, then you are at third normal form.

Now let's review the various normal forms and what each does for you.

Where to Begin

The concepts of relational database design are founded on the notion of *entities* and *relations*. If you're familiar with object-oriented programming, then you can liken most top-level entities to objects in an object model. Much as a parent object might contain other objects that further describe it, tables may have a child or other table that further describe the rows in the original table.

An entity will generally tie to one "parent" table. That table will usually have one and only one row per instance of entity you're describing (for example, a table that is the top table for tracking orders in a system will have only one row per individual order). The one entity may, however, require multiple tables to provide additional descriptive information (for example, a details or line item table to carry a list of all the things that were purchased on that particular order).

A relation is a representation of how two entities relate to each other logically. For example, a customer is a different entity from an order, but they are related. You cannot have so much as one order without at least one customer. Furthermore, your order relates to only one customer.

As you start the process of "normalizing" these entities and relations into tables, some things about your data are assumed even before you get to the first of the normal forms:

❑   The table should describe one and only one entity. (No trying to shortcut and combine things!)

❑   All rows must be unique, and there must be a primary key.

❑   The column and row order must not matter.

As you gain experience, this will become less of a "process" and more of the natural starting point for your tables. You will find that creating a normalized set of tables will be the way things flow from your mind to start with rather than anything special that you have to do.

Getting to Third Normal Form

As I indicated earlier, there are, from a practical point of view, three normal forms:

❑   **The first normal form (1NF)** is all about eliminating repeating groups of data and guaranteeing *atomicity* (the data is self-contained and independent). At a high level, it works by creating a primary key (which you already have), then moving any repeating data groups into new tables, creating new keys for those tables, and so on. In addition, you break out any columns that combine data into separate rows for each piece of data.

❑   **Second normal form (2NF)** further reduces the incidence of repeated data (not necessarily groups). Second normal form has two rules to it:

    ❑   The table must meet the rules for first normal form. (Normalization is a building block kind of process — you can't stack the third block on if you don't have the first two there already.)

    ❑   Each column must depend on the *whole* key.

❑   **Third normal form (3NF)** deals with the issue of having all the columns in your table not just be dependent on something — but the right thing. Third normal form has just three rules to it:

    ❑   The table must be in 2NF (I told you this was a building block thing).

    ❑   No column can have any dependency on any other non-key column.

    ❑   You cannot have derived data (that is, data that can be inferred from other data in your tables).

Other Normal Forms

There are a few other forms out there that are considered, at least by academics, to be part of the normalization model. These include:

❑ **Boyce-Codd** (considered to really just be a variation on third normal form) — This one tries to address situations where you have multiple overlapping candidate keys. This can only happen if:

    a. All the candidate keys are composite keys (that is, it takes more than one column to make up the key).

    b. There is more than one candidate key.

    c. The candidate keys each have at least one column that is in common with another candidate key.

    This is typically a situation where any number of solutions works, and almost never gets thought of outside the academic community (and I think I'll stop thinking about it right now . . . .).

❑ **Fourth normal form** — This one tries to deal with issues surrounding multi-valued dependence. This is the situation where, for an individual row, no column depends on a column other than the primary key and depends on the whole primary key (meeting third normal form). However, there can be rather odd situations where one column in the primary key can depend separately on other columns in the primary key. These are rare and don't usually cause any real problem. Thus, they are largely ignored in the database world, and we will not address them any further here.

❑ **Fifth normal form** — Deals with non-loss and loss decompositions. Essentially, there are certain situations where you can decompose a relationship such that you cannot logically recompose it into its original form. Again, these are rare, largely academic, and, again, we won't deal with them any further here.

This is, of course, just a really quick look at these — and that's deliberate on my part. The main reason you need to know these in the real world is either to impress your friends (or prove to them you're a "know it all") and to not sound like an idiot when some database guru comes to town and starts talking about them. However you choose to use this knowledge, I do recommend against using it to get dates.

Relationships

Well, I've always heard from women that men immediately leave the room if you even mention the word "relationship." With that in mind, I hope that I didn't just lose about half my readers.

I am, of course, kidding — but not by as much as you might think. Experts say the key to successful relationships is that you know the role of both parties and that everyone understands the boundaries and rules of the relationship that they are in. I can be talking about database relationships with that statement every bit as much as people relationships.

There are three different kinds of major relationships:

❑ **One-to-one** — This is exactly what it says it is. A one-to-one relationship is one where the fact that you have a record in one table means that you have exactly one matching record in another table.

❑ **One-to-many** — This is one form of your run-of-the-mill, average, everyday foreign key kind of relationship. Usually, this is found in some form of header/detail relationship, and generally implements some idea of a parent to child hierarchy. For example, for every one customer, you might have several orders.

❑ **Many-to-many** — In this type of relationship, both sides of the relationship may have several records that match. An example of this would be the relationship of products to orders — an order may contain several products, and, likewise, a product will appear on many orders. SQL Server has no way of physically establishing a direct many-to-many relationship, so you cheat by having an intermediate table to organize the relationship.

Each of these has some variations depending on whether one side of the relationship is nullable or not. For example, instead of a one-to-one relationship, you might have a zero- or one-to-one relationship.

Diagramming

Entity-relationship diagrams (ERDs) are an important tool in good database design. Small databases can usually be easily created from a few scripts and implemented directly without drawing things out at all. The larger your database gets, however, the faster it becomes very problematic to just do things "in your head." ERDs solve a ton of problems because they allow you to quickly visualize and understand both the entities and their relationships.

For this book, I've decided to do things somewhat in reverse of how I've done things before. SQL Server includes a very basic diagramming tool that you can use as a starting point for building rudimentary ERDs. Unfortunately, it employs a proprietary diagramming methodology that does not look remotely like any standard I'm aware of out there. In addition, it does not allow for the use of logical modeling — something I consider a rather important concept. Therefore, I'm going to start off talking about the more standard diagramming methodologies first — later in the chapter we'll look at SQL Server's built-in tools and how to use them.

There are two reasonably common diagramming paradigms — IE and IDEF1X. You'll find both of these in widespread use, but I'm going to limit things here to a once over of the basics of IE (also called Information Engineering). For the record, IDEF1X is a perfectly good diagramming paradigm, and was first put forth by the U.S. Air Force. IE (again, Information Engineering — *not* Internet Explorer) is, however, the method I use personally, and I do so for just one reason — it is far more intuitive for the inexperienced reviewer of your diagrams. I also find it to be the far more common of the two.

> **I can't say enough about the importance of having the right tools. While the built-in tools at least give you "something," they are a long way away from "what you need."**

> ER tools are anything but cheap — running from somewhere over $1,000 to just under $5,000 (that's per seat!). They are also something of a language unto themselves. Don't plan on just sitting down and going to work with any of the major ER tools — you had better figure on some spin-up time to get it to do what you expect.

> Don't let the high price of these tools keep you from building a logical model. While Visio continues to fall somewhat short in terms of answering the world's database design problems, it does do okay in a pinch for light logical modeling and can do some degree of synchronization and physical modeling. That said, if you're serious about database design, and going to be doing a lot of it, you really need to find the budget for a real ER tool.

Expense aside, there is no comparison between the productivity possible in the third-party tools out there and the built-in tools. Depending on the ER tool you select, they give you the capability to do things like:

- ❑ Create logical models, and then switch back and forth between the logical and physical model.

- ❑ Work on the diagram offline — then propagate all your changes to the physical database at one time (when you're ready, as opposed to when you need to log off).

- ❑ Reverse engineer your database from any one of a number of mainstream RDBMS systems (even some ISAM databases), and then forward engineer them to a completely different RDBMS.

- ❑ Create your physical model on numerous different systems.

This really just scratches the surface.

A Couple of Relationship Types

Before you get going too far in more diagramming concepts, I want to explore two types of relationships: identifying and non-identifying.

Identifying Relationships

For some of you, I'm sure the term *identifying relationship* brings back memories of some boyfriend or girlfriend you've had in the past who got just a little over possessive — this is not that kind of relationship. Instead, you're dealing with the relationships that are defined by foreign keys.

An *identifying relationship* is one where the column or columns (remember, there can be more than one) being referenced (in the parent table) are used as all or part of the referencing (child) table's primary key. Since a primary key serves as the identity for the rows in a table, and all or part of the primary key for the child table is dependent on the parent table — the child table can be said to, at least in part, be "identified" by the parent table.

Non-Identifying Relationships

Non-identifying relationships are those that are created when you establish a foreign key that does not serve as part of the referencing (child) table's primary key. This is extremely common in situations where you are referencing a domain table — where essentially the sole purpose of the referenced table is to limit the referencing field to a set list of possible choices.

The Entity Box

One of the many big differences you'll see in both IE and IDEF1X versus SQL Server's own brand of diagramming comes in the *entity box*. The entity box, depending on whether you're dealing with logical or physical models, equates roughly to a table. By looking over the entity box, you should be able to easily identify the entity's name, primary key, and any attributes (effectively columns) that entity has. In addition, the diagram may expose other information such as the attribute's data type or whether it has a foreign key defined for it. As an example, consider the entity box in Figure 5-1.

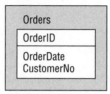

Figure 5-1

The name of our entity is kept on the top outside the box. Then, in the top area of the overall box, but in a separate box of its own, you have the primary key (you'll look at an example with more than one column in the primary key shortly), and last, but not least, come the attributes of the entity.

Take a look at a slightly different entity (Figure 5-2).

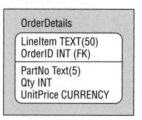

Figure 5-2

Several new things appear:

❑ The data types (I've turned on the appropriate option).

❑ Foreign keys (if any — again I've turned on the option to make this show).

❑ You have multiple columns in the primary key (everything above the line is part of the primary key).

❑ This time, the entity is rounded on the corners. This tells you that this table is identified (remember identifying relationships?) by at least one other table.

Depending on the ER tool, the data types can be defined right within the ER diagram. Also, as you draw the lines that form your relationships (you'll look at those shortly), you are able to define foreign keys, which can also be shown. For most available ER tools, you can even tell the tool to automatically define the referenced field(s) in the foreign key relationship as being part (or possibly all) of the primary key in the referencing table.

The Relationship Line

There are two kinds, and they match 100 percent with our relationship types:

A solid line indicates an identifying relationship:

_____

A broken or dashed line indicates a non-identifying relationship:

Again, an identifying relationship is one where the column that is referencing another table serves as all or part of the primary key of the referencing table. In a non-identifying relationship, the foreign key column has nothing to do with the primary key in the referencing table.

Terminators

Ahh, this is where things become slightly more interesting. The terminators we're talking about here are, of course, not the kind you'd see Arnold Schwarzenegger play in a movie — they are the end caps that we put on our relationship lines.

The terminators on our lines will communicate as much or more about the nature of our database as the entities themselves will. They are the thing that will tell you the most information about the true nature of the relationship, including the cardinality of the relationship.

Cardinality is, in its most basic form, the number of records on both sides of the relationship. When you say it is a one-to-many relationship, then you are indicating cardinality. Cardinality can, however, be much more specific than the zero, one, or many naming convention that you use more generically. Cardinality can address specifics, and is often augmented in a diagram with two numbers and a colon, such as:

❑　　1:M
❑　　1:6 (which, while meeting a one-to-many criteria, is more specific and says there is a maximum of 6 records on that side of the relationship).

Walk through a couple of the parts of a terminator and examine what they mean.

> Just as a reminder, the terminators that follow are the ones from the IE diagramming methodology. As I have indicated, there is another diagramming standard that is in widespread use (though I see it much less than IE) called IDEF1X. While its entity boxes are much like IE's, its terminators on the relationship lines are entirely different.

In the top half of the terminator shown in Figure 5-3, it is indicating the first half of our relationship. In this case, we have a zero. For the bottom half, we are indicating the second half of our relationship — in this case, a many. In this example, then, we have a zero, one, or many side of a relationship.

Figure 5-3

In Figure 5-4, you're not allowing nulls at this end of the relationship — this is a one or many end to a relationship.

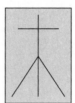

Figure 5-4

In Figure 5-5, you're back to allowing a zero at this end of the relationship, but you are now allowing a maximum of one. This is a zero or one side of a relationship.

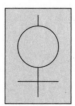

Figure 5-5

And last, but not least, you have Figure 5-6. This one is pretty restrictive — it's simply a "one" (no more, no less) side of a relationship.

Figure 5-6

121

Since it's probably pretty confusing to look at these just by themselves, take a look at a couple of example tables and relationships (Figure 5-7).

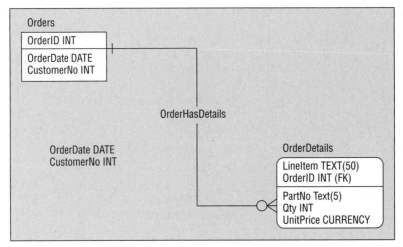

Figure 5-7

Figure 5-7 is a diagram that shows two tables that support the notion of just one logical entity — an order. You have an `Orders` table to keep track of information that is global to the order (this has just a `CustomerNo`, but it may have contained things like a shipping address, a date of the order, a due date, and so on). You also have an `OrderDetails` table to track the individual line items' place on this order. The diagram depicts not only your `Orders` and `OrderDetails` tables but also the one (the `Orders` side) to zero, one, or many (the `OrderDetails` side) relationship between the two tables. The relationship is an identifying relationship (solid, rather than dashed line), and the relationship is called `OrderHasDetails`.

In Figure 5-8, you add in a `Products` table.

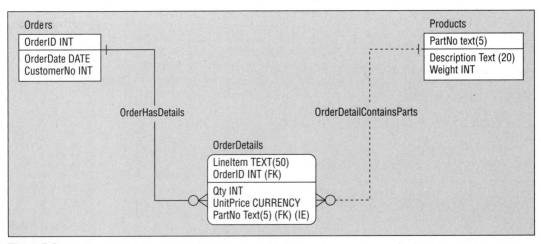

Figure 5-8

This new relationship is very similar to the relationship that you already looked at. It is again a one (`Products` this time) to zero, one, or many (`OrderDetails` again) relationship, but this one is non-identifying (as represented by the broken line). The `IE` indicates that, for this table, `PartNo` is an *Inversion Entry*, or an index that is not associated with anything other than a foreign key. The Inversion Entry has been added as it usually makes sense to have an index on a field that is a foreign key (since it is a frequent target of lookups).

By looking at all three together, you can see that there is a many-to-many relationship between `Orders` and `Products` by virtue of their relationship through the `OrderDetails` table.

> *Note that an Inversion Entry does not have to be associated with anything at all — it just happened to be associated with a foreign key in this particular case. An Inversion Entry is essentially any index that is not unique or associated with a primary key.*

As I've indicated before, you are still really only scratching the surface of the different information that your ER diagrams can convey. Still, as you look later in the chapter at the SQL Server diagramming tools, you will be able to see that the more accepted methodologies out there have an awful lot more information to convey than the included tools do. In addition, just the nature of how tables are displayed makes information such as keys more visible and easier to read.

Logical versus Physical Design

In your database work, you may have already heard about the concepts of logical versus physical models. In this section, we'll be exploring the differences between the two.

The physical model is one that's probably pretty easy to grasp. It is essentially what you have been working with up to this point in the book. You can think of anything that you can perform a `CREATE` statement on as being part of the physical model. Indeed — if you run any statements in SQL Server on it at all then it must be part of the physical model.

That being said, a logical model is a means to a number of different things — the physical model in particular. This means that, as you work on the logical model, you are working your way toward being able to generate DDL (Data Definition Language — or things like `CREATE`, `ALTER`, and `DROP` statements). Think of the logical model as being like the planning stages for an artist. The artist figures out what to paint, gets out the paints and brushes, and picks out an appropriately sized canvas, but he hasn't painted anything yet. The physical model is the actual painting. The painting is, of course, what everyone sees and notices, but the painting couldn't exist without the decision of what to paint and the gathering of the paints and other supplies needed. Likewise, the best physical models are generally put together as a progression from a solid logical model.

Purpose of a Logical Model

The first thing to understand about logical models is that they have somewhat different goals than physical models do. A logical model does several things for you:

❑ Allows you to begin to build abstracts of complex, data-related business issues as well as provide a high-level effort at identifying your entities

❑ Allows you to use these abstracts to effectively communicate business rules and content as relates to data

- ❑ Represents the purest form of the data (before you start introducing the realities of what will really work)

- ❑ Serves as a major piece of documentation in the data requirements portion of your project

Because logical models aren't strictly rooted in the exact syntax to create the database, they give you a flexibility that you can't obtain from a physical model. You can attach dialog and rules to the logical model regardless of whether your particular RDBMS will support those rules or not. In short, it allows you to squeeze in all the facts before you start paring down your design to a specific implementation.

What's nice about this is that logical models allow you to capture all of your data rules in one place regardless of where that rule will be actually implemented. You will frequently run into situations where you cannot sensibly implement your rules in the database. The rules in question may be data related, but due to some constraint or requirement, you need to implement them using more procedural code in your client or in some form of middle tier. With logical models, you go ahead and include the data-related rules anyway.

Regardless of its source, you include all data-related information in a logical design to create one or more abstracts of the data in your system. These abstracts can then be used as a representation to your customer about what you really are intending to store and what rules you believe you have captured. Using such a representation early (and often) can save valuable time and money in your projects by opening extra doors of communication. Even a customer who is not very data savvy can often look at the highest level diagrams and say things like "Where are the purchase requisitions?" Usually, you have some handy dandy explanation of why you called them something else and you can point to them on the diagram — other times, however, you find yourself uttering that most fearsome of words — "Oops!" I don't know about you, but I'd rather utter that word in the first weeks of a project rather than the first weeks of deployment. Logical modeling, when properly shared with the customer, can help avoid those deployment-time Oops statements.

I can't do enough to stress the importance of sharing your logical design (there had better be one!) with your customer both early and often. With a little education of the customer in how to read your logical model (this should also include good documentation on cause and purpose of the entities and relationships of the model), you can save a fortune in both time and money.

I haven't met a developer with any real experience who hasn't, at least once (and probably far more often than that), learned the hard way about the cost of late changes to your system. Changing code is very expensive, but that typically doesn't even begin to touch what happens when you need to change your database late in a project. If you haven't done a good job of abstracting your database, then every change you make to your database is going to cascade through tons of code. In other words, one little change in your database can potentially cost several hundred or even thousands (depending on the size of the system) of changes in the code that accesses the database.

In short, communication is everything, and logical modeling should be a huge part of your tool set for communicating with your customer.

Parts of a Logical Model

A logical model contains three major parts:

❑   Structure

❑   Constraints

❑   Rules

The combination of these three should completely describe the requirements of the data in your system, but they may not translate entirely to the physical model. Some of the issues identified in the logical model may need to be implemented in some procedural form (such as in a middle-tier component). Other times, the entire logical model can be implemented through the various features of your RDBMS.

> This is a really important point, and I want to stress it again — just because it's in your logical model doesn't mean that it will be in your physical database. A logical model should take into account *all* of your data requirements — even those that are not possible to implement in your RDBMS (for example, data that you might be retrieving from a third-party source — perhaps in an XML document or some other storage medium). Having everything in your logical model allows you to plan the physical design in such a way that you can be sure that you have addressed all data issues — not just those that will physically reside in the database.

Structure

Structure is that part of the logical design that deals with the concept of actually storing the data. When you deal with the structure of the database, you're talking about entities — most of which will translate to tables that will store your data — and the particular columns you are going to need to maintain the atomicity of your data.

Constraints

Constraints, from a logical model standpoint, are a bit broader than the way that you've used the word *constraint* up until now. Prior to now, when you used the word *constraint*, you were talking about a specific set of features to limit data to certain values. From a logical standpoint, a constraint is anything that defines the "what" question for our data — that is, what data is valid. A logical model includes constraints, which is to say that it includes things like:

❑   Data types (notice that this is really a separate thought from the notion that a column needs to exist or what the name of that column should be).

❑   Constraints in the form you're used to up until now — that is, CHECK constraints, foreign keys, or even primary keys and UNIQUE constraints (alternate keys). Each of these provides a logical definition of what data can exist in our database. This area would also include things like domain tables (which you would reference using foreign keys) — which restrict the values in a column to a particular "domain" list.

Rules

If constraints were the "what" in our data, then *rules* are the "when and how much" in our data.

When we define logical rules, we're defining things like "Do we require a value on this one?" (which equates to "Do we allow nulls?") and "How many of these do we allow?" (which defines the cardinality of our data — do we accept one or many?).

It's worth noting yet again that any of these parts may not be implemented in the physical part of your database — we may decide that the restrictions that we want to place on things will be handled entirely at the client — regardless of where the requirement is implemented, it should still be part of our comprehensive logical data model. It is only when we achieve this complete modeling of our data that we can really know that we have addressed all the issues (regardless of where we addressed them).

Dealing with File-Based Information Via Classic BLOBs

BLOBs. You probably haven't seen enough of them to hate them yet. Whether that's a "yet" or not largely depends on whether or not you need to support backward compatibility.

Back in SQL Server 2005, Microsoft added some new data types (`varchar(max)`, `nvarchar(max)`, and `varbinary(max)`) that greatly simplify dealing with Binary large objects — or BLOBs. SQL Server 2008 adds yet another option to the mix in the form of supporting a special file-level storage option called filestreams (these are a lot more complex, and require a very cohesive design effort with your client-side coders as well as special network considerations). Other than a quick glance at them, we'll largely defer the discussion of filestreams to the next chapter (advanced data structures) and our more advanced performance design chapter (Chapter 21).

When used with a compatible data access model (ADO.NET 2.0 or higher), you can access BLOB data through the more standard methods (that is, without using filestreams) as though it were the same as its smaller base data type (`varchar`, `nvarchar`, or `varbinary`). For those of you still needing to deal with backward compatibility issues, you'll have to use the older (and even slower) "chunking" method to access your data. Regardless of which access method you're using, BLOBs are slow — very slow and big. Using the new access methods can really help BLOB handling performance though, so let me encourage you to migrate as soon as possible to at least SQL Server 2005 as your bottom level of support.

> The oldest version of SQL Server you're supporting is the critical factor — not the data access method — when using the newer BLOB data types. SQL Server will automatically translate the newer data types to appear like the old ones when dealing with the older connectivity methods. Note, however, that use of filestreams does require very specific client-side code.

BLOBs are nice in the sense that they let you break the 8K barrier on row size (BLOBs can be up to about 2GB in size). The first problem is that they can be clumsy to use under the old data types and access methods. Perhaps the larger problem, however, is that they are painfully slow (I know, I'm repeating myself, but I suspect I'm also making a point here). In the race between the BLOB and the tortoise (the sequel to the tortoise and the hare), the BLOB won only after the tortoise stopped for a nap.

Okay, okay, so I've beaten the slow thing into the ground. Indeed, there have been substantial performance improvements in BLOB handling over the years, and the difference is not what it used to be, but at the risk of mentioning it one too many times, BLOBs are still relatively slow.

All right, so now you've heard me say BLOBs are slow and you still need to store large blocks of text or binary information. Normally, you'd do that using a BLOB — and, with the recent performance improvements in BLOB handling, that's probably best — but you do have the option of doing it another way. You can go around the problem by storing things as files instead.

> **Okay, so by now some of you have to be asking the question of "isn't a database going to be a faster way of accessing data than the file system?" My answer is quite simply — "Usually not."**

There are two ways to do this without going to filestreams. We'll start with the method that has traditionally been implemented, and then we'll talk about another potential (it requires very application-specific design on your part) way to do it in the .NET era.

I'm going to warn you right up front that, in order to pull the typical way of doing this off, you need to be planning for it in your client — this isn't a database server–only kind of thing to do. Indeed, you'll be removing most of the work from the database server and putting it into your middle tier and file system. You can start by looking at what you need to do on the server's file system side. The only thing that you need is to make sure that you have at least one directory to store the information in. Depending on the nature of your application, you may also need to have logic in a middle-tier object that will allow it to create additional directories as needed.

All Windows operating systems have limits on the number of files they can store in one directory. With the 64-bit operating systems out, the maximum number of files per directory has increased such that the maximum isn't so much the issue, as raw performance. (Windows still tends to get very slow in file access as the number of files in a particular directory rises.) As such, you still need to think about how many files you're going to be storing. If it will be many (say, over 500), then you'll want to create a mechanism in the object that stores your BLOB so that it can create new directories either on an as-needed basis, or based on some other logical criteria.

Your business component will be in charge of copying the BLOB information to the file you're going to store it in. If it is already is some defined file format, you're on easy street — just run your language's equivalent to a copy command (with a twist we'll go over shortly), and you're in business. If it is streamed data, then you'll need to put the logic in your component to store the information in a logical format for later retrieval.

> **One big issue with this implementation is that of security. Since you're storing the information in a file that's outside of SQL Server's realm, it is also outside SQL Server's protection security-wise. Instead, you have to rely on your network security.**

There are several "Wow, that's scary!" things that should come to mind for you here. First, if someone's going to read data out of the directory that you're storing all this in, doesn't that mean they can see other files that are stored in there? Yes, it does (if you wanted to get really tricky, you could get around this by changing the Windows security for each file, but it would be very tedious indeed — in the case of a Web application, you would need to do something like implementing a DLL on your Web server). Second, since you'd have to give people rights to copy the file into the directory, wouldn't there be a risk of someone altering the file directly rather than using the database (potentially causing your database to be out of sync with the file)? Absolutely.

The answer to these and the many other questions that you could probably come up with lies in your data access layer. (I'm assuming an n-tier approach here.) You can, for example, have the access component run under a different security context than the end user. This means that you can create a situation where the users can access their data — but only when they are using the data access component to do it (they don't have any rights to the directory themselves — indeed, they probably don't even know where the files are stored).

So then, where does SQL Server come into play in all this? It keeps track of where you stored the information in question. Theoretically, the reason why you were trying to store this information in the databases in the first place is because it relates to some other information in the row you were going to store it as part of. But instead of saving the actual data in the row in the form of a BLOB, you will now store a path to the file that you saved. The process for storage will look something like this:

1. Determine the name you're going to store it as.

2. Copy the file to the location that you're going to store it at.

3. Save the full name and path in a `varchar` along with the rest of the data for that row.

4. To retrieve the data, run your query much as you would have if you were going to retrieve the data direction from the table, only this time, retrieve the path to where the actual BLOB data is stored.

5. Retrieve the data from the file system.

In general, this approach will run somewhat faster than if you were using BLOBs. There are, however, some exceptions to the rule when using this approach:

❑ The BLOBs you are saving are consistently small (less than 8K) in size.

❑ The data is text or some format that MS Search has a filter for, and you want to be able to perform full-text searches against it.

If the size of your BLOBs is consistently less than 8K, then the data may be able to fit entirely on one data page. This significantly minimizes the overhead in dealing with your BLOB. While the file system approach may still be faster, the benefits will be sharply reduced such that it doesn't make as much sense. If you're in this scenario, and speed is everything, then all I can suggest is to experiment.

If you want to perform full-text searches, you're probably going to be better off going ahead and storing the large blocks of text as a TEXT data type (which is a BLOB) in SQL Server. If the text is stored in a binary format that has an MS Search filter available (or you could write your own if you're desperate enough), then you can store the file in an image data type and MS Search will automatically use the filter to build the full-text index. Don't get me wrong; it's still very possible to do full-text searches against the text in the file, but you're going to have to do substantially more coding to keep your relationships intact if you want non-BLOB data from the same functional row. In addition, you're most likely going to wind up having to program your middle tier to make use of index server.

If push comes to shove, and you need to make a full-text search against file system–based information, you could take a look at accessing the index server via a query directly. SQL Server can issue remote queries such that you can potentially access any OLE DB (a Microsoft originated data access API — we'll see a bit more about it in Chapter 25) data source. The MS Search service has an OLE DB provider and can be used at the target as a linked server or in an OPENQUERY. The bad news, however, is that performing an index server query against an index server that is not on the same physical box as your SQL Server really doesn't work. (Feel free to e-mail me if you've found a workaround to this.) The only workaround is to have an index server on the system local to SQL Server, but have it catalog files stored on another system. The problem with this is the network chatter during the cataloging process and the fact that it doesn't let you offload the cataloging work (which hurts scalability).

Okay, so that was way #1 (you may recall I said there were two). The second leverages the .NET assembly architecture that was added back in SQL Server 2005. We haven't really gotten to a discussion of .NET integration yet, so we'll keep this fairly high level.

This approach actually leverages many of the same concepts that were used in the middle-tier file access approach. The only real change is in what server or component takes charge of the file access.

With the advent of Common Language Runtime (CLR) integration, we have the ability to create user-defined functions far more complex than those previously possible. As part of that, we have the ability to define table-valued functions that can retrieve data from nearly any base source. Indeed, in Chapter 10 we will take a look at how we can enumerate files in a directory and return them as a table-valued function, but we could just as easily return a varbinary(max) column that contains the file. Under this model, all file access would be performed under whatever network security context we establish for that assembly to run under, but it would only be performed as part of the table-valued function.

> It is important to note that the file system–based method mentioned earlier can be considered as something of a predecessor to the filestream feature introduced with this release. Filestreams implement a somewhat advanced version of this approach — one that includes coordinated backups among other things. That said, filestreams also add substantial complexity over even this approach — thus why I have deferred detailed discussion of them to the advanced data structures and performance chapters.

Subcategories

Subcategories are a logical construct that provides you another type of relationship (sometimes called a "Supertype" or "Subtype" relationship) to work with. On the physical side of the model, a subcategory is implemented using a mix of the types of relationships that I've already talked about (you'll see the specifics of that before you're done).

A subcategory deals with the situation where you have a number of what may first seem like different entities but which share some, although not all, things in common.

I think the best way to get across the concept of a subcategory is to show you one. To do this, we'll take the example of a document in a company.

A document has a number of attributes that are common to any kind of document. For example:

- ❑ Title
- ❑ Author
- ❑ Date created
- ❑ Date last modified
- ❑ Storage location

I'm sure there are more. Note that I'm not saying that every document has the same title, rather that every document has a title. Every document has an author (possibly more than one actually, but, for this example, we'll assume a limit of one). Every document was created on some date. You get the picture — you're dealing with the attributes of the concept of a document, not any particular instance of a document.

But there are lots of different kinds of documents. From things like legal forms (say your mortgage documents) to office memos, to report cards — there are lots of document types. Still, each of these can still be considered to be a document — or a subcategory of a document. Consider a few examples.

For our first example, we'll look at a lease. A lease has all the characteristics that we expect to find in our documents category, but it also has information that is particular to a lease. A lease has things like:

- ❑ Lessor
- ❑ Lessee
- ❑ Term (how long the lease is for)
- ❑ Rate (how much per month or week)
- ❑ Security deposit
- ❑ Start date
- ❑ Expiration date
- ❑ Option (which usually offers an extension at a set price for a set additional term)

The fact that a lease has all of these attributes does not preclude the fact that it is still a document.

We can come up with a few more examples, and I'll stay with my legal document trend — start with a divorce document. It has attributes such as:

- ❑ Petitioner (the person suing for a divorce)
- ❑ Respondent (the plaintiff's spouse)
- ❑ Separation date
- ❑ Date the petitioner files for the divorce
- ❑ Date the divorce was considered "final"

❑ Alimony (if any)

❑ Child support (if any)

We could also have a bill of sale — our bill of sale might include attributes such as:

❑ Date of sale

❑ Amount of the sale

❑ Seller

❑ Purchaser

❑ Warranty period (if any)

Again, the fact that divorces and bills of sale both have their own attributes does not change the fact that they are documents.

In each case — leases, divorces, and bills of sale — we have what is really a subcategory of the category of "documents." A document really has little or no meaning without also belonging to a subcategory. Likewise, any instance of a subcategory has little meaning without the parent information that is found only in the supercategory — documents.

Types of Subcategories

Subcategories fall into two separate classifications of their own — exclusive and non-exclusive.

When you refer to a subcategory as simply a "subcategory," then you are usually referring to a subcategory arrangement where you have a record in a table that represents the supercategory (a document in our previous example), and a matching record in at least one of the subcategories.

This kind of subcategory is represented with a symbol that appears rather odd as compared to those you've seen thus far (Figure 5-9).

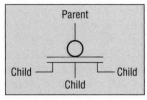

Figure 5-9

Even though there are three subcategories depicted both here and in the document example, don't misconstrue this as being any kind of official limit to the number of subcategories — there isn't one. You could have a single subcategory or 10 of them — it doesn't really make any difference.

Far more common is the situation where you have an exclusive subcategory. An exclusive subcategory works exactly as a category did with only one exception — for every record in the supercategory, there is only one matching record in any of the subcategories. Each subcategory is deemed to be mutually exclusive, so a record to match the supercategory exists as exactly one row in exactly one of the subcategory tables.

The diagramming for an exclusive sub-type looks even a little odder yet (Figure 5-10).

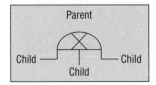

Figure 5-10

Keeping Track of What's What — Implementing Subcategories

The thing that's really cool about subcategories is that they allow you to store all of a similar construct in one place. Before learning this concept, you would have taken one of two approaches to implement our document model:

❑   Add all of the attributes into one column and just leave the columns null for the information that doesn't fit the specific type of document you're interested in for a given record.

❑   Have separate tables for each type of document. The columns that are essentially the same between document types would be repeated for each table (each table stores its own copy of the document information as it applies to the records in that particular table).

Using the notion of a subcategory, you can now store all documents, regardless of type, such that they all begin in one place. Any query that you have that is looking for information about all the documents in your system can now run against just one table instead of having to do something like using the UNION operator on three (maybe more, maybe less) different tables. It probably goes without saying, then, that implementing this kind of situation using a subcategory can provide a serious performance enhancement over the other options.

There is a catch though (you knew there would be, right?) — you need to provide some mechanism to point to the rest of the information for that document. Your query of all documents may provide the base information on the specific document that you're looking for, but when you want the rest of the information for that document (the things that are unique to that document type), then how does your application know which of the subcategory tables to search for the matching record in? To do this, just add a field to your supercategory that indicates what the subcategory is for that record. In our example, you would probably implement another column in our documents table called "DocumentType." From that type, you would know which of your other tables to look through for the matching record with more information. Furthermore, you might implement this using a domain table — a table to limit the values in your DocumentType column to just those types that you have subcategories for — and a foreign key to that table.

Keep in mind that while what I'm talking about here is the physical storage and retrieval of the data, there is no reason why you couldn't abstract this using either a sproc or a series of views (or both). For example, you could have a stored procedure call that would pull together the information from the Documents *table and then join to the appropriate subcategory.*

Oh — for those of you who are thinking, "Wait, didn't that other text that I read about n-tier architecture say to never use sprocs?" Well, that's a garbage recommendation in my not so humble opinion (you'll look more at sprocs in Chapter 10). It's foolish not to use the performance tools available — just remember to access them only through your data access layer — don't allow middle-tier or client components to even know your sprocs exist. Follow this advice, and you'll get better performance, improved overall encapsulation, shorter dev times, and, even with all that, still live within the real theory of a separate data access layer that is so fundamental to n-tier design.

In addition to establishing a pointer to the type of document, you also need to determine whether you're dealing with a plain subcategory or an exclusive subcategory. In our document example, you have what should be designed as an exclusive subcategory. You may have lots of documents, but you do not have documents that are both a lease and a divorce (a non-exclusive subcategory would allow any mix of our subcategories). Even if you had a lease with a purchase option, the bill of sale would be a separate document created at the time the lease option was exercised.

Figure 5-11 shows an implementation of our logical model.

Okay, so you have an entity called documents. These documents are of a specific type, and that type is limited to a domain — the boundaries of that domain are set by `DocumentType`. In addition, each of the types is represented by its own entity — or subcategory. The symbol in the middle of it all (the half-circle with an "X" through it), tells you that the three subcategories are exclusive in nature (you have one, and only one, for each instance of a document).

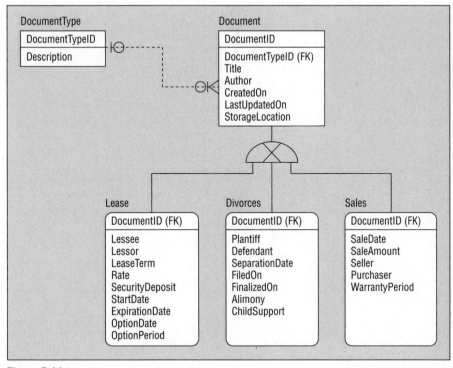

Figure 5-11

This is an excellent place to step back and reflect on what your logical model can do for you. As I discussed earlier in the chapter, our logical model, among other things, provides you with a way to communicate the business rules and requirements of our data. In this case, with a little explanation, someone (a customer perhaps?) can look at this and recognize the concept that you are saying that Leases, Divorces, and Sales are all variations on a theme — that they are really the same thing. This gives the viewer the chance to say, "Wait — no, those aren't really the same thing." Or perhaps something like, "Oh, I see — you know, you also have will and power-of-attorney documents — they are pretty much the same, aren't they?" These are little pieces of information that can save you a bundle of time and money later.

Getting Physical — The Physical Implementation of Subcategories

On the physical side of things, there's nothing quite as neat and clean as it looks in the logical model. Indeed, all you do for the physical side is implement a series of one-to-zero or -one relationships. You do, however, draw them out as being part of a single, multi-table relationship (Figure 5-12).

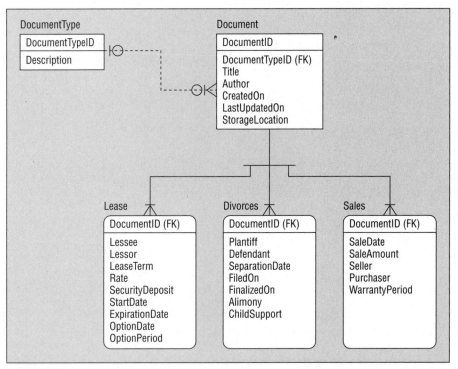

Figure 5-12

The only real trick in the game occurs if you have an exclusive subcategory (which is actually the case much more often than not). In this case, you also need to put some logic into the subcategory tables (in the form of triggers) to ensure that, if any row is to be inserted, there is not already another matching row in one of the other subcategories. For example, you would need to place an insert trigger in Leases that queried the `Divorces` and `Sales` tables for records with the same `DocumentID`. If one was found, then the trigger should reject inserted record with an appropriate error message and a `ROLLBACK`.

Adding to Extensibility with Subcategories

Subcategories are one of those concepts that can make a huge difference in the success of your database design. If used when appropriate, you can cut significant time off your queries and significantly simplify pulling together aggregate information for related but different pieces of information. Yet these aren't the only benefits to subcategories.

Subcategories can provide a pathway to making your database more extensible. If you need to add another subcategory, the only queries you need to deal with are those that are specific to your new subcategory. Any of your queries that worked only with the parent table will still work fine — what's more, they'll pick up the information on your new subcategory without any changes!

In short, you're picking up two major scalability benefits:

❑ The information for your supercategory (documents in the example) can be scanned from just one table rather than using a `UNION` operator. This means fewer joins and faster relative query performance — especially as your tables grow larger or you have more and more subcategories.

❑ Adding new subcategories often does not take as much development time as it would have if you where developing the framework for those categories from scratch.

Now, just as with most things, you do need to keep in mind one downside — subcategories can create a bottleneck at the parent table. Every query that you run against all the tables and data involved in the overall set of categories is probably going to need to access the parent table. Think about the locking implications there. (If you're new to locking considerations, they are discussed in full in Chapter 12.) If you are not careful about your index and query strategies, this can lead to some very bad blocking and/or deadlocking problems. That said, with intelligent planning and query writing, this is usually not a problem. Also, if the sheer size of the parent table becomes a problem, SQL Server now gives us the option of using partitioned tables to scale to larger sizes.

Database Reuse

This is almost never thought of, but you can create databases that facilitate reusability. Why do I say that it's almost never thought of? Well, just trust me on this — developers think of things like reusable components. Things such as objects to validate credit cards, distribute mail, and stream binary information in and out are all things that you would immediately think about placing in a repository and using over and over again. For whatever reason, however, databases just don't seem to get thought of in that way.

Perhaps one reason for this is that databases, by definition, store data. Data is normally thought of as being unique to one company or industry and, most of all, as being private. I'm guessing that you then automatically think of the storage container for that data as also being personal — who knows?

Contrary to popular belief, however, databases can be built to be reusable. Surprisingly, to do this you apply a lot of the same concepts that make code components reusable — most of all compartmentalization and the use of common interfaces.

Just remember to make sure you have a really good fit before you try to reuse an existing database structure. Much like most things in programming that I've seen reuse of, it's very possible to have your reuse become a situation where you are trying to use the wrong tool for the job, and things can actually become even more expensive than they would have been if you had written things from scratch to begin with.

Candidates for Reusable Databases

The databases that have the best chance at being reusable are those that can be broken up into separate subject areas (much as components are usually broken up into functional groupings). Each subject area is kept as generic as is feasible. An example would be something like an accounting database. You could have separate subject areas that match up with the functional areas in accounting:

- ❑ Purchasing

- ❑ Accounts receivable (which in turn may be broken up into invoicing and cash receipts)

- ❑ Inventory

- ❑ Accounts payable

- ❑ General ledger

- ❑ Cash management

The list could go on. You can also take the approach down to a more granular level and create many, many databases, down to the level of things like persons, commercial entities (ever noticed how similar customers are to vendors?), orders — there are lots of things that have base constructs that are used repeatedly. You can roll these up into their own "mini-database," and then plug them into a larger logical model (tied together using sprocs, views, or other components of your data access layer).

How to Break Things Up

This is where the logical versus physical modeling really starts to show its stuff. When you're dealing with databases that you're trying to make reusable, you often have one logical database (that contains all the different subject areas) that contains many physical databases. Sometimes you'll choose to implement your logical design by referencing each of the physical implementations directly. Other times you may choose an approach that does a better job of hiding the way that you've implemented the database — you can create what amounts to a "virtual" database in that it holds nothing but views that reference the data from the appropriate physical database.

Let me digress long enough to point out that this process is essentially just like encapsulation in object-oriented programming. By using the views, you are hiding the actual implementation of your database from the users of the view. This means that you can remove one subject area in your database and replace it with an entirely different design — the only trick in doing this is to map the new design to your views — from that point on, the client application and users are oblivious to the change in implementation.

Breaking things up into separate physical databases and/or virtualizing the database places certain restrictions on you, and many of these restrictions contribute to the idea of being able to separate one subject area from the whole, and reuse it in another environment.

Some of the things to do include:

❏ Minimize or eliminate direct references to other functional areas. If you've implemented the view approach, connect each physically separate piece of the database to the logical whole only through the views.

❏ Don't use foreign key constraints — where necessary, use triggers instead. Triggers can span databases; foreign key constraints can't.

The High Price of Reusability

All this reuse comes at a price. Many of the adjustments that you make to your design in order to facilitate reuse have negative performance impacts. Some of these include:

❏ Foreign key constraints are faster than triggers overall, but triggers are the only way to enforce referential integrity that crosses database boundaries.

❏ Using views means two levels of optimization run on all your queries (one to get at the underlying query and mesh that into your original query, another to sort out the best way to provide the end result) — that's more overhead, and it slows things down.

❏ If not using the virtual database approach (one database that has views that map to all the other databases), maintaining user rights across many databases can be problematic.

In short, don't look for things to run as fast unless you're dealing with splitting the data across more servers than you can with the single database model.

Reusing your database can make lots of sense in terms of reduced development time and cost, but you need to balance those benefits against the fact that you may suffer to some degree in the performance category.

De-Normalization

I'm going to keep this relatively short, since this tends to get into fairly advanced concepts, but remember not to get carried away with the normalization of your data.

As I stated early in this chapter, normalization is one of those things that database designers sometimes wear like a cross. It's somehow turned into a religion for them, and they begin normalizing data for the sake of normalization rather than for the good things it does to their database. Here are a couple of things to think about in this regard:

❏ If declaring a computed column or storing some derived data is going to allow you to run a report more effectively, then by all means put it in. Just remember to take into account the benefit versus the risk. (For example, what if your "summary" data gets out of sync with the data it can be derived from? How will you determine that it happened, and how will you fix it if it does happen?)

❏ Sometimes, by including just one (or more) de-normalized column in a table, you can eliminate or significantly cut down the number of joins necessary to retrieve information. Watch for these scenarios — they actually come up reasonably frequently. I've dealt with situations where adding one column to one commonly used base table cut a nine-table join down to just three, and cut the query time by about 90 percent in the process.

❑ If you are keeping historical data — data that will largely go unchanged and is just used for reporting — then the integrity issue becomes a much smaller consideration. Once the data is written to a read-only area and verified, you can be reasonably certain that you won't have the kind of "out of sync" problems that is one of the major things that data normalization addresses. At that point, it may be much nicer (and faster) to just "flatten" (de-normalize) the data out into a few tables, and speed things up.

❑ The fewer tables that have to be joined, the happier your users who do their own reports are going to be. The user base out there continues to get more and more savvy with the tools they are using. Increasingly, users are coming to their DBA and asking for direct access to the database to be able to do their own custom reporting. For these users, a highly normalized database can look like a maze and become virtually useless. De-normalizing your data can make life much easier for these users.

All that said, if in doubt, normalize things. There is a reason why that is the way relational systems are typically designed. When you err on the side of normalizing, you are erring on the side of better data integrity, and on the side of better performance in a transactional environment.

Partitioning for Scalability

Beginning with SQL Server 2000, SQL Server picked up the marvelous ability to create one logical table from multiple physical tables — partitioned views. That is, the data from one logical table is partitioned such that it is stored in a separate well-defined set of physical tables. But the notion of partitioning your data has been around a lot longer than partitioned views have been. Indeed, keeping your main accounting system on one server and your order entry and inventory systems on another is a form of partitioning — you are making sure that the load of handling the two activities is spread across multiple servers. SQL Server 2005 took an additional step by adding what are called partitioned tables.

Partitioned tables are a bit different from partitioned views in a way that is implied in their name — they truly remain a table throughout. Whereas a partitioned view could not support some of the functionality found in tables (constraints, defaults, identity columns, and so on), a partitioned table supports all these.

There is, of course, a catch — partitioned tables are limited to just one server (it is a means of separating a table across multiple filegroups and, therefore, drive volumes). Note that the limitation to one server doesn't mean you're limited to one physical storage device — there is nothing stopping you from linking multiple storage devices (including multiple SANs) to the one SQL Server.

> **Partitioned tables do not allow unique indexes on columns that are not part of the partitioning key — this can be critical when the column you want to partition on is not the one you want to use as a primarykey or you have other columns that need unique constraint enforcement.**

Partitioned views are still an option when the load is such that you need to span multiple servers. For purposes of this chapter, you're going to stick with the basic notions of partitioning that apply to both the view and table models.

Regardless of which partitioning method you're using, the concepts are pretty much the same. You utilize one or more columns in the logical table as a divider to physically separate your data. This allows you to use multiple I/O pathways and even multiple servers to process your query for you. The question of just *how* to partition your data should be a very big one. The tendency is going to be to take the hyper-simplistic approach and just divide things up equally based on the possible values in a partitioning column. This approach may work fine, but it is also a little shortsighted for two big reasons:

❑ Data rarely falls into nice, evenly distributed piles. Often, predicting the distribution requires a lot of research and sampling up front.

❑ It fails to take into account the way the data will actually be used once stored.

The way that you partition your data does a lot more than determine the volume of data that each partition will receive — much more importantly, it makes a positively huge difference in how well your overall system is going to perform. Keep in mind:

❑ Tables rarely live in a bubble. Most of the time you are going to be joining data from any given table with other data in the system — is how the "other" data is partitioned compatible (from a performance perspective)?

❑ Network bandwidth tends to be a huge bottleneck in overall system performance — how are you taking that into account when designing your partitions? This is not that big of a deal if dealing with a partitioned table scheme (which will be local to just one server) but can be huge for a portioned view model.

So, with all this in mind, here are a couple of rules for you:

❑ If using partitioned views to spread data across servers, keep data that will be used together stored together. That is, if certain tables are going to be used together frequently in queries, then try to partition those tables such that data that is likely to be returned as part of a query will most likely reside on the same server. Obviously, you won't be able to make that happen 100 percent of the time, but, with careful thought and recognition of how your data gets used, you should find that you can arrange things so that most queries will happen local to just one server. For example, for a given order, all the related order detail rows will be on the same server.

❑ When you design your application, you should ideally make it partition aware — that is, you should code the routines that execute the queries such that they know which server most likely has their data. The data may be broken out across multiple machines — wouldn't it be nice if the database server your application made the request to was the right one from the start, and there was no need for the request to be forwarded to another server?

If you've gotten as far as deciding that you need to go with a partitioned system, then you must really have one heck of a load you're planning on dealing with. How you partition your data is going to have a huge impact on how well your system is going to deal with that load. Remember to take the time to fully plan out your partitioning scheme. After you think you've decided what you're going to do — Test! Test! Test!

The SQL Server Diagramming Tools

You can open up SQL Server's built-in tools by navigating to the Diagrams node of the database you want to build a diagram for (expand your server first, then the database). Some of what you are going to see you'll find familiar — some of the dialogs are the same as you saw in Chapter 4 when you were creating tables. The SQL Server diagramming tools don't give you all that many options, so you'll find that you'll get to know them fairly quickly.

You can start by creating your first diagram. You can create your new diagram by right-clicking the Diagrams node underneath the AdventureWorks database and choosing the New Database Diagram option.

> *You may (if it's the first time you've tried to create a diagram) see a dialog come up warning you that some of the objects needed to support diagramming aren't in the database and asking if you want to create them — choose yes.*

SQL Server starts you out with an Add Table dialog (see Figure 5-13) that lists the available tables you can add to your diagram.

Figure 5-13

Select the following tables (remember to hold down the control key to select more than one table):

- ❑ Address
- ❑ Customer
- ❑ CustomerAddress
- ❑ SalesOrderHeader
- ❑ SalesOrderDetail

Then click Add. After a brief pause while SQL Server draws all the tables you selected, click the Close button. SQL Server has added our tables to the diagram, as shown in Figure 5-14.

I've rearranged my layout slightly from what SQL Server came up with by default to make more of it fit into this book. Depending on your screen resolution, it may be difficult to see the entire diagram at once due to the zoom. To pull more of the tables into view, change the zoom setting in the toolbar.

SQL Server enumerates through each table you have said you want to add and analyzes what other objects are associated with those tables. The various other items you see beyond the table itself are some of the many other objects that tie into tables — primary keys, foreign keys.

So, having gotten a start, I'll use this diagram as a launching point for explaining how the diagramming tool works and building a few tables here and there.

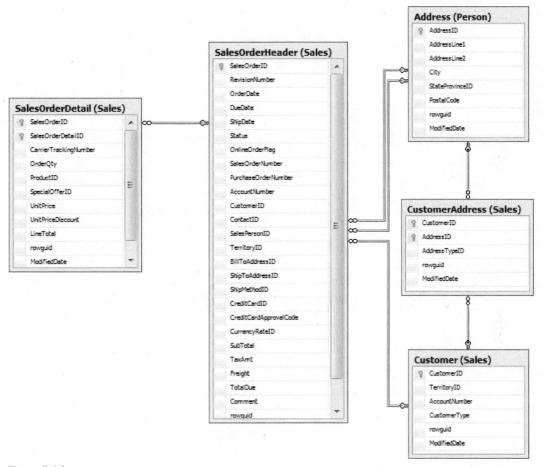

Figure 5-14

Tables

Each table has its own window you can move around. The primary key is shown with the little symbol of a key in the column to the left of the name like the one next to the `CustomerID`. This is just the default view for the table; you can select from several others that allow you to edit the very make-up of the table. To check out your options for views of a table, right-click the table that you're interested in. The default is column names only, but you should also take an interest in the choice of Custom; this or "standard" is what you would use when you want to edit the table from right within the diagram (very nice!).

Adding Tables

You can add a new table to the diagram in one of two ways:

❑ If you have a table that already exists in the database (but not in the diagram), but now you want to add it to your diagram, you simply click the Add Table button on the diagramming window's toolbar, or right-click anywhere in the diagram and choose Add Table. You'll be presented with a list of all the tables in the database; just choose the one that you want to add, and it will appear along with any relationships it has to other tables in the diagram.

❑ If you want to add a completely new table, click the New Table button on the diagramming window's toolbar or right-click in the diagram and choose New Table. You'll be asked for a name for the new table, and the table will be added to the diagram in Column Properties view. Simply edit the properties to have the column names, data types, and so on that you want, and you have a new table in the database.

Let me take a moment to point out a couple of gotchas in this process.

First, don't forget to add a primary key to your table. SQL Server does not automatically do this, nor does it even prompt you. This is a somewhat less than intuitive process. To add a primary key, you must select the columns that you want to have in the key. Then right-click and choose Set Primary Key.

Next, be aware that your new table is not actually added to the database until you choose to save — this is also true of any edits that you make along the way.

Go ahead and quickly add a table to see how this works and set you up for some later examples.

First, right-click anywhere in the diagramming pane, and choose New Table. You'll be prompted for a table name — call this one CustomerNotes. Now add just three columns as shown in Figure 5-15.

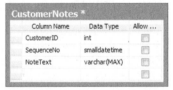

Figure 5-15

Notice the asterisk in the title bar for the table — that means there are unsaved changes to this table (specifically, the table has yet to be saved at all). Go ahead and save the diagram, and that will also create the table in the physical database. You now have a table with three NOT NULL columns. There is not, as yet, any primary key for this table. (We'll deal with that in our section on adding constraints.)

Dropping Tables from Either the Database or Diagram

Dropping tables is a bit confusing since there is a vague distinction between deleting them from the diagram versus deleting them from the database. You can drop a table from the diagram either of two ways:

❑ Select the table and press your Delete key.

❑ Select the table and choose the Remove from Diagram button on the toolbar.

To entirely drop the table from the database, you have three choices:

❑ Select the table, and choose Edit➤Delete Tables from Database

❑ Select the table, and click the Delete Tables from Database icon on the toolbar

❑ Right-click the table header, and choose Delete Tables from Database

> **Note that, while deleting a table from the diagram does not become permanent until you save the diagram, deleting it from the database happens *immediately* after you confirm the deletion.**

Dealing with Constraints

If you're using the diagram tools at all, you'll want to do more than create just the basic table — you'll want to be able to establish constraints as well. The diagramming tools make these relatively easy.

Primary Keys

This really couldn't be much simpler. To create a primary key, just select the column(s) you want to participate in the key (again, hold down the control key if you need to select multiple columns), right-click and select Set Primary Key, as shown in Figure 5-16.

I'm adding a primary key to the CustomerNotes table we created in the previous section. As you choose the Set Primary Key option, you'll see it add a key icon to each of the fields that participate in your column. To change the primary key, just select a new set of columns and again choose Set Primary Key. To remove it, just choose Remove Primary Key from the same menu. (It does not show in my figure, because no primary key had been set yet.)

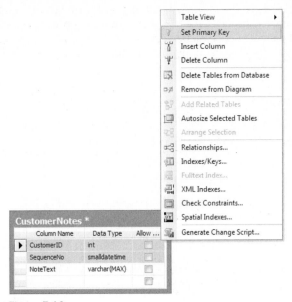

Figure 5-16

Foreign Keys

Foreign keys are nearly as easy as primary keys were — they use a simple drag-and-drop model.

In our `CustomerNotes` example, you'll notice I used `CustomerID` — this is intended to be the same `CustomerID` that is used elsewhere in the AdventureWorks database, so it makes sense that you would want a foreign key to the base table for `CustomerID`'s (`Customer`). To do this, simply click the `CustomerID` column in the `Customer` table, and drag it onto the `CustomerNotes` table. Management Studio will then give you the dialog in Figure 5-17 to confirm the foreign key you're after.

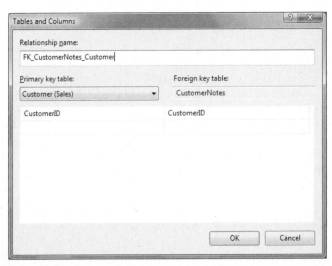

Figure 5-17

From here, you can change what the columns are in both the referenced and referencing tables, and even add additional columns if you need to. Click OK, and you move on to the dialog in Figure 5-18, which allows you to set the other properties that go with a foreign key definition, including such things as cascading actions and whether this foreign key should be propagated to any replicated databases you have out there.

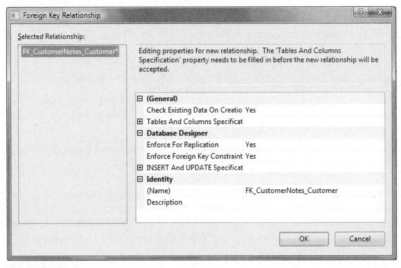

Figure 5-18

To edit the foreign key after you've created it, select it (by clicking it), and you will see properties in the pane on the right-hand side of the screen.

Note that the properties pane is a dockable window, so it's possible you have moved it away from the default right-hand side.

To delete a foreign key, simply right-click the relationship and choose Delete Relationships from Database.

CHECK Constraints

To work on the CHECK constraints for your table, simply right-click the table and choose Check Constraints. This brings up a dialog that allows you to either create a new constraint or to select from those already defined for the table. After you create a new one or select one of the existing ones, Management Studio brings up a dialog that is not all that different from that used for foreign keys.

As when you created tables, you can see the asterisk next to the CK_CustomerNotes name — this lets you know that there are unsaved changes. The primary thing you want to focus on in this dialog is the Expression field; this is where you would enter in the conditions of your constraint.

Do not confuse the Identity box in this dialog with an IDENTITY column — this section of the dialog is only there for providing the name and, optionally, a description of the constraint.

To edit an existing constraint, just change the properties as desired. To remove it, just select the constraint you're interested in and click the Delete button.

Regarding Date Columns

Normally I wouldn't spend much time on specific data types, but with SQL Server 2008 the new data types require some special attention. Of particular issue is how the new `Date` and `Time` data types alter things. We'll hold off on the performance and space ramifications for our designing for performance chapter (Chapter 21), but the new `Date` data type in particular deserves a brief moment of discussion.

Previous versions of SQL Server supported only the notions of date and time as one combined data type. The `datetime` data type takes up a whopping 8 bytes, and the combination often creates hassles in development — among these are:

❑ Wasted space when there is no need to track a specific time (or when time of day is all you need).

❑ Hassles in comparing dates when there is time also attached. (You want to see if it's on the same day, but they don't compare equally due to different times of day; you can get around this, but it's a hassle and muddles your code).

❑ Occasional compatibility hassles when interacting with client data types that expect just the date or just the time.

The new date and time data types address these issues by making date and time data discrete and adding flexibility to each type (you can even set precision). Dates are now easily compared to other dates, and times are not only easily compared to other times, but also precision settable to either save space or capture time down to the nanosecond (we were limited to roughly 3 milliseconds previously).

In addition, we have new data types that are meant to deal with the increasing need to standardize time. Allowances have been made to keep track of time offsets versus Coordinated Universal Time, or UTC, which is an abbreviation for the French, *Temps Universel Coordonné*. This means you can accept times submitted from all around the world and easily reconcile them for more genuine time comparisons.

We will touch on these new data types more as we continue through the book, but given the legacy of the `datetime` data type, it is important to recognize these new data types and plan for how they will affect your applications moving forward.

Summary

Database design is a huge concept, and one that has many excellent books dedicated to it as their sole subject. It is essentially impossible to get across every database design notion in just a chapter or two.

In this chapter, you have, however, gotten off to a solid start. You've gotten a bit of review of normalization. You have, however, also seen that normalization is not always the right answer — strategic de-normalization of our data can simplify the database for users and speed reporting performance. Finally, you've looked at some non-normalization-related concepts in database design, plus how to make use of the diagramming tools to design our database.

In the next chapter, you will be taking a very close look at how SQL Server stores information and how to make the best use of indexes.

6

Core Storage and Index Structure

Indexes. They may well be the second most important part (to tables) of your database planning and system maintenance. Why is it then that they are, all too often, an afterthought in many designs?

Think about it for a minute. Most database systems are based on the notion of fast and efficient data retrieval and maintenance. Indexes provide your database system with additional ways to look up data and take shortcuts to that data's physical location. The right index can cut huge percentages of time off your query executions. So, if efficient data retrieval and maintenance are why we build databases, and indexes are critical to the efficient access and maintenance of the data in databases, why is it that so many software architects move straight from determining a table layout to stored procedures or client code? Silly.

Now, don't get me wrong: thinking about stored procedures, client code, and other non-table elements is important, and most developers aren't going to leave a database with zero indexes. Indeed, at least a few indexes will show up in your database without you having to specify them. (Creating a primary key or unique constraint creates an implied index required to enforce those constraints.) It is, however, amazing just how often indexes are applied based on only a few minutes worth of guesses or purely to address a specific performance bug that showed up in QA (or worse, as a patch to a released product). In still other scenarios, developers will take an "index everything" approach, failing to realize the additional storage required or how too many poorly planned indexes can actually *increase* the time it takes for your query to run.

In this chapter, we will be focusing on the core index structures in SQL Server from both a developer's and an administrator's point of view. We will also look at how data is stored in SQL Server so that we may better understand how SQL Server makes optimization choices, and, from that, what indexes make sense in what situations.

SQL Server Storage

Storage is an area that has undergone some minor changes in SQL Server 2008. (Well, technically they showed up in a service pack for SQL Server 2005.) These changes, primarily centered around the compression of fixed-length storage types, are discussed in the next chapter.

Data in SQL Server can be thought of as existing in something of a hierarchy of structures. The hierarchy is pretty simple. Some of the objects within the hierarchy are things that you will deal with directly and will therefore know easily. A few others exist under the cover, and while they can be directly addressed in some cases, they usually are not. Take a look at them one by one.

The Database

Okay — this one is easy. I can just hear people out there saying, "Duh! I knew that." Yes, you probably did, but I point it out as a unique entity here because it is the highest level of the definition of storage (for a given server). This is the highest level that a *lock* can be established at, although you cannot explicitly create a database level lock.

A lock is something of both a hold and a place marker that is used by the system. We will be looking into locking extensively in Chapter 11, but we will see the lockability of objects within SQL Server discussed in passing as we look at storage.

The File

By default, your database has two files associated with it:

❑ The first is the primary physical database file — that's where your data is ultimately stored. This file should be named with an *.mdf extension (this is a recommendation, not a requirement — but I think you'll find doing it in other ways will become confusing over time). "Secondary" files can be added (and should use an *.ndf extension), and do not need to be on the same physical drive as the primary (which means you can use them to distribute I/O load — we will explore these further in Chapter 21).

❑ The second is something of an offshoot to the database file — the log. We'll dive into the log quite a bit when we deal with transactions and locks in Chapter 11, but you should be aware that it resides in its own file (which should end with an *.ldf extension), and that your database will not operate without it. The log is the serial recording of what's happened to your database since the last time that data was "committed" to the database. The database isn't really your complete set of data. The log isn't your complete set of data. Instead, if you start with the database and "apply" (add in all the activities from the last point the two synched up) the log, you have your complete set of data.

There is no restriction about where these files are located relative to each other. It is possible (actually, it's even quite desirable) to place each file on a separate physical device. This not only allows for the activity in one file not to interfere with that in the other file, but it also creates a situation where losing the file with the database does not cause you to lose your work — you can restore a backup and then reapply the log (that was safe on the other drive). Likewise, if you lose the drive with the log, you'll still have a valid database up through the time of the last *checkpoint* (checkpoints are fully covered in Chapter 11).

The Extent

An *extent* is the basic unit of storage used to allocate space for tables and indexes within a given file. It is made up of eight contiguous 64KB data *pages*.

The concept of allocating space based on extents, rather than actual space used, can be somewhat difficult to understand for people used to operating system storage principles. The important points about an extent include:

❑ Once an extent is full, the next record will take up not just the size of the record but the size of a whole new extent. Many people who are new to SQL Server get tripped up in their space estimations in part due to the allocation of an extent at a time rather than a record at a time.

❑ By pre-allocating this space, SQL Server saves the time of allocating new space with each record.

It may seem like a waste that a whole extent is taken up just because one too many rows were added to fit on the currently allocated extent(s), but the amount of space wasted this way is typically not that much as a percentage of the entire database. Still, it can add up — particularly in a highly fragmented environment — so it's definitely something you should keep in mind.

The good news in taking up all this space is that SQL Server skips some of the allocation time overhead. Instead of worrying about allocation issues every time it writes a row, SQL Server deals with additional space allocation only when a new extent is needed.

Don't confuse the space that an extent is taking up with the space that a database takes up. Whatever space is allocated to the database is what you'll see disappear from your disk drive's available space number. An extent is merely how things are, in turn, allocated within the total space reserved by an individual database file.

The Page

Much like an extent is a unit of allocation within the database, a page is the unit of allocation within a specific extent. There are eight pages to every extent.

A page is the last level you reach before you are at the actual data row. Whereas the number of pages per extent is fixed, the number of rows per page is not — that depends entirely on the size of the row, which can vary. You can think of a page as being something of a container for both table and index row data. A row is not allowed to be split between pages.

Figure 6-1 illustrates how data gets put into a page. Notice how, for every row you insert, you have to place the row offset down at the end of the page to indicate where in the page that particular row's data begins.

There are a number of different *page types*. For purposes of this book, the types we care about are:

❑ Data

❑ Index

❑ Binary Large Object (BLOB) (for Image, most Text and Ntext data, and `varchar(max)`/`nvarchar(max)` data that is larger than about 8k)

- ❑ Global and Shared Global Allocation Map (GAM, or SGAM)
- ❑ Page Free Space (PFS)
- ❑ Index Allocation Map (IAM)
- ❑ Bulk Changed Map
- ❑ Differential Changed Map

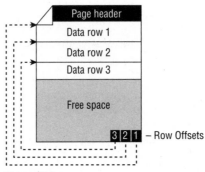

Figure 6-1

Data Pages

Data pages are pretty self-explanatory — they are the actual data in your table, with the exception of any BLOB data that is not stored "in row" (more on this in the BLOB pages section). In the case of a row that has a column that contains BLOB data, the regular data is stored in a data page, and the BLOB data may be stored in page (if small enough to fit). If the BLOB data can't fit on the page, then a 16-byte pointer is used to show where to find the BLOB page that contains the start of the BLOB.

Index Pages

Index pages are also pretty straightforward: They hold both the non-leaf and leaf level pages (we'll examine what these are later in the chapter) of a non-clustered index, as well as the non-leaf level pages of a clustered index. These index types will become much clearer as we continue through this chapter.

BLOB Pages

BLOB pages are for storing Binary Large Objects. For SQL Server, these amount to data stored in `varbinary(max)`, `varchar(max)`, or `nvarchar(max)` columns. BLOB pages are special as far as data storage pages go, in that they don't have any rows as such. Since a BLOB can be as large as 2GB, they have to be able to go on more than one page — for this portion of things it doesn't matter what the version is. SQL Server will allocate as many pages as it needs in order to store the entire BLOB, but there is no guarantee that these pages will be contiguous — the pages could be located anywhere within the database file(s).

As mentioned before, the connection between the non-BLOB data for a row and any BLOB-related to that row comes in the form of a pointer. The nature of that pointer and how SQL Server navigates to the BLOB data was changed for version 7.0 of SQL Server. In version 6.5 and before, the BLOB pages were put together in a chain — similar to a linked list. In order to find any page that was part of the BLOB, you needed to start at the beginning and navigate through the BLOB page by page. If you were trying to perform some form of text or binary search, this kind of arrangement would be deadly, given that you were forced into a serial scan of the data. Beginning with version 7.0, however, the pages were changed to be organized into a B-Tree structure (which I will discuss fully a little later in the chapter). B-Trees provide more of a branching structure, and, therefore, a more direct path for larger BLOBs. This has made quite a difference in how quickly text operations can be performed.

Even with the significant improvements made across several versions over the years, BLOBs are very slow performance-wise, so we will talk about alternative storage methods when we look at advanced design issues later on.

Global Allocation Map, Shared Global Allocation Map, and Page Free Space Pages

Global Allocation Map (GAM), Shared Global Allocation Map (SGAM), and Page Free Space (PFS) page types are involved with figuring out which extents and pages are in use, and which are not. Essentially, these pages store records that indicate where there is space available. Understanding these page types is not really necessary to do high-quality development or systems administration, and is beyond the scope of this book. If, however, you're just dying to know about them (or you're having problems with insomnia), then you can find more information on them in the Books Online — just look up GAM in the index.

Bulk Changed Map

Hmmm. How to address this one, since we haven't addressed bulk operations yet . . . .

SQL Server has the concept of "bulk operations." Bulk operations are very high-speed changes to the database (usually a mass import of data or a truncation of a table). Part of this speed comes from the idea that they don't "log" every single thing they do. The log is a critical part of the backup and recovery system, and bulk operations mean that unlogged activity (well, it logs that it did an operation, but not the specifics, and so the log cannot reconstruct what you did) has occurred in your database.

The Bulk Changed Map — or BCM — is a set of pages that track what extents have been altered via bulk operations. It cares nothing about the specifics of the changes — merely that you messed with that particular extent. Since it knows you altered that extent, it provides more options when you back up your database. More specifically, when backing up the log, you can supplement the log backup with backing up of the physical data in the extents that were affected by bulk operations.

Differential Changed Map

This is nearly the same thing as the Bulk Changed Map, but, instead of tracking only those extents changed by bulk operations, it instead tracks any extents that were changed since the last full backup of your database.

When you request a differential backup, the Differential Changed Map — or DCM — supplies information about what extents need to be backed up. You wind up with a much smaller and faster running (albeit only partial) backup as only those extents that have changed since the prior backups are included.

Page Splits

When a page becomes full, it splits. This means more than just a new page being allocated — it also means that approximately half the data from the existing page is moved to the new page.

The exception to this process is when a clustered index is in use. If there is a clustered index, and the next inserted row would be physically located as the last record in the table, then a new page is created, and the new row is added to the new page without relocating any of the existing data. We will see much more on page splits as we investigate indexes.

Rows

You will hear much about "Row Level Locking," so it shouldn't be a surprise to hear this term. Rows typically can be up to 8K.

In addition to the limit of 8,060 characters, there is also a maximum of 1,024 columns. In practice, you'll find it very unusual to run into a situation where you run out of columns before you run into the 8,060-character limit. 1,024 gives you an average column width of 8 bytes. For most uses, you'll easily exceed that. The exception to this tends to be in measurement and statistical information — where you have a large number of different things that you are storing numeric samples of. Still, even those applications will find it a rare day when they bump into the 1,024 column count limit.

I did, as you may have noted, use the term *typically* when I mentioned the 8KB limit. This limit is based on a row being limited to a single page, and the page having an 8KB size, but it can be exceeded in a few circumstances — specifically, with `varchar(max)` or `varbinary(max)` as well as traditional BLOB data types like `image` and `text`. If a row contains too much data in one of these types to fit within the single page, then these special data types know how to make your data span multiple pages (up to 2GB in a single row). In this case, the original row is used to keep track of where the actual data for that column is stored (all other columns are still stored in the original row).

Full-Text Catalogs

Prior to SQL Server 2008, these were a separate storage mechanism outside of your normal database. While you could associate a full-text catalog as being the default for a given database, and even back up your full-text catalogs together with your database (in 2005 — prior to that even the backups were decoupled), they were stored completely separately. With SQL Server 2008, the Full-Text Catalog no longer has relevance as a storage unit — instead, it is merely a logical grouping of full-text indexes. I mention them here solely for historical reference. (We discuss full text in Chapter 18.)

> Coordinated backups between full-text index files and the core database did not exist prior to SQL Server 2005. Keep this in mind if you have backward compatibility concerns with prior versions.

File Streams

File streams are a special storage method meant to address the performance issues with the storage of very large BLOBs. Instead of storing the file's stream in a set of BLOB pages, the file is stored in an NT File System (NTFS) directory that is created explicitly for use by the particular SQL Server database you're storing data in. Unlike client-controlled systems that store binary data in the file system and a pointer in the database, SQL Server coordinates file versioning for you — allowing the file stream to participate in transactions and backups.

File streams are something of a niche area, but a rather important one. We will explore their structure more fully in the next chapter, and further still in our chapter on designing for performance (Chapter 21).

Understanding Indexes

Webster's dictionary defines an index as:

A list (as of bibliographical information or citations to a body of literature) arranged usually in alphabetical order of some specified datum (as author, subject, or keyword).

I'll take a simpler approach in the context of databases and say it's a way of potentially getting to data a heck of a lot quicker. Still, the Webster's definition isn't too bad — even for our specific purposes.

Perhaps the key thing to point out in the Webster's definition is the word *usually* that's in there. The definition of "alphabetical order" changes depending on a number of rules. For example, in SQL Server, we have a number of different *collation* options available to us. Among these options are:

❑ **Binary:** Sorts by the numeric representation of the character (for example, in ASCII, a space is represented by the number 32, the letter *D* is 68, but the letter *d* is 100). Because everything is numeric, this is the fastest option; unfortunately, it's also not at all the way in which people think, and can also really wreak havoc with comparisons in your WHERE clause.

❑ **Dictionary order:** This sorts things just as you would expect to see in a dictionary, with a twist; you can set a number of different additional options to determine sensitivity to case, accent, and character set. Keep in mind that every language can add its own notion of what constitutes dictionary order, so, if you choose a collation that's oriented around a non-English language, you may see sort order altered somewhat.

It's fairly easy to understand that, if we tell SQL Server to pay attention to case, then *A* is not going to be equal to *a*. Likewise, if we tell it to be case insensitive, then *A* will be equal to *a*. Things get a bit more confusing when we add accent sensitivity — that is, SQL Server pays attention to diacritical marks, and therefore *a* is different from *á*, which is different from *à*. Where many people get even more confused is in how collation order affects not only the equality of data but also the sort order (and, therefore, the way it is stored in indexes).

By way of example, let's look at the equality of a couple of collation options in the following table, and what they do to our sort order and equality information:

Collation Order	Comparison Values	Index Storage Order
Dictionary order, case insensitive, accent insensitive (the default)	A = a = à = á = â = Ä = ä = Å = å	a, A, à, â, á, Ä, ä, Å, å
Dictionary order, case insensitive, accent insensitive, uppercase preference	A = a = à = á = â = Ä = ä = Å = å	A, a, à, â, á, Ä, ä, Å, å
Dictionary order, case sensitive	A ≠ a, Ä ≠ ä, Å ≠ å, a ≠ à ≠ á ≠ â ≠ ä ≠ å, A ≠ Ä ≠ Å	A, a, à, á, â, Ä, ä, Å, å

The point here is that what happens in your indexes depends on the collation information you have established for your data. Collation can be set at the database and column level, so you have a fairly fine granularity in your level of control. If you're going to assume that your server is case insensitive, then you need to be sure that the documentation for your system deals with this or you had better plan on a lot of tech support calls — particularly if you're selling outside of the United States. Imagine you're an independent software vendor (ISV) and you sell your product to a customer who installs it on an existing server (which is going to seem like an entirely reasonable thing to the customer), but that existing server happens to be an older server that's set up as case sensitive. You're going to get a support call from one very unhappy customer.

> **Once the collation order has been set, changing it is very non-trivial (but possible), so be certain of the collation order you want before you set it.**

To "B," or Not to "B": B-Trees

The concept of a *Balanced Tree*, or *B-Tree*, is certainly not one that was created with SQL Server. Indeed, B-Trees are used in a very large number of indexing systems both in and out of the database world.

A B-Tree simply attempts to provide a consistent and relatively low-cost method of finding your way to a particular piece of information. The *Balanced* in the name is pretty much self-descriptive — a B-Tree is, with the odd exception, self-balancing, meaning that every time the tree branches, approximately half the data is on one side, and half on the other side. The *Tree* in the name is also probably pretty obvious at this point. (Hint: tree, branch — see a trend here?) It's there because, when you draw the structure, then turn it upside down, it has the general form of a tree.

A B-Tree starts at the *root node* (another stab at the tree analogy there, but not the last). This root node can, if there is a small amount of data, point directly to the actual location of the data. In such a case, you would end up with a structure that looked something like Figure 6-2.

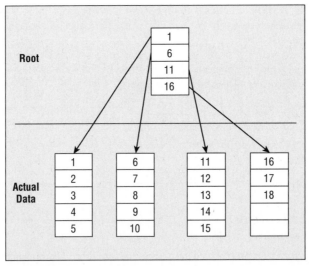

Figure 6-2

So, we start at the root and look through the records until we find the last page that starts with a value less than what we're looking for. We then obtain a pointer to that node, and look through it until we find the row that we want.

In most situations though, there is too much data to reference from the root node, so the root node points at intermediate nodes — or what are called *non-leaf level nodes*. Non-leaf level nodes are nodes that are somewhere in between the root and the node that tells you where the data is physically stored. Non-leaf level nodes can then point to other non-leaf level nodes, or to *leaf level nodes* (last tree analogy reference — I promise). Leaf level nodes are the nodes where you obtain the real reference to the actual physical data. Much like the leaf is the end of the line for navigating the tree, the node we get to at the leaf level is the end of the line for our index — from here, we can go straight to the actual data node that has our data on it.

As you can see in Figure 6-3, we start with the root node just as before, then move to the node that starts with the highest value that is equal to or less than what we're looking for and is also in the next level down. We then repeat the process — look for the node that has the highest starting value at or below the value for which we're looking. We keep doing this, level by level down the tree, until we get to the leaf level — from there we know the physical location of the data and can quickly navigate to it.

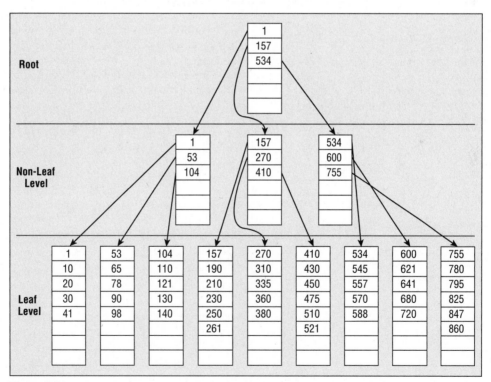

Figure 6-3

Page Splits — A Deeper Look

All of this works quite nicely on the read side of the equation; it's the insert that gets a little tricky. Recall that the *B* in B-Tree stands for *balanced*. You may also recall that I mentioned that a B-Tree is balanced because about half the data is on either side every time you run into a branch in the tree. B-Trees are sometimes referred to as *self-balancing* because the way new data is added to the tree generally prevents them from becoming lopsided.

When data is added to the tree, a node will eventually become full, and will need to split. Because, in SQL Server, a node equates to a page — this is called a *page split*, illustrated in Figure 6-4.

When a page split occurs, data is automatically moved around to keep things balanced. The first half of the data is left on the old page, and the rest of the data is added to a new page — thus you have about a 50–50 split, and your tree remains balanced.

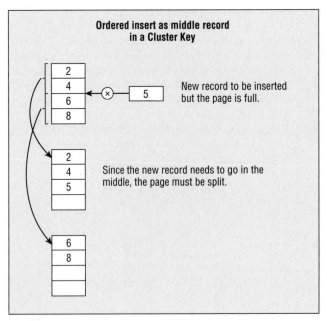

Figure 6-4

If you think about this splitting process a bit, you'll realize that it adds a substantial amount of overhead at the time of the split. Instead of inserting just one page, you are:

❑   Creating a new page

❑   Migrating rows from the existing page to the new page

❑   Adding your new row to one of the pages

❑   Adding another entry in the parent node

But the overhead doesn't stop there. Since you're in a tree arrangement, you have the possibility for something of a cascading action. When you create the new page (because of the split), you need to make another entry in the parent node. This entry in the parent node also has the potential to cause a page split at that level, and the process starts all over again. Indeed, this possibility extends all the way up to and can even affect the root node.

If the root node splits, then you actually end up creating two additional pages. Because there can be only one root node, the page that was formerly the root node is split into two pages, and becomes a new intermediate level of the tree. An entirely new root node is then created, and will have two entries (one to the old root node, one to the split page).

Needless to say, page splits can have a very negative impact on system performance and are characterized by behavior where your process on the server seems to just pause for a few seconds (while the pages are being split and rewritten).

We will talk about page-split prevention before we're done with this chapter.

> While page splits at the leaf level are a common fact of life, page splits at intermediate nodes happen far less frequently. As your table grows, every layer of the index will experience page splits, but, because the intermediate nodes have only one entry for several entries on the next lower node, the number of page splits gets less and less frequent as you move further up the tree. Still, for a split to occur above the leaf level, there must have already been a split at the next lowest level — this means that page splits up the tree are cumulative (and expensive performance-wise) in nature.

SQL Server has a number of different types of indexes (which we will discuss shortly), but they all make use of this B-Tree approach in some way or another. Indeed, they are all very similar in structure thanks to the flexible nature of a B-Tree. Still, we shall see that there are indeed some significant differences, and these can have an impact on the performance of our system.

> For a SQL Server index, the nodes of the tree come in the form of pages, but you can actually apply this concept of a root node, the non-leaf level, the leaf level, and the tree structure to more than just SQL Server or even just databases.

How Data Is Accessed in SQL Server

In the broadest sense, there are only two ways in which SQL Server retrieves the data you request:

❑   Using a table scan

❑   Using an index

Which method SQL Server will use to run your particular query will depend on what indexes are available, what columns you are asking about, what kind of joins you are doing, and the size of your tables.

Use of Table Scans

A table scan is a pretty straightforward process. When a table scan is performed, SQL Server starts at the physical beginning of the table looking through every row in the table. As it finds rows that match the criteria of your query, it includes them in the result set.

You may hear lots of bad things about table scans, and in general, they will be true. However, table scans can actually be the fastest method of access in some instances. Typically, this is the case when retrieving data from rather small tables. The exact size where this becomes the case will vary widely according to the width of your table and what the specific nature of the query is.

See if you can spot why the use of EXISTS *in the* WHERE *clause of your queries has so much to offer performance-wise where it fits the problem. When you use the* EXISTS *operator, SQL Server stops as soon as it finds one record that matches the criteria. If you had a million record table, and it found a matching record on the third record, then use of the* EXISTS *option would have saved you the reading of 999,997 records!* NOT EXISTS *works in much the same way.*

Use of Indexes

When SQL Server decides to use an index, the process actually works somewhat similarly to a table scan, but with a few shortcuts.

During the query optimization process, the Optimizer takes a look at all the available indexes and chooses the best one (this is primarily based on the information you specify in your joins and WHERE clause, combined with statistical information SQL Server keeps on index make-up). Once that index is chosen, SQL Server navigates the tree structure to the point of data that matches your criteria and again extracts only the records it needs. The difference is that, since the data is sorted, the query engine knows when it has reached the end of the current range it is looking for. It can then end the query, or move on to the next range of data as necessary.

If you ponder the query topics you've worked with and studied thus far, you may notice some striking resemblances to how the EXISTS option works. The EXISTS keyword allows a query to quit running the instant that it finds a match. The performance gains of using an index are similar or even better since the process of searching for data can work in a similar fashion — that is, the server is able to know when there is nothing left that's relevant, and can stop things right there. Even better, however, is that by using an index, you don't have to limit yourself to Boolean situations (does the piece of data I was after exist — yes or no?). You can apply this same notion to both the beginning and end of a range — you are able to gather ranges of data with essentially the same benefits that using an index gives to finding data. What's more, you can do a very fast lookup (called a SEEK) of your data rather than hunting through the entire table.

Don't get the impression from my comparing what indexes do for you to the EXISTS *operator that indexes replace the* EXISTS *operator altogether (or vice versa). The two are not mutually exclusive; they can be used together, and often are. I mention them here together only because they have the similarity of being able to tell when their work is done, and quit before getting to the physical end of the table.*

Index Types and Index Navigation

Although there are nominally two types of indexes in SQL Server (*clustered* and *non-clustered*), there are actually, internally speaking, three different types:

❑   Clustered indexes

❑   Non-clustered indexes — which comprise:

   ❑   Non-clustered indexes on a heap

   ❑   Non-clustered indexes on a clustered index

The way the physical data is stored varies between clustered and non-clustered indexes. The way SQL Server traverses the B-Tree to get to the end data varies between all three index types.

All SQL Server indexes have leaf level and non-leaf level pages. As I mentioned when I discussed B-Trees, the leaf level is the level that holds the "key" to identifying the record, and the non-leaf level pages are guides to the leaf level.

The indexes are built over either a clustered table (if the table has a clustered index) or what is called a heap (what's used for a table without a clustered index).

❑　A *clustered table* is any table that has a clustered index on it. Clustered indexes are discussed in detail shortly, but what they mean to the table is that the data is physically stored in a designated order. Individual rows are uniquely identified through the use of the *cluster key* — the columns that define the clustered index.

   This should bring to mind the question, "What if the clustered index is not unique?" That is, how can a clustered index be used to uniquely identify a row if the index is not a unique index? The answer lies under the covers — SQL Server forces any clustered indexes to be unique — even if you don't define it that way. Fortunately, it does this in a way that doesn't change how you use the index. You can still insert duplicate rows if you wish, but SQL Server will add a suffix to the key internally to ensure that the row has a unique identifier.

❑　A *heap* is any table that does not have a clustered index on it. In this case, a unique identifier, or row ID (RID) is created based on a combination of the extent, pages, and row offset (places from the top of the page) for that row. A RID is necessary only if there is no cluster key available (no clustered index).

Clustered Indexes

A *clustered index* is unique for any given table — you can have only one per table. You don't have to have a clustered index, but you'll find it to be one of the most commonly chosen types as the first index, for a variety of reasons that will become apparent as you look at your index types.

What makes a clustered index special is that the leaf level of a clustered index is the actual data — that is, the data is resorted to be stored in the physical order defined in the index or related key command. This means that once you get to the leaf level of the index, you're done — you're at the data. Any new record is inserted according to its correct physical order in the clustered index. How new pages are created changes depending on where the record needs to be inserted.

In the case of a new record that needs to be inserted into the middle of the index structure, a normal page split occurs. The last half of the records from the old page are moved to the new page and the new record is inserted into the new or old page as appropriate.

In the case of a new record that is logically at the end of the index structure, a new page is created, but only the new record is added to the new page, as shown in Figure 6-5.

Navigating the Tree

As I've indicated previously, even the indexes in SQL Server are stored in a B-Tree. Theoretically, a B-Tree always has half of the remaining information in each possible direction as the tree branches. Take a look at a visualization of what a B-Tree looks like for a clustered index (Figure 6-6).

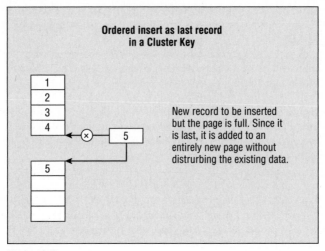

Figure 6-5

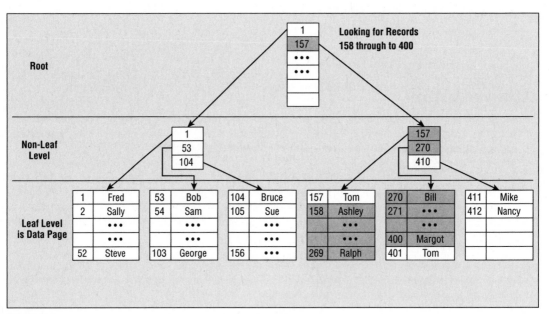

Figure 6-6

As you can see, it looks essentially identical to the more generic B-Trees we discussed earlier in the chapter. In this case, we're doing a range search (something clustered indexes are particularly good at) for numbers 158–400. All we have to do is the following:

Navigate to the first record, and include all remaining records on that page — we know we need the rest of that page because the information from one node up lets us know that we'll also need data from a few other pages. Because this is an ordered list, we can be sure it's continuous — that means if the next page has records that should be included, then the rest of this page must be included. We can just start spewing out data from those pages without having to do the verification side of things.

We start by navigating to the root node. SQL Server is able to locate the root node based on an entry that is kept a system table. You can look at the logical content of that table by querying sys.indexes.

> Every index in your database has an entry in **sys.indexes**. This system view is part of your database (as opposed to being in the master database) and shows the stored location information for all the indexes in your database as well as which columns they are based on.

> In older versions of SQL Server, you could query against the underlying table (technically you still can, but I highly recommend against such direct queries at this point) which is called **sysindexes**.

By looking through the page that serves as the root node, we can figure out what the next page we need to examine is (the second page on the second level as we have it drawn here). We then continue the process. With each step we take down the tree, we are getting to smaller and smaller subsets of data.

Eventually, we will get to the leaf level of the index. In the case of our clustered index, getting to the leaf level of the index means that we are also at our desired row(s) and our desired data.

> I can't stress enough the importance of the distinction that, with a clustered index, when you've fully navigated the index, you've fully navigated to your data. How much of a performance difference this can make will really show its head as you look at non-clustered indexes — particularly when the non-clustered index is built over a clustered index.

Non-Clustered Indexes on a Heap

Non-clustered indexes on a heap work very similarly to clustered indexes in most ways. They do, however, have a few notable differences:

The leaf level is not the data — instead, it is the level at which you are able to obtain a pointer to that data. This pointer comes in the form of the RID, which, as described earlier in the chapter, is made up of the extent, page, and row offset for the particular row being pointed to by the index. Even though the leaf level is not the actual data (instead, it has the RID), you have only one more step than with a clustered index — because the RID has the full information on the location of the row, you can go directly to the data.

Don't, however, misunderstand this "one more step" to mean that there's only a small amount of over-head difference, and that non-clustered indexes on a heap will run close to as fast as a clustered index. With a clustered index, the data is physically in the order of the index. That means, for a range of data, when you find the row that has the beginning of your data on it, there's a good chance that the other rows are on that page with it (that is, you're already physically almost to the next record since they are stored together). With a heap, the data is not linked together in any way other than through the index. From a physical standpoint, there is absolutely no sorting of any kind. This means that, from a physical read standpoint, your system may have to retrieve records from all over the file. Indeed, it's quite possible (possibly even probable) that you will wind up fetching data from the same page several separate times. SQL Server has no way of knowing it will have to come back to that physical location because there was no link between the data. With the clustered index, it knows that's the physical sort, and can therefore grab it all in just one visit to the page.

> *Just to be fair to the non-clustered index on a heap here versus the clustered index, the odds are extremely high that any page that was already read once will still be in the memory cache, and, thus, will be retrieved extremely quickly. Still, it does add some additional logical operations to retrieve the data.*

Figure 6-7 shows the same search you did with the clustered index, only with a non-clustered index on a heap this time.

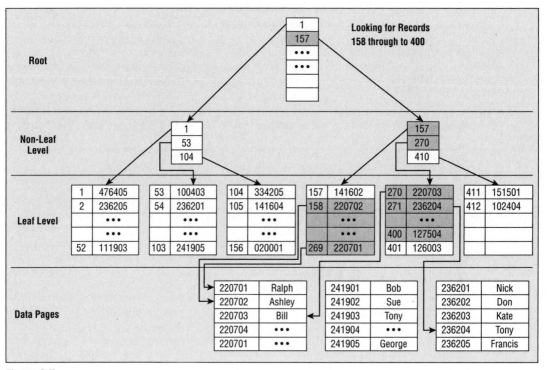

Figure 6-7

Through most of the index navigation, things work exactly as they did before. You start out at the same root node, and you traverse the tree dealing with more and more focused pages until you get to the leaf level of your index. This is where you run into the difference. With a clustered index, you could have stopped right here, but, with a non-clustered index, you have more work to do. If the non-clustered index is on a heap, then you have just one more level to go. You take the Row ID from the leaf-level page, and navigate to it — it is not until that point that you are at your actual data.

Non-Clustered Indexes on a Clustered Table

With *non-clustered indexes on a clustered table*, the similarities continue — but so do the differences. Just as with non-clustered indexes on a heap, the non-leaf level of the index looks pretty much as it did for a clustered index. The difference does not come until you get to the leaf level.

> At the leaf level, you have a rather sharp difference from what you've seen with the other two index structures — you have yet another index to look over. With clustered indexes, when you got to the leaf level, you found the actual data. With non-clustered indexes on a heap, you didn't find the actual data, but did find an identifier that let you go right to the data (you were just one step away). With non-clustered indexes on a clustered table, you find the cluster key. That is, you find enough information to go and make use of the clustered index.

You end up with something that looks like Figure 6-8.

What you end up with is two entirely different kinds of lookups.

In the example from your diagram, you start off with a ranged search — you do one single lookup in your index and are able to look through the non-clustered index to find a continuous range of data that meets your criterion (LIKE 'T%'). This kind of lookup, where you can go right to a particular spot in the index, is called a *seek*.

The second kind of lookup then starts — the lookup using the clustered index. This second lookup is very fast; the problem lies in the fact that it must happen multiple times. You see, SQL Server retrieved a list from the first index lookup (a list of all the names that start with "T"), but that list doesn't logically match up with the cluster key in any continuous fashion — each record needs to be looked up individually as shown in Figure 6-9.

Needless to say, this multiple lookup situation introduces more overhead than if you had just been able to use the clustered index from the beginning. The first index search — the one through your non-clustered index — is going to require very few logical reads.

For example, if I have a table with 1,000 bytes per row, and I did a lookup similar to the one in our drawing (say, something that would return 5 or 6 rows); it would take only something to the order of 8–10 logical reads to get the information from the non-clustered index. However, that gets me only as far as being ready to look up the rows in the clustered index. Those lookups would cost approximately 3–4 logical reads *each*, or 15–24 additional reads. That probably doesn't seem like that big a deal at first, but look at it this way:

Logical reads went from 3 minimum to 24 maximum — that's an 800 percent increase in the amount of work that had to be done.

Now expand this thought out to something where the range of values from the non-clustered index wasn't just five or six rows, but five or six thousand, or five or six *hundred* thousand rows — that's going to be a huge impact.

> Don't let the extra overhead versus a clustered index scare you. The point isn't meant to scare you away from using indexes, but rather to point out that a non-clustered index is not going to be as efficient as a clustered index from a read perspective (it can, in some instances, actually be a better choice at insertion time). An index of any kind is usually (there are exceptions) the fastest way to do a lookup. I'll explain what index to use and why later in the chapter.

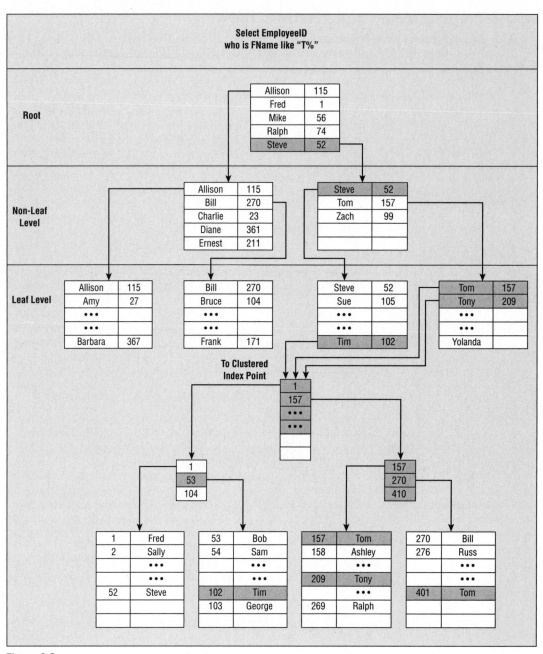

Figure 6-8

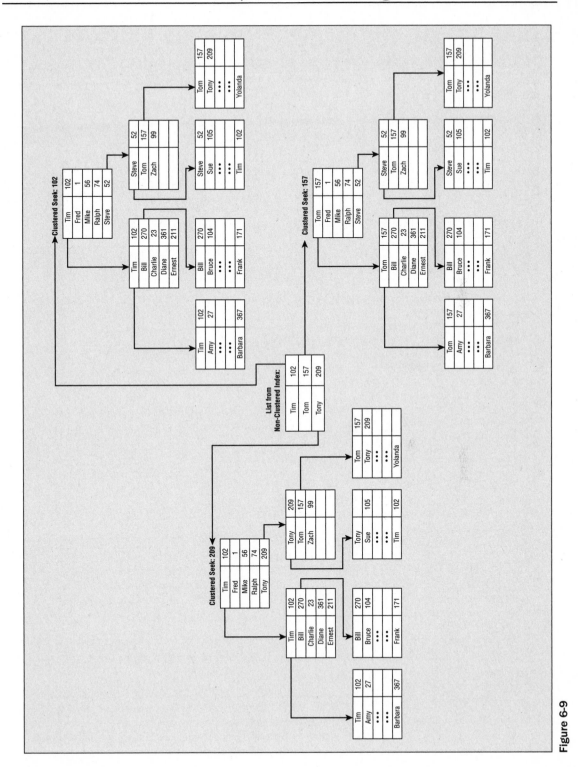

Figure 6-9

Creating, Altering, and Dropping Indexes

These work much as they do on other objects such as tables. Take a look at each, starting with CREATE.

Indexes can be created in two ways:

❑ Through an explicit CREATE INDEX command

❑ As an implied object when a constraint is created

Each of these has its own quirks about what it can and can't do, so take a look at each of them individually.

The CREATE INDEX Statement

The CREATE INDEX statement does exactly what it sounds like; it creates an index on the specified table or view based on the stated columns.

The syntax to create an index is somewhat drawn out, and introduces several items that I haven't really talked about up to this point:

```
CREATE [UNIQUE] [CLUSTERED|NONCLUSTERED]
INDEX <index name> ON <table or view name>(<column name> [ASC|DESC] [,...n])
INCLUDE (<column name> [, ...n])
[WITH
[PAD_INDEX = { ON | OFF }]
[[,] FILLFACTOR = <fillfactor>]
[[,] IGNORE_DUP_KEY  = { ON | OFF }]
[[,] DROP_EXISTING = { ON | OFF }]
[[,] STATISTICS_NORECOMPUTE = { ON | OFF }]
[[,] SORT_IN_TEMPDB = { ON | OFF }]
[[,] ONLINE = { ON | OFF }
[[,] ALLOW_ROW_LOCKS = { ON | OFF }
[[,] ALLOW_PAGE_LOCKS = { ON | OFF }
[[,] MAXDOP = <maximum degree of parallelism>
]
[ON {<filegroup> | <partition scheme name> | DEFAULT }]
```

There is legacy syntax available for many of these options, and so you may see that syntax put into use to support prior versions of SQL Server. That syntax is, however, considered deprecated and will be removed at some point. I highly recommend that you stay with the newer syntax where possible.

> **There is a similar but sufficiently different syntax for creating XML and spatial indexes. These will be handled separately in the next chapter.**

Loosely speaking, this statement follows the same CREATE <object type> <object name> syntax that you've seen plenty of already (and will see even more of). The primary hitch in things is that you have a few intervening parameters that you haven't seen elsewhere.

Just as you'll see with views in Chapter 8, you do have to add an extra clause onto your CREATE statement to deal with the fact that an index isn't really a standalone kind of object. It has to go together with a table or view, and you need to state the table that your column(s) are "ON."

After the ON <table or view name>(<column name>) clause, everything is optional. You can mix and match these options. Many of them are seldom used, but some (such as FILLFACTOR) can have a significant impact on system performance and behavior, so take a look at them one by one.

ASC/DESC

These two allow you to choose between an ascending and a descending sort order for your index. The default is ASC, which is, as you might guess, ascending order.

A question that might come to mind is why ascending versus descending matters: You see, SQL Server can just look at an index backwards if it needs the reverse sort order. Life is not, however, always quite so simple. Looking at the index in reverse order works just fine if you're dealing with only one column, or if your sort is always the same for all columns, but what if you needed to mix sort orders within an index? That is, what if you need one column to be sorted ascending, but the other descending? Since the indexed columns are stored together, reversing the way you look at the index for one column would also reverse the order for the additional columns. If you explicitly state that one column is ascending, and the other is descending, then you invert the second column right within the physical data. There is suddenly no reason to change the way that you access your data.

As a quick example, imagine a reporting scenario where you want to order your employee list by the hire date, beginning with the most recent (a descending order), but you also want to order by their last name (an ascending order). In previous versions, SQL Server would have to do two operations: one for the first column and one for the second. By having control over the physical sort order of your data, you gain flexibility in the way you combine columns.

Generally speaking, you'll want to leave this one alone (again, remember backward compatibility). Some likely exceptions are:

- ❑ You need to mix ascending and descending order across multiple columns.
- ❑ Backward compatibility is not an issue.

INCLUDE

This was first added with SQL Server 2005. Its purpose is to provide better support for what are called *covered queries*. A query is considered to be "covered" when all of the data the query needs is covered in the index that is being used. If all the data needed is already in the index, then there is no need to go to the actual data page; as soon as it has gotten to the leaf level of the index, it has all it needs and can stop there (saving a bunch of I/O operations).

When you INCLUDE columns as opposed to placing them in the ON list, SQL Server adds them only at the leaf level of the index. Because each row at the leaf level of an index corresponds to a data row, what you're doing is essentially including more of just the raw *data* in the leaf level of your index. If you think about this, you can probably guess that INCLUDE really applies only to non-clustered indexes. (Clustered indexes already *are* the data at the leaf level, so there would be no point.)

Why does this matter? Well, as we'll discuss further as the book goes on, SQL Server stops working as soon as it has what it actually needs. So, if while traversing the index, it can find all the data that it needs without continuing on to the actual data row, then it won't bother going to the data row (what would be the point?). By including a particular column in the index, you may "cover" a query that utilizes that particular index at the leaf level and save the I/O associated with using that index pointer to go to the data page.

> **Careful not to abuse this one! When you INCLUDE columns, you are enlarging the size of the leaf level of your index pages. That means fewer rows will fit per page, and, therefore, more I/O may be required to see the same number of rows. The result may be that your effort to speed up one query may slow down others. To quote an old film from the eighties, "Balance Danielson — balance!" Think about the effects on all parts of your system, not just the particular query you're working on that moment.**

WITH

WITH is an easy one — it just tells SQL Server that you will indeed be supplying one or more of the options that follow.

PAD_INDEX

In the syntax list, this one comes first — but that will seem odd when you understand what PAD_INDEX does. In short, it determines just how full the non-leaf level pages of your index are going to be (as a percentage), when the index is first created. You don't state a percentage on PAD_INDEX because it will use whatever percentage is specified in the FILLFACTOR option that follows. Setting PAD_INDEX = ON would be meaningless without a FILLFACTOR (which is why it seems odd that it comes first).

FILLFACTOR

When SQL Server first creates an index, the pages are, by default, filled as full as they can be, minus two records. You can set the FILLFACTOR to be any value between 1 and 100. This number will be how full your pages are as a percentage after index construction is completed. Keep in mind, however, that as your pages split, your data will still be distributed 50–50 between the two pages. You cannot control the fill percentage on an ongoing basis other than regularly rebuilding the indexes (something you should do — setting up a maintenance schedule for this is covered in Chapter 23).

You use a FILLFACTOR when you need to adjust the page densities. Think about things this way:

- ❑   If it's an OLTP system, you want the FILLFACTOR to be low.
- ❑   If it's an OLAP or other very stable (in terms of changes — very few additions and deletions) system, you want the FILLFACTOR to be as high as possible.
- ❑   If you have something that has a medium transaction rate and a lot of report type queries against it, then you probably want something in the middle (not too low, not too high).

If you don't provide a value, then SQL Server will fill your pages to two rows short of full, with a minimum of one row per page. (For example, if your row is 8,000 characters wide, you can fit only one row per page, so leaving things two rows short wouldn't work).

IGNORE_DUP_KEY

The IGNORE_DUP_KEY option is a way of doing little more than circumventing the system. In short, it causes a UNIQUE constraint to have a slightly different action from that which it would otherwise have.

Normally, a unique constraint, or unique index, does not allow duplicates of any kind. If a transaction tried to create a duplicate based on a column that is defined as unique, then that transaction would be rolled back and rejected. Once you set the IGNORE_DUP_KEY option, however, you'll get mixed behavior. You will still receive an error message, but the error will be only of a warning level. The record is still not inserted.

This last line — the record is still not inserted — is a critical concept from an IGNORE_DUP_KEY standpoint. A rollback isn't issued for the transaction (the error is a warning error rather than a critical error), but the duplicate row will have been rejected.

Why would you do this? Well, it's a way of storing unique values, but not disturbing a transaction that tries to insert a duplicate. For whatever process is inserting the would-be duplicate, it may not matter at all that it's a duplicate row (no logical error from it). Instead, that process may have an attitude that's more along the lines of, "Well, as long as I know there's one row like that in there, I'm happy. I don't care whether it's the specific row that I tried to insert or not."

DROP_EXISTING

If you specify the DROP_EXISTING option, any existing index with the name in question will be dropped prior to construction of the new index. This option is much more efficient than simply dropping and re-creating an existing index when you use it with a clustered index. If you rebuild an exact match of the existing index, SQL Server knows that it need not touch the non-clustered indexes, while an explicit drop and create would involve rebuilding all of the non-clustered indexes twice in order to accommodate the different row locations. If you change the structure of the index using DROP_EXISTING, the NCIs are rebuilt only once instead of twice. Furthermore, you cannot simply drop and re-create an index created by a constraint, for example, to implement a certain fill factor. DROP_EXISTING is a workaround to this.

STATISTICS_NORECOMPUTE

By default, SQL Server attempts to automate the process of updating the statistics on your tables and indexes. By selecting the STATISTICS_NORECOMPUTE option, you are saying that you will take responsibility for the updating of the statistics. To turn this option off, you need to run the UPDATE STATISTICS command, but not use the NORECOMPUTE option.

I strongly recommend against using this option. Why? Well, the statistics on your index are what the Query Optimizer uses to figure out just how helpful your index is going to be for a given query. The statistics on an index are changing constantly as the data in your table goes up and down in volume and as the specific values in a column change. When you combine these two facts, you should be able to see that not updating your statistics means that the Query Optimizer is going to be running your queries based on out-of-date information. Leaving the automatic statistics feature on means that the statistics will be updated regularly. (Just how often depends on the nature and frequency of your updates to the table.) Conversely, turning automatic statistics off means that you will either be out of date or you will need to set up a schedule to manually run the UPDATE STATISTICS command.

SORT_IN_TEMPDB

This option makes sense only when your `tempdb` is stored on a physically separate drive from the database that is to contain the new index. This is largely an administrative function, so I'm not going to linger on this topic for more than a brief overview of what it is and why it makes sense only when `tempdb` is on a separate physical device.

When SQL Server builds an index, it has to perform multiple reads to take care of the various index construction steps:

1. Read through all the data, constructing a leaf row corresponding to each row of actual data. Just like the actual data and final index, these go into pages for interim storage. These intermediate pages are not the final index pages but rather a holding place to temporarily store things every time the sort buffers fill up.

2. A separate run is made through these intermediate pages to merge them into the final leaf pages of the index.

3. Non-leaf pages are built as the leaf pages are being populated.

If the SORT_IN_TEMPDB option is not used, then the intermediate pages are written out to the same physical files that the database is stored in. This means that the reads of the actual data have to compete with the writes of the build process. The two cause the disk heads to move to different places from those the other (read versus write) needs. The result is that the disk heads are constantly moving back and forth; this takes time.

If, on the other hand, SORT_IN_TEMPDB is used, then the intermediate pages will be written to `tempdb` rather than the database's own file. If they are on separate physical drives, this means that there is no competition between the read and write operations of the index build. Keep in mind, however, that this works only if `tempdb` is on a separate physical drive from your database file; otherwise, the change is only in name, and the competition for I/O is still a factor.

> *If you're going to use* SORT_IN_TEMPDB, *make sure that there is enough space in* `tempdb` *for large operations.*

ONLINE

If you set this to ON, it forces the table to remain available for general access and does not create any locks that block users from the index and/or table. By default, full index operations will grab the locks (eventually a table lock) it needs to have full and efficient access to the table. The side effect, however, is that your users are blocked out. (Yeah, it's a paradox; you're likely building an index to make the database more usable, but you essentially make the table unusable while you do it.)

Now, you're probably thinking something like: "Oh, that sounds like a good idea. I'll do that every time so my users are unaffected." Poor thinking. Keep in mind that any index construction like that is probably a very highly I/O-intensive operation, so it is affecting your users one way or the other. Now, add that there is a lot of additional overhead required in the index build for it to make sure that it doesn't step on the toes of any of your users. If you let SQL Server have free reign over the table while it's building the index, then the index will be built much faster, and the overall time that the build is affecting your system will be much smaller.

ONLINE index operations are supported only in the Enterprise Edition of SQL Server. You can execute the index command with the ONLINE directive in other editions, but it will be ignored, so don't be surprised if you use ONLINE and find your users still being blocked out by the index operation if you're using a lesser edition of SQL Server.

ALLOW ROW/PAGE LOCKS

This is a longer term directive than ONLINE is, and is a very, very advanced topic. For purposes of this book and given how much we've introduced so far on locking, I want to stick with a pretty simple explanation.

Through much of the book thus far I have repeatedly used the term *lock*. As explained early on, this is something of a placeholder to avoid conflicts in data integrity. The ALLOW settings you're looking at here are setting directives regarding whether this index will allow those styles of locks or not. This falls under the heading of *extreme* performance tweak.

MAXDOP

This is overriding the system setting for the maximum degree of parallelism for purposes of building this index. Parallelism is not something I talk about in this book, so I'll give you a mini-dose of it here.

In short, the degree of parallelism is how many processes are put to use for one database operation (in this case, the construction of an index). There is a system setting called the max degree of parallelism that allows you to set a limit on how many processes can run in parallel per logical operation. The MAXDOP option in the index creation options allows you to set the degree of parallelism to be either higher or lower than the base system setting as you deem appropriate.

ON

SQL Server gives you the option of storing your indexes separately from the data by using the ON option. This can be nice from a couple of perspectives:

- ❑ The space that is required for the indexes can be spread across other drives.
- ❑ The I/O for index operations does not burden the physical data retrieval.

There's more to this, but this is *highly* advanced stuff. It is very data- and use-dependent, and so we'll consider it out of the scope of this book.

Implied Indexes Created with Constraints

I guess I call this one "index by accident." It's not that the index shouldn't be there. It has to be there if you want the constraint that created the index. It's just that I've seen an awful lot of situations where the only indexes on the system were those created in this fashion. Usually, this implies that the administrators and/or designers of the system are virtually oblivious to the concept of indexes.

However, you'll also find another bizarre twist on this one — the situation where the administrator or designer knows how to create indexes but doesn't really know how to tell what indexes are already on the system and what they are doing. This kind of situation is typified by duplicate indexes. As long as they have different names, SQL Server will be more than happy to create them for you.

Implied indexes are created when one of two constraints is added to a table:

❑   A PRIMARY KEY

❑   A UNIQUE constraint (a.k.a. an *alternate key*)

You've seen plenty of the CREATE syntax up to this point, so I won't belabor it; however, it should be noted that all the options except for {CLUSTERED|NONCLUSTERED} and FILLFACTOR are not allowed when creating an index as an implied index to a constraint.

ALTER INDEX

The command ALTER INDEX is somewhat deceptive. Up until now, ALTER commands have always been about changing the definition of your object. You ALTER tables to add or disable constraints and columns for example. ALTER INDEX is different. It is all about maintenance and zero about structure. If you need to change the make-up of your index, you still need either to DROP and CREATE it or to CREATE and use the index with the DROP_EXISTING=ON option.

As you saw earlier in the chapter, SQL Server gives you an option for controlling just how full your leaf level pages are, and, if you choose, another option to deal with non-leaf level pages. Unfortunately, these are proactive options. They are applied once, and then you need to reapply them as necessary by rebuilding your indexes and reapplying the options.

In the upcoming section on maintenance, you'll learn more on the wheres and whys of utilizing this command, but for now take it on faith that you'll use maintenance commands like ALTER INDEX as part of your regular maintenance routine.

The ALTER INDEX syntax looks like this:

```
ALTER INDEX { <name of index> | ALL }
    ON <table or view name>
    { REBUILD
        [ [ WITH (
        [ PAD_INDEX  = { ON | OFF } ]
      | [[,] FILLFACTOR = <fillfactor>
      | [[,] SORT_IN_TEMPDB = { ON | OFF } ]
      | [[,] IGNORE_DUP_KEY = { ON | OFF } ]
      | [[,] STATISTICS_NORECOMPUTE = { ON | OFF } ]
      | [[,] ONLINE = { ON | OFF } ]
      | [[,] ALLOW_ROW_LOCKS = { ON | OFF } ]
      | [[,] ALLOW_PAGE_LOCKS = { ON | OFF } ]
      | [[,] MAXDOP = <max degree of parallelism>
              ) ]
        | [ PARTITION = <partition number>
            [ WITH ( <partition rebuild index option>
                  [ ,...n ] ) ] ] ]
    | DISABLE
    | REORGANIZE
      [ PARTITION = <partition number> ]
```

```
        [ WITH ( LOB_COMPACTION = { ON | OFF } ) ]
   | SET ([ ALLOW_ROW_LOCKS= { ON | OFF } ]
        | [[,] ALLOW_PAGE_LOCKS = { ON | OFF } ]
        | [[,] IGNORE_DUP_KEY = { ON | OFF } ]
        | [[,] STATISTICS_NORECOMPUTE = { ON | OFF } ]
        )
   } [ ; ]
```

Several of the options are common to the CREATE INDEX command, so I will skip redefining those particular ones here. Beyond that, a fair amount of the ALTER-specific options are fairly detailed and relate to dealing with things like fragmentation (you'll get to fragmentation and maintenance shortly) or are more DBA oriented and usually used on an ad hoc basis to deal with very specific problems. The core elements here should, however, be part of your regular maintenance planning.

You'll start by looking at a couple of top parameters and then look at the options that are part of your larger maintenance planning needs

Index Name

You can name a specific index if you want to maintain one specific index, or use ALL to indicate that you want to perform this maintenance on every index associated with the named table.

Table or View Name

Pretty much just what it sounds like — the name of the specific object (table or view) that you want to perform the maintenance on. Note that it needs to be one specific table. (You can feed it a list and say, "do all of these please!").

REBUILD

This is the "industrial-strength" approach to fixing an index. If you run ALTER INDEX with this option, the old index is completely thrown away and a new one reconstructed from scratch. The result is a truly optimized index, where every page in both the leaf and non-leaf levels of the index has been reconstructed as you have defined it (either with the defaults, or using switches to change things like the fill factor). If the index in question is a clustered index, then the physical data is also reorganized.

By default, the pages will be reconstituted to be full minus two records. Just as with the CREATE TABLE syntax, you can set the FILLFACTOR to be any value between 0 and 100. This number will be the percent full that your pages are once the database reorganization is complete. Remember though that, as your pages split, your data will still be distributed 50–50 between the two pages. You cannot control the fill percentage on an ongoing basis other than regularly rebuilding the indexes.

> Careful on this one. As soon as you kick off a REBUILD, the index you are working on is essentially gone until the rebuild is complete. Any queries that relied on that index may become exceptionally slow (potentially by orders of magnitude). This is the sort of thing you want to test on an offline system first to have an idea how long it's going to take, and then schedule to run in off hours (preferably with someone monitoring it to be sure it's back online when peak hours come along).

This one can have major side effects while it runs, and thus it falls squarely in the domain of the database administrator in my not so humble opinion.

DISABLE

This one does what it says, only in somewhat drastic fashion. It would be nice if all this command did was take your index offline until you decided further what you want to do, but instead it essentially marks the index as unusable. Once an index has been disabled, it must be rebuilt (not reorganized, but rebuilt) before it will be active again.

This is one you're very, very rarely going to do yourself (you would more likely just drop the index) — it is far more likely to happen during a SQL Server upgrade or some other oddball situation.

> **Yet another BE CAREFUL!!! warning on this one. If you disable the clustered index for your table, it has the effect of disabling the table. The data will remain, but will be inaccessible by all indexes (since they all depend on the clustered index) until you rebuild the clustered index.**

REORGANIZE

BINGO!!! from the developer perspective. With REORGANIZE you hit much more of a happy medium in life. When you reorganize your index, you get a slightly less complete optimization than you get with a full rebuild, but one that occurs online. (Users can still utilize the index.)

This should, if you're paying attention, bring about the question "What exactly do you mean by '*slightly less complete*'?" Well, REORGANIZE works only on the leaf level of your index; non-leaf levels of the index go untouched. This means that you're not quite getting a full optimization, but, for the lion's share of indexes, that is not where your real cost of fragmentation is (though it can happen and your mileage may vary).

Given its much lower impact on users, this is usually the tool you'll want to use as part of your regular maintenance plan. We'll look into this a bit more later when talking fragmentation.

DROP INDEX

This one returns to most of the simplicity of prior DROP statements. The only real trick to it is that, since an index is not a standalone object (it is essentially contained within the definition of a table), you must name not only the index but also the table that is belongs to. The syntax looks like this:

```
DROP INDEX <table name>.<index name>
```

As you can see, there's not really much to it. You can use full four-part naming (I guess it turns into five part if you include the index) if you need to.

Choosing Wisely: Deciding What Index Goes Where and When

By now, you're probably thinking to yourself, "Gee, I'm always going to create clustered indexes!" There are plenty of good reasons to think that way. Just keep in mind that there are also some reasons not to.

Choosing which indexes to include and which not to include can be a tough process, and, in case that wasn't enough, you have to make some decisions about what type you want them to be. The latter decision is made simultaneously easier and harder by the fact that you can only have one clustered index. It means that you have to choose wisely to get the most out of it.

Selectivity

Indexes, particularly non-clustered indexes, are primarily beneficial when there is a reasonably high level of *selectivity* within the index. By selectivity, I'm referring to the percentage of values in the column that are unique. The higher the percentage of unique values within a column, the higher the selectivity is said to be, and the greater the benefit of indexing.

If you think back to the sections on non-clustered indexes — particularly the section on non-clustered indexes over a clustered index — you will recall that the lookup in the non-clustered index is really only the beginning. You still need to make another loop through the clustered index to find the real data. Even with the non-clustered index on a heap, you still end up with multiple physically separate reads to perform.

If one lookup in your non-clustered index is going to generate multiple additional lookups in a clustered index, then you are probably better off with the table scan. The exponential effect that's possible here is actually quite amazing. Consider that the looping process created by the non-clustered index is not worth it if you don't have somewhere in the area of 90–95 percent uniqueness in the indexed column.

Clustered indexes are substantially less affected by this because, once you're at the start of your range of data — unique or not — you're there. There are no additional index pages to read. Still, more than likely, your clustered index has other things that it could be put to greater use on.

> One other exception to the rule of selectivity has to do with foreign keys. If your table has a column that is a foreign key, then, in all likelihood, you're going to benefit from having an index on that column. Why foreign keys and not other columns? Well, foreign keys are frequently the target of joins with the table they reference. Indexes, regardless of selectivity, can be very instrumental in join performance because they allow what is called a merge join. A merge join obtains a row from each table and compares them to see if they match the join criteria (what you're joining on). Since there are indexes on the related columns in both tables, the seek for both rows is very fast.

> The point here is that selectivity is not everything, but it is a big issue to consider. If the column in question is not in a foreign key situation, then it is almost certainly second only to the, "How often will this be used?" question in terms of issues you need to consider.

Watching Costs: When Less Is More

Remember that, while indexes speed up performance when reading data, they are actually very costly when modifying data. Indexes are not maintained by magic. Every time that you make a modification to your data, any indexes related to that data also need to be updated.

When you insert a new row, a new entry must be made into every index on your table. Remember, too, that when you update a row, this is handled as a delete and insert; again, your indexes have to be updated. But wait! There's more! (Feeling like a late night infomercial here.) When you delete records, again, you must update all the indexes, not just the data. For every index that you create, you are creating one more block of entries that has to be updated.

Notice, by the way, that I said entries plural — not just one. Remember that a B-Tree has multiple levels to it. Every time that you make a modification to the leaf level, there is a chance that a page split will occur, and that one or more non-leaf level pages must also be modified to have the reference to the proper leaf page.

Sometimes — quite often actually — not creating that extra index is the thing to do. Sometimes, the best thing to do is choose your indexes based on the transactions that are critical to your system and use the table in question. Does the code for the transaction have a WHERE clause in it? What column(s) does it use? Is there a sorting required?

Choosing That Clustered Index

Remember that you can have only one, so you need to choose it wisely.

By default, your primary key is created with a clustered index. This is often the best place to have it, but not always (indeed, it can seriously hurt you in some situations), and if you leave things this way, you won't be able to use a clustered index anywhere else. The point here is don't just accept the default. Think about it when you are defining your primary key: Do you really want it to be a clustered index?

If you decide that you indeed want to change things — that is, you don't want to declare things as being clustered — just add the NONCLUSTERED keyword when you create your table. For example:

```
CREATE TABLE MyTableKeyExample
(
   Column1    intIDENTITY
     PRIMARY KEY NONCLUSTERED,
   Column2    int
)
```

Once the index is created, the only way to change it is to drop and rebuild it, so you want to get it set correctly up front.

Keep in mind that, if you change which column(s) your clustered index is on, SQL Server will need to do a complete resorting of your entire table. (Remember, for a clustered index, the table sort order and the index order are the same.) Now, consider a table you have that is 5,000 characters wide and has a million rows in it. That is an awful lot of data that has to be reordered. Several questions should come to mind from this:

❑ How long will it take? It could be a long time, and there really isn't a good way to estimate that time.

❑ Do I have enough space? Figure that in order to do a resort on a clustered index you will, on average, need an *additional* 1.2 times (the working space plus the new index) the amount of space your table is already taking up. This can turn out to be a very significant amount of space if you're dealing with a large table. Make sure you have the room to do it in. All this activity will, by the way, happen in the database itself, so this will also be affected by how you have your maximum size and growth options set for your database.

❑ Should I use the SORT_IN_TEMPDB option? If tempdb is on a separate physical array from your main database and it has enough room, then the answer is probably yes.

The Pros

Clustered indexes are best for queries when the column(s) in question will frequently be the subject of a ranged query. This kind of query is typified by use of the BETWEEN statement or the < or > symbols. Queries that use a GROUP BY and make use of the MAX, MIN, and COUNT aggregators are also great examples of queries that use ranges and love clustered indexes. Clustering works well here, because the search can go straight to a particular point in the physical data, keep reading until it gets to the end of the range, and then stop. It is extremely efficient.

Clusters can also be excellent when you want your data sorted (using ORDER BY) based on the cluster key.

The Cons

There are two situations where you don't want to create that clustered index. The first is fairly obvious — when there's a better place to use it. I know I'm sounding repetitive here, but don't use a clustered index on a column just because it seems like the thing to do. (Primary keys are the common culprit here.) Be sure that you don't have another column that it's better suited to first.

Perhaps the much bigger no-no use for clustered indexes, however, is when you are going to be doing a lot of inserts in a non-sequential order. Remember that concept of page splits? Well, here's where it can come back and haunt you big time.

Imagine this scenario: You are creating an accounting system. You would like to make use of the concept of a transaction number for your primary key in your transaction files, but you would also like those transaction numbers to be somewhat indicative of what kind of transaction it is. (It really helps troubleshooting by your accountants.) So, you come up with something of a scheme: You'll place a prefix on all the transactions indicating what sub-system they come out of. They will look something like this:

```
ARXXXXXX          Accounts Receivable Transactions
GLXXXXXX          General Ledger Transactions
APXXXXXX          Accounts Payable Transactions
```

where XXXXXX will be a sequential numeric value.

This seems like a great idea, so you implement it, leaving the default of the clustered index going on the primary key.

At first look, everything about this setup looks fine. You're going to have unique values, and the accountants will love the fact that they can infer where something came from based on the transaction number. The clustered index seems to make sense since they will often be querying for ranges of transaction IDs.

Ah, if only it were that simple. Think about your inserts for a bit. With a clustered index, you originally had a nice mechanism to avoid much of the overhead of page splits. When a new record was inserted that was to go after the last record in the table, then, even if there was a page split, only that record would go to the new page, SQL Server wouldn't try to move around any of the old data. Now you've messed things up though.

New records inserted from the General Ledger will wind up going on the end of the file just fine. (GL is last alphabetically, and the numbers will be sequential.) The AR and AP transactions have a major problem though; they are going to be doing non-sequential inserts. When AP000025 gets inserted and there isn't room on the page, SQL Server is going to see AR000001 in the table, and know that it's not a sequential insert. Half the records from the old page will be copied to a new page before AP000025 is inserted.

The overhead of this can be staggering. Remember that you're dealing with a clustered index, and that the clustered index is the data. The data is in index order. This means that, when you move the index to a new page, you are also moving the data. Now imagine that you're running this accounting system in a typical OLTP environment (you don't get much more OLTP-like than an accounting system) with a bunch of data-entry people keying in vendor invoices or customer orders as fast as they can. You're going to have page splits occurring constantly, and every time you do, you're going to see a brief hesitation for users of that table while the system moves data around.

Fortunately, there are a couple of ways to avoid this scenario:

❑ Choose a cluster key that is going to be sequential in its inserting. You can either create an identity column for this or you may have another column that logically is sequential to any transaction entered regardless of system.

❑ Choose not to use a clustered index on this table. This is often the best option in a situation like that in this example, since an insert into a non-clustered index on a heap is usually faster than one on a cluster key.

Even though I've told you to lean toward sequential cluster keys to avoid page splits, you also have to realize that there's a cost there. Among the downsides of sequential cluster keys are concurrency (two or more people trying to get to the same object at the same time). It's all about balancing what you want, what you're doing, and what it's going to cost you elsewhere.

This is perhaps one of the best examples of why I have gone into so much depth as to how things work. You need to think through how things are actually going to get done before you have a good feel for what the right index to use (or not to use) is.

Column Order Matters

Just because an index has two columns, it doesn't mean that the index is useful for any query that refers to either column.

An index is considered for use only if the first column listed in the index is used in the query. The bright side is that there doesn't have to be an exact one-for-one match to every column — just the first. Naturally, the more columns that match (in order), the better, but only the first creates a definite do-not-use situation.

Think about things this way. Imagine that you are using a phone book. Everything is indexed by last name and then first name. Does this sorting do you any good if all you know is that the person you want to call is named Fred? On the other hand, if all you know is that his last name is Blake, the index will still serve to narrow the field for you.

One of the more common mistakes that I see in index construction is to think that one index that includes all the columns is going to be helpful for all situations. Indeed, what you're really doing is storing all the data a second time. The index will totally be ignored if the first column of the index isn't mentioned in the JOIN, ORDER BY, or WHERE clauses of the query.

Dropping Indexes

If you're constantly re-analyzing the situation and adding indexes, don't forget to drop indexes, too. Remember the overhead on inserts. It doesn't make much sense to look at the indexes that you need and not also think about which indexes you do not need. Always ask yourself: "Can I get rid of any of these?"

The syntax to drop an index is pretty much the same as that for dropping a table. The only hitch is that you need to qualify the index name with the table or view it is attached to:

```
DROP INDEX <table or view name>.<index name>
```

And it's gone.

Use the Database Engine Tuning Advisor

It would be my hope that you'll learn enough about indexes not to need the *Database Engine Tuning Advisor*, but it still can be quite handy. It works by taking a workload file, which you generate using the SQL Server Profiler (discussed in Chapter 22), and looking over that information for what indexes will work best on your system.

The Database Engine Tuning Advisor is found as part of the Tools menu of the SQL Server Management Studio. It can also be reached as a separate program item in the Start Menu of Windows (under Microsoft SQL Server 2008 ➤ Performance Tools). As with most tuning tools, I don't recommend using this tool as the sole way you decide what indexes to build, but it can be quite handy in terms of making some suggestions that you may not have thought of.

Maintaining Your Indexes

As developers, we often tend to forget about our product after it goes out the door. For many kinds of software, that's something you can get away with just fine. You ship it and then you move on to the next product or next release. However, with database-driven projects, it's virtually impossible to get away with. You need to take responsibility for the product well beyond the delivery date.

Please don't take me to mean that you have to go serve a stint in the tech support department. I'm actually talking about something even more important: *maintenance planning*.

There are really two issues to be dealt with in terms of the maintenance of indexes:

❑ Page splits
❑ Fragmentation

Both are related to page density and, while the symptoms are substantially different, the troubleshooting tool is the same, as is the cure.

Fragmentation

We've already talked about page splits quite a bit, but we haven't really touched on fragmentation. I'm not talking about the fragmentation that you may have heard of with your O/S files and the defrag tool you use, because that won't help with database fragmentation.

Fragmentation happens when your database grows, pages split, and then data is eventually deleted. While the B-Tree mechanism is really not that bad at keeping things balanced from a growth point of view, it doesn't really have a whole lot to offer as you delete data. Eventually, you may get down to a situation where you have one record on this page, a few records on that page — a situation where many of your data pages are holding only a small fraction of the amount of data that they could hold.

The first problem with this is probably the first you would think about — wasted space. Remember that SQL Server allocates an extent of space at a time. If only one page has one record on it, then that extent is still allocated. In the case of the empty pages in the extent, SQL Server will see those pages as available for reuse in the same table or index, but if, for example, that table or index is decreasing in size, the free pages in the extent will remain unused.

The second problem is the one that is more likely to cause you grief: Records that are spread all over the place cause additional overhead in data retrieval. Instead of just loading up one page and grabbing the 10 rows it requires, SQL Server may have to load 10 separate pages in order to get that same information. It isn't just reading the row that causes effort, SQL Server has to read that page in first. More pages equals more work on reads.

That being said, database fragmentation does have its good side. OLTP systems positively love fragmentation. Any guesses as to why? Page splits. Pages that don't have much data in them can have data inserted with little or no fear of page splits.

So, high fragmentation equates to poor read performance, but it also equates to excellent insert performance. As you might expect, this means that OLAP systems really don't like fragmentation, but OLTP systems do.

Identifying Fragmentation

SQL Server has always had commands to help you identify just how full the pages and extents in your database are. In SQL Server 2005, Microsoft greatly expanded the options and, in particular, the usability of management tools for indexes, and those increased options continue to become more mainstream as we move into the SQL Server 2008 era and slowly become less concerned about compatibility with SQL Server 2000 and earlier. We can use the information provided by these commands and tools to make some decisions about what we want to do to maintain our database.

sys.dm_db_index_physical_stats

The `sys.dm_db_index_physical_stats` function is one of several metadata functions that were added back in SQL Server 2005. (There is a discussion of these in Appendix B.) The idea behind these and similar metadata functions is to allow developers and administrators alike more flexible access to data on the condition of our server, the database, and the tables and indexes within. Whereas before we were stuck with different functions within the *Database Consistency Checker* (DBCC), which gave free-form output that was difficult to use programmatically (you were pretty much stuck parsing the results to find what you need), we now have both scalar and table-valued functions, as appropriate, that return usable data to us that we can build conditions around, grab values to use in variables, and otherwise manipulate as discrete pieces of data. When talking indexes, the metadata function we're most likely interested in is `sys.dm_db_index_physical_stats`. It is a table-valued function that requires several parameters, and the syntax looks like this:

```
sys.dm_db_index_physical_stats (
    { <database id> | NULL | 0 | DEFAULT }
    , { <object id> | NULL | 0 | DEFAULT }
    , { <index id> | NULL | 0 | -1 | DEFAULT }
    , { <partition number>| NULL | 0 | DEFAULT }
    , { LIMITED | SAMPLED | DETAILED | NULL | DEFAULT }
)
```

Again, this is a table-valued function, so you need to use it in conjunction with a SELECT statement. Let's look at the input parameters individually.

Parameter	Description
Database ID	SQL Server's internal identifier for the database you want containing the tables and indexes you want physical statistics for. Use the DB_ID() function to easily retrieve the database id for your database. The default for this parameter is NULL (technically the same as 0 in use), which means supply information for all databases.
Object ID	The internal identifier for the particular object you want physical statistical information on. Use the OBJECT_ID() function to easily retrieve the object id for the table or view you're interested in. The default is NULL (again, functionally the equivalent of 0) and implies that you want data for all objects in the database(s) you've indicated.
Index ID	The internal identifier for the particular index you're interested in physical statistics for. Fetching a particular index identifier is more of a challenge, as there is no system function to retrieve it. (You would need to query it from sys.indexes using the name and the object id it belongs to.) As with the other parameters so far, this one defaults to -1. Unlike previous parameters, this is not functionally equivalent to 0 (which is only valid if the table is built on a heap, and then indicates you want data on the heap itself).
Partition number	For the vast majority of tables, there is only going to be one partition (and its number will be 1). The default is NULL, which returns all partitions and is functionally equivalent to 0.
Mode	Determines the level of scanning performed to establish the statistics returned. Scan modes include LIMITED, SAMPLED, and DETAILED in order of increasing accuracy but increasing overhead (and slower response).

What is returned is a very wide table with an array of different physical statistics on your index or table. We won't address every one of them here, but let's take a look at some of the highlights:

Column	Description
index_type_desc	Indicates the nature of the index this row relates to. If the result is HEAP or CLUSTERED INDEX, then it relates to the physical data for the table. Other possible results include NONCLUSTERED INDEX, PRIMARY XML INDEX, XML INDEX, and SPATIAL INDEX.
index_depth	Number of levels to the index. If it's a heap or a set of LOB pages, then this will always be 1; otherwise, it will represent how many levels there are in the index. (For example, back in Figure 8-7, there are three levels to the non-clustered index.)
index_level	This one is somewhat counterintuitive in that it counts from the bottom of the index up. The leaf level of the index will be zero (also zero for a heap or LOB), and the number will go up as one navigates backwards up the tree. This value is only supplied when the mode is DETAILED
avg_fragmentation_ in_percent	This indicates the degree of fragmentation in the index tree based on pages or extents that are out of order (the pointer to the logical next page is not the same as the physical next page). You're usually looking for a low number here, though how low depends on the specifics of your row makeup and the purpose of the index.
avg_record_ size_in_bytes	Just what it says it is. The average size of a record in the index. This can be a highly useful number when doing space planning (If I add another 100,000 rows, how much space will it take up?).
record_count	Another somewhat tricky one. This value will *generally* match what you would get from a SELECT COUNT(*). The exception is when dealing with a heap that has a forwarding record. Forwarding records occur when a record is written onto a page, and then is later updated such that a given column no longer fits on the page (so they store a pointer to where the data is instead).

Let's take a look at a quick example of using this system function. Imagine for a moment that we want to see the fragmentation on the clustered index for the Sales.SalesOrderDetail table. We could get key pieces of information with the following query:

```
SELECT index_type_desc AS Type,
       index_id,
       avg_fragmentation_in_percent,
       forwarded_record_count
FROM sys.dm_db_index_physical_stats(
    DB_ID(),
    OBJECT_ID('Sales.SalesOrderDetail'),
```

```
            DEFAULT,
            DEFAULT,
            'DETAILED' )
    WHERE index_id = 1
        AND index_level = 0;
```

Which yields a fairly straightforward result set:

```
Type              index_id  avg_fragmentation_in_percent forwarded_record_count
----------------  --------- ---------------------------- ------------------
CLUSTERED INDEX   1         0.0810372771474878           NULL

(1 row(s) affected)
```

Note that I've used the index_id = 1 in my WHERE clause to force it to be the clustered index. (I would choose zero had this been on a heap.) I've chosen index_level = 0 to force it to give me information on just the leaf level of the index.

By placing an additional WHERE condition on the fragmentation percentage, I could use the information provided here to build a list of indexes that I thought required maintenance (more on that in Chapter 23).

Backward Compatibility

So we've now seen the metadata way of getting information, but what about when we're working with older releases (prior to SQL Server 2005)? The "old standby" command is actually an option for the DBCC. This is the command you're likely to find utilized in some fashion in virtually every installation today and for years to come. This is the pre-2005 way of doing things, and any pre-2005 database installation that had any maintenance going at all utilized it. What's more, there continue to be tons and tons of articles and "how-tos" on the Web that show you how to use this tool.

> Before I get too far into extolling the praises of DBCC SHOWCONTIG, let me remind you that this is the "old," and, dare I say, "inflexible" way of doing things. The system views give us many more possibilities in terms of being able to more specifically query data and manage indexes on a more global level. We explore much more of that functionality in Appendix B at the end of this book. With that said, DBCC has done the job for years, and it is the thing to use if you are monitoring indexes in a server environment that contains pre–SQL Server 2005 installations, and is what you will likely find in much of the existing management code out there.

The syntax is pretty simple:

```
DBCC SHOWCONTIG
    [({<table name>|<table id>|<view name>|<view id>}
     [, <index name>|<index id>])]
    [WITH { [ ALL_INDEXES ]
          | [, FAST ]
          | [, TABLERESULTS ]
          | [, ALL_LEVELS } ]
          | [, NO_INFOMSGS ]
```

Some of this is self-describing (such as the table name), but I want address the items beyond the names:

`table id/view id/index id`	The is the internal object `id` for the table, view, or index. In prior versions of SQL Server, `DBCC SHOWCONTIG` operated solely off this identifier, so you had to look it up using the `OBJECT_ID()` function prior to making your DBCC call.
`ALL_INDEXES`	This is one of those "what it sounds like" things. If you specify this option, you can skip providing a specific index, as all indexes will be analyzed and data returned.
`FAST`	This is about getting a return as fast as possible, and it therefore skips analyzing the actual pages of the index and will output only minimal information.
`TABLERESULTS`	A very cool feature — this one returns the results as a table rather than text. This means it's much easier to parse the results and take automated actions.
`ALL_LEVELS`	This really only has one relevance in SQL Server 2005, as what it used to do it now ignores. The relevance? Backward compatibility. Basically, you can include this option and the command will still run, but it won't be any different.
`NO_INFOMSGS`	This just trims out informational-only messages. Basically, if you have any significant errors in your table (error level 11 or higher), then messages will still come through, but error level 10 and lower will be excluded.

As an example, to again get the information from the `PK_SalesOrderDetail_SalesOrderID_ SalesOrderDetailID` index in the `Sales.SalesOrderDetail` table, we could run:

```
USE AdventureWorks2008;
GO

DBCC SHOWCONTIG ('Sales.SalesOrderDetail',
    PK_SalesOrderDetail_SalesOrderID_SalesOrderDetailID);
```

Notice the single quotation marks around the table name. These are only required because I'm using two-part naming; if I had only specified the name of the table (`SalesOrderDetail`), then the quotation marks would not have been required. The problem here is that, depending on how your user is set up for use of different schemas or the existence of other tables with the same name in a different schema, leaving out the schema name may generate an error or perform the operation on a different table than you expected.

The output is not really all that self-describing:

```
DBCC SHOWCONTIG scanning 'SalesOrderDetail' table...
Table: 'SalesOrderDetail' (898102240); index ID: 1, database ID: 7
TABLE level scan performed.
- Pages Scanned................................: 1234
- Extents Scanned..............................: 155
```

```
- Extent Switches............................: 154
- Avg. Pages per Extent.......................: 8.0
- Scan Density [Best Count:Actual Count].......: 100.00% [155:155]
- Logical Scan Fragmentation .................: 0.08%
- Extent Scan Fragmentation ..................: 3.23%
- Avg. Bytes Free per Page....................: 28.5
- Avg. Page Density (full)....................: 99.65%
DBCC execution completed. If DBCC printed error messages, contact your
system administrator.
```

Some of this is probably pretty straightforward, but the following table will walk you through what everything means:

Stat	What It Means
Pages Scanned	The number of pages in the table (for a clustered index) or index.
Extents Scanned	The number of extents in the table or index. This will be a minimum of the number of pages divided by 8 and then rounded up. The more extents for the same number of pages, the higher the fragmentation.
Extent Switches	The number of times DBCC moved from one extent to another as it traversed the pages of the table or index. This is another one for fragmentation — the more switches it has to make to see the same amount of pages, the more fragmented you are.
Avg. Pages per Extent	The average number of pages per extent. A fully populated extent would have eight.
Scan Density [Best Count: Actual Count]	The best count is the ideal number of extent changes if everything is perfectly linked. Actual count is the actual number of extent changes. Scan density is the percentage found by dividing the best count by the actual count.
Logical Scan Fragmentation	The percentage of pages that are out-of-order as checked by scanning the leaf pages of an index. Only relevant to scans related to a clustered table. An out-of-order page is one for which the next page indicated in the index allocation map (IAM) is different from that pointed to by the next page pointer in the leaf page.
Extent Scan Fragmentation	This one is telling you if an extent is not physically located next to the extent that it is logically located next to. This just means that the leaf pages of your index are not physically in order (though they still can be logically), and just what percentage of the extents this problem pertains to.
Avg. Bytes free per page	Average number of free bytes on the pages scanned. This number can get artificially high if you have large row sizes. For example, if your row size was 4,040 bytes, then every page could only hold one row, and you would always have an average number of free bytes of about 4,020 bytes. That would seem like a lot, but, given your row size, it can't be any less than that.
Avg. Page density (full)	Average page density (as a percentage). This value takes into account row size and is, therefore, a more accurate indication of how full your pages are. The higher the percentage, the better.

Now, the question is how do we use this information once we have it? The answer is, of course, that it depends.

Using the output from our SHOWCONTIG, we have a decent idea of whether our database is full, fragmented, or somewhere in between (the latter is, most likely, what we want to see). If we're running an OLAP system, then seeing our pages full would be great; fragmentation would bring on depression. For an OLTP system, we would want much the opposite (although only to a point).

So, how do we take care of the problem? To answer that, we need to look into the concept of index rebuilding and fillfactors.

DBREINDEX — That Other Way of Maintaining Your Indexes

Earlier in the chapter, we looked at the ALTER INDEX command. This should be your first line command for performing index reorganization and managing your fragmentation levels. While I highly recommend the use of ALTER INDEX moving forward, DBREINDEX is the way things have been done in the past, and, much like DBCC SHOWCONTIG, there is far, far too much code and use out there already for me to just skip it.

DBREINDEX is another DBCC command, and the syntax looks like this:

```
DBCC DBREINDEX (<'database.owner.table_name'>[, <index name>
[, <fillfactor>]]) [WITH NO_INFOMSGS]
```

Executing this command completely rebuilds the requested index. If you supply a table name with no index name, then it rebuilds all the indexes for the requested table. There is no single command to rebuild all the indexes in a database.

Rebuilding your indexes restructures all the information in those indexes, and reestablishes a base percentage that your pages are full. If the index in question is a clustered index, then the physical data is also reorganized.

As with ALTER INDEX, the pages will, by default, be reconstituted to be full minus two records. Just as with the CREATE TABLE syntax, you can set the FILLFACTOR to be any value between 0 and 100. This number will be the percent full that your pages are once the database reorganization is complete. Remember though that, as your pages split, your data will still be distributed 50–50 between the two pages. You cannot control the fill percentage on an ongoing basis other than regularly rebuilding the indexes.

> There is something of an exception on the number matching the percent full that occurs if you use zero as your percentage. It will go to full minus two rows (it's a little deceiving — don't you think?).

We use a FILLFACTOR when we need to adjust the page densities. As we've already discussed, lower page densities (and therefore lower FILLFACTORs) are ideal for OLTP systems where there are a lot of insertions; this helps prevent page splits. Higher page densities are desirable with OLAP systems (fewer pages to read, but no real risk of page splitting due to few to no inserts).

If we wanted to rebuild the index that serves as the primary key for the `Order Details` table we were looking at earlier with a fill factor of 65, we would issue a DBCC command as follows:

```
DBCC DBREINDEX ('Sales.SalesOrderDetail',
    PK_SalesOrderDetail_SalesOrderID_SalesOrderDetailID, 65)
```

We can then re-run the `DBCC SHOWCONTIG` to see the effect:

```
DBCC SHOWCONTIG scanning 'SalesOrderDetail' table...
Table: 'SalesOrderDetail' (898102240); index ID: 1, database ID: 7
TABLE level scan performed.
- Pages Scanned...............................: 1883
- Extents Scanned............................: 236
- Extent Switches............................: 235
- Avg. Pages per Extent.......................: 8.0
- Scan Density [Best Count:Actual Count].......: 100.00% [236:236]
- Logical Scan Fragmentation ..................: 0.05%
- Extent Scan Fragmentation ...................: 1.27%
- Avg. Bytes Free per Page....................: 2809.1
- Avg. Page Density (full)....................: 65.29%
DBCC execution completed. If DBCC printed error messages, contact your
system administrator.
```

The big one to notice here is the change in `Avg. Page Density`. The number didn't quite reach 65 percent because SQL Server has to deal with page and row sizing, but it gets as close as it can.

Several things to note about `DBREINDEX` and `FILLFACTOR`:

❑ If a `FILLFACTOR` isn't provided, then the `DBREINDEX` will use whatever setting was used to build the index previously. If one has never been specified, then the fill factor will make the page full less two records (which is too full for most situations).

❑ If a `FILLFACTOR` is provided, then that value becomes the default `FILLFACTOR` for that index.

❑ While `DBREINDEX` can be done live, I strongly recommend against it. It locks resources and can cause a host of problems. At the very least, look at doing it at non-peak hours. Better still, if you're going to do it online, use `ALTER INDEX` instead and just do a `REORGANIZE` rather than a rebuild.

❑ I've said it before, but it bears repeating: `DBREINDEX` is now considered deprecated, and you should avoid it in situations where you do not need that backward compatibility. (Use `ALTER INDEX` instead.)

Summary

Indexes are sort of a cornerstone topic in SQL Server or any other database environment, and are not something to be taken lightly. They can drive your performance successes, but they can also drive your performance failures.

Top-level things to think about with indexes:

❑ Clustered indexes are usually faster than non-clustered indexes (one could come very close to saying always, but there are exceptions).

❑ Only place non-clustered indexes on columns where you are going to get a high level of selectivity (that is, 95 percent or more of the rows are unique).

❑ All Data Manipulation Language (DML: INSERT, UPDATE, DELETE, SELECT) statements can benefit from indexes, but inserts, deletes, and updates (remember, they use a delete and insert approach) are slowed by indexes. The lookup part of a query is helped by the index, but anything that modifies data will have extra work to do (to maintain the index in addition to the actual data).

❑ Indexes take up space.

❑ Indexes are used only if the first column in the index is relevant to your query.

❑ Indexes can hurt as much as they help — know why you're building the index, and don't build indexes you don't need.

❑ Indexes can provide structured data performance to your unstructured XML data, but keep in mind that, like other indexes, there is overhead involved.

When you're thinking about indexes, ask yourself these questions:

Question	Response
Are there a lot of inserts or modifications to this table?	If yes, keep indexes to a minimum. This kind of table usually has modifications done through single record lookups of the primary key — usually, this is the only index you want on the table. If the inserts are non-sequential, think about not having a clustered index.
Is this a reporting table? That is, relatively few inserts, but reports that run many different ways?	More indexes are fine. Target the clustered index to frequently used information that is likely to be extracted in ranges. OLAP installations will often have many times the number of indexes seen in an OLTP environment.
Is there a high level of selectivity on the data?	If yes, and it is frequently the target of a WHERE clause, then add that index.
Have I dropped the indexes I no longer need?	If not, why not?
Do I have a maintenance strategy established?	If not, why not?

7

More Advanced Index Structures

Alright, so we've walked through the basics of design. Heck, we've even walked through the advanced stages of traditional indexing. There are, however, some even more advanced things to think about in indexing and other storage. Among these are some of the atypical index and storage structures including:

- ❑ XML indexes

- ❑ Spatial data and their associated indexes

- ❑ User-defined data types

- ❑ Filestreams

- ❑ Table compression

- ❑ Hierarchical data

In this chapter, we'll take a look at each of these. Some of it will build on things you already know (like the XML data type and methods we've already talked about extensively), and some will likely be totally new. (Indeed, the remaining items are new with SQL Server 2008.)

The choice to group these particular items into one chapter may seem a bit crazy (even to me), but the thing they have in common is pretty simple. They are all somewhat out of the mainstream and require a bit of extra thinking to see how they work.

XML Indexes

XML indexes first appeared in SQL Server 2005, and I have to admit that I continue to be mildly amazed that Microsoft pulled it off. I've known some of that team for a very long time now, and I have a lot of confidence in them, but the indexing of something as unstructured as XML has been a problem that many have tried to address, but few have done with any real success. Kudos to the SQL Server team for pulling this one off. Enough gushing though. I want to get down to the business of what XML indexes are all about.

Perhaps the most amazing thing about XML indexes is that they are really not all that different from indexes of more typical relational data. Indeed, the XML CREATE syntax supports all the same options you saw in the previous chapter for the CREATE INDEX statement with the exception of IGNORE_DUP_KEY and ONLINE. Why is this such a big deal? Well, while an index would seem to be a basic structure that could support anything, the nature of what's being indexed can have a significant impact in how well traditional indexes support the underlying data. Unlike the relational data that you may be more accustomed to, XML tends to be very unstructured. It utilizes tags to identify data, and can be far more variable in nature than typical relational data. The unstructured nature of XML requires the notion of "navigating" or "path" information to find a data "node" in an XML document. Now indexes, on the other hand, try to provide very specific structure and order to data. This poses something of a conflict.

You can create indexes on columns in SQL Server that are of type XML. The requirements of doing this are:

❑ The table containing the XML you want to index *must* have a clustered index on it, and that clustered index must be on the table's primary key; furthermore, the primary key can not include more than 15 columns.

❑ A "primary" XML index must exist on the XML data column before you can create "secondary" indexes (more on this in a moment).

❑ XML indexes can be created only on columns of XML type (and an XML index is the only kind of index you can create on columns of that type).

❑ The XML column must be part of a base table. You cannot create the index on a view, table variable, or table user-defined data type.

Creating one or more XML indexes on a table also implies an important restriction on your table: You cannot modify the primary key or (as a result) the clustered index while any XML indexes exist on the table. If you need to modify the primary key, you must first drop all the XML indexes. (You can rebuild them after the modification to the primary key is complete.)

The Primary XML Index

The first index you create on an XML index must be declared as a "primary" index. When you create a primary index, SQL Server "shreds" the XML (converting it to tabular form) and creates a new clustered index that combines the clustered index of the base table with data from whatever XML node you specify. In addition to the cluster key information, the primary XML index will also store:

❑ The tag name of the node being indexed (its element or attribute name)

❑ The value of the node

❑ The type of the node (element, attribute, or text)

❑   An internal node identifier (order information)

❑   The path from the node to the document root

All this is the result of shredding the XML out into an internal table. This internal table is how the XML data is persisted in a form that allows the traditional index model to work. You can get a look at what internal tables are being stored in your system by querying `sys.internal_tables` (which also shows other types of internal tables) or `sys.xml_indexes`. For example, we can check out the XML indexes in the AdventureWorks2008 database:

```
SELECT * FROM sys.xml_indexes;
```

This yields us several primary XML indexes and a few secondary XML indexes. (We'll look at secondary XML indexes shortly.)

```
object_id    name                                              index_id    type
-----------  ------------------------------------------------  ----------  ----
162099618    PXML_ProductModel_CatalogDescription              256000      3 ...
162099618    PXML_ProductModel_Instructions                    256001      3 ...
270624007    PXML_Store_Demographics                           256000      3 ...
1509580416   PXML_Person_AddContact                            256000      3 ...
1509580416   PXML_Person_Demographics                          256001      3 ...
1509580416   XMLPATH_Person_Demographics                       256002      3 ...
1509580416   XMLPROPERTY_Person_Demographics                   256003      3 ...
1509580416   XMLVALUE_Person_Demographics                      256004      3 ...

(8 row(s) affected)
```

The result here has been truncated on the right side to allow it to fit in the book, but if you run the query for yourself, you'll see a wealth of additional information about the nature of each XML index listed.

We'll defer discussion of the shredding process for a bit, and move, for the moment, to secondary XML indexes and how they differ from primary indexes.

Secondary XML Indexes

Much like non-clustered indexes point to the cluster key of the clustered index, secondary XML indexes point at the various columns that are part of the internal table of the primary XML index. Secondary XML indexes are merely separate, and far more specialized than the primary XML index they depend on or any other index for that matter. You can have up to 248 secondary XML indexes against a given column.

Secondary XML indexes are special in the sense that they come in three different sub-types:

❑   **PATH**: This secondary index type focuses on providing fast access based on a path-based search criteria. This index is based on the reverse path of the internal table, plus the value.

❑   **VALUE**: As the name suggests, this index type provides an index oriented around searching for a specific node value. This one can be considered to be the inverse of the PATH secondary index type, indexing first on the value, and then on the reverse path.

❑   **PROPERTY**: Similar to VALUE, but oriented around multivalued scenarios.

It follows then that the key thing to understand with secondary XML indexes is that your index choice is not targeted just around what data you're indexing, but also specific types of queries you'll be issuing against that data.

Let's take a look at each of the three types.

PATH XML Indexes

The first of the secondary XML index types is targeted toward queries that are searching based on a specific path. If most of your queries will include a specific path in your WHERE clause, then the PATH style secondary index is for you. While the primary XML index will greatly aid in the search for a specific path (likely via .exist()), it carries with it the overhead of the identifying information for the blob (the node information we discussed earlier). As a secondary index, the PATH-based index focuses solely on the path information, and is, therefore, more compact (and therefore more efficient when simply searching).

The key of using a PATH index's efficiency is making sure that a particular path is specified. Your XPath designation of the path can also include a value (if you so choose), but including a path is what will cause this kind of index to be used.

For example, let's look at the Person.Person table in the AdventureWorks2008 database. We can issue a relatively straightforward XPath-oriented query against the table's Demographics column:

```
WITH XMLNAMESPACES
  ('http://schemas.microsoft.com/sqlserver/2004/07/adventure-
works/IndividualSurvey' AS "IS")

SELECT Demographics.query('
  /IS:IndividualSurvey/IS:TotalPurchaseYTD
') AS Result
FROM Person.Person
WHERE Demographics.exist ('/IS:IndividualSurvey/IS:TotalPurchaseYTD') = 1;
```

The search for a specific path creates a situation that is optimal for the PATH secondary index type. To see that SQL Server is indeed using it, check out the query plan, as shown in Figure 7-1.

Indeed, we can see that the XMLPATH_Person_Demographics index is in use.

VALUE XML Indexes

This one is all about ordering by — wait for it .... — value. You knew it was coming, right?

The columns used for this index are based on the Primary node value and the path. The type of the value is not important. The important thing to remember when considering this is that you may not know the entire path. In particular, you may know only the element and/or attribute that actually contains the value.

Since the index is primarily focused on the value, it finds a match there first, and then concerns itself with whether or not the path matches. The path is actually stored in reverse order, which allows you to find a match to the leaf portion of a path regardless of what is the parent to the partial path you supply.

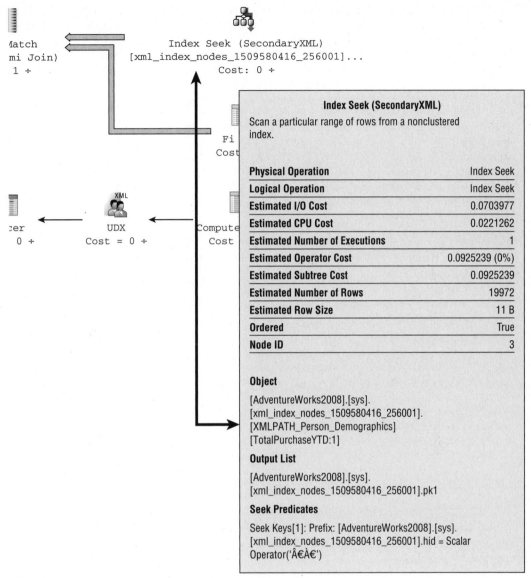

Figure 7-1

PROPERTY XML Indexes

PROPERTY indexes are meant to combine values from two different kinds of columns — whatever the primary key is, and, of course, the XML column. PROPERTY indexes are first oriented around the primary key of the row, and then on the path (again, stored in reverse) and value of individual XML nodes. As you might surmise from the first value being the primary key for the row, this index is useful only for situations where the primary key is known. After that, it acts somewhat like the PATH secondary index type.

Creating XML Indexes

So, now that we have all the different types of XML indexes figured out, we're probably set to see how to create them. Much of the syntax isn't that different from creating standard indexes, but there are a few twists. The overall syntax looks like this:

```
CREATE [ PRIMARY ] XML INDEX <index name>
    ON <table> (<name of the xml column to index> )
    [ USING XML INDEX <name of primary xml index if creating a secondary>
        [ FOR { PATH | VALUE | PROPERTY } ] ]
    [ WITH ( PAD_INDEX   = { ON | OFF }
           | FILLFACTOR = <fill factor>
           | SORT_IN_TEMPDB = { ON | OFF }
           | IGNORE_DUP_KEY = OFF
           | STATISTICS_NORECOMPUTE = { ON | OFF }
           | DROP_EXISTING = { ON | OFF }
           | ONLINE = OFF
           | ALLOW_ROW_LOCKS = { ON | OFF }
           | ALLOW_PAGE_LOCKS = { ON | OFF }
           | MAXDOP = <max degree of parallelism>
           [ ,...n ]
          ) ][ ; ]
```

Notice that both the IGNORE_DUP_KEY and ONLINE options have only one setting. I honestly can't tell you why Microsoft decided to keep them in there at all (I suspect just to keep it more in line with the basic CREATE INDEX statement, but it still seems odd), but they are there for now. (Perhaps they will have additional options later.) As you can see, most of the other options are the same, so let's focus on the main syntax items.

First, XML indexes must be explicitly called out in the CREATE INDEX line via the XML keyword. The PRIMARY keyword is only necessary for primary XML indexes. The XML index is otherwise assumed to be a secondary index.

Moving on, notice that we do not have the option of supplying multiple columns. Instead, we just name which index of type xml we plan on indexing.

The USING clause is mutually exclusive with the PRIMARY keyword and applies only in the case of (and in such case is required) for secondary indexes. Use this clause along with the FOR keyword to indicate the type of secondary index you want to create (PATH, VALUE, or PROPERTY).

So, were we to put this to use, we might create a primary XML index on the Production. ProductModel table:

```
CREATE PRIMARY XML INDEX PXProductModelInstructions
  ON Production.ProductModel (Instructions)
    WITH (PAD_INDEX  = OFF,
          SORT_IN_TEMPDB = OFF,
          DROP_EXISTING = OFF,
          ALLOW_ROW_LOCKS  = ON,
          ALLOW_PAGE_LOCKS  = ON
          );
```

Note that, if you want to actually run the previous script, you would need to drop the existing XML index that came with the AdventureWorks2008 sample.

Or to create a secondary index utilizing the primary we just created, we would do something like:

```
CREATE XML INDEX SXProductModelInstructionsPATH
  ON Production.ProductModel (Instructions)
  USING XML INDEX PXProductModelInstructions
        FOR PATH
    WITH (PAD_INDEX  = OFF,
          SORT_IN_TEMPDB = OFF,
          DROP_EXISTING = OFF,
          ALLOW_ROW_LOCKS  = ON,
          ALLOW_PAGE_LOCKS  = ON
         );
```

Note that either of the preceding CREATE XML INDEX *statements will fail in Adventure-Works2008 because the sample already has a default primary XML index. The second of the two examples will run if you change the* USING *clause to reference the existing primary XML index* (PXML_ProductModel_Instructions).

Again, the syntax differences versus standard indexes are relatively subtle in nature.

User-Defined Data Types

Ah, the awesome potential of user-defined data types or UDTs.

This is a little bit of the classic "What came first, the chicken or the egg?" thing. You see, part of what has made UDTs interesting since SQL Server 2005 is the addition of .NET objects as a possible source for a UDT. For various reasons, however, I'd prefer to hold up on the addition of .NET until we're talking the procedural side of things in Chapter 10.

With this in mind, I've decided to compromise a bit. We'll start our discussion of UDTs here, and finish the .NET side of it in Chapter 10 (call it a little bit of both worlds . . . .).

So, all, with the organizational stuff disposed of, let's address the issue of what exactly a user-defined data type is. If you're a true SQL Server "Pro," then the fundamentals of a UDT may well be old news. After all, UDTs have been part of SQL Server since long before anyone had even thought of .NET. Then again, until the .NET era, they had only minimal value. Even with the advent of .NET, the flexibility of .NET data types requires an exorbitant amount of complexity and requires you to turn on some things in the server configuration that may violate some security policies. (Many DBAs see a great deal of risk in turning on SQLCLR and .NET for SQL Server.) You may well have just ignored UDTs altogether, and given the changes in UDTs for SQL Server 2008, it's worth a look at UDTs as they are today.

Classic UDTs

The classic UDT is founded on existing data types. Indeed, it can be considered to be nothing more than an alias for the base types already found in SQL Server. Historically, it has been used primarily to aid consistency in a frequently used attribute, or in conjunction with rules and defaults (which can be bound directly to a UDT and apply anywhere the classic UDT is used).

Let's start with a fairly basic example — an account number. The AdventureWorks2008 database makes use of a user-defined data type called AccountNumber that is created *from* the base type of nvarchar — in this case, an nvarchar(15). Using the AccountNumber UDT rather than directly using the nvarchar(15) base type ensures consistency across all instances where you want to make use of the account number concept.

The syntax for creating classic UDTs (UDTs that source from built-in data types and are not tabular in nature) is pretty simple:

```
CREATE TYPE [<schema name>.]<type name>
    FROM <base type>
    [ ( precision[, scale]) ]
    [ NULL | NOT NULL ]
```

So, the AccountNumber data type used in AdventureWorks2008 would look like this:

```
CREATE TYPE dbo.AccountNumber
    FROM nvarchar(15) NULL;
```

As you can see, there isn't a whole lot to creating what amounts to a simple alias to an existing type. You may see these relatively simple types extended via the use of rules and defaults, but I recommend against this as Microsoft has said for the last four releases that rules and defaults are considered deprecated and will be removed from the product at some point.

> *It's probably worth noting that I've been told by members on the team that Microsoft is getting more serious about "truly" following up on removing deprecated features. When SQL Server 11 (currently code named Kilimanjaro) eventually ships, expect to see some long deprecated features finally disappear from the product.*

.NET UDTs

I'm going to defer most of our discussion of .NET-based UDTs until Chapter 10 when we will fully explore .NET-based development, but at least a cursory look at .NET-based UDTs has to be included here if for no other reason than context.

As you might expect, .NET UDTs make use of a .NET assembly to implement a custom data type. These have been around since .NET first appeared in SQL Server as part of SQL Server 2005, and can implement some very complex custom types. How complex? Well, complex enough that the new geospatial data types that will be discussed a bit later in this chapter were implemented using .NET. Indeed, they are essentially the same as any .NET data type you might develop and deploy yourself, save that they are flagged as a system type and do not require explicitly enabling .NET in order for geospatial data types to be used.

Just to make sure we have a copy of our syntax examples in the same place, here's the syntax for .NET UDTs:

```
CREATE TYPE [<schema name>.]<type name>
    EXTERNAL NAME <assembly name>[.<class name>]
```

So, as a preview of the example we'll use in Chapter 10 (don't actually execute this code — we'll get to it in due time!), we could add a .NET assembly called `ComplexNumber` with code such as:

```
CREATE TYPE ComplexNumber
    EXTERNAL NAME [ComplexNumber].[Microsoft.Samples.SqlServer.ComplexNumber];
```

Again, we will more fully explore .NET-based UDTs in Chapter 10, including creating our own type.

Tabular UDTs

These are new in SQL Server 2008, and they are the start of something big that I suspect will evolve over the next few releases.

What are they? Well, largely what they sound like: a user-defined data type that accepts tabular data. You create them with a syntax that mostly matches the syntax used for table-valued variables or in the CREATE TABLE command. After creation, you can then utilize them in scripts or, perhaps more importantly, as a table-valued parameter in a stored procedure.

Note that I did not mention using them as a type you can use *within* a table. Unlike other user-defined data types, user-defined data types based on the notion of a table are not usable within other table type objects (that is, a table object or table variable).

> **Unlike other user-defined data types, tabular UDTs cannot be embedded within other tabular objects such as a table variable or table object.**

As of this writing, Microsoft has not yet made a commitment about how far they are going to take tabular UDTs. Right now, it would appear that we are on a path that is taking us closer and closer to a more fully functioning tabular UDT similar to that found in competitive products — such as Oracle — where you have long been able to embed a table within a table.

For now, we're going to focus on how exactly we create tabular UDTs. In Chapter 10, we'll examine the most likely use for tabular UDTs: table-valued parameters for stored procedures.

Creating a Table User-Defined Data Type

Creating a table user-defined data type works as something of a combination of the classic CREATE TYPE and table variable syntax. The tabular CREATE TYPE syntax looks like this:

```
CREATE TYPE [<schema name>.]<type name>
    AS TABLE
    (
      { <column name> <data type>
        [ COLLATE <collation name> ]
        [ NULL | NOT NULL ]
        [ DEFAULT <expression> ]
        [ IDENTITY [ ( <seed>, <increment> ) ]
        [ ROWGUIDCOL ] [<column constraint> [ ...n ] ]
        [<table constraint>]}
```

```
|    <computed column definition> }
)[;]
```

As an example, we're going to create a user-defined table type that will represent addresses. Later in the book (in Chapter 10), we'll see how we can pass an instance of this data type into a stored procedure or function for further processing.

Long ago, it seemed one address was generally enough for most people. The majority of systems out there stored a single address for most business entities they worked with. Today, however, one doesn't seem to be enough. Between dealing with companies that have multiple locations, and even individuals deciding to receive bills at one location, but ship to a different location, many business entities we work with have multiple addresses. The AdventureWorks2008 database represents this by separating addresses out into their own table (Person.Address). We've decided that we want to represent this notion of an address in a consistent way across our systems, so we create our custom type:

```
USE AdventureWorks2008;
GO

CREATE TYPE Person.Address
AS TABLE(
  AddressID int NULL,
  AddressLine1 nvarchar(60) NOT NULL,
  AddressLine2 nvarchar(60) NULL,
  City nvarchar(30) NOT NULL,
  StateProvinceID int NOT NULL,
  PostalCode nvarchar(15) NOT NULL,
  SpatialLocation geography NULL
);
```

There are a host of items to notice about this script:

- ❑ I used the exact name of an existing object in the database (there is a table called Person.Address). The type can be considered to be much like the difference between a class and an object — that is, a type is a definition, and a table is an actual instance of something (though, the table is not an instance of the type definition the way an object is an instance of a class).

- ❑ The syntax for creating the actual definition is very similar to the CREATE TABLE syntax.

- ❑ The layout maps very closely to the Person.Address table in order to support moving data between the two relatively easily.

Note that I created my user-defined type with the same name as a table just to prove the point. I would not recommend duplicating names in practice, as it is likely to lead to far more confusion than it is worth.

With my type now created, I can reference it as a valid data type for variable declarations, or function or sproc parameters (more on the latter two in Chapter 10).

Let's further our example just a bit by utilizing our new type:

```
DECLARE @Address Person.Address;

INSERT INTO @Address
```

```
        (AddressID,
         AddressLine1,
         City,
         StateProvinceID,
         PostalCode
        )
    VALUES
        (
           1,
           'My first address',
           'MyTown',
           1,
           '21212'
        ),
        (
           1,
           'My second address',
           'OtherTown',
           5,
           '43434'
        ),
        (
           1,
           'My third address',
           'MyTown',
           1,
           '21214'
        );

    SELECT *
    FROM @Address;
```

Notice that, with a simple declaration of our `Person.Address` user-defined type, we gained access to all the columns for that tabular type. We're able to insert rows, and select them back out:

```
(3 row(s) affected)
AddressID    AddressLine1
-----------  --------------------
1            My first address  ...
1            My second address ...
1            My third address  ...

(3 row(s) affected)
```

Again, we'll take a further look at uses for this in Chapter 10 as part of our table-valued parameter discussion.

Dropping a User-Defined Type

It's fairly intuitive, but just to make sure we've addressed the point, all varieties of UDTs are dropped using the very common `DROP <object type> <object name>` syntax:

```
DROP TYPE [<schema name>.]<type name>[;]
```

Hierarchical Data

This area is somewhat more revolutionary than most of the other items we discuss during this chapter. While spatial data has been around in other products for some time now (and the lack of spatial support had been something SQL Server was often derided for), the addition of the new HierarchyID data type and its embedded functions brings a new realm of functionality to the database that was somewhat unexpected.

So what is HierarchyID? Simply put, it is a special data type that is optimized to the needs of representing a single node in a hierarchical structure (usually a tree). The real horsepower here is in the idea that it is able to analyze the concepts of hierarchical ancestry (parent/child relationships) as well as understand the notion of depth and siblings (for example, all departmental managers versus operational staff or executives).

> A given instance of **HierarchyID** data does not represent a tree. Instead it is merely information about the properties of a single node of a tree, including that node's ancestry. Only by making use of a collection of related nodes can one represent a true hierarchy tree.

The need for hierarchical representation of data is not new. Indeed, the version of AdventureWorks that shipped back in SQL Server 2005 included a fairly typical modeling of one of the more common hierarchical problems: employee reporting structures. (Indeed, we created a similar mapping to this when we created the Employee2 table to show off CTEs back in Chapter 3.) The typical solution was what is called a unary relationship — that is, a table that has a foreign key to itself. "Kits" are another common hierarchical problem. (For example, a part that is nothing more than a collection of other parts, with some of those, perhaps, being kits with other parts.) XML is naturally hierarchical, and has also been a frequent solution to storing hierarchies even for non-XML applications.

Let's take a look at how it works, and then we'll explore some of the functionality that comes with the data type and its associated methods.

Understanding Depth Versus Fanout

Before getting too much into the structure of the HierarchyID type and the methods and index type that support it, it is important to understand the concepts of depth (or level) versus the idea of what is called *fan out* (for the moment, think about this as being horizontal).

The depth — or levels deep — of a hierarchy node is based on the number of direct and indirect ancestor nodes. Note that this yields us a zero-based set — that is, the root node of a hierarchy has a level of zero, its direct descendants have a level of 1, and so on. So, for example, the node labeled E in Figure 7-1 has a level of 2. The root node labeled A in Figure 7-1 has a level of zero.

The HierarchyID type gives us a special method call to tell us what level (not surprisingly called GetLevel) a given node is within a hierarchy. Levels are used primarily for comparisons with siblings, and will become important later in the chapter when we discuss breadth-first indexes on HierarchyID columns.

The *fanout* of a hierarchy refers to the idea of how many children a given parent node has. In a tree representation such as the one in Figure 7-1, you can think of the fanout as governing the width of the hierarchy. In Figure 7-1, the E node has a fanout of 3, the B node has a fanout of 4, and the A node has a fanout of 11. In our next section, we'll take a look at how we store all this information.

HierarchyID Type Structure

The HierarchyID data type is stored internally as a variable-length binary representation of a node. Indeed, if we retrieve an instance of HierarchyID type data, it will come back in a hexadecimal representation. So, for example, if we execute:

```
SELECT e.OrganizationNode
FROM HumanResources.Employee e;
```

it give us back some numbers in hex:

```
OrganizationNode
---------------------------
0x
0x58
0x68
...
...
0x85EBA6
0x85EBAA
0x85EBAE

(290 row(s) affected)
```

You can use the ToString method (we'll explore the various method calls in the next section) to render it a bit more human readable:

```
SELECT e.OrganizationNode.ToString() AS OrganizationNode

FROM HumanResources.Employee e;
```

This gets us back something that, at first blush, probably doesn't seem all that much more readable:

```
OrganizationNode
/
/1/
/2/
/3/
/4/
/5/
/6/
/1/1/
/2/1/
/2/2/
...
...
/4/3/1/9/
```

```
/4/3/1/10/
/4/3/1/11/

(290 row(s) affected)
```

There are several items of note in this string representation:

❑   Each forward slash (/) separates a representation of a node in the current node's lineage

❑   The numbers are largely arbitrary. You can assign them yourself, or SQL Server can find a place to insert them for you. If you have SQL Server generate the number for you, then the number will be the next available whole number unless you explicitly state that you want the new value to be between existing nodes. In which case you need to supply the points you want the value to lay between. (More on this when we look at the GetDescendant method in the next section.) Only by explicitly managing the values for a given level can you provide any form of ranking within a given level.

❑   The numeric order does not matter within a specific node, only the position in the series matters. Each set of numbers matters only within that particular level. (Notice that the first 1 in /1/1/ is a different item than the second 1 is. The number sequencing is maintained separately within each level of the hierarchy.)

❑   The solitary forward slash (/) represents what is being seen as the root node. (The equivalent in hex was 0x0.) This is, however, also arbitrary, as nothing prevents you from having multiple root nodes.

> There is nothing inherent in the **HierarchyID** data type that ensures that you only have a single root node. Indeed, there is no guarantee of uniqueness at all unless you explicitly enforce that constraint (via primary key or unique constraint).

As indicated earlier, the inner workings of the HierarchyID type represent the node in a variable-length bit field (thus all the hex output). Unlike other variable-length data types, you do not explicitly define the length. Instead, SQL Server adjusts the length as required to address the depth and fanout found in the various nodes. Microsoft hasn't really said much about the specifics of how each bit is manipulated, but based on what Microsoft has said publically, you can figure that most installations are going to average 5–6 bytes per node.

Working with HierarchyID Values — HierarchyID Methods

So, all these concepts and theories are great, but anyone who has read much from my books knows that I'm more of a fan of showing specific examples. With that in mind, we're going to use this next section to cover the various methods that are supported by the type. These work much like the methods we used with the XML data. We'll address each method based on the function they help us perform (inserts, positions, grafting, and the like), but just to get them all into one place for reference, here is the quick list of methods and what they are used for:

❑   **GetAncestor(n)**: This fetches the node value for the parent node that is *n* number of nodes up the tree. So, for example, GetAncestor(1) would fetch the immediate parent.

❑ **GetDescendant(<*child 1*>, <*child 2*>)**: This varies in behavior depending on the specific values provided for the child arguments, but the name is a bit misleading. Contrary to what you might expect, GetDescendant() is not used to fetch a specific child node, which would be hard since there may be multiple children at any level of the hierarchy. Instead, it is used to calculate a value to use in inserting a new node into the hierarchy.

❑ **GetLevel()**: Returns the level of the current node where the root node is considered level 0 and each child level below the root adds one to the reported level.

❑ **GetReparentedValue(<*old root*>, <*new root*>)**: This is another deceptively named one. Despite using the Get moniker in the name, GetReparentedValue() actually performs a task — that is, pruning a given node or set of child nodes from a given parent (old root) and grafting them to a new parent (new root). Do not let the use of the term "root" confuse you here. This does not need to be the primary root for the entire hierarchy, but rather the common parent that all the grafted nodes share.

❑ **GetRoot()**: Supplies the constant value of the root node of a hierarchy (which is always 0x0). Unlike most of the other methods discussed here, GetRoot() is a static method and thus only callable against the base type and not an individual node instance. We'll explore the specifics of this a little later when we discuss fetching the root.

❑ **IsDescendantOf(<*node*>)**: Provides a true/false indication as to whether or not the current node is a descendent of the provided node. Note that a parent *is* considered a child of itself (so if you perform a IsDescendantOf() on a given node referencing itself, the result will be true).

❑ **Parse()**: Loosely speaking, this can be considered the opposite of the ToString() method. This receives a string-based representation of a node and converts it to the internal binary representation. Like GetRoot(), this is a static method, and can be called only against the base type (for example, HierarchyID::GetRoot()).

❑ **Read()**: This is a CLR or client language only function (it is not callable from within T-SQL), and is used to receive a stream of a HierarchyID instance in its native binary representation. In general, the database developer would utilize this only while doing extremely complex CLR programming or manipulating the hierarchy in a client language.

❑ **ToString()**: This does what it says — that is, it converts the binary representation into a more human-readable string.

❑ **Write()**: This is the functional opposite of Read(). Like Read() it is CLR/.NET only, and cannot be called from T-SQL. It is used to take a client-side binary representation of a HierarchyID instance and write it directly back to SQL Server without the need for a string conversion.

So, with the introductions done, let's take a look at things from a more functional standpoint, and discuss the many things we might want to do with an instance of the HierarchyID data type.

Methods Related to Retrieving a Given Level of Hierarchy Data

There are a few examples of the HierarchyID data type in the AdventureWorks2008 database (one each in the Address, Document, Employee, and ProductDocument tables). We'll focus on the Employee table here as it is the easiest to get the concept of, but each of the other HierarchyID usages provides a further example of a potential hierarchy.

Let's start out with retrieving a simple user-readable selection of the `Employee` table. For this, we use the `ToString()` method we saw earlier in the section. `ToString()` takes no arguments and is used relative to an instance of data (usually a row or variable) of type `HierarchyID`. So, to formalize the syntax, it would look like this:

```
<instance of hierarchical data>.ToString()
```

To keep things manageable, we're going to limit the results using the OrganizationLevel column:

```
SELECT e.BusinessEntityID,
       p.LastName + ', ' + p.FirstName AS Name,
       e.OrganizationNode.ToString() AS Hierarchy
FROM HumanResources.Employee e
JOIN Person.Person p
  ON e.BusinessEntityID = p.BusinessEntityID
WHERE e.OrganizationLevel BETWEEN 1 AND 2;
```

This gives us list of a set of parents and their respective children:

```
BusinessEntityID Name                             Hierarchy
---------------- ------------------------------   ----------
2                Duffy, Terri                     /1/
16               Bradley, David                   /2/
25               Hamilton, James                  /3/
234              Norman, Laura                    /4/
263              Trenary, Jean                    /5/
273              Welcker, Brian                   /6/
3                Tamburello, Roberto              /1/1/
17               Brown, Kevin                     /2/1/
18               Wood, John                       /2/2/
19               Dempsey, Mary                    /2/3/
20               Benshoof, Wanida                 /2/4/
21               Eminhizer, Terry                 /2/5/
22               Harnpadoungsataya, Sariya        /2/6/
23               Gibson, Mary                     /2/7/
24               Williams, Jill                   /2/8/
26               Krebs, Peter                     /3/1/
211              Abolrous, Hazem                  /3/2/
222              Wright, A. Scott                 /3/3/
227              Altman, Gary                     /3/4/
235              Barreto de Mattos, Paula         /4/1/
241              Liu, David                       /4/2/
249              Kahn, Wendy                      /4/3/
262              Barber, David                    /4/4/
264              Conroy, Stephanie                /5/1/
267              Berg, Karen                      /5/2/
268              Meyyappan, Ramesh                /5/3/
269              Bacon, Dan                       /5/4/
270              Ajenstat, François               /5/5/
271              Wilson, Dan                      /5/6/
272              Bueno, Janaina                   /5/7/
274              Jiang, Stephen                   /6/1/
285              Abbas, Syed                      /6/2/
```

```
287              Alberts, Amy                    /6/3/
```

```
(33 row(s) affected)
```

Notice that nothing about the numbers used in the HierarchyID column has anything to do with the other columns. BusinessEntityID is the primary key for the table, but it is not utilized in the hierarchy representation at all. Taking a look at Roberto Tamburello, we can see that he reports to Terri Duffy. The number "1" is reused at each level of the hierarchy, and implies no relationship to how it might be used in other levels of the hierarchy. The number sequences we see here happen to be sequential at each level, but that is an arbitrary fact of this particular data set. There is no requirement that it be this way. (Decimals can and will occur, as can negative numbers.)

Next, take note of the OrganizationLevel column that we used in the previous query. If you look at the definition of this column in the database, you'll see that this is a computed column. Indeed, it utilizes the next method we want to look at: GetLevel().

GetLevel() takes no arguments. (It is assumed to be operating on the instance of hierarchy data you used the method with, and passes back just how deep that node is in the hierarchy with the root node considered to be zero, the first level of children of the root being level 1, their children being 2, and so on.) So, the syntax would look like this:

```
<instance of hierarchical data>.GetLevel()
```

So, if we wanted to do a comparison of the OrganizationLevel we used in our previous query to what we would see using GetLevel() directly, we could rewrite it as:

```
SELECT e.OrganizationNode.ToString() AS Hierarchy,
       OrganizationLevel,
       e.OrganizationNode.GetLevel() AS ComputedLevel
FROM HumanResources.Employee e
WHERE e.OrganizationLevel BETWEEN 1 AND 2;
```

Which would, as expected, yield identical values for OrganizationLevel and our use of GetLevel():

```
Hierarchy   OrganizationLevel ComputedLevel
----------  ----------------- -------------
/1/         1                 1
/2/         1                 1
/3/         1                 1
...
...
/6/1/       2                 2
/6/2/       2                 2
/6/3/       2                 2
```

```
(33 row(s) affected)
```

We can use this in a wide variety of ways, but the most notable would be:

❑ Returning all rows of data related to a certain level in a hierarchy. For example, all CxO level employees might be found by looking for level 1 or 2, or a regional manager might be at level 3. It just depends on how you set up your hierarchy.

❑ Indexing for horizontal comparisons.

Methods Related to Retrieving Parent or Child Hierarchy Data

Looking at the information for a specific level or node of a hierarchy is all well and good, but it doesn't really show off the horsepower of the HierarchyID data type. For that, you need to expand more fully out to the parent/child relationships that are the cornerstone of what hierarchical data is all about. The real centerpiece of this functionality are the GetAncestor() and IsDescendantOf() methods.

Let's start with the syntax for GetAncestor(), which takes a single argument. It looks like this:

```
<instance of HierarchyID data>.GetAncestor(n):
```

The method is assumed to be operating against the instance of hierarchical data it was called as a method of, and uses the single argument to indicate how many levels up the tree you want to go.

> The value returned by **GetAncestor()** is of type **HierarchyID**, which means you can further extend the **GetAncestor()** call with other **HierarchyID** methods.

Let's see what we get if we fetch a few different ancestor levels for the employee named Roberto Tamburello that we saw in one of our first hierarchy example queries. You may recall his hierarchy node looked like this:

```
/1/1/
```

So let's run a few instances of the GetAncestor() method to see what gets returned:

```
SELECT e.BusinessEntityID,
       p.LastName + ', ' + p.FirstName AS Name,
       e.OrganizationNode.ToString() AS Hierarchy,
       e.OrganizationNode.GetAncestor(0).ToString() AS Self,
       e.OrganizationNode.GetAncestor(1).ToString() AS OneUp,
       e.OrganizationNode.GetAncestor(2).ToString() AS TwoUp,
       e.OrganizationNode.GetAncestor(3).ToString() AS TooFar
FROM HumanResources.Employee e
JOIN Person.Person p
  ON e.BusinessEntityID = p.BusinessEntityID
WHERE e.BusinessEntityID = 3
```

If you look at this closely, you'll see that I'm fetching the same node several times, but, with each separate column, I'm stepping further up the hierarchy until I've stepped beyond the level that I happen to know that this particular piece of data lays at. Run this, and we get back a single row:

```
BusinessEntityID Name                  Hierarchy Self  OneUp TwoUp TooFar
---------------- --------------------- --------- ----- ----- ----- ------
3                Tamburello, Roberto   /1/1/     /1/1/ /1/   /     NULL

(1 row(s) affected)
```

Several things are of note in this result:

❑   Although it provides little value, zero was a valid argument (it returns the calling node).

❑　　Each increase in the argument to GetAncestor() moved us further up the hierarchy tree.

❑　　Using a value that goes beyond the root of the hierarchy list returns a NULL.

This is great for going *up* the hierarchy tree, but what if we want to return the children, or simply know if a specific child has a given parent anywhere in its ancestry? For that, the right answer depends on whether we know how far down the chain we want to go (all reports or only direct reports). If it is all reports, we have IsDescendantOf(). This one takes a single node as an argument and returns a Boolean result that is, as you might expect, a simple true/false as to whether the node you pass into the method has the node are calling the method from as a child (directly or indirectly). The syntax looks like this:

```
<instance of HierarchyID data>.IsDescendantOf(n):
```

For this, let's look at how it can be used in either direction. For example, let's say we want to return all superiors to Mr. Tamburello. This translates to us wanting to return any row with a node that considers Mr. Tamburello's node to be a descendant. For example:

```
DECLARE @ChildNode HierarchyID

SELECT @ChildNode = OrganizationNode
FROM HumanResources.Employee e
WHERE e.BusinessEntityID = 3

SELECT e.BusinessEntityID,
       p.LastName + ', ' + p.FirstName AS Name,
       e.OrganizationNode.ToString() AS Hierarchy
FROM HumanResources.Employee e
JOIN Person.Person p
  ON e.BusinessEntityID = p.BusinessEntityID
WHERE @ChildNode.IsDescendantOf(e.OrganizationNode) = 1;
```

First, note that we were able to move a node into a variable of type HierarchyID, and we were still able to make a method call from that variable. Why use a query like this one instead of using GetAncestor()? If you think about this for a moment, I suspect you'll see that it has to do with how open ended the question was. GetAncestor() really expects you to know how many ancestors you have. You could figure that out using GetLevel() or rig up some test for NULL values, but that is far more complicated than simply returning all rows where IsDescendant() is true.

```
BusinessEntityID Name                                 Hierarchy
---------------- ----------------------------- ----------
1                Sanchez, Ken                         /
2                Duffy, Terri                         /1/
3                Tamburello, Roberto                  /1/1/

(3 row(s) affected)
```

> **Much as a node can consider itself its own ancestor (with a level input of zero), a node is also considered its own descendant.**

That showed us how to check what ancestors are above us, but what about the children below us? For that, we can ask an even more open-ended question. For example, listing all people that report directly or indirectly to Mr. Tamburello requires a simple reversal of the WHERE condition in our previous query:

```
DECLARE @ChildNode HierarchyID

SELECT @ChildNode = OrganizationNode
FROM HumanResources.Employee e
WHERE e.BusinessEntityID = 3

SELECT e.BusinessEntityID,
       p.LastName + ', ' + p.FirstName AS Name,
       e.OrganizationNode.ToString() AS Hierarchy
FROM HumanResources.Employee e
JOIN Person.Person p
  ON e.BusinessEntityID = p.BusinessEntityID
WHERE e.OrganizationNode.IsDescendantOf(@ChildNode) = 1;
```

And just that quick we have all of Mr. Tamburello's reports:

BusinessEntityID	Name	Hierarchy
3	Tamburello, Roberto	/1/1/
4	Walters, Rob	/1/1/1/
5	Erickson, Gail	/1/1/2/
6	Goldberg, Jossef	/1/1/3/
7	Miller, Dylan	/1/1/4/
8	Margheim, Diane	/1/1/4/1/
9	Matthew, Gigi	/1/1/4/2/
10	Raheem, Michael	/1/1/4/3/
11	Cracium, Ovidiu	/1/1/5/
12	D'Hers, Thierry	/1/1/5/1/
13	Galvin, Janice	/1/1/5/2/
14	Sullivan, Michael	/1/1/6/
15	Salavaria, Sharon	/1/1/7/

```
(13 row(s) affected)
```

To get his direct reports, we use pretty much the same query, but return to the GetAncestor() method:

```
DECLARE @ChildNode HierarchyID;

SELECT @ChildNode = OrganizationNode
FROM HumanResources.Employee e
WHERE e.BusinessEntityID = 3;

SELECT e.BusinessEntityID,
       LEFT((p.LastName + ', ' + p.FirstName), 30) AS Name,
       LEFT(e.OrganizationNode.ToString(), 10) AS Hierarchy
FROM HumanResources.Employee e
JOIN Person.Person p
  ON e.BusinessEntityID = p.BusinessEntityID
WHERE e.OrganizationNode.GetAncestor(1) = @ChildNode;
```

Which limits us to just the specific level below us (or, as GetAncestor() looks at it, the level that we are currently 1 above).

Inserting New Hierarchical Data

At its most basic level, inserting new hierarchical data isn't unlike inserting any other data in SQL Server. The real trick to inserting new hierarchy nodes lies in understanding what the representation should look like for the new row.

Remember that SQL Server has no preconceived notions about your hierarchy. Indeed, SQL Server doesn't necessarily even look at it as a tree or that a given node is unique. So, while SQL Server can't build your hierarchy for you, it can help you generate values based on information you provide. The functionality for this is provided by the GetDescendant() method.

GetDescendant() would probably have been more accurately named if they had called it something like "GenerateHierarchyNodeRepresentation()" or something like that. Its purpose is to generate a valid representation of a hierarchy node that falls between two optionally set parameters. The syntax looks like this:

```
<parent node>.GetDescendant({<Low Child> | NULL}, {<High Child> | NULL})
```

The low and high child nodes specify a range that the generated value must fall *between* (it is non-inclusive). The generated value may contain decimals or even be a negative value as long as it falls within the specified range. While both arguments are required, you can explicitly specify NULL as the value for either, effectively putting no bound on that side of the generation.

- ❑ If parent is NULL, returns NULL.
- ❑ If parent is not NULL, and both low and high children are NULL, returns a child of parent.
- ❑ If parent and the low child are not NULL, and the high child is NULL, returns a child of parent greater than the low child.
- ❑ If parent and the high child are not NULL and the low child is NULL, returns a child of parent less than the high child.
- ❑ If the parent, the low child, and the high child are not NULL, returns a child of parent greater than the low child and less than the high child.
- ❑ If the low child is not NULL and not a child of parent, an exception is raised.
- ❑ If high child is not NULL and not a child of parent, an exception is raised.
- ❑ If the low child is equal to or greater than the high child, an exception is raised.

For this particular method call, we'll generate a bit more custom example using the following script:

```
CREATE TABLE NodeTest
(
  NodeID    int           NOT NULL IDENTITY  PRIMARY KEY,
  Node      hierarchyid NOT NULL,
  NodeLevel AS Node.GetLevel(),
  Name      varchar(50) NOT NULL
);
```

```
INSERT NodeTest
VALUES
  ('/', 'Manager');

DECLARE @Manager hierarchyid;
SELECT @Manager = Node
FROM NodeTest
WHERE NodeID = 1;

INSERT NodeTest
VALUES
  (@Manager.GetDescendant(NULL, NULL), 'ReportAAA'),
  (@Manager.GetDescendant(NULL, NULL), 'ReportBBB'),
  (@Manager.GetDescendant(NULL, '/1000/'), 'ReportCCC'),
  (@Manager.GetDescendant(NULL, '/1000/'), 'ReportDDD'),
  (@Manager.GetDescendant('/1000/', NULL), 'ReportEEE'),
  ('/547/', 'ReportFFF'),
  (@Manager.GetDescendant('/3/', '/547/'), 'ReportGGG'),
  (@Manager.GetDescendant('/1/', '/2/'), 'ReportHHH'),
  (@Manager.GetDescendant('/-10/', '/-1/'), 'ReportIII'),
  ('/547/345/', 'SecondLevelAA'),
  ('/547/346/', 'SecondLevelBB'),
  ('/547/345/1/', 'ThirdLevelAA'),
  ('/785/294/386/925/','RandomEntry');


SELECT NodeID,
       Node.ToString(),
       Name
FROM NodeTest;
```

With this script, we've stuck a wide variety of data in, but the output may surprise you in several places:

```
NodeID                             Name
----------- -------------------- --------------------------------
1           /                    Manager
2           /1/                  ReportAAA
3           /1/                  ReportBBB
4           /999/                ReportCCC
5           /999/                ReportDDD
6           /1001/               ReportEEE
7           /547/                ReportFFF
8           /4/                  ReportGGG
9           /1.1/                ReportHHH
10          /-9/                 ReportIII
11          /547/345/            SecondLevelAA
12          /547/346/            SecondLevelBB
13          /547/345/1/          ThirdLevelAA
14          /785/294/386/925/    RandomEntry

(14 row(s) affected)
```

Note that we were able to insert data randomly. For example, we have a fourth-level node called RandomEntry that is just that — random. It has no parent. SQL Server does nothing to enforce a tree representation or the validity of your hierarchy; it only provides the tools for making nodes work together in a way you are most likely to use to create hierarchy trees.

Next, note that we inserted decimal-based values. Our ninth entry was inserting between 1 and 2, so there was no way to squeeze it in there without going to decimals (and so that's exactly what SQL Server did).

Continuing on, we have negative values. Again, we provided SQL Server no real choice, as our low and high children were both negative.

Finally, we inserted duplicate rows. HierarchyID columns are not any more inherently unique than any other data type. If you want to avoid duplicate node values, you'll need to utilize a unique or primary key constraint. Note also that given a specific high and low child, GetDescendant() will generate the same value over and over again without regard to whether or not there is a duplicate (and regardless of whether there is a unique or primary key constraint). You need to plan for the values you're going to insert. For the vast majority of hierarchies, horizontal position is not important, so you can usually use whatever the max node is for the level you're inserting into.

Moving Sub-Trees Between Parents

The HierarchyID data type also provides for the concept of a coordinated prune and graft of a node and its children to a new parent using the GetReparentedValue() method. Like GetDescendant(), the name of GetReparentedValue() seems to imply that its main function is getting data back. While returning data is indeed technically what it does, GetReparentedValue() is largely about moving data around. It requires two arguments: the old "root" and the new "root." So the basic syntax looks like this:

```
<node to be moved>.GetReparentedValue(<old root>, <new root>)
```

Note that "root" in this case doesn't mean the top-level root of the entire hierarchy. Instead, it is just the root of the particular sub-tree you're wanting to move.

> GetReparentedValue() does not necessarily make the represented move. It is merely a way to show a "what if?" scenario. When used with an UPDATE statement, it performs the actual move.

Let's go back to the NodeTest table we created in the previous example. We want to see what things would look like if we took the children of node /547/ and moved them to node /1001/. We can do this by combining our GetReparentedValue() method with the IsDescendantOf() method:

```
SELECT NodeID,
       Node.GetReparentedValue('/547/', '/1001/').ToString() AS New,
       Node.ToString() AS Old,
       Name
FROM NodeTest
WHERE Node.IsDescendantOf('/547/') = 1;
```

This code shows what things would look like if we pruned the /547/ sub-tree (included the /547/ node itself) and grafted all related nodes to the /1001/ node. Let's take a look at the results:

```
NodeID       New                   Old                   Name
-----------  --------------------  --------------------  --------------------
7            /1001/                /547/                 ReportFFF
11           /1001/345/            /547/345/             SecondLevelAA
12           /1001/346/            /547/346/             SecondLevelBB
13           /1001/345/1/          /547/345/1/           ThirdLevelAA

(4 row(s) affected)
```

At first blush, this looks perfect, but there is one potential problem: the actual /547/ node. In our original data, we already have a /1001/ node. If we are ok with duplicates (and thus the nodes appearing to have two parents), then there is no problem here. Most of the time, however, a node is going to have one and only one parent. To change things so that we only move the *children* of /547/, we just need to exclude it from the result set using the WHERE clause:

```
SELECT NodeID,
       Node.GetReparentedValue('/547/', '/1001/').ToString() AS New,
       Node.ToString() AS Old,
       Name
FROM NodeTest
WHERE Node.IsDescendantOf('/547/') = 1
  AND Node.ToString() != '/547/';
```

And we've quickly cleaned our errant node out of the results:

```
NodeID       New                   Old                   Name
-----------  --------------------  --------------------  --------------------
11           /1001/345/            /547/345/             SecondLevelAA
12           /1001/346/            /547/346/             SecondLevelBB
13           /1001/345/1/          /547/345/1/           ThirdLevelAA

(3 row(s) affected)
```

With that all figured out, we're ready to actually move our data around using an UPDATE statement:

```
UPDATE NodeTest
SET Node = Node.GetReparentedValue('/547/', '/1001/')

WHERE Node.IsDescendantOf('/547/') = 1
  AND Node.ToString() != '/547/';
```

Execute this, and then reselect all the data from our NodeTest table:

```
NodeID       Name
-----------  --------------------  --------------------------------------
1            /                     Manager
2            /1/                   ReportAAA
3            /1/                   ReportBBB
4            /999/                 ReportCCC
5            /999/                 ReportDDD
```

```
6              /1001/                ReportEEE
7              /547/                 ReportFFF
8              /4/                   ReportGGG
9              /1.1/                 ReportHHH
10             /-9/                  ReportIII
11             /1001/345/            SecondLevelAA
12             /1001/346/            SecondLevelBB
13             /1001/345/1/          ThirdLevelAA
14             /785/294/386/925/     RandomEntry

(14 row(s) affected)
```

As planned, all of our nodes that were previously descendants of /547/ have been moved to /1001/. /547/ has been left in its original state as planned.

Getting the Root of a Hierarchy

Well, it deserves mentioning I guess, but it's probably going to be a bit anti-climactic. The last method we're going to cover here (I'm limiting myself to those that are T-SQL addressable) is for retrieving the root of a hierarchy. The odd thing about this method is that it is returning a constant. Since it is a static member of the HierarchyID type, you reference it using the HierarchyID type rather than a specific instance. You can, if you so choose, skip this, as the value will always be the same ("/" if you do a ToString() on it). The syntax is straightforward, and does not vary by specific implementation:

```
HierarchyID::GetRoot()
```

As I said, there is no real magic to this one. You can always select it to see:

```
SELECT HierarchyID::GetRoot().ToString();
```

which will yield you the now familiar simple forward slash:

```
--------------
/

(1 row(s) affected)
```

Indexing Hierarchy Data

There are two likely ways for you to want your hierarchical data indexed:

❏   **Vertically (also referred to as "Depth First")**: This is what is inherent to the base indexing of a HierarchyID column. It starts at the highest node it can find (the root node assuming you have one), and drills downward into the tree. As shown in Figure 7-2, when it reaches a bottom node it indexes everything at that level, and then returns to the lowest node part of the same general branch that hasn't been indexed yet, and then again starts downward. Creating the index uses the standard index syntax we covered in the previous chapter. If you index with a HierarchyID column as your first column, then you're sure to be getting a depth-first traversal index.

❏   **Horizontally (usually referred to as a "Breadth-First" index)**: Creating a breadth-first index requires a little extra effort, but, before we worry about that, let's focus on what exactly it does.

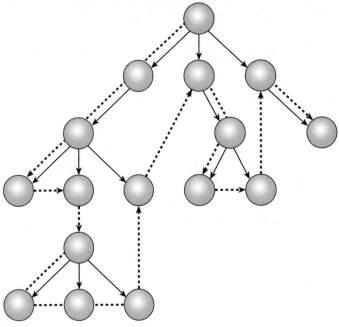

Figure 7-2

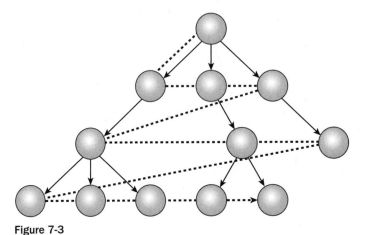

Figure 7-3

A breadth-first index stores siblings close together (as shown in Figure 7-3). This is created for comparisons that are oriented around things like the GetAncestor() method. To create an index with this treatment order, you need to create a computed column based on the GetLevel() method just as the AdventureWorks2008 database has for the OrganizationLevel column of the Employee table (and as I created in our NodeTest). You can then index the Level column followed by the HierarchyID column to have a breadth-first index.

Other than considering the difference in depth versus breadth on first traversal, HierarchyID indexes work much like any other index in SQL Server.

Performance Considerations

In general, the HierarchyID approach is going to give you the best overall performance and functionality for hierarchical data. However, as is the case with so many things in software development, there are other approaches and exceptions to the best performance rule. We discussed some of the alternatives at the beginning of our hierarchy discussion, but let's quickly explore some of the performance ramifications of each choice by utilizing a table approach.

I'm told that people love it when I build the "Best performance by the numbers" and "If this, then that" tables I occasionally have in my books. While I do put these things forward based on experience or other research, keep in mind that they are "best guess" suggestions as to approach. In short, they are what works for the listed situations "most of the time." Your mileage may vary, and you really should, as I say all too often, test, test, test!

| | Likely Best Approach | | |
Situation	HierarchyID	Parent/Child	XML
Sub-tree queries are common (this is the most common scenario)	X		
Most sub-tree queries are only for direct descendants		X	
Most queries are to a known, single node in the hierarchy		X	
Parent nodes change frequently		X	
The entire data set is consumed at once (ideally in XML format)			X

Don't confuse the number of squares indicating parent/child relationships as being a good fit as being an endorsement as parent/child continuing to be the likely best solution. Treat each case individually, and realize that sub-tree and ancestry queries are generally very common in hierarchies, and such queries are where the HierarchyID data type excels.

Spatial Data

The addition of spatial data handling has been one of the most touted features of SQL Server 2008. Perhaps the most interesting thing to me is that such a feature can be touted to an audience who mostly has no basis for understanding what the feature is even about.

What am I trying to get at here? Well, the new geospatial data types that are part of SQL Server have been a relatively highly requested feature for perhaps the last ten years or so. (It is one of the things often focused on by the Oracle crowd, since Oracle has handled geospatial data for some time now.) While very powerful, it is addressing an area that many database developers don't even realize they may need, let alone actually understand.

The geospatial data types require a grasp of a style of data that is much different than other forms of data we deal with. For example, when dealing with the new `HierarchyID` type that we looked at in the previous section, we were working with a style of data most developers already have some concept of. (We've dealt with hierarchies such as org charts for years.) So the new thing was simply the way we went about manipulating data and we already understood the nature of that. With geospatial data, however, many developers will be asking themselves many questions regarding what geospatial data is all about. For example:

- ❑ Is this just defining a specific location (for example an address)?
- ❑ Is it defining the boundaries of a property?
- ❑ Is it mapping a road?
- ❑ How many of my customers live within 5 miles of this point?
- ❑ How many bridges are there in Madison County?

The reality is a bit larger than any one of these questions. Indeed, it encompasses all of the concepts just listed and more. How would we have designed for these kinds of questions in the past? For some of them we could have taken a relatively simple (and low power) approach, such as including a simple address. We might even have passed the address to an external application that kept geospatial data and utilized feedback from that application to ask bigger questions. Today's end users, however, expect more. It is, for example, nearly impossible to find a retail or restaurant chain website that does not include a "find a store near you" feature. They use geospatial functionality to supply that.

With some of these needs in mind, let's explore the two types of geospatial data (planar or geodetic) and the functionality supporting each.

Spatial Concepts

To figure out the peculiarities of the specific type of geospatial data you need to work with, we are going to first get a bit of grounding in the more commonly accepted methods of representing spatial data. As you might imagine, there are standards surrounding how spatial data should be represented. Unfortunately, there isn't just one standard (indeed, SQL Server supports several "models").

To begin understanding geospatial data, we must first grasp that there are two different major models of representing geospatial data: planar (flat earth) and geodetic (round earth). Both have the same basic goal: to represent space via a set of data points (points, lines, curves). Planar representations are generally more simplistic and, therefore, easier to grasp and manage. Planar data is often used for relatively "local" data — that is, data that does not need to cover a particularly large area and does not need to have precision adjustments for the curvature of the earth's surface. Geodetic representations offer a more "real world" depiction, and are generally used when you need to represent a larger area that is more likely to be affected by the curvature of the earth.

Planar (Flat Earth) Data

Planar data is known by several names, such as geoplaner, geometric, or flat earth. You can think of this as mapping reasonably well to the Euclidian geometry that you likely studied in high school. With planar data, everything is represented on, as you might guess, a plane or series of planes. The space being presented is assumed to be flat. This is, for smaller areas, a very practical method of looking at spatial data, as it is easy to visualize and most functionality does not require particularly complex math (for example, distance is the same as a straight line). Planar data can be represented using the sort of x, y, z data points you might have used in graphics in geometry class by mixing a collection of point data into lines and polygonal shapes; one can use basic geometry to represent complex shapes, and still handle things like overlapping objects.

No matter how well we draw our planar mapping though, we are often representing something that is not truly flat by using points on a flat surface. This can introduce some problems. There are a number of approaches to minimizing the effects of a flat representation of a round earth. Figures 7-4 through 7-5 are examples of some common projections of the earth. Planar representations of the earth make use of the concept of a "projection" — that is, the round earth gets projected onto a flat surface.
As it turns out, these projects are generally "good enough" for many applications of spatial data. Indeed, most local maps for government tracking of properties, roads, and other needs are done using planar models such as latitude and longitude.

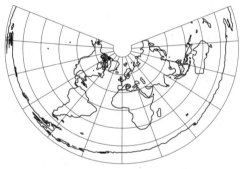

Figure 7-4

Figure 7-5

Be careful with your assumptions regarding latitude and longitude. While these may seem like well understood and agreed on concepts, there are actually multiple mappings of latitude and longitude used in the world today. For example, the longitude used in the Global Positioning System (GPS) is a noticeable distance (more than 100 meters or more depending on what part of the earth you're standing on when you measure it) different than most other representations of longitude (which are generally based on the Royal Observatory's definition of zero longitude).

Planar data is supported in SQL Server by the GEOMETRY data type (which will serve as the core type for most of our upcoming examples).

> **There are multiple accepted models of the earth. Make certain when supplying or receiving spatial data that the models being used are compatible or that you know how to adjust for differences between the two.**

Geodetic (Round Earth) Data

Geodetic data, as shown in Figure 7-5, represents the more realistic (far more complex) model based on a round earth. Geodetic representation of data is supported by the GEOGRAPHY data type.

Under the planar data model, it is assumed that the surface of the earth is flat. This works just fine for areas measured in relatively small distances (say, as much as several miles), but begins to fall apart as the distances grow larger. For example, when measuring the distance between Portland, Oregon and Beijing, China, the straight line used in a planar model would improperly represent the distance by many miles less than it actually is. Why? Well, under the flat model, the distance is a straight line rather than the more appropriate arc (which would follow the curvature of the earth's surface). Indeed, the issue can get even more complex, as the earth is not a perfect sphere (it bulges in places) with the circumference varying by literally hundreds of miles depending on which direction you're measuring. Geodetic data models the curve of the earth, and is supported in SQL Server via the GEOGRAPHY data type.

> **It is important to note that SQL Server can only represent geographic data that resides within a single *hemisphere*. A hemisphere can be considered as any half of a sphere — regardless of what plane you cut the sphere along.**

Representing Spatial Data

There are several key notions that are common to representing both planar and geodetic data and work together to allow you to represent a given type of data in different ways. The Open Geospatial Consortium (OGC) — an organization specializing in geometric data standards — defines several formats that you can utilize to represent spatial data. SQL Server 2008 implements three of these:

❑ **Well Known Text (WKT):** This is very plain-text looking, and simply sequentially names a series of objects (such as a point or a line) followed by coordinate information for each object.

❑ **Well Known Binary (WKB):** Implementing the same general notion as WKT, this representation encodes the same kind of information in a binary stream rather than plain text.

❑ **Geography Markup Language (GML)**: An XML schema designed to represent geometric data. GML leverages the self-defining nature of XML data to allow additional (non-coordinate) information to be encoded along with the coordinate data. Examples of the kind of extended information that might be included with GML data would be things like a description of what is found at the location or, perhaps, sensor information (say, an ozone measurement at a specific point in Los Angeles, CA versus a similar measurement taken in Lisbon, Portugal).

> We will utilize WKT for the examples in this book, but this is largely a readability decision, and does not imply that WKT is a better choice in general use (the right choice will vary by situation).

Regardless of which data representation is being utilized, the general objects required will be the same. Each format recognizes a set of three base objects that can be used individually or as a collection to represent spatial data. The objects are:

❑ **Point**: This is a specific point in space. It has no length, no width, and no height. It is the equivalent of the spot you mark with a thumb tack on a map to represent a place you are or have been. A point requires a simple X, Y notation.

❑ **Line**: In each of the formats SQL Server recognizes, a line is represented using a `LINESTRING` object. Note the relevance of the term `STRING` that is embedded. This recognizes that a line is represented as a series of two or more points. The use of multiple points in the line definition allows for the idea that the line may not be straight. Since each *segment* of the line string is the shortest path between the two points, increasing the number of points representing the same conceptual line will increase the accuracy of that line's representation.

❑ A line is considered "simple" if it does not cross over itself, and is considered to be a one-dimensional object even if it is curved or forms a *ring* (a line that has the same ending and starting point).

> Note that a ring does not mean that a polygon is round — only that it creates some form of enclosed space.

❑ **Polygon**: Although it is defined by one or more rings (again, a line with the same ending and starting points), defining what is individually a linestring that forms a ring as a polygon instead changes the treatment of the would-be linestring. Unlike the base ring definition, which is one dimensional and has no area, a polygon does have area. In addition, the ring that defines the outer boundary of the polygon can contain additional polygons that can define areas in the outer polygon that are *hollow*. The space defined by these inner hollow polygons is not considered to be part of the area of the parent polygon.

❑ **Collection**: This is a collection of the other three objects (point, line, polygon).

Regardless of which spatial data type you're using within SQL Server — GEOMETRY or GEOGRAPHY — all three of these base objects (or a collection of them) are available and can be used in any mix within a given table. For example, a table of world landmarks might store a complex polygon to represent Yellowstone Park, a line to represent the equator, and a simple point to indicate the highest point on the earth. Each of these (or a collection of them) could be represented within the same column in the same table.

In addition to these base concepts, the OGC defines a set of methods that should be supported to work with our spatial data. We'll explore some of these that are supported by SQL Server as we go through the examples, but it's worth noting that many of the methods exist for both types of spatial data (using the same name or just a slight name change) and have the same general functionality between the types. The OGC functions all start with a prefix of ST followed by a verb that indicates what the function does. They are implemented as a method for each instance of spatial data. Key examples are discussed in the following table.

> Note that, for each ST method call, the spatial reference id — or SRID — must match in order to perform a valid comparison. The SRID indicates what recognized (by the European Petroleum Survey Group) spatial model this particular spatial instance is referencing. If the SRIDs of two instances do not match, then any comparison will return NULL.

Method	Use
.STArea()	Calculates the area of a spatial instance that is a polygon and accounts for hollow spaces created by contained polygons.
.STContains(<spatial instance>)	Returns a bit indicating whether the supplied instance is entirely contained within the calling instance.
.STDistance(<spatial instance>)	Provides a numeric value indicating the distance between the supplied instance and the calling instance.
.STEquals(<spatial instance>)	Returns a bit indicating whether the supplied and calling instance are qualitatively equal. Note that this does not require them to be defined in exactly the same way, but, rather, to wind up with the same result (for example, defining a square with 8 line segments, and another with 4, but with the same resulting side lengths and position would return a 1).
.STIntersects(<spatial instance>)	Returns a bit indicating whether the supplied instance crosses the calling instance at any point
.STOverlaps(<spatial instance>)	Returns a bit indicating whether the supplied instance overlaps the calling instance (for example, a line starting within a polygon, and then ending outside of it).
.STTouches(<spatial instance>)	Returns a bit indicating whether the supplied instance touches the calling instance in any way.
.STWithin(<spatial instance>)	Returns a bit indicating whether the supplied instance lies entirely within the calling instance; if any portion of the supplied instance falls outside of the calling instance, then STWithin will return a zero.

The OGC function list is actually much, much longer and does vary somewhat between the GEOMETRY and GEOGRAPHY types, but these provide a taste of what's available and, among other things, includes those supported for indexes against spatial data. You can find a more complete list in the Books Online by looking under each spatial type (GEOMETRY and GEOGRAPHY).

Implementing Planar Data Representations — The GEOMETRY Data Type

As previously mentioned, the data type that implements the concept of planar, or flat earth, data is called GEOMETRY. Using the GEOMETRY data type not only provides a means to contain the types of geometric object definitions (point, linestring, polygon) we discussed earlier, but also a series of methods that can be utilized against that data. Like the HierarchyID data type we discussed earlier in the chapter (and the GEOGRAPHY type we'll discuss next), GEOMETRY is implemented via a CLR user-defined function (then flagged as system so it doesn't require the security considerations that true CLR UDTs require). Like other .NET classes, you can make use of a number of properties and static members of the class.

The GEOMETRY type can accept any of the geometric types we just discussed. Let's check this out with a quick example that not only instantiates a geometric data type, but loads it with data.

> Note that SQL Server will attempt to represent some spatial data in Management Studio. The representation will, however, become visible only when you are in the Results to Grid mode in the Query Editor Window.

We'll start by examining the way to get our WKT data into our data type:

```
DECLARE @MyGeometry     GEOMETRY;

SET @MyGeometry = Geometry::STGeomFromText('LINESTRING(-3 3, 3 3, 3 -3, -3 -3,
 -3 3)', 0)
SET @MyGeometry = Geometry::Parse('LINESTRING(-3 3, 3 3, 3 -3, -3 -3, -3 3)')
SET @MyGeometry = 'LINESTRING(-3 3, 3 3, 3 -3, -3 -3, -3 3)'

SELECT @MyGeometry;

SET @MyGeometry = 'POLYGON((-3 3, 3 3, 3 -3, -3 -3, -3 3))'

SELECT @MyGeometry;
```

In this code, we've declared an instance of geometric data in a variable called @MyGeometry. We then assign linestring data to our variable in three different ways. These are all functionally the same, with the final assignment using the Parse function implicitly.

We then select out our newly assigned line. When this is executed, Management Studio shows us not only a binary representation, but also the visual representation shown in Figure 7-6.

> Note that, in order to see the spatial data tab, you must be using the "Results to Grid" mode in the Query Editor Window.

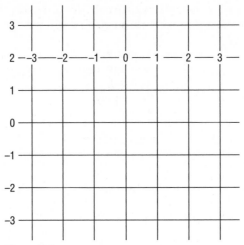

Figure 7-6

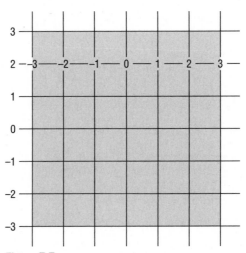

Figure 7-7

We then go on to repeat the assignment and selection, but this time for a polygon instead of a linestring. This winds up yielding us slightly different results (shown in Figure 7-7).

Notice the slightly different representation of two objects based on the same series of points. Why are they different? Well, recall that a linestring is always considered one dimensional. Although they can curve and even cross over themselves, they are still considered to lack area (which requires two dimensions). SQL Server represents the linestring — even though it forms a ring — as hollow to represent the lack of area. For the polygon, however, SQL Server fills in the square to represent the enclosure of two-dimensional space. SQL Server is aware that the two, though based on the same series of points, have a fundamental difference distinguishing them. This difference will become more apparent later on, as various methods of the GEOGRAPHY data type are only relevant to specific object types (for example, the method that calculates area only makes sense on polygons, not on lines).

Our polygons are, of course, not limited to squares or even rectangles. Indeed, they can be virtually any shape as long as they eventually are enclosed into a ring by ending at the same point they started at. (A linestring simply crossing itself is not enough to form a ring, and, therefore, a polygon. It must start and end at the same point.) In addition, we can use polygons embedded inside other polygons to represent hollow space. Let's check all these concepts out.

First, we need a few different instances of the GEOMETRY data type to compare against each other. We'll also go ahead and establish a simple square again, but this time we'll call the STArea() method of the GEOMETRY type to get the area of our square:

```
DECLARE @First     GEOMETRY,
        @Second    GEOMETRY,
        @Merged    GEOMETRY;

SET @First = 'POLYGON((-3 3, 3 3, 3 -3, -3 -3, -3 3))';

SELECT 'First polygon area: ', @First.STArea();

SELECT @First;
```

The STArea() method is an example of a method that is part of the OGC list of spatial data methods. Execute this code, and we get a representation of our square (the same as we showed in Figure 7-7), but we also get a calculated area of 36.

Moving on, let's expand our script to add another polygon, but this time we'll add something that has a slightly more complex linestring:

```
DECLARE @First     GEOMETRY,
        @Second    GEOMETRY,
        @Merged    GEOMETRY;

SET @First = 'POLYGON((-3 3, 3 3, 3 -3, -3 -3, -3 3))'

SELECT 'First polygon area: ', @First.STArea();

SELECT @First;

SET @Second =
    'POLYGON((-1 .4, -.4 1, .4 1, 1 .4, 1 -.4, .4 -1, -1 -1, -.4 -1, -1 -.4, -1 .4))';

SELECT @Second;

SET @Second= @Second.MakeValid();
SELECT 'Second polygon area: ', @Second.STArea();
```

As the more complex linestring in @Second would imply, we are shown a more complex shape: an octagon (shown in Figure 7-8).

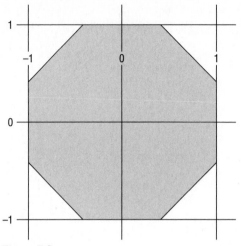

Figure 7-8

Note also, though, that we had to perform an additional action on our polygon to make it valid — that done, we are able to call the area calculation and receive our result (3.28000022888182).

Continuing the example, we can build a polygon that utilizes both linestrings, with the second becoming a hollow area in the first:

```
DECLARE @First    GEOMETRY,
        @Second   GEOMETRY,
        @Merged   GEOMETRY;

SET @First = 'POLYGON((-3 3, 3 3, 3 -3, -3 -3, -3 3))'

SELECT 'First polygon area: ', @First.STArea();

SELECT @First;

SET @Second =
    'POLYGON((-1 .4, -.4 1, .4 1, 1 .4, 1 -.4, .4 -1, -1 -1, -.4 -1, -1 -.4, -
1 .4))';

SELECT @Second;

SET @Second= @Second.MakeValid();
SELECT 'Second polygon area: ', @Second.STArea();
SET @Merged = 'POLYGON((-3 3, 3 3, 3 -3, -3 -3, -3 3),
    (-1 .4, -.4 1, .4 1, 1 .4, 1 -.4, .4 -1, -1 -1, -.4 -1, -1 .4, -1 .4))'

SELECT @Merged;

SET @Merged = @Merged.MakeValid();
SELECT 'Merged polygon area: ', @Merged.STArea();
```

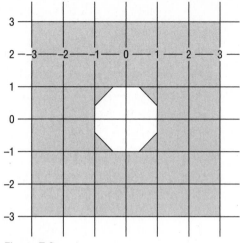

Figure 7-9

This time SQL Server shows both polygons — inverting the color fill to show the hollow space (shown in Figure 7-9).

The calculated area for the merged polygon has properly taken into account the hollow area (that is, it subtracts it from the larger polygon) and gives us the correct area of 32.7200009155276.

Let's make one last addition to this script, this time adding yet another polygon into the mix to see how SQL Server handles overlapping areas. We'll add another octagon to the merged polygon:

```
DECLARE @First     GEOMETRY,
        @Second    GEOMETRY,
        @Merged    GEOMETRY;

SET @First = 'POLYGON((-3 3, 3 3, 3 -3, -3 -3, -3 3))'

SELECT 'First polygon area: ', @First.STArea();

SELECT @First;

SET @Second =
  'POLYGON((-1 .4, -.4 1, .4 1, 1 .4, 1 -.4, .4 -1, -1 -1, -.4 -1, -1 -.4, -1
.4))';

SELECT @Second;

SET @Second= @Second.MakeValid();
SELECT 'Second polygon area: ', @Second.STArea();

SET @Merged = 'POLYGON((-3 3, 3 3, 3 -3, -3 -3, -3 3),
          (-1 .4, -.4 1, .4 1, 1 .4, 1 -.4, .4 -1, -1 -1, -.4 -1, -1 -.4, -
1 .4))'

SET @Merged = @Merged.MakeValid();
```

```
SELECT 'Merged polygon area: ', @Merged.STArea();
SET @Merged = 'POLYGON((-3 3, 3 3, 3 -3, -3 -3, -3 3),
  (-1 .4, -.4 1, .4 1, 1 .4, 1 -.4, .4 -1, -1 -1, -.4 -1, -1 -.4, -1 .4),
  (-2.5 .4, -1.9 1, -1.1 1, -.5 .4, -.5 -.4, -1.1 -1, -2.5 -1, -1.9 -1, -2.5 -
.4, -2.5 .4))'

SELECT @Merged;

SET @Merged = @Merged.MakeValid();
SELECT 'Second Merged polygon area: ', @Merged.STArea();
```

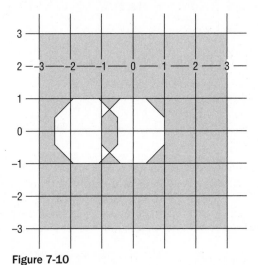

Figure 7-10

Pay attention to both the third figure (shown in Figure 7-10) and the area of 30.4900010681158. Note that both polygons are shown (including their overlap area), and that the area result subtracted the hollow area only once — that is, the area that overlaps between the two inner polygons was only removed once.

Last, but not least, let's take a quick visit of the ToString() method. For this, we'll use the same merged GEOMETRY, activate the MakeValid() method, and then output the slightly modified result:

```
DECLARE @Merged    GEOMETRY;

SET @Merged = 'POLYGON((-3 3, 3 3, 3 -3, -3 -3, -3 3),
                (-1 .4, -.4 1, .4 1, 1 .4, 1 -.4, .4 -1, -1 -1, -.4 -1, -1 -.4,
-1 .4))'

SET @Merged = @Merged.MakeValid();
SELECT 'Merged polygon area: ', @Merged.STArea();

SELECT @Merged;
SELECT @Merged.ToString()
```

Notice the changes to the output:

```
POLYGON ((-3 -3, 3 -3, 3 3, -3 3, -3 -3), (-0.39999961853027344 -1, -1 -
0.39999961853027344, -1 0.39999961853027344, -0.39999961853027344 1,
0.39999961853027344 1, 1 0.39999961853027344, 1 -0.39999961853027344,
0.39999961853027344 -1, -0.39999961853027344 -1))
```

The changes away from our relatively round numbers is a byproduct of the `MakeValid()` command, but, other than that change, we got back almost exactly the layout we put in.

Implementing Geodetic Representations — The GEOGRAPHY Type

The type that implements the concept of geodetic, or round earth, data is called GEOGRAPHY. The GEOGRAPHY data type works, in most ways, just like the GEOMETRY type did. (Indeed, they share many of the same functions.) Like the last two data types we've discussed, GEOMETRY is implemented via a CLR user-defined function.

The GEOGRAPHY type can also accept any of the geometric types we discussed earlier in the section, but it also applies the notion of a hemisphere.

> While the geometric data type would apply a default SRID to spatial instances (the default is zero), the **GEOGRAPHY** data type does not generally have a default value (some individual geography methods do assume a SRID of 4326), and must be supplied each time you redefine a geographic instance.

Let's start by utilizing a near duplicate of our first geometry example, only using the GEOGRAPHY type this time:

```
DECLARE @First    GEOGRAPHY;

SET @First = GEOGRAPHY::STGeomFromText('LINESTRING(-3 3, 3 3, 3 -3, -3 -3, -3
3)', 4326)
SET @First = GEOGRAPHY::Parse('LINESTRING(-3 3, 3 3, 3 -3, -3 -3, -3 3)')
SET @First = 'LINESTRING(-3 3, 3 3, 3 -3, -3 -3, -3 3)'

SELECT @First;
```

This all works fine, with only the `STGeomFromText()` function working differently than its geometric counterpart (and, even then, the only difference is that it requires a second parameter instead of using a default).

Things get a bit more interesting when we get to a polygon though, as we must fit within a given *hemisphere*. A hemisphere is, just as in the dictionary definition, half of a sphere. The starting and stopping points of each hemisphere vary depending on what SRID you're referencing, but, regardless of which you've chosen, all polygons, lines, and points referenced for a given spatial instance must fit within that hemisphere.

I would imagine this to provoke the question of "Why?" I know it did for me. The issue has to do with eliminating ambiguity on what is considered "inside" versus "outside" a polygon. There are functions that look to see if something is contained within a spatial instance, but how do you know if something is inside an object if you don't know which side of the defining ring is considered inside versus outside?

There is, of course, more than one way to address the inside versus outside problem with spatial data in general, but the SQL Server team had to pick one, and they went with an approach that requires you to stay within a single hemisphere. If you need to map an object that crosses a hemisphere boundary, consider mapping it as two adjacent objects (sharing the hemisphere border), and utilizing them as a pair.

To check this out, we'll continue to run through what is largely the same example as we used for geometry, but mapped to the curve aware data type (GEOGRAPHY):

```
DECLARE @First    GEOGRAPHY;

SET @First = 'POLYGON((-3 3, 3 3, 3 -3, -3 -3, -3 3))';

SELECT @First;
```

But when you try and execute this, you run into trouble that you didn't have under the GEOGRAPHY data type:

```
Msg 6522, Level 16, State 1, Line 3
A .NET Framework error occurred during execution of user-defined routine or
aggregate "geography":
Microsoft.SqlServer.Types.GLArgumentException: 24205: The specified input does
 not represent a valid geography instance because it exceeds a single
hemisphere. Each geography instance must fit inside a single hemisphere. A
common reason for this error is that a polygon has the wrong ring orientation.
Microsoft.SqlServer.Types.GLArgumentException:
    at Microsoft.SqlServer.Types.GLNativeMethods.ThrowExceptionForHr(GL_HResult
errorCode)
    at Microsoft.SqlServer.Types.GLNativeMethods.GeodeticIsValid(GeoData g)
    at Microsoft.SqlServer.Types.SqlGeography.IsValidExpensive()
    at Microsoft.SqlServer.Types.SqlGeography.ConstructGeographyFromUserInput(GeoData
g, Int32 srid)
    at Microsoft.SqlServer.Types.SqlGeography.GeographyFromText(OpenGisType
type, SqlChars taggedText, Int32 srid)
    at Microsoft.SqlServer.Types.SqlGeography.Parse(SqlString s)
.

(1 row(s) affected)
```

The extra stack of error lines is a result of the .NET implementation that is behind all of the new data types that are covered in this chapter. The key item, however, is the GLArgumentException line; we are in more than one hemisphere.

When I first started learning about the hemisphere issue, my assumption was that it must have to do with negative and positive numbers — not so. Instead, the issue is more of a simplistic test of whether the "inside" of our polygon fits inside a hemisphere. We've defined a box that seems fairly straightforward and small here, so it's easy to see why one might be confused at how it is in more than one hemisphere.

The problem is, however, also fairly simple. Our inside and outside are backwards. That is, what you likely perceive as being "outside" the square is considered to be inside as we've defined the box to SQL Server.

To address this issue, we have to think of the polygon in terms of the ring that draws it — that is, as a series of connected lines that eventually ends where it started. The "inside" is always deemed to be the side that is on the *left* of the line as you draw it. In general, this means that, when you draw an object, you'll want to lay out the lines that enclose it in a *counterclockwise* direction. In our example, we were going clockwise, so we created a situation where the "outside" was the area that was bounded by our line, and the inside was unbounded. We can fix our error by simply reversing the order we draw the polygon in:

```
DECLARE @First    GEOGRAPHY;

SET @First = 'POLYGON((-3 3, -3 -3, 3 -3, 3 3, -3 3))';


SELECT @First;
```

Now if we execute it, things return and look pretty much as they did when we were working with the GEOMETRY type.

The set of methods implemented in the GEOMETRY and GEOGRAPHY types has significant overlap between them, but is not identical. (All the ones we've seen in this chapter, except for MakeValid() are implemented in both types). Spatial data is its own area of study, so I recommend exploring information well outside the SQL Server–specific community to understand what is expected in each implementation.

Filestreams

This is something of a "high-octane" feature that is new in SQL Server 2008. Indeed, it is relatively fringe in nature, and even requires you to take special steps to enable it. (It is not enabled in the default installation.) Still, while I consider this feature to still be solidly in its infancy, it has started a path to something that is potentially very special. So that should bring about the question: "OK then, what exactly do filestreams do?" Glad you asked.

There has long been a series of problems in the database realm regarding what to do with storage of unstructured data files (for example, images, documents, spreadsheets, movies, and so on). The files are often an integral part of a large piece of data we are storing in a database (let's say something like photos of a crash and a scanned image of a claim form on an insurance claim).

With this is mind, we would like to:

❑ Store all that data together and in a space-efficient manner

❑ Read and write the data with maximum performance

❑ Utilize transactions

❑ Secure the data effectively and under one model

❑ Have consistent state on the data when backing up and restoring

The methods of addressing these problems have varied depending on which of these issues were considered the priority for a particular installation. The balancing act has gone something like this:

❑ **Performance is key**: The data was generally kept in individual files at the file system level.

❑ **Consistent state is key**: The data was generally stored as binary large objects (blobs) in the database. Often the blobs were kept on a separate drive array through the use of filegroups.

The specifics vary by installation, but, while SQL Server's performance in blob handling has improved substantially over the years, it was still slow enough that the most common installation was to store files at the file system level and just store the path to the file in SQL Server. This has several risks, including:

❑ Files can get moved without the database knowing, breaking the link between data with no history that might allow recovery.

❑ Updates to the files are made without the database being directly aware of the change, making auditing ineffective at best.

❑ There was no means of co-enrolling data changes in the same transaction. This means you can overwrite a file, but have the associated database changes rolled back (or vice versa), destroying the proper state of your data.

❑ The lack of coordinated transactions created a time latency between changes in the file system and backup/recovery work in the database.

Other installations did go the SQL Server blob route, fixing the preceding issues, but creating other problems:

❑ Storage was inefficient, with space loss due to SQL Server's page storage model overhead as relates to blob data.

❑ Performance suffered. In general, this performance hit occurred in a manner that affected all the data being accessed, not just the blob.

❑ Accessing blob data from the database required special handling versus other data in the database — adding complexity. What's more, the access model was generally seen as more complex than the relatively simple stream handling of files from the file system.

Filestreams in SQL Server address virtually all of these problems by coordinating storage between the database and the file system into one cohesive solution, with both systems doing what they do best (SQL Server coordinating the transactions and storing the structured data, and the file system storing the unstructured data).

Under a filestream model, SQL Server integrates with NTFS (the file system used in Windows). For tables and columns that are configured to do so, data for columns defined as type varbinary(max) are redirected to the file system. Access from within SQL Server is relatively transparent, and standard T-SQL statements will work against the data. For client languages, however, they can utilize a special SqlFileStream object that is derived from the Stream class in .NET, making much of the functionality very familiar to client developers that are already used to the Stream object for file handling and other stream access. Through this integration of the best parts of SQL Server and NTFS, several key problems are solved:

❑ **Security is coordinated between SQL Server and NTFS**: The directory used to store the SQL Server filestream data can only be accessed within a SQL Server granted context. This means that those who do not have appropriate access to the `varbinary(max)` column in SQL Server cannot gain access to the underlying file in NTFS.

❑ **Transactions are fully supported**: Stream updates are fully enrolled in any active transaction (indeed, clients using a filestream are required to enroll in a transaction context in order to gain access to the data at all), and will honor commits and rollbacks as appropriate. This means updates to an existing file will be rolled back as appropriate, restoring the file to its original state if the transaction did not complete.

❑ **Backups are also coordinated**: This means that backups of the database include the NTFS handled files in a state consistent with the rest of the backup data.

❑ **Access to the file information is handled through virtually identical means as it would have been had the file been stored within NTFS directly**: Only minimal coordination overhead is incurred, so performance differences versus direct NTFS storage is negligible.

The ramifications of this bode very well for the future of unstructured data in otherwise structured environments. Let's take a quick look at what's involved from a development perspective.

Enabling Filestreaming

By default, filestream access is turned off when you install SQL Server. There is an option to set this up during the installation process, and I recommend using that option if you remember it. If, however, you forget (or just didn't, at the time, think you needed it), you can enable filestreaming for the server by using the SQL Server Configuration Manager. Go to the SQL Server Services node, and right-click the SQL Server services for your instance (the default instance is labeled MSSQLSERVER). This should bring up the dialog shown in Figure 7-11. (Notice that I've changed to the FILESTREAM tab).

Figure 7-11

Installation of the AdventureWorks2008 database requires that filestream be turned on for the server you install it on, so, if you've made it this far in the book, you're certain to have filestream access turned on for the server you've been working examples with. That said, you may want to play around with a system that doesn't have filestream turned on so you can understand what's involved in turning it on after the fact.

In this dialog, you can define the level of access you want the filestream exposed to. Be sure and note that what you are setting up here is for the *server*, and your database(s) will need additional configuration to be able to store stream data.

Enabling a Database for Filestreams

To enable filestreaming for a database, you just need to create a filegroup using the CONTAINS FILESTREAM option. This will set the path that you want to place under SQL Server access control and enable tables to be configured for filestream access. Let's try this out by creating a database we'll use for examples in this section:

```
CREATE DATABASE FileStreamDB
ON
PRIMARY ( NAME = FSDBPrimary, FILENAME = 'C:\FSDB\DB\fsdb.mdf'),
FILEGROUP FSDBStream CONTAINS FILESTREAM
   ( NAME = FSDBStream, FILENAME = 'C:\FSDB\STREAM')
LOG ON  ( NAME = FSDBLog, FILENAME = 'C:\FSDB\fsdb.ldf')
GO
```

> Note that, unlike the data and log file paths, which must exist when you run the **CREATE DATABASE** statement, the filegroup you're using for the filestream must *not* yet exist. SQL Server creates the directory as part of the database creation, coordinating with NTFS regarding permissions and ownership of the directory.

Run this (changing the file paths to something that works on your particular system) and you should get a confirmation that your database has been created.

You can use the ALTER DATABASE command to add a filestream filegroup if you need to enable an existing database for filestream access.

Creating a Filestream-Enabled Table

There are no special settings required to enable a table for filestream. Instead, you just need to make sure that your table has a unique constrained column of type rowguidcol (a special data type that uses the uniqueidentifer type but also defines it as a row identifier for SQL Server) defined. After that, filestream access is defined on a per-column basis based on options for any varbinary(max) columns in the table.

Again, let's try this out by creating a table we'll use later to store an object on our SQL Server:

```
CREATE TABLE FSTable
(
   FileKey   int            NOT NULL    IDENTITY  PRIMARY KEY,
```

```
    rowguid    uniqueidentifier  rowguidcol  NOT NULL  UNIQUE,
    filedata   varbinary(max)    FILESTREAM
);
```

Again, this should get you a simple confirmation that the command ran successfully, but, with this created, we should be ready to manipulate stream data.

Using T-SQL with Filestreams

Filestream data is relatively transparent to T-SQL access. We can, for example, run a simple INSERT statement just as we would any other row that had binary data:

```
DECLARE @Ident  int

INSERT FSTable
VALUES
   (NEWID(), 0x0A);

SET @Ident = @@IDENTITY;

SELECT FileKey, filedata
FROM FSTable
WHERE FileKey = @Ident;

UPDATE FSTable
SET filedata = 0x49276D206C6561726E696E672066696C6573747265616D73
WHERE FileKey = @Ident;

SELECT FileKey, filedata
FROM FSTable
WHERE FileKey = @Ident;

DELETE FSTable
WHERE FileKey = @Ident;

SELECT FileKey, filedata
FROM FSTable
WHERE FileKey = @Ident;
```

This explores all the main statements of SQL:

```
(1 row(s) affected)
FileKey      filedata
----------- -----------------------------------------------------------------------
1            0x0A

(1 row(s) affected)

(1 row(s) affected)
```

```
FileKey      filedata
----------   -----------------------------------------------------------------------
1                    0x49276D206C6561726E696E672066696C6573747265616D73

(1 row(s) affected)

(1 row(s) affected)

FileKey      filedata
----------   -----------------------------------------------------------------------

(0 row(s) affected)
```

As you can see, there really isn't a lot to it from a T-SQL perspective. Indeed, all the major statements work pretty much as they would with non-filestream data. There is a small amount of additional information using the `PathName()` property that is added to the `varbinary(max)` data type when filestream is enabled, for example:

```
DECLARE @Ident  int;

INSERT FSTable
VALUES
    (NEWID(), 0x0A);

SELECT @Ident = @@IDENTITY;

SET @Ident = @@IDENTITY;

SELECT rowguid, fs.filedata.PathName() AS Path
FROM FSTable fs
WHERE FileKey = @Ident;
```

Run this, and you should see a single row back. (It is, unfortunately, too wide to fit gracefully in this book.) First, notice the rowguid column. Now compare it with the final portion of the Path column, and you should see a match.

As you can see, the column we identify as the rowguidcol is critically important in terms of setting a unique path for our stored filestreams.

Using Filestreams with .NET

I'm going to defer much of our discussion of .NET with filestreams until we discuss connectivity in Chapter 25 (which is a web-only release, so don't skip right to the back of the book!). However, I think it important to understand some key points early, as they have design ramifications that you may not otherwise think of before you get in the middle of some .NET code.

Any work with a filestream requires a *transaction context*. Even if you're just reading data, you need the transaction context from the SQL Server side to govern issues of concurrency and consistency of your data. Unfortunately, you *cannot* make use of the T-SQL keyword BEGIN TRANSACTION (there are some rules for multiple active result set — or MARS — enabled connections that BEGIN TRANSACTION does not live up to), so you must use your client's data access API's method of enlisting transactions prior to accessing data via a filestream.

Other than that, the primary difference between handling a SQL Server related filestream and the more generic `Stream` object in .NET is mostly one of what you instantiate. (For SQL Server filestreams, a `SqlFileStream` object takes care of most of the differences transparently.)

Again, we will look at an example filestream connection in Chapter 25.

> **Again, as an important reminder, Chapter 25 is a web release chapter, and one I hope to occasionally update during the life of this book to keep it somewhat in line with the ever changing world of connectivity.**

Table Compression

> **It is important to note that, as of this writing, the data compression features in SQL Server 2008 are limited to the Enterprise edition.**

This one is, again, new with SQL Server 2008, but some early indications of what was to come first appeared in a SQL Server 2005 service pack. From a programming standpoint, there is actually relatively little to be done here. (It's largely about table settings.) But it's worth a visit in this "advanced" data structures chapter for three simple reasons:

❑ **Planning**: The compression feature fundamentally alters the page/row storage format of data on disk, and can significantly reduce the footprint of your data. This is done on a table-by-table basis (again, it is a table-level setting), and therefore requires an adjustment to how you plan for the required storage volume and growth in your database.

❑ **Performance**: There is a performance trade-off when you deal with table compression that can work for or against you. It depends on the particular scenario. There is extra overhead to managing the compression, but the compression may also sharply reduce I/O requirements, and thus gain back any performance lost to the compression overhead.

❑ **Structure Knowledge**: I went so far as to tell you about the traditional page/row storage methods, so anything that fundamentally alters those default storage methods probably deserves something of a look.

Enabling Compression

In the previous chapter, we took a look at the CREATE INDEX syntax. This, along with CREATE TABLE, is where the DATA_COMPRESSION option is available. The CREATE INDEX version is highlighted in the following code (it works the same in the CREATE TABLE statement).

```
CREATE [UNIQUE] [CLUSTERED|NONCLUSTERED]
INDEX <index name> ON <table or view name>(<column name> [ASC|DESC] [,...n])
INCLUDE (<column name> [, ...n])
[WITH
[PAD_INDEX = { ON | OFF }]
[[,] FILLFACTOR = <fillfactor>]
```

```
[[,] IGNORE_DUP_KEY  = { ON | OFF }]
[[,] DROP_EXISTING = { ON | OFF }]
[[,] STATISTICS_NORECOMPUTE = { ON | OFF }]
[[,] SORT_IN_TEMPDB = { ON | OFF }]
[[,] ONLINE = { ON | OFF }
[[,] ALLOW_ROW_LOCKS = { ON | OFF }
[[,] ALLOW_PAGE_LOCKS = { ON | OFF }
[[,] DATA_COMPRESSION = { NONE | ROW | PAGE}
     [ ON PARTITIONS ( { <partition number expression> | <range> }

[[,] MAXDOP = <maximum degree of parallelism>
]
[ON {<filegroup> | <partition scheme name> | DEFAULT }]
```

As mentioned before, you can turn on data compression as part of the CREATE TABLE statement by adding an identical line to that used in the CREATE INDEX statement.

Summary

Virtually everything seen in this chapter is new with SQL Server 2008 (XML indexes being the notable exception). Most of it is highly specialized, but each does what it does very well with data structures that have been optimized for that specific task.

If you're dealing with XML data, consider your index carefully, but experiment with indexes and realize that they can greatly speed XML queries. For hierarchical data, consider the new HierarchyID data type. Not only does it include hierarchy-specific methods, but, for many developers, the notion that a given node knows its entire lineage is going to be much easier to grasp than the recursive calls that are generally required for the parent child approach to hierarchies.

Spatial data is finally here, but brings SQL Server developers into a realm that they have likely not been in before. There is support for both flat and round earth models, and the ability to recognize proximity, irregular shapes, intersections, and similar spatial-specific concepts is a huge boon for many that didn't realize they had a special need — let alone conceive of a way to address that need.

Filestreams address a long-standing need in SQL Server. Most of the functionality supported by filestreams has been supported in some other fashion for a long time, but filestreams integrate that functionality in a manner that allows for more coordinated backup processes and, perhaps more important, transaction-based handling of large binary files. While filestream access is largely a client application–only process, it requires substantial design and security consideration by the database architect.

Data compression is finally here at the database level. While the compression is largely transparent to the application, compression can affect performance in both good and bad ways, and needs to be carefully considered prior to activating the compression feature.

In our next chapter, we'll explore an old mainstay of SQL Server — views.

8

Views

Since we're assuming, in this book, that you already know something about SQL Server, I am going to minimize the discussion of the basics and focus primarily on the more meaty uses of views. That said, we'll touch ever so briefly on view basics before moving on.

Views have a tendency to be used either too much, or not enough — rarely just right. When we're done with this chapter, you should be able to use views to:

❑ Be more comfortable with view basics

❑ Add additional indexing to your database to speed query performance — even when you're not using the view the index is based on

❑ Understand and utilize the notion of partitioned views and federated servers

A view is, at its core, really nothing more than a stored query. You can create a simple query that selects from only one table and leaves some columns out, or you can create a complex query that joins several tables and makes them appear as one.

Reviewing View Syntax

The most basic syntax for a view looks something like this:

```
CREATE VIEW <view name>
AS
<SELECT statement>
```

It utilizes that basic CREATE <object type> <object name> syntax that exists for most SQL Server objects. It is just the minimum, of course, but it's still all we need in a large percentage of the situations. The more extended syntax looks like this:

```
CREATE VIEW [<schema name>].<view name> [(<column name list>)]
[WITH [ENCRYPTION] [, SCHEMABINDING] [, VIEW_METADATA]]
```

```
AS
<SELECT statement>
[WITH CHECK OPTION]
```

So, an extremely simple view on the `Person.Person` table in the AdventureWorks2008 database might look something like:

```
USE AdventureWorks2008;
GO

CREATE VIEW Person.PersonView
AS
    SELECT FirstName, MiddleName, LastName
    FROM Person.Person;
```

So, when you run:

```
SELECT * FROM Person.PersonView;
```

You get back exactly the same thing as:

```
SELECT FirstName, MiddleName, LastName
FROM Person.Person;
```

You are essentially saying to SQL Server: "Give me all of the rows and columns you get when you run the statement `SELECT FirstName, MiddleName, LastName FROM Person.Person`."

We've created something of a pass-through situation — that is, our view hasn't really changed anything, but rather just "passed through" a filtered version of the data it was accessing. Think about the uses for this a bit, and you should be able to see how this concept can be utilized to do things like simplify the data for inexperienced users (show them only the columns they care about to keep from confusing them) or to proactively hide sensitive data (such as profit or salary numbers) by granting the user rights to a view that doesn't include that data, but not giving them rights to the underlying table.

> Be aware that, by default, there is nothing special done for a view. The view runs just as if it were a query run from the command line — there is no pre-optimization of any kind. This means that you are adding one more layer of overhead between the request for data and the data being delivered. That means that a view is never going to run as fast as if you had just run the underlying SELECT statement directly. That said, views exist for a reason — be it security or simplification for the user — balance your need against the overhead as would seem to fit your particular situation.

> How much overhead? Well, it depends both on how complex the view is and on the calling code. It can range from milliseconds to much longer impacts (though usually the former) depending on the specifics.

Let's take this one step further.

You've already seen how to create a simple view — you just use any SELECT statement. How do you filter the results of your queries? With a WHERE clause. Views are no different.

More Complex Views

Perhaps one of the most common uses of views is to flatten data — that is, the removal of complexity that we outlined at the beginning of the chapter. Imagine that we are providing a view for management to make it easier to check on sales information. No offense to managers who are reading this book, but managers who write their own complex queries are still a rather rare breed — even in the information age.

For an example, our manager would like to be able to do simple queries that will tell him or her what orders have been placed for what items and how many sold on each order and related pricing information. So, we create a view that he or she can perform very simple queries on:

```
USE AdventureWorks2008;
GO

CREATE VIEW CustomerOrders_vw
AS
SELECT    o.SalesOrderID,
          o.OrderDate,
          od.ProductID,
          p.Name,
          od.OrderQty,
          od.UnitPrice,
          od.LineTotal
FROM Sales.SalesOrderHeader AS o
JOIN    Sales.SalesOrderDetail AS od
    ON o.SalesOrderID = od.SalesOrderID
JOIN    Production.Product AS p
    ON od.ProductID = p.ProductID;
```

Now do a SELECT:

```
SELECT *
FROM CustomerOrders_vw;
```

You wind up with a bunch of rows — over 100,000 — but you also wind up with information that is far simpler for the average manager to comprehend and sort out. What's more, with not that much training, the manager (or whoever the user might be) can get right to the heart of what he or she is looking for:

```
SELECT ProductID, OrderQty, LineTotal
FROM CustomerOrders_vw
WHERE OrderDate = '5/15/2003';
```

The user didn't need to know how to do a four-table join — that was hidden in the view. Instead, he or she needs only limited skill (and limited imagination for that matter) in order to get the job done.

```
ProductID   OrderQty LineTotal
----------- -------- ---------------------------------------
791         1        2443.350000
781         1        2071.419600
794         1        2181.562500
798         1        1000.437500
783         1        2049.098200
801         1        1000.437500
784         1        2049.098200
779         1        2071.419600
797         1        1000.437500

(9 row(s) affected)
```

However, we could make our query even more targeted. Let's say that we want our view to return only yesterday's sales. We'll make only slight changes to our query:

```
USE AdventureWorks2008;
GO

CREATE VIEW YesterdaysCustomerOrders_vw
AS
SELECT    o.SalesOrderID,
          o.OrderDate,
          od.ProductID,
          p.Name,
          od.OrderQty,
          od.UnitPrice,
          od.LineTotal
FROM Sales.SalesOrderHeader AS o
JOIN    Sales.SalesOrderDetail AS od
    ON o.SalesOrderID = od.SalesOrderID
JOIN    Production.Product AS p
    ON od.ProductID = p.ProductID
WHERE CONVERT(varchar(12),o.OrderDate,101) =
      CONVERT(varchar(12),DATEADD(day,-1,GETDATE()),101)
```

All the dates in the AdventureWorks database are old enough that this view wouldn't return any data, so let's add a row to test it. Execute the following script all at one time:

```
USE AdventureWorks2008;

DECLARE @Ident int;

INSERT INTO Sales.SalesOrderHeader
    (
    CustomerID,
    OrderDate,
    DueDate,
    BillToAddressID,
    ShipToAddressID,
    ShipMethodID
    )
VALUES
    (
```

```
      1,                           -- CustomerID
      DATEADD(day,-1,GETDATE()),  -- OrderDate (Yesterday)
      GETDATE(),                   -- Due Date (today)
      1,                           -- BillToAddressID
      1,                           -- ShipToAddressID
      1                            -- ShipMethodID
   );

SELECT @Ident = @@IDENTITY;

INSERT INTO Sales.SalesOrderDetail
    (SalesOrderID,
     OrderQty,
     ProductID,
     SpecialOfferID,
     UnitPrice,
     UnitPriceDiscount)
VALUES
(@Ident, 4, 765, 1, 50, 0);

SELECT 'The OrderID of the INSERTed row is ' + CONVERT(varchar(8),@Ident);
```

Most of what's going on in this script shouldn't be a big mystery for non-beginners, but I'll be explaining all of what is going on here in Chapter 9. For now, just trust me that we'll need to run all of this in order for us to have a value in AdventureWorks2008 that will come up for our view. You should see a result from the Management Studio that looks something like this:

```
(1 row(s) affected)

(1 row(s) affected)


-------------------------------------------
The OrderID of the INSERTed row is 75124

(1 row(s) affected)
```

Be aware that some of the messages shown in the preceding code will appear only on the Messages *tab if you are using the Management Studio's* Results In Grid *mode. Also remember that your particular OrderID may be different from mine depending what experimenting you've already been doing in the AdventureWorks2008 database.*

The SalesOrderID might vary, but the rest should hold pretty true.

Now let's run a query against our view and see what we get:

```
SELECT SalesOrderID, OrderDate FROM YesterdaysCustomerOrders_vw
```

You can see that the 75124 does indeed show up:

```
SalesOrderID OrderDate
------------ ----------------------
75124        2008-12-31 01:00:00.000

(1 row(s) affected)
```

> Don't get stuck on the notion that your `SalesOrderID` numbers are going to be the same as mine — these are set by the system (since `SalesOrderID` is an identity column) and are dependent on just how many rows have already been inserted into the table. As such, your numbers will vary.

Using a View to Change Data — Before INSTEAD OF Triggers

As we've said before, a view works *mostly* like a table does from an in-use perspective (obviously, creating them works quite a bit differently). Now we're going to come across some differences, however.

It's surprising to many, but you can run INSERT, UPDATE, and DELETE statements against a view successfully. There are several things, however, that you need to keep in mind when changing data through a view:

❑ If the view contains a join, you won't, in most cases, be able to INSERT or DELETE data unless you make use of an INSTEAD OF trigger. An UPDATE can, in some cases (as long as you are only updating columns that are sourced from a single table), work without INSTEAD OF triggers, but it requires some planning, or you'll bump into problems very quickly.

❑ If your view references only a single table, then you can INSERT data using a view without the use of an INSTEAD OF trigger provided all the required fields in the table are exposed in the view or have defaults. Even for single-table views, if there is a column not represented in the view that does not have a default value, then you must use an INSTEAD OF trigger if you want to allow an INSERT.

❑ You can, to a limited extent, restrict what is and isn't inserted or updated in a view.

Now, I've already mentioned INSTEAD OF triggers several times. INSTEAD OF triggers are a special, fairly complex kind of trigger we will look at extensively in Chapter 12. The problem here is that we haven't discussed triggers to any significant extent yet. As is often the case in SQL Server items, we have something of the old chicken versus egg thing going ("Which came first?"). I need to discuss INSTEAD OF triggers because of their relevance to views, but we're also not ready to talk about INSTEAD OF triggers unless we understand both of the objects (tables and views) that they can be created against.

The way we are going to handle things for this chapter is to address views the way they used to be — before there was such a thing as INSTEAD OF triggers. While we won't deal with the specifics of INSTEAD OF triggers in this chapter, we'll make sure we understand when they must be used. We'll then come back and address these issues more fully when we look at INSTEAD OF triggers in Chapter 12.

Having said that, I will provide this bit of context — an INSTEAD OF trigger is a special kind of trigger that essentially runs "instead" of whatever statement caused the trigger to fire. The result is that it can see what your statement would have done, and then make decisions right in the trigger about how to resolve any conflicts or other issues that might have come up. It's very powerful but also fairly complex stuff, which is why we defer it for now.

Dealing with Changes in Views with Joined Data

If the view has more than one table, then using a view to modify data is, in many cases, out — sort of anyway — unless you use an INSTEAD OF trigger. Since it creates some ambiguities in the key arrangements, Microsoft locks you out by default when there are multiple tables. To resolve this, you can use an INSTEAD OF trigger to examine the altered data and explicitly tell SQL Server what you want to do with it.

Required Fields Must Appear in the View or Have the Default Value

By default, if you are using a view to insert data (there must be a single table SELECT in the underlying query or at least you must limit the insert to affecting just one table and have all required columns represented), then you must be able to supply some value for all required fields (fields that don't allow NULLs). Note that by "supply some value" I don't mean that it has to be in the SELECT list — a default covers the bill rather nicely. Just be aware that any columns that do not have defaults and do not accept NULL values will need to appear in the view in order to perform INSERTs through the view. The only way to get around this is — you guessed it — with an INSTEAD OF trigger.

Limit What's Inserted into Views — WITH CHECK OPTION

The WITH CHECK OPTION is one of those lesser-known to almost completely unknown features in SQL Server. The rules are simple — in order to update or insert data using the view, the resulting row must qualify to appear in the view results. Restated, the inserted or updated row must meet any WHERE criterion that's used in the SELECT statement that underlies your view.

Editing Views with T-SQL

The main thing to remember when you edit views with T-SQL is that you are completely replacing the existing view. The only differences between using the ALTER VIEW statement and the CREATE VIEW statement are:

- ❑ ALTER VIEW expects to find an existing view, whereas CREATE doesn't.
- ❑ ALTER VIEW retains any permissions that have been established for the view.
- ❑ ALTER VIEW retains any dependency information.

The second of these is the biggie. If you perform a DROP and then use a CREATE, you have *almost* the same effect as using an ALTER VIEW statement. The problem is that you will need to entirely reestablish your permissions on who can and can't use the view.

Dropping Views

It doesn't get much easier than this:

```
DROP VIEW <view name>, [<view name>,[ ...n]]
```

And it (or they) is gone.

Auditing: Displaying Existing Code

What do you do when you have a view, but you're not sure what it does? The first option should be easy at this point — just go into the Management Studio as if you're going to edit the view. Go to the Views sub-node, select the view you want to edit, right-click, and either choose Design or Script View As and then choose the specific type of script you want. Either way, you'll see the code behind the view complete with color-coding.

> *Note that the Design feature brings up a special view builder utility. While the view builder is fabulous for those with little SQL experience (it works much like a similar tool in Access), I find it to be overly invasive about the way I want my view formatted, and inevitably leaves me with a view that is much more wordy (and therefore harder to read) than I would like; therefore, I usually stick to using the scripting tool and my own SQL writing skills.*

Unfortunately, we don't always have the option of having the Management Studio around to hold our hand through this stuff (we may be using a lighter-weight tool of some sort, or we may need to build the actual requests into our own application). The bright side is that we have a few ways of getting at the actual view definition:

- ❑   `sp_helptext`
- ❑   The `OBJECT_DEFINITION()` system function
- ❑   The `sys.comments` system view

Let's look at the first of these by running `sp_helptext` against one of the supplied views in the AdventureWorks2008 database — `vStateProvinceCountryRegion`:

```
EXEC sp_helptext 'Person.vStateProvinceCountryRegion';
```

> *Note the quotes. This is because this stored proc expects only one argument, and the period is a delimiter of sorts — if you pass `Person.vStateProvinceCountryRegion` in without the quotes, it sees the period and isn't sure what to do with it and therefore errors out. If the view was in our default schema, we could supply just the view name (no schema) and would not need to wrap it in quotes.*

SQL Server obliges us with the code for the view:

```
Text
--------------------------------------------------------------------------------

CREATE VIEW [Person].[vStateProvinceCountryRegion]
WITH SCHEMABINDING
AS
SELECT
    sp.[StateProvinceID]
    ,sp.[StateProvinceCode]
    ,sp.[IsOnlyStateProvinceFlag]
    ,sp.[Name] AS [StateProvinceName]
    ,sp.[TerritoryID]
    ,cr.[CountryRegionCode]
    ,cr.[Name] AS [CountryRegionName]
```

```
FROM [Person].[StateProvince] sp
    INNER JOIN [Person].[CountryRegion] cr
    ON sp.[CountryRegionCode] = cr.[CountryRegionCode];
```

Now, sp_helptext is great, but I would classify it as somewhat antiquated at this point. Why? Well, since sp_helptext is a stored procedure, you can't easily include the result set as part of a more complex data operation. Fortunately, Microsoft has given us OBJECT_DEFINITON() to deal with that issue.

OBJECT_DEFINITION() should be your preferred choice for a couple of reasons:

❑   When new releases come out, it will automatically be updated for changes to the system tables (so you don't have to worry about such things)

❑   The value returned can easily be used within a broader query (for example, as one column, with the source code for many objects being returned)

The syntax looks like this:

```
OBJECT_DEFINITION(<object id>)
```

The negative in this is that we rarely know what our object's id is without doing special lookup. Fortunately, SQL Server provides us a simple way to look up an object's id by using the OBJECT_ID() function. For example, if we wanted to use OBJECT_DEFINITION() to get the code for the same view we looked at earlier, we could write:

```
SELECT OBJECT_DEFINITION (OBJECT_ID(N'Person.vStateProvinceCountryRegion'));
```

> **Object IDs are SQL Server's internal way of keeping track of things. They are integer values rather than the names that you're used to for your objects. In general, they are outside the scope of this book, but it is good to realize they are there, as you will find them used by scripts you may copy from other people or just bump into them later in your SQL endeavors.**

Try it, and you'll see the result is nearly identical to when we used sp_helptext (it just doesn't name the column for us unless we provide an alias in our query definition).

We can take this a bit further and easily return the code for every view in our database:

```
SELECT '------------------------', OBJECT_DEFINITION(so.object_id)
FROM sys.objects so
WHERE so.type = 'V';
```

I've omitted the results here in the book lest thousands of trees die needlessly — it's that lengthy. That said, running the previous query should give you all of the views in the AdventureWorks2008 database.

We couldn't have done that with sp_helptext without utilizing a cursor — making it easy to see the usefulness of system functions such as OBJECT_DEFINITION versus the system stored procedure objects we had in earlier versions of SQL Server.

Now let's try it the last of our ways — using sys.comments.

> *You may see* sys.comments *(a system view) used interchangeably with the older, but not far less desirable* syscomments *(a system table).* syscomments *is one of many system tables that gave us most of our system information in SQL Server versions of old. Microsoft has been trying to move us away from direct calls to system tables for years, and they have finally given us the set of tools that allows us to comply with their wish.*
>
> *Even when system tables were the only directly queryable way to get system information, their use was somewhat risky, as Microsoft has always warned that system tables can change at any time (even service packs, though I've never seen that actually happen). Now that Microsoft has given us the views in the* sys *schema and a wide variety of table valued functions for metadata (see Appendix B for more on those), it is downright silly to go directly against the system tables. I highly recommend that you migrate old code that may be accessing the system tables directly to utilize the equivalent view (usually easily found by just adding a period after the "sys" in the old system table name).*

sys.comments provides an actual view to your underlying source code, and thus provides something you can join directly to if you so choose. Like OBJECT_DEFINITION(), any use of sys.comments is going to require you to know your object's id. You can either join to the sys.objects system view, much as I did in the previous example, or utilize the OBJECT_ID() function as I did in the example before that. Note, however, that, when using sys.objects, you need to treat the object name and schema name separately (which means that you also need to involve the sys.schemas system view). For example:

```
SELECT sc.text
FROM sys.syscomments sc
JOIN sys.objects so
    ON sc.id = so.object_id
JOIN sys.schemas ss
    ON so.schema_id = ss.schema_id
WHERE so.name = 'vStateProvinceCountryRegion'
  AND ss.name = 'Person';
```

Again, you get the same block of code we saw in the previous two methods.

Protecting Code: Encrypting Views

If you're building any kind of commercial software product, odds are that you're interested in protecting your source code. All you have to do to encrypt your view (and most other forms of server stored code) is use the WITH ENCRYPTION option. This one has a couple of tricks to it if you're used to the WITH CHECK OPTION clause:

❑   WITH ENCRYPTION goes after the name of the view, but *before* the AS keyword.

❑   WITH ENCRYPTION does not use the OPTION keyword.

In addition, remember that if you use an ALTER VIEW statement, you are entirely replacing the existing view except for access rights. This means that the encryption is also replaced. If you want the altered view to be encrypted, then you must use the WITH ENCRYPTION clause in the ALTER VIEW statement.

Let's do an ALTER VIEW on the CustomerOrders_vw view that we created earlier in the chapter. If you haven't yet created the CustomerOrders_vw view, then just change the ALTER to CREATE (don't forget to run this against AdventureWorks):

```
ALTER VIEW CustomerOrders_vw
WITH ENCRYPTION

AS
SELECT    o.SalesOrderID,
          o.OrderDate,
          od.ProductID,
          p.Name,
          od.OrderQty,
          od.UnitPrice,
          od.LineTotal
FROM Sales.SalesOrderHeader AS o
JOIN    Sales.SalesOrderDetail AS od
    ON o.SalesOrderID = od.SalesOrderID
JOIN    Production.Product AS p
    ON od.ProductID = p.ProductID;
```

Now do an sp_helptext on our CustomerOrders_vw:

```
EXEC sp_helptext CustomerOrders_vw;
```

SQL Server promptly tells us that it can't do what we're asking:

```
The text for object 'CustomerOrders_vw' is encrypted.
```

The heck you say, and promptly go to the sys.comments view:

```
SELECT sc.text
FROM syscomments sc
JOIN sys.objects so
    ON sc.id = so.object_id
JOIN sys.schemas ss
    ON so.schema_id = ss.schema_id
WHERE so.name = 'CustomerOrders_vw'
  AND ss.name = 'dbo';
```

But that doesn't get you very far either — SQL Server recognizes that the table was encrypted and will give you a NULL result.

In short — your code is safe and sound. Even if you pull it up in other viewers (such as Management Studio, which actually won't even give you the Design option on an encrypted table), you'll find it useless.

> Make sure you store your source code somewhere before using the WITH ENCRYPTION option. Once it's been encrypted, there is no way to get it back. If you haven't stored your code away somewhere and you need to change it, then you may find yourself rewriting it from scratch.

About Schema Binding

Schema binding essentially takes the things that your view is dependent upon (tables or other views), and "binds" them to that view. The significance of this is that no one can make alterations to those objects (CREATE, ALTER) unless they drop the schema-bound view first.

Why would you want to do this? Well, there are a few reasons why this can come in handy:

❑ It prevents your view from becoming "orphaned" by alterations in underlying objects. Imagine, for a moment, that someone performs a DROP or makes some other change (even deleting a column could cause your view grief) but doesn't pay attention to your view. Oops. If the view is schema bound, then this is prevented from happening.

❑ To allow indexed views. If you want an index on your view, you *must* create it using the SCHEMABINDING option. (We'll look at indexed views just a few paragraphs from now.)

❑ If you are going to create a schema-bound user-defined function (and there are instances where your UDF *must* be schema bound) that references your view, then your view must also be schema bound.

Keep these in mind as you are building your views.

Making Your View Look Like a Table with VIEW_METADATA

This option has the effect of making your view look very much like an actual table to DB-LIB, ODBC, and OLE-DB clients. Without this option, the metadata passed back to the client API is that of the base table(s) that your view relies on.

Providing this metadata information is required to allow for any client-side cursors (cursors your client application manages) to be updatable. Note that, if you want to support such cursors, you're also going to need to use an INSTEAD OF trigger.

Indexed (Materialized) Views

In SQL Server 2000, this one was supported only in the Enterprise Edition (okay, the Developer and Evaluation Editions also supported it, but you aren't allowed to use test and development editions in production systems). It is, however, supported in all editions since SQL Server 2005.

When a view is referred to, the logic in the query that makes up the view is essentially incorpora[te] the calling query. Unfortunately, this means that the calling query just gets that much more compl[ex] extra overhead of figuring out the impact of the view (and what data it represents) on the fly can a[dd] get very high. What's more, you're often adding additional joins into your query in the form of the [tables] that are joined in the view. Indexed views give you a way of taking care of some of this impact befo[re the] query is ever run.

An indexed view is essentially a view that has had a set of unique values "materialized" into the for[m] of a clustered index. The advantage of this is that it provides a very quick lookup in terms of pullin[g] the information behind a view together. After the first index (which must be a clustered index against a unique set of values), SQL Server can also build additional indexes on the view using the cluster key from the first index as a reference point. That said, nothing comes for free — there are some restrictions about when you can and can't build indexes on views (I hope you're ready for this one — it's an awfully long list!):

❑ The view must use the SCHEMABINDING option.

❑ If it references any user-defined functions (more on these later in the book), then these must also be schema bound.

❑ The view must not reference any other views — just tables and UDFs.

❑ All tables and UDFs referenced in the view must utilize a two-part (not even three-part and four-part names are allowed) naming convention (for example, dbo.Customers, BillyBob.SomeUDF) and must also have the same owner as the view.

❑ The view must be in the same database as all objects referenced by the view.

❑ The ANSI_NULLS and QUOTED_IDENTIFIER options must have been turned on (using the SET command) at the time the view and all underlying tables were created.

❑ Any functions referenced by the view must be deterministic.

To create an example indexed view, let's start by reviewing the CustomerOrders_vw object that we created earlier in the chapter. I'm showing this using the ALTER statement we used in the section on encryption, but, really, it could just as easily be the original version we created very early in the chapter as long as the WITH SCHEMABINDING is properly added.

```
ALTER VIEW CustomerOrders_vw
WITH SCHEMABINDING
AS
SELECT    o.SalesOrderID,
          o.OrderDate,
          od.ProductID,
          p.Name,
          od.OrderQty,
          od.UnitPrice,
          od.LineTotal
FROM Sales.SalesOrderHeader AS o
JOIN   Sales.SalesOrderDetail AS od
    ON o.SalesOrderID = od.SalesOrderID
JOIN   Production.Product AS p
    ON od.ProductID = p.ProductID;
```

he important things to notice here are:

❑   We had to make our view use the SCHEMABINDING option.

❑   In order to utilize the SCHEMABINDING option, we must have two-part naming for the objects (in this case, all tables) that we reference (in this case, we did anyway, but not all views you come across will already be configured that way).

This is really just the beginning — we don't have an indexed view as yet. Instead, what we have is a view that *can* be indexed. When we create the index, the first index created on the view must be both clustered and unique.

```
CREATE UNIQUE CLUSTERED INDEX ivCustomerOrders
ON CustomerOrders_vw(SalesOrderID, ProductID, Name);
```

Once this command has executed, we have a clustered view. We also, however, have a small problem that will become clear in just a moment.

Let's test our view by running a simple SELECT against it:

```
SELECT * FROM CustomerOrders_vw;
```

If you execute this, you'll see that the graphical showplan as shown in Figure 8-1 (Display Estimated Execution Plan is the tooltip for this, and you'll find it toward the center of the toolbar; you can also find it in the menus at Query ➤ Display Estimated Execution Plan) shows us using our new index.

> The index supporting an indexed view may be utilized by SQL Server even if you do not explicitly use the view. For example, if you are performing joins that are similar to those the index is supporting for the view, SQL Server may recognize this and utilize the index.

Partitioned Views

These have been in use just since SQL Server 2000, but Microsoft has, since 2005, considered partitioned tables to be the preferred partitioning method. I bring them up here because they were one of the leading scalability options put forth by Microsoft for many years, and you need to know how they work in case you run into them in legacy code. In addition, there are some partitioning problems that are difficult to unsolvable utilizing partitioned tables, so it's good to know and understand another option.

A partitioned view is a view that unifies multiple identical (in terms of structure — not actual data) tables and makes them appear to be a single table. At first, this seems like an easy thing to do with simple UNION clauses, but the concept actually becomes somewhat tricky when you go to handle insert and update scenarios.

With partitioned views, we define a constraint on one of the tables in our view. We then define a similar, but mutually exclusive, constraint on a second (and possibly many more) table. When you build the view that unifies these mutually exclusive tables, SQL Server is able to sort out the exclusive nature of the tables in a logical manner. By doing this, SQL Server can determine exactly which table is to get the new data (by determining which table *can* accept the data — if you created them as mutually exclusive as you should have, then the data will be able to get into only one table and there is no conflict). The only catch is that the so called "partitioning column" must participate in the primary key. Let's see how this works by building our own little mini-sample.

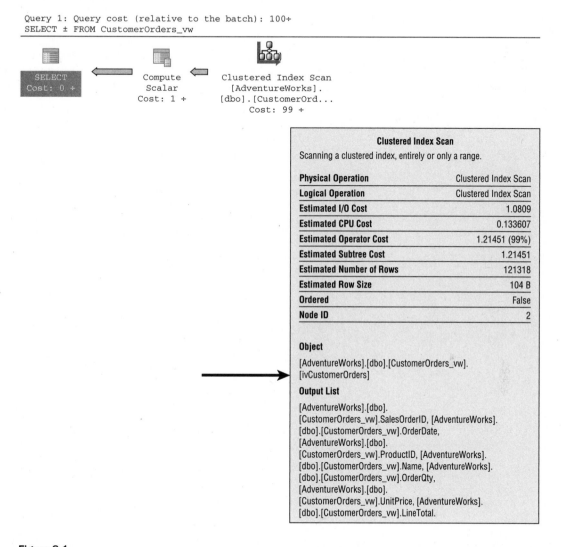

Figure 8-1

Imagine for a moment that you are running a very large Internet site, and you are taking in thousands of orders daily. Your Orders table is getting to be huge, and you are having issues where your purge job (to delete older records) is causing blocking issues while the DELETE statement is running.

By utilizing partitioned views (or as we'll learn later, partitioned tables), we can essentially silo our data such that we can spread the data out physically (by using different filegroups, or even different servers for each table) and have SQL Server sort out where everything is supposed to go.

Here's what a two-month set of data might look:

```
CREATE TABLE OrderPartitionJan08
(OrderID     int      NOT NULL,
 OrderDate   date     NOT NULL
   CONSTRAINT CKIsJanOrder
     CHECK (OrderDate >= '2008/01/01'
       AND  OrderDate <  '2008/02/01'),
 CustomerID int     NOT NULL,
 CONSTRAINT PKOrderIDOrderDateJan
   PRIMARY KEY (OrderID, OrderDate)
);

CREATE TABLE OrderPartitionFeb08
(OrderID     int      NOT NULL,
 OrderDate   date     NOT NULL
   CONSTRAINT CKIsFebOrder
     CHECK (OrderDate >= '2008/02/01'
       AND  OrderDate <  '2008/03/01'),
 CustomerID int     NOT NULL,
 CONSTRAINT PKOrderIDOrderDateFeb
   PRIMARY KEY (OrderID, OrderDate)
);

GO

CREATE VIEW Orders
AS
SELECT *
FROM OrderPartitionJan08

UNION ALL

SELECT *
FROM OrderPartitionFeb08;
```

Once we have created these tables along with the view that unites them into a partitioned view, we're ready to insert a few rows of data:

```
INSERT INTO Orders
VALUES
    (1, '2008-01-15', 1),
    (2, '2008-02-15', 1);
```

Orders is a view, and therefore has no data of its own — so where does the data go? Under the covers, SQL Server analyzes the data being inserted and figures out that, based on the constraints in our table, the data can, in each case, go to one and only one table. Let's check that out with a few queries:

```
SELECT * FROM Orders;
SELECT * FROM OrderPartitionJan08;
SELECT * FROM OrderPartitionFeb08;
```

This gets us, in order, both rows we inserted, then the row from January, then the one from February.

```
OrderID     OrderDate   CustomerID
----------- ----------- -----------
1           2008-01-15  1
2           2008-02-15  1

(2 row(s) affected)

OrderID     OrderDate   CustomerID
----------- ----------- -----------
1           2008-01-15  1

(1 row(s) affected)

OrderID     OrderDate   CustomerID
----------- ----------- -----------
2           2008-02-15  1

(1 row(s) affected)
```

As you can see, our data has been split up into separate tables based on the partitioning column. We can easily create additional tables to partition our data into (for example, an `OrderPartitionMar08` table) and then alter our view to union in the additional table. Likewise, we can easily remove a block of data by excluding it from the view and then dropping the table.

> **You can also spread the tables that support the partitioned view over multiple servers utilizing linked servers. This distributes the query load for those tables out to the various servers that house them, and is usually referred to as a "distributed partitioned view." The servers that support a given distributed partitioned view are said to be "federated."**

Summary

Views tend to be either the most overused or most underused tools in most of the databases I've seen. Some people like to use them to abstract seemingly everything (often forgetting that they are adding another layer to the process when they do this). Others just seem to forget that views are even an option. Personally, like most things, I think you should use a view when it's the right tool to use — not before, not after.

Common uses for views include:

❑   Filtering rows

❑   Protecting sensitive data

❑   Reducing database complexity

❑   Abstracting multiple physical databases into one logical database

❑   Creating indexes that effectively pre-join data between tables

Things to remember with views include:

- ❏ Stay away from building views based on views — instead, adapt the appropriate query information from the first view into your new view.

- ❏ Remember that a view using the WITH CHECK OPTION provides some flexibility that can't be duplicated with a normal CHECK constraint.

- ❏ Encrypt views when you don't want others to be able to see your source code — either for commercial products or general security reasons.

- ❏ Using an ALTER VIEW completely replaces the existing view other than permissions. This means you must include the WITH ENCRYPTION and WITH CHECK OPTION clauses in the ALTER statement if you want encryption and restrictions to be in effect in the altered view.

- ❏ Use the OBJECT_DEFINITION() system function to display the supporting code for a view — avoid using system tables.

- ❏ Minimize the use of views for production queries — they can add additional overhead and hurt performance.

- ❏ Indexing a view puts additional load on any data modification process that affects the data participating in the indexed view.

- ❏ Distributed partitioned views can be utilized to distribute data and query load across multiple servers, but, for single server partitioning, partitioned tables is typically a better choice.

In our next chapter, we'll take a look at batches and scripting. Batches and scripting will lead us right into stored procedures and user defined functions — the closest thing that SQL Server has to its own programs.

Scripts and Batches

Geez. I've been writing too long. For some reason, when I see the phrase "Scripts and Batches" it reminds me of the old song "Love and Marriage" (Frank Sinatra for the curious). While scripts and batches do go together like a horse and carriage, they are hardly as lyrical — but I digress . . . .

We have, of course, already written many SQL scripts in this book. My assumption, given that this is a "Professional" level book, is that you already have most of the script basics down. After all, every CREATE statement that you write, every ALTER, every SELECT is all (if you're running a single statement) or part (multiple statements) of a script. It is, however, rather difficult to get excited about a script with one line in it. Could you imagine Hamlet's "To be, or not to be . . . ?" if it had never had the following lines. We wouldn't have any context for what he was talking about.

SQL scripts are much the same way. Things get quite a bit more interesting when we string several commands together into a longer script — a full play or at least an act to finish our Shakespeare analogy. Now imagine that we add a richer set of language elements from .NET to the equation. Now we're ready to write an epic!

Scripts generally have a unified goal. That is, all the commands that are in a script are usually building up to one overall purpose. Examples include scripts to build a database (these might be used for a system installation), scripts for system maintenance, such as backups, Database Consistency Checker utilities (DBCCs), and scripts for anything where several commands are usually run together.

We will be reviewing the notion of scripts during this chapter, and adding in the notion of *batches*, which control how SQL Server groups your commands together. In addition, we will take a look at *SQLCMD*, the command-line utility, and how it relates to scripts.

> *SQLCMD was introduced as the new command-line scripting tool in SQL Server 2005. For backward compatibility only, SQL Server continues to support osql.exe (the previous tool that did command-line work). You may also see references to isql.exe, which served this same function in earlier releases. (Do not confuse this with isqlw.exe.) Isql.exe is no longer supported, but, since the options are pretty much the same, migration to osql or SQLCMD is generally not that difficult.*

Script Basics

A script technically isn't a script until you store it in a file where it can be pulled up and reused. SQL scripts are stored as text files. SQL Server Management Studio provides many tools to help you with your script writing, but, technically, you can do the writing in any text editor. Keep in mind, however, that to actually test your script, it's going to have to be something that can connect to a SQL Server. With SQL Server 2008, the Management Studio gains the additional advantage of supporting IntelliSense.

I continue to occasionally make use of a highly robust text editor for its ability to handle real expressions and other text-editing features that Management Studio, and even Visual Studio, will likely never have. That said, the Management Studio has, as it has added more features, become my preferred tool for editing SQL scripts for SQL Server.

Scripts are usually treated as a unit. That is, you are normally executing the entire script or nothing at all. They can make use of both system functions and local variables. As an example, let's look at a simple script that could be used to INSERT order records into a typical order header and order detail table scenario:

```
USE SomeDatabase

DECLARE @Ident int

INSERT INTO Orders
(CustomerID,OrderDate)
VALUES
(25, DATEADD(day,-1,GETDATE()))   -- this always sets the OrderDate to yesterday

SELECT @Ident = @@IDENTITY

INSERT INTO Details
(OrderID, ProductID, UnitPrice, Quantity)
VALUES
(@Ident, 1, 50, 25)

SELECT 'The OrderID of the INSERTed row is ' + CONVERT(varchar(8),@Ident)
```

We have six distinct commands working here, covering a range of different things that we might do in a script. We're using both system functions and local variables, the USE statement, INSERT statements, and both assignment and regular versions of the SELECT statement. They are all working in unison to accomplish one task — to insert complete orders into the database.

Batches

A *batch* is a grouping of T-SQL statements into one logical unit, and, while this seems a pretty basic concept (indeed, I cover it at length in my *Beginning* title), I find it to be one of the more frequently misunderstood concepts in SQL Server, even among experienced administrators and developers.

All of the statements within a batch are combined into one execution plan, so all statements are parsed together and must pass a validation of the syntax or none of the statements will execute. Note, however, that this does not prevent runtime errors from happening. In the event of a runtime error, any statement that has been executed prior to the runtime error will still be in effect. To summarize, if a statement fails at parse-time, then nothing runs. If a statement fails at runtime, then all statements until the statement that generated the error have already run.

All the scripts we have run up to this point are made up of one batch each. Even the script we've been analyzing so far in this chapter is just one batch. To separate a script into multiple batches, we make use of the GO statement. The GO statement:

❑   Must be on its own line (nothing other than a comment can be on the same line); there is an exception to this discussed shortly, but think of a GO as needing to be on a line to itself

❑   Causes all statements since the beginning of the script or the last GO statement (whichever is closer) to be compiled into one execution plan and sent to the server independently of any other batches

❑   Is not a T-SQL command, but, rather, a command recognized by the various SQL Server command utilities (OSQL, ISQL, and the Query Analyzer)

A Line to Itself

The GO command should stand alone on its own line. Technically, you can start a new batch on the same line after the GO command, but you'll find this puts a serious damper on readability. T-SQL statements cannot precede the GO statement, or the GO statement will often be misinterpreted and cause either a parsing error or some other unexpected result. For example, if I use a GO statement after a WHERE clause:

```
SELECT * FROM Customers WHERE CustomerID = 2 GO
```

The parser becomes somewhat confused:

```
Msg 102, Level 15, State 1, Line 1
Incorrect syntax near 'GO'.
```

Each Batch Is Sent to the Server Separately

Because each batch is processed independently, an error in one batch does not preclude another batch from running. To illustrate, take a look at some code:

```
USE AdventureWorks2008;

DECLARE @MyVarchar varchar(50);  --This DECLARE only lasts for this batch!

SELECT @MyVarchar = 'Honey, I''m home...';

PRINT 'Done with first Batch...';

GO

PRINT @MyVarchar;  --This generates an error since @MyVarchar
                   --isn't declared in this batch
PRINT 'Done with second Batch';

GO

PRINT 'Done with third batch';   -- Notice that this still gets executed
                                 -- even after the error
```

```
GO
```

If there were any dependencies between these batches, then either everything would fail — or, at the very least, everything after the point of error would fail — but it doesn't. Look at the results if you run the preceding script:

```
Done with first Batch...
Msg 137, Level 15, State 2, Line 2
Must declare the scalar variable "@MyVarchar".
Done with third batch
```

Again, each batch is completely autonomous in terms of runtime issues. Keep in mind though that you can build in dependencies in the sense that one batch may try to perform work that depends on the first batch being complete. We'll see some of this in the next section when we talk about what can and can't span batches.

GO Is Not a T-SQL Command

Thinking that GO is a T-SQL command is a common mistake. GO is a command that is recognized only by the editing tools (Management Studio, SQLCMD). If you use a third-party tool, then it may or may not support the GO command, but most that claim SQL Server support will.

When the editing tool encounters a GO statement, it sees it as a flag to terminate that batch, package it up, and send it as a single unit to the server, *without* including the GO. That's right; the server itself has absolutely no idea what GO is supposed to mean.

> If you try to execute a GO command in a pass-through query using ODBC, OLE DB, ADO, ADO.NET, or any other access method, you'll get an error message back from the server. The GO is merely an indicator to the tool that it is time to end the current batch, and time, if appropriate, to start a new one. In the case of the aforementioned access methods, they each have the concept of a "command" object. That command object may include multiple statements, but each execution of the command object is implied to represent exactly one batch.

> Keep this notion in mind if you are building scripts you want to be compatible with other RDBMSs. Your non-SQL Server target system will likely fail if you pass it the GO keyword.

Errors in Batches

Errors in batches fall into two categories:

❑   Syntax errors

❑   Runtime errors

If the query parser finds a *syntax error*, the processing of that batch is canceled immediately. Since syntax checking happens before the batch is compiled or executed, a failure during the syntax check means none of the batch will be executed, regardless of the position of the syntax error within the batch.

Runtime errors work quite a bit differently. Any statement that has already executed before the runtime error was encountered is already done, so anything that statement did will remain intact unless it is part of an uncommitted transaction. (Transactions are covered in Chapter 11, but the relevance here is that they imply an all or nothing situation.) What happens beyond the point of the runtime error depends on the nature of the error. Generally speaking, runtime errors will terminate execution of the batch from the point where the error occurred to the end of the batch. Some runtime errors, such as a referential-integrity violation will prevent only the offending statement from executing; all other statements in the batch will still be executed. This latter scenario is why error checking is so important. We will cover error checking in full in our chapter on stored procedures (see Chapter 10).

When to Use Batches

Batches have several purposes, but they all have one thing in common: They are used when something has to happen either before or separately from everything else in your script.

Statements That Require Their Own Batch

There are several commands that absolutely must be part of their own batch. These include:

- ❑   CREATE DEFAULT
- ❑   CREATE FUNCTION
- ❑   CREATE PROCEDURE
- ❑   CREATE RULE
- ❑   CREATE SCHEMA
- ❑   CREATE TRIGGER
- ❑   CREATE VIEW

If you want to combine any of these statements with other statements in a single script, then you will need to break them up into their own batch by using a GO statement.

> Note that, if you DROP an object, you may want to place the DROP in its own batch or at least with a batch of other DROP statements. Why? Well, if you're going to create an object later with the same name, the CREATE will fail during the parsing of your batch unless the DROP has already happened. That means you need to run the DROP in a separate and prior batch so it will be complete when the batch with the CREATE statement executes.

Using Batches to Establish Precedence

Perhaps the most likely scenario for using batches is when precedence is required — that is, you need one task to be completely done before the next task starts. Most of the time, SQL Server deals with this kind of situation just fine. The first statement in the script is the first executed, and the second statement in the script can rely on the server being in the proper state when the second statement runs. There are times, however, when SQL Server can't resolve this kind of issue.

Let's take the example of creating a database together with some tables:

```
CREATE DATABASE Test;

CREATE TABLE TestTable
(
    col1    int,
    col2    int
);
```

Execute this and, at first, it appears that everything has gone well:

```
Command(s) completed successfully.
```

However, things are not as they seem. Check out the INFORMATION_SCHEMA in the Test database, and you'll notice something is missing:

```
SELECT TABLE_CATALOG
FROM INFORMATION_SCHEMA.TABLES
WHERE TABLE_NAME = 'TestTable'
TABLE_CATALOG
---------------------------------------------------------------------------
master

(1 row(s) affected)
```

Hey! Why was the table created in the wrong database? The answer lies in what database was current when we ran the CREATE TABLE statement. In our case, it happened to be the master database, so that's where our table was created.

Note that you may have been somewhere other than the master database when you ran this, so you may get a different result. That's kind of the point though. You could be in pretty much any database. That's why making use of the USE statement is so important.

When you think about it, this seems like an easy thing to fix. Just make use of the USE statement, but before we test our new theory, we have to get rid of the old (okay, not that old) database:

```
USE MASTER;
DROP DATABASE Test;
```

We can then run our newly modified script:

```
CREATE DATABASE Test;

USE Test;

CREATE TABLE TestTable
(
    col1    int,
```

```
    col2    int
);
```

Unfortunately, this has its own problems:

```
Msg 911, Level 16, State 1, Line 3
Database 'Test' does not exist. Make sure that the name is entered correctly.
```

The parser tries to validate our code and finds that we are referencing a database with a USE command that doesn't exist. Ahh, now we see the need for our batches. We need the CREATE DATABASE statement to be completed before we try to use the new database:

```
CREATE DATABASE Test;
GO


USE Test;

CREATE TABLE TestTable
(
    col1    int,
    col2    int
);
```

Now things work a lot better. Our immediate results look the same:

```
Command(s) completed successfully.
```

But when we run our INFORMATION_SCHEMA query, things are confirmed:

```
TABLE_CATALOG
---------------------------------------------------------------------------
Test
(1 row(s) affected)
```

Let's move on to another example that shows an even more explicit need for precedence.

When you use an ALTER TABLE statement that significantly changes the type of a column or adds columns, you cannot make use of those changes until the batch that makes the changes has completed.

If we add a column to our TestTable table in our Test database and then try to reference that column without ending the first batch:

```
USE Test;

ALTER TABLE TestTable
    ADD col3 int;

INSERT INTO TestTable
(col1, col2, col3)
VALUES
(1,1,1);
```

We get an error message. SQL Server cannot resolve the new column name and therefore complains:

```
Msg 207, Level 16, State 1, Line 6
Invalid column name 'col3'.
```

Add one simple GO statement after the ADD col3 int though, and everything is working fine:

```
(1 row(s) affected)
```

SQLCMD

SQLCMD is a utility that allows you to run scripts from a command prompt in a Windows command box. This can be very nice for executing conversion or maintenance scripts, as well as a quick-and-dirty way to capture a text file.

SQLCMD replaces the older OSQL. OSQL is still included with SQL Server for backward compatibility only. An even older command-line utility — ISQL — is no longer supported.

The syntax for running SQLCMD from the command line includes a large number of different switches, and looks like this:

```
sqlcmd
[
{ { -U <login id> [ -P <password> ] } | -E }
]
[-S <server> [ \<instance > ] ] [ -H <workstation> ] [ -d <database> ]
[ -l <time out> ] [ -t <time out> ] [ -h <headers> ]
[ -s <col separator> ] [ -w <col width> ] [ -a <packet size> ]
[ -e ] [ -I ]
[ -c <cmd end> ] [ -L [ c ] ] [ -q "<query>" ] [ -Q "<query>" ]
[ -m <error level> ] [ -V ] [ -W ] [ -u ] [ -r [ 0 | 1 ] ]
[ -i <input file> ] [ -o <output file> ]
[ -f <codepage> | i:<codepage> [ <, o: <codepage> ]
[ -k [ 1 | 2 ] ]
[ -y <display width> ] [-Y <display width> ]
[ -p [ 1 ] ] [ -R ] [ -b ] [ -v ] [ -A ] [ -X [ 1 ] ] [ -x ]
[ -? ]
]
```

The single biggest thing to keep in mind with these flags is that many of them (but, oddly enough, not all of them) are case sensitive. For example, both -Q and -q will execute queries, but the first will exit SQLCMD when the query is complete, and the second won't.

So, let's try a quick query direct from the command line. Again, remember that this is meant to be run from the Windows command prompt (don't use the Management Console):

```
SQLCMD -Usa -Pmypass -Q "SELECT * FROM AdventureWorks2008.HumanResources.Employee"
```

The -P is the flag that indicates the password. If your server is configured with something other than a blank password (and it should be!), then you'll need to provide that password immediately following the -P with no space in between.

If you run this from a command prompt, you should get something like 290 rows back. Now, let's create a quick text file to see how it works when including a file. At the command prompt, type the following:

```
C:\>copy con testsql.sql
```

This should take you down to a blank line (with no prompt of any kind), where you can enter this:

```
SELECT * FROM AdventureWorks2008.HumanResources.Employee
```

Then press F6 and Return (this ends the creation of our text file). You should get back a message like:

```
1 file(s) copied.
```

Now let's retry our earlier query, using a script file this time. The command line at the prompt only has a slight change to it:

```
C:\>sqlcmd -Usa -Pmypass -i testsql.sql
```

This should get us exactly the same results as when we ran the query using -Q. The major difference is, of course, that we took the command from a file. The file could have had hundreds — if not thousands — of different commands in it.

There are a wide variety of different parameters for SQLCMD, but the most important are the login, the password, and the one that says what you want to do (straight query or input file). You can mix and match many of these parameters to obtain fairly complex behavior from this seemingly simple command-line tool.

Dynamic SQL: Generating Your Code on the Fly with the EXEC Command

Okay, so all this saving stuff away in scripts is all fine and dandy, but what if you don't know what code you need to execute until runtime?

As a side note, notice that we are done with SQLCMD for now. The following examples should be run utilizing the Management Console.

SQL Server allows us, with a few gotchas, to build our SQL statement on the fly using string manipulation. The need to do this usually stems from not being able to know the details about something until runtime. The syntax looks like this:

```
EXEC ({<string variable>|'<literal command string>'})
```

Or:

```
EXECUTE ({<string variable>|'<literal command string>'})
```

As with executing a stored proc, whether you use the EXEC or EXECUTE makes no difference.

Let's build an example in the AdventureWorks2008 database by creating a dummy table from which to grab our dynamic information:

```
USE AdventureWorks2008;
GO


--Create The Table. We'll pull info from here for our dynamic SQL
CREATE TABLE DynamicSQLExample
(
    TableID     int    IDENTITY   NOT NULL
        CONSTRAINT PKDynamicSQLExample
                PRIMARY KEY,
    SchemaName  varchar(128)    NOT NULL,
    TableName   varchar(128)    NOT NULL
);
GO


/* Populate the table. In this case, We're grabbing every user
** table object in this database                          */
INSERT INTO DynamicSQLExample
SELECT s.name AS SchemaName, t.name AS TableName
    FROM sys.schemas s
    JOIN sys.tables t
     ON s.schema_id = t.schema_id;
```

This should get us a response something like:

```
(78 row(s) affected)
```

To quote the old advertising disclaimer: "actual results may vary." It's going to depend on which examples you've already followed along with in the book, which ones you haven't, and for which ones you took the initiative and did a DROP on once you were done with them. In any case, don't sweat it too much.

Okay, so what we now have is a list of all the tables in our current database. Now let's say that we wanted to select some data from one of the tables, but we wanted to identify the table only at runtime by using its ID. For example, I'll pull out all the data for the table with an ID of 15:

```
DECLARE @SchemaName     varchar(128)
DECLARE @TableName      varchar(128)

-- Now, grab the table name that goes with our ID
SELECT @SchemaName = SchemaName, @TableName = TableName
    FROM DynamicSQLExample
    WHERE TableID = 15

-- Finally, pass that value into the EXEC statement
EXEC ('SELECT * FROM ' + @SchemaName + '.' + @TableName)
```

If your table names went into the DynamicSQLExample table the way mine did, then a TableID of 15 should equate to the ProductProductPhoto table. If so, you should wind up with something like this:

```
ProductID    ProductPhotoID Primary ModifiedDate
-----------  -------------- ------- -----------------------
1            1              1       1998-05-02 00:00:00.000
2            1              1       1998-05-02 00:00:00.000
3            1              1       1998-05-02 00:00:00.000

 ...
 ...
997          102            1       2003-06-01 00:00:00.000
998          102            1       2003-06-01 00:00:00.000
999          102            1       2003-06-01 00:00:00.000

(504 row(s) affected)
```

The Gotchas of EXEC

Like most things that are of interest, using EXEC is not without its little trials and tribulations. Among the gotchas of EXEC are:

❑   It runs under a separate scope than the code that calls it — that is, the calling code can't reference variables inside the EXEC statement, and the EXEC can't reference variables in the calling code after they are resolved into the string for the EXEC statement.

❑   By default, it runs under the same security context as the current user — not that of the calling object. Use the EXECUTE AS option to override this.

❑   It runs under the same connection and transaction context as the calling object (we'll discuss this further with transactions in Chapter 11).

❑   Concatenation that requires a function call must be performed on the EXEC string prior to actually calling the EXEC statement. You can't do the concatenation of function in the same statement as the EXEC call.

❑   EXEC cannot be used inside a user-defined function.

Each of these can be a little difficult to grasp, so let's look at each individually.

The Scope of EXEC

Determining variable scope with the EXEC statement is something less than intuitive. The actual statement line that calls the EXEC statement has the same scope as the rest of the batch or procedure that the EXEC statement is running in, but the code that is performed as a result of the EXEC statement is considered to be in its own batch. As is so often the case, this is best shown with an example:

```
USE AdventureWorks2008;

/* First, we'll declare to variables. One for stuff we're putting into
** the EXEC, and one that we think will get something back out (it won't)
*/
DECLARE @InVar    varchar(50);
DECLARE @OutVar   varchar(50);

-- Set up our string to feed into the EXEC command
```

```
SET @InVar = 'SELECT @OutVar = FirstName FROM Person.Person
    WHERE ContactID = 1';

-- Now run it
EXEC (@Invar);

-- Now, just to show there's no difference, run the select without using a in variable
EXEC ('SELECT @OutVar = FirstName FROM Person.Person WHERE BusinessEntityID = 1');

-- @OutVar will still be NULL because we haven't been able to put anything in it
SELECT @OutVar;
```

Now, look at the output from this:

```
Msg 137, Level 15, State 1, Line 1
Must declare the scalar variable '@OutVar'.
Msg 137, Level 15, State 1, Line 1
Must declare the scalar variable '@OutVar'.


-------------------------------------------------
NULL
(1 row(s) affected)
```

SQL Server wastes no time in telling us that we are scoundrels and clearly don't know what we're doing. Why do we get a "Must Declare" error message when we have already declared @OutVar? Because we've declared it in the outer scope — not within the EXEC itself.

Let's look at what happens if we run things a little differently:

```
USE AdventureWorks2008;

-- This time, we only need one variable. It does need to be longer though.
DECLARE @InVar    varchar(200);

/* Set up our string to feed into the EXEC command. This time we're going
** to feed it several statements at a time. They will all execute as one
** batch.
*/
SET @InVar = 'DECLARE @OutVar varchar(50)
            SELECT @OutVar = FirstName FROM Person.Person
                WHERE BusinessEntityID = 1
            SELECT ''The Value Is '' + @OutVar';

-- Now run it
EXEC (@Invar);
```

This time we get back results closer to what we expect:

```
-----------------------------------------------------------
The Value Is Ken
```

Notice the way that I'm using two quotation marks right next to each other to indicate that I really want a quotation mark rather than to terminate my string.

So, what we've seen here is that we have two different scopes operating, and nary the two shall meet. There is, unfortunately, no way to pass information between the inside and outside scopes without using an external mechanism such as a temporary table. If you decide to use a `temp` table to communicate between scopes, just remember that any temporary table created within the scope of your EXEC statement will live only for the life of that EXEC statement.

> This behavior of a `temp` table only lasting the life of the scope it is created in will show up again when we are dealing with triggers and sprocs.

A Small Exception to the Rule

There is one thing that happens inside the scope of the EXEC that can be seen after the EXEC is done — system functions. So, things like @@ROWCOUNT can still be used. Again, let's look at a quick example:

```
USE AdventureWorks2008;

EXEC('SELECT * FROM Sales.Customer');
SELECT 'The Rowcount is ' + CAST(@@ROWCOUNT as varchar);
```

This yields us (after the result set):

```
The Rowcount is 19820
```

Security Contexts and EXEC

When you give someone the right to run a stored procedure, you imply that he or she also gains the right to perform the actions called for within the sproc. For example, let's say we had a stored procedure that lists all the employees hired within the last year. Someone who has rights to execute the sproc can do so (and get results back) even if he or she does not have rights to the HumanResources.Employee table directly. This is really handy as it allows you to grant access to information for a very specific need without granting more general access to the underlying object.

Developers usually assume that this same implied right is valid for an EXEC statement also — not necessarily. Indeed, by default, any reference made inside an EXEC statement will be run under the security context of the current user. So, let's say I have the right to run a procedure called spNewEmployee, but I do not have rights to the Employee table. If spNewEmployee gets the values by running a simple SELECT statement, then everything is fine. If, however, spNewEmployee uses an EXEC statement to execute that SELECT statement, the EXEC statement will fail because I don't have the rights to perform a SELECT on the Employee table.

Fortunately, we now have some (albeit limited) options to get around this by utilizing the EXECUTE AS option that was added beginning in SQL Server 2005. We'll discuss the specifics of how to do so as we work with security in Chapter 19, when we will discuss how to run under a specific user context.

> The security context of an EXEC statement run within a stored procedure, user-defined function, or trigger can be overridden using the EXECUTE AS clause within the sproc, function, or trigger. EXECUTE AS will be discussed more fully when we discuss security in Chapter 19.

Use of Functions in Concatenation and EXEC

This one is actually more of a nuisance than anything else, since there is a reasonably easy workaround. Simply put, you can't run a function against your EXEC string in the argument for an EXEC. For example:

```
USE AdventureWorks2008;

-- This won't work
DECLARE @NumberOfLetters int;
SET @NumberOfLetters = 3;
EXEC('SELECT LEFT(LastName,' + CAST(@NumberOfLetters AS varchar) + ') AS FilingName
FROM Person.Person');
GO

-- But this does
DECLARE @NumberOfLetters AS int;
SET @NumberOfLetters = 3;
DECLARE @str AS varchar(255);
SET @str = 'SELECT LEFT(LastName,' + CAST(@NumberOfLetters AS varchar) + ') AS
FilingName FROM Person.Person';
EXEC(@str);
```

The first instance gets us an error message because the CAST function needs to be fully resolved prior to the EXEC line:

```
Msg 102, Level 15, State 1, Line 6
Incorrect syntax near 'CAST'.
```

But the second line works just fine because it is already a complete string:

```
FilingName
----------
Abb
Abe
Abe
...
Zuk
Zwi
Zwi
(19972 row(s) affected)
```

EXEC and UDFs

In short, you can't get there from here. You are not allowed to use EXEC to run dynamic SQL within a UDF — period. (Using EXEC to run a sproc is, however, legal in a few cases.)

Control-of-Flow Statements

Control-of-flow statements are a veritable must for any programming language these days. I can't imagine having to write my code where I couldn't change what commands to run depending on a condition.

Given that we're assuming at least an intermediate knowledge of both programming and SQL, we're not going to dwell on these a lot, but since "intermediate" means different things to different people, we had best give these the once over.

T-SQL offers most of the classic choices for control-of-flow situations, including:

- ❏ IF...ELSE
- ❏ GOTO
- ❏ WHILE
- ❏ WAITFOR
- ❏ TRY/CATCH

We also have the CASE statement (a.k.a. SELECT CASE, DO CASE, and SWITCH/BREAK in other languages), but it doesn't have quite the level of control of flow capabilities that you've come to expect from other languages.

The IF . . . ELSE Statement

IF...ELSE statements work much as they do in any language, although I equate them most closely to C in the way they are implemented. The basic syntax is:

```
IF <Boolean Expression>
    <SQL statement> | BEGIN <code series> END
[ELSE
    <SQL statement> | BEGIN <code series> END]
```

The expression can be pretty much any expression that evaluates to a Boolean.

This brings us back to one of the most common traps that I see SQL programmers fall into — improper use of NULLs. I can't tell you how often I have debugged stored procedures only to find a statement like:

```
IF @myvar = NULL
```

This will, of course, never be true on most systems (see the exception shortly) and will wind up bypassing all their NULL values. Instead, it needs to read:

```
IF @myvar IS NULL
```

The exception to this is dependent on whether you have set the ANSI_NULLS option ON or OFF. The default is that this is ON, in which case you'll see the behavior described previously. You can change this behavior by setting ANSI_NULLS to OFF. I strongly recommend against this since it violates the ANSI standard (it's also just plain wrong).

Note that only the very next statement after the IF will be considered to be conditional (as per the IF). You can include multiple statements as part of your control-of-flow block using BEGIN...END, but we'll discuss that one a little later in the chapter.

To show off a simple version of this, let's run an example that's very common to build scripts. Imagine for a moment that we want to CREATE a table if it's not there, but to leave it alone if it already exists. We could make use of the EXISTS operator. (You may recall my complaint that the Books Online calls EXISTS a keyword when I consider it an operator.)

```
-- We'll run a SELECT for our table to start with to prove it's not there
SELECT 'Found Table ' + s.name + '.' + t.name
   FROM sys.schemas s
   JOIN sys.tables t
       ON s.schema_id = t.schema_id
   WHERE s.name = 'dbo'
     AND t.name = 'OurIFTest';


-- Now we're run our conditional CREATE statement
IF NOT EXISTS (
    SELECT s.name AS SchemaName, t.name AS TableName
       FROM sys.schemas s
       JOIN sys.tables t
           ON s.schema_id = t.schema_id
       WHERE s.name = 'dbo'
         AND t.name = 'OurIFTest'
             )
    CREATE TABLE OurIFTest(
       Col1    int        PRIMARY KEY
       );

-- And now look again to prove that it's been created.
SELECT 'Found Table ' + s.name + '.' + t.name
   FROM sys.schemas s
   JOIN sys.tables t
       ON s.schema_id = t.schema_id
   WHERE s.name = 'dbo'
     AND t.name = 'OurIFTest';
```

The meat of this is in the middle. Notice that our CREATE TABLE statement runs only if no matching table already exists:

```
-----------------------------------------------------------------------------

(0 row(s) affected)


-----------------------------------------------------------------------------
Found Table dbo.OurIFTest

(1 row(s) affected)
```

The ELSE Clause

Now this thing about being able to run a statement conditionally is just great, but it doesn't really deal with all the scenarios we might want to deal with. Quite often — indeed, most of the time — when we deal with an IF condition, we have specific statements we want to execute not just for the true condition, but also a separate set of statements that we want to run if the condition is false — or the ELSE condition.

> You will run into situations where a Boolean cannot be evaluated — that is, the result is unknown (for example, if you are comparing to a NULL). Any expression that returns a result that would be considered as an unknown result will be treated as FALSE.

The ELSE statement works pretty much as it does in any other language. The exact syntax may vary slightly, but the nuts and bolts are still the same. The statements in the ELSE clause are executed if the statements in the IF clause are not.

To expand our earlier example just a bit, let's actually print a warning message out if we do not create our table:

```
-- Now we're run our conditional CREATE statement
IF NOT EXISTS (
    SELECT s.name AS SchemaName, t.name AS TableName
        FROM sys.schemas s
        JOIN sys.tables t
            ON s.schema_id = t.schema_id
        WHERE s.name = 'dbo'
          AND t.name = 'OurIFTest'
            )
    CREATE TABLE OurIFTest(
        Col1    int        PRIMARY KEY
        );
ELSE
    PRINT 'WARNING: Skipping CREATE as table already exists';
```

If you have already run the preceding example, then the table will already exist, and running this second example should get you the warning message:

```
WARNING: Skipping CREATE as table already exists
```

Grouping Code into Blocks

Sometimes you need to treat a group of statements as though they were all one statement. (If you execute one, then you execute them all, otherwise, you don't execute any of them.) For instance, the IF statement will, by default, consider only the very next statement after the IF to be part of the conditional code. What if you want the condition to require several statements to run? Life would be pretty miserable if you had to create a separate IF statement for each line of code you wanted to run if the condition holds.

Thankfully, like most any language with an IF statement, SQL Server gives us a way to group code into blocks that are considered to all belong together. The block is started when you issue a BEGIN statement and continues until you issue an END statement. It works like this:

```
IF <Expression>
BEGIN    --First block of code starts here -- executes only if
         --expression is TRUE
    Statement that executes if expression is TRUE
    Additional statements
    ...
    ...
```

```
    Still going with statements from TRUE expression
    IF <Expression>   --Only executes if this block is active
        BEGIN
            Statement that executes if both outside and inside
                expressions are TRUE
            Additional statements
            ...
            ...
            Still statements from both TRUE expressions
        END
    Out of the condition from inner condition, but still
        part of first block
END     --First block of code ends here
ELSE
BEGIN
    Statement that executes if expression is FALSE
    Additional statements
    ...
    ...
    Still going with statements from FALSE expression
END
```

Notice our ability to nest blocks of code. In each case, the inner blocks are considered to be part of the outer block of code. I have never heard of there being a limit to how many levels deep you can nest your BEGIN...END blocks, but I would suggest that you minimize them. There are definitely practical limits to how deep you can keep them readable — even if you are particularly careful about the formatting of your code.

Just to put this notion into play, let's make yet another modification to table creation. This time, we're going to provide an informational message regardless of whether the table was created or not:

```
-- This time we're adding a check to see if the table DOES already exist
-- We'll remove it if it does so that the rest of our example can test the
-- IF condition. Just remove this first IF EXISTS block if you want to test
-- the ELSE condition below again.
IF EXISTS (
    SELECT s.name AS SchemaName, t.name AS TableName
        FROM sys.schemas s
        JOIN sys.tables t
            ON s.schema_id = t.schema_id
        WHERE s.name = 'dbo'
          AND t.name = 'OurIFTest'
            )
    DROP TABLE OurIFTest;

-- Now we're run our conditional CREATE statement
IF NOT EXISTS (
    SELECT s.name AS SchemaName, t.name AS TableName
        FROM sys.schemas s
        JOIN sys.tables t
            ON s.schema_id = t.schema_id
        WHERE s.name = 'dbo'
            AND t.name = 'OurIFTest'
            )
```

```
    BEGIN
        PRINT 'Table dbo.OurIFTest not found.'
        PRINT 'CREATING: Table dbo.OurIFTest'
        CREATE TABLE OurIFTest(
            Col1    int    PRIMARY KEY
            );
    END
ELSE
        PRINT 'WARNING: Skipping CREATE as table already exists';
```

Now, we've mixed all sorts of uses of the IF statement there. We have the most basic IF statement — with no BEGIN...END or ELSE. In our other IF statement, the IF portion uses a BEGIN...END block, but the ELSE does not.

I did one this way just to illustrate how you can mix them. That said, I recommend you go back to my old axiom of "be consistent." It can be really hard to deal with what statement is being controlled by what IF...ELSE condition if you are mixing the way you group things. In practice, if I'm using BEGIN...END on any statement within a given IF, then I use them for every block of code in that IF statement even if there is only one statement for that particular condition.

The CASE Statement

The CASE statement is, in some ways, the equivalent of one of several different statements depending on the language from which you're coming. Statements in procedural programming languages that work in a similar way to CASE include:

- ❑ Switch: C, C++, C#, Delphi
- ❑ Select Case: Visual Basic
- ❑ Do Case: Xbase
- ❑ Evaluate: COBOL

I'm sure there are others; these are just from the languages that I've worked with in some form or another over the years. The big drawback in using a CASE statement in T-SQL is that it is, in many ways, more of a substitution operator than a control-of-flow statement.

There is more than one way to write a CASE statement: with an input expression or a Boolean expression. The first option is to use an input expression that will be compared with the value used in each WHEN clause. The SQL Server documentation refers to this as a simple CASE:

```
CASE <input expression>
WHEN <when expression> THEN <result expression>
[...n]
[ELSE <result expression>]
END
```

Option number two is to provide an expression with each WHEN clause that will evaluate to TRUE/FALSE. The docs refer to this as a searched CASE:

```
CASE
WHEN <Boolean expression> THEN <result expression>
```

```
    [...n]
    [ELSE <result expression>]
END
```

Perhaps what's nicest about CASE is that you can use it "inline" with (that is, as an integral part of) a SELECT statement. This can actually be quite powerful.

A Simple CASE

A simple CASE takes an expression that equates to a Boolean result. Let's get right to an example:

```
USE AdventureWorks2008;
GO

SELECT TOP 10 SalesOrderID, SalesOrderID % 10 AS 'Last Digit', Position =
CASE SalesOrderID % 10
    WHEN 1 THEN 'First'
    WHEN 2 THEN 'Second'
    WHEN 3 THEN 'Third'
    WHEN 4 THEN 'Fourth'
    ELSE 'Something Else'
END
FROM Sales.SalesOrderHeader;
```

For those of you who aren't familiar with it, the % operator is for a *modulus*. A modulus works in a similar manner to the divide by (/), but it gives you only the remainder. Therefore, 16 % 4 = 0 (4 goes into 16 evenly), but 16 % 5 = 1. (16 divided by 5 has a remainder of 1.) In the example, since we're dividing by 10, using the modulus is giving us the last digit of the number we're evaluating.

Let's see what we got with this:

```
SalesOrderID Last Digit  Position
------------ ----------- --------------
75124        4           Fourth
43793        3           Third
51522        2           Second
57418        8           Something Else
43767        7           Something Else
51493        3           Third
72773        3           Third
43736        6           Something Else
51238        8           Something Else
53237        7           Something Else

(10 row(s) affected)
```

Notice that whenever there is a matching value in the list, the THEN clause is invoked. Since we have an ELSE clause, any value that doesn't match one of the previous values will be assigned whatever we've put in our ELSE. If we had left the ELSE out, then any such value would be given a NULL.

Let's go with one more example that expands on what we can use as an expression. This time, we'll use another column from our query:

```
USE AdventureWorks2008;
GO

SELECT TOP 10 SalesOrderID % 10 AS 'OrderLastDigit',
    ProductID % 10 AS 'ProductLastDigit',
    "How Close?" = CASE SalesOrderID % 10
        WHEN ProductID % 1 THEN 'Exact Match!'
        WHEN ProductID % 1 - 1 THEN 'Within 1'
        WHEN ProductID % 1 + 1 THEN 'Within 1'
        ELSE 'More Than One Apart'
    END
FROM Sales.SalesOrderDetail
ORDER BY SalesOrderID DESC;
```

Notice that we've used equations at every step of the way on this one, yet it still works . . . .

```
OrderLastDigit ProductLastDigit How Close?
-------------- ---------------- --------------------
4              5                More Than One Apart
3              2                More Than One Apart
3              9                More Than One Apart
3              8                More Than One Apart
2              2                More Than One Apart
2              8                More Than One Apart
1              7                Within 1
1              0                Within 1
1              1                Within 1
0              2                Exact Match!

(10 row(s) affected)
```

As long as the expression evaluates to a specific value that is of compatible type to the input expression, it can be analyzed, and the proper THEN clause applied.

A Searched CASE

This one works pretty much the same as a simple CASE, with only two slight twists:

❑   There is no input expression. (Remember, that's the part between the CASE and the first WHEN.)

❑   The WHEN expression must evaluate to a Boolean value (whereas in the simple CASE examples we've just looked at, we used values such as 1, 3, and ProductID + 1).

Perhaps what I find the coolest about this kind of CASE is that we can completely change around what is forming the basis of our expression — mixing and matching column expressions, depending on our different possible situations.

As usual, I find the best way to get across how this works is via an example:

```
SELECT TOP 10 SalesOrderID % 10 AS 'OrderLastDigit',
```

```
        ProductID % 10 AS 'ProductLastDigit',
        "How Close?" = CASE
            WHEN (SalesOrderID % 10) < 3 THEN 'Ends With Less Than Three'
            WHEN ProductID = 6 THEN 'ProductID is 6'
            WHEN ABS(SalesOrderID % 10 - ProductID) <= 1 THEN 'Within 1'

            ELSE 'More Than One Apart'
        END
    FROM Sales.SalesOrderDetail
    ORDER BY SalesOrderID DESC;
```

This is substantially different from our simple CASE examples, but it still works:

```
OrderLastDigit ProductLastDigit How Close?
-------------- ---------------- ------------------------
4              5                More Than One Apart
3              2                More Than One Apart
3              9                More Than One Apart
3              8                More Than One Apart
2              2                Ends With Less Than Three
2              8                Ends With Less Than Three
1              7                Ends With Less Than Three
1              0                Ends With Less Than Three
1              1                Ends With Less Than Three
0              2                Ends With Less Than Three

(10 row(s) affected)
```

These are a few of the things to pay particular attention to in how SQL Server evaluated things:

❏   Even when two conditions evaluate to TRUE, only the first condition is used. For example, the second-to-last row meets both the first (the last digit is smaller than 3) and third (the last digit is within 1 of the ProductID) conditions. For many languages, including Visual Basic, this kind of statement always works this way. If you're from the C world, however, you'll need to remember this when you are coding; no "break" statement is required. A CASE statement always terminates after one condition is met.

❏   You can mix and match what fields you're using in your condition expressions. In this case, we used SalesOrderID, ProductID, and both together.

❏   You can perform pretty much any expression as long as, in the end, it evaluates to a Boolean result.

Looping with the WHILE Statement

The WHILE statement works much as it does in other languages to which you have probably been exposed. Essentially, a condition is tested each time you come to the top of the loop. If the condition is still TRUE, then the loop executes again; if not, you exit.

The syntax looks like this:

```
WHILE <Boolean expression>
    <sql statement> |
```

```
[BEGIN
     <statement block>
     [BREAK]
     <sql statement> | <statement block>
     [CONTINUE]
END]
```

While you can just execute one statement (much as you do with an IF statement), you'll almost never see a WHILE that isn't followed by a BEGIN...END with a full statement block.

The BREAK statement is a way of exiting the loop without waiting for the bottom of the loop to come and the expression to be re-evaluated.

I'm sure I won't be the last to tell you this, but using a BREAK is generally thought of as something of bad form in the classical sense. I tend to sit on the fence on this one. I avoid using them if reasonably possible. Most of the time, I can indeed avoid them just by moving a statement or two around, while still coming up with the same results. The advantage of this is usually more readable code. It is simply easier to handle a looping structure (or any structure for that matter) if you have a single point of entry and a single exit. Using a BREAK violates this notion.

All that being said, sometimes you can actually make things worse by reformatting the code to avoid a BREAK. In addition, I've seen people write much slower code for the sake of not using a BREAK statement — bad idea.

The CONTINUE statement is something of the opposite of a BREAK statement. In short, it tells the WHILE loop to go back to the beginning. Regardless of where you are in the loop, you immediately go back to the top and re-evaluate the expression (exiting if the expression is no longer TRUE).

We'll go ahead and do something of a short example here just to get our feet wet. As I mentioned before, WHILE loops tend to be rare in non-cursor situations, so forgive me if this example seems lame.

What we're going to do is create something of a monitoring process using our WHILE loop and a WAITFOR command. (We'll look at the specifics of WAITFOR in our next section.) We're going to be automatically updating our statistics once per day:

```
WHILE 1 = 1
BEGIN
   WAITFOR TIME '01:00'
   EXEC sp_updatestats
   RAISERROR('Statistics Updated for Database', 1, 1) WITH LOG
END
```

This would update the statistics for every table in our database every night at 1 AM and write a log entry of that fact to both the SQL Server log and the Windows application log. If you want to check to see if this works, leave this running all night and then check your logs in the morning.

Note that using an infinite loop like this isn't the way that you would normally want to schedule a task. If you want something to run every day, set up a job using Management Studio. In addition to not keeping a connection open all the time (which the preceding example would do), you also get the capability to make follow up actions dependent on the success or failure of your script. Also, you can e-mail or netsend messages regarding the completion status.

The WAITFOR Statement

There are often things that you either don't want to or simply can't have happen right this moment, but you also don't want to have to hang around waiting for the right time to execute something.

No problem — use the WAITFOR statement and have SQL Server wait for you. The syntax is incredibly simple:

```
WAITFOR
    DELAY <'time'> | TIME <'time'>
```

The WAITFOR statement does exactly what it says it does. It waits for whatever you specify as the argument to occur. You can specify either an explicit time of day for something to happen, or you can specify an amount of time to wait before doing something.

The DELAY Parameter

The DELAY parameter choice specifies an amount of time to wait. You cannot specify a number of days — just time in hours, minutes, and seconds. The maximum allowed delay is 24 hours. So, for example:

```
WAITFOR DELAY '01:00'
```

would run any code prior to the WAITFOR, then reach the WAITFOR statement, and stop for one hour, after which execution of the code would continue with whatever the next statement was.

The TIME Parameter

The TIME parameter choice specifies to wait until a specific time of day. Again, we cannot specify any kind of date — just the time of day using a 24-hour clock. Once more, this gives us a one-day time limit for the maximum amount of delay. For example:

```
WAITFOR TIME '01:00'
```

would run any code prior to the WAITFOR, then reach the WAITFOR statement, and stop until 1 AM, after which execution of the code would continue with whatever the next statement was after the WAITFOR.

TRY/CATCH Blocks

This is yet another one of those areas that I would consider to be critical learning when learning your basics, so, in theory, you should know it well by the time you get to the "Professional" level. That said, TRY/CATCH is still relatively new (it was added in SQL Server 2005), and, if you've grown up supporting an older application, you may not have seen this lovely new addition or may have been avoiding it for backward compatibility reasons.

In days of yore (meaning anything before SQL Server 2005), our error-handling options were pretty limited. We could check for error conditions, but we had to do so proactively. Indeed, in some cases we could have errors that would cause us to leave our procedure or script without an opportunity to trap it at all. (This can still happen, but is much more limited.) We're going to save a more full discussion of error handling for our stored procedures discussion in Chapter 10, but we'll touch on the fundamentals of the new TRY/CATCH blocks here.

A `TRY/CATCH` block in SQL Server works remarkably similarly to those used in any C-derived languages (C, C++, C#, Delphi, and a host of others). The syntax looks like this:

```
BEGIN TRY
     { <sql statement(s)> }
END TRY
BEGIN CATCH
     { <sql statement(s)> }
END CATCH [ ; ]
```

In short, SQL Server will "try" to run anything within the `BEGIN...END` that goes with your `TRY` block. If, and only if, you have an error condition that has an error level of 11–19, then SQL Server will exit the `TRY` block immediately and begin with the first line in your `CATCH` block. Since there are more possible error levels than just 11–19, take a look at what we have there:

Error Level	Nature
1–10	Informational only. This would include things like context changes such as settings being adjusted or `NULL` values found while calculating aggregates. These will not trigger a `CATCH` block, so if you need to test for this level of error, you'll need to do so manually by checking `@@ERROR`.
11–19	Relatively severe errors, but ones that can be handled by your code (foreign key violations, as an example). Some of these can be severe enough that you are unlikely to want to continue processing (such as a memory exceeded error), but at least you can trap them and exit gracefully.
20–25	Very severe. These are generally system-level errors. Your server-side code will never know this kind of error happened, as the script and connection will be terminated immediately, and the `CATCH` block will never execute.

Keep these in mind — if you need to handle errors outside the 11–19 level range, then you'll need to make other plans. The good news is that most errors that we need to trap fall in that 11–19 range.

Now, to test this out, we'll make some alterations to our `CREATE` script that we built back when we were looking at `IF...ELSE` statements. You may recall that part of the reason for our original test to see whether the table already existed was to avoid creating an error condition that might have caused our script to fail. That kind of test is the way things have been done historically (and there really wasn't much in the way of other options). With the advent of `TRY/CATCH` blocks, we could just try the `CREATE` and then handle the error if one were given:

```
BEGIN TRY
    -- Try and create our table
    CREATE TABLE OurIFTest(
        Col1    int         PRIMARY KEY
        )
END TRY
BEGIN CATCH
    -- Uh oh, something went wrong, see if it's something
    -- we know what to do with
    DECLARE @ErrorNo    int,
            @Severity   tinyint,
            @State      smallint,
            @LineNo     int,
```

```
           @Message     nvarchar(4000)
    SELECT
        @ErrorNo = ERROR_NUMBER(),
        @Severity = ERROR_SEVERITY(),
        @State = ERROR_STATE(),
        @LineNo = ERROR_LINE (),
        @Message = ERROR_MESSAGE()

    IF @ErrorNo = 2714 -- Object exists error, we knew this might happen
        PRINT 'WARNING: Skipping CREATE as table already exists'
    ELSE -- hmm, we don't recognize it, so report it and bail
        RAISERROR(@Message, 16, 1 )
END CATCH
```

Notice I used some special functions to retrieve the error condition, so let's take a look at those.

Also note that I moved them into variables that were controlled by me so they would not be lost. I must admit this is a holdover habit that I have from the days before TRY/CATCH, *when you would lose the error code on the next statement. The functions used here persist within the scope of the particular* CATCH *block, so you are relatively safe against losing their values. The primary reason to move the values over, at this point, is if you want to utilize the error values after you exit the* CATCH *block.*

Function	Returns
ERROR_NUMBER()	The actual error number. If this is a system error, there will be an entry in the sys.messages that matches that error and contains some of the information you'll get from the other error-related functions.
ERROR_SEVERITY()	This equates to what is sometimes called "error level" in other parts of this book and Books Online. My apologies for the inconsistency. I'm guilty of perpetuating something that Microsoft started doing a version or two ago. Again, the "severity" must be 11–19 before the error will wind up in a catch block. (See the previous table in this chapter for further discussion on this.)
ERROR_STATE()	I use this as something of a place mark. This will always be 1 for system errors. When we discuss error handling in more depth in Chapter 10, you'll see how to raise your own errors. At that point, you can use state to indicate things like at what point in your stored procedure, function, or trigger the error occurred (this helps with situations where a given error can be handled in any one of many places).
ERROR_PROCEDURE()	We did not use this in the preceding example, as it is only relevant to stored procedures, functions, and triggers. This supplies the name of the procedure that caused the error — very handy if your procedures are nested at all, as the procedure that causes the error may not be the one to actually handle that error.
ERROR_LINE()	Just what it says — the line number of the error.
ERROR_MESSAGE()	The text that goes with the message. For system messages, this is the same as what you'll see if you select the message from the sys.messages function. For user-defined errors, it will be the text supplied to the RAISERROR function.

In our example, I utilized a known error id that SQL Server raises if we attempt to create an object that already exists. You can see all system error messages by selecting them from the sys.messages table function.

> *Beginning with SQL Server 2005, the* sys.messages *output grew so lengthy that it's hard to find what you're looking for by just scanning it. My solution is less than elegant but is rather effective. I just artificially create the error I'm looking for and see what error number it gives me (simple solutions for simple minds like mine!).*
>
> *I simply execute the code I want to execute (in this case, the* CREATE *statement) and handle the error if there is one; there really isn't much more to it than that.*

We will look at error handling in a far more thorough fashion in Chapter 10. In the meantime, you can use TRY/CATCH to give basic error handling to your scripts.

Summary

Understanding scripts and batches is the cornerstone to an understanding of programming with SQL Server. The concepts of scripts and batches lay the foundation for a variety of functions from scripting complete database builds to programming stored procedures and triggers.

Local variables have scope for only one batch. Even if you have declared the variable within the same overall script, you will still get an error message if you don't redeclare it (and start over with assigning values) before referencing it in a new batch.

You can use batches to create precedence between different parts of your scripts. The first batch starts at the beginning of the script and ends at the end of the script or the first GO statement, whichever comes first. The next batch (if there is another) starts on the line after the first one ends and continues to the end of the script or the next GO statement — again, whichever comes first. The process continues to the end of the script. The first batch from the top of the script is executed first, the second is executed second, and so on. All commands within each batch must pass validation in the query parser, or none of that batch will be executed; however, any other batches will be parsed separately and will still be executed (if they pass the parser).

In addition, we reviewed the constructs to deal with control of flow and error-handling conditions. We can use this to build complex scripts that are able to adapt to different runtime environments (such as recognizing that it needs to process an upgrade of a database instead of an installation, or even determine what version of your schema it is upgraded from).

Finally, we also saw how we can create and execute SQL dynamically. This can afford us the opportunity to deal with scenarios that aren't always 100 percent predictable or situations where something we need to construct our statement is actually itself a piece of data.

In the next couple of chapters, we will take the notions of scripting and batches to the next level, and apply them to stored procedures and triggers — the closest things that SQL Server has to actual programs. We will also see how we can utilize any .NET language to add more complex language functionality to our stored procedures, functions, and triggers.

10

Advanced Programmability

When deciding on where the cutoff should be between my *Beginning* and *Professional* titles, this was, perhaps, the most difficult area for me to reconcile. The thing is, how much a supposed "SQL Server jock" knows about things beyond basic DML really varies a lot, so what exactly qualifies someone as ready to do the "Professional" level title?

In this chapter, I'm going to assume that you already know the basics of stored procedures and user-defined functions (the differences between them, types of SQL-based user-defined functions, parameterization, and basic control of flow statements). After all, if they are "the basics," then they seem more appropriate for a beginning title (and, indeed, I cover them at length in *Beginning SQL Server 2008 Programming*). So what, then, is this chapter all about? Well, it's about all the things that go beyond the basics. In this section, we'll cover:

❑   OUTPUT parameters (often misunderstood by even advanced SQL programmers)

❑   Error handling (again, I cover this somewhat in the *Beginning* title, but it's so often misunderstood even amongst advanced SQL programmers that it deserves revisiting)

❑   Table-valued parameters (new with SQL Server 2008)

❑   .NET-based stored procedures and user-defined functions

Even paring out the so called basics, there is a lot to be covered, so let's get to it.

> *Most of the concepts provided in this chapter apply relatively equally to both stored procedures and user-defined functions.*

A More Advanced Look At Stored Procedures

Stored procedures — or "sprocs" — have long been fundamental to truly "programming" in SQL Server. Prior to SQL Server 2005, they could be complex, but even the most complex was still relatively mundane given the limitations of T-SQL. With each release, however, Microsoft has added more to the puzzle. It was a rather big leap in the case of .NET assemblies (again, beginning with SQL Server 2005 — we'll cover those a little later in this chapter), and the addition of table-valued parameters in SQL Server 2008 brings a lot of continuity to what we can do inside of a stored procedure.

Let's start this section off with a review of the general sproc syntax:

```
CREATE PROCEDURE|PROC <sproc name>
   [<parameter name> [<schema>.]<data type> [VARYING]
         [= <default value>] [OUT[PUT]] [READONLY]
 [, n...]
[WITH
    RECOMPILE| ENCRYPTION | [EXECUTE AS { CALLER|SELF|OWNER|'<user name>'}]
[FOR REPLICATION]
AS
    <code> | EXTERNAL NAME <assembly name>.<assembly class>.<method>
```

Most of this should be second nature at this point, but, before this chapter is done, we will have captured any elements of the syntax that you may not be as comfortable with.

Let's start by taking a look at output parameters.

Output Parameters

Sometimes, you want to pass non-recordset information out to whatever called your sproc. Perhaps one of the most common uses for this is with sprocs that do inserts into tables with identity values. Often the code calling the sproc wants to know what the identity value was when the process is complete.

To show this off, we'll utilize a stored procedure that is already in the AdventureWorks2008 database — uspLogError. It looks like this:

```
-- uspLogError logs error information in the ErrorLog table about the
-- error that caused execution to jump to the CATCH block of a
-- TRY...CATCH construct. This should be executed from within the scope
-- of a CATCH block otherwise it will return without inserting error
-- information.
CREATE PROCEDURE [dbo].[uspLogError]
    @ErrorLogID [int] = 0 OUTPUT -- contains the ErrorLogID of the row inserted
                                 -- by uspLogError in the ErrorLog table
AS
BEGIN
    SET NOCOUNT ON;

    -- Output parameter value of 0 indicates that error
    -- information was not logged
    SET @ErrorLogID = 0;

    BEGIN TRY
        -- Return if there is no error information to log
        IF ERROR_NUMBER() IS NULL
            RETURN;
```

```
        -- Return if inside an uncommittable transaction.
        -- Data insertion/modification is not allowed when
        -- a transaction is in an uncommittable state.
        IF XACT_STATE() = -1
        BEGIN
            PRINT 'Cannot log error since the current transaction is in an
uncommittable state. '
                + 'Rollback the transaction before executing uspLogError in order to
successfully log error information.';
            RETURN;
        END
        INSERT [dbo].[ErrorLog]
            (
            [UserName],
            [ErrorNumber],
            [ErrorSeverity],
            [ErrorState],
            [ErrorProcedure],
            [ErrorLine],
            [ErrorMessage]
            )
        VALUES
            (
            CONVERT(sysname, CURRENT_USER),
            ERROR_NUMBER(),
            ERROR_SEVERITY(),
            ERROR_STATE(),
            ERROR_PROCEDURE(),
            ERROR_LINE(),
            ERROR_MESSAGE()
            );

        -- Pass back the ErrorLogID of the row inserted
        SET @ErrorLogID = @@IDENTITY;

    END TRY
    BEGIN CATCH
        PRINT 'An error occurred in stored procedure uspLogError: ';
        EXECUTE [dbo].[uspPrintError];
        RETURN -1;
    END CATCH
END;
```

Note the sections that I've highlighted here — these are the core to our output parameter. The first declares the parameter as being an output parameter. The second makes the insert that utilizes the identity value, and finally the SET statement captures the identity value. When the procedure exits, the value in @ErrorLogID is passed to the calling script.

Let's utilize our TRY/CATCH example from the tail end of the previous chapter, but this time we'll make the call to uspLogError:

```
USE AdventureWorks2008;

BEGIN TRY
```

```
-- Try and create our table
CREATE TABLE OurIFTest(
    Col1    int     PRIMARY KEY
    )
END TRY
BEGIN CATCH
    -- Uh oh, something went wrong, see if it's something
    -- we know what to do with
    DECLARE @MyOutputParameter int;

    IF ERROR_NUMBER() = 2714 -- Object exists error, we knew this might happen
    BEGIN
        PRINT 'WARNING: Skipping CREATE as table already exists';
        EXEC dbo.uspLogError @ErrorLogID = @MyOutputParameter OUTPUT;
        PRINT 'A error was logged. The Log ID for our error was '
            + CAST(@MyOutputParameter AS varchar);
    END
    ELSE    -- hmm, we don't recognize it, so report it and bail
        RAISERROR('something not good happened this time around', 16, 1 );

END CATCH
```

If you run this in a database that does not already have the OurIFTest table, then you will get a simple:

```
Command(s) completed successfully.
```

But run it where the OurIFTest table already exists (for example, run it twice if you haven't run the CREATE code before), and you get something to indicate the error:

```
WARNING: Skipping CREATE as table already exists
A error was logged. The Log ID for our error was 1
```

Now run a little select against the error log table:

```
SELECT ErrorLogID, UserName, ErrorMessage
FROM ErrorLog
WHERE ErrorLogID = 1; -- change this value to whatever your
                      -- results said it was logged as
```

And you can see that the error was indeed properly logged:

```
ErrorLogID  UserName    ErrorMessage
----------- ----------- -------------------------------------------------
1           dbo         There is already an object named 'OurIFTest' ...

(1 row(s) affected)
```

There are several things that you should take note of between the sproc itself, and the usage of it by the calling script:

❑   The OUTPUT keyword was required for the output parameter in the sproc declaration.

❑ You must use the OUTPUT keyword when you call the sproc, much as you did when you declared the sproc. This gives SQL Server advance warning about the special handling that parameter will require. Be aware, however, that forgetting to include the OUTPUT keyword won't create a runtime error (you won't get any messages about it), but the value for the output parameter won't be moved into your variable (you'll just wind up with what was already there — most likely a NULL value). This means that you'll have what I consider to be the most dreaded of all computer terms — unpredictable results.

❑ The variable you assign the output result to does *not* have to have the same name as the internal parameter in the sproc. For example, in our previous sproc, the internal parameter in the error logging sproc was called @ErrorLogID, but the variable the value was passed to was called @MyOutputParameter.

❑ The EXEC (or EXECUTE) keyword was required since the call to the sproc wasn't the first thing in the batch (you can leave off the EXEC if the sproc call is the first thing in a batch) — personally, I recommend that you train yourself to use it regardless.

Dealing with Errors

This is one of those sections that squarely overlaps with my "Beginning" title. If you think about it a while, I hope you won't be that surprised.

The problem is fairly simple: Many who learn SQL do so almost by accident. That is, they either don't have a beginning book to read at all, or, at best, they skim an SQL title enough to get some statements crammed into their client language and eventually move on to some basic sprocs. While they know error handling in their client environment, they suddenly find themselves writing fairly complex stored procedures having learned the things required to actually make a sproc run, but not much about how a sproc really should be written. I overlap here to back up and catch a spot that a lot of intermediate to fairly advanced stored procedure authors often have very little real exposure to.

If you already have the whole error handling in SQL thing down cold, then I'd suggest just skimming through this section for new ideas, and otherwise moving on to the coverage of table-valued parameters and .NET programming in SQL Server.

Four common types of errors can happen in SQL Server:

❑ Errors that create runtime errors and stop your code from proceeding further.

❑ Errors that are informational in nature and do not create runtime errors. A non-zero error number is returned (if you ask), but no error is raised (and so no error trapping will be activated unless you are testing for that specific error).

❑ Errors that create runtime errors but continue execution within SQL Server such that you can trap them and respond in the manner of your choosing.

❑ Errors that are more logical in nature and to which SQL Server is essentially oblivious.

Now, here things get a bit sticky, and versions become important, so hang with me as I lead you down a winding road.

We touched on TRY/CATCH blocks some in our last chapter, and examined how to make use of them, but they weren't always a part of T-SQL. The possibilities for error handling have changed a lot over the years, and particularly so back in SQL Server 2005. Today, we have genuine error traps in the form of the aforementioned TRY/CATCH blocks. There is, as you might expect, backward compatibility to consider, but that continues to be less of a consideration as SQL Server 2000 fades in support.

One thing remains common between the old and new error-handling models: higher-level runtime errors. Some general errors cause SQL Server to terminate the script immediately. This was true prior to TRY/CATCH, and it remains true even in the TRY/CATCH era. Errors that have enough severity to generate a runtime error are problematic from the SQL Server side of the equation. The new TRY/CATCH logic is a bit more flexible for some errors than the error trapping model that preceded it, but even now your sproc won't necessarily know when something bad happens (it just depends how bad "bad" is). On the bright side, all the current data access object models pass through the message on such errors, so you know about them in your client application and can do something about them there.

The Way We Were

In older versions of SQL Server (prior to 2005), there was no formal error handler. You didn't have an option that essentially said, "If any error happens, go run this code over in this other spot." Instead, you had to monitor for error conditions within your own code and then decide what to do at the point you detected the error — possibly well after the actual error occurred. Let's go ahead and take a look at how we handle errors in that model.

In case you're in the "since we have the new TRY/CATCH blocks, why do I even care about this?" frame of mind, let me point out that there is tons of code out there written for those earlier versions of SQL Server (before TRY/CATCH), and continues to be older style code written by developers that either don't know the newer way or are just too much creatures of habit to use it. In short, it's important to understand this way of doing things, so you understand other code that you will see in your career.

Handling Inline Errors

Inline errors are those pesky little things where SQL Server keeps running as such, but hasn't, for some reason, succeeded in doing what you wanted it to do. For example, try to insert a record into the Person.EmailAddress table that doesn't have a corresponding record in the Person.BusinessEntity table:

```
USE AdventureWorks2008;
GO

INSERT INTO Person.EmailAddress
    (BusinessEntityID, EmailAddress)
VALUES
    (0, 'robv@professionalsql.com');
```

SQL Server won't perform this insert for you because there is a FOREIGN KEY constraint on BusinessEntityID that references another table. Since there is not a matching record in that table, the record we are trying to insert into Person.EmailAddress violates that foreign key constraint and is rejected:

```
Msg 547, Level 16, State 0, Line 2
The INSERT statement conflicted with the FOREIGN KEY constraint
```

```
"FK_EmailAddress_Person_BusinessEntityID". The conflict occurred in database
"AdventureWorks2008", table "Person.Person", column 'BusinessEntityID'.
The statement has been terminated.
```

Pay attention to that error 547 up there. That's something you can use.

Using @@ERROR

@@ERROR contains the error number of the last T-SQL statement executed. If the value is zero, then no error occurred. This is somewhat similar to the ERROR_NUMBER() function we saw in the previous chapter when we first discussed TRY/CATCH blocks. While ERROR_NUMBER() is only valid and remains the same regardless of where you are within a CATCH block, @@ERROR receives a new value with each statement you execute.

> The caveat with @@ERROR is that it is reset with each new statement. This means that if you want to defer analyzing the value, or you want to use it more than once, you need to move the value into some other holding bin — a local variable that you have declared for this purpose.

Play with this just a bit using the INSERT example from before:

```
USE AdventureWorks2008;
GO

DECLARE    @Error   int;

-- Bogus INSERT - there is no BusinessEntityID of 0.

INSERT INTO Person.EmailAddress
    (BusinessEntityID, EmailAddress)
VALUES
    (0, 'robv@professionalsql.com');

-- Move our error code into safekeeping. Note that, after this statement,
-- @@Error will be reset to whatever error number applies to this statement
SELECT @Error = @@ERROR;

-- Print out a blank separator line
PRINT '';

-- The value of our holding variable is just what we would expect
PRINT 'The Value of @Error is ' + CONVERT(varchar, @Error);

-- The value of @@ERROR has been reset - it's back to zero
PRINT 'The Value of @@ERROR is ' + CONVERT(varchar, @@ERROR);
```

Now execute your script, and you can examine how @@ERROR is affected:

```
Msg 547, Level 16, State 0, Line 6
The INSERT statement conflicted with the FOREIGN KEY constraint
"FK_EmailAddress_Person_BusinessEntityID". The conflict occurred in database
"AdventureWorks2008", table "Person.Person", column 'BusinessEntityID'.
The statement has been terminated.

The Value of @Error is 547
The Value of @@ERROR is 0
```

This illustrates pretty quickly the issue of saving the value from @@ERROR. The first error statement is only informational in nature. SQL Server has thrown that error, but hasn't stopped the code from executing. Indeed, the only part of that message that your sproc has access to is the error number. That error number resides in @@ERROR for just that next T-SQL statement; after that it's gone.

> Notice that **@Error** and **@@ERROR** are two separate and distinct variables, and can be referred to separately. This isn't just because of the case difference. (Depending on how you have your server configured, case sensitivity can affect your variable names.) It's because of the difference in scope. The **@** or **@@** is part of the name, so the number of **@** symbols on the front makes each one separate and distinct from the other.

Using @@ERROR in a Sproc

OK, so let's start with an assumption here: If you're using @@ERROR, then the likelihood is that you are not using TRY/CATCH blocks. If you have not made this choice for backward compatibility reasons, I'm going to bop you upside the head and suggest you reconsider — TRY/CATCH is much cleaner and all around better.

> **TRY/CATCH** will handle varieties of errors that in previous versions would have terminated the execution of your script.

That said, TRY/CATCH is out of the equation if backward compatibility with SQL Server 2000 or prior is what you need, so let's take a quick look.

What we're going to do is look at two short procedures to take a look at how inline error checking works when it works, and how it doesn't when it doesn't (in particular, when inline does not work, but TRY/CATCH would).

Let's start with the referential integrity example we did a moment ago:

```
USE AdventureWorks2008;
GO
```

```
INSERT INTO Person.EmailAddress
    (BusinessEntityID, EmailAddress)
VALUES
    (0, 'robv@professionalsql.com');
```

You may recall this got us a simple 547 error. This is one of those that is trappable. We could trap this in a simple script, but let's do it as a sproc since procedural stuff is supposedly what we're working on here . . . .

```
USE AdventureWorks2008;
GO

CREATE PROC spInsertValidatedEmailAddress
    @BusinessEntityID int,
    @EmailAddress nvarchar(50)
AS
BEGIN

    DECLARE @Error int;

    INSERT INTO Person.EmailAddress
        (BusinessEntityID, EmailAddress)
    VALUES
        (@BusinessEntityID, @EmailAddress);

    SET @Error = @@ERROR;

    IF @Error = 0
        PRINT 'New Record Inserted';
    ELSE
    BEGIN
        IF @Error = 547 -- Foreign Key violation. Tell them about it.
            PRINT 'At least one provided parameter was not found. Correct and retry';
        ELSE -- something unknown
            PRINT 'Unknown error occurred. Please contact your system admin';
    END
END
```

Now try executing this with values that work:

```
EXEC spInsertValidatedEmailAddress 1, 'robv@professionalsql.com';
```

Our insert happens correctly, so no error condition is detected (because there isn't one):

```
(1 row(s) affected)
New Record Inserted
```

Now, try something that should blow up:

```
EXEC spInsertValidatedEmailAddress 0, 'robv@professionalsql.com';
```

And you see not only the actual SQL Server message but the message from our error trap (note that there is no way of squelching the SQL Server message):

```
Msg 547, Level 16, State 0, Procedure spInsertValidatedEmailAddress, Line 10
The INSERT statement conflicted with the FOREIGN KEY constraint
"FK_EmailAddress_Person_BusinessEntityID". The conflict occurred in database
"AdventureWorks2008", table "Person.Person", column 'BusinessEntityID'.
The statement has been terminated.
At least one provided parameter was not found. Correct and retry
```

As you can see, we were able to detect our error without a TRY/CATCH block.

Now, let's move on to an example of why TRY/CATCH is better — a situation where a TRY/CATCH works fine, but where inline error checking fails. To show this one off, all we need to do is use our example for TRY/CATCH that we used in the scripting chapter. It looked like this:

```
BEGIN TRY
    -- Try and create our table
    CREATE TABLE OurIFTest(
        Col1    int         PRIMARY KEY
        )
END TRY
BEGIN CATCH
    -- Uh oh, something went wrong, see if it's something
    -- we know what to do with
    DECLARE @ErrorNo    int,
            @Severity    tinyint,
            @State       smallint,
            @LineNo      int,
            @Message     nvarchar(4000)
    SELECT
        @ErrorNo = ERROR_NUMBER(),
        @Severity = ERROR_SEVERITY(),
        @State = ERROR_STATE(),
        @LineNo = ERROR_LINE (),
        @Message = ERROR_MESSAGE()

    IF @ErrorNo = 2714 -- Object exists error, we knew this might happen
        PRINT 'WARNING: Skipping CREATE as table already exists'
    ELSE -- hmm, we don't recognize it, so report it and bail
        RAISERROR(@Message, 16, 1 )
END CATCH
```

It worked just fine. But if I try and do this using inline error checking, I have a problem:

```
CREATE TABLE OurIFTest(
    Col1    int         PRIMARY KEY
    );
IF @@ERROR != 0
    PRINT 'Problems!';
ELSE
    PRINT 'Everything went OK!';
```

Run this (you'll need to run it twice to generate the error if the table isn't already there), and we quickly find out that, without the TRY block, SQL Server aborts the script entirely on the particular error we're generating here:

```
Msg 2714, Level 16, State 6, Line 2
There is already an object named 'OurIFTest' in the database.
```

Notice that our PRINT statements never got a chance to execute — SQL Server had already terminated processing. With TRY/CATCH we were able to trap and handle this error, but using inline error checking, our attempts to trap an error like this fail.

Manually Raising Errors

Sometimes you have errors that SQL Server doesn't really know about, but you wish it did. For example, perhaps in the previous example you don't want to return −1000. Instead, you'd like to be able to create a runtime error at the client end that the client would then use to invoke an error handler and act accordingly. To do this, you use the RAISERROR command in T-SQL. The syntax is pretty straightforward:

```
RAISERROR (<message ID | message string>, <severity>, <state>
[, <argument>
[,<...n>]] )
[WITH option[,...n]]
```

Message ID/Message String

The message ID or message string you provide determines which message is sent to the client.

Using a message ID creates a manually raised error with the ID that you specified and the message that is associated with that ID as found in the sys.messages system view.

If you want to see what your SQL Server has as predefined messages, you can always perform a SELECT * FROM sys.messages. This includes any messages you've manually added to your system using the sp_addmessage stored procedure or through Management Studio.

You can also just supply a message string in the form of ad hoc text without creating a more permanent message in sys.messages:

```
RAISERROR ('Hi there, I''m an error', 1, 1);
```

This raises a rather simple error message:

```
Hi there, I'm an error
Msg 50000, Level 1, State 50000
```

Notice that the assigned message number, even though you didn't supply one, is 50000. This is the default error value for any ad hoc error. It can be overridden using the WITH SETERROR option. (We'll look at that briefly in a moment.)

Severity

We got a quick overview of this when looking at TRY/CATCH in the chapter on scripting. For those of you already familiar with Windows servers, severity should be an old friend. *Severity* is an indication of just how bad things really are based on this error. For SQL Server, however, what severity codes mean can get a little bizarre. They can range from informational (severities 1–18), to system level (19–25), and even catastrophic (20–25). If you raise an error of severity 19 or higher (system level), the WITH LOG option must also be specified. 20 and higher automatically terminates the users' connections. (They *hate* that!)

So, get back to what I meant by bizarre. SQL Server actually varies its behavior into more ranges than Windows does, or even than the Books Online will tell you about. Errors fall into five major groupings, as shown in the following table:

1–10	Purely informational but will return the specific error code in the message information.
11–16	If you do not have a TRY/CATCH block set up, then these terminate execution of the procedure and raise an error at the client. The state is shown to be whatever value you set it to. If you have a TRY/CATCH block defined, then that handler will be called rather than raising an error at the client.
17	Usually, only SQL Server should use this severity. Basically, it indicates that SQL Server has run out of resources — for example tempdb was full — and can't complete the request. Again, a TRY/CATCH block will get this before the client does.
18–19	Both of these are severe errors and imply that the underlying cause requires system administrator attention. With 19, the WITH LOG option is required, and the event will show up in the NT or Windows Event Log if you are using that OS family. These are the final levels at which you can trap the error with a TRY/CATCH block — after this, it will go straight to the client.
20–25	Your world has just caved in as has the user's connection. Essentially, this is a fatal error. The connection is terminated. As with 19, you must use the WITH LOG option, and a message will, if applicable, show up in the Event Log.

State

State is an ad hoc value. It's something that recognizes that exactly the same error may occur at multiple places within your code. The notion is that this gives you an opportunity to send something of a place marker for where exactly the error occurred.

State values can be between 1 and 127. If you are troubleshooting an error with Microsoft tech support, they apparently have some arcane knowledge that hasn't been shared with us about what some of these mean. I'm told that if you make a tech support call to Microsoft, they are likely to ask about and make use of this state information.

> *One way I make use of State when raising my own errors is as a location tool. There will be instances where your procedure has the potential to raise the same error in multiple places in the sproc — I will change the State information in my RAISERROR to provide an extra indication of which specific line raised the error.*

Error Arguments

Some predefined errors accept arguments. These allow you to make the error to be somewhat more dynamic by changing to the specific nature of the error. You can also format your error messages to accept arguments.

When you want to use dynamic information in what is otherwise a static error message, you need to format the fixed portion of your message so that it leaves room for the parameterized section of the message. You do so by using placeholders. If you're coming from the C or C++ world, then you'll recognize the parameter placeholders immediately; they are similar to the `printf` command arguments. If you're not from the C world, these may seem a little odd to you. All the placeholders start with the % sign and are then coded for the kind of information you'll be passing to them, as shown in the following table.

Placeholder Type Indicator	Type of Value
d	Signed integer. Books Online indicates that i is an acceptable choice, but I've had problems getting it to work as expected.
o	Unsigned octal.
p	Pointer.
s	String.
u	Unsigned integer.
X or x	Unsigned hexadecimal.

In addition, there is the option to prefix any of these placeholder indicators with some additional flag and width information:

Flag	What It Does
– (dash or minus sign)	Left-justify. Only makes a difference when you supply a fixed width.
+ (plus sign)	Indicates the positive or negative nature if the parameter is a signed numeric type.
0	Tells SQL Server to pad the left side of a numeric value with zeros until it reaches the width specified in the width option.
# (pound sign)	Applies only to octal and hex values. Tells SQL Server to use the appropriate prefix (0 or 0x) depending on whether it is octal or hex.
' '	Pads the left of a numeric value with spaces if positive.

Last, but not least, you can also set the width, precision, and long/short status of a parameter:

- ❑ **Width** — Set by simply supplying an integer value for the amount of space you want to hold for the parameterized value. You can also specify a *, in which case SQL Server will automatically determine the width according to the value you've set for precision.

- ❑ **Precision** — Determines the maximum number of digits output for numeric data.

❑ **Long/Short** — Set by using an h (short) or I (long) when the type of the parameter is an integer, octal, or hex value.

Use this in an example:

```
RAISERROR ('This is a sample parameterized %s, along with a zero
padding and a sign%+010d',1,1, 'string', 12121);
```

If you execute this, you get back something that looks a little different from what's in the quotation marks:

```
This is a sample parameterized string, along with a zero
padding and a sign+000012121
Msg 50000, Level 1, State 1
```

The extra values supplied were inserted, in order, into your placeholders, with the final value being reformatted as specified.

WITH <option>

Currently, you can mix and match three options when you raise an error:

❑ LOG

❑ SETERROR

❑ NOWAIT

WITH LOG

This tells SQL Server to log the error to the SQL Server error log and the Windows Application Log. This option is required with severity levels that are 19 or higher.

WITH SETERROR

By default, a RAISERROR command doesn't set @@ERROR with the value of the error you generated. Instead, @@ERROR reflects the success or failure of your actual RAISERROR command. SETERROR overrides this and sets the value of @@ERROR to be equal to your error ID.

WITH NOWAIT

Immediately notifies the client of the error.

Adding Your Own Custom Error Messages

You can make use of a special system stored procedure to add messages to the system. The sproc is called sp_addmessage, and the syntax looks like this:

```
sp_addmessage [@msgnum =] <message id>,
[@severity =] <severity>,
[@msgtext =] <'msg'>
[, [@lang =] <'language'>]
```

```
[, [@with_log =] [TRUE|FALSE]]
[, [@replace =] 'replace']
```

All the parameters mean pretty much the same thing that they did with RAISERROR, except for the addition of the language and replace parameters and a slight difference with the WITH LOG option.

> Custom error messages added using sp_addmessage are shared by all databases on the server. Take this into account when defining message identifiers, as conflicts are possible.

@lang

This specifies the language to which this message applies. What's cool here is that you can specify a separate version of your message for any language supported. This equates to the alias if you select the language list from sys.syslanguages.

@with_log

This works just the same as it does in RAISERROR in that, if set to TRUE the message will be automatically logged to the SQL Server error log and the Windows Application Log when raised. The only trick here is that you indicate that you want this message to be logged by setting this parameter to TRUE rather than using the WITH LOG option.

@replace

If you are editing an existing message rather than creating a new one, you must set the @replace parameter to 'REPLACE'. If you leave this off, you'll get an error if the message already exists.

> Creating a set list of additional messages for use by your applications can greatly enhance reuse, but more importantly, it can significantly improve readability of your application. Imagine if every one of your database applications made use of a constant list of custom error codes. You could then easily establish a constants file (a resource or include library, for example) that had a listing of the appropriate errors. You could even create an include library that had generic handling of some or all of the errors. In short, if you're going to be building multiple SQL Server applications in the same environment, consider using a set list of errors that is common to all your applications.

Using sp_addmessage

As has already been indicated, sp_addmessage creates messages in much the same way as you create ad hoc messages using RAISERROR.

As an example, add your own custom message that tells users about the issues with their order date:

```
sp_addmessage
  @msgnum = 60000,
```

```
        @severity = 10,
        @msgtext = '%s is not a valid Order date.
Order date must be within 7 days of current date.';
```

Execute the sproc and it confirms the addition of the new message:

```
(1 row(s) affected)
```

> No matter what database you're working with when you run **sp_addmessage**, the
> actual message is added to a table in the master database (you can, however, see all
> the messages available on the server by simply querying **sys.messages** no matter
> what database you happen to be in). The significance of this is that, if you migrate
> your database to a new server, the messages need to be added again to that new
> server. The old ones will still be in the master database of the old server. As such, I
> strongly recommend keeping all your custom messages stored in a script
> somewhere, so they can easily be added into a new system.

Removing an Existing Custom Message

To get rid of the custom message, use the following:

```
sp_dropmessage <msg num>
```

And it's gone.

Table-Valued Parameters (TVPs)

TABLE as a data type first appeared in SQL Server 2005, but was limited to variables. They were a natural
extension of table-valued user-defined functions (first introduced in SQL Server 2000), allowing you
to declare tables as variables rather than necessarily creating a temporary table. Unfortunately, table
variables were not usable as parameters; the new user-defined table type we discussed back in Chapter 7
supplies the framework for extending table-valued variables functionality to parameters.

Why would we need a TVP? Primarily to deal with many to one constructs. In Chapter 7, we had the
concept of multiple addresses: what if we wanted to update all the addresses for a particular customer
or business entity? How about orders? Wouldn't it be nice to pass an entire order to a single sproc rather
than call one sproc for the order header and a separate sproc once for each line item?

With TVPs, we could pass an order as a single unit — scalar parameters for the various pieces of order
header information, and a TVP to represent each line item. We could then do our one insert into the
order header table, and, more importantly, insert all rows into the details table in a single pass rather
than repeating individual calls for each separate line item (consider the performance ramifications of a
single connection to the database and single pass over the data).

To take a look at a relatively simple example of how a single call to a sproc can now perform actions with
multiple rows, let's revisit the user-defined table type we created back in Chapter 7 — it looked like this:

```
USE AdventureWorks2008;
GO
```

```
CREATE TYPE Person.Address
AS TABLE(
  AddressID int NULL,
  AddressLine1 nvarchar(60) NOT NULL,
  AddressLine2 nvarchar(60) NULL,
  City nvarchar(30) NOT NULL,
  StateProvinceID int NOT NULL,
  PostalCode nvarchar(15) NOT NULL,
  SpatialLocation geography NULL
);
```

We can now use this new type as part of a stored procedure. In our case, we'll create a procedure that is going to accept a list of addresses, and MERGE them into the Address table. The use of a TVP is relatively straightforward. You simply declare it as you would any other parameter type. The sole exception is that you must mark your table parameter(s) as READONLY. Our merge example would look something like this:

```
CREATE PROC spAddressTVPExample
  @AddressesIn   Person.Address READONLY
AS

-- MERGE our data
MERGE Person.Address AS pa
USING
(
  SELECT AddressID,
         AddressLine1,
         AddressLine2,
         City,
         StateProvinceID,
         PostalCode,
         SpatialLocation
  FROM @AddressesIn
) AS a
ON (pa.AddressID = a.AddressID)
WHEN MATCHED THEN
  UPDATE SET pa.AddressLine1 = a.AddressLine1,
             pa.AddressLine2 = a.AddressLine2,
             pa.City = a.City,
             pa.StateProvinceID = a.StateProvinceID,
             pa.PostalCode = a.PostalCode,
             pa.SpatialLocation = a.SpatialLocation
WHEN NOT MATCHED THEN
  INSERT (
          AddressLine1,
          AddressLine2,
          City,
          StateProvinceID,
          PostalCode,
          SpatialLocation
          )
  VALUES (
          a.AddressLine1,
          a.AddressLine2,
```

```
                a.City,
                a.StateProvinceID,
                a.PostalCode,
                a.SpatialLocation
            );
```

We declare the type of parameter we're expecting, just as we do for any other parameter type. The primary difference is that our parameter is read only; that is, it must be explicitly defined as being unavailable for use as an OUTPUT parameter, and no changes can be made to the inbound data.

So, with our sproc created, let's pass it in some data and see what happens:

```
-- Create the instance of our user defined type
DECLARE @Address Person.Address;

-- Now populate it. One row will match existing data,
-- and the other three will be new rows.
INSERT INTO @Address
    (AddressID,
     AddressLine1,
     City,
     StateProvinceID,
     PostalCode,
     SpatialLocation
    )
VALUES
    (
      1,
      '1970 Napa Ct. - ALTERED',
      'Bothell',
      79,
      '98011',
      0xE6100000010CAE8BFC28BCE4474067A89189898A5EC0
    ),
    (
      NULL,
      'My first address',
      'MyTown',
      1,
      '21212',
      NULL
    ),
    (
      NULL,
      'My second address',
      'OtherTown',
      5,
      '43434',
      NULL
    ),
    (
      NULL,
      'My third address',
      'MyTown',
```

```
     1,
     '21214',
     NULL
     );

  -- Start a transaction just to make it easy to roll this back and
  -- keep our AdventureWorks2008 database looking as it did originally
  BEGIN TRAN;

  -- Now feed our table to the sproc we created earlier by
  -- utilizing the TVP
  EXEC spAddressTVPExample @Address

  -- Show the outcome. Note that my > 32521 number limits to rows
  -- that would be beyond those included in the stock sample
  SELECT *
  FROM Person.Address
  WHERE AddressID = 1 OR AddressID > 32521;

  -- Roll things back to keep our database a bit more pristine
  ROLLBACK TRAN;
```

We were able to address many individual addresses in a single pass. We could further expand on this notion to accept a particular BusinessEntityID and use the TVP to update, insert, or delete for all related rows in both the Address table and the associate table that links the BusinessEntityID and its related addresses.

Debugging

Long ago and far away (SQL Server 2000), the Management Studio had real-live debugging tools. They were a little clunky in the sense that they really only worked around stored procedures (there wasn't a way to debug just a script, and debugging triggers required you to create a sproc that would fire the trigger), but, with some workarounds here and there, we had the long sought after debugger. SQL Server 2005 came along and removed all debugging functionality out of the Management Studio. (It was in the product, but you had to use the Visual Studio installation that is part of the Business Intelligence Development Studio in order to get at them — not real handy in any case, but non-existent if you didn't install BIDS for some reason). I'm happy to say that debugging is back in the Management Studio, and it's better than ever!

Starting the Debugger

Unlike with previous versions, the debugger in SQL Server 2008 is pretty easy to find. Much of using the debugger works as it does in VB or C# — probably like most modern debuggers for that matter. Simply choose the Debug menu (available when a query window is active). You can then choose from options to get things started: Start Debugging (Alt+F5) or Step Into (F11).

Let's do a little bit of setup to show the debugger in action both in a standard script, and in a stored procedure scenario. To do this, we'll use a recursive procedure that I find to be ideal for showing off the call stack. To work through this example, you'll need to create it using the following code:

```
CREATE PROC spTriangular
    @ValueIn int,
```

```
        @ValueOut int OUTPUT
AS

DECLARE @InWorking int;
DECLARE @OutWorking int;

IF @ValueIn != 1
BEGIN
  SELECT @InWorking = @ValueIn - 1;
  EXEC spTriangular @InWorking, @OutWorking OUTPUT;
  SELECT @ValueOut = @ValueIn + @OutWorking;
END
ELSE
BEGIN
  SELECT @ValueOut = 1;
END

RETURN;
GO
```

Now that our recursive sproc is created, we just need a little code to set up our debugging test:

```
DECLARE @WorkingOut int
DECLARE @WorkingIn int = 5

EXEC spTriangular @WorkingIn, @WorkingOut OUTPUT

PRINT CAST(@WorkingIn AS varchar) + ' Triangular is '
    + CAST(@WorkingOut AS varchar)
```

With this script as the active query window, let's start a debugging run with the Step Into option (choose it from the Debug menu or simply press F11).

Parts of the Debugger

Several things are worth noticing when the Debugger window first comes up (See Figures 10-1 and 10-2):

❑   The yellow arrow on the left of your screen (shown in Figure 10-1) indicates the *current execution line* — this is the next line of code that will be executed if we do a "go" or we start stepping through the code.

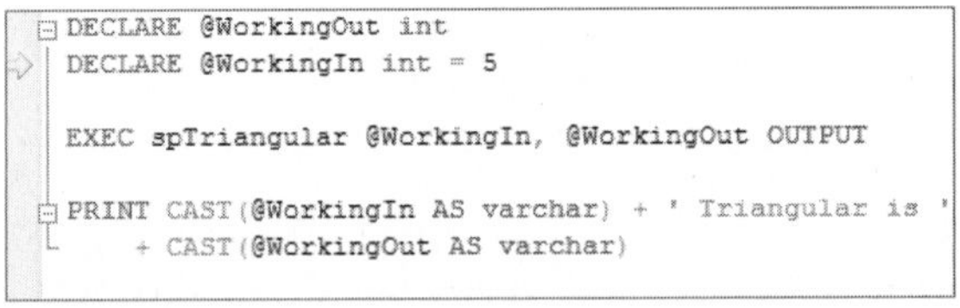

```
  ⊟ DECLARE @WorkingOut int
⇨ |   DECLARE @WorkingIn int = 5

  |   EXEC spTriangular @WorkingIn, @WorkingOut OUTPUT

  ⊟ PRINT CAST(@WorkingIn AS varchar) + ' Triangular is '
  └       + CAST(@WorkingOut AS varchar)
```

Figure 10-1

Figure 10-2

❑ There are icons at the top (see Figure 10-2) to indicate our different options, including:

❑ **Continue**: This will run to the end of the sproc or the next breakpoint (including a watch condition).

❑ **Stop Debugging**: Again, this does what it says — it stops execution immediately. The debugging window does remain open, however.

❑ **Step Into**: This executes the next line of code and stops prior to running the next line of code regardless of what procedure or function that code is in. If the line of code being executed is calling a sproc or function, then Step Into has the effect of calling that sproc or function, adding it to the call stack, changing the Locals window to represent the newly nested sproc rather than the parent, and then stopping at the first line of code in the nested sproc.

❑ **Step Over**: This executes every line of code required to take us to the next statement that is at the same level in the call stack. If you are not calling another sproc or a UDF, then this command will act just like a Step Into. If, however, you are calling another sproc or a UDF, then a Step Over will take you to the statement immediately following where that sproc or UDF returned its value.

❑ **Step Out**: This executes every line of code up to the next line of code at the next highest point in the call stack. That is, we will keep running until we reach the same level as whatever code called the level we are currently at.

❑ **Toggle Breakpoints and Remove All Breakpoints**: In addition, you can set breakpoints by clicking in the left margin of the code window. Breakpoints are points that you set to tell SQL Server to stop here! when the code is running in debug mode. This is handy in big sprocs or functions where you don't want to have to deal with every line — you just want it to run up to a point and stop every time it gets there.

In addition, there is a choice that brings up the Breakpoints window, which is a list of all breakpoints that are currently set (again, handy in larger blocks of code). There are also a few of what we'll call "status" windows; let's go through a few of the more important of these.

The Locals Window

As I indicated back at the beginning of the book, I'm pretty much assuming that you have experience with some procedural language out there. As such, the Locals window (shown in Figure 10-3 as it matches with the current statement shown in Figure 10-2) probably isn't all that new of a concept to you. Simply put, it shows you the current value of all the variables that are currently in scope. The list of variables in the Locals window may change (as may their values) as you step into nested sprocs and back out again. Remember — these are only those variables that are in scope as of the next statement to run.

In Figure 10-3, we're at the start of our first run through this sproc, so the value for the @ValueIn parameter has been set, but all other variables and parameters are not yet set and thus are effectively null.

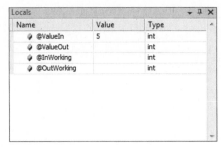

Figure 10-3

Three pieces of information are provided for each variable or parameter:

❑ The name

❑ The current value

❑ The data type

However, perhaps the best part to the Locals window is that you can edit the values in each variable. That means it's a lot easier to change things on the fly to test certain behaviors in your sproc.

The Watch Window

Here you can set up variables that you want to keep track of regardless of where you currently are in the call stack. You can either manually type in the name of the variable you want to watch, or you can select that variable in code, right-click, and then select Add Watch. In Figure 10-4, I've added a watch for @ValueOut, but, since we haven't addressed that variable in code, you can see that no value has been set for it as yet.

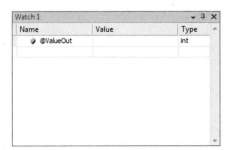

Figure 10-4

The Call Stack Window

The Call Stack window provides a listing of all the sprocs and functions that are currently active in the process that you are running. The handy thing here is that you can see how far in you are when you are running in a nested situation, and you can change between the nesting levels to verify what current variable values are at each level.

Figure 10-5

In Figure 10-5, I've stepped into the code for spTriangular such that we're down to it processing the working value of 3. If you're following along, you can just watch the @ValueIn variable in your Locals window and see how it changes as we step in. Our call stack now has several instances of spTriangular running as we've stepped into it (one for 5, one for 4, and now one for 3) as well as providing information on what statement is next in the current scope.

The Output Window

Much as it sounds, the Output window is the spot where SQL Server prints any output. This includes result sets as well as the return value when your sproc has completed running, but also provides debug information from attaching to the process we're debugging. Some example output from the middle of a debug run is shown in Figure 10-6.

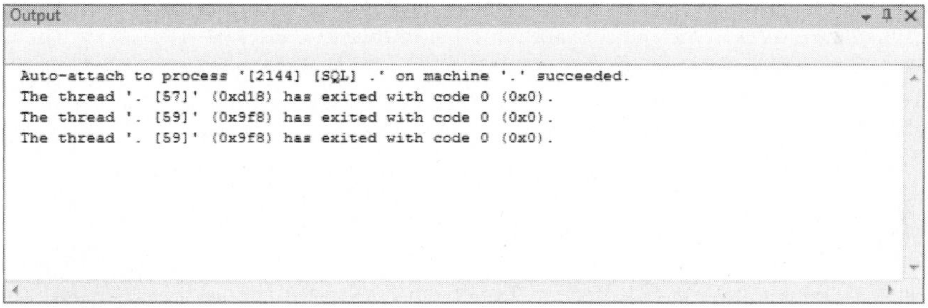

```
Output                                                              ▾ ₽ ×
Auto-attach to process '[2144] [SQL] .' on machine '.' succeeded.
The thread '. [57]' (0xd18) has exited with code 0 (0x0).
The thread '. [59]' (0x9f8) has exited with code 0 (0x0).
The thread '. [59]' (0x9f8) has exited with code 0 (0x0).
```

Figure 10-6

The Command Window

The Command window is probably going to be beyond common use as it is in SQL Server 2008. In short, it allows you something of a command-line mode to access debugger commands and other objects. It is, however, cryptic at best and, as of this writing, relatively undocumented. To see examples of commands you could issue would be something like:

```
>Debug.StepInto
```

There are a whole host of commands available to IntelliSense, but you'll find that most of these are not actually available when debugging.

Using the Debugger Once It's Started

Now that we have the preliminaries out of the way and the Debugger window up, we're ready to start walking through our code. If you were walking through some of the descriptions before, stop the debugger and restart it so we're in the same place.

The first executable line of our sproc is a bit deceptive. It is the DECLARE statement for @WorkingIn. Normally variable declarations are not considered executable, but, in this case, we are initializing the variable as part of the declaration, so the initialization code is seen by the debugger. You should notice that none of our variables has yet been set (the initialization code will be next to run, but has not actually executed yet. Step forward (using the menu choice, the tool tip, or simply press F11), and you should see (via the Locals window) @WorkingIn get initialized to our value of 5: @WorkingOut is not initialized as part of the declaration.

Use the Step Into key one more time and we enter into our first execution of the spTriangular stored procedure and land at the first executable line in the sproc — our IF statement.

Since the value of @ValueIn is indeed not equal to 1, we step into the BEGIN...END block specified by our IF statement. Specifically, we move to our SELECT statement that initializes the @InWorking parameter for this particular execution of the procedure. As we'll see later, if the value of @ValueIn had indeed been one, we would have immediately dropped down to our ELSE statement.

Again, step forward one line by pressing F11 or using the Step Into icon or menu choice until just *before* you enter the next instance of spTriangular.

Pay particular attention to the value of @InWorking in the Locals window. Notice that it changed to the correct value (@ValueIn is currently 5, so 5–1 is 4) as set by our SELECT statement. Also notice that our Call Stack window has only the current instance of our sproc in it (plus the current statement) — since we haven't stepped down into our nested versions of the sproc yet, we only see one instance.

Now go ahead and step into our next statement. Since this is the execution of a sproc, we're going to see a number of different things change in the debugger. Notice that it *appears* that our arrow that indicates the current statement jumped back up to the IF statement. Why? Well, this is a new instance of what is otherwise the same sproc. We can tell this based on our Call Stack window — notice that it now has two instances of our sproc listed. The one at the top (with the yellow arrow) is the current instance, and the one with the red breakpoint dot is a parent instance that is now waiting for something further up in the call stack. Notice also that the @ValueIn parameter has the value of 4 – that is the value we passed in from the outer instance of the sproc.

If you want to see the value of variables in the scope of the outer instance of the sproc, just double-click that instance's line in the Call Stack window (the one with the green arrow) and you'll see several things changed in our debugging windows.

There are two things to notice here. First, the values of our variables have changed back to those in the scope of the outer (and currently selected) instance of the sproc. Second, the icon for our current execution line is different. This new green arrow is meant to show that this is the current line in this instance of the sproc, but it is not the current line in the overall call stack.

Go back to the current instance by clicking the top item in the Call Stack window. Then step in three more times. This should bring you to the top line (the IF statement) in our third instance of the sproc.

Notice that our call stack has become three deep, and that the values of our variables and parameters in the Locals window have changed again. Last, but not least, notice that this time our @ValueIn parameter has a value of 3. Repeat this process until the @ValueIn parameter has a value of 1.

Step into the code one more time, and you'll see a slight change in behavior. This time, since the value in @ValueIn is equal to 1, we move into the BEGIN...END block defined with our ELSE statement.

Since we've reached the bottom, we're ready to start going back up the call stack. Use Step Into through the last line of our procedure, and you'll find that our call stack is back to only four levels. Also, notice that our output parameter (@OutWorking) has been appropriately set.

This time, let's do something different and do a Step Out (Shift+F11). If you're not paying attention, it will look like absolutely nothing has changed.

> In this case, to use the old cliché, looks are deceiving. Again, notice the change in the Call Stack window and in the values in the Locals window — we stepped *out* of what was then the current instance of the sproc and moved up a level in the call stack. If we now keep stepping into the code (*F11*), then our sproc has finished running and we'll see the final version of our status windows and their respective finishing values. A *big* word of caution here! If you want to be able to see the truly final values (such as an output parameter being set), make *sure* that you use the Step Into option to execute the last line of code.

> If you use an option that executes several lines at once, such as a Go or Step Out, all you will get is the Output window without any final variable information.

> A workaround is to place a breakpoint on the last point at which you expect to perform a RETURN in the outermost instance of your sproc. That way, you can run in whatever debug mode you want, but still have execution halt in the end so you can inspect your final variables.

So, you should now be able to see how the debugger can be very handy indeed.

Understanding the SQLCLR and .NET Programming in SQL Server

So, since you're reading this book, we're almost ready to proclaim you a "Pro" with SQL Server, but no notion of a pro is going to be complete without at least a solid concept of what is involved .NET programming in SQL Server. With that in mind, it's time to take a look at some of the major elements that .NET brought to SQL Server, and, where appropriate, provide some mention of what's new in SQL Server 2008. We'll see such things utilizing .NET as:

❑ Creating basic assemblies — including non T-SQL-based stored procedures, functions, and triggers

❑ Defining aggregate functions (something T-SQL user-defined functions can't do)

❑ Complex data types

❑ External calls (and with it, some security considerations)

.NET is something of a wide-ranging topic that will delve into many different areas we've already touched on in this book and take them even farther, so, with that said, let's get going!

> Note that several of the examples in this chapter utilize the existing Microsoft Sample set. You must install the sample scripts during SQL Server installation or download the SQL Server .NET development SDK to access these samples. In addition, there is a significant reliance on Visual Studio .NET (2008 is used in the examples).

Assemblies 101

All the.NET functionality is surrounded by the term *assembly*. So, a reasonable question might be: "What exactly is an assembly?" An assembly is a DLL that has been created using managed code (what .NET language does not matter). The assembly may have been built using Visual Studio .NET or some other development environment, but the .NET Framework SDK also provides a command-line compiler for those of you who do not have Visual Studio available.

> Not all custom attributes or .NET Framework APIs are legal for assemblies used in SQL Server. You can consult Books Online for a full list, but, in general, anything that supports windowing is not allowed, nor is anything marked UNSAFE, unless your assembly is to be granted access at an UNSAFE level.

Compiling an Assembly

Use of .NET assemblies requires that you enable the Common Language Runtime (CLR) in SQL Server, which is disabled by default. You can enable the CLR by executing the following in the Management Studio:

```
sp_configure 'clr enabled', 1;
GO

RECONFIGURE;
```

There really isn't that much to this beyond compiling a normal DLL. The real key points to compiling a DLL that is going to be utilized as a SQL Server .NET assembly are:

❑ You cannot reference any assemblies that include functions related to windowing (dialogs and so on).

❑ How the assembly is marked (safe, external access, unsafe) will make a large difference to whether or not the assembly is allowed to execute some functions.

From there, most things are not all that different from any other DLL you might create to make a set of classes available. You can either compile the project using Visual Studio (if you have it), or you can use the compiler that is included in the .NET SDK.

Let's go ahead and work through a relatively simple example for an assembly we'll use as a stored procedure example a little later in the chapter.

Create a new SQL Server project in Visual Studio using C# (you can translate this to VB if you wish) called `ExampleProc`. You'll find the SQL Server project type under the "Database" project group (under C#). When it comes up, cancel out of any database instance dialogs you get.

> **The actual project type you start with does not really matter other than what references it starts with. While this example suggests starting with a SQL Server project, you could start with a simple class project and add the appropriate references manually.**

Now add a new stored procedure by right-clicking the project and selecting Add ➢ Stored Procedure ... as shown in Figure 10-7.

In this new stored proc, we need to set a few references; Visual Studio should already have them done for you:

```
using System;
using System.Data;
using System.Data.SqlClient;
using System.Data.SqlTypes;
using Microsoft.SqlServer.Server;
```

And then we're ready to get down to writing some real code. Code you want to put in a .NET assembly is implemented through a public class. I've chosen to call my class `StoredProcedures`, but, really, I could have called it most anything. I'm ready to add my method declaration:

```
public partial class StoredProcedures
{
    [Microsoft.SqlServer.Server.SqlProcedure]
    public static void ExampleSP(out int outval)
    {
```

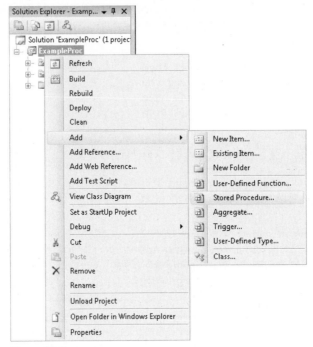

Figure 10-7

The method has, like the class, been declared as `public`. I can also have private classes if I so choose. (They would, of course, need to be supporting methods, as they would not be exposed externally.) The `void` indicates that I do not intend to supply a return value (when we run it in SQL Server, it will always return the default of zero). I could, however, declare it as returning type `int` and supply a value as appropriate in my code (most likely zero for no error, and non-zero if there was an error).

Notice also the `Microsoft.SqlServer.Server.SqlProcedure` directive. This is completely optional and is utilized by Visual Studio's deployment tool to know that the following method is a stored procedure. I left it in there primarily to show you that it is there. (We're going to manually deploy the proc rather than use the deployment functionality of Visual Studio.)

From there, we're ready to grab a reference to a connection. Pay particular attention to this one, as it is different from what you will see in typical .NET database connections. Everything about it is the same as a typical connection, except for the connect string. With that, we are using a special syntax that indicates that we want to utilize the same connection that called the stored procedure. The beauty of this is that we can assume a login context and do not need to explicitly provide a server or even a username.

```
// This causes the connection to use the existing connection context
// that the stored procedure is operating in. We could also create a
// completely new connection to fetch data from external sources.
using (SqlConnection cn = new SqlConnection("context connection=true"))
{
    cn.Open();
```

So, now we have a connection. Technically, we didn't really open a new connection (remember, we're utilizing the one that was already opened to call this stored procedure). Instead, we're really creating a new reference to the existing connection.

We're now ready to create a command object. There really isn't anything mysterious about this at all. It is created using a fairly typical syntax. (Indeed, you can create the command object in any of the typical ways you would if you were doing this from a typical .NET client.) I've chosen to define the `CommandText` and connection properties as part of my object declaration.

```
// set up a simple command that is going to return two columns.
SqlCommand cmd = new SqlCommand("SELECT @@SERVERNAME, @@SPID", cn);
```

And then we're ready to execute the command. This is one of the spots I'm utilizing something assembly specific, as I am not only executing the command, but also I'm explicitly saying to go ahead and send it to the client.

> Unlike a T-SQL-based stored procedure, queries you execute are not defaulted as going to the client. Instead, the assumption is that you want to work with the result set locally. Therefore, you need to explicitly issue a command to send anything out to the client.

The object that does this is the `.Pipe` object within the `SqlContext`:

```
// The following actually sends the row for the select.
// It could have been multiple rows, and that would be fine too.
SqlContext.Pipe.ExecuteAndSend(cmd);
```

Last, but not least, I'm populating my output variable. In this procedure, I haven't really done anything special with it, but I'm tossing something into it just so we can see that it really does work.

```
            // Set the output value to something. It could have been anything
            // including some form of computed value, but we're just showing
            // that we can output some value for now.
            outval = 12345;
        }
    }
};
```

Now simply build your project, and you have your first assembly ready to be uploaded to your SQL Server. Later, we'll take a look at how to define the assembly for use as a stored procedure.

Uploading Your Assembly to SQL Server

That's right — I used the term *upload*. When you "create" an assembly in SQL Server, you're both creating a copy of the DLL within SQL Server as well as something of a handle that defines the assembly and the permissions associated with it.

```
CREATE ASSEMBLY <assembly name>
[ AUTHORIZATION <owner name> ]
```

```
FROM { <client assembly specifier> | <assembly bits> [ ,...n ] }
[ WITH PERMISSION_SET = { SAFE | EXTERNAL_ACCESS | UNSAFE } ]
[ ; ]
```

The CREATE portion of things adheres to the standard CREATE <object type> <object name> notion that we've seen throughout SQL. From there, we have a few different things to digest:

Option	Description
AUTHORIZATION	The authorization is the name of the user this assembly will be considered to belong to. If this parameter is not supplied, then the current user is assumed to be the owner. You can use this to alias to a user with appropriate network access to execute any file actions defined by the assembly.
FROM	The fully qualified path to the physical DLL file. This can be a local file or a UNC path. You can, if you so choose, provide the actual byte sequence to build the file right on the line in the place of a file. (I have to admit I've never tried that one.)
WITH PERMISSION_SET	You have three options for this. SAFE is the default and implies that the object is not utilizing anything that requires access outside of the SQL Server process (no file access, no external database access). EXTERNAL_ACCESS indicates that your assembly requires access outside of the SQL Server process (to files in the operating system or UNC path, or perhaps an external ODBC/OLEDB connection). UNSAFE implies that your assembly has free access to the SQL Server memory space without regard to the CLR managed code facilities. This means your assembly has the potential to destabilize your SQL Server through improper access.

So, with all this in mind, we're ready to upload our assembly:

```
USE AdventureWorks2008;

CREATE ASSEMBLY ExampleProc
    FROM '<solution path>\ExampleProc\bin\Debug\ExampleProc.dll'
```

Assuming that you have the path to your compiled DLL correct, you shouldn't see any messages except for the typical "Command(s) completed successfully" message, and, with that, you are ready to create the SQL Server stored procedure that will reference this assembly.

Creating Your Assembly-Based Stored Procedure

All right then; all the tough stuff is done. (If you're looking for how to actually create the assembly that is the code for the stored proc, take a look back two sections.) We have a compiled assembly, and we have uploaded it to SQL Server; it's time to put it to use.

To do this, we use the same CREATE PROCEDURE command we used for the more classic T-SQL-based stored procedures. The difference is that, in the place of T-SQL code, we reference our assembly. For review, the syntax looks like this:

```
CREATE PROCEDURE|PROC <sproc name>
    [<parameter name> [<schema>.]<data type> [VARYING] [= <default value>] [OUT
```

```
[PUT]][,
    <parameter name> [<schema>.]<data type> [VARYING] [= <default value>]
[OUT[PUT]][,
    ...
    ...
    ]]
[WITH
    RECOMPILE| ENCRYPTION | [EXECUTE AS { CALLER|SELF|OWNER|<'user name'>}]
[FOR REPLICATION]
AS
    <code> | EXTERNAL NAME <assembly name>.<assembly class>
```

Some of this we can ignore when doing assemblies. The key things are:

❑   We use the EXTERNAL NAME option instead of the <code> section we used in our main chapter on
    stored procedures. The EXTERNAL NAME is done in a format of

    `<assembly name>.<class name>.<method name>`

❑   We still need to define all parameters (in an order that matches the order our assembly method).

Now let's apply that to the assembly we created in the previous section:

```
CREATE PROC spCLRExample
    (
        @outval int = NULL OUTPUT
    )
AS EXTERNAL NAME ExampleProc.StoredProcedures.ExampleSP;
```

It is not until this point that we actually have a stored procedure that utilizes our assembly. Notice that
the stored procedure name is completely different from the name of the method that implements the
stored procedure.

Now go ahead and make a test call to our new stored procedure:

```
DECLARE @OutVal int;
EXEC spCLRExample @OutVal OUTPUT;

SELECT @OutVal;
```

We're declaring a holding variable to receive the results from our output variable. We then execute the
procedure and select the value for our holding variable. When you check the results, however, you'll find
not one result set — but two:

```
------------------- ------
KIERKEGAARD           52

(1 row(s) affected)


-----------
```

```
12345

(1 row(s) affected)
```

The first of these is the result set we sent down the `SqlContext.Pipe`. When we executed the `cmd` object, the results were directed down the pipe, and so the client received them. The second result set represents the `SELECT` of our `@OutVal` variable.

This is, of course, a pretty simplistic example, but realize the possibilities here. The connection could have been, assuming we were set to `EXTERNAL_ACCESS`, to any data source. We could access files and even Web services. We can add in complex libraries to perform things like regular expressions (careful on performance considerations there).

We will look at adding some of these kinds of things in as we explore more types of assembly-based SQL programming.

Creating Scalar User-Defined Functions from Assemblies

Scalar functions are not much different from stored procedures. Indeed, for the most part, they have the very same differences as the T-SQL versions. Much as with stored procedures, we utilize the same core `CREATE` syntax used in standard T-SQL user-defined functions (UDFs):

```
CREATE FUNCTION [<schema name>.]<function name>
    ([<@parameter name> [AS] [<schema name>.]<data type>
         [ = <default value>]   [READONLY]
      [ ,...n ] ] )
RETURNS {<type>|TABLE [(<table definition>)]}
    [ WITH [ENCRYPTION]|[SCHEMABINDING] |
        [ RETURNS NULL ON NULL INPUT | CALLED ON NULL INPUT ] | [EXECUTE AS {
        CALLER|SELF|OWNER|<'user name'>} ]
]
[AS] { EXTERNAL NAME <external method> |
BEGIN
    [<function statements>]
    {RETURN <type as defined in RETURNS clause>|RETURN (<SELECT statement>)}
END }[;]
```

There are one or two new things once you get inside of the .NET code. Of particular note is that there are some properties that you can set for your function. Among those, probably the most significant is that you must indicate whether the function is deterministic. (The default is nondeterministic.) We'll see an example of this in use shortly.

For the example this time, start a new SQL Server project in Visual Studio, but instead of adding a stored procedure as we did in our original assembly example, add a user-defined function.

SQL Server starts you out with a simple template:

```
using System;
using System.Data;
using System.Data.SqlClient;
using System.Data.SqlTypes;
using Microsoft.SqlServer.Server;
```

```
public partial class UserDefinedFunctions
{
    [Microsoft.SqlServer.Server.SqlFunction]
    public static SqlString ExampleUDF()
    {
        // Put your code here
        return new SqlString("Hello");
    }
};
```

This is actually a workable template "as is." You could compile it and add it to SQL Server as an assembly, and it would work right out of the box (although getting back nothing but the string "Hello" is probably not all that useful).

We'll replace that, but this time we're going to write something that is still amazingly simple. In the end, we'll see that, while simple, it is much more powerful than our stored procedure example.

In previous books, I have often lamented the issues with trying to validate e-mail fields in tables. E-mail, when you think about it, is a strongly typed notion, but one that SQL Server has only been able to perform minimal validation of. What we need are regular expressions.

We could approach this issue by writing a validation function and implementing it as a user-defined data type. This approach would have some validity, but has a problem: the rules for validating e-mails change on occasion (such as when new country codes are added, or when the .biz and .info top domains were added several years ago). Instead, we're going to implement simple regex functionality and then utilize a call to that function in a constraint.

We can do this with relatively minimal changes to the function template that SQL Server gave us. First, we can get rid of a few library declarations, since we won't be really working with SQL Server data to speak of, and add back two of our own. We wind up with just three using declarations:

```
using System;
using System.Text.RegularExpressions;
using Microsoft.SqlServer.Server;
```

We're then ready to implement our function with very few changes:

```
[SqlFunction(IsDeterministic = true, IsPrecise = true)]
public static bool RegExIsMatch(string pattern, string matchString)
{
    Regex reg = new Regex(pattern.TrimEnd(null));
    return reg.Match(matchString.TrimEnd(null)).Success;
}
```

Oh sure, we completely replaced the old function, but it didn't take a lot to do it. Indeed, we only have two more lines of code — and that's including the determinism declaration!

I'm not going to review it much here, but take a look earlier in the chapter if you need to be reminded of how determinism works The key thing is that, given the same inputs, the function must always yield the same outputs.

Go ahead and compile this, and we're ready to upload the assembly:

```
USE AdventureWorks2008;

CREATE ASSEMBLY ExampleUDF
FROM '<solution path>\ExampleUDF\bin\Debug\ExampleUDF.dll';
```

And then create the function reference:

```
CREATE FUNCTION fCLRExample
    (
        @Pattern nvarchar(max),
        @MatchString nvarchar(max)
    )
RETURNS BIT
AS EXTERNAL NAME ExampleUDF.UserDefinedFunctions.RegExIsMatch;
```

Notice the use of the nvarchar type instead of varchar. The string data type is a Unicode data type, and our function data type declaration needs to match.

This done, we're ready to test things out a bit:

```
SELECT pp.BusinessEntityID, pp.FirstName, pp.LastName, pe.EmailAddress
FROM Person.Person pp
JOIN Person.EmailAddress pe
    ON pp.BusinessEntityID = pe.BusinessEntityID
WHERE dbo.fCLRExample('[a-zA-Z0-9_\-]+@([a-zA-Z0-9_\-
]+\.)+(com|org|edu|mil|info|biz|net)',
                    EmailAddress) = 1;
```

If you have the default data, then this will actually return every row in the table since they all are adventure-works.com addresses. So, let's try a simple test to show what works versus what doesn't:

```
DECLARE @GoodTestMail varchar(100),
        @BadTestMail varchar(100);

SET @GoodTestMail = 'robv@professionalsql.com';
SET @BadTestMail = 'misc. text';

SELECT dbo.fCLRExample('[a-zA-Z0-9_\-]+@([a-zA-Z0-9_\-]+\.)+(com|org|edu|nz|au)',
                    @GoodTestMail) AS ShouldBe1
SELECT dbo.fCLRExample('[a-zA-Z0-9_\-]+@([a-zA-Z0-9_\-]+\.)+(com|org|edu|nz|au)',
                    @BadTestMail) AS ShouldBe0;
```

For the sake of brevity, I have not built the full e-mail regex string here. It would need to include all of the valid country code top domains such as au, ca, uk, and us. There are a couple hundred of these, so it wouldn't fit all that well. That said, the basic construct is just fine; you can tweak it to meet your particular needs.

This gets us back what we would expect:

```
ShouldBe1
---------
1
```

```
(1 row(s) affected)

ShouldBe0
---------
0

(1 row(s) affected)
```

But let's not stop there. We have this nice function, let's apply it a little further by actually applying it as a constraint to the table:

```
ALTER TABLE Person.EmailAddress
ADD CONSTRAINT ExampleFunction
CHECK (dbo.fCLRExample('[a-zA-Z0-9_\-]+@([a-zA-Z0-9_\-
]+\.)+(com|org|edu|nz|au)',
                       EmailAddress) = 1);
```

Now we try to update a row to insert some bad data into our column, and it will be rejected:

```
UPDATE Person.EmailAddress
SET EmailAddress = 'blah blah'
WHERE BusinessEntityID = 1
AND EmailAddressID = 1;
```

And SQL Server tells you the equivalent of "no way!":

```
Msg 547, Level 16, State 0, Line 2
The UPDATE statement conflicted with the CHECK constraint "ExampleFunction". The
conflict occurred in database "AdventureWorks2008", table "Person.EmailAddress",
column 'EmailAddress'.
The statement has been terminated.
```

Creating Table-Valued Functions

Functions are going to continue to be a focus of our look at .NET for a bit. Why? Well, functions have a few more twists to them than some of the other assembly uses.

In this section, we're going to focus in on table-valued functions. They are among the more complex things we need to deal with in this chapter, but, as they are in the T-SQL version, they were also among the more powerful. The uses range far and wide. They can be as simple as special treatment of a column in something you could have otherwise done in a typical T-SQL function or can be as complex as a merge of data from several disparate and external data sources.

Go ahead and start another Visual Studio project called ExampleTVF, using the SQL Server project template. Also add a new user-defined function. We're going to be demonstrating accessing the file system this time, so add the following references:

```
using System;
using System.IO;
using System.Collections;
using Microsoft.SqlServer.Server;
```

Before we get too far into the code, let's look ahead a bit at some of the things a table-valued function — or TVF — requires:

The entry function must implement the `IEnumerable` interface. This is a special, widely used, interface in .NET that essentially allows for the iteration over some form of row (be it in an array, collection, table, or whatever). As part of this concept, we must also define the `FillRowMethodName` property. The function specified in this special property will be implicitly called by SQL Server every time SQL Server has the need to move between rows. You will find that a good many developers call whatever function they implement this in `FillRow`. For me it will vary depending on the situation and whether or not I feel it warrants something more descriptive of what it's doing.

So, with those items described, let's look at the opening of our function. Our function is going to be providing a directory listing, but one based on information that must be retrieved from individual files. This means that we have to enumerate the directory to retrieve each file's information. Just to add to the flavor of things a bit, we will also support the notion of subdirectories, which means we have to understand the notion of directories within directories.

We'll start with our top-level function call. This accepts the search filter criteria, including the directory we are considering the root directory for our list, the filename criteria for the search, and a Boolean indicator of whether or not to include subdirectories:

```
public partial class UserDefinedFunctions
{

    [SqlFunction(FillRowMethodName = "FillRow")]

    public static IEnumerable DirectoryList(string sRootDir, string sWildCard,
 bool bIncludeSubDirs)
    {
        // retrieve an array of directory entries. Where this an object of our
 own making,
        // it would need to be one that supports IEnumerable, but since
 ArrayList already
        // does that, we have nothing special to do here.
        ArrayList aFileArray = new ArrayList();
        DirectorySearch(sRootDir, sWildCard, bIncludeSubDirs, aFileArray);

        return aFileArray;
    }
```

This has done little other than establish an array that will hold our file list and call to internal functions to populate it. Next, we need to implement the function that is enumerating the directory list to get the files in each directory:

```
    private static void DirectorySearch(string directory, string sWildCard,
 bool bIncludeSubDirs, ArrayList aFileArray)
    {
        GetFiles(directory, sWildCard, aFileArray);

        if (bIncludeSubDirs)
        {
            foreach (string d in Directory.GetDirectories(directory))
```

```
            {
                DirectorySearch(d, sWildCard, bIncludeSubDirs,
aFileArray);
            }
        }
    }
```

For each directory we file, we make a simple call of the `GetFiles` method (it is implemented in `System.IO`) and enumerate the results for the current directory. As we enumerate, we populate our array with the `FullName` and a `LastWriteTime` properties from the file:

```
    private static void GetFiles(string d, string sWildCard, ArrayList aFileArray)
    {
        foreach (string f in Directory.GetFiles(d, sWildCard))
        {
            FileInfo fi = new FileInfo(f);

            object[] column = new object[2];
            column[0] = fi.FullName;
            column[1] = fi.LastWriteTime;

            aFileArray.Add(column);
        }

    }
```

From there, we're ready to bring it all home by actually implementing our `FillRow` function, which does nothing more than serve as a conduit between our array and the outside world — managing the feed of data to one row at a time:

```
    private static void FillRow(Object obj, out string filename, out DateTime
date)
    {
        object[] row = (object[])obj;

        filename = (string)row[0];
        date = (DateTime)row[1];
    }
};
```

With all that done, we should be ready to compile and upload our assembly. We use the same CREATE ASSEMBLY command we've used all chapter long, but there is a small change: We must declare the assembly as having the EXTERNAL_ACCESS permission set. One of two conditions that must be met in order to do this:

❑   The assembly is signed with a certificate (more on these in Chapter 19) that corresponds to a user with proper EXTERNAL_ACCESS rights.

❑   The database owner has EXTERNAL_ACCESS rights *and* the database has been marked as being TRUSTWORTHY in the database properties.

We're going to take the unsigned option, so we need to set the database to be marked as trustworthy:

```
ALTER DATABASE AdventureWorks2008
SET TRUSTWORTHY ON;
```

And we're now ready to finish uploading our assembly with proper access:

```
USE AdventureWorks2008;

CREATE ASSEMBLY fExampleTVF
FROM '<solution path>\ExampleTVF\bin\Debug\ExampleTVF.dll'
WITH PERMISSION_SET = EXTERNAL_ACCESS;
```

The actual creation of the function reference that utilizes our assembly is not bad but is slightly trickier than the one for the simple scalar function. We must define the table that is to be returned in addition to the input parameters:

```
CREATE FUNCTION fTVFExample
    (
        @RootDir nvarchar(max),
        @WildCard nvarchar(max),
        @IncludeSubDirs bit
    )
RETURNS TABLE
    (
        FileName nvarchar(max),
        LastWriteTime datetime
    )
AS EXTERNAL NAME fExampleTVF.UserDefinedFunctions.DirectoryList;
```

And, with that, we're ready to test:

```
SELECT FileName, LastWriteTime
FROM dbo.fTVFExample('C:\', '*.sys', 0);
```

What you get back when you run this will vary a bit depending on what components and examples you have installed, but, in general, it should look something like:

```
FileName                                           LastWriteTime
-------------------------------------------------- -----------------------
C:\CONFIG.SYS                                      2006-04-01 00:21:43.470
C:\IO.SYS                                          2006-04-01 00:21:43.470
C:\MSDOS.SYS                                       2006-04-01 00:21:43.470
C:\pagefile.sys                                    2008-12-31 00:00:00.000

(4 row(s) affected)
```

We've now shown not only how we can do table-valued functions but also how we can access external data — powerful stuff!

Creating Aggregate Functions

Now this one is going to be the one thing in this chapter that's really new. When we look at user-defined data types a little later, we'll see something with a bigger shift than some of the other constructs we've looked at here, but aggregate functions are something that you can't do any other way. The T-SQL version of a UDF does not allow for aggregation.

So, what am I talking about here? Well, examples are SUM, AVG, MIN, and MAX. These all look over a set of data and then return a value that is based on some analysis of the whole. It may be based on your entire result set or on some criteria defined in the GROUP BY clause.

Performing the analysis required to support your aggregate gets rather tricky. Unlike other functions, where everything can be contained in a single call to your procedure, aggregates require mixing activities your function does (the actual aggregation part) with activities SQL Server is doing at essentially the same time (organizing the groups for the GROUP BY, for example). The result is something of staged calls to your assembly class. Your class can be called at any of four times and can support methods for each of these calls:

- ❑ **Init** — This supports the initialization of your function. Since you're aggregating, there's a good chance that you are setting some sort of accumulator or other holding value — this is the method where you would initialize variables that support the accumulation or holding value.

- ❑ **Accumulate** — This is called by SQL Server once for every row that is to be aggregated. How you choose to utilize the function is up to you, but presumably it will implement whatever accumulation logic you need to support your aggregate.

- ❑ **Merge** — SQL Server is a multithreaded application, and it may very well utilize multiple threads that can each be calling into your function. As such, you utilize this function to deal with merging the results from different threads into one final result. Depending on the type of aggregate you're doing, this can make things rather tricky. You can, however, make use of private members in your class to keep track of how many threads were running and reconcile the differences. It's worth noticing that this function receives a copy of your class as an argument (consider it to be what amounts to recursive when you are in this method) rather than whatever other type of value you've been accumulating — this is so you get the proper results that were calculated by the other thread.

- ❑ **Terminate** — This is essentially the opposite of Init. This is the call that actually returns the end result.

Now, let's see what this looks like in practice.

To start things off, create a new project in Visual Studio (I'm calling mine ExampleAggregate), and then add a new aggregate to the project (right-click the project in the solution and choose Add ➤ Aggregate). SQL Server builds you a stock template that includes all four of the methods we just discussed:

```
using System;
using System.Data;
using System.Data.SqlClient;
using System.Data.SqlTypes;
using Microsoft.SqlServer.Server;


[Serializable]
[Microsoft.SqlServer.Server.SqlUserDefinedAggregate(Format.Native)]
public struct ExampleAggregate
{
    public void Init()
    {
        // Put your code here
    }
```

```
public void Accumulate(SqlString Value)
{
    // Put your code here
}

public void Merge(ExampleAggregate Group)
{
    // Put your code here
}

public SqlString Terminate()
{
    // Put your code here
    return new SqlString("");
}

// This is a place-holder member field
private int var1;

}
```

This is the genuine foundation — complete with templates for all four method calls.

What we're going to be doing for an example in this section is to build an implementation of a PRODUCT function, which is essentially the same concept as SUM but multiplying instead of adding. Like the SUM function, we will ignore NULL values (unless they are all NULL, and then we will return NULL), but we will warn the user about the NULL being found and ignored should we encounter one.

We need to start with some simple changes. First, I'm going to change the class name to Product instead of ExampleAggregate, which we called the project. In addition, I need to declare some member variables to hold our accumulator and some flags.

```
using System;
using System.Data;
using System.Data.SqlClient;
using System.Data.SqlTypes;
using Microsoft.SqlServer.Server;


[Serializable]
[Microsoft.SqlServer.Server.SqlUserDefinedAggregate(Format.Native)]
public struct Product
{
    private SqlDouble dAccumulator;
    private bool fContainsNull;
    private bool fAllNull;
```

The fContainsNull variable will be used to tell us if we need to warn the user about any values being ignored. The fAllNull is used to tell if every value received was null — in which case we want to return null as our result.

We then need to initialize our member variables as part of the Init function:

```
public void Init()
{
        // Initialize our flags and accumulator
        dAccumulator = 1;
        fContainsNull = false;
        fAllNull = true;


}
```

We are then ready to build the main accumulator function:

```
public void Accumulate(SqlDouble Value)
{
        // This is the meat of things. This one is where we actually apply
        // whatever logic is appropriate for our accumulation. In our example,
        // we simply multiply whatever value is already in the accumulator by
        // the new input value. If the input value is null, then we set the
        // flag that indicates that we've seen null values and then ignore
        // the value we just received and maintain the existing accumulation.

        if (Value.IsNull)
        {
            fContainsNull = true;
        }
        else
        {
            fAllNull = false;
            dAccumulator *= Value;
        }

}
```

The comments pretty much tell the tale here. We need to watch to make sure that none of our flag conditions have changed. Other than that, we simply need to continue accumulating by multiplying the current value (assuming it's not null) by the existing accumulator value.

With the accumulator fully implemented, we can move on to dealing with the merge scenario:

```
public void Merge(Product Group)
{
        // For this particular example, the logic of merging isn't that hard.
        // We simply multiply what we already have by the results of any other
        // instances of our Product class.

        if (Group.dAccumulator.IsNull)
        {
            if (Group.fContainsNull)
```

```
                    fContainsNull = true;
            if (!Group.fAllNull)
                fAllNull = false;
            dAccumulator *= dAccumulator;
        }


    }
```

For this particular function, the implementation of a merge is essentially just applying the same checks that we did in the `Accumulate` function.

Finally, we're ready to implement our `Terminate` function to close out our aggregation when it's done:

```
public SqlDouble Terminate()
{
    // And this is where we wrap it all up and output our results
    if (fAllNull)
    {
        return SqlDouble.Null;
    }
    else
    {
        SqlContext.Pipe.Send("WARNING: Aggregate values exist and were ignored");
        return dAccumulator;
    }
}
```

With all that done, we should be ready to compile our procedure and upload it:

```
CREATE ASSEMBLY ExampleAggregate
FROM '<solution path>\ExampleAggregate\bin\Debug\ExampleAggregate.dll';
```

And create the aggregate. Note that while an aggregate is a type of function, we use a different syntax to create it. The basic syntax looks like this:

```
CREATE AGGREGATE [ <schema name> . ] <aggregate name>
        (@param_name <input sql type> )
RETURNS <SQL Type of Return Value>
EXTERNAL NAME <assembly name> [ .<class name> ]
```

So, to create the aggregate from our assembly, we would do something like:

```
CREATE AGGREGATE dbo.Product(@input float)
RETURNS float
EXTERNAL NAME ExampleAggregate.Product;
```

And, with that, we're ready to try it out. To test it, we'll create a small sample table that includes some data that can be multiplied along with a grouping column, so we can test out how our aggregate works with a GROUP BY scenario.

```
CREATE TABLE TestAggregate
(
    PK          int         NOT NULL    PRIMARY KEY,
    GroupKey    int         NOT NULL,
    Value       float       NOT NULL
);
```

Now we just need some test data:

```
INSERT INTO TestAggregate(PK, GroupKey, Value)
    VALUES (1, 1, 2),
           (2, 1, 6),
           (3, 1, 1.5),
           (4, 2, 2),
           (5, 2, 6);
```

And we're ready to give our aggregate a try. What we're going to be doing is returning the PRODUCT of all the rows within each group (our sample data has two groups, so this should work out to two rows).

```
SELECT GroupKey, dbo.Product(Value) AS Product
FROM TestAggregate
GROUP BY GroupKey;
```

Run this and we get back two rows (just as we expected):

```
GroupKey    Product
----------- ----------------------
1           18
2           12

(2 row(s) affected)
```

Do the match on our sample data, and you'll see we got back just what we wanted.

> *If you're thinking about it, you should be asking yourself "OK, this is great, but how often am I really going to use this?" For most of you, the answer will be "never." There are, however, those times where what's included just isn't ever going to do the job. Aggregates are one of those places where special cases come rarely, but when they come, they really need exactly what they need and nothing else. In short, I wouldn't crowd your brain cells by memorizing every little thing about this section, but do take the time to learn what's involved and get a concept for what it can and can't do so you know what's available should you need it.*

Creating Triggers from Assemblies

> *Note that we have a bit of a "chicken or the egg" (which came first?) thing going on with triggers and .NET. Triggers are not covered until Chapter 12, but I wanted to keep all .NET items close together for reference reasons. If you understand the basics of triggers, you'll be fine with this — if not, you may want to read Chapter 12 first, and then come back to this.*

Much like the other assembly types we've worked with so far in this chapter, triggers have a lot in common with the rest, but also their own little smattering of special things.

The differences will probably come to mind quickly if you think about it for any length of time:

❑ How do we deal with the contextual nature of triggers? That is, how do we know to handle things differently if it's an INSERT trigger situation versus a DELETE or UPDATE trigger?

❑ How do we access the inserted and deleted tables?

You may recall from earlier examples, how we can obtain the "context" of the current connection — it is by utilizing this context that we are able to gain access to different objects that we are interested in. For example, the SqlContext object that we've obtained a connection from in prior examples also contains a SqlTriggerContext object — we can use that to get properties such as whether we are dealing with an insert, update, or delete scenario (the first question we had). The fact that we have access to the current connections also implies that we are able to access the inserted and deleted tables simply by querying them. Let's get right to putting this to use in an example.

Start by creating a new SQL Server project in Visual Studio (I've called mine ExampleTrigger this time). Once your project is up, right-click the project in the Solution Explorer and select Add ➤ Trigger.

Visual Studio is nice enough to provide you with what is, for the most part, a working template. Indeed, it would run right as provided except for one issue:

```
using System;
using System.Data;
using System.Data.SqlClient;
using Microsoft.SqlServer.Server;


public partial class Triggers
{
    // Enter existing table or view for the target and uncomment the attribute
  line
    // [Microsoft.SqlServer.Server.SqlTrigger (Name="ExampleTrigger",
Target="Table1", Event="FOR UPDATE")]

    public static void ExampleTrigger()
    {
        // Replace with your own code
        SqlContext.Pipe.Send("Trigger FIRED");
    }
}
```

I've highlighted the key code line for you. At issue is that we must provide more information to SQL Server than we do in our other object types. Specifically, we must identify what table and events we're going to be executing our trigger against. We're actually going to create a special demonstration table for this before the trigger is actually put into action, so we can just use the table name TriggerTable for now.

```
[Microsoft.SqlServer.Server.SqlTrigger (Name="ExampleTrigger",
 Target="TriggerTable", Event="FOR INSERT, UPDATE, DELETE")]
```

Notice that I've also altered what events will fire our trigger to include all event types.

Now we'll update the meat of things just a bit, so we can show off different actions we might take in our trigger and, perhaps more importantly, how we can check the context of things and make our actions specific to what has happened to our table. We'll start by getting our class going:

```
public static void ExampleTrigger()
{
    // Get a handle to our current connection
    SqlConnection cn = new SqlConnection("context connection=true");
    cn.Open();

    SqlTriggerContext ctxt = SqlContext.TriggerContext;
    SqlCommand cmd = new SqlCommand();
    cmd.Connection = cn;
```

So far, this isn't much different from what we've used in our other .NET examples. Perhaps the only significant difference from things we've seen already is the `SqlTriggerContext` object — we will use this later on to determine what action caused the trigger to fire.

We're ready to start code that is conditional on the action the trigger is firing for (based on the `TriggerAction` property of the `TriggerContext` of the `SqlContext`). For this, I'm going to use a simple `switch` command (though there are those that will call me a programming charlatan for using a `switch` statement — to them I say "deal with it!"). I'm also going to pipe out various things to the client to report what we're doing.

In practice, you generally do not want to be outputting information from a trigger — figure that they should usually run silently as far as the client is concerned. I've gone ahead and output several items in this example just to make it readily apparent what the trigger is doing under what scenario.

```
switch (ctxt.TriggerAction)
{
    case TriggerAction.Insert:
        cmd.CommandText = "SELECT COUNT(*) AS NumRows FROM INSERTED";
        SqlContext.Pipe.Send("Insert Trigger Fired");
        SqlContext.Pipe.ExecuteAndSend(cmd);
        break;

    case TriggerAction.Update:
        // This time, we'll use datareaders to show how we can
        // access the data from the inserted/deleted tables

        SqlContext.Pipe.Send("Update Trigger Fired");
        SqlContext.Pipe.Send("inserted rows...");
        cmd.CommandText = "SELECT * FROM INSERTED";
        SqlContext.Pipe.Send(cmd.ExecuteReader());
        break;

    case TriggerAction.Delete:
```

```
                    // And now we'll go back to what we did with the inserted rows...
                    cmd.CommandText = "SELECT COUNT(*) AS NumRows FROM DELETED";
                    SqlContext.Pipe.Send("Delete Trigger Fired");
                    SqlContext.Pipe.ExecuteAndSend(cmd);
                    break;
            }

            SqlContext.Pipe.Send("Trigger Complete");
        }
    }
```

And, with that, we're ready to compile and upload it. The assembly upload works just as most of them have so far (we're back to not needing anything other than the default PERMISSION_SET).

```
CREATE ASSEMBLY ExampleTrigger
FROM '<solution path>\ExampleTrigger\bin\Debug\ExampleTrigger.dll';
```

Before we get to creating the reference to the trigger, however, we need a table. For this example, we'll just create something very simple:

```
CREATE TABLE TestTrigger
(
    PK          int             NOT NULL PRIMARY KEY,
    Value       varchar(max)    NOT NULL
);
```

With the assembly uploaded and the table created, we're ready to create our trigger reference.

Much like stored procedures and functions, a .NET trigger creation is made from the same statement as T-SQL-based triggers. We eliminate the T-SQL side of things and replace it with the EXTERNAL NAME declaration:

```
CREATE TRIGGER trgExampleTrigger
ON TestTrigger
FOR INSERT, UPDATE, DELETE
AS EXTERNAL NAME ExampleTrigger.Triggers.ExampleTrigger;
```

And with that, our trigger should be in place on our table and ready to be fired whenever one of its trigger actions is fired (which happens to be for every trigger action), so let's test it.

We'll start by getting a few rows inserted into our table. And, wouldn't you just know it? That will allow us to test the insert part of our trigger.

```
INSERT INTO TestTrigger
    (PK, Value)
VALUES
    (1, 'first row'),
    (2, 'second row');
```

Run this, and we not only get our rows in but we also get a little bit of feedback that is coming out of our trigger:

```
Insert Trigger Fired
NumRows
```

```
-----------
1

(1 row(s) affected)

Trigger Complete

(1 row(s) affected)
Insert Trigger Fired
NumRows
-----------
1

(1 row(s) affected)

Trigger Complete

(1 row(s) affected)
```

As you can see, we're getting output from our trigger. Notice that we're getting the "(1 row(s) affected)" both from the query running inside the trigger and from the one that actually inserted the data. We could have taken any action that could have been done in a T-SQL trigger (though many are more efficient if you stay in the T-SQL world). The key is that we could do so much more if we had the need. We could, for example, make an external call or perform a calculation that isn't doable in the T-SQL world.

There is an old saying: "Caution is the better part of valor." This could have been written with triggers in mind. I can't possibly express enough about the "be careful" when it comes to what you're doing in triggers. Just because you can make an external call doesn't make it a smart thing to do. Assess the need — is it really that important that the call be made right then? Realize that these things can be slow, and whatever transaction that trigger is participating in will not complete until the trigger completes — this means you may be severely damaging performance.

Okay, so with all that done, let's try an update:

```
UPDATE TestTrigger
SET Value = 'Updated second row'
WHERE PK = 2;
```

And let's see what we get back:

```
Update Trigger Fired
inserted rows...
PK          Value
----------- -------------------------------------
2           Updated second row

(1 row(s) affected)

Trigger Complete

(1 row(s) affected)
```

The result set we're getting back is the one our trigger is outputting. That's followed by some of our other output as well as the base "(1 row(s) affected)" that we would normally expect from our single row update. Just as with the insert statement, we were able to see what had happened and could have adapted accordingly.

And so, that leaves us with just the delete statement. This time, we'll delete all the rows, and we'll see how the count of our deleted table does indeed reflect both of the deleted rows.

```
DELETE TestTrigger;
```

And again check the results:

```
Delete Trigger Fired
NumRows
-----------
2

(1 row(s) affected)

Trigger Complete

(2 row(s) affected)
```

Now, these results may be just a little confusing, so let's look at what we have.

We start with the notification that our trigger fired. That comes from our trigger. (Remember, we send that message down the pipe ourselves.) Then comes the result set from our SELECT COUNT(*). Notice the "(1 row(s) affected)" — that's from our result set rather than the UPDATE that started it all. We then get to the end of execution of our trigger (again, we dropped that message in the pipe), and, finally, the "(2 row(s) affected)" that was from the original UPDATE statement.

And there we have it. We've done something to address every action scenario, and we could have, of course, done a lot more within each. We could also do something to address a BEFORE trigger if we needed to.

Custom Data Types

Sometimes you have the need to store data that you want to be strongly typed, but that SQL Server doesn't fit within SQL Server's simple data type list. Indeed, you may need to invoke a complex set of rules in order to determine whether or not the data properly meets the type requirement.

Requests for support of complex data types have been around a very long time. Indeed, I can recall being at the Sphinx Beta 2.0 — known to most as Beta 2 for SQL Server 7.0 — event in 1998, and having that come up as something like the second most requested item in a request session I was at. Well, it took a lot of years, but it's finally here.

By utilizing a .NET assembly, we can achieve a virtually limitless number of possibilities in our data types. The type can have complex rules or even contain multiple properties.

Before we get to the syntax for adding assemblies, let's get an assembly constructed.

> The sample used here will be the `ComplexNumber.sln` solution included in the SQL Server samples. You will need to locate the base directory for the solution — the location of which will vary depending on your particular installation.

We need to start by creating the signature keys for this project. To do this, I recommend starting with your solution directory being current and then calling `sn.exe` using a fully qualified path (or, if your .NET Framework directory is already in your PATH, then it's that much easier!). For me, it looks like this:

```
C:\Program Files\Microsoft.NET\SDK\v2.0
64bit\LateBreaking\SQLCLR\UserDefinedDat
aType>"C:\Program Files (x86)\Microsoft Visual Studio 8\SDK\v2.0\Bin\sn" -k
temp
.snk
```

And with that, you're ready to build your DLL.

Let's go ahead and upload the actual assembly (alter this to match the paths on your particular system):

```
CREATE ASSEMBLY ComplexNumber
   FROM '<solution path>\ComplexNumber\bin\debug\ComplexNumber.dll'
WITH PERMISSION_SET = SAFE;
```

And with the assembly loaded, we're ready to begin.

Creating Your Data Type from Your Assembly

So, you have an assembly that implements your complex data type and have uploaded it to SQL Server using the CREATE ASSEMBLY command. You're ready to instruct SQL Server to use it. This works pretty much as other assemblies have. The syntax (you may recall from Chapter 7) looks like this:

```
CREATE TYPE [<schema name>.]<type name>
    EXTERNAL NAME <assembly name>[.<class name>][;]
```

You'll notice immediately that it looks like our previous assembly-related constructs, and, indeed, the use is the same.

So, utilizing our complex type created in the last section, it would look like this:

```
CREATE TYPE ComplexNumber
   EXTERNAL NAME [ComplexNumber].[Microsoft.Samples.SqlServer.ComplexNumber];
```

Accessing Your Complex Data Type

Microsoft has provided a file called `test.sql` for testing the assembly we just defined as our complex data type, but I find it falls just slightly short of where we want to be in our learning here. What I want to emphasize is how the various functions of the supporting class for our data type are still available. In addition, each individual property of the variable is fully addressable. So, let's run a modified version of the provided script:

```
USE AdventureWorks2008;
GO

-- create a variable of the type, create a value of the type and invoke
-- a behavior over it

DECLARE @c ComplexNumber;

SET @c = CONVERT(ComplexNumber, '(1, 2i)');


SELECT @c.ToString() AS FullValueAsString;

SELECT @c.Real AS JustRealProperty'
GO
```

Now run it, and check out the results:

```
FullValueAsString
------------------
  (1,2i)

(1 row(s) affected)

JustRealProperty
------------------
1

(1 row(s) affected)
```

In the first result that was returned, the ToString function was called as defined as a method of our class. The string is formatted just as our method desires. If we had wanted to reverse the order of the numbers or some silly thing like that, we would only have needed to change the ToString function in the class, recompile it, and re-import it our database.

In our second result, we address just one property of our complex data type. The simple dot "." delimiter told SQL Server that we were looking for a property — just as it would in C# or VB.NET.

Dropping Data Types

As you might expect, the syntax for dropping a user-defined data type works just like other drop statements:

```
DROP TYPE [<schema name>.]<type name>[;]
```

And it's gone — maybe.

Okay, so why a "maybe" this time? Well, if there is most any object out there that references this data type, then the DROP will be disallowed and will fail. So, if you have a table that has a column of this type, then an attempt to drop it would fail. Likewise, if you have a schema bound view, stored procedure, trigger, or function defined that utilizes this type, then a drop would also fail.

> *Note that this form of restriction appears in other places in SQL Server — such as dropping a table when it is the target of a foreign key reference — but those restrictions tend to be less all-encompassing than this one is (virtually any use of it in your database at all will block the drop), so I haven't felt as much need to point it out (they were more self-explanatory).*

Summary

Well, if you aren't thinking to yourself something along the lines of "Wow, some of that stuff is pretty powerful," then I can only guess you somehow skipped straight to the summary without reading the rest of the chapter. That's what this chapter is all about — giving you the power to do very complex things (or, in a few cases, simple things that still weren't possible before).

There is a lot to think about out of this chapter. You have table-valued parameters, which allow a sharp reduction in round trips from the client and further allows you to bundle more logic in a single parent sproc.

When using assemblies, you need to be careful. Think about what you're doing, and analyze each of the steps that your assembly is going to be taking even more thoroughly than you already do. Consider latency you're going to be adding if you create long-running processes. Consider external dependencies you are creating if you make external calls — how reliable are those external processes? You need to know, as your system is now only as reliable as the external systems you're calling.

As always, think about what you need, and don't make your solution any more complex than it needs to be. Keep in mind, however, that what seems at first to be the more complex solution may actually be simpler in the end. I've seen stored procedures that solved the seemingly unsolvable T-SQL problem. Keeping your system away from assemblies would seem to make it simpler, but what's better: a 300-line, complex T-SQL stored proc or an assembly that is concise and takes only 25 lines including declarations?

Choose wisely.

Transactions and Locks

What to do . . . ? What to do . . . ? This I pondered when considering this chapter. Since I usually teach this topic even to so-called "beginners" (and I have coverage of it in *Beginning SQL Server 2008 Programming*), I seriously debated removing this subject from the *Professional* title. The problem with that, however, is that, while fundamental in nature, transactions and locks are a fundamental that even lots of fairly advanced users don't quite "get." You see, while nothing in this chapter is wildly difficult, transactions and locks tend to be two of the most misunderstood areas in the database world.

This is one of those chapters that, when you go back to work, will make you sound like you've had your Wheaties today. As such, this "beginning" (or at least I think it's a basic) concept is going to make you start to look like a real pro.

In this chapter, we're going to:

❑ Examine transactions

❑ Examine how the SQL Server log and "checkpoints" work

❑ Unlock your understanding of locks

Now, lest you think that I've suddenly decided to treat you like a rookie, rest assured, we will look a tad more in depth in several places than I necessarily do for beginning readers.

Transactions

Transactions are all about *atomicity*. Atomicity is the concept that something should act as a unit. From our database standpoint, it's about the smallest grouping of one or more statements that should be considered to be "all or nothing."

Often, when dealing with data, we want to make sure that if one thing happens, another thing happens, or that neither of them do. Indeed, this can be carried out to the degree where 20 things (or more) all have to happen together or nothing happens. Let's look at a classic example.

Imagine that you are a banker. Sally comes in and wants to transfer $1,000 from checking to savings. You are, of course, happy to oblige, so you process her request.

Behind the scenes, we have something like this happening:

```
UPDATE checking
   SET Balance = Balance - 1000
   WHERE Account = 'Sally'
UPDATE savings
   SET Balance = Balance + 1000
   WHERE Account = 'Sally'
```

This is a hypersimplification of what's going on, but it captures the main thrust of things: you need to issue two different statements — one for each account.

Now, what if the first statement executes and the second one doesn't? Sally would be out of a thousand dollars! That might, for a short time, seem okay from your perspective (heck, you just made a thousand bucks!), but not for long. By that afternoon you'd have a steady stream of customers leaving your bank. It's hard to stay in the bank business with no depositors.

What you need is a way to be certain that if the first statement executes, the second statement executes. At first, it would seem that there really isn't a way that we can be certain of that. All sorts of things can go wrong, from hardware failures to simple things such as violations of data integrity rules. Fortunately, however, there is a way to do something that serves the same overall purpose. We can essentially forget that the first statement ever happened. We can enforce at least the notion that if one thing didn't happen, then nothing did — at least within the scope of our *transaction*.

In order to capture this notion of a transaction, however, we need to be able to define boundaries. A transaction has to have very definitive begin and end points. Actually, every SELECT, INSERT, UPDATE, and DELETE statement you issue in SQL Server is part of an implicit transaction. Even if you issue only one statement, that one statement is considered to be a transaction. Everything about the statement will be executed, or none of it will. Indeed, by default, that is the length of a transaction — one statement.

> Again: Every **SELECT**, **INSERT**, **UPDATE**, and **DELETE** statement you issue in SQL Server is part of an implicit transaction. Even if you issue only one statement, that one statement is considered to be a transaction. Everything about the statement will be executed, or none of it will.

But what if we need to have more than one statement be all or nothing — such as our preceding bank example? In such a case, we need a way of marking the beginning and end of a transaction, as well as the success or failure of that transaction. To that end, there are several T-SQL statements that we can use to "mark" these points in a transaction. We can:

❏ **BEGIN a transaction:** Set the starting point.

❏ **COMMIT a transaction:** Make the transaction a permanent, irreversible part of the database.

❑ **ROLLBACK a transaction:** Essentially saying that you want to forget that it ever happened.

❑ **SAVE a transaction:** Establish a specific marker to allow us to do only a partial rollback.

Let's look over all of these individually before we put them together into our first transaction.

BEGIN TRAN

The beginning of the transaction is probably one of the easiest concepts to understand in the transaction process. Its sole purpose in life is to denote the point that is the beginning of a unit. If, for some reason, we are unable to or do not want to commit the transaction, this is the point to which all database activity will be rolled back. That is, everything beyond this point that is not eventually committed will effectively be forgotten as far as the database is concerned.

The syntax is:

```
BEGIN TRAN[SACTION] [<transaction name>|<@transaction variable>]
    [WITH MARK ['<description>']][;]
```

The WITH MARK section is optional, and is, in practice, rarely used, but don't discount it as unimportant — quite the contrary!

If you're marking the transaction, you must include the transaction *name*. (Note that it's the name, not the description that is required. The name is optional if you're not marking the transaction.) If supplied the description should be a maximum of 255 characters. (It can be longer, but, if so, it will be truncated to 255.)

Regarding Marking Transactions

Beginning back in SQL Server 2005, we gained the ability, when restoring a database from backups and logs, to restore to a specific point in time. You could specify an exact time that you wanted a backup rolled forward to (utilizing a log), and SQL Server would recover everything up to that point, and nothing beyond. A marked transaction expands this capability by creating a special notation in the transaction log. When performing a point-in-time recovery, you can specify the marked transaction as the point you want to recover to, instead of the time, by simply specifying the description of the mark. You can use this for things such as:

❑ Marking a point when a critical action took place so that, if necessary, you can recover to just that point

❑ Marking activity in two databases so that those databases can be restored to a synchronized point in time

This concept of marking your point in time can be a handy thing to have available. While it is something of an extreme use, you will find scenarios where you need to synchronize with external systems (not even necessarily a SQL Server) on backups.

COMMIT TRAN

The committing of a transaction is the end of a completed transaction. At the point that you issue the COMMIT TRAN, the transaction is considered to be what is called *durable*. That is, the effect of the transaction is now permanent and will last even if you have a system failure (as long as you have a backup or the database files haven't been physically destroyed). The only way to "undo" whatever the transaction accomplished is to issue a new transaction that, functionally speaking, is a reverse of your first transaction.

The syntax for a COMMIT looks pretty similar to a BEGIN:

```
COMMIT [TRAN[SACTION] [<transaction name>|<@transaction variable>]][;]
```

Note that, similar to the way EXECUTE *can be truncated to* EXEC, TRANSACTION *can be truncated down to* TRAN. *While* TRANSACTION *is the more full and clear form of the word, you'll find, in practice, that most developers use the shortened* TRAN. *(What can I say? We're apparently a rather lazy bunch.)*

SQL Server also supports a more ANSI-compliant syntax in the form of:

```
COMMIT [WORK][;]
```

The notion of a transaction name moniker is not supported under this syntax, and, while it is more ANSI compliant, it has, for whatever reason (probably its late addition to the product), been virtually nonutilized with SQL Server in actual practice.

ROLLBACK TRAN

Whenever I think of a ROLLBACK, I think of the old movie *The Princess Bride*. If you've ever seen the film (if you haven't, I highly recommend it), you'll know that the character Vizzini (considered a genius in the film) always said, "If anything goes wrong, go back to the beginning."

That was some mighty good advice. A ROLLBACK does just what Vizzini suggested. It goes back to the beginning. In this case, it's your transaction that goes back to the beginning. Anything that happened since the associated BEGIN statement is effectively forgotten. The only exception to going back to the beginning occurs when using what are called *savepoints*, which I'll describe shortly.

The syntax for a ROLLBACK again looks pretty much the same, with the exception of allowance for a savepoint:

```
ROLLBACK TRAN[SACTION] [<transaction name>|<save point name>|
    <@transaction variable>|<@savepoint variable>][;]
```

Alternatively, you can use the ANSI syntax similar to what we saw with COMMIT:

```
ROLLBACK [WORK][;]
```

SAVE TRAN

To save a transaction is essentially to create something of a bookmark. You establish a name for your bookmark. (You can have more than one.) After this "bookmark" is established, you can reference it in a rollback. What's nice about this is that you can roll back to the exact spot in the code that you want to just by naming a savepoint to which you want to roll back.

> Names for savepoints must conform to the rules for identifiers that we discussed back in Chapter 1. There is, however, a difference; savepoint names are limited to 32 characters in length.

The syntax is simple enough:

```
SAVE TRAN[SACTION] [<save point name>| <@savepoint variable>][;]
```

The thing to remember about savepoints is that they are cleared on ROLLBACK — that is, even if you save five savepoints, once you perform one ROLLBACK they are all gone. You can start setting new savepoints again, and rolling back to those, but whatever savepoints you had when the ROLLBACK was issued are gone.

Savepoints were something of a major confusion area for me when I first came across them. Books Online *indicates that, after rolling back to a savepoint, you must run the transaction to a logical conclusion. (This is technically correct.) Where the confusion came was in the* Books Online *implication that seemed to indicate that you had to go to a* ROLLBACK *or* COMMIT *without using any more savepoints. This is not the case. You just can't use the savepoints that you declared prior to the* ROLLBACK. *Savepoints after this are just fine.*

Let's test this out with a bit of code to see what happens when we mix the different types of TRAN commands. Type the following code in and then we'll run through an explanation of it:

```
USE AdventureWorks2008; -- We're making our own table - what DB doesn't matter

-- Create table to work with
CREATE TABLE MyTranTest
(
    OrderID    INT    PRIMARY KEY    IDENTITY
);
-- Start the transaction
BEGIN TRAN TranStart;

-- Insert our first piece of data using default values.
-- Consider this record No1. It is also the 1st record that stays
-- after all the rollbacks are done.
INSERT INTO MyTranTest
    DEFAULT VALUES;

-- Create a "Bookmark" to come back to later if need be
SAVE TRAN FirstPoint;

-- Insert some more default data (this one will disappear
-- after the rollback).
-- Consider this record No2.
INSERT INTO MyTranTest
    DEFAULT VALUES;
```

```
-- Roll back to the first savepoint. Anything up to that
-- point will still be part of the transaction. Anything
-- beyond is now toast.
ROLLBACK TRAN FirstPoint;

-- Insert some more default data.
-- Consider this record No3 It is the 2nd record that stays
-- after all the rollbacks are done.

INSERT INTO MyTranTest
    DEFAULT VALUES;

-- Create another point to roll back to.
SAVE TRAN SecondPoint;

-- Yet more data. This one will also disappear,
-- only after the second rollback this time.
-- Consider this record No4.
INSERT INTO MyTranTest
    DEFAULT VALUES;

-- Go back to second savepoint
ROLLBACK TRAN SecondPoint;

-- Insert a little more data to show that things
-- are still happening.
-- Consider this record No5. It is the 3rd record that stays
-- after all the rollbacks are done.
INSERT INTO MyTranTest
    DEFAULT VALUES;

-- Commit the transaction
COMMIT TRAN TranStart;

-- See what records were finally committed.
SELECT TOP 3 OrderID
FROM MyTranTest
ORDER BY OrderID DESC;

-- Clean up after ourselves
DROP TABLE MyTranTest;
```

First, we create a table to work with for our test:

```
-- Create table to work with
CREATE TABLE MyTranTest
(
    OrderID    INT    PRIMARY KEY    IDENTITY
);
```

Since we're creating our own table to play with, what database we are using doesn't really matter for this demonstration.

Then it's time to begin the transaction. This starts our grouping of "all or nothing" statements. We then INSERT a row. At this juncture, we have just one row inserted:

```
-- Start the transaction
BEGIN TRAN TranStart;


-- Insert our first piece of data using default values.
-- Consider this record No1. It is also the 1st record that stays
-- after all the rollbacks are done.
INSERT INTO MyTranTest
    DEFAULT VALUES;
```

Next, we establish a savepoint called FirstPoint and insert yet another row. At this point, we have two rows inserted, but remember, they are not committed yet, so the database doesn't consider them to be part of the database:

```
-- Create a "Bookmark" to come back to later if need be
SAVE TRAN FirstPoint;


-- Insert some more default data (this one will disappear
-- after the rollback).
-- Consider this record No2.
INSERT INTO MyTranTest
    DEFAULT VALUES;
```

We then ROLLBACK — explicitly saying that it is *not* the beginning that we want to rollback to, but just to FirstPoint. With the ROLLBACK, everything between ROLLBACK and the FirstPoint savepoint is undone. Since we have one INSERT statement between the ROLLBACK and the SAVE, that statement is rolled back. At this juncture, we are back down to just one row inserted. Any attempt to reference a savepoint would now fail since all savepoints have been reset with our ROLLBACK:

```
-- Roll back to the first savepoint. Anything up to that
-- point will still be part of the transaction. Anything
-- beyond is now toast.
ROLLBACK TRAN FirstPoint;
```

We add another row, putting us back up to a total of two rows inserted at this point. We also create a brand new savepoint. This is perfectly valid, and we can now refer to this savepoint since it is established after the ROLLBACK:

```
-- Insert some more default data.
-- Consider this record No3. It is the 2nd record that stays
-- after all the rollbacks are done.

INSERT INTO MyTranTest
    DEFAULT VALUES;


-- Create another point to roll back to.
SAVE TRAN SecondPoint;
```

Time for yet another row to be inserted, bringing our total number of still-valid inserts up to three:

```
-- Yet more data. This one will also disappear,
-- only after the second rollback this time.
```

```
-- Consider this record No4.
INSERT INTO MyTranTest
    DEFAULT VALUES;
```

Now we perform another ROLLBACK, this time referencing our new savepoint (which happens to be the only one valid at this point since FirstPoint was reset after the first ROLLBACK). This one undoes everything between it and the savepoint it refers to — in this case just one INSERT statement. That puts us back at two INSERT statements that are still valid:

```
-- Go back to second savepoint
ROLLBACK TRAN SecondPoint;
```

We then issue yet another INSERT statement, bringing our total number of INSERT statements that are still part of the transaction back up to three:

```
-- Insert a little more data to show that things
-- are still happening.
-- Consider this record No5. It is the 3rd record that stays
-- after all the rollbacks are done.
INSERT INTO MyTranTest
    DEFAULT VALUES;
```

Last (for our transaction anyway), but certainly not least, we issue the COMMIT TRAN statement that locks our transaction in and makes it a permanent part of the history of the database:

```
-- Commit the transaction
COMMIT TRAN TranStart

-- See what records were finally committed.
SELECT TOP 3 OrderID
FROM MyTranTest
ORDER BY OrderID DESC;
```

> Note that if either of these ROLLBACK statements had not included the name of a savepoint, or had included a name that had been set with the BEGIN statement, then the entire transaction would have been rolled back, and the transaction would be considered to be closed.

With the transaction complete, we can issue a little statement that shows us our three rows. When you look at this, you'll be able to see what's happened in terms of rows being added and then removed from the transaction:

```
OrderID
-----------
5
3
1

(3 row(s) affected)
```

Sure enough, every other row was inserted.

Finally, we clean up after ourselves. This really has nothing to do with the transaction.

```
DROP TABLE MyTranTest;
```

How the SQL Server Log Works

You definitely must have the concept of transactions down before you get into trying to figure out the way that SQL Server tracks what's in your database. You see, what you *think* of as your database is only rarely a complete version of all the data. Except for rare moments when it happens that everything has been written to disk, the data in your database is made up of not only the data in the physical database file(s) but also any transactions that have been committed to the *log* since the last checkpoint.

In the normal operation of your database, most activities that you perform are "logged" to the *transaction log* rather than written directly to the database. A *checkpoint* is a periodic operation that forces all dirty pages for the database currently in use to be written to disk. Dirty pages are log or data pages that have been modified after they were read into the cache, but the modifications have not yet been written to disk. Without a checkpoint the log would fill up and/or use all the available disk space. The process works something like the diagram in Figure 11-1.

> *Don't mistake all this as meaning that you have to do something special to get your data out of the cache. SQL Server handles all of this for you. This information is only provided here to facilitate your understanding of how the log works, and, from there, the steps required to handle a transaction. Whether something is in cache or not can make a big difference to performance, so understanding when things are logged and when things go in and out of the cache can be a big deal when you are seeking maximum performance.*

Note that the need to read data into a cache that is already full is not the only reason that a checkpoint would be issued. Checkpoints can be issued under the following circumstances:

❑ By a manual statement — using the CHECKPOINT command.

❑ At normal shutdown of the server (unless the WITH NOWAIT option is used).

❑ When you change any database option (for example, single user only, dbo only, and so on).

❑ When the Simple Recovery option is used and the log becomes 70 percent full.

❑ When the amount of data in the log since the last checkpoint (often called the *active* portion of the log) exceeds the size that the server could recover in the amount of time specified in the *recovery interval* option.

Let's look at each of these more carefully.

Using the CHECKPOINT Command

One way — but probably the least often used way — for the database to have a checkpoint issued is for it to be done manually. You can do this anytime by just typing in the word:

```
CHECKPOINT
```

It's just that simple.

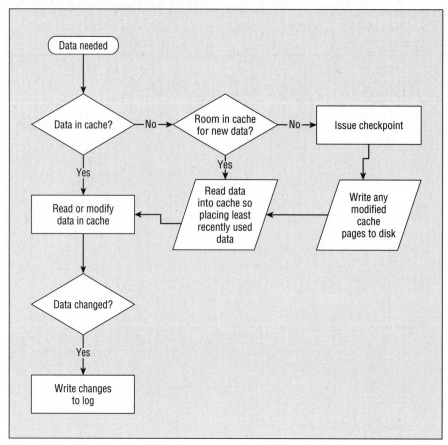

Figure 11-1

SQL Server does a very good job of managing itself in the area of checkpoints, so the times when issuing a manual checkpoint makes sense are fairly rare.

One place that I will do this is during the development cycle when I have the simple recovery model turned on for my database (you are very unlikely to want that for a production database). It's not at all uncommon during the development stage of your database to perform actions that are long running and fill up the log rather quickly. While I could always just issue the appropriate command to truncate the log myself, CHECKPOINT is a little shorter and faster and, when using the simple recovery model, has the same effect.

At Normal Server Shutdown

Ever wonder why SQL Server can sometimes take a very long time to shut down? Besides the dealloca-tion of memory and other destructor routines that have to run to unload the system, SQL Server must also first issue a checkpoint before the shutdown process can begin. This means that you'll have to wait for any data that's been committed in the log to be written out to the physical database before your shutdown can continue. Checkpoints also occur when the server is stopped:

❑ Using the Management Studio

❑ Using the NET STOP MSSQLSERVER instruction at a command window (a DOS box some would call it) prompt

❑ Using the Services icon in the Windows control panel, selecting the MSSQLSERVER service, and clicking the stop button

> Unlike Checkpoint on Recovery, this is something that I like. I like the fact that all my committed transactions are in the physical database (not split between the log and database), which just strikes me as being cleaner, with less chance of data corruption.

There is a way you can get around the delay if you so choose. To use it, you must be shutting down using the SHUTDOWN command in T-SQL. To eliminate the delay associated with the checkpoint (and the checkpoint itself for that matter), you just add the WITH NO WAIT key phrase to your shutdown statement:

```
SHUTDOWN [WITH NO WAIT]
```

Note that I recommend highly *against* using this unless you have some programmatic need to shut down your server. It will cause the subsequent restart to take a longer time than usual to recover the databases on the server, and it means that your shutdown is not as clean. (Some data is only in the log rather than all of it being in the database file.)

At a Change of Database Options

A checkpoint is issued anytime you issue a change to your database options regardless of how the option gets changed (such as using sp_dboption or ALTER DATABASE). The checkpoint is issued prior to making the actual change in the database.

When the Truncate on Checkpoint Option Is Active

If you have turned on the Truncate On Checkpoint database option (which is a common practice during the development phase of your database), then SQL Server will automatically issue a checkpoint any time the log becomes more than 70 percent full.

When Recovery Time Would Exceed the Recovery Interval Option Setting

As we saw briefly earlier (and will see more closely next), SQL Server performs a process called recovery every time the SQL Server is started up. SQL Server will automatically issue a checkpoint any time the estimated time to run the recovery process would exceed the amount of time set in a database option called recovery interval. By default, the recovery interval is set to zero, which means that SQL Server will decide for you. (In practice, this means about one minute.)

Failure and Recovery

A recovery happens every time that SQL Server starts up. SQL Server takes the database file and then applies (by writing them out to the physical database file) any committed changes that are in the log since the last checkpoint. Any changes in the log that do not have a corresponding commit are rolled back — that is, they are essentially forgotten about.

Let's take a look at how this works depending on how transactions have occurred in your database. Imagine five transactions that span the log, as pictured in Figure 11-2.

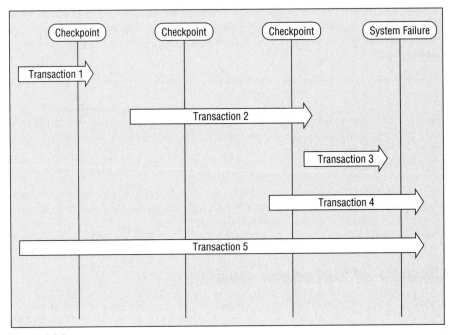

Figure 11-2

Let's look at what would happen to these transactions one by one.

Transaction 1

Absolutely nothing would happen. The transaction has already been through a checkpoint and has been fully committed to the database. There is no need to do anything at recovery, because any data that is read into the data cache would already reflect the committed transaction.

Transaction 2

Even though the transaction existed at the time that a checkpoint was issued, the transaction had not been committed (the transaction was still going). Without that commitment, the transaction does not actually participate in the checkpoint. This transaction would, therefore, be "rolled forward." This is just a fancy way of saying that we would need to read all the related pages back into cache and then use the information in the log to re-run all the statements that we ran in this transaction. When that's finished, the transaction should look exactly as it did before the system failed.

Transaction 3

It may not look the part, but this transaction is exactly the same as Transaction 2 from the standpoint of what needs to be done. Again, because Transaction 3 wasn't finished at the time of the last checkpoint, it did not participate in that checkpoint, just like Transaction 2 didn't. The only difference is that Transaction 3 didn't even exist at that time, but, from a recovery stand-point it makes no difference — it's where the commit is issued that makes all the difference.

Transaction 4

This transaction wasn't completed at the time of system failure, and must, therefore, be rolled back. In effect, it never happened from a row data perspective. The user would have to re-enter any data, and any process would need to start from the beginning.

Transaction 5

This one is no different than Transaction 4. It appears to be different because the transaction has been running longer, but that makes no difference. The transaction was not committed at the time of system failure, and must therefore be rolled back.

Implicit Transactions

Primarily for compatibility with other major RDBMS systems, such as Oracle or DB2, SQL Server supports (it is off by default but can be turned on if you choose) the notion of what is called an *implicit transaction*. Implicit transactions do not require a BEGIN TRAN statement — instead, they are automatically started with your first statement. They then continue until you issue a COMMIT TRAN or ROLLBACK TRAN statement. The next transaction then begins with your next statement.

Theoretically, the purpose behind this is to make sure that every statement is part of a transaction. SQL Server also wants every statement to be part of a transaction, but, by default, takes a different approach — if there is no BEGIN TRAN, then SQL Server assumes you have a transaction of just one statement, and automatically begins and ends that transaction for you. With some other systems though, you'll find the implied transaction approach. Those systems will assume that any one statement is only the beginning of the transaction and therefore require that you explicitly end the every transaction with a COMMIT or ROLLBACK.

By default, the IMPLICIT_TRANSACTIONS option is turned off (and the connection is in autocommit transaction mode). You can turn it on by issuing the command:

```
SET IMPLICIT_TRANSACTIONS ON;
```

After that, any of the following statements will initiate a transaction:

```
CREATE
ALTER TABLE
GRANT
REVOKE
SELECT
UPDATE
DELETE
INSERT
```

```
TRUNCATE TABLE
DROP
OPEN
FETCH
```

The transaction will continue until you COMMIT or ROLLBACK. Note that the implicit transactions option will affect only the current connection — any other users will still have the option turned off unless they have also executed the SET statement.

> The implicit transactions option is dangerous territory, and I highly recommend that you leave this option off unless you have a very specific reason to turn it on (such as compatibility with code written in another system).

> Here's a common scenario: A user calls up and says, "I've been inserting data for the last half hour, and none of my changes are showing." So, you go run a DBCC OPENTRAN, and discover that there's a transaction that's been there for a while — you can take a guess at what's happened. The user has a transaction open, and his or her changes won't appear until that transaction is committed. The user may have done it using an explicit BEGIN TRANS statement, but he or she may also have executed some code that turned implicit transactions on and then didn't turn it off. A mess follows.

Locks and Concurrency

Concurrency is a major issue for any database system. It addresses the notion of two or more users trying to interact with the same object at the same time. The nature of that interaction may be different for each user (updating, deleting, reading, inserting), and the ideal way to handle the competition for control of the object changes depending on just what all the users in question are doing and just how important their actions are. The more users — more specifically, the more transactions — that you can run with reasonable success at the same time, the higher your concurrency is said to be.

In the Online Transaction Processing (OLTP) environment, concurrency is usually the first thing we deal with in data, and it is the focus of most of the database notions put forward in this book. (Online Analytical Processing [OLAP] is usually something of an afterthought; it shouldn't necessarily be that way, but it is.) Dealing with the issue of concurrency can be critical to the performance of your system. At the foundation of dealing with concurrency in databases is a process called *locking*.

Locks are mechanisms for preventing a process from performing an action on an object that conflicts with something already being done on that object. That is, you can't do some things to an object if someone else got there first. What you can and cannot do depends on what the other user is doing. It is also a means of describing what is being done, so the system knows whether or not the second process action is compatible with the first process. For example, 1, 2, 10, 100, 1,000, or whatever number of user connections the system can handle are usually all able to share the same piece of data at the same time as long as they all only want the record on a read-only basis. Think of it as being like a crystal shop: Lots of people can be in looking at things — even the same thing — as long as they don't move it, buy it, or otherwise change it. If more than one person does that at the same time, you're liable to wind up with broken crystal. That's why the shopkeeper usually keeps a close eye on things, and they will usually decide who gets to handle it first.

The SQL Server *lock manager* is that shopkeeper. When you come into the SQL Server "store," the lock manager asks what is your intent — what it is you're going to be doing. If you say "just looking," and no one else already there is doing anything but "just looking," then the lock manager will let you in. If you want to "buy" (update or delete) something, then the lock manager will check to see if anyone's already there. If so, then you must wait, and everyone who comes in behind you will also wait. When you are let in to "buy," no one else will be let in until you are done.

By doing things this way, SQL Server is able to help us avoid a mix of different problems that can be created by concurrency issues. We will examine the possible concurrency problems and how to set a *transaction isolation level* that will prevent each, but for now, let's move on to what can and cannot be locked, and what kinds of locks are available.

What Problems Can Be Prevented by Locks

Locks can address four major problems:

- ❑ Dirty reads
- ❑ Non-repeatable reads
- ❑ Phantoms
- ❑ Lost updates

Each of these presents a separate set of problems, and can be handled by mix of solutions that usually includes proper setting of the transaction isolation level. Just to help make things useful as you look back at this chapter later, I'm going to include information on which transaction isolation level is appropriate for each of these problems. We'll take a complete look at isolation levels shortly, but for now, let's first make sure that we understand what each of these problems is all about.

Dirty Reads

Dirty reads occur when a transaction reads a record that is part of another transaction that isn't complete yet. If the first transaction completes normally, then it's unlikely there's a problem. But what if the transaction were rolled back? You would have information from a transaction that never happened from the database's perspective!

Let's look at it in an example series of steps:

Transaction 1 Command	Transaction 2 Command	Logical Database Value	Uncommitted Database Value	What Transaction 2 Shows
BEGIN TRAN		3		
UPDATE col = 5	BEGIN TRAN	3	5	
SELECT anything	SELECT @var = col	3	5	5
ROLLBACK	UPDATE anything SET whatever = @var	3		5

Oops — problem!!!

Transaction 2 has now made use of a value that isn't valid! If you try to go back and audit to find where this number came from, you'll wind up with no trace and an extremely large headache.

Fortunately, this scenario can't happen if you're using the SQL Server default for the transaction isolation level (called READ COMMITTED, which will be explained later in the section "Setting the Isolation Level").

Non-Repeatable Reads

It's really easy to get this one mixed up with a dirty read. Don't worry about that — it's only terminology. Just get the concept.

A *non-repeatable read* is caused when you read the record twice in a transaction, and a separate transaction alters the data in the interim. For this one, let's go back to our bank example. Remember that we don't want the value of the account to go below 0 dollars:

Transaction 1	Transaction 2	@Var	What Transaction 1 *Thinks* Is in The Table	Value in Table
BEGIN TRAN		NULL		125
SELECT @Var = value FROM table	BEGIN TRAN	125	125	125
	UPDATE value, SET value = value – 50			75
IF @Var >=100	END TRAN	125	125	75
UPDATE value, SET value = value – 100		125	125 (waiting for lock to clear)	75
(Finish, wait for lock to clear, then continue)		125	75	Either: –25 (If there isn't a CHECK constraint enforcing > 0) Or: Error 547 (If there is a CHECK)

Again, we have a problem. Transaction 1 has prescanned (which can be a good practice in some instances) to make sure that the value is valid and that the transaction can go through (there's enough money in the account). The problem is that, before the UPDATE was made, Transaction 2 beat Transaction 1 to the punch. If there isn't any CHECK constraint on the table to prevent the negative value, then it will indeed be set to –25 — even though it logically appeared that we prevented this through the use of our IF statement.

We can prevent this problem in only two ways:

❑ Create a CHECK constraint and monitor for the 547 Error.

❑ Set our ISOLATION LEVEL to be REPEATABLE READ or SERIALIZABLE.

The CHECK constraint seems fairly obvious. The thing to realize here is that you are taking something of a reactive rather than a proactive approach with this method. Nonetheless, in most situations we have a potential for non-repeatable reads, so this would be my preferred choice in most circumstances.

We'll be taking a full look at isolation levels shortly, but for now, suffice to say that there's a good chance that setting it to REPEATABLE READ or SERIALIZABLE is going to cause you as many headaches (or more) as it solves. Still — it's an option.

Phantoms

No — we're not talking the "of the opera" kind here — what we're talking about are records that appear mysteriously, as if unaffected by an UPDATE or DELETE statement that you've issued. This can happen quite legitimately in the normal course of operating your system, and doesn't require any kind of elaborate scenario to illustrate. Here's a classic example of how this happens.

Let's say you are running a fastfood restaurant. If you're typical of that kind of establishment, you probably have a fair number of employees working at the "minimum wage" as defined by the government. The government has just decided to raise the minimum wage from $6.55 to $7.25 per hour, and you want to run an update on a table called Employees to move anyone making less than $7.25 per hour up to the new minimum wage. No problem, you say, and you issue the rather simple statement:

```
UPDATE Employees
SET HourlyRate = 7.25
WHERE HourlyRate < 7.25;

ALTER TABLE Employees
    ADD CONSTRAINT ckWage CHECK (HourlyRate >= 7.25);
GO
```

That was a breeze, right? *Wrong!* Just for illustration, we're going to say that you get an error message back:

```
Msg 547, Level 16, State 1, Line 1
ALTER TABLE statement conflicted with COLUMN CHECK constraint 'ckWage'. The
conflict occurred in database 'FastFood', table 'Employees', column 'HourlyRate'.
```

So, you run a quick SELECT statement checking for values below $7.25, and sure enough you find one. The question is likely to come rather quickly, "How did that get there? I just did the UPDATE which should have fixed that!" You did run the statement, and it ran just fine — you just got a *phantom*.

The instances of phantom reads are rare and require just the right circumstances to happen. In short, someone performed an INSERT statement at the very same time your UPDATE was running. Since it was an entirely new row, it didn't have a lock on it, and it proceeded just fine.

The only cure for this is setting your transaction isolation level to SERIALIZABLE, in which case any updates to the table must not fall within your WHERE clause, or they will be locked out.

Lost Updates

Lost updates happen when one update is successfully written to the database but is accidentally overwritten by another transaction. I can just hear you right about now, "Yikes! How could that happen?"

Lost updates can happen when two transactions read an entire record, then one writes updated information back to the record, and the other writes updated information back to the record. Let's look at an example.

Let's say that you are a credit analyst for your company. You get a call that customer X has reached his or her credit limit and would like an extension, so you pull up the customer information to take a look. You see that they have a credit limit of $5,000, and that they appear to always pay on time.

While you're looking, Sally, another person in your credit department, pulls up customer X's record to enter a change in the address. The record she pulls up also shows the credit limit of $5,000.

At this point, you decide to go ahead and raise customer X's credit limit to $7,500, and press enter. The database now shows $7,500 as the credit limit for customer X.

Sally now completes her update to the address, but she's using the same edit screen that you are — that is, she updates the entire record. Remember what her screen showed as the credit limit? $5,000. Oops, the database now shows customer X with a credit limit of $5,000 again. Your update has been lost!

The solution to this depends on your code somehow recognizing that another connection has updated your record between the time when you read the data and when you went to update it. How this recognition happens varies depending on what access method you're using.

Lockable Resources

There are six different *lockable resources* for SQL Server, and they form a hierarchy. The higher level the lock, the less *granularity* it has (that is, you're choosing a higher and higher number of objects to be locked in something of a cascading action just because the object that contains them has been locked). The more relevant of these include, in ascending order of granularity:

- ❑ **Database:** The entire database is locked. This happens usually during database schema changes.

- ❑ **Table:** The entire table is locked. This includes all the data-related objects associated with that table, including the actual data rows (every one of them) and all the keys in all the indexes associated with the table in question.

- ❑ **Extent:** The entire extent is locked. Remember that an extent is made up of eight pages, so an extent lock means that the lock has control of the extent, the eight data or index pages in that extent, and all the rows of data in those eight pages.

- ❑ **Page:** All the data or index keys on that page are locked.

- ❑ **Key:** There is a lock on a particular key or series of keys in an index. Other keys in the same index page may be unaffected.

- ❑ **Row or Row Identifier (RID):** Although the lock is technically placed on the row identifier (an internal SQL Server construct), it essentially locks the entire row.

Lock Escalation and Lock Effects on Performance

Escalation is all about recognizing that maintaining a finer level of granularity (say a row lock instead of a page lock) makes a lot of sense when the number of items being locked is small. However, as we get more and more items locked, the overhead associated with maintaining those locks actually hinders performance. It can cause the lock to be in place longer, thus creating contention issues; the longer the lock is in place, the more likely that someone will want that particular record. When you think about this for a bit, you'll realize there's probably a balancing act to be done somewhere, and that's exactly what the lock manager uses escalation to do.

When the number of locks being maintained reaches a certain threshold, the lock is escalated to the next highest level, and the lower-level locks do not have to be so tightly managed (freeing resources and helping speed over contention).

Note that the escalation is based on the number of locks rather than the number of users. The importance here is that you can single-handedly lock a table by performing a mass update. A row lock can graduate to a page lock, which then escalates to a table lock. That means that you could potentially be locking every other user out of the table. If your query makes use of multiple tables, it's actually quite possible to wind up locking everyone out of all of those tables.

While you certainly would prefer not to lock all the other users out of your object, there are times when you still need to perform updates that are going to have that effect. There is very little you can do about escalation other than to keep your queries as targeted as possible. Recognize that escalations will happen, so make sure you've thought about what the possible ramifications of your query are.

Lock Modes

Beyond considering just what resource level you're locking, you also should consider what lock mode your query is going to acquire. Just as there are a variety of resources to lock, there are also a variety of *lock modes*.

Some modes are exclusive of each other (which means they don't work together). Some modes do nothing more than essentially modify other modes. Whether modes can work together is based on whether they are *compatible*. We'll take a closer look at compatibility between locks later in this chapter.

Just as we did with lockable resources, let's take a look at lock modes one by one.

Shared Locks

This is the most basic type of lock there is. A *shared lock* is used when you only need to read the data — that is, when you won't be changing anything. A shared lock wants to be your friend, as it is compatible with other shared locks. That doesn't mean that it still won't cause you grief — while a shared lock doesn't mind any other kind of lock, there are other locks that don't like shared locks.

Shared locks tell other locks that you're out there. It's the old, "Look at me! Ain't I special?" thing. They don't serve much of a purpose, yet they can't really be ignored. However, one thing that shared locks do is to prevent users from performing dirty reads.

Exclusive Locks

Exclusive locks are just what they sound like. Exclusive locks are not compatible with any other lock. They cannot be achieved if any other lock exists, nor will they allow a new lock of any form to be created on the resource while the exclusive lock is still active. This prevents two people from updating, deleting, or doing whatever at the same time.

Update Locks

Update locks are something of a hybrid between shared locks and exclusive locks. An update lock is a special kind of placeholder. Think about it — in order to do an UPDATE, you need to validate your WHERE clause (assuming there is one) to figure out just what rows you're going to be updating. That means that you only need a shared lock, until you actually go to make the physical update. At the time of the physical update, you'll need an exclusive lock.

Update locks indicate that you have a shared lock that's going to become an exclusive lock after you've done your initial scan of the data to figure out what exactly needs to be updated. This acknowledges the fact that there are two distinct stages to an update:

❑   First, the stage where you are figuring out what meets the WHERE clause criteria (what's going to be updated). This is the part of an update query that has an update lock.

❑   Second, the stage where, if you actually decide to perform the update, the lock is upgraded to an exclusive lock. Otherwise, the lock is converted to a shared lock.

What's nice about this is that it forms a barrier against one variety of *deadlock*. A deadlock is not a type of lock in itself but rather a situation where a paradox has been formed. A deadlock would arise if one lock can't do what it needs to do in order to clear because another lock is holding that resource. The problem is that the opposite resource is itself stuck waiting for the lock to clear on the first transaction.

Without update locks, these deadlocks would crop up all the time. Two update queries would be running in shared mode. Query A completes its query and is ready for the physical update. It wants to escalate to an exclusive lock, but it can't because Query B is finishing its query. Query B then finishes the query, except that it needs to do the physical update. To do that, Query B must escalate to an exclusive lock, but it can't because Query A is still waiting. This creates an impasse.

An update lock prevents any other update locks from being established. The instant that the second transaction attempts to achieve an update lock, the new transaction will be put into a wait status for whatever the lock timeout is; the lock will not be granted. If the first lock clears before the lock timeout is reached, then the lock will be granted to the new requester, and that process can continue. If not, an error will be generated.

Update locks are compatible only with shared locks and intent shared locks.

Intent Locks

An *intent lock* is a true placeholder and is meant to deal with the issue of object hierarchies. Imagine a situation where you have a lock established on a row, but someone wants to establish a lock on a page or extent, or to modify a table. You wouldn't want another transaction to go around yours by going higher up the hierarchy, would you?

Without intent locks, the higher-level objects wouldn't even know that you had the lock at the lower level. Intent locks improve performance, as SQL Server needs to examine intent locks only at the table level, and not check every row or page lock on the table, to determine if a transaction can safely lock the entire table. Intent locks come in three different varieties:

❑   **Intent shared lock:** A shared lock has or is going to be established at some lower point in the hierarchy. For example, a page is about to have a page level shared lock established on it. This type of lock applies only to tables and pages.

❑ **Intent exclusive lock:** This is the same as intent shared, but with an exclusive lock about to be placed on the lower-level item.

❑ **Shared with intent exclusive lock:** A shared lock has or is about to be established lower down the object hierarchy, but the intent is to modify data, so it will become an intent exclusive at some point.

Schema Locks

These come in two flavors:

❑ **Schema modification lock (Sch-M):** A schema change is being made to the object. No queries or other CREATE, ALTER, or DROP statements can be run against this object for the duration of the Sch-M lock.

❑ **Schema stability lock (Sch-S):** This is very similar to a shared lock; this lock's sole purpose is to prevent a Sch-M since there are already locks for other queries (or CREATE, ALTER, DROP statements) active on the object. This is compatible with all other lock types.

Bulk Update Locks

A *bulk update lock (BU)* is really just a variant of a table lock with one little (but significant) difference. Bulk update locks allow parallel loading of data — that is, the table is locked from any other "normal" (T-SQL Statements) activity, but multiple BULK INSERT or bcp operations can be performed at the same time.

Ranged Keylocks

Ranged keylocks are merely a way for SQL Server to control internally individual locks more efficiently. Rather than being its own lock, it is, instead, just a method of tracking which locks are being held. Instead of holding an individual lock for each row in a range being accessed, SQL Server is able to maintain one lock that addressed the entire range (thus saving memory and lock operations).

Lock Compatibility

The table that follows shows the compatibility of the resource lock modes (listed in increasing lock strength). Existing locks are shown by the columns; requested locks by the rows:

	IS	S	U	IX	SIX	X
Intent Shared (IS)	YES	YES	YES	YES	YES	NO
Shared (S)	YES	YES	YES	NO	NO	NO
Update (U)	YES	YES	NO	NO	NO	NO
Intent Exclusive (IX)	YES	NO	NO	YES	NO	NO
Shared with Intent Exclusive (SIX)	YES	NO	NO	NO	NO	NO
Exclusive (X)	NO	NO	NO	NO	NO	NO

Also:

- ❏ The Sch-S is compatible with all lock modes except the Sch-M.
- ❏ The Sch-M is incompatible with all lock modes.
- ❏ The BU is compatible only with schema stability and other bulk update locks.
- ❏ RangeS-S, RangeS-U, RangeI-N, and RangeX-X are range locks that match with the corresponding S, U, and X lock types where applicable, and, in the case of RangeI-N (the N stands for null), lock a range of *potential* rows to prevent phantoms.

Specifying a Specific Lock Type — Optimizer Hints

Sometimes you want to have more control over how the locking goes either in your query, or perhaps in your entire transaction. You can do this by making use of what are called *optimizer hints*.

Optimizer hints are ways of explicitly telling SQL Server to escalate a lock to a specific level. They are included right after the name of the table (in your SQL Statement) that they are to act against, and are designated as follows:

Hint	Description
SERIALIZABLE/HOLDLOCK	Once a lock is established by a statement in a transaction, that lock is not released until the transaction is ended (via ROLLBACK or COMMIT). Inserts are also prevented if the inserted record would match the criteria in the WHERE clause in the query that established the lock (no phantoms). This is the highest isolation level, and guarantees absolute consistency of data.
READUNCOMMITTED/NOLOCK	Obtains no lock (not even a shared lock) and does not honor other locks. While a very fast option, it can generate dirty reads as well as a host of other problems.
READCOMMITTED	The default. Honors all locks, but how it handles acquiring locks depends on the database option READ_COMMITTED_SNAPSHOT. If that setting is on, then READCOMMITTED will *not* acquire locks, and will instead use a row versioning scheme to determine whether any conflicts have occurred. In practice, this should work just fine, and READCOMMITTED should be the way for you to go for both backward compatibility and what is likely better performance.
READCOMMITTEDLOCK	This is nuance stuff here. Consider this one to be largely the same as READCOMMITTED in most situations. (Indeed, this one works exactly as READCOMMITTED did in prior versions of SQL Server.) It honors all locks but releases any locks held as soon as the object in question is no longer needed. Performs the same as the READ COMMITTED isolation level.

Hint	Description
REPEATABLEREAD	Once a lock is established by a statement in a transaction, that lock is not released until the transaction is ended (via ROLLBACK or COMMIT). New data can be inserted, however.
READPAST	Rather than waiting for a lock to clear, skips all locked rows. The skip is limited to row locks (still waits for page, extent, and table locks) and can only be used with a SELECT statement.
NOWAIT	Causes the query to fail immediately rather than wait if any locks are detected.
ROWLOCK	This forces the initial level of the lock to be at the row level, even if the optimizer would have otherwise selected a less granular locking strategy. It does not prevent the lock from being escalated to those less granular levels if the number of locks reaches the system's lock threshold.
PAGLOCK	Uses a page-level lock regardless of the choice that otherwise would have been made by the optimizer. The usefulness of this can go both ways — sometimes you know that a page lock is more appropriate than a row lock for resource conservation — other times you want to minimize contention where the optimizer might have chosen a table lock.
TABLOCK	Forces a full table lock rather than whatever the lock manager would have used. Can really speed up known table scan situations but creates big contention problems if other users want to modify data in the table.
TABLOCKX	Similar to TABLOCK, but creates an exclusive lock — locks all other users out of the table for the duration of the statement or transaction depending on how the TRANSACTION ISOLATION LEVEL is set.
UPDLOCK	Uses an update lock instead of a shared lock. This is a highly underutilized tool in the war against deadlocks, as it still allows other users to obtain shared locks but ensures that no data modification (other update locks) are established until you end the statement or transaction (presumably after going ahead and updating the rows).
XLOCK	With its roots in TABLOCKX, this one first appeared in SQL Server 2000. The advantage here is that you can specify an exclusive lock regardless of what lock granularity you have chosen (or not chosen) to specify.

Most of these can be very useful in specific situations, but, before you get too attached to using these, make sure that you also check out the concept of isolation levels later in the chapter.

The syntax for using locks is fairly easy — just add it after the table name, or after the alias if you're using one:

```
....
FROM <table name> [AS <alias>][[WITH](<hint>)]
```

So, to put this into a couple of examples, any of these would be legal, and all would force a table lock (rather than the more likely key or row lock) on the SalesOrderHeader table:

```
SELECT * FROM Sales.SalesOrderHeader AS ord WITH (TABLOCKX)
```

```
SELECT * FROM Sales.SalesOrderHeader AS ord (TABLOCKX)
```

```
SELECT * FROM Sales.SalesOrderHeader WITH (TABLOCKX)
```

```
SELECT * FROM Sales.SalesOrderHeader (TABLOCKX)
```

Now look at it from a multiple-table perspective. The following queries would do the same thing as the previous ones in terms of locking. They would force an exclusive table lock on the SalesOrderHeader table. The thing to note, though, is that they do *not* place any kind of special lock on the SalesOrderDetail table. The SQL Server lock manager still is in complete control of that table.

```
SELECT *
FROM Sales.SalesOrderHeader AS ord WITH (TABLOCKX)
JOIN Sales.SalesOrderDetail AS od
  ON ord.SalesOrderID = od.SalesOrderID;

SELECT *
FROM Sales.SalesOrderHeader AS ord (TABLOCKX)
JOIN Sales.SalesOrderDetail AS od
  ON ord.SalesOrderID = od.SalesOrderID;

SELECT *
FROM Sales.SalesOrderHeader WITH (TABLOCKX);
JOIN Sales.SalesOrderDetail AS od
  ON Sales.SalesOrderHeader.SalesOrderID = od.SalesOrderID;

SELECT *
FROM Sales.SalesOrderHeader (TABLOCKX)
JOIN Sales.SalesOrderDetail AS od
  ON Sales.SalesOrderHeader.SalesOrderID = od.SalesOrderID;
```

We also could have done something completely different here and placed a totally separate hint on the SalesOrderDetail table. It's all up to you.

Determining Locks Using the Management Studio

Perhaps the nicest way of all to take a look at your locks is by using Management Studio. Management Studio will show you locks in two different sorts — by *process ID* or by *object* — by utilizing the Activity Monitor.

To make use of Management Studio's lock display, just navigate to the Server and right-click, then choose Activity Monitor. You should come up with a new window that looks something like Figure 11-3 (I've expanded the Processes frame).

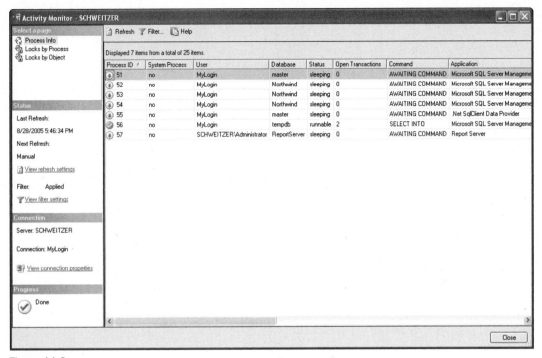

Figure 11-3

Just expand the node that you're interested in (either the `Process ID` or the `Object`), and you'll see various locks.

Perhaps the coolest feature in Management Studio shows itself when you double-click a specific lock in the right-hand side of the window. A dialog box will come up and tell you the last statement that was run by that process ID. This can be very handy when you are troubleshooting deadlock situations.

Setting the Isolation Level

We've seen that several different kinds of problems can be prevented by different locking strategies. We've also seen what kinds of locks are available and how they have an impact on the availability of resources. Now it's time to take a closer look at how these process management pieces work together to ensure overall data integrity and to make certain that you can get the results you expect.

The first thing to understand about the relationship between transactions and locks is that they are inextricably linked with each other. By default, any lock that is data modification related will, once created, be held for the duration of the transaction. If you have a long transaction, this means that your locks may be preventing other processes from accessing the objects you have a lock on for a long time. It probably goes without saying that this can be rather problematic.

However, that's only the default. In fact, there are actually five different *isolation levels* that you can set at the transaction level:

❑ READ COMMITTED (the default)

❑ READ UNCOMMITTED

❑ REPEATABLE READ

❑ SERIALIZABLE

❑ SNAPSHOT

The syntax for switching between them is pretty straightforward:

```
SET TRANSACTION ISOLATION LEVEL <READ COMMITTED|READ UNCOMMITTED
    |REPEATABLE READ|SERIALIZABLE|SNAPSHOT>
```

The change in isolation level will affect only the current connection. So you don't need to worry about adversely affecting other users (or them affecting you).

Let's start by looking at the default situation (READ COMMITTED) a little more closely.

READ COMMITTED

With READ COMMITTED, any shared locks you create will be automatically released as soon as the statement that created them is complete. That is, if you start a transaction, run several statements, run a SELECT statement, and then run several more statements, the locks associated with the SELECT statement are freed as soon as the SELECT statement is complete. SQL Server doesn't wait for the end of the transaction.

Action queries (UPDATE, DELETE, and INSERT) are a little different. If your transaction performs a query that modifies data, then those locks will be held for the duration of the transaction (in case you need to roll back).

By keeping this level of default, with READ COMMITTED, you can be sure that you have enough data integrity to prevent dirty reads. However, non-repeatable reads and phantoms can still occur.

READ UNCOMMITTED

READ UNCOMMITTED is the most dangerous of all isolation level choices but also has the highest performance in terms of speed.

Setting the isolation level to READ UNCOMMITTED tells SQL Server not to set any locks, and not to honor any locks. With this isolation level, it is possible to experience any of the various concurrency issues we discussed earlier in the chapter (most notably a dirty read).

Why would one ever want to risk a dirty read? When I watch the newsgroups on Usenet, I see the question come up on a regular basis. It's surprising to a fair number of people, but there are actually good reasons to have this isolation level, and they are almost always to do with reporting.

In an OLTP environment, locks are both your protector and your enemy. They prevent data integrity problems, but they also often prevent, or block, you from getting at the data you want. It is extremely commonplace to see a situation where the management wants to run reports regularly, but the data entry people are often prevented from or delayed in entering data because of locks held by the manager's reports.

By using READ UNCOMMITTED, you can often get around this problem — at least for reports where the numbers don't have to be exact. For example, let's say that a sales manager wants to know just how much has been done in sales so far today. Indeed, we'll say he's a micro-manager and asks this same question (in the form of re-running the report) several times a day.

If the report happened to be a long-running one, then there's a high chance that his running it would damage the productivity of other users due to locking considerations. What's nice about this report though, is that it is a truly nebulous report. The exact values are probably meaningless. The manager is really just looking for ballpark numbers.

By having an isolation level of READ UNCOMMITTED, we do not set any locks, so we don't block any other transactions. Our numbers will be somewhat suspect (because of the risk of dirty reads), but we don't need exact numbers anyway, and we know that the numbers are still going to be close even on the off chance that a dirty read is rolled back.

You can get the same effect as READ UNCOMMITTED by adding the NOLOCK optimizer hint in your query. The advantage to setting the isolation level is that you don't have to use a hint for every table in your query, or use it in multiple queries. The advantage to using the NOLOCK optimizer hint is that you don't need to remember to set the isolation level back to the default for the connection. (With READ UNCOMMITTED you do.)

REPEATABLE READ

The REPEATABLE READ escalates your isolation level somewhat, and provides an extra level of concurrency protection by preventing not only dirty reads (the default already does that) but also preventing non-repeatable reads.

That prevention of non-repeatable reads is a big upside, but holding even shared locks until the end of the transaction can block users' access to objects, and therefore hurt productivity. Personally, I prefer to use other data integrity options (such as a CHECK constraint together with error handling) rather than this choice, but it remains an available option.

The equivalent optimizer hint for the REPEATABLE READ isolation level is REPEATABLEREAD (these are the same, only no space).

SERIALIZABLE

SERIALIZABLE is something of the fortress of isolation levels. It prevents all forms of concurrency issues except for a lost update. Even phantoms are prevented.

When you set your isolation to SERIALIZABLE, you're saying that any UPDATE, DELETE, or INSERT to the table or tables used by your transaction must not meet the WHERE clause of any statement in that transaction. Essentially, if the user was going to do something that your transaction would be interested in, then it must wait until your transaction has been completed.

The SERIALIZABLE isolation level can also be simulated by using the SERIALIZABLE or HOLDLOCK optimizer hint in your query. Again, as with the READ UNCOMMITTED and NOLOCK debate, the option of not having to set it every time versus not having to remember to change the isolation level back is the big issue.

> *Going with an isolation level of SERIALIZABLE would, on the surface, appear to be the way you want to do everything. Indeed, it does provide your database with the highest level of what is called consistency — that is, the update process works the same for multiple users as it would if all your users did one transaction at a time (processed things serially).*

> *As with most things in life, however, there is a trade-off. Consistency and concurrency can, in a practical sense, be thought of as polar opposites. Making things SERIALIZABLE can prevent other users from getting to the objects they need; that equates to lower concurrency. The reverse is also true: Increasing concurrency (by going to a REPEATABLE READ for example) reduces the consistency of your database.*

> *My personal recommendation on this is to stick with the default (READ COMMITTED) unless you have a specific reason not to.*

SNAPSHOT

> Note that the SNAPSHOT transaction isolation level is not available by default. To utilize it, you must enable the ALLOW_SNAPSHOT_ISOLATION option for your database utilizing the ALTER DATABASE command.

This was first added in SQL Server 2005, and was not particularly well publicized (and still isn't well documented if you ask me!). SNAPSHOT utilizes what is referred to as "row versioning." Transactions that would have been blocked from a given record are instead allowed read access to that record in its last known good state, which is to say, the way it was before whatever transaction is blocking began its modifications to the row.

SNAPSHOT is something of a mixed blessing. On one hand, concurrency is increased as read transactions are allowed to continue forward unabated with a value that is technically the correct value for that moment in time (at least in terms of what data has been truly committed). The down side, however, is that those transactions are being allowed to continue with data that has a significant chance of being inaccurate soon.

Which should you use? Well, as you can imagine, my answer would be "It depends." The safer answer is to stick with the default of READ COMMITTED. Sometimes, however, we don't need that safety, and higher concurrency is the better choice.

> The default isolation level of READ COMMITTED can be switched over to a version that utilizes row versioning, effectively the same as SNAPSHOT, by enabling the READ_COMMITTED_SNAPSHOT database option with the ALTER DATABASE command. Make *certain* however, that you know what you fully understand the differences between the two READ COMMITTED implementations before making such a change.

Dealing with Deadlocks (a.k.a. "A 1205")

Okay. So now you've seen locks, and you've also seen transactions. Now that you've got both, we can move on to the rather pesky problem of dealing with *deadlocks*.

As we've already mentioned, a deadlock is not a type of lock in itself, but rather a situation where a paradox has been formed by other locks. Like it or not, you'll bump into these on a regular basis (particularly when you're just starting out), and you'll be greeted with an *error number 1205*. So prolific is this particular problem that you'll hear many a database developer refer to them simply by the number.

Deadlocks are caused when one lock can't do what it needs to do in order to clear because a second lock is holding that resource, and vice versa. When this happens, somebody has to win the battle, so SQL Server chooses a deadlock *victim*. The deadlock victim's transaction is then rolled back and is notified that this happened through the 1205 error. The other transaction can continue normally. (Indeed, it will be entirely unaware that there was a problem, other than seeing an increased execution time.)

How SQL Server Figures Out There's a Deadlock

Every 5 seconds SQL Server checks all the current transactions for what locks they are waiting for but haven't yet been granted. As it does this, it essentially makes a note that the request exists. It will then re-check the status of all open lock requests again, and, if one of the previous requests has still not been granted, it will recursively check all open transactions for a circular chain of lock requests. If it finds such a chain, then one or more deadlock victims will be chosen.

How Deadlock Victims Are Chosen

By default, a deadlock victim is chosen based on the "cost" of the transactions involved. The transaction that costs the least to roll back will be chosen (in other words, SQL Server has to do the least number of things to undo it). You can, to some degree, override this by using the DEADLOCK_PRIORITY SET option available in SQL Server; this is, however, generally both ill-advised and out of the scope of this book. (I consider this to be very much in the camp of the administrator rather than the developer.)

Avoiding Deadlocks

Deadlocks can't be avoided 100 percent of the time in complex systems, but you can almost always totally eliminate them from a practical standpoint — that is, make them so rare that they have little relevance to your system.

To cut down or eliminate deadlocks, follow these simple (okay, usually simple) rules:

- ❑ Use your objects in the same order.
- ❑ Keep your transactions as short as possible and in one batch.
- ❑ Use the lowest transaction isolation level necessary.
- ❑ Do not allow open-ended interruptions (user interactions, batch separations) within the same transaction.
- ❑ In controlled environments, use bound connections.

Nearly every time I run across deadlocking problems, at least one (usually more) of these rules has been violated. Let's look at each one individually.

Using Objects in the Same Order

This is the most common problem area within the few rules that I consider to be basic. What's great about using this rule is that it almost never costs you anything to speak of; it's more a way of thinking. You decide early in your design process how you want to access your database objects, including order, and it becomes a habit in every query, procedure, or trigger that you write for that project.

Think about it for a minute. If our problem is that our two connections each have what the other wants, then it implies that we're dealing with the problem too late in the game. Let's look at a simple example.

Consider that we have two tables: Suppliers and Products. Now say that we have two processes that make use of both of these tables. Process 1 accepts inventory entries, updates Products with the new amount of product on hand, and then updates Suppliers with the total amount of product that we've purchased. Process 2 records sales; it updates the total amount of product sold in the Suppliers table and then decreases the inventory quantity in Products.

If we run these two processes at the same time, we're begging for trouble. Process 1 will grab an exclusive lock on the Products table. Process 2 grabs an exclusive lock on the Suppliers table. Process 1 then attempts to grab a lock on the Suppliers table, but it will be forced to wait for Process 2 to clear its existing lock. In the meantime, Process 2 tries to create a lock on the Products table, but it will have to wait for Process 1 to clear its existing lock. We now have a paradox: Both processes are waiting for each other. SQL Server will have to pick a deadlock victim.

Now let's rearrange that scenario, with Process 2 changed to first decrease the inventory quantity in Products and then update the total amount of product sold in the Suppliers table. This is a functional equivalent to the first way we organized the processes, and it will cost us nothing to perform it this new way. The impact though, will be stunning. No more deadlocks (at least not between these two processes)! Let's walk through what will now happen.

When we run these two processes at the same time, Process 1 will grab an exclusive lock on the Products table (so far, it's the same). Process 2 then also tries to grab a lock on the Products table but will be forced to wait for Process 1 to finish. (Notice that we haven't done anything with Suppliers yet.) Process 1 finishes with the Products table but doesn't release the lock because the transaction isn't complete yet. Process 2 is still waiting for the lock on Products to clear. Process 1 now moves on to grab a lock on the Suppliers table. Process 2 continues to wait for the lock to clear on Products. Process 1 finishes and commits or rolls back the transaction as required but frees all locks in either case. Process 2 now is able to obtain its lock on the Products table and moves through the rest of its transaction without further incident.

Just swapping the order in which these two queries are run has eliminated a potential deadlock problem. Keep things in the same order wherever possible and you, too, will experience far fewer deadlocks.

Keeping Transactions As Short As Possible

This is another of the basics. Again, it should become just an instinct — something you don't really think about, something you just do.

This is one that never has to cost you anything really. Put what you need to put in the transaction, and keep everything else out. It's just that simple. The reason this works isn't rocket science. The longer the transaction is open, and the more it touches (within the transaction), the higher the likelihood that you're going to run into some other process that wants one or more of the objects that you're using (reducing concurrency). If you keep your transaction short, you minimize the number of objects that can potentially cause a deadlock, plus you cut down on the time that you have your lock on them. It's as simple as that.

Keeping transactions in one batch minimizes network round-trips during a transaction, reducing possible delays in completing the transaction and releasing locks.

Using the Lowest Transaction Isolation Level Possible

This one is considerably less basic, and requires some serious thought. As such, it isn't surprising just how often it isn't thought of at all. Consider it Rob's axiom: That which requires thought is likely not to be thought of. Be different — think about it.

We have several different transaction isolation levels available. The default is READ COMMITTED. Using a lower isolation level holds shared locks for a shorter duration than a higher isolation level, thereby reducing locking contention.

Allowing No Open-Ended Transactions

This one probably makes the most common sense out of all the recommendations here, but it's one that's often violated because of past practices.

One of the ways we used to prevent lost updates (mainframe days here, folks!) was just to grab the lock and hold it until we were done with it. I can't tell you how problematic this was. (Can you say *yuck*!)

Imagine this real-life example: Someone in your service department likes to use update (exclusive locks) screens instead of display (shared locks) screens to look at data. "After all," he says. "That way I'm right there ready to edit if I see something that needs to be changed." He goes on to look at a work order. Now his buddy calls and asks if he's ready for lunch. "Sure!" comes the reply, and the service clerk heads off to a rather long lunch (1–2 hours). Everyone who is interested in this record is now locked out of it for the duration of this clerk's lunch.

Wait — it gets worse. In the days of the mainframe, you used to see the concept of queuing far more often. (It actually can be quite efficient.) Now someone submits a print job (which is queued) for this work order. It sits in the queue waiting for the record lock to clear. Since it's a queue environment, every print job your company has for work orders now piles up behind that first print job (which is going to wait for that person's lunch before clearing).

This is a rather extreme example, but it is a real-life scenario I've seen many times, and I hope that it clearly illustrates the point. Don't ever create locks that will still be open when you begin some form of open-ended process. Usually we're talking user interaction (like our lunch lover), but it could be any process that has an open-ended wait to it.

Using Bound Connections

Hmm. I had to debate even including this one, because it's something of a can of worms. Once you open it, you're never going to get them all back in. I'll just say that this is one which is used extremely rarely and is not for the faint of heart.

It's not that it doesn't have its uses; it's just that things can become convoluted rather quickly, so you need to manage things well. It's my personal opinion that there is usually a better solution.

That brings on the question of what is a bound connection. *Bound connections* are connections that have been associated and are essentially allowed to share the same set of locks. What that means is that the two transactions can operate in tandem without any fear of deadlocking each other or being blocked by one another. The flip side of this means that you essentially are on your own in terms of dealing with most concurrency issues. Locks aren't keeping you safe anymore.

Given my distaste for these for 99.9 percent of situations, we're going to forget that these exist now that we've seen that they are an option. If you're going to insist on using them, just remember that you're going to be dealing with an extremely complex relationship between connections, and you need to manage the activities in those connections rather closely if you are going to maintain data integrity within the system.

Summary

Transactions and locks are both cornerstone items to how SQL Server works and, therefore, to maximizing your development of solutions in SQL Server.

By using transactions, you can make sure that everything you need to have happen as a unit happens, or none of it does. SQL Server's use of locks ensures that we avoid the pitfalls of concurrency to the maximum extent possible. (You'll never avoid them entirely, but it's amazing how close you can come with a little — OK a lot — of planning.) By using the two together, you are able to pass what the database industry calls the *ACID* test. If a transaction is ACID, then it has:

- ❑ **Atomicity:** The transaction is all or nothing.

- ❑ **Consistency:** All constraints and other data integrity rules have been adhered to, and all related objects (data pages, index pages) have been updated completely.

- ❑ **Isolation:** Each transaction is completely isolated from any other transaction. The actions of one transaction cannot be interfered with by the actions of a separate transaction.

- ❑ **Durability:** After a transaction is completed, its effects are permanently in place in the system. The data is "safe," in the sense that things such as a power outage or other non-disk system failure will not lead to data that is only half-written.

In short, by using transactions and locks, you can minimize deadlocks, ensure data integrity, and improve the overall efficiency of your system.

In our next chapter, we'll be looking at triggers. Indeed, we'll see that, for many of the likely uses of triggers, the concepts of transactions and rollbacks will be at the very center of the trigger.

12

Triggers

I am often asked, "Should I use triggers?" The answer is, as with most things in SQL, "It depends." There's little that's black and white in the wonderful world of SQL Server; triggers are definitely a very plain shade of gray.

Know what you're doing before you go the triggers route; it's important for the health and performance of your database. The good news is that's what we're here to learn.

As with most of the core subjects we've covered in this book (save for a few that were just too important to rush), we're going to be moving along quickly in the assumption that you already know the basics. Still, this also happens to be one of those topics where you can have become a relatively advanced user of SQL Server, and never hit this particular topic. That is, triggers can be needed by the beginner for some installations, and yet never been touched by the "Pro" in others (SQL is just that way ...). The result is that, if you've read my *Beginning SQL Server 2008 Programming* title, then you'll definitely notice some overlap (but you'll find much more depth here). If you're in that group of people, feel free to skip ahead to the INSTEAD OF triggers section.

In this chapter, we'll try to look at triggers in all of their colors — from black all the way to white and a whole lot in between. The main issues we'll be dealing with include:

- ❏ What is a trigger (the *very* quick and dirty version)?

- ❏ Using triggers for more flexible referential integrity

- ❏ Using triggers to create flexible data integrity rules

- ❏ Using INSTEAD OF triggers to create more flexible updatable views

- ❏ Other common uses for triggers

- ❏ Controlling the firing order of triggers

- ❏ Performance considerations

By the time we're done, you should have an idea of just how complex is the decision about when and where not to use triggers. You'll also have an inkling of just how powerful and flexible they can be.

Most of all, if I've done my job well, you won't be a trigger extremist (which *so* many SQL Server people I meet are) with the distorted notion that triggers are evil and should never be used. Neither will you side with the other end of the spectrum: those who think that triggers are the solution to all the world's problems. The right answer in this respect is that triggers can do a lot for you, but they can also cause a lot of problems. The trick is to use them when they are the right things to use, and not to use them when they aren't.

Some common uses of triggers include:

- ❑ Enforcement of referential integrity: Although I recommend using declarative referential integrity (DRI) whenever possible, there are many things that DRI won't do (for example, referential integrity across databases or even servers, many complex types of relationships, and so on). The use of triggers for RI is becoming very special case, but it's still out there.

- ❑ Creating audit trails, which means writing out records that keep track of not just the most current data but also the actual change history for each record.

- ❑ Functionality similar to a CHECK constraint, but which works across tables, databases, or even servers.

- ❑ Substituting your own statements in the place of a user's action statement (usually used to enable inserts in complex views).

In addition, you have the new but likely much more rare case (as I said, they are new, so only time will tell for sure) DDL trigger — which is about monitoring changes in the structure of your table.

And these are just a few. So, with no further ado, let's look at exactly what a trigger is.

What Is a Trigger?

A trigger is a special kind of stored procedure that responds to specific events. There are two kinds of triggers: Data Definition Language (DDL) triggers and Data Manipulation Language (DML) triggers.

DDL triggers fire in response to someone changing the structure of your database in some way (CREATE, ALTER, DROP, and similar statements). These were first added back in SQL Server 2005 and are critical to some installations (particularly high-security installations) but are pretty narrow in use. In general, you will need to look into using these only where you need extreme auditing of changes/history of your database structure. We will save these until last.

DML triggers are pieces of code that you attach to a particular table or view. Unlike sprocs, where you needed to explicitly invoke the code, the code in triggers is automatically run whenever the event(s) you attached the trigger to occurs in the table. Indeed, you *can't* explicitly invoke triggers — the only way to do this is by performing the required action in the table that they are assigned to.

> *Beyond not being able to explicitly invoke a trigger, you'll find two other things that exist for sprocs but are missing from triggers: parameters and return codes.*

While triggers take no parameters, they do have a mechanism for figuring out what records they are supposed to act on (we'll investigate this further later in the chapter). And, while you can use the RETURN keyword, you cannot return a specific return code (because you didn't explicitly call the trigger, what would you return a return code to?).

What events can you attach triggers to? The three "action" query types you use in SQL. So, you wind up with triggers based in inserts, updates, and/or deletes (you can mix and match to what events you want the trigger to be attached).

It's worth noting that there are times when a trigger will not fire — even though it seems that the action you are performing falls into one of the preceding categories. At issue is whether or not the operation you are doing is in a logged activity. For example, a DELETE statement is a normal, logged activity that would fire any delete trigger, but a TRUNCATE TABLE, which has the effect of deleting rows, just deallocates the space used by the table. There is no individual deletion of rows logged, and no trigger is fired.

The syntax for creating triggers looks an awful lot like all of our other CREATE syntax, except that it has to be attached to a table somewhat similar to an index; a trigger can't stand on its own.

Let's take a look:

```
CREATE TRIGGER <trigger name>
    ON [<schema name>.]<table or view name>
    [WITH ENCRYPTION | EXECUTE AS <CALLER | SELF | <user> >]
    {{{FOR|AFTER} <[DELETE] [,] [INSERT] [,] [UPDATE]>} |INSTEAD OF}
    [WITH APPEND]
    [NOT FOR REPLICATION]
AS
    <sql statements> | EXTERNAL NAME <assembly method specifier>
```

As you can see, the all too familiar CREATE <object type> <object name> is still there as well as the execution stuff we've seen in many other objects — we've just added the ON clause to indicate the table to which this trigger is going to be attached, as well as when and under what conditions it fires.

ON

This part just names what object you are creating the trigger against. Keep in mind that if the type of the trigger is an AFTER trigger (if it uses FOR or AFTER to declare the trigger), then the target of the ON clause must be a table — AFTER triggers are not supported for views.

WITH ENCRYPTION

This works just as it does for views and sprocs. If you add this option, you can be certain that no one will be able to view your code (not even you!). This is particularly useful if you are going to be building software for commercial distribution, or if you are concerned about security and don't want your users to be able to see what data you're modifying or accessing. Obviously, you should keep a copy of the code required to create the trigger somewhere else, in case you want to re-create it sometime later.

As with views and sprocs, the thing to remember when using the WITH ENCRYPTION option is that you must reapply it every time you ALTER your trigger. If you make use of an ALTER TRIGGER statement and do not include the WITH ENCRYPTION option, then the trigger will no longer be encrypted.

The FOR|AFTER versus the INSTEAD OF Clause

In addition to deciding what kind of queries will fire your trigger (INSERT, UPDATE, and/or DELETE), you also have some choice as to when the trigger fires. While the FOR (alternatively, you can use the keyword AFTER if you choose) trigger is the one that has been around a long time and is the one people generally think of, you also have the ability to run what is called an INSTEAD OF trigger. Choosing between these two will affect whether you enter your trigger before or after the data has been modified. In either case, you will be in your trigger before any changes are truly committed to the database.

Confusing? Probably. Let's try it a different way with a diagram that shows where each choice fires (see Figure 12-1).

The thing to note here is that, regardless of which choice you make, SQL Server will put together two working tables — one holding a copy of the records that were inserted (and, incidentally, called INSERTED) and one holding a copy of any records that were deleted (called DELETED). We'll look into the details of the uses of these working tables a little later. For now realize that with INSTEAD OF triggers the creation of these working tables will happen *before* any constraints are checked, and with FOR triggers, these tables will be created after constraints are checked.

The key to INSTEAD OF triggers is that you can actually run your own code in the place of whatever the user requested. This means we can clean up ambiguous insert problems in views (remember the problem back in Chapter 8 with inserting when there was a JOIN in the view?). It also means that we can take action to clean up constraint violations before the constraint is even checked.

Triggers using the FOR and AFTER declaration behave identically to each other. The big difference between them and INSTEAD OF triggers is that they build their working tables *after* any constraints have been checked.

The AFTER (or, alternatively, you can use FOR) clause indicates under what type of action(s) you want this trigger to fire. You can have the trigger fire whenever there is an INSERT, UPDATE, or DELETE, or any mix of the three. So, for example, your FOR clause could look something like:

```
AFTER INSERT, DELETE
```

... or:

```
AFTER UPDATE, INSERT
```

... or:

```
AFTER DELETE
```

As was stated in the section about the ON clause, triggers declared using the AFTER or FOR clause can only be attached to tables — no views are allowed (see INSTEAD OF triggers for those).

It's worth noting that, unlike prior editions of this book, I actually do advise a specific choice between AFTER and FOR. While both are equally usable, and there is no indication that either will be deprecated, the AFTER clause is the "standard" way of doing things, so it is more likely to be supported by other database vendors.

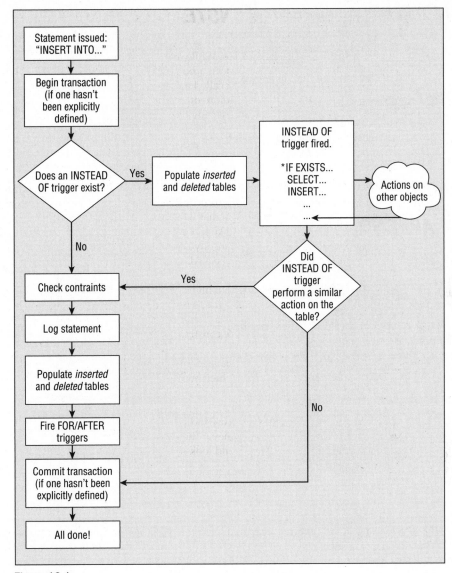

Figure 12-1

INSERT Trigger

The code for any trigger that you mark as being FOR INSERT will be executed any time that someone inserts a new row into your table. For each row that is inserted, SQL Server will create a copy of that new row and insert it in a special table that exists only within the scope of your trigger. That table is called INSERTED, and we'll see much more of it over the course of this chapter. The big thing to understand is that the INSERTED table only lives as long as your trigger does. Think of it as not existing before your trigger starts or after your trigger completes.

DELETE Trigger

This works much the same as an INSERT trigger does, save that the INSERTED table will be empty (after all, you deleted rather than inserted, so there are no records for the INSERTED table). Instead, a copy of each record that was deleted is inserted into another table called DELETED. That table, like the INSERTED table, is limited in scope to just the life of your trigger.

UPDATE Trigger

More of the same, save for a twist. The code in a trigger declared as being FOR UPDATE will be fired whenever an existing record in your table is changed. The twist is that there's no such table as UPDATED. Instead, SQL Server treats each row as if the existing record had been deleted, and a totally new record was inserted. As you can probably guess from that, a trigger declared as FOR UPDATE contains not one but two special tables called INSERTED and DELETED. The two tables have exactly the same number of rows, of course.

WITH APPEND

WITH APPEND is something of an oddball and, in all honesty, you're pretty unlikely to use it; nonetheless, and since this is, after all, a "Professional" title, we'll cover it here for that "just-in-case" scenario. WITH APPEND applies only when you are running in 6.5 compatibility mode (which can be set using sp_dbcmptlevel).

SQL Server 6.5 and prior did not allow multiple triggers of the same type on any single table. For example, if you had already declared a trigger called trgCheck to enforce data integrity on updates and inserts, then you couldn't create a separate trigger for cascading updates. Once one update (or insert, or delete) trigger was created, that was it — you couldn't create another trigger for the same type of action.

This was a real pain. It meant that you had to combine logically different activities into one trigger. Trying to get what amounted to two entirely different procedures to play nicely together could, at times, be quite a challenge. In addition, it made reading the code something of an arduous task.

Along came SQL Server 7.0 and the rules changed substantially. No longer do we have to worry about how many triggers we have for one type of action query — you can have several if you like. When running our database in 6.5 compatibility mode, though, we run into a problem: Our database is still working on the notion that there can only be one trigger of a given type on a given table.

WITH APPEND gets around this problem by explicitly telling SQL Server that we want to add this new trigger even though we already have a trigger of that type on the table; both will be fired when the appropriate trigger action (INSERT, UPDATE, DELETE) occurs. It's a way of having a bit of both worlds.

Again, this option is not really needed unless you're running SQL Server in the "way back machine" version, that is, 6.5 compatibility mode. Do not use this unless you know you have a very specific reason you need it.

> At this juncture, running in 6.5 compatibility mode means that you are asking SQL Server to run as it was more than a decade ago, and with a version compatibility level that is now four versions old. If the code is important enough to still be running after this much time has passed, it would seem important enough to warrant updating to a more recent version of support.

NOT FOR REPLICATION

Adding this option slightly alters the rules as to when the trigger is fired. With this option in place, the trigger will not be fired whenever a replication-related task modifies your table. Usually a trigger is fired (to do the housekeeping/cascading/and so on) when the original table is modified and there is no point in doing it again.

AS

Exactly as it was with sprocs, this is the meat of the matter. The AS keyword tells SQL Server that your code is about to start. From this point forward, we're into the scripted portion of your trigger.

Using Triggers for Data Integrity Rules

Although they shouldn't be your first option, triggers can also perform the same functionality as a CHECK constraint or even a DEFAULT. The answer to the question "Should I use triggers or CHECK constraints?" is the rather definitive: "It depends." If a CHECK can do the job, then it's probably the preferable choice. There are times, however, when a CHECK constraint just won't do the job, or when something inherent in the CHECK process makes it less desirable than a trigger. Examples of where you would want to use a trigger over a CHECK include:

❑   Your business rule needs to reference data in a separate table.

❑   Your business rule needs to check the *delta* (difference between before and after) of an update.

❑   You require a customized error message.

This really just scratches the surface of things. Since triggers are highly flexible, deciding when to use them really just comes down to whenever you need something special done. To provide at least *some* guidance though, here's a comparison table I've included in past books:

Restriction	Pros	Cons
Constraints	Fast.	Must be redefined for each table.
	Can reference other columns.	Can't reference other tables.
	Happens before the command occurs.	Can't be bound to data types.
	ANSI compliant.	
Triggers	Ultimate flexibility.	Happens after the command occurs.
	Can reference other columns and other tables.	High overhead.
	Can even use .NET to reference information that is external to your SQL Server.	

Note that this is deliberately non-specific. Every situation varies, so what I've tried to provide here is a set of guidelines about where either option either succeeds or fails.

Some of you may have noticed that, when I included the preceding table, I did not include the option for Rules and Defaults as I have in previous editions. Why not? Well, because Rules and Defaults (Default the object, not default the constraint) have been considered deprecated for several releases now, so I am gradually intensifying my presentation of the idea that they are there for backward compatibility only.

Dealing with Requirements Sourced from Other Tables

CHECK constraints are great — fast and efficient — but they don't do everything you'd like them to. Perhaps the biggest shortcoming shows up when you need to verify data across tables.

To illustrate this, let's take a look at the Products and SalesOrderDetail tables in AdventureWorks2008 as well as the related SpecialOfferProduct table. The relationship looks like Figure 12-2.

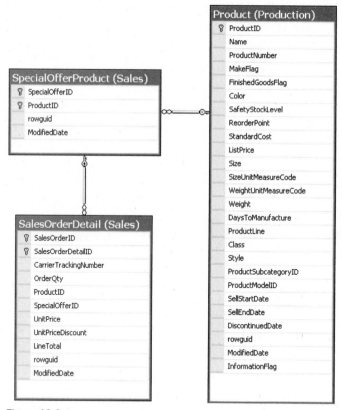

Figure 12-2

So, under normal DRI, you can be certain that no order line item can be entered into the SalesOrderDetail table unless there is a matching ProductID in the Products table (via the chain through the `SpecialOfferProduct` table). We are, however, looking for something more than just the "norm" here.

Our Inventory department has been complaining that our Customer Support people keep placing orders for products that are discontinued. They would like to have such orders rejected before they get into the system.

We can't deal with this using a `CHECK` constraint because the place where we know about the discontinued status (the `Products` table) is in a separate table from where we are placing the restriction (the `SalesOrderDetail` table). Don't sweat it though; you can tell the Inventory department, "No problem!" You just need to use a trigger:

```
USE AdventureWorks2008;
GO

CREATE TRIGGER OrderDetailNotDiscontinued
    ON Sales.SalesOrderDetail
    AFTER INSERT, UPDATE
AS
    IF EXISTS
        (
        SELECT 'True'
        FROM Inserted i
        JOIN Production.Product p
            ON i.ProductID = p.ProductID
        WHERE p.DiscontinuedDate IS NOT NULL
        )
    BEGIN
        RAISERROR('Order Item is discontinued. Transaction Failed.',16,1);
        ROLLBACK TRAN;
    END
```

Let's go ahead and test our handiwork. First, we need at least one record that will fail when it hits our trigger. That means we need a discontinued item in the `Products` table; the problem is, there is no such record currently.

```
SELECT ProductID, Name
FROM Production.Product
WHERE DiscontinuedDate IS NOT NULL;
```

```
ProductID   Name
----------- --------------------------------------------------

(0 row(s) affected)
```

So, we'll pick one and change it ourselves for test purposes:

```
UPDATE Production.Product
SET DiscontinuedDate = GETDATE()
WHERE ProductID = 680;
```

With that done, we're ready to see if our trigger works, so let's go ahead and add a line item that violates this constraint. I'm going to make use of a `SalesOrderHeader` that already exists, so we don't have to get over elaborate building up a full order:

```
INSERT Sales.SalesOrderDetail
   (
    SalesOrderID,
    OrderQty,
    ProductID,
    SpecialOfferID,
    UnitPrice,
    UnitPriceDiscount
   )
VALUES
   (
    43660,
    5,
    680,
    1,
    1431,
    0
   );
```

This gets the rejection that we expect:

```
Msg 50000, Level 16, State 1, Procedure OrderDetailNotDiscontinued, Line 14
Order Item is discontinued. Transaction Failed.
Msg 3609, Level 16, State 1, Line 1
The transaction ended in the trigger. The batch has been aborted.
```

Remember that we could, if desired, also create a custom error message to raise, instead of the ad hoc message that we used with the RAISERROR command.

Using Triggers to Check the Delta of an Update

Sometimes, you're not interested as much in what the value was or is as you are in how much it changed. While there isn't any one column or table that gives you that information, you can calculate it by making use of both the Inserted and Deleted tables in your trigger.

A quick example of this might be to write records for security reasons. Let's say, for example, that you wanted to track every adjustment to inventory regardless of what initiated it for auditing purposes (for example, inventory adjustments might be made directly against inventory tables rather than via an order item).

To implement something like this, we would need an audit table to make use of both the Inserted and Deleted tables:

```
USE AdventureWorks2008;

CREATE TABLE Production.InventoryAudit
```

```
(
    TransactionID    int         IDENTITY PRIMARY KEY,
    ProductID        int         NOT NULL
        REFERENCES Production.Product(ProductID),
    NetAdjustment    smallint    NOT NULL,
    ModifiedDate     datetime    DEFAULT(CURRENT_TIMESTAMP)
);

GO

CREATE TRIGGER ProductAudit
    ON Production.ProductInventory
    FOR INSERT, UPDATE, DELETE
AS
INSERT INTO Production.InventoryAudit
(ProductID, NetAdjustment)
        SELECT COALESCE(i.ProductID, d.ProductID),
            ISNULL(i.Quantity, 0) - ISNULL(d.Quantity, 0) AS NetAdjustment
        FROM Inserted i
        FULL JOIN Deleted d
            ON i.ProductID = d.ProductID
          AND i.LocationID = d.LocationID
        WHERE ISNULL(i.Quantity, 0) - ISNULL(d.Quantity, 0) != 0;
```

Before we test this, let's analyze what we're doing here. I've started by adding an audit table to receive information about changes to our base table. From there, I've created a trigger that will fire on any change to the table and will write the next change out to our new audit table.

Now, let's check this out by running a test script:

```
PRINT 'The values before the change are:'
SELECT ProductID, LocationID, Quantity
FROM Production.ProductInventory
WHERE ProductID = 1
  AND LocationID = 50;

PRINT 'Now making the change'
UPDATE Production.ProductInventory
SET Quantity = Quantity + 7
WHERE ProductID = 1
  AND LocationID = 50;

UPDATE Production.ProductInventory
SET Quantity = Quantity - 7
WHERE ProductID = 1
  AND LocationID = 50;

PRINT 'The values after the change are:'
SELECT ProductID, LocationID, Quantity
FROM Production.ProductInventory
WHERE ProductID = 1
  AND LocationID = 50;

SELECT * FROM Production.InventoryAudit;
```

And we can use the before and after output to verify that our audit records were properly written:

```
The values before the change are:
ProductID    LocationID Quantity
----------- ---------- --------
1               50          353

(1 row(s) affected)

Now making the change

(1 row(s) affected)

(1 row(s) affected)

(1 row(s) affected)

(1 row(s) affected)

(1 row(s) affected)
The values after the change are:
ProductID    LocationID Quantity
----------- ---------- --------
1               50          353

(1 row(s) affected)

TransactionID ProductID    NetAdjustment ModifiedDate
------------- ----------- ------------- -----------------------
1               1           7             2008-12-15 22:29:11.900
2               1           -7            2008-12-15 22:29:11.900

(2 row(s) affected)
```

Using Triggers for Custom Error Messages

We've already touched on this in some of our other examples, but remember that triggers can be handy for retaining control over the error message or number that gets passed out to your user or client application.

With a CHECK constraint, for example, you're just going to get the standard 547 error along with its rather nondescript explanation. As often as not, this is less than helpful in terms of the user really figuring out what went wrong; indeed, your client application often doesn't have enough information to make an intelligent and helpful response on behalf of the user.

In short, sometimes you create triggers when there is already something that would give you the data integrity that you want but won't give you enough information to handle it.

Other Common Uses for Triggers

In addition to the straight data integrity uses, triggers have a number of other uses. Indeed, the possibilities are fairly limitless, but here are a few common examples:

- ❑ Updating summary information
- ❑ Feeding de-normalized tables for reporting
- ❑ Setting condition flags

Updating Summary Information

Sometimes we like to keep aggregate information around to help with reporting or to speed performance when checking conditions.

Take, for instance, the example of a customer's credit limit versus their current balance. The limit is a fairly static thing and is easily stored with the rest of the customer information. The current balance is another matter. We can always figure out the current balance by running a query to total all of the unpaid balances for any orders the customer has, but think about that for a moment. Let's say that you work for Sears, and you do literally millions of transactions every year. Now think about how your table is going to have many millions of records for your query to sort through and that you're going to be competing with many other transactions in order to run your query. Things would perform an awful lot better if we could just go to a single place to get that total — but how to maintain it?

We certainly could just make sure that we always use a stored procedure for adding and paying order records, and then have the sproc update the customer's current balance. But that would mean that we would have to be sure that every sproc that has a potential effect on the customer's balance would have the update code. If just one sproc leaves it out, then we have a major problem, and figuring out which sproc is the offending one is a hassle at best, and problematic at worst. By using a trigger, however, the updating of the customer balance becomes pretty easy.

We could maintain virtually any aggregation we want to keep track of. Keep in mind, however, that every trigger that you add increases the amount of work that has to be done to complete your transactions. That means that you are placing an additional burden on your system and increasing the chances that you will run into deadlock problems.

Feeding Data into De-normalized Tables for Reporting

I'm going to start right off by saying this isn't the way you should do things in most circumstances. Usually, this kind of data transfer should be handled as part of a batch process run at night or during non-peak hours for your system — depending on the nature of what you are moving, replication may also be an excellent answer. We will be discussing replication in detail in Chapter 17.

That being said, sometimes you need the data in your reporting tables to be right up-to-the-minute. The only real ways to take care of this is to modify all your sprocs and other access points into your system, to update the reporting tables at the same time as they update the Online Transaction Processing (OLTP) tables (YUCK!), or to use triggers to propagate any updates to records.

What's nice about using this method to propagate data is that you are always certain to be up-to-the-minute on what's happening in the OLTP tables. That being said, it defeats a large part of the purpose of keeping separate reporting tables. While keeping the data in a de-normalized format can greatly improve query performance, one of its main goals, in most installations, is to clear reporting needs out of the main OLTP database and minimize concurrency issues. If all your OLTP updates still have to update information in your reporting tables, then all you've done is to move the database in which the actual deadlock or other concurrency issue is happening. From the OLTP standpoint, you've added work without gaining any benefits.

The thing you have to weigh here is whether you're going to gain enough performance in your reporting to make it worth the damage you're going to do to performance on your OLTP system.

Setting Condition Flags

This situation is typically used much as aggregation is — to maintain a flag as changes are made rather than having to look for a certain condition across a complete table. Lookup flags are one of the little things that, while they usually break the rules of normalization (you're not supposed to store data that can be derived elsewhere), they can really boost system performance substantially.

For the example on this topic, let's assume that we maintain a variety of information on the products that we sell. Material Safety Data Sheets (MSDS), information on suppliers — imagine there can be an unlimited number of different documents that all provide some sort of information on our products. Now, further imagine that we have something more than the mere 504 products that are in the AdventureWorks2008 database (it's not at all uncommon for businesses to have 50,000 or more different line items in their catalog). The number of possible informational records could get extremely high.

We want to be able to put a flag on our Customer Support screens that tell the order taker whether there is any additional information available for this product. If we were living by the rules of a normalized database, we would have to look in the ProductDocument table to see if it had any records that matched up with our ProductID.

Rather than do those lookups, we can just place a bit field in our Products table that is a yes/no indicator on whether other information is available. We would then put a trigger on the ProductInformation table that updates the bit flag in the Products table. If a record is inserted into ProductInformation, then we set the bit flag to TRUE for the corresponding product. When a ProductInformation record is deleted, we look to see whether it was the last one, and, if so, set the bit flag in the Products table back to FALSE.

We'll go for an ultra-quick example. First, we need to set up by creating the bit flag field and ProductDocument table:

```
ALTER TABLE Production.Product
    ADD InformationFlag    bit    NOT NULL
    CONSTRAINT InformationFlagDefault
        DEFAULT 0 WITH VALUES;
```

Then we need to fix the data in the table to allow for documentation we already have:

```
UPDATE p
SET p.InformationFlag = 1
FROM Production.Product p
WHERE EXISTS
    (
        SELECT 1
        FROM Production.ProductDocument pd
        WHERE pd.ProductID = p.ProductID
    );
```

Then we're ready to add our trigger:

```
CREATE TRIGGER DocumentBelongsToProduct
    ON Production.ProductDocument
    FOR INSERT, DELETE
AS
    DECLARE @Count    int;

    SELECT @Count = COUNT(*) FROM Inserted;

    IF @Count > 0
        BEGIN
            UPDATE p
                SET p.InformationFlag = 1
                FROM Inserted i
                JOIN Production.Product p
                    ON i.ProductID = p.ProductID;
        END

    IF @@ERROR != 0
        ROLLBACK TRAN;

    SELECT @Count = COUNT(*) FROM Deleted
    IF @Count > 0
    BEGIN
        UPDATE p
            SET p.InformationFlag = 0
            FROM Inserted i
            RIGHT JOIN Production.Product p
                ON i.ProductID = p.ProductID
            WHERE i.ProductID IS NULL
    END

    IF @@ERROR != 0
        ROLLBACK TRAN;
```

And we're ready to test:

```
SELECT ProductID, InformationFlag
FROM Production.Product p
WHERE p.ProductID = 1;
```

```
INSERT INTO Production.ProductDocument
    (ProductID, DocumentNode)
VALUES
    (1, 0x);

SELECT ProductID, InformationFlag
FROM Production.Product p
WHERE p.ProductID = 1;
```

This yields the proper update:

```
ProductID    InformationFlag
-----------  ---------------
1                0

(1 row(s) affected)

(1 row(s) affected)


(1 row(s) affected)
ProductID    InformationFlag
-----------  ---------------
1                1

(1 row(s) affected)
```

And the delete:

```
DELETE Production.ProductDocument
WHERE ProductID = 1
   AND DocumentNode = 0x;

SELECT ProductID, InformationFlag
FROM Production.Product p
WHERE p.ProductID = 1;
```

Again, this gets the proper update:

```
ProductID    InformationFlag
-----------  ---------------
1                0

(1 row(s) affected)
```

Now we can find out whether there's product documentation right in the very same query with which we grab the base information on the product. We won't incur the overhead of the query to the ProductDocument table unless there really is something out there for us to retrieve.

Other Trigger Issues

You have most of it now, but if you're thinking you are finished with triggers, then think again. As I indicated early in the chapter, triggers create an awful lot to think about. The sections that follow attempt to point out some of the biggest issues you need to consider, plus they provide some information on additional trigger features and possibilities.

Triggers Can Be Nested

A nested trigger is one that does not fire directly as a result of a statement that you issued but rather because of a statement that was issued by another trigger.

This can actually set off quite a chain of events — with one trigger causing another trigger to fire which, in turn, causes yet another trigger to fire, and so on. Just how deep the triggers can fire depends on:

❑ Whether nested triggers are turned on for your system (this is a system-wide, not database-level option; it is set using Management Studio or `sp_configure`, and defaults to on).

❑ Whether there is a limit of nesting to 32 levels deep.

❑ Whether a trigger has already been fired. A trigger can, by default, only be fired once per trigger transaction. Once fired, it will ignore any other calls as a result of activity that is part of the same trigger action. Once you move on to an entirely new statement (even within the same overall transaction), the process can start all over again.

In most circumstances, you actually want your triggers to nest (thus the default), but you need to think about what's going to happen if you get into a circle of triggers firing triggers. If it comes back around to the same table twice, then the trigger will not fire the second time, and something you think is important may not happen; for example, a data integrity violation may get through. It's also worth noting that, if you do a `ROLLBACK` anywhere in the nesting chain, then the entire chain is rolled back. In other words, the entire nested trigger chain behaves as a transaction.

Triggers Can Be Recursive

What is a recursive trigger? A trigger is said to be recursive when something the trigger does eventually causes that same trigger to be fired. It may be directly (by an action query done to the table on which the trigger is set), or indirectly (through the nesting process).

Recursive triggers are rare. Indeed, by default, recursive triggers are turned off. This is, however, a way of dealing with the situation just described, where you are nesting triggers and you want the update to happen the second time around. Recursion, unlike nesting, is a database-level option and can be set using the `sp_dboption` system sproc.

The danger in recursive triggers is that you'll get into some form of unintended loop. As such, you'll need to make sure that you get some form of recursion check in place to stop the process if necessary.

Debugging Triggers

Debugging triggers is a hassle at best. Since you have something of a level of indirection (you write a statement that causes the trigger to fire, rather than explicitly firing it yourself), it always seems like you have to second-guess what's going on.

You can utilize the same debugger we utilized in Chapter 10 — you just need to get tricky to do it. The trick? The trick is to create a block of code (stored procedure or batch) that will cause your trigger to fire, and then step into that block of code. You can then step your way right into the trigger.

When debugging with the built-in tool is a trial, use PRINT and SELECT statements to output your values in the triggers. Beyond telling you what your variables are doing along the way, they can also tip you off to recursion and, in some cases, nesting problems.

Nesting issues can be one of the biggest gotchas of trigger design. You will find it not at all uncommon to see situations where you execute a command and wind up with unexpected results because you didn't realize how many other triggers were, in turn, going to be fired. What's more, if the nested triggers perform updates to the initiating table, the trigger will not fire a second time — this creates data integrity problems in tables where you are certain that your trigger is correct in preventing them. It probably has the right code for the first firing, but it doesn't even run the second time around in a nested situation.

You can also make use of SELECT @@NESTLEVEL to show just how deep into a nesting situation you've got.

Keep in mind though, that PRINT and result set generating SELECT statements don't really have anywhere to send their data other than the screen (in Management Studio) or as an informational message (data access models). This is usually far more confusing than anything else. As such, I highly recommend removing these statements once you've finished debugging, and before you go to production release.

Triggers Don't Get in the Way of Architecture Changes

This is a classic good news/bad news story.

Using triggers is positively great in terms of making it easy to make architecture changes. Indeed, I often use triggers for referential integrity early in the development cycle (when I'm more likely to be making lots of changes to the design of the database) and then change to DRI late in the cycle when I'm close to production.

When you want to drop a table and re-create it using DRI, you must first drop all of the constraints before dropping the table. This can create quite a maze in terms of dropping multiple constraints, making your changes, and then adding the constraints again. It can be quite a wild ride trying to make sure that everything drops that is supposed to so that your changed scripts will run. Then it's just as wild a ride to make sure that you've got everything back on that needs to be. Triggers take care of all this because they don't care that anything has changed until they actually run.

There's the rub though — when they run. You see, it means that you may change architecture and break several triggers without even realizing that you've done it. It won't be until the first time that those triggers try to address the object(s) in question that you find the error of your ways. By that time, you may find difficulty in piecing together exactly what you did and why.

Both sides have their hassles; just keep the hassles in mind no matter which method you're employing.

Triggers Can Be Turned Off without Being Removed

Sometimes, just like with CHECK constraints, you want to turn off the integrity feature, so you can do something that will violate the constraint but still has a valid reason for happening (importation of data is probably the most common of these).

Another common reason for doing this is when you are performing some sort of bulk insert (importation again), but you are already 100 percent certain the data is valid. In this case, you may want to turn off the triggers to eliminate their overhead and speed up the insert process.

You can turn a trigger off and on by using an ALTER TABLE statement. The syntax looks like this:

```
ALTER TABLE <table name>
    <ENABLE|DISABLE> TRIGGER <ALL|<trigger name>>
```

As you might expect, my biggest words of caution in this area are, "Don't forget to re-enable your triggers!"

One last thing. If you're turning them off to do some form of mass importation of data, I highly recommend that you kick out all your users and go to RESTRICTED_USER mode. This will make sure that no one sneaks in behind you while you have the triggers turned off.

> Be sure to consider the ability to disable triggers when addressing security concerns. If you are counting on triggers to perform audits for you, but you are allowing the disabling of triggers (granted, they would have to have some degree of security already, but you still need to fully consider the possibilities), then you have a loophole in your auditing.

Trigger Firing Order

In long ago releases of SQL Server (7.0 and prior), we had no control over firing order. Indeed, you may recall me discussing how there was only one of any particular kind of trigger (INSERT, UPDATE, DELETE) prior to 7.0, so firing order was something of a moot point. Later releases of SQL Server provide a limited amount of control over which triggers go in what order. For any given table (not views, since firing order can only be specified for AFTER triggers and views accept only INSTEAD OF triggers), you can elect to have one (and only one) trigger fired first. Likewise, you may elect to have one (and only one) trigger fired last. All other triggers are considered to have no preference on firing order — that is, you have no guarantee in what order a trigger with a firing order of "none" will fire, other than that it will fire after the FIRST trigger (if there is one) is complete and before the LAST trigger (again, if there is one) begins (see Figure 12-3).

The creation of a trigger that is to be first or last works just the same as any other trigger. You state the firing order preference after the trigger has already been created by using a special system stored procedure, sp_settriggerorder.

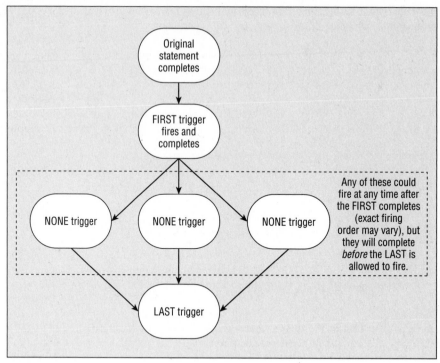

Figure 12-3

The syntax of sp_settriggerorder looks like this:

```
sp_settriggerorder[@triggername =] '<trigger name>',
    [@order =] '{FIRST|LAST|NONE}',
    [@stmttype =] '{INSERT|UPDATE|DELETE}'
```

There can be only one trigger that is considered to be "first" for any particular action (INSERT, UPDATE, or DELETE). Likewise, there can be only one "last" trigger for any particular action. Any number of triggers can be considered to be "none" — that is, the number of triggers that don't have a particular firing order is unlimited.

So, the question should be, "Why do I care what order they fire in?" Well, often you won't care at all. At other times, it can be important logic-wise or just a good performance idea. Let's consider what I mean in a bit more detail.

Controlling Firing Order for Logic Reasons

Why would you *need* to have one trigger fire before another? The most common reason would be that the first trigger lays some sort of foundation for, or otherwise validates, what will come afterward. Under SQL Server 6.5 and earlier, we didn't have to think about this kind of thing much — we were only allowed one trigger of any particular type (UPDATE, DELETE, or INSERT) for a given table. This meant that having one thing happen before another wasn't really a problem. Because you combined all logic into one trigger, you just put the first thing that needed to happen first in the code and the last part last (no real rocket science there at all).

Version 7.0 came along and made things both better and worse than they were before. You were no longer forced to jam all of your logic into one trigger. This was really cool because it meant that you could physically separate parts of your trigger code that were logically different, which, in turn, both made the code much easier to manage and allowed one part of the code to be disabled (remember that NO CHECK thing we did a few sections ago?) while other parts of the code continued to function. The downside was that if you went ahead and separated out your code that way, you lost the logical stepping order that the code had when it was in one trigger.

By gaining at least a rudimentary level of control over firing order, we now have something of the best of both worlds: we can logically separate our triggers but still maintain necessary order of precedence on what piece of code runs first or last.

Controlling Firing Order for Performance Reasons

On the performance front, a FIRST trigger is the only one that really has any big thing going for it. If you have multiple triggers, but only one of them is likely to generate a rollback (for example, it may be enforcing a complex data integrity rule that a constraint can't handle), you would want to consider making such a trigger a FIRST trigger. This ensures that the most likely cause of a rollback is already complete before you invest any more activity in your transaction. The more you do before the rollback is detected, the more that will have to be rolled back. Determine the highest possibility of that rollback happening before performing additional activity.

INSTEAD OF Triggers

While it can work against tables, the primary purpose of an INSTEAD OF trigger is usually to allow updates to views in places where it was previously not possible.

Essentially, an INSTEAD OF trigger is a block of code we can use as something of an interceptor for anything that anyone tries to do to our table or view. We can either elect to go ahead and do whatever the user requests or, if we choose, we can go so far as doing something entirely different.

As with FOR/AFTER triggers, INSTEAD OF triggers come in three different flavors — INSERT, UPDATE, and DELETE. Unlike FOR/AFTER triggers, however, you can only have one trigger per table or view for each of the different flavors (one each for INSERT, UPDATE, DELETE).

If we're going to explore these, we need to get some appropriate sample tables out there. To that end, let's take the following four tables (you can change the script to use an existing database if you wish):

```
CREATE DATABASE OurInsteadOfTest;
GO

USE OurInsteadOfTest;

CREATE TABLE dbo.Customers
    (
    CustomerID varchar(5) NOT NULL PRIMARY KEY ,
    Name varchar(40) NOT NULL
```

```
    );

CREATE TABLE dbo.Orders
    (
    OrderID int IDENTITY NOT NULL PRIMARY KEY,
    CustomerID varchar(5) NOT NULL
        REFERENCES Customers(CustomerID),
    OrderDate datetime NOT NULL
    );

CREATE TABLE dbo.Products
    (
    ProductID int IDENTITY NOT NULL PRIMARY KEY,
    Name varchar(40) NOT NULL,
    UnitPrice money NOT NULL
    );

CREATE TABLE dbo.OrderItems
    (
    OrderID int NOT NULL
        REFERENCES dbo.Orders(OrderID),
    ProductID int NOT NULL
        REFERENCES dbo.Products(ProductID),
    UnitPrice money NOT NULL,
    Quantity int NOT NULL
        CONSTRAINT PKOrderItem PRIMARY KEY CLUSTERED
            (OrderID, ProductID)
    );

-- INSERT sample records
INSERT dbo.Customers
    VALUES ('ABCDE', 'Bob''s Pretty Good Garage');

INSERT dbo.Orders
    VALUES ('ABCDE', CURRENT_TIMESTAMP);

INSERT dbo.Products
    VALUES ('Widget', 5.55),
           ('Thingamajig', 8.88)

INSERT dbo.OrderItems
    VALUES (1, 1, 5.55, 3);
```

We will use these tables for all three of the upcoming examples of INSTEAD OF triggers.

INSTEAD OF INSERT Triggers

The INSTEAD OF INSERT trigger allows us to examine the data that is about to go into our table or view, and decide what we want to do with it prior to the insert physically occurring. The typical use of this will usually be on a view — in which manipulating the data before the actual physical insert is attempted can mean the difference between the insert succeeding or failing.

Let's look at an example by creating an updatable view — specifically, one that will accept INSERTs where, before INSTEAD OF INSERT triggers, we wouldn't have been able to do it.

In this case, we'll create a view that demonstrates the update problem and then look at how to fix it. Let's take the case of showing some order line items, but with more full information about the customer and products (be sure you're using the database you created the sample tables in):

```
USE OurInsteadOfTest;
GO

CREATE VIEW CustomerOrders_vw
WITH SCHEMABINDING
AS
SELECT    o.OrderID,
          o.OrderDate,
          od.ProductID,
          p.Name,
          od.Quantity,
          od.UnitPrice
FROM dbo.Orders AS o
JOIN    dbo.OrderItems AS od
    ON o.OrderID = od.OrderID
JOIN    dbo.Products AS p
    ON od.ProductID = p.ProductID;
```

```
CREATE VIEW CustomerOrders_vw
WITH SCHEMABINDING
AS
SELECT    o.SalesOrderID,
          o.OrderDate,
          od.ProductID,
          p.Name,
          od.OrderQty,
          od.UnitPrice,
          od.LineTotal
FROM Sales.SalesOrderHeader AS o
JOIN    Sales.SalesOrderDetail AS od
    ON o.SalesOrderID = od.SalesOrderID
JOIN    Production.Product AS p
    ON od.ProductID = p.ProductID
```

The view is not fully updatable in its current state. How would SQL Server know which data went to which table? Sure, one could make a case for a straight update statement working, but we don't have the primary key for every table here. Even worse, what if we wanted to do an insert (which, as it happens, we do)?

The answer is something that SQL Server can't give you by itself — you need to provide more instructions as to what you want to do in such complex situations. That's where INSTEAD OF triggers really shine.

Let's take a look at our example order:

```
SELECT *
FROM CustomerOrders_vw
WHERE OrderID = 1;
```

This gets us back the one row we used to prime our sample:

```
Bob's Pretty Good Garage...1...2006-04-13 05:14:22.780...1...Widget...3...5.55
```

Now, just to prove it doesn't work, let's try to INSERT a new order item:

```
INSERT INTO CustomerOrders_vw
    (
    OrderID,
    OrderDate,
    ProductID,
    Quantity,
    UnitPrice
    )
VALUES
    (
    1,
    '1998-04-06',
    2,
    10,
    6.00
    )
```

As expected, it doesn't work:

```
Server: Msg 4405, Level 16, State 1, Line 2
View or function 'CustomerOrders_vw' is not updatable because the modification affects
multiple base tables.
```

It's time for us to take care of this with an INSTEAD OF trigger. What we need to do here is decide ahead of time what scenarios we want to handle (in this case, just the insert of new OrderItem records) and what we want to do about it.

We're going to treat any INSERT as an attempt to add a new order item. We're going to assume for this example that the customer already exists (if we wanted to get complex, we could break things up further) and that we have an OrderID available. Our trigger might look something like:

```
CREATE TRIGGER trCustomerOrderInsert ON CustomerOrders_vw
INSTEAD OF INSERT
AS
BEGIN
    -- Check to see whether the INSERT actually tried to feed us any rows.
    -- (A WHERE clause might have filtered everything out)
    IF (SELECT COUNT(*) FROM Inserted) > 0
    BEGIN
        INSERT INTO dbo.OrderItems
```

```
              SELECT  i.OrderID,
                      i.ProductID,
                      i.UnitPrice,
                      i.Quantity
              FROM Inserted AS i
              JOIN Orders AS o
                  ON i.OrderID = o.OrderID;
        -- If we have records in Inserted, but no records could join to
        -- the orders table, then there must not be a matching order
        IF @@ROWCOUNT = 0
              RAISERROR('No matching Orders. Cannot perform insert',10,1);
    END
END
```

So, let's try that insert again:

```
INSERT INTO CustomerOrders_vw
    (
    OrderID,
    OrderDate,
    ProductID,
    Quantity,
    UnitPrice
    )
VALUES
    (
    1,
    '1998-04-06',
    2,
    10,
    6.00
    )
```

We've explicitly addressed what table we're going to insert into, and so SQL Server is happy. We could easily extend this to address non-nullable columns that don't participate in the view if we needed to. (The customer can't provide values to those columns because they are not in the view the customer is using.)

INSTEAD OF UPDATE Triggers

We've now seen how INSERT statements against views can lead to ambiguous situations and also how to fix them with an INSTEAD OF INSERT trigger — but what about updates?

Even on the update side of things our statements can become ambiguous; if we update the ProductName in CustomerOrders_vw, does that mean we want to change the actual name on the product or does it mean that we want to change what product this line item is selling? The answer, of course, is that it depends on the situation. For one system, changing the ProductName might be the correct answer. For another system, changing the product sold might be the thing.

Much like INSTEAD OF INSERT triggers, INSTEAD OF UPDATE triggers give us the chance to trap what is coming in and address it explicitly. In our ProductName example, we could have chosen to do it either way. By default, SQL Server would update the name in the Products table. We could, however, use an

INSTEAD OF UPDATE trigger to trap it and explicitly look up the ProductName to find the ProductID if that is what the user intended. From there, we could generate an error if the provided ProductID did not make the one that went with the name.

INSTEAD OF DELETE Triggers

Okay, this is the last of our INSTEAD OF triggers and, most likely, the one that you'll run into the least often. As with the other two INSTEAD OF trigger types, these are used almost exclusively to allow views to delete data in one or more underlying tables.

So, continuing with our CustomerOrders_vw example, we'll add some delete functionality. This time, however, we're going to raise the complexity bar a bit. We want to delete all the rows for a given order, but if deleting those rows means that the order has no detail items left, then we also want to delete the order header.

We know from our last section (assuming you've been playing along) that we have two rows in Order 1 (the one we seeded when we built the table and the one we inserted in the INSTEAD OF INSERT example) but, before we start trying to delete things, let's build our trigger:

```
CREATE TRIGGER trCustomerOrderDelete ON CustomerOrders_vw
INSTEAD OF DELETE
AS
BEGIN

    -- Check to see whether the DELETE actually tried to feed us any rows
    -- (A WHERE clause might have filtered everything out)
    IF (SELECT COUNT(*) FROM Deleted) > 0
    BEGIN
        DELETE oi
            FROM dbo.OrderItems AS oi
            JOIN Deleted AS d
                ON d.OrderID = oi.OrderID
                AND d.ProductID = oi.ProductID;

        DELETE Orders
            FROM Orders AS o
            JOIN Deleted AS d
                ON o.OrderID = d.OrderID
            LEFT JOIN OrderItems AS oi
                ON oi.OrderID = d.OrderID
                AND oi.ProductID = d.OrderID
            WHERE oi.OrderID IS NULL;
    END
END
```

And now we're ready to test. We'll start off by deleting just a single row from our CustomerOrders_vw view:

```
DELETE CustomerOrders_vw
WHERE OrderID = 1
  AND ProductID = 2;
```

We're ready to run our select again:

```
SELECT ProductID, UnitPrice, Quantity
FROM CustomerOrders_vw
WHERE OrderID = 1;
```

Sure enough, the row that we first inserted in our INSTEAD OF INSERT section is now gone:

```
ProductID   UnitPrice            Quantity
----------- -------------------- -----------
1           5.55                 3

(1 row(s) affected)
```

So, our deleting of individual detail lines is working just fine. Now let's get a bit more cavalier and delete the entire order:

```
DELETE CustomerOrders_vw
WHERE OrderID = 1
```

To really check that this worked okay, we need to go all the way to our Orders table:

```
SELECT * FROM Orders WHERE OrderID = 1;
```

Sure enough — the order has been removed.

> While we don't have to think about individual columns with INSTEAD OF DELETE triggers (you delete by row, not by column), we do need to be aware of what referential integrity actions exist on any table (not view) for which we are defining an INSTEAD OF DELETE trigger. Just like INSTEAD OF UPDATE triggers, INSTEAD OF DELETE triggers are not allowed on tables that have referential integrity actions.

IF UPDATE() and COLUMNS_UPDATED()

In an UPDATE trigger, we can often limit the amount of code that actually executes within the trigger by checking to see whether the column(s) we are interested in are the ones that have been changed. To do this, we make use of the UPDATE() or COLUMNS_UPDATED() functions. Let's look at each.

The UPDATE() Function

The UPDATE() function has relevance only within the scope of a trigger. Its sole purpose in life is to provide a Boolean response (true/false) to whether a particular column has been updated or not. You can use this function to decide whether or not a particular block of code needs to run — for example, if that code is only relevant when a particular column is updated.

Let's run a quick example of this by modifying one of our earlier triggers:

```
USE AdventureWorks2008;
GO

ALTER TRIGGER Production.ProductAudit
    ON Production.ProductInventory
    FOR INSERT, UPDATE, DELETE
AS
IF UPDATE(Quantity)
BEGIN
    INSERT INTO Production.InventoryAudit
    (ProductID, NetAdjustment)
        SELECT COALESCE(i.ProductID, d.ProductID),
            ISNULL(i.Quantity, 0) - ISNULL(d.Quantity, 0) AS NetAdjustment
        FROM Inserted i
        FULL JOIN Deleted d
            ON i.ProductID = d.ProductID
          AND i.LocationID = d.LocationID
        WHERE ISNULL(i.Quantity, 0) - ISNULL(d.Quantity, 0) != 0;
END
```

With this change, we will now limit the rest of the code to run only when the Quantity column (the one we care about) has been changed. The user can change the value of any other column, and we don't care. This means that we'll be executing fewer lines of code and, therefore, this trigger will perform slightly better than our previous version.

The COLUMNS_UPDATED() Function

This one works somewhat differently from UPDATE() but has the same general purpose. What COLUMNS_UPDATED() gives us is the ability to check multiple columns at one time. In order to do this, the function uses a bit mask that relates individual bits in one or more bytes of varbinary data to individual columns in the table. It ends up looking something like Figure 12-4.

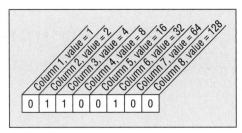

Figure 12-4

In this case, our single byte of data is telling us that the second, third, and sixth columns were updated — the rest were not.

In the event that there are more than eight columns, SQL Server just adds another byte on the right-hand side and keeps counting (see Figure 12-5).

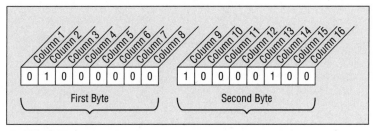

Figure 12-5

This time the second, ninth, and fourteenth columns were updated.

I can hear you out there: "Gee, that's nice — but how do I make any use of this?" Well, to answer that, we have to get into the world of Boolean algebra.

Making use of this information means that you need to add up the binary value of all the bytes, considering the leftmost digit to be the least significant. So, if you want your comparison to take into account 2, 5, and 7, then you need to add the binary value of each bit: 2 + 16 + 64. Then you need to compare the sum of the binary values of your columns to the bit mask by using bitwise operators:

❑ | Represents bitwise OR

❑   & Represents bitwise AND

❑   ^ Represents bitwise Exclusive OR

As I read back over what I've just written, I realize that it is correct, but about as clear as mud, so let's look a little closer at what I mean with a couple of examples.

Imagine that we updated a table that contained five columns. If we updated the first, third, and fifth columns, the bit mask used by COLUMNS_UPDATED would contain 10101000, from 1 + 4 + 16 = 21. We could use:

❑   COLUMNS_UPDATED() > 0 to find out if any column was updated

❑   COLUMNS_UPDATED() ^ 21 = 0 to find out if *all* of the columns specified (in this case 1, 3, and 5) were updated and nothing else was

❑   COLUMNS_UPDATED() & 21 = 21 to find out if all of the columns specified were updated, but the state of other columns doesn't matter

❑   COLUMNS_UPDATED | 21 != 21 to find out if any column *other* than those we're interested in was updated

Understand that this is tough stuff — Boolean math is not exactly the easiest of concepts to grasp for most people, so check things carefully and TEST, TEST, TEST!

Performance Considerations

I've seen what appear almost like holy wars happen over the pros and cons, evil and good, and light and dark of triggers. The worst of it tends to come from purists — people who love the theory, and that's all they want to deal with, or people that have figured out how flexible triggers are and want to use them for seemingly everything.

My two bits worth on this is, as I stated early in the chapter, use them when they are the right things to use. If that sounds sort of noncommittal and ambiguous — good! Programming is rarely black and white, and databases are almost never that way. I will, however, point out some facts for you to think about.

Triggers Are Reactive Rather Than Proactive

What I mean here is that triggers happen after the fact. By the time that your trigger fires, the entire query has run and your transaction has been logged (but not committed and only to the point of the statement that fired your trigger). This means that, if the trigger needs to roll things back, it has to undo what is potentially a ton of work that's already been done. *Slow!* Keep this knowledge in balance though. How big an impact this adds up to depends strongly on how big your query is.

"So what?" you say. Well, compare this to the notion of constraints, which are proactive — that is, they happen before your statement is really executed. That means that they prevent things that will eventually fail from happening before the majority of the work has been done. This will usually mean that they will run at least slightly faster — much faster on more complex queries. Note that this extra speed really only shows itself to any significant extent when a rollback occurs.

What's the end analysis here? Well, if you're dealing with very few rollbacks, and/or the complexity and runtime of the statements affected are low, then there probably isn't much of a difference between triggers and constraints. There's some, but probably not much. If, however, the number of rollbacks is unpredictable or if you know it's going to be high, you'll want to stick with constraints if you can (and frankly, I suggest sticking with constraints unless you have a very specific reason not to).

Triggers Don't Have Concurrency Issues with the Process That Fires Them

You may have noticed throughout this chapter that we often make use of the ROLLBACK statement, even though we don't issue a BEGIN TRAN. That's because a trigger is always implicitly part of the same transaction as the statement that caused the trigger to fire.

If the firing statement was not part of an explicit transaction (one where there was a BEGIN TRAN), then it would still be part of its own one-statement transaction. In either case, a ROLLBACK TRAN issued inside the trigger will still roll back the entire transaction.

Another upshot of this part-of-the-same-transaction business is that triggers inherit the locks already open on the transaction they are part of. This means that we don't have to do anything special to make sure that we don't bump into the locks created by the other statements in the transaction. We have free access within the scope of the transaction, and we see the database based on the modifications already placed by previous statements within the transaction.

Keep It Short and Sweet

I feel like I'm stating the obvious here, but it's for a good reason.

I can't tell you how often I see bloated, stupid code in sprocs and triggers. I don't know whether it's that people get in a hurry, or if they just think that the medium they are using is fast anyway, so it won't matter.

Remember that a trigger is part of the same transaction as the statement in which it is called. This means the statement is not complete until your trigger is complete. Think about it — if you write long-running code in your trigger, this means that every piece of code that you create that causes that trigger to fire will, in turn, be long running. This can really cause heartache in terms of trying to figure out why your code is taking so long to run. You write what appears to be a very efficient sproc, but it performs terribly. You may spend weeks and yet never figure out that your sproc is fine — it just fires a trigger that isn't.

Don't Forget Triggers When Choosing Indexes

Another common mistake. You look through all your sprocs and views figuring out what the best mix of indexes is — and totally forget that you have significant code running in your triggers.

This is the same notion as the "Short and Sweet" section — long-running queries make for long-running statements which, in turn, lead to long-running everything. Don't forget your triggers when you optimize!

Try Not to Roll Back within Triggers

This one's hard since rollbacks are so often a major part of what you want to accomplish with your triggers.

Just remember that AFTER triggers (which are far and away the most common type of trigger) happen after most of the work is already done — that means a rollback is expensive. This is where DRI picks up almost all of its performance advantage. If you are using many ROLLBACK TRAN statements in your triggers, then make sure that you pre-process looking for errors before you execute the statement that fires the trigger. That is, because SQL Server can't be proactive in this situation, be proactive for it. Test for errors beforehand rather than waiting for the rollback.

Dropping Triggers

Dropping triggers is as easy as it has been for almost everything else this far:

```
DROP TRIGGER <trigger name>
```

And it's gone.

Summary

Triggers are an extremely powerful tool that can add tremendous flexibility to both your data integrity and the overall operation of your system. That being said, they are not something to take lightly. Triggers can greatly enhance the performance of your system if you use them for proper summarization of data, but they can also be the bane of your existence. They can be very difficult to debug (even now that we have the debugger), and a poorly written trigger affects not only the trigger itself but any statement that causes that trigger to fire.

13

SQL Cursors

Throughout this book thus far, we've been dealing with data in sets. This tends to go against the way that the more procedure-driven languages go about things. Indeed, when the data gets to the client end, they almost always have to take our set and then deal with it row by row. What they are dealing with is a *cursor*. Indeed, even in traditional SQL Server tools, we can wind up in something of a cursor mode if we utilize a non-SQL-oriented language in our scripts using the new CLR-based language support.

In this chapter, we will be looking at:

❑   What a cursor is

❑   The life span of a cursor

❑   Cursor types (sensitivity and scrollability)

❑   Uses for cursors

We'll discover that there's a lot to think about when creating cursors.

> Perhaps the biggest thing to think about when creating cursors is, "Is there a way I can get out of doing this?" If you ask yourself that question every time you're about to create a cursor, then you will be on the road to a better performing system. That being said, we shall see that there are times when nothing else will do.

What Is a Cursor?

Cursors are a way of taking a set of data and being able to interact with a single record at a time. It doesn't happen nearly as often as one tends to think, but there are indeed times where you just can't obtain the results you want to by modifying or even selecting the data in an entire set. The set is generated by something all of the rows have in common (as defined by a SELECT statement), but then you need to deal with those rows on a one-by-one basis.

The result set that you place in a cursor has several distinct features that set it apart from a normal SELECT statement:

❑   You declare the cursor separately from actually executing it.

❑   The cursor and, therefore, its result set are named at declaration; you then refer to it by name.

❑   The result set in a cursor, once opened, stays open until you close it.

❑   Cursors have a special set of commands used to navigate the recordset.

While SQL Server has its own engine to deal with cursors, there are actually a few different object libraries that can also create cursors in SQL Server:

❑   SQL Native Client (used by ADO.NET)

❑   OLE DB (used by ADO)

❑   ODBC (used by RDO, DAO, and in some cases, OLE DB/ADO)

❑   JDBC (used by Java)

❑   DB-Lib (now a distant legacy offering, but still used in some older apps)

These are the libraries that client applications will typically use to access individual records. Each provides it own syntax for navigating the recordset and otherwise managing the cursor. Each, however, shares in the same set of basic concepts, so, once you have got one object model down for cursors, you're most of the way there for all of them.

> *Every data access API out there (ADO.NET, ADO, ODBC, OLE DB, JDBC, and so on) returns data to a client application or component in a cursor. It's simply the only way that non-SQL programming languages can currently deal with things. This is the source of a big difference between this kind of cursor and SQL Server cursors. With SQL Server cursors, you usually have a choice to perform things as a set operation, which is what SQL Server was designed to do. With the API-based cursors, all you have is cursors, so you don't have the same cursor versus no cursor debate that you have in your server-side activities.*

> *The client-side part of your data handling is going to be done using cursors. That's a given, so don't worry about it. Instead, worry about making the server side of your data access as efficient as possible; that means not using cursors on the server side if you can possibly help it.*

The Life Span of a Cursor

Cursors have lots of little pieces to them, but I think that it's best if we get right into looking first at the most basic form of cursor and then build up from there.

Before we get into the actual syntax though, we need to understand that using a cursor requires more than one statement. Indeed, it takes several. The main parts include:

❑   The declaration

❑   Opening

❑   Utilizing/navigating

❑   Closing

❑   Deallocating

That being said, the basic syntax for declaring a cursor looks like this:

```
DECLARE <cursor name> CURSOR
FOR <select statement>
```

Keep in mind that this is the super-simple rendition. Create a cursor using defaults wherever possible. We'll look at more advanced cursors a little later in the chapter.

The cursor name is just like any other variable name, and, other than not requiring the @ prefix, they must obey the rules for SQL Server naming. The SELECT statement can be any valid SELECT statement that returns a result set. Note that some result sets will not, however, be updatable. (For example, if you use a GROUP BY, then what part of the group is updated? The same holds true for calculated fields for much the same reason.)

We'll go ahead and start building a reasonably simple example. For now, we're not really going to use it for much, but we'll see later that it will be the beginning of what used to be a rather handy tool for administering your indexes (still is handy if you need to support older versions of SQL Server — more on that later):

```
USE AdventureWorks2008;

DECLARE @SchemaName varchar(255);
DECLARE @TableName varchar(255);
DECLARE @IndexName varchar(255);
DECLARE @Fragmentation float;
DECLARE TableCursor CURSOR FOR
  SELECT SCHEMA_NAME(CAST(OBJECTPROPERTYEX(i.object_id, 'SchemaId') AS int)),
         OBJECT_NAME(i.object_id),
         i.name,
         ps.avg_fragmentation_in_percent
  FROM sys.dm_db_index_physical_stats (DB_ID(), NULL, NULL, NULL, NULL) AS ps
  JOIN sys.indexes AS i
    ON ps.object_id = i.object_id
   AND ps.index_id = i.index_id
  WHERE avg_fragmentation_in_percent > 30;
```

Note that this is just the beginning of what you will be building. One of the first things you should notice about cursors is that they require a lot more code than the usual SELECT statement.

We've just declared a cursor called TableCursor that is based on a SELECT statement that will select all of the tables in our database. We also declare a holding variable that will contain the values of our current row while we are working with the cursor.

Just declaring the cursor isn't enough though. We need to actually open it:

```
OPEN TableCursor;
```

This actually executes the query that was the subject of the FOR clause, but we still don't have anything in place we can work with. For that, we need to do a couple of things:

❑ Grab — or FETCH — our first record

❑ Loop through, as necessary, FETCHing the remaining records

We issue our first FETCH. This is the command that says to retrieve a particular record. We must also say into which variables we want to place the values:

```
FETCH NEXT FROM TableCursor INTO @TableName, @IndexName, @Fragmentation
```

Now that we have a first record, we're ready to move onto performing actions against the cursor set:

```
WHILE @@FETCH_STATUS = 0
BEGIN
   PRINT @SchemaName + '.' + @TableName + '.' + @IndexName + ' is '
       + CAST(@Fragmentation AS varchar) + '% Fragmentented';
   FETCH NEXT FROM TableCursor INTO @SchemaName, @TableName, @IndexName,
       @Fragmentation;
END
```

Every time we fetch a row, @@FETCH_STATUS is updated to tell us how our fetch went. The possible values are:

❑ **0 Fetch succeeded:** Everything's fine.

❑ **−1 Fetch failed:** Record missing (you're not at the end, but a record has been deleted since you opened the cursor). We'll look at this closer later in the chapter.

❑ **−2 Fetch failed:** This time it's because you're beyond the last (or before the first) record in the cursor. We'll also see more of this later in the chapter.

Once we exit this loop, we are, for our purposes here, done with the cursor, so we'll close it:

```
CLOSE TableCursor;
```

Closing the cursor, does not, however, free up the memory associated with that cursor. It does free up the locks associated with it. To be sure that you've totally freed up the resources used by the cursor, you must deallocate it:

```
DEALLOCATE TableCursor;
```

So, let's bring it all together just for clarity:

```
DECLARE @SchemaName varchar(255)
DECLARE @TableName varchar(255)
DECLARE @IndexName varchar(255)
DECLARE @Fragmentation float
DECLARE TableCursor CURSOR FOR
   SELECT SCHEMA_NAME(CAST(OBJECTPROPERTYEX(i.object_id, 'SchemaId') AS int)),
```

```
            OBJECT_NAME(i.object_id),
            i.name,
            ps.avg_fragmentation_in_percent
    FROM sys.dm_db_index_physical_stats (DB_ID(), NULL, NULL, NULL, NULL) AS ps
    JOIN sys.indexes AS i
      ON ps.object_id = i.object_id
     AND ps.index_id = i.index_id
    WHERE avg_fragmentation_in_percent > 30
OPEN TableCursor
FETCH NEXT FROM TableCursor INTO @SchemaName, @TableName, @IndexName,
      @Fragmentation

WHILE @@FETCH_STATUS = 0
BEGIN
    PRINT @SchemaName + '.' + @TableName + '.' +
@IndexName + ' is '            + CAST(@Fragmentation AS varchar) + '% Fragmentented'
    FETCH NEXT FROM TableCursor INTO @SchemaName, @TableName, @IndexName,
          @Fragmentation
END
CLOSE TableCursor
DEALLOCATE TableCursor
```

We now have something that runs, but as we've created it at the moment, it's really nothing more than if we had just run the SELECT statement by itself. (Technically, this isn't true since we can't "PRINT" a SELECT statement, but you could do what amounts to the same thing.)

```
Production.ProductInventory.PK_ProductInventory_ProductID_LocationID is 42 ...
Production.ProductListPriceHistory.PK_ProductListPriceHistory_ProductID_St ...
Sales.SpecialOfferProduct.PK_SpecialOfferProduct_SpecialOfferID_ProductID ...
Sales.SpecialOfferProduct.AK_SpecialOfferProduct_rowguid is 50% Fragmenten ...
    ...
    ...
    ...
Production.ProductCostHistory.PK_ProductCostHistory_ProductID_StartDate is ...
Production.ProductDescription.AK_ProductDescription_rowguid is 66.6667% Fr ...
dbo.DatabaseLog.PK_DatabaseLog_DatabaseLogID is 33.3333% Fragmentented
```

What's different is that, if we so chose, we could have done nearly anything to the individual rows. Let's go ahead and illustrate this by completing our little utility.

In days of old, there was no single statement that would rebuild all the indexes in an entire database. (Fortunately, we now have an option in DBCC INDEXDEFRAG to do an entire database.) Keeping your indexes defragmented is, however, a core part of administering your system. The cursor example we're using here is something of a descendant of what was the common way of getting this kind of index defragmentation done. In this newer version, however, we're making use of specific fragmentation information, and we're making it possible to allow for the use of ALTER INDEX (which allows for more options in how exactly to do our defragmentation) instead of DBCC INDEXDEFRAG.

Okay, so we have a few different methods for rebuilding or reorganizing indexes without entirely dropping and re-creating them. ALTER INDEX is the most flexible in terms of letting you select different underlying methods of defragmenting (online or offline, complete rebuild or just a reorganization of what's there, and so on), so we're going to leverage this way of doing things. The simple version of the syntax for ALTER INDEX looks like this:

```
ALTER INDEX <index name> | ALL
  ON <object>
  {[REBUILD] | [REORGANIZE]}
```

Again, this is the hyper-simple version of ALTER INDEX. There are a ton of other little switches and options for it that are described in Chapter 6.

The problem with trying to use this statement to rebuild all the indexes on all of your tables is that it is designed to work on one table at a time. You can use the ALL option instead of the index name if you want to build all the indexes for a table, but you can't leave off the table name to build all the indexes for all the tables. Indeed, even if we had used a tool like DBCC INDEXDEFRAG — which can do an entire database, but just doesn't have as many options — it would still be an all-or-nothing thing. That is, we can't tell it to do just the tables above a certain level of fragmentation, or to exclude particular tables that we may *want* to have fragmentation in.

Remember that there are occasionally times when fragmentation is a good thing. In particular, it can be helpful on tables where we are doing a large number of random inserts as it reduces the number of page splits.

Our cursor can get us around this by just dynamically building the DBCC command:

```
USE AdventureWorks2008;

DECLARE @SchemaName varchar(255);
DECLARE @TableName varchar(255);
DECLARE @IndexName varchar(255);
DECLARE @Fragmentation float;
DECLARE @Command varchar(max);
DECLARE TableCursor CURSOR FOR
  SELECT SCHEMA_NAME(CAST(OBJECTPROPERTYEX(i.object_id, 'SchemaId') AS int)),
         OBJECT_NAME(i.object_id),
         i.name,
         ps.avg_fragmentation_in_percent
  FROM sys.dm_db_index_physical_stats (DB_ID(), NULL, NULL, NULL, NULL) AS ps
  JOIN sys.indexes AS i
    ON ps.object_id = i.object_id
   AND ps.index_id = i.index_id
  WHERE avg_fragmentation_in_percent > 30;
OPEN TableCursor;
FETCH NEXT FROM TableCursor INTO @SchemaName, @TableName, @IndexName,
    @Fragmentation;

WHILE @@FETCH_STATUS = 0
BEGIN
    PRINT 'Reindexing ' + ISNULL(@SchemaName, 'dbo') + '.' +
        @TableName + '.' + @IndexName;
    SET @Command = 'ALTER INDEX [' + @IndexName + '] ON [' +
        ISNULL(@SchemaName, 'dbo') + '.' + @TableName + '] REBUILD';
    EXEC (@Command);
```

```
      FETCH NEXT FROM TableCursor
            INTO @SchemaName, @TableName, @IndexName, @Fragmentation;
END
CLOSE TableCursor;
DEALLOCATE TableCursor;
```

We've now done what would be impossible using only set-based commands. The ALTER INDEX command is expecting a single argument. Providing it a recordset won't work. We get around the problem by combining the notion of a set operation (the SELECT that forms the basis for the cursor) with single-data-point operations (the data in the cursor).

In order to mix these set-based and individual data point operations, we had to walk through a series of steps. First, we declared the cursor and any necessary holding variables. We then "opened" the cursor. It was not until this point that the data was actually retrieved from the database. Next, we utilized the cursor by navigating through it. In this case, we only navigated forward, but, as we shall see, we could have created a cursor that could scroll forward and backward. Moving on, we closed the cursor (if the cursor had still had any open locks, they were released at this point), but memory continues to be allocated for the cursor. Finally, we deallocated the cursor. At this point, all resources in use by the cursor are freed for use by other objects in the system.

So just that quick, we have our first cursor. Still, this is really only the beginning. There is much more to cursors than meets the eye in this particular example. Next, we'll go on and take a closer look at some of the powerful features that give cursors additional flexibility.

Types of Cursors and Extended Declaration Syntax

Cursors come in a variety of different flavors. (We'll visit them all before we're done.) The default cursor is forward-only. (You can only move forward through the records, not backward.) It is also read-only, but cursors can also be scrollable and updatable. They can also have a varying level of sensitivity to changes that are made to the underlying data by other processes.

The forward-only, read-only cursor is the default type of cursor in not only the native SQL Server cursor engine, but also in pretty much all the cursor models I've ever bumped into. It is extremely low in overhead, by comparison, to the other cursor choices, and is usually referred to as being a "firehose" cursor because of the sheer speed with which you can enumerate the data. Like a fire hose, it knows how to dump its contents in just one direction though. (You can't put the water back in a fire hose now can you?) Firehose cursors simply blow away the other cursor-based options in most cases, but don't mistake this as a performance choice over set operations. Even a firehose cursor is slow by comparison to most equivalent set operations.

Let's start out by taking a look at a more extended syntax for cursors, and then we'll look at all of the options individually:

```
DECLARE <cursor name> CURSOR
[LOCAL|GLOBAL]
[FORWARD_ONLY|SCROLL]
[STATIC|KEYSET|DYNAMIC|FAST_FORWARD]
```

```
[READ_ONLY|SCROLL_LOCKS|OPTIMISTIC]
[TYPE_WARNING]
FOR <SELECT statement>
[FOR UPDATE [OF <column name >[,...n]]][;]
```

Or for better ANSI/ISO support:

```
DECLARE <cursor name> [INSENSITIVE|SCROLL] CURSOR
FOR <SELECT statement>
[FOR [READ ONLY|UPDATE [OF <column name >[,...n]]][;]
```

Note that the ANSI/ISO version of the syntax was added long after cursors were added to the product (cursors first made an appearance in SQL Server 6.0 in the mid-'90s). It is probably for this reason (well, that and more features) that virtually all cursors I've seen on SQL Server utilize the syntax I listed first as opposed to the somewhat more portable ANSI/ISO version.

At first glance, it really looks like a handful, and indeed, there are a good many things to think about when declaring cursors. (As I've said, probably the most important is along the lines of, "Do I really need to be doing this in a cursor?") The bright side is that several of these options imply one another, so once you've made one choice the others often start to fall into place quickly.

Let's go ahead and apply the specific syntax in a step-by-step manner that attaches each part to the important concepts that go with it.

Scope

The LOCAL versus GLOBAL option determines the scope of the cursor, that is, what connections and processes can "see" the cursor. Most items that have scope will default to the more conservative approach, that is, the minimum scope (which would be LOCAL in this case). SQL Server cursors are something of an exception to this. The default is actually GLOBAL. Before we get too far into the ramifications of the LOCAL versus GLOBAL scope question, we had better digress for a moment to cover what I mean by local and global in this context.

We are already dealing with something of an exception in that the default scope is set to what we're calling global rather than the more conservative option of local. The exception doesn't stop there though. In SQL Server, the notion of something being global versus local usually indicates that it can be seen by all connections rather than just the current connection. For the purposes of our cursor declaration, however, it refers to whether all processes (batches, triggers, sprocs) in the current connection can see it versus just the current process.

Figure 13-1 illustrates this.

Now let's think about what this means and test it a bit.

The ramifications to the global default fall, as you might expect, on both the pro and the con side of the things. Being global, it means that you can create a cursor within one sproc and refer to it from within a separate sproc — you don't necessarily have to pass references to it. The downside of this though is that, if you try to create another cursor with the same name, you're going to get an error.

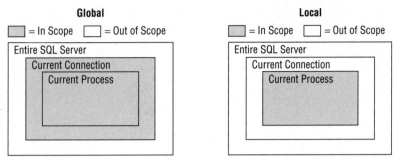

Figure 13-1

Let's test this out with a brief sample. What we're going to do here is create a sproc that will create a cursor for us:

```
USE AdventureWorks2008;
GO

CREATE PROCEDURE spCursorScope
AS

DECLARE @Counter      int,
        @OrderID      int,
        @CustomerID   int

DECLARE CursorTest  CURSOR
GLOBAL
FOR
    SELECT SalesOrderID, CustomerID
    FROM Sales.SalesOrderHeader;

SELECT @Counter = 1;
OPEN CursorTest;
FETCH NEXT FROM CursorTest INTO @OrderID, @CustomerID;
PRINT 'Row ' + CAST(@Counter AS varchar) + ' has a SalesOrderID of ' +
    CONVERT(varchar,@OrderID) + ' and a CustomerID of ' + CAST(@CustomerID AS
varchar);

WHILE (@Counter<=5) AND (@@FETCH_STATUS=0)
BEGIN
    SELECT @Counter = @Counter + 1;
    FETCH NEXT FROM CursorTest INTO @OrderID, @CustomerID;
    PRINT 'Row ' + CAST(@Counter AS varchar) + ' has a SalesOrderID of ' +
        CONVERT(varchar,@OrderID) + ' and a CustomerID of ' + CAST(@CustomerID
AS varchar);
END
```

Notice several things in this sproc. First, I've declared holding variables to do a few things for us. The first, @Counter, will just keep tabs on things so we have to move through only a few records rather than through the entire recordset. The second and third, @OrderID and @CustomerID, respectively, will hold the values retrieved from the query as we go row by row through the result set.

Next, we declare the actual cursor. Note that I've explicitly set the scope. By default, if I had left off the GLOBAL keyword, then I would have still received a cursor that was global in scope.

> You do not have to live by this default. You can use **sp_dboption** or **ALTER DATABASE** to set the Default to local cursor option to **True**. (Set it back to **False** if you want to go back to global.)

> This happens to be yet another great example of why it makes sense to always explicitly state the options that you want. Don't rely on defaults. Imagine if you were just relying on the default of **GLOBAL** and then someone changed that option in the system! I can just hear plenty of you out there saying, "Oh, no one would ever change that." WRONG! This is exactly the kind of "small change" that people make to fix some problem somewhere. Depending on the obscurity of your cursor usage, it may be weeks before you run into the problem, by which time you'll have totally forgotten that the change was made.

We then go ahead and open the cursor and step through several records. Notice, however, that we do not close or deallocate the cursor. We just leave it open and available as we exit the sproc.

I can't help but think of the old show Lost in Space here, with the robot constantly yelling "DANGER Will Robinson! DANGER!" Leaving cursors open like this willy-nilly will lead you to a life of sorrow, frustration, and severe depression.

I'm doing it here to illustrate fully the concept of scope, but you would want to be extremely careful about this kind of usage. The danger lies in the notion that you would call this sproc without realizing that it doesn't clean up after itself. If you don't clean up (close and deallocate) the cursor outside the sproc, then you will create something of a resource leak in the form of this abandoned, but still active, cursor. You will also expose yourself to the possibility of errors should you call the same sproc again. (It will try to declare and open the cursor again, but it already exists.)

When we look into declaring our cursor for output, we will see a much more explicit and better choice for situations where we want to allow outside interaction with our cursors.

Now that we've enumerated several records and proven that our sproc is operating, we will then exit the sproc. (Remember, we haven't closed or deallocated the cursor.) We'll then refer to the cursor from outside the sproc:

```
EXEC spCursorScope;

DECLARE @Counter      int,
        @OrderID      int,
        @CustomerID   int;

SET @Counter=6;

WHILE (@Counter<=10) AND (@@FETCH_STATUS=0)
BEGIN
```

```
    PRINT 'Row ' + CAST(@Counter AS varchar) + ' has a SalesOrderID of ' +
    CAST(@OrderID AS varchar) + ' and a CustomerID of ' +
    CAST(@CustomerID AS varchar);
        SELECT @Counter = @Counter + 1;
        FETCH NEXT FROM CursorTest INTO @OrderID, @CustomerID;
    END

    CLOSE CursorTest;
    DEALLOCATE CursorTest;
```

Okay, so let's walk through what's happening here.

First, we execute the sproc. As we've already seen, this sproc builds the cursor and then enumerates several rows. It exits, leaving the cursor open.

Next, we declare the very same variables that were declared in the sproc. Why do we have to declare them again, but not the cursor? Because it is only the cursor that is global by default. That is, our variables went away as soon as the sproc went out of scope. We can't refer to them anymore, or we'll get a variable undefined error. We must redeclare them.

The next code structure looks almost identical to one in our sproc. We're again looping through to enumerate several records.

Finally, once we've proven our point that the cursor is still alive outside the realm of the sproc, we're ready to close and deallocate the cursor. It is not until we close the cursor that we free up the memory or `tempdb` space from the result set used in the cursor, and it is not until we deallocate that the memory taken up by the cursor variable and its query definition is freed.

Now, go ahead and create the sproc in the system (if you haven't already) and execute the script. You should wind up with a result that looks like this:

```
Row 1 has a SalesOrderID of 43659 and a CustomerID of 29825
Row 2 has a SalesOrderID of 43660 and a CustomerID of 29672
Row 3 has a SalesOrderID of 43661 and a CustomerID of 29734
Row 4 has a SalesOrderID of 43662 and a CustomerID of 29994
Row 5 has a SalesOrderID of 43663 and a CustomerID of 29565
Row 6 has a SalesOrderID of 43664 and a CustomerID of 29898

Row 7 has a SalesOrderID of 43665 and a CustomerID of 29580
Row 8 has a SalesOrderID of 43666 and a CustomerID of 30052
Row 9 has a SalesOrderID of 43667 and a CustomerID of 29974
Row 10 has a SalesOrderID of 43668 and a CustomerID of 29614
```

So, you can see that the cursor stayed open, and our loop outside the sproc was able to pick up right where the code inside the sproc had left off.

Now let's see what happens if we alter our sproc to have local scope:

```
USE AdventureWorks2008;
GO

ALTER PROCEDURE spCursorScope
```

```
AS

DECLARE @Counter      int,
        @OrderID      int,
        @CustomerID   int;

DECLARE CursorTest   CURSOR
LOCAL
FOR
    SELECT SalesOrderID, CustomerID
    FROM Sales.SalesOrderHeader;

SELECT @Counter = 1;
OPEN CursorTest;
FETCH NEXT FROM CursorTest INTO @OrderID, @CustomerID;
PRINT 'Row ' + CAST(@Counter AS varchar) + ' has a SalesOrderID of ' +
    CAST(@OrderID AS varchar) + ' and a CustomerID of ' + CAST(@CustomerID AS varchar);

WHILE (@Counter<=5) AND (@@FETCH_STATUS=0)
BEGIN
    SELECT @Counter = @Counter + 1;
    FETCH NEXT FROM CursorTest INTO @OrderID, @CustomerID;
    PRINT 'Row ' + CAST(@Counter AS varchar) + ' has a SalesOrderID of ' +
        CAST(@OrderID AS varchar) + ' and a CustomerID of ' + CAST(@CustomerID
AS varchar);
END
```

It seems like only a minor change, but the effects are significant when we execute our script again:

```
Row 1 has a SalesOrderID of 43659 and a CustomerID of 29825
Row 2 has a SalesOrderID of 43660 and a CustomerID of 29672
Row 3 has a SalesOrderID of 43661 and a CustomerID of 29734
Row 4 has a SalesOrderID of 43662 and a CustomerID of 29994
Row 5 has a SalesOrderID of 43663 and a CustomerID of 29565
Row 6 has a SalesOrderID of 43664 and a CustomerID of 29898

Msg 16916, Level 16, State 1, Line 14
A cursor with the name 'CursorTest' does not exist.
Msg 16916, Level 16, State 1, Line 18
A cursor with the name 'CursorTest' does not exist.
Msg 16916, Level 16, State 1, Line 19
A cursor with the name 'CursorTest' does not exist.
```

Things ran just as they did before until we got out of the sproc. This time the cursor was no longer in scope as we came out of the sproc, so we were unable to refer to it, and our script ran into several errors. Later on in the chapter, we'll take a look at how to have a cursor with local scope but still be able to access it from outside the procedure in which it was created.

The big thing that you should have gotten out of this section is that you need to think about the scope of your cursors. They do not behave quite the way that other items for which you use the DECLARE statement do.

Scrollability

Like most of the concepts we'll be talking about throughout this chapter, *scrollability* applies to pretty much any cursor model you might face. The notion is actually fairly simple: Can I navigate in relatively any direction, or am I limited to only moving forward? The default is no. You can only move forward.

FORWARD_ONLY

A forward-only cursor is exactly what it sounds like. Since it is the default method, it probably doesn't surprise you to hear that it is the only type of cursor that we've been using up to this point. When you are using a forward-only cursor, the only navigation option that is valid is FETCH NEXT. You need to be sure that you're done with each record before you move onto the next because, once it's gone, there's no getting back to the previous record unless you close and reopen the cursor.

SCROLLABLE

Again, this is just as it sounds. You can "scroll" the cursor backward and forward as necessary. If you're using one of the APIs (ODBC, OLE DB, JDBC, and so on), then, depending on what object model you're dealing with, you can often navigate right to a specific record. Indeed, with ADO, ADO.NET, and LINQ you can even easily resort the data and add additional filters.

The cornerstone of scrolling is the FETCH keyword. You can use FETCH to move forward and backward through the cursor, as well as move to specific positions. The main arguments to FETCH are:

- ❑   NEXT: Move to the next record.
- ❑   PRIOR: Move to the previous record.
- ❑   FIRST: Move to the first record.
- ❑   LAST: Move to the last record.

We'll take a more in-depth look at FETCH later in this chapter, but for now, be aware that FETCH exists and is what controls your navigation through the cursor set.

Let's do a brief example to get across the concept of a scrollable cursor. We'll actually just use a slight variation of the sproc we created a little earlier in the chapter:

```
USE AdventureWorks2008;
GO

CREATE PROCEDURE spCursorScroll
AS

DECLARE @Counter      int,
        @OrderID      int,
        @CustomerID   int

DECLARE CursorTest  CURSOR
LOCAL
SCROLL
```

```
FOR
    SELECT SalesOrderID, CustomerID
    FROM Sales.SalesOrderHeader;

SELECT @Counter = 1;
OPEN CursorTest;
FETCH NEXT FROM CursorTest INTO @OrderID, @CustomerID;
PRINT 'Row ' + CAST(@Counter AS varchar) + ' has a SalesOrderID of ' +
    CAST(@OrderID AS varchar) + ' and a CustomerID of ' + CAST(@CustomerID AS
varchar);

WHILE (@Counter<=5) AND (@@FETCH_STATUS=0)
BEGIN
    SELECT @Counter = @Counter + 1;
    FETCH NEXT FROM CursorTest INTO @OrderID, @CustomerID;
    PRINT 'Row ' + CAST(@Counter AS varchar) + ' has a SalesOrderID of ' +
        CAST(@OrderID AS varchar) + ' and a CustomerID of ' + CAST(@CustomerID
AS varchar);
END

WHILE (@Counter > 1) AND (@@FETCH_STATUS = 0)
BEGIN
    SELECT @Counter = @Counter - 1;
    FETCH PRIOR FROM CursorTest INTO @OrderID, @CustomerID;
    PRINT 'Row ' + CONVERT(varchar,@Counter) + ' has an SalesOrderID of ' +
    CAST(@OrderID AS varchar) + ' and a CustomerID of ' + CAST(@CustomerID
AS varchar);
END

CLOSE CursorTest;
DEALLOCATE CursorTest;
```

The big differences are:

❑   The cursor is declared with the SCROLL option.

❑   We added a new navigation keyword — PRIOR — in the place of NEXT.

❑   We went ahead and closed and deallocated the cursor in the sproc rather than using an outside procedure (been there, done that).

The interesting part comes in the results. This one doesn't require the fancy test script. Simply execute it:

```
EXEC spCursorScroll;
```

and you'll see how the order values scroll forward and back:

```
Row 1 has a SalesOrderID of 43659 and a CustomerID of 29825
Row 2 has a SalesOrderID of 43660 and a CustomerID of 29672
Row 3 has a SalesOrderID of 43661 and a CustomerID of 29734
Row 4 has a SalesOrderID of 43662 and a CustomerID of 29994
Row 5 has a SalesOrderID of 43663 and a CustomerID of 29565
Row 6 has a SalesOrderID of 43664 and a CustomerID of 29898
```

```
Row 5 has an SalesOrderID of 43663 and a CustomerID of 29565
Row 4 has an SalesOrderID of 43662 and a CustomerID of 29994
Row 3 has an SalesOrderID of 43661 and a CustomerID of 29734
Row 2 has an SalesOrderID of 43660 and a CustomerID of 29672
Row 1 has an SalesOrderID of 43659 and a CustomerID of 29825
```

As you can see, we were able to successfully navigate not only forward, as we did before, but also backward.

A forward-only cursor is far and away the more efficient choice of the two options. Think about the overhead for a moment: If it is read-only, then SQL Server really needs to keep track of the next record only — á la a linked list. In a situation where you may reposition the cursor in other ways, extra information must be stored in order to reasonably seek out the requested row. How exactly this is implemented depends on the specific cursor options you choose.

Some types of cursors imply scrollability; others do not. Some types of cursors are sensitive to changes in the data, and some are not. We'll look at some of these issues in the next section.

Cursor Types

The various APIs generally break cursors into four types:

❑   Static

❑   Keyset driven

❑   Dynamic

❑   Forward-only

How exactly these four types are implemented (and what they're called) will sometimes vary slightly among the various APIs and object models, but their general nature is usually pretty much the same.

What makes the various cursor types different is their ability to be scrollable and their *sensitivity* to changes in the database over the life of the cursor. We've already seen what scrollability is all about, but the term "sensitivity" probably sounds like something you'd be more likely to read in *Men Are from Mars, Women Are from Venus* than in a programming book. Actually though, the concept of sensitivity is a rather critical one to think about when choosing your cursor type.

Whether or not a cursor is sensitive defines whether or not it notices changes in the database after the cursor is opened. It also defines just what it does about it once the change is detected. Let's look at this in its most extreme versions — static versus dynamic cursors. The static cursor, once created, is absolutely oblivious to any change to the database. The dynamic cursor, however, is effectively aware of every change (inserted records, deletions, updates, you name it) to the database as long as the cursor remains open. We'll explore the sensitivity issue as we look at each of the cursor types.

Static Cursors

A static cursor is one that represents a "snapshot" in time. Indeed, at least one of the data access object models refers to it as a snapshot recordset rather than a static one.

When a static cursor is created, the entire recordset is created in what amounts to a temporary table in tempdb. After the time that it's created, a static cursor changes for no one and nothing. That is, it is set in stone. Some of the different object models will let you update information in a static cursor, some won't, but the bottom line is always the same: you cannot write updates to the database via a static cursor.

Before we get too far into this brand of cursor, I'm going to go ahead and tell you that the situations where it makes sense to use a static cursor on the server side are extremely rare. I'm not saying they don't exist. They do, but they are very rare indeed.

Before you get into the notion of using a static cursor on the server side, ask yourself:

- ❏   Can I do this with a temporary table?
- ❏   Can I do this entirely on the client side?

Remember that a static cursor is kept by SQL Server in a private table in tempdb. If that's how SQL Server is going to be storing it anyway, why not just use a temporary table yourself? There are times when that won't give you what you need (record rather than set operations). However, if you are just after the concept of a snapshot in time, rather than record-based operations, build your own temp table using SELECT INTO or CREATE TABLE and INSERT INTO and save yourself (and SQL Server) a lot of overhead.

If you're working in a client-server arrangement, static cursors are often better dealt with on the client side. By moving the entire operation to the client, you can cut the number of network roundtrips to the server substantially. Since you know that your cursor isn't going to be affected by changes to the database (after all, isn't that why you chose a static cursor in the first place?), there's no reason to make contact with the server again regarding the cursor after it is created.

Okay, so let's move on to an example of a static cursor. What we're going to do in this example is play around with the notion of creating a static cursor, then make changes and see what happens. We'll play with variations of this throughout the remainder of this part of the chapter as we look at each cursor type.

We'll start with building a table to test with, and then we'll build our cursor and manipulate it to see what's in it:

```
USE AdventureWorks2008;
/* Build the table that we'll be playing with this time */
SELECT SalesOrderID, CustomerID
INTO CursorTable
FROM Sales.SalesOrderHeader
WHERE SalesOrderID BETWEEN 43661 AND 43665;

-- Declare our cursor
DECLARE CursorTest CURSOR
GLOBAL                    -- So we can manipulate it outside the batch
SCROLL                    -- So we can scroll back and see the changes
STATIC                    -- This is what we're testing this time
FOR
SELECT SalesOrderID, CustomerID
FROM CursorTable;

-- Declare our two holding variables
DECLARE @SalesOrderID       int;
```

```
DECLARE @CustomerID    varchar(5);

-- Get the cursor open and the first record fetched
OPEN CursorTest;
FETCH NEXT FROM CursorTest INTO @SalesOrderID, @CustomerID;

-- Now loop through them all
WHILE @@FETCH_STATUS = 0
BEGIN
     PRINT CAST(@SalesOrderID AS varchar) + '    ' + @CustomerID;
     FETCH NEXT FROM CursorTest INTO @SalesOrderID, @CustomerID;
END

-- Make a change. We'll see in a bit that this won't affect the cursor.
UPDATE CursorTable
     SET CustomerID = -111
     WHERE SalesOrderID = 43663;

-- Now look at the table to show that the update is really there.
SELECT SalesOrderID, CustomerID
FROM CursorTable;

-- Now go back to the top. We can do this since we have a scrollable cursor
FETCH FIRST FROM CursorTest INTO @SalesOrderID, @CustomerID;

-- And loop through again.
WHILE @@FETCH_STATUS=0
BEGIN
     PRINT CONVERT(varchar(5),@SalesOrderID) + '    ' + @CustomerID;
     FETCH NEXT FROM CursorTest INTO @SalesOrderID, @CustomerID;
END

-- Now it's time to clean up after ourselves
CLOSE CursorTest;

DEALLOCATE CursorTest;

DROP TABLE CursorTable;
```

Let's take a look at what this gets us. (Note that I've switched over to the Results in Text option to make it easier to see my result sets and my PRINT messages together):

```
(5 row(s) affected)
43661   29734
43662   29994
43663   29565
43664   29898
43665   29580

(1 row(s) affected)
SalesOrderID CustomerID
------------ -----------
43661        29734
43662        29994
```

```
43663          -111
43664          29898
43665          29580

(5 row(s) affected)

43661    29734
43662    29994
43663    29565
43664    29898
43665    29580
```

There are several things to notice about what happened during the run on this script:

❑   First, even though we had a result set open against the table, we were able to perform the update. In this case, it's because we have a static cursor. Once it was created, it was disconnected from the actual records and no longer maintains any locks.

❑   Second, although we can clearly see that our update did indeed take place in the actual table, it did not affect the data in our cursor. Again, this is because, once created, our cursor took on something of a life of its own. It is no longer associated with the original data in any way.

❑   Under the heading of "one more thing," you could also notice that we made use of a new argument to the FETCH keyword. This time we went back to the top of our result set by using FETCH FIRST.

Keyset-Driven Cursors

When we talk about keysets with cursors, we're not talking your local locksmith. Instead, we're talking about maintaining a set of data that uniquely identifies the entire row in the database.

Keyset-driven cursors have the following high points:

❑   They require a unique index to exist on the table in question.

❑   Only the keyset is stored in tempdb — not the entire dataset.

❑   They are sensitive to changes to the rows that are already part of the keyset, including the possibility that they have been deleted.

❑   They are, however, not sensitive to new rows that are added after the cursor is created.

❑   Keyset cursors can be used as the basis for a cursor that is going to perform updates to the data.

Given that it has a name of "keyset" and that I've already said that the keyset uniquely identifies each row, it probably doesn't shock you in any way that you must have a unique index of some kind (usually a primary key, but it could also be any index that is explicitly defined as unique) to create the keyset from.

The keys are all stored in a private table in tempdb. SQL Server uses this key as a method to find its way back to the data as you ask for a specific row in the cursor. The point to take note of here is that the actual data is being fetched, based on the key, at the time that you issue the FETCH. The great part about this is that the data for that particular row is up to date as of when the specific row is fetched. The downside (or upside depending on what you're using the cursor for) is that it uses the keyset that is already created to do the lookup. This means that once the keyset is created, that is all the rows that will be included in your cursor. Any rows that were added after the cursor was created — even if they meet the conditions of the WHERE clause in the SELECT statement — will not be seen by the cursor. The rows that are already part of the cursor can, depending on the cursor options you chose, be updated by a cursor operation.

Let's modify our earlier script to illustrate the sensitivity issue when we are making use of keyset-driven cursors:

```
USE AdventureWorks2008;
/* Build the table that we'll be playing with this time */
SELECT SalesOrderID, CustomerID
INTO CursorTable
FROM Sales.SalesOrderHeader
WHERE SalesOrderID BETWEEN 43661 AND 43665;

-- Now create a unique index on it in the form of a primary key
ALTER TABLE CursorTable
      ADD CONSTRAINT PKCursor
      PRIMARY KEY (SalesOrderID);

/* The IDENTITY property was automatically brought over when
** we did our SELECT INTO, but I want to use my own SalesOrderID
** value, so I'm going to turn IDENTITY_INSERT on so that I
** can override the identity value.
*/
SET IDENTITY_INSERT CursorTable ON;


-- Declare our cursor
DECLARE CursorTest CURSOR
GLOBAL                      -- So we can manipulate it outside the batch
SCROLL                      -- So we can scroll back and see the changes
KEYSET                      -- This is what we're testing this time
FOR
SELECT SalesOrderID, CustomerID
FROM CursorTable;

-- Declare our two holding variables
DECLARE @SalesOrderID     int;
DECLARE @CustomerID    varchar(5);

-- Get the cursor open and the first record fetched
OPEN CursorTest;
FETCH NEXT FROM CursorTest INTO @SalesOrderID, @CustomerID;

-- Now loop through them all
WHILE @@FETCH_STATUS = 0
BEGIN
     PRINT CAST(@SalesOrderID AS varchar) + '   ' + @CustomerID;
     FETCH NEXT FROM CursorTest INTO @SalesOrderID, @CustomerID;
END

-- Make a change. We'll see that does affect the cursor this time.
UPDATE CursorTable
     SET CustomerID = -111
```

```
        WHERE SalesOrderID = 43663;

-- Now we'll delete a record so we can see how to deal with that
DELETE CursorTable
        WHERE SalesOrderID = 43664;

-- Now Insert a record. We'll see that the cursor is oblivious to it.
INSERT INTO CursorTable
        (SalesOrderID, CustomerID)
VALUES
        (-99999, -99999);

-- Now look at the table to show that the changes are really there.
SELECT SalesOrderID, CustomerID
FROM CursorTable;

-- Now go back to the top. We can do this since we have a scrollable cursor
FETCH FIRST FROM CursorTest INTO @SalesOrderID, @CustomerID;

/* And loop through again.
** This time, notice that we changed what we're testing for.
** Since we have the possibility of rows being missing (deleted)
** before we get to the end of the actual cursor, we need to do
** a little bit more refined testing of the status of the cursor.
*/
WHILE @@FETCH_STATUS != -1
BEGIN
        IF @@FETCH_STATUS = -2
        BEGIN
            PRINT '  MISSING! It probably was deleted.';
        END
        ELSE
        BEGIN
            PRINT CAST(@SalesOrderID AS varchar) + '   ' + CAST(@CustomerID AS varchar);

        END
        FETCH NEXT FROM CursorTest INTO @SalesOrderID, @CustomerID;
END

-- Now it's time to clean up after ourselves
CLOSE CursorTest;

DEALLOCATE CursorTest;

DROP TABLE CursorTable;
```

The changes aren't really all that remarkable. We've gone ahead and added the required unique index. I happened to choose to do it as a primary key since that's what matches up best with the table we got this information out of, but it also could have been a unique index without the primary key. We also added something to insert a row of data so we can clearly see that the keyset doesn't see the row in question.

Perhaps the most important thing that we've changed is the condition for the WHILE loop on the final run through the cursor. Technically speaking, we should have made this change to both loops, but there is zero risk of a deleted record the first time around in this example, and I wanted the difference to be visible right within the same script.

The change was made to deal with something new we've added — the possibility that we might get to a record only to find that it's now missing. More than likely, someone has deleted it.

Let's take a look then at the results we get after running this:

```
(5 row(s) affected)
43661    29734
43662    29994
43663    29565
43664    29898
43665    29580

(1 row(s) affected)

(1 row(s) affected)

(1 row(s) affected)
SalesOrderID CustomerID
------------ -----------
-99999       -99999
43661        29734
43662        29994
43663        -111
43665        29580

(5 row(s) affected)

43661    29734
43662    29994
43663    -111
    MISSING! It probably was deleted.
43665    29580
```

Okay, let's walk through the highlights here.

Everything starts out pretty much as it did before. We see the same five rows in the first result set as we did last time. We then see an extra couple of "affected by" messages. These are for the INSERT, UPDATE, and DELETE statements that we added. Next comes the second result set. It's at this point that things get a bit more interesting.

In this next result set, we see the actual results of our UPDATE, INSERT, and DELETE statements. Just as we think we're done, SalesOrderID 43664 has been deleted, and a new order with the SalesOrderID of –99999 has been inserted. That's what's in the table, but things don't appear quite as cozy in the cursor.

The next (and final) result set tells the tale on some differences in the way that things are presented in the cursor versus actually re-running the query. As it happens, we have exactly five rows — just like we started out with and just like our SELECT statement showed are in the actual table. But that's entirely coincidental.

In reality, there are a couple of key differences between what the cursor is showing and what the table is showing. The first presents itself rather boldly. Our result set actually knows that a record is missing. You see, the cursor continues to show the key position in the keyset, but, when it went to do the lookup on the data, the data wasn't there anymore. Our @@FETCH_STATUS was set to -2, and we were able to test for it and report it. The SELECT statement showed us what data was actually there without any remembrance of the record ever having been there. The INSERT, on the other hand, is an entirely unknown quantity to the cursor. The record wasn't there when the cursor was created, so the cursor has no knowledge of its existence. It doesn't show up in our result set.

Keyset cursors can be very handy for dealing with situations where you need some sensitivity to changes in the data, but don't need to know about every insert right up to the minute. They can, depending on the nature of the result set you're after and the keyset, also provide some substantial savings in the amount of data that has to be duplicated and stored into tempdb. This can have some favorable performance impacts for your overall server.

> **WARNING!!!** If you define a cursor as being of type **KEYSET** but do so on a table with no unique index, then SQL Server will implicitly convert your cursor to be **STATIC**. The fact that the behavior gets changed would probably be enough to ruffle your feathers a bit, but it doesn't stop there. It doesn't tell you about it. That's right; by default you get absolutely no warning about this conversion. Fortunately, you can watch out for this sort of thing by using the **TYPE_WARNING** option in your cursor. We'll look at this option briefly toward the end of the chapter.

Dynamic Cursors

Don't you just wish that you could be on a quiz show and have them answer a question like, "What's so special about a dynamic cursor?" Hmmm, then again, I suppose their pool of possible contestants would be small, but those that decided to go for it would probably have the answer right away, "They are *dynamic*, right?" Exactly.

Well, almost exactly. Dynamic cursors fall just short of what I would call dynamic in the sense that they won't proactively tell you about changes to the underlying data. What gets them close enough to be called dynamic is that they are sensitive toward all changes to the underlying data. Of course, like most things in life, all this extra power comes with a high price tag.

If you want inserted records to be added to the cursor — no problem. If you want updated rows to appear properly updated in the cursor — no problem. If you want deleted records to be removed from the cursor set — no problem (although you can't really tell that something's been deleted since you won't see the missing record that you saw with a keyset cursor type). If, however, you want to have concurrency — uh oh, big problem. (You're holding things open longer, so collisions with other users are more likely.) If you want this to be low overhead — uh oh, big problem again. (You are effectively requerying with every FETCH.) Yes, dynamic cursors can be the bane of your performance existence, but, hey, that's life isn't it?

The long and the short of it is that you usually should avoid dynamic cursors.

Why all the hype and hoopla? Well, in order to understand some of the impacts that a dynamic cursor can have, you need to realize a bit about how they work. You see, with a dynamic cursor, your cursor is essentially rebuilt every single time you issue a FETCH. That's right, the SELECT statement that forms the basis of your query, complete with its associated WHERE clause is effectively re-run. Think about that when dealing with large data sets. It brings just one word to mind — ugly. Very ugly indeed.

One of the things I've been taught since the dawn of my RDBMS time is that dynamic cursors are performance pigs — I've found this not to always be the case. This seems to be particularly true when the underlying tables are not very large in size. If you think about it for a bit, you might be able to come up with why a dynamic cursor can actually be slightly faster in terms of raw speed.

My guess as to what's driving this is the use of tempdb for keyset cursors. While a lot more work has to be done with each FETCH in order to deal with a dynamic cursor, the data for the requery will often be completely in cache (depending on the sizing and loading of your system). This means the dynamic cursor gets to work largely from RAM. The keyset cursor, on the other hand, is stored in tempdb, which is on disk (that is, much, much slower) for most systems.

As your table size gets larger, there is more diverse traffic hitting your server, the memory allocated to SQL Server gets smaller, and the more that keyset-driven cursors are going to have something of an advantage over dynamic cursors. In addition, raw speed isn't everything. You really need to think about concurrency issues too (we will look at the options for concurrency in detail later in the chapter), which can be more problematic in dynamic cursors. Still, don't count out dynamic cursors for speed alone if you're dealing with a server-side cursor with small data sets.

Let's go ahead and re-run our last script with only one modification — the change from KEYSET to DYNAMIC:

```
USE AdventureWorks2008;
/* Build the table that we'll be playing with this time */
SELECT SalesOrderID, CustomerID
INTO CursorTable
FROM Sales.SalesOrderHeader
WHERE SalesOrderID BETWEEN 43661 AND 43665;

-- Now create a unique index on it in the form of a primary key
ALTER TABLE CursorTable
      ADD CONSTRAINT PKCursor
      PRIMARY KEY (SalesOrderID);

/* The IDENTITY property was automatically brought over when
** we did our SELECT INTO, but I want to use my own SalesOrderID
** value, so I'm going to turn IDENTITY_INSERT on so that I
** can override the identity value.
*/
SET IDENTITY_INSERT CursorTable ON;

-- Declare our cursor
DECLARE CursorTest CURSOR
    GLOBAL                      -- So we can manipulate it outside the batch
    SCROLL                      -- So we can scroll back and see the changes
    DYNAMIC                     -- This is what we're testing this time
FOR
SELECT SalesOrderID, CustomerID
FROM CursorTable;
```

```
-- Declare our two holding variables
DECLARE @SalesOrderID    int;
DECLARE @CustomerID   varchar(5);

-- Get the cursor open and the first record fetched
OPEN CursorTest;
FETCH NEXT FROM CursorTest INTO @SalesOrderID, @CustomerID;

-- Now loop through them all
WHILE @@FETCH_STATUS = 0
BEGIN
    PRINT CAST(@SalesOrderID AS varchar) + '   ' +  @CustomerID;
    FETCH NEXT FROM CursorTest INTO @SalesOrderID, @CustomerID;
END

-- Make a change. We'll see that does affect the cursor this time.
UPDATE CursorTable
    SET CustomerID = -111
    WHERE SalesOrderID = 43663;

-- Now we'll delete a record so we can see how to deal with that
DELETE CursorTable
    WHERE SalesOrderID = 43664;

-- Now Insert a record. We'll see that the cursor is oblivious to it.
INSERT INTO CursorTable
    (SalesOrderID, CustomerID)
VALUES
    (-99999, -99999);

-- Now look at the table to show that the changes are really there.
SELECT SalesOrderID, CustomerID
FROM CursorTable;

-- Now go back to the top. We can do this since we have a scrollable cursor
FETCH FIRST FROM CursorTest INTO @SalesOrderID, @CustomerID;

/* And loop through again.
** This time, notice that we changed what we're testing for.
** Since we have the possibility of rows being missing (deleted)
** before we get to the end of the actual cursor, we need to do
** a little bit more refined testing of the status of the cursor.
*/
WHILE @@FETCH_STATUS != -1
BEGIN
    IF @@FETCH_STATUS = -2
    BEGIN
        PRINT '  MISSING! It probably was deleted.';
    END
    ELSE
    BEGIN
        PRINT CAST(@SalesOrderID AS varchar) + '   ' +  CAST(@CustomerID AS varchar);
    END
```

```
        FETCH NEXT FROM CursorTest INTO @SalesOrderID, @CustomerID;
END

-- Now it's time to clean up after ourselves
CLOSE CursorTest;

DEALLOCATE CursorTest;

DROP TABLE CursorTable;
```

And the results:

```
(5 row(s) affected)
43661   29734
43662   29994
43663   29565
43664   29898
43665   29580

(1 row(s) affected)

(1 row(s) affected)

(1 row(s) affected)
SalesOrderID CustomerID
------------ -----------
-99999       -99999
43661        29734
43662        29994
43663        -111
43665        29580

(5 row(s) affected)

-99999   *
43661    29734
43662    29994
43663    -111
43665    29580
```

The first two recordsets look exactly as they did last time. The change comes when we get to the third (and final) result set:

❑   There is no indication of a failed fetch, even though we deleted a record (no notification).

❑   The updated record shows the update (just as it did with a keyset).

❑   The inserted record now shows up in the cursor set.

Dynamic cursors are the most sensitive of all cursors. They are affected by everything you do to the underlying data. The downside is that they can provide some extra concurrency problems, and they can pound the system when dealing with larger data sets.

Technically speaking, and unlike a keyset cursor, a dynamic cursor can operate on a non-unique index. Avoid this at all costs. (In my opinion, it should prevent you from doing this and throw an error.) Under certain circumstances, it is quite possible to create an infinite loop because the dynamic cursor cannot keep track of where it is in the cursor set. The only sure-fire way of avoiding this is to either stay away from dynamic cursors or only work on tables with a truly unique index available.

FAST_FORWARD Cursors

Fast (from a cursor standpoint — queries make this or any other cursor look like a snail) is the operative word on this one. This one is the epitome of the term "firehose cursor" that is often used around forward-only cursors. I've always taken the analogy to imply the way that the data sort of spews forth. Once out, you can't put it back in. In short, you're simply awash with data. With FAST_FORWARD cursors, you open the cursor, and do nothing but deal with the data, move forward, and deallocate it. (Note that I didn't say close it.)

Now, it's safe to say that calling this a cursor "type" is something of a misnomer. This kind of cursor has several different circumstances where it is automatically converted to other cursor types, but I think of them as being most like a keyset-driven cursor in the sense that membership is fixed. Once the members of the cursor are established, no new records are added. Deleted rows show up as a missing record (@@FETCH_STATUS of -2). Keep in mind though that, if the cursor is converted to something else (via automatic conversion), it will take on the behavior of that new cursor type.

> The nasty side here is that SQL Server doesn't tell you that the conversion has happened unless you have the **TYPE_WARNING** option added to your cursor definition.

As I said before, there are a number of circumstances where a FAST_FORWARD cursor is implicitly converted to another cursor type. The following table outlines these conversions.

Condition	Converted to
The underlying query requires that a temporary table be built	Static
The underlying query is distributed in nature	Keyset
The cursor is declared as FOR UPDATE	Dynamic
A condition exists that would convert to keyset driven, but at least one underlying table does not have a unique index	Static

I've heard that there are other circumstances where a cursor will be converted, but I haven't seen any documentation of this, and I haven't run into it myself.

> If you find that you are getting that most dreaded of all computer-related terms (unpredictable results), you can make use of **sp_describe_cursor** (a system stored procedure) to list all the currently active options for your cursor.

It's worth noting that all FAST_FORWARD cursors are read-only in nature. You can explicitly set the cursor to have the FOR UPDATE option, but, as suggested in the preceding implicit conversion table, the cursor will be implicitly converted to dynamic.

Okay, so what exactly does a FAST_FORWARD cursor have that any of the other cursors wouldn't have if they were declared as being FORWARD_ONLY? Well, a FAST_FORWARD cursor will implement at least one of two tricks to help things along:

❑ The first is to pre-fetch data. That is, at the same time that you open the cursor, it automatically fetches the first row. This means that you save a roundtrip to the server if you are operating in a client-server environment using ODBC. Unfortunately, this is available only under ODBC.

❑ The second is the one that is a sure thing — auto-closing of the cursor. Since you are running a cursor that is forward-only, SQL Server can assume that you want the cursor closed once you reach the end of the recordset. Again, this saves a roundtrip and squeezes out a tiny bit of additional performance.

Choosing a cursor type is one of the most critical decisions when structuring a cursor. Choices that have little apparent difference in the actual output of the cursor task can have major differences in performance. Other effects can be seen in sensitivity to changes, concurrency issues, and updatability.

Concurrency Options

We got our first taste of concurrency issues back in our chapter on transactions and locks. As you recall, we deal with concurrency issues whenever there are issues surrounding two or more processes trying to get to the same data at essentially the same time. When dealing with cursors, however, the issue becomes just slightly stickier.

The problem is multifold:

❑ The operation tends to last longer (more time to have a concurrency problem).

❑ Each row is read at the time of the fetch, but someone may try to edit it before you get a chance to do your update.

❑ You may scroll forward and backward through the result set for what could be an essentially unlimited about of time (I hope you never do that, but it's possible to do).

As with all concurrency issues, this tends to be more of a problem in a transaction environment than when running in a single statement situation. The longer the transaction, the more likely you are to have concurrency problems.

SQL Server gives us three different options for dealing with this issue:

❑ READ_ONLY

❑ SCROLL_LOCKS (equates to Pessimistic in most terminologies)

❑ OPTIMISTIC

Each of these has their own thing they bring to the party, so let's look at them one by one.

READ_ONLY

In a read-only situation, you don't have to worry about whether your cursor is going to try and obtain any kind of update or exclusive lock. You also don't have to worry about whether anyone has edited the data while you've been busy making changes of your own. Both of these make life considerably easier.

READ_ONLY is just what it sounds like. When you choose this option, you cannot update any of the data, but you also skip most (but not all) of the notion of concurrency entirely.

SCROLL_LOCKS

Scroll locks equate to what is more typically referred to as pessimistic locking in the various APIs and object models. In its simplest form, it means that, as long as you are editing this record, no one else is allowed to edit it. The specifics of implementation of duration of this vary depending on:

❑ Whether or not you're in a transaction

❑ What transaction isolation level you've set

Note that this can be different from what we saw with update locks back in our locking and transaction chapter.

With update locks, we prevented other users from updating the data. This lock was held for the duration of the transaction. If it was a single statement transaction, then the lock was not released until every row affected by the update was complete.

Scroll locks work identically to update locks with only one significant exception — the duration the lock is held. With scroll locks, there is much more of a variance depending on whether or not the cursor is participating in a multi-statement transaction. Assuming for the moment that you do not have a transaction wrapped around the cursor, then the lock is held only on the current record in the cursor — that is, from the time the record is first fetched until the next record (or end of the result set) is fetched. Once you move on to the next record, the lock is removed from the prior record.

Let's take a look at this through a significantly pared-down version of the script we've been using through much of this chapter:

```
USE AdventureWorks2008;
/* Build the table that we'll be playing with this time */
SELECT SalesOrderID, CustomerID
INTO CursorTable
FROM Sales.SalesOrderHeader
WHERE SalesOrderID BETWEEN 43661 AND 43665;

-- Now create a unique index on it in the form of a primary key
ALTER TABLE CursorTable
     ADD CONSTRAINT PKCursor
     PRIMARY KEY (SalesOrderID);

/* The IDENTITY property was automatically brought over when
** we did our SELECT INTO, but I want to use my own SalesOrderID
** value, so I'm going to turn IDENTITY_INSERT on so that I
** can override the identity value.
*/
```

```
SET IDENTITY_INSERT CursorTable ON;

-- Declare our cursor
DECLARE CursorTest CURSOR
GLOBAL                          -- So we can manipulate it outside the batch
SCROLL                          -- So we can scroll back and see the changes
DYNAMIC                         -- This is what we're testing this time
SCROLL_LOCKS
FOR
SELECT SalesOrderID, CustomerID
FROM CursorTable;

-- Declare our two holding variables
DECLARE @SalesOrderID     int;
DECLARE @CustomerID   varchar(5);

-- Get the cursor open and the first record fetched
OPEN CursorTest;
FETCH NEXT FROM CursorTest INTO @SalesOrderID, @CustomerID;
```

You'll not see much gray in the preceding code block (to indicate that changes were made on that line) because only one line was added. The remainder of the changes were deletions of lines, so there's nothing for me to make gray for you. Just make sure that you've made the appropriate changes if you're going to try and run this one.

What we've done is toss out most of the things that were happening, and we've refocused ourselves back on the cursor. Perhaps the biggest thing to notice though is a couple of key things that we have deliberately omitted even though they are things that would normally cause problems if we try to operate without them:

❑   We do not have a CLOSE on our cursor, nor do we deallocate it at this point.

❑   We don't even scroll any farther than getting the first row fetched.

The reason we've left the cursor open is to create a situation where the state of the cursor being open lasts long enough to play around with the locks somewhat. In addition, we fetch only the first row because we want to make sure that there is an active row. (The way we had things before, we would have been to the end of the set before we started running with other, possibly conflicting, statements.)

What you want to do is execute the preceding and then open a completely separate connection window with AdventureWorks2008 active. Then run a simple test in the new connection window:

```
SELECT * FROM CursorTable;
```

If you haven't been grasping what I've been saying in this section, you might be a tad surprised by the results:

```
SalesOrderID CustomerID
------------ -----------
43661        29734
43662        29994
43663        29565
```

```
43664         29898
43665         29580

(5 row(s) affected)
```

Based on what we know about locks (from Chapter 11), you would probably expect the preceding SELECT statement to be blocked by the locks on the current record. Not so with scroll locks. The lock is only on the record that is currently in the cursor, and, perhaps more importantly, the lock only prevents updates to the record. Any SELECT statements (such as ours) can see the contents of the cursor without any problems.

Now that we've seen how things work, go back to the original window and run the code to clean things up. This is back to the same code we've worked with for much of this chapter:

```
-- Now it's time to clean up after ourselves
CLOSE CursorTest;

DEALLOCATE CursorTest;

DROP TABLE CursorTable;
```

Don't forget to run the preceding clean-up code!!! If you forget, then you'll have an open transaction sitting in your system until you terminate the connection. SQL Server should clean up any open transactions (by rolling them back) when the connection is broken, but I've seen situations where you run the database consistency checker (DBCC) and find that you have some really old transactions. SQL Server missed cleaning up after itself.

OPTIMISTIC

Optimistic locking creates a situation where no scroll locks of any kind are set on the cursor. The assumption is that, if you do an update, you want people to still be able to get at your data. You're being optimistic because you are essentially guessing (hoping may be a better word) that no one will edit your data between when you fetched it into the cursor and when you applied your update.

The optimism is not necessarily misplaced. If you have a lot of records and not that many users, then the chances of two people trying to edit the same record at the same time are very small (depending on the nature of your business processes). Still, if you get this optimistic, then you need to also be prepared for the possibility that you will be wrong — that is, that someone has altered the data in between when you performed the fetch and when you went to actually update the database.

If you happen to run into this problem, SQL Server will issue an error with a value in @@ERROR of 16394. When this happens, you need to completely refetch the data from the cursor (so you know what changes were being made) and either rollback the transaction or try the update again.

Detecting Conversion of Cursor Types: TYPE_WARNING

This one is really pretty simple. If you add this option to your cursor, then you will be notified if an implicit conversion is made on your cursor. Without this statement, the conversion just happens with no notification. If the conversion wasn't an anticipated behavior, then there's a good chance that you're going to see the most dreaded of all computer terms (unpredictable results).

This is perhaps best understood with an example, so let's go back and run a variation again of the cursor that we've been using throughout most of the chapter.

In this instance, we're going to take out the piece of code that creates a key for the table. Remember that without a unique index on a table, a keyset will be implicitly converted to a static cursor:

```
USE AdventureWorks2008;

/* Build the table that we'll be playing with this time */
SELECT SalesOrderID, CustomerID
INTO CursorTable
FROM Sales.SalesOrderHeader
WHERE SalesOrderID BETWEEN 43661 AND 43665;

-- Declare our cursor
DECLARE CursorTest CURSOR
GLOBAL                  -- So we can manipulate it outside the batch
SCROLL                  -- So we can scroll back and see the changes
KEYSET
TYPE_WARNING
FOR
SELECT SalesOrderID, CustomerID
FROM CursorTable;

-- Declare our two holding variables
DECLARE @SalesOrderID     int;
DECLARE @CustomerID   varchar(5);

-- Get the cursor open and the first record fetched
OPEN CursorTest;
FETCH NEXT FROM CursorTest INTO @SalesOrderID, @CustomerID;

-- Now loop through them all
WHILE @@FETCH_STATUS=0
BEGIN
        PRINT CAST(@SalesOrderID AS varchar) + '   ' + CAST(@CustomerID AS varchar);
    FETCH NEXT FROM CursorTest INTO @SalesOrderID, @CustomerID;
END

-- Now it's time to clean up after ourselves
CLOSE CursorTest;

DEALLOCATE CursorTest;

DROP TABLE CursorTable;
```

There's nothing particularly special about this one. I'm considering it to be something of a complete rewrite only because we've deleted so much from the original and it's been so long since we've seen it. The creation of the table and cursor is pretty much the same as when we did our keyset-driven cursor much earlier in the chapter. The major changes are the removal of blocks of code that we don't need for this illustration along with the addition of the TYPE_WARNING option in the cursor declaration.

Now we come up with some interesting results:

```
(5 row(s) affected)
The created cursor is not of the requested type.
43661   29734
43662   29994
43663   29565
43664   29898
43665   29580
```

Everything ran okay. We just saw a statement that was meant solely as a warning. The results may not be what you expected given that the cursor was converted.

The downside here is that you get a message sent out, but no error. Programmatically speaking, there is essentially no way to tell that you received this message — which makes this option fairly useless in a production environment. Still, it can often be quite handy when you're trying to debug a cursor to determine why it isn't behaving in the expected fashion.

FOR <SELECT>

This section of the cursor declaration is at the very heart of the matter. This is a section that is required under even the most basic of cursor syntax, and that's because it's the one and only clause that determines what data should be placed in the cursor.

Almost any SELECT statement is valid — even those including an ORDER BY clause. As long as your SELECT statement provides a single result set, you should be fine. Examples of options that would create problems would be any of the summary options such as a CUBE or ROLLUP.

FOR UPDATE

By default, any cursor that is updatable at all is completely updatable — that is, if one column can be edited then any of them can.

The FOR UPDATE <column list> option allows you to specify that only certain columns are to be editable within this cursor. If you include this option, then only the columns in your column list will be allowed to be updatable. Any columns not explicitly mentioned will be considered to be read-only.

Navigating the Cursor: The FETCH Statement

I figure that whoever first created the SQL cursor syntax must have really liked dogs. They probably decided to think of the data they were after as being the bone, with SQL Server the faithful bloodhound. From this, I'm guessing, the FETCH keyword was born.

It's an apt term if you think about it. In a nutshell, it tells SQL Server to "go get it boy!" With that, our faithful mutt (in the form of SQL Server) is off to find the particular bone (row) we were after. We've gotten a bit of a taste of the FETCH statement in some of the previous cursors in this chapter, but it's time to look at this very important statement more closely.

FETCH actually has many more options than what we've seen so far. Up to this point, we've seen three different options for FETCH (NEXT, PREVIOUS, and FIRST). These really aren't a bad start. Indeed, we really only need to add one more for the most basic set of cursor navigation commands, and a few after that for the complete set.

Let's look at each of the cursor navigation commands and see what they do for us:

FETCH Option	Description
NEXT	This moves you forward exactly one row in the result set and is the backbone option. Ninety percent or more of your cursors won't need any more than this. Keep this in mind when deciding to declare as FORWARD_ONLY or not. When you try to do a FETCH NEXT and it results in moving beyond the last record, you will have a @@FETCH_STATUS of –1.
PRIOR	As you have probably surmised, this one is the functional opposite of NEXT. This moves backward exactly one row. If you performed a FETCH PRIOR when you were at the first row in the result set, then you will get a @@FETCH_STATUS of –1 just as if you had moved beyond the end of the file.
FIRST	Like most cursor options, this one says what it is pretty clearly. If you perform a FETCH FIRST, then you will be at the first record in the recordset. The only time this option should generate a @@FETCH_STATUS of –1 is if the result set is empty.
LAST	The functional opposite of FIRST, FETCH LAST moves you to the last record in the result set. Again, the only way you'll get a –1 for @@FETCH_STATUS on this one is if you have an empty result set.
ABSOLUTE	With this one, you supply an integer value that indicates how many rows you want from the beginning of the cursor. If the value supplied is negative, then it is that many rows from the end of the cursor. Note that this option is not supported with dynamic cursors (since the membership in the cursor is redone with every fetch, you can "really know where you're at"). This equates roughly to navigating to a specific "absolute position" in a few of the client access object models.
RELATIVE	No — this isn't your mother-in-law kind of thing. Instead, this is about navigating by moving a specified number of rows forward or backward relative to the current row.

We've already gotten a fair look at a few of these in our previous cursors. The other navigational choices work pretty much the same.

Altering Data within Your Cursor

Up until now, we've kind of glossed over the notion of changing data directly in the cursor. Now it's time to take a look at updating and deleting records within a cursor.

Since we're dealing with a specific row rather than set data, we need some special syntax to tell SQL Server that we want to update. Happily, this syntax is quite easy given that you already know how to perform an UPDATE or DELETE.

Essentially, we're going to update or delete data in the table that is underlying our cursor. Doing this is as simple as running the same UPDATE and DELETE statements that we're now used to, but qualifying them with a WHERE clause that matches our cursor row. We just add one line of syntax to our DELETE or UPDATE statement:

```
WHERE CURRENT OF <cursor name>
```

Nothing remarkable about it at all. Just for grins though, we'll go ahead and implement a cursor using this syntax:

```
USE AdventureWorks2008;
/* Build the table that we'll be playing with this time */
SELECT SalesOrderID, CustomerID
INTO CursorTable
FROM Sales.SalesOrderHeader
WHERE SalesOrderID BETWEEN 43661 AND 43665;

-- Now create a unique index on it in the form of a primary key
ALTER TABLE CursorTable
     ADD CONSTRAINT PKCursor
     PRIMARY KEY (SalesOrderID);

/* The IDENTITY property was automatically brought over when
** we did our SELECT INTO, but I want to use my own OrderID
** value, so I'm going to turn IDENTITY_INSERT on so that I
** can override the identity value.
*/
SET IDENTITY_INSERT CursorTable ON;

-- Declare our cursor
DECLARE CursorTest CURSOR
SCROLL              -- So we can scroll back and see if the changes are there
KEYSET
FOR
SELECT SalesOrderID, CustomerID
FROM CursorTable;

-- Declare our two holding variables
DECLARE @SalesOrderID    int;
DECLARE @CustomerID      varchar(5);

-- Get the cursor open and the first record fetched
OPEN CursorTest;
FETCH NEXT FROM CursorTest INTO @SalesOrderID, @CustomerID;

-- Now loop through them all
WHILE @@FETCH_STATUS=0
BEGIN
    IF (@SalesOrderID % 2 = 0)    -- Even number, so we'll update it
    BEGIN
        -- Make a change. This time though, we'll do it using cursor syntax
        UPDATE CursorTable
            SET CustomerID = -99999
```

```
                        WHERE CURRENT OF CursorTest;
        END
        ELSE                            -- Must be odd, so we'll delete it.
        BEGIN
            -- Now we'll delete a record so we can see how to deal with that
            DELETE CursorTable
                    WHERE CURRENT OF CursorTest;
        END
        FETCH NEXT FROM CursorTest INTO @SalesOrderID, @CustomerID;
END


-- Now go back to the top. We can do this since we have a scrollable cursor
FETCH FIRST FROM CursorTest INTO @SalesOrderID, @CustomerID;

-- And loop through again.
WHILE @@FETCH_STATUS != -1
BEGIN
    IF @@FETCH_STATUS = -2
    BEGIN
        PRINT '  MISSING! It probably was deleted.';
    END
    ELSE
    BEGIN
        PRINT CAST(@SalesOrderID AS varchar) + ' ' + CAST(@CustomerID AS varchar);
    END
    FETCH NEXT FROM CursorTest INTO @SalesOrderID, @CustomerID;
END
```

```
-- Now it's time to clean up after ourselves
CLOSE CursorTest;

DEALLOCATE CursorTest;

DROP TABLE CursorTable;
```

Again, I'm treating this one as an entirely new cursor. We've done enough deletions, additions, and updates that I suspect you'll find it easier to just key things in a second time rather than having to look through row by row to see what you might have missed.

We are also again using the modulus operator (%) that we saw earlier in the book. Remember that it gives us nothing but the remainder. Therefore, if the remainder of any number divided by 2 is zero, then we know the number was an even number.

The rest of the nuts and bolts of this don't require any rocket science, yet we can quickly tell that we got some results:

```
(5 row(s) affected)

(1 row(s) affected)

(1 row(s) affected)

(1 row(s) affected)
```

```
(1 row(s) affected)

(1 row(s) affected)
  MISSING! It probably was deleted.
43662 *
  MISSING! It probably was deleted.
43664 *
  MISSING! It probably was deleted.
```

You can see the multiple "1 row affected" that is the returned message for any row that was affected by the UPDATE and DELETE statements. When we get down to the last result set enumeration, you can quickly tell that we deleted all the odd numbers (which is what we told our code to do), and that we updated the even numbered rows with a new CustomerID.

No tricks — just a WHERE clause that makes use of the WHERE CURRENT argument.

Summary

Cursors give us those memories of the old days when we could address things row by row. Ahhh, it sounds so romantic with that "old days" kind of thought. WRONG! I'd stick to set operations any day if I thought I could get away with it.

The fact is that set operations can't do everything. Cursors are going to be the answer any time a solution must be done on a row-by-row basis. Notice that I used the word "must" in there, and that's the way you should think of it. Cursors are great for taking care of some problems that can't be solved by any other means.

That being said, remember to avoid cursor use wherever possible. Cursors are resource pigs and will almost always produce 100 times or worse negative performance impact. It is extremely tempting — especially if you come from the mainframe world or from a dBase background — to just keep thinking in that row-by-row method. Don't fall into that trap! Cursors are meant to be used only when no other options are available.

14

Reporting Services

There are a few chapters in my books where I've chosen to overlap content between the *Beginning* and *Professional* titles. Now, it may seem like beginning and professional topics would be mutually exclusive, but that holds true only in a perfect world where everyone is gaining experience in the same way and in the same order, and where everyone has the same definition of beginning and professional.

In case you haven't already guessed it, this is one of those chapters where, if you've read my *Beginning* title, you're going to notice a little bit of overlap. In the case of Reporting Services, the reasons are multifold, but a couple of the key ones are:

❑ Some people get into database development specifically driven by the need to control more of their own reporting destiny (in which case they may have almost started with Reporting Services, and then started learning the queries they need to support the data in the report). Others are long-term database "experts" who are just getting around to using one of those "extras" that SQL Server provides.

❑ It's a relatively new feature (in the grand life of SQL Server as a product), so it's "new" to many professional-level people.

Now, don't go rushing off yet if you read the chapter on Reporting in the *Beginning* title. While we do repeat *some* key items, we go a bit deeper here, and focus on more of the true developer-oriented items (and less on the model-driven aspects). Feel free, however, to skip ahead to the section on the data sources and data source views, where we will take a far more "Pro" look at things including parameterization, drill-throughs, and charting.

A Quick Look at Reports as a Concept

After all the queries have been written, and after all the stored procedures have been run, there remains a rather important thing we need to do in order to make our data useful — make it available to end users.

Reporting is one of those things that seems incredibly simple, but turns out to be rather tricky. You see, you can't simply start sticking numbers in front of people's faces. The numbers must make sense and, if at all possible, capture the attention of the person you're reporting for. To produce reports that actually get used and, therefore, are useful, there are a few things to keep in mind:

❑ **Use just the right amount of data:** Do not try to do too much in one report; nor should you do too little. A report that is a jumble of numbers is going to lose a reader's attention quickly, and you'll find that it doesn't get utilized after the first few times it is generated. Likewise, a barren report will get just a glance and get tossed without any real thought. Find a balance of mixing the right amount of data with the right data.

❑ **Make it appealing:** Sad as it is to say, another important element in reporting is what one of my daughters would call making it "prettiful," which is to say, making it look nice and pleasing to the eye. An ugly report is a dead report.

In this chapter, we're going to be taking a look at a few key concepts of Reporting Services (often referred to as SSRS), and then moving on to some more advanced aspects. While I do indeed skip some of the "basics," I cover some fundamental items necessary to make any sense out of the more advanced topics, but then quickly move on to the Report Designer, which allows for the most advanced reporting options Reporting Services has to offer.

> *For the sake of brevity (and to minimize overlap), I cover report models in this book only with a discussion of what they are there for, not with a specific example. This is one of the places where I draw the line between Beginning- and Pro-level information. That said, even if you did not already understand report models before reading this chapter, you'll find that learning about core items such as data sources and the Report Designer will make learning how to use the Report Modeler and the Report Model designer largely intuitive. The building of actual reports will be similarly easy.*

Reporting Services 101

Odds are that you've already generated some reports in your day. They may have been paper reports off a printer (perhaps in something as rudimentary as Access's reporting area, which is actually one of the best parts of Access to me). Or perhaps you have used a rather robust reporting engine such as Crystal Reports. Even if you haven't used tools that fancy, one can argue that handing your boss the printout from a stored procedure is essentially a very simple (albeit not necessarily nice-looking) report. I would tend to agree with that argument.

The reality, however, is that our managers and coworkers today expect something more. This is where Reporting Services comes in. Reporting Services really has two different varieties of operation:

❑ **Report Models:** This is making use of a relatively simple, Web-driven interface that is meant to allow end users to create their own simple reports.

❑ **Reports generated in the Business Intelligence Development Studio:** While this doesn't necessarily mean you have to write code (you can actually create some fairly robust reports using drag-and-drop functionality), you can get pretty fancy and do very complex things depending on just how far you want to take it.

Note that, while your users can eventually access these reports from the same Reporting Services Web host, they are based on somewhat different architectures (and are created in different fashions).

In addition, Reporting Services provides features for pre-generating reports (handy if the queries that underlie the report take a while to run) as well as for distributing the report via e-mail. Exported reports can be rendered in PDF, Excel, and Word formats.

Tools Used with Reporting Services

Reporting Services has several tools to help you create, use, and manage reports. These include:

❑ **Reporting Services Configuration Manager:** This tool can be found in the Configuration Tools subfolder under the main SQL Server. This allows you to configure such things as the account Reporting Services runs under, the IP addresses and ports the supporting Web server will respond to, the virtual directory names used for Reporting Services, e-mail accounts to be used, and the database used to keep track of Reporting Services information, as well as encryption keys and scalability configuration information.

❑ **Business Intelligence Development Studio (BIDS):** This is essentially Visual Studio with a set of templates installed that focus on Reporting Services, Analytics, Integration Services, and Data Mining. If you already have Visual Studio 2008 installed, BIDS just adds some more templates and shortcuts to get to Visual Studio. We will be utilizing the Development Studio extensively over several of the remaining chapters of this book (sometimes in its base SQL Server installed form, and sometimes as part of a full Visual Studio installation).

❑ **SQL Server Management Studio:** In the Management Studio, you can connect to virtually all of the different SQL Server–related services in order to (can you see this one coming? Of course you can!), *manage* things about that particular service. While only the base data engine has what I would consider "full functionality" entirely wrapped up in the Management Studio, the Studio is the place to perform most security-related tasks as well as anything tied to job scheduling.

❑ **The Report Server Website:** This is where you go to actually run most of the reports you'll want executed in Reporting Services, but through the Site Settings link (in the upper-right side of the browser). It is also a place to manage some elements of your server (in particular, caching, assigning roles, and scheduling).

Unfortunately, no individual tool does everything involved in Reporting Services. Indeed, none of them even comes close (as Management Studio does for the database engine). But by utilizing a combination of the various tools, we're able to manage all the aspects of our Report Server.

Other Means of Accessing Reporting Services

Reporting Services also supports a fairly robust Web service model. There is a set of libraries provided to support .NET projects accessing the Reporting Services Web Service API. We will take a look at the basics of that toward the end of the chapter.

Report Server Projects

Report Models (the primary discussion of Reporting Services in my *Beginning* title) can be considered as "scratching the surface" of things. Reporting Services has much more flexibility than that. (Indeed, there are entire books solely about Reporting Services; there is that much to it.) In addition to the Report Modeler, the Business Intelligence Development Studio will allow you to create Report Server Projects.

As I said earlier, there are entire books about this subject, so the approach we're going to take here is to start with a little taste of the possibilities through a simple example. We'll then expand on things a bit.

> *A lot has changed with the look and feel of Report Service Projects for this release. Microsoft bought licenses to a number of the Dundas (a component development company) Reporting Service Components. These are a significant upgrade in the componentry for Reporting Services.*

In our journey to look at Report Server Projects, we'll start with several core items that are common to both the Report Modeler and Report Server Projects. If you are already familiar with data sources and data source views, you can scan the next two sections to pick up the relevant parts of the project example, but otherwise skip to the section where we are discussing the actual report layout.

So, let's get started with a Report Server Project. Start by opening the Business Intelligence Development Studio, and opening a new project. You'll want to use the Business Intelligence using the Report Server Project template in the Business Intelligence Development Studio, as shown in Figure 14-1.

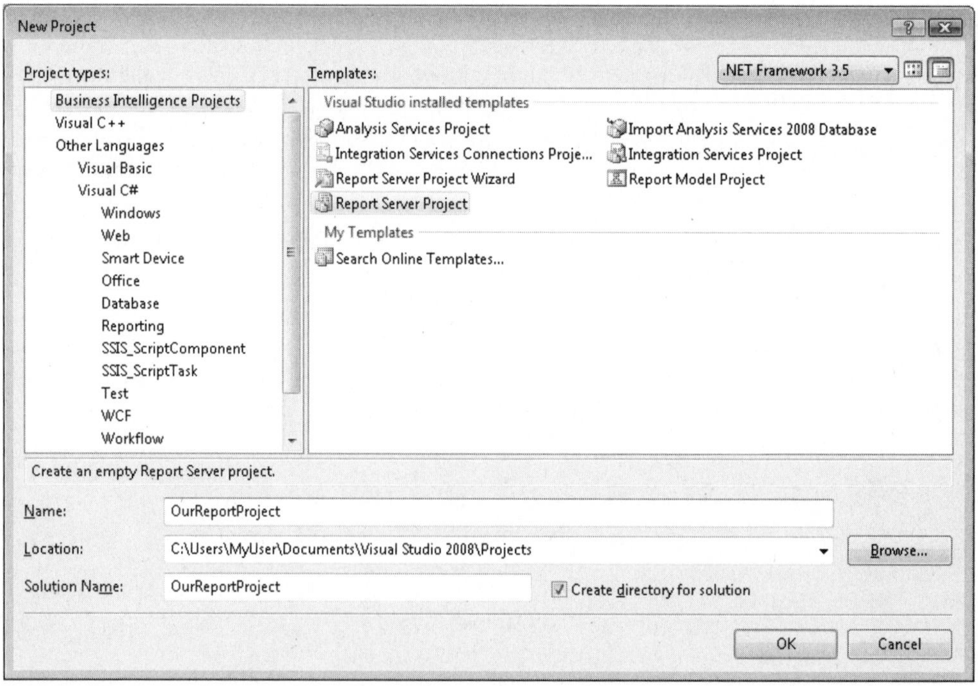

Figure 14-1

> Note that the exact appearance of this dialog may vary somewhat depending on whether you have Visual Studio installed and, if so, which specific languages and templates you've installed. The image shown is of a full version of Visual Studio, as it is required for some of the more advanced topics of this book.

This will serve as the project for most of what we are going to do in this chapter. With our project now created, we're ready to get into some of the key concepts of a report. Some of these will be a review if you've read my *Beginning* title, but you'll want to get this first report together to have it available for some of the more robust examples later.

Data Sources

Data sources and data source views (we'll be looking at those next) are perhaps the most central items in Reporting Services. Each serves in some fashion regardless of what specific type of report you're building and regardless of whether it's using the Report Modeler or a Report Project. Although they have similar names, they serve slightly different levels in the hierarchy of pulling data together into a report.

A data source is essentially the definition required for connecting to wherever you're getting your data from. This can be a connection to a SQL Server or any OLE DB or ODBC data source. If you ponder the possibilities of that for a moment, you should quickly come to the conclusion that, although Reporting Services is associated with SQL Server, you have the prospect of using a wide variety of non–SQL Server data sources in your reports. This is a very powerful concept indeed.

There are two types of data sources:

❑ **Embedded:** This type of data source is stored within the same file that defined the report. We will take a look at the XML (called Report Definition Language — or RDL) a little later in the chapter, but suffice to say that all the relevant information for the data source is stored in an XML block within the report definition file. Access to this kind of data source definition is limited to the report with which it is embedded.

❑ **Shared:** This is largely the same as an embedded data source, except that the definition for the data source is stored in its own file (usually with the extension .ds).

We will be making use of a shared data source later in the chapter.

Regardless of the type, data sources store several pieces of required information, and optionally store additional items to deal with security scenarios.

Creating a Data Source

Let's go ahead and create a data source that we will use throughout the remainder of this chapter.

If your Visual Studio environment is still in its default configuration, you should see the Solution Explorer on the upper-right side. Right-click Shared Data Sources and choose Add New Data Source, as show in Figure 14-2.

This will bring you up to the Shared Data Source Properties dialog (as shown in Figure 14-3).

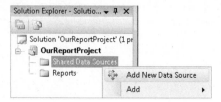

Figure 14-2

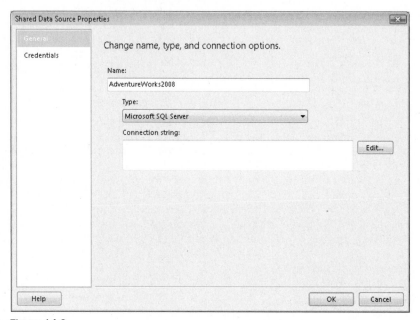

Figure 14-3

The dialog has two major elements, the first of which allows us to define the name (I've named mine for the database we're going to connect to) as well as the connection string for our data source. (For those not familiar with connection strings, it tells whatever object is connecting to your data source where to go and how to log in.). You can either edit the connection string directly or click the Edit button to bring up the Connection Properties dialog shown in Figure 14-4.

The first time I saw this dialog, I was mildly surprised to see that it was different than the connection dialog that had been used repeatedly in the Management Studio; nonetheless, it does contain the same basic elements, just in a slightly different visual package (in short, don't worry if it looks a little different).

In my case, I've selected the local server, the system administrator account (sa), and our old friend, the AdventureWorks2008 database.

Go ahead and click OK, and then the Credentials option in the Data Source Properties dialog, and we get the security options for our data source (see Figure 14-5).

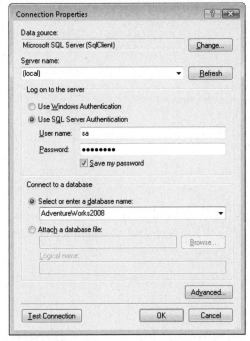

Figure 14-4

Figure 14-5

We have several options here worth discussing — they include:

❑ **Use Windows Authentication:** This is what it sounds like. It authenticates based on the user who executes the report. This means that the related Windows user account must have access to not only the report, but all underlying data related to the report.

❑ **Use this user name and password:** The user name and password referenced will be SQL Server login information (not Windows).

❑ **Prompt for credentials:** Again, this is predictable. Credentials are obtained from the user at run time. The credentials supplied will be passed to whatever data provider the report utilizes.

❑ **No credentials:** This forces anonymous access, so the data provider needs to support such access or you will get an authentication error when you run the report.

In Figure 14-5, I've chosen to use the sa and provided the related password. This means that the supplied login and password will be persisted (in an encrypted form) with the data source in the ds file.

When we click OK for this dialog, we wind up back at our relatively generic Visual Studio project, but we have our new data source, and are ready to create more of the required pieces for our report.

Using the Report Wizard

Even though we didn't choose the Report Wizard project type when we created this project, elements of the Report Wizard are still available as we create reports. Indeed, the simple act of asking for a new report will, by default, bring up the Report Wizard. You can cancel out of the wizard to create a blank report, but, unless you do, Visual Studio will try and use the wizard to do some of the work for you.

To move on with the example we're building, we'll go ahead and add a report to walk through the Report Wizard process. For our example, we'll say that our manager has asked us for a summary report showing the total sales by category for all the sales invoices sold by David Campbell in July 2003. She has warned us that she may ask about other salespeople and periods later, but, for now, the information on Mr. Campbell for July 2003 is all she needs.

To get started, right-click the Reports node in the Solution Explorer, select Add New Report as shown in Figure 14-6, and it should bring up the Report Wizard Welcome dialog.

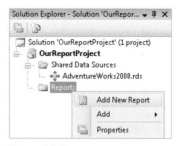

Figure 14-6

Figure 14-7

Click Next to move on to the data source selection dialog shown in Figure 14-7. Note that, while I've chosen to use the shared data source we created a few moments ago, I could also create a new data source as part of this dialog. (The new data source would be embedded, but could be converted to shared later if we so chose.)

Again click Next to move on to the Query Builder dialog shown in Figure 14-8. I've already created a query and the query looks like this:

```
SELECT per.FirstName + ' ' + per.LastName AS Employee,
    ps.Name AS Subcategory,
    SUM(sod.LineTotal) AS Sales,
    soh.SalesOrderID,
    soh.SalesOrderNumber,
    p.Name AS Product,
    SUM(sod.OrderQty) AS OrderQty,
    sod.UnitPrice,
    pc.Name AS Category
FROM Sales.SalesOrderHeader soh
JOIN Sales.SalesPerson SP
  ON sp.BusinessEntityID = soh.SalesPersonID
JOIN Sales.SalesOrderDetail sod
```

```
  ON soh.SalesOrderID = sod.SalesOrderID
JOIN HumanResources.Employee e
  ON soh.SalesPersonID = e.BusinessEntityID
JOIN Person.Person per
  ON per.BusinessEntityID = sp.BusinessEntityID
JOIN Production.Product p
  ON sod.ProductID = p.ProductID
JOIN Production.ProductSubcategory ps
  ON p.ProductSubcategoryID = ps.ProductSubcategoryID
JOIN Production.ProductCategory pc
  ON ps.ProductCategoryID = pc.ProductCategoryID
WHERE (DATEPART(Year, soh.OrderDate) = 2003)
  AND (DATEPART(Month, soh.OrderDate) = 7)
  AND (soh.SalesPersonID = 283)
GROUP BY per.FirstName + ' ' + per.LastName,
    DATEPART(Month, soh.OrderDate),
    soh.SalesOrderID,
    soh.SalesOrderNumber,
    p.Name,
    ps.Name,
    sod.UnitPrice,
    pc.Name
```

Figure 14-8

There isn't any real rocket science to this query. It is simply gathering up sales totals for the salesperson with an ID of 283 (which happens to be David Campbell) in July of 2003. We will look at how to make this selectable later in the chapter, but, for now, we'll go with the simple, hard coded query.

Paste in this query code (you can find it in the downloadable sample code on the `wrox.com` or `www.professionalsql.com` websites), and click Next to choose between a tabular or matrix report. A tabular report is a classic row-by-row of data layout. A matrix looks for an intersection of data, and is more oriented around displaying totals at the intersection of a column and row. For this particular report, we'll go with the tabular option, and then click Next to move on to the dialog shown in Figure 14-9.

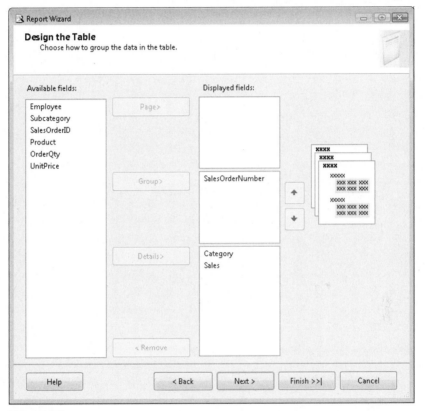

Figure 14-9

The sales report we're generating is going to be showing the total for each sales order that Mr. Campbell issued in July 2003. The selections we're making now will have the wizard create part of the formatting we need. Choose the `SalesOrderNumber` as a Group By item, and the `Category` and `Sales` fields for detail items, and click Next. In this next dialog (shown in Figure 14-10), I've chosen a block format. There isn't any real magic in it. I've just chosen it because I think it suits this particular data best. I've also chosen to include subtotals. Since we're grouping by `SalesOrderNumber`, it means we will get a total for each `SalesOrderNumber` value.

Again click Next to choose a style for the wizard with which to configure the report. I happen to be choosing Ocean, but anything will work. Click Next one last time to see a summary, as shown in Figure 14-11, of what the wizard is going to do and to name your report. (I've chosen SalesOrderSummary. I'd suggest using that name since we will alter this report as we go through the chapter.) You're then ready to click Finish to generate the actual report.

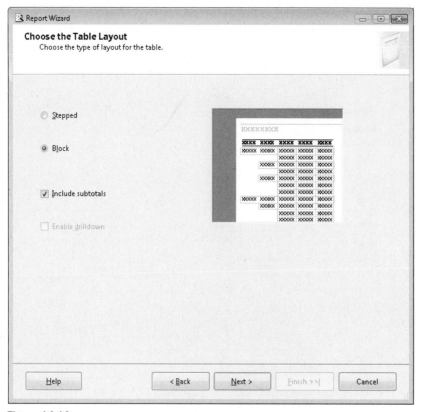

Figure 14-10

The report that first comes up (shown in Figure 14-12) doesn't look that complex.

Go ahead and choose the Preview tab to see what the report looks like with real data (shown in Figure 14-13).

This is indeed a nice start, but has some significant flaws, so let's look at editing the report.

Editing Reports

To edit a report, we move back to the Design tab for the report in Visual Studio. Continuing our example, we have a few issues we would like to take care of to clean up the look of the report:

- ❑ The title should reflect a more proper title format.
- ❑ The number values should look more like currency values.
- ❑ We're seeing each instance of a category sale, not a total as was requested.

Figure 14-11

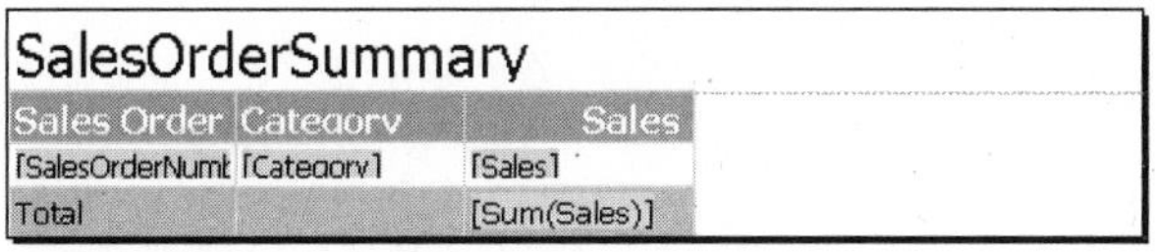

SalesOrderSummary		
Sales Order	Category	Sales
[SalesOrderNumt	[Category]	[Sales]
Total		[Sum(Sales)]

Figure 14-12

Let's take each of these in turn.

First up, let's change the title. This is the easiest of the changes we'll make. Simply click the area of the title once to select it, and a second time to make your cursor active so you can edit it much as you would any other label object. Double-clicking has the same effect. Go ahead and select it and change the title to **D. Campbell, July 2003 Summary**.

Next, we'll take on the number formatting issue. Again, this isn't that difficult. Simply right-click the field that holds our Sales information, and select Text Box Properties as shown in Figure 14-14.

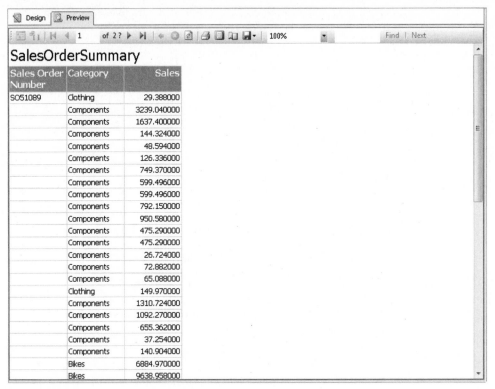

Figure 14-13

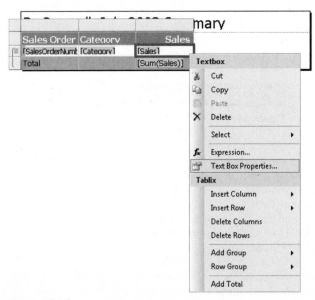

Figure 14-14

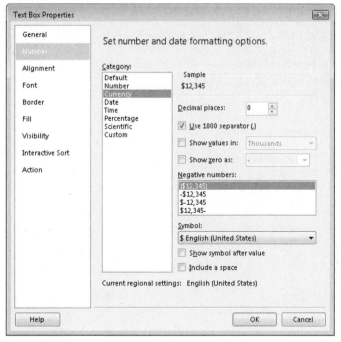

Figure 14-15

This brings us up the dialog shown in Figure 14-15, which allows us to set a wide variety of properties for the cell of our report table (which, incidentally, is called a tablix). In Figure 14-15, I've chosen the Numbers node, and set our number display to round to the nearest whole unit of currency, and to use a separator for thousands.

Notice that it doesn't ask what you want to use as a thousands separator, nor does it just assume that you want to use a comma. The thousands separator will vary based on what localization your report server is configured for, and can be overridden on a report-by-report basis.

That takes us to the last, and trickiest of the changes we decided to make: rolling up each category to a total within each sales order. To do this, we again right-click the cell that contains the [Sales] value as shown in Figure 14-16. We choose the row group, and modify the properties using the dialog shown in Figure 14-17. This will limit the rows returned to just one per category within the larger SalesOrderNumber group. (Notice the brackets on the far left of the tablix. Remember we added that one by selecting it when we were in the Report Wizard.) We're not quite done in here, though. Since we're focused on categories, we should probably sort the categories to make them a bit more readable. To do that, we can choose the Sorting node in the current dialog, as shown in Figure 14-18.

So, with all that accomplished, it would seem that we're ready to preview our report again, but, when we do, we see that, while things are vastly improved, we still have a few problems (as shown in Figure 14-19).

While our report is starting to *look* good, we have some problems with our numbers. If you were to compare it with the earlier values that were returned (you can go back to Figure 14-13 to see those), you should quickly see that our numbers don't add up. Indeed, the report is not showing the totals for each category, but rather the first row returned in each category. We can't have that!

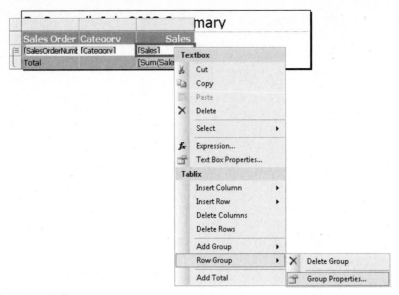

Figure 14-16

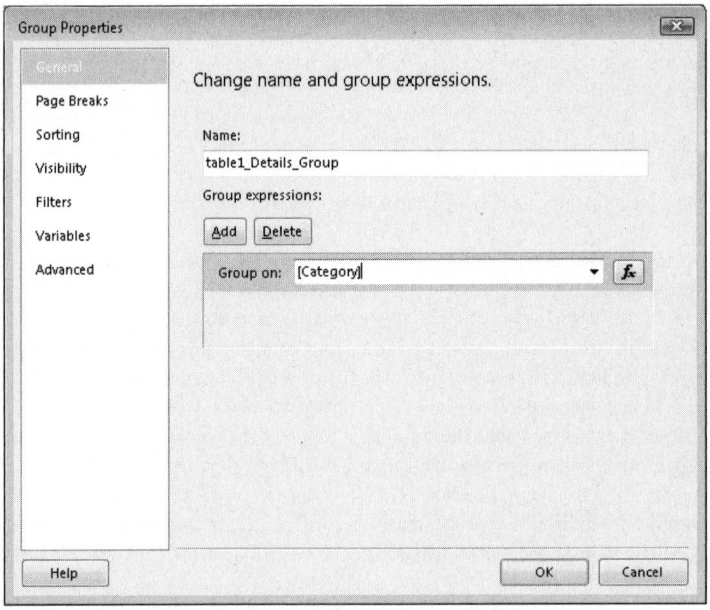

Figure 14-17

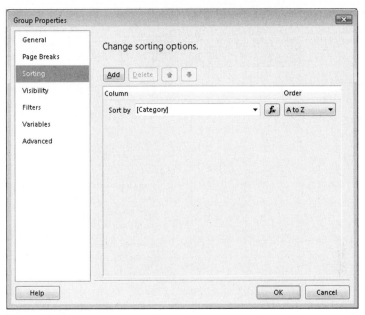

Figure 14-18

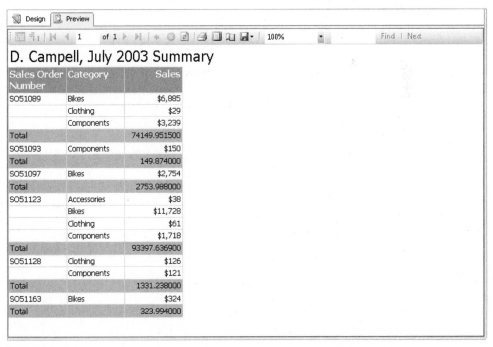

Figure 14-19

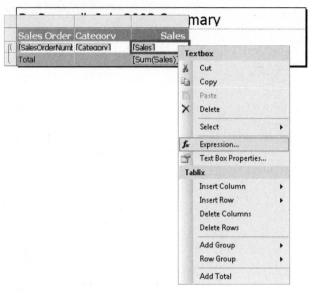

Figure 14-20

To fix this, we need to explicitly indicate what we want done for each cell. Once again, right-click our [Sales] cell, but, this time, click Expression as shown in Figure 14-20.

The dialog returned shows that we are currently returning the exact value from the Sales field in the data set:

    =Fields!Sales.Value

What we need, however, is a total — or a Sum — for the field within the group. To do this, we can use one of the many built-in functions of Reporting Services. In this case, the Sum function:

    =Sum(Fields!Sales.Value)

So, to see how this looks in the dialog, check out Figure 14-21.

Click OK, and preview the report again, and we now have a reasonably well-formatted report (don't get too carried away formatting it — we're just getting started with this report!) shown in Figure 14-22, and we're ready to run it, print it (or export it to another format), and deliver it to our manager.

Parameterizing Reports

Getting this report on David Campbell is all well and good, but it is pretty limiting. Recall that our manager warned us that she might want it for other people and for other times, later on. It's time to implement that functionality.

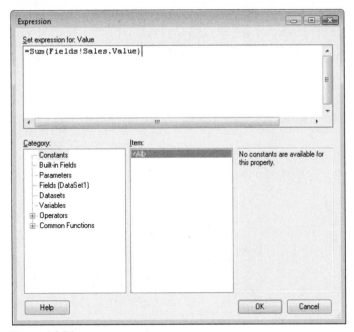

Figure 14-21

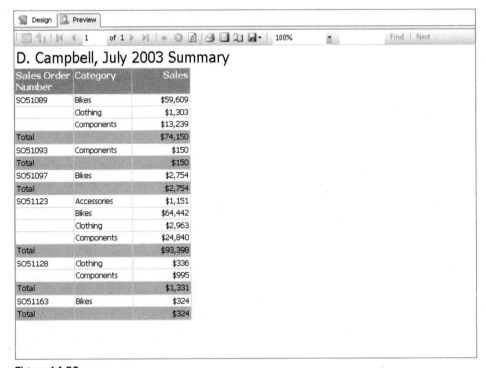

Figure 14-22

Parameterization is a vital part of most reporting projects. Fortunately, making SQL Server recognize a report as parameterized is relatively easy. Once a report is parameterized, SQL Server will prompt the user in some fashion to supply a parameter value. As we'll learn in this section, we have many options for making parameter choices easy on the user.

As our first step, we will add the most rudimentary parameterization to our report. Making our report reliant on parameters starts with simply altering our query to expect those parameters. We'll then just need to tell the report to request the parameters before the report is executed. Let's start by editing our query. Go to the Report Data item in the View menu for the project. (It's also available as a tab in the Solution Explorer pane.) The Report Data tab is shown in Figure 14-23. Just double-click our one data set for this report to bring up the dialog shown in Figure 14-24, which will, among other things, allow us to edit our query. (Some reports can have several data sets. This particular report just has one.)

Note that you can also edit the query in a separate Query Editor Window by right-clicking the data set and selecting Query.

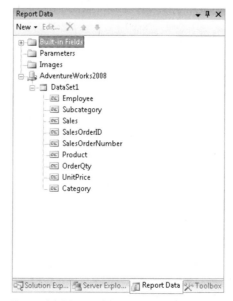

Figure 14-23

I have already changed our hard-coded values for Darren Campbell's BusinessEntityID, the month of July, and the year of 2003 to be parameter values (@BusinessEntityID, @Month, and @Year, respectively). With this complete, we're ready to move on to the Parameters node of the dialog as shown in Figure 14-25.

I've added each of the parameters in this dialog, so I can now click OK, and I'm ready to preview (or just downright run) the report. In Figure 14-26, I have run it via the Preview tab. Notice at the top of the pane how it has asked for (and I have provided) the three parameters.

In looking over the report, you can see that we wound up with exactly the same values that we had in our original report, only now we could run the report for a different time period, or for a sales rep. Our report just became a lot more flexible.

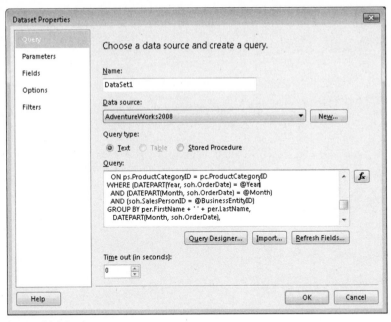

Figure 14-24

Figure 14-25

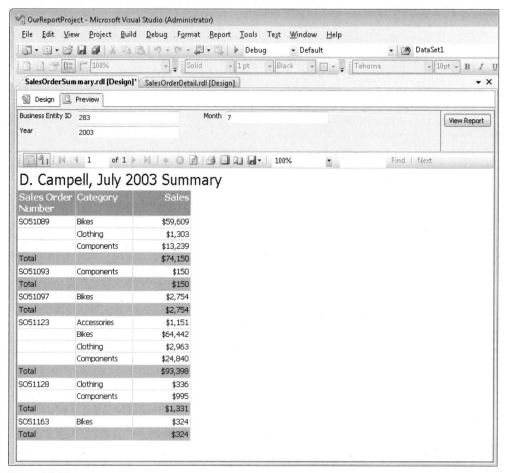

Figure 14-26

Providing/Controlling Parameter Values and How They Are Used

Well, the report as we have it seems pretty nice. We cannot only provide a report on David Campbell as we could before, but now we can input different parameters including a different employee's BusinessEntityID, and a completely different time period. We do, however, still have several usability issues. Some of these include:

❑   The input values are free-form, which means users may input illegal values.

❑   There are no hints at what might be a proper input value, so the user is left to know ahead of time, or guess. This is not too horrible for the date and year, but would be problematic in terms of getting the right salesperson's BusinessEntityID.

❑   No matter which sales person you input, the header is hard-coded to say David Campbell. A similar issue exists for the month and year.

Let's take a look at how to fix these issues.

Creating Pre-set Parameter Lists

Reporting Services gives you the ability to create pre-defined value lists for your parameters. This functionality utilizes the parameters that we've already defined, and simply adds additional properties to them.

To add fixed lists to our @Month and @Year parameters, we navigate to the Parameters node of the Report Data tab, expand the list, and then double-click the parameter for which we're interested in supplying values. (You could also right-click the parameter and then select Parameter Properties.) Go ahead and try this for the @Month parameter, which should bring up the dialog shown in Figure 14-27.

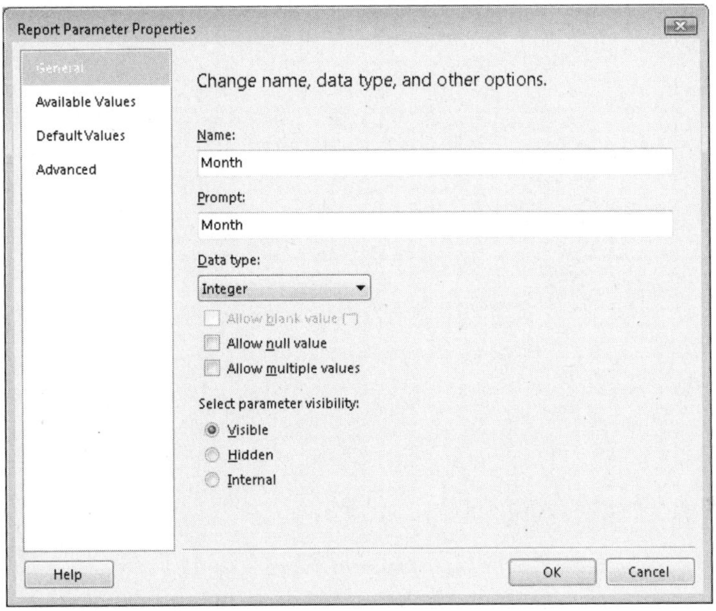

Figure 14-27

Notice that I could set a custom prompt for my parameter. (It doesn't have to be the parameter name.) I can also control the initial visibility of the parameter (perhaps for a parameter that is only valid if another parameter is set to a specific value) as well as the nullability or acceptance of blank values.

I've mostly stuck with the defaults here, but I did change the data type to be an Integer. (Remember we are taking the month number as a parameter.) We're then ready to move on to the Available Values node shown in Figure 14-28.

I've made several modifications in this dialog — most notably supplying separate labels and values. The label indicates what the user will be shown to choose from, and the value will be what is passed to the parameter when the report is executed. I was given the ability to create this list as part of choosing the Specify Values option. Note, however, that I could also have made the list query driven. (We'll get to one of those shortly.)

Go ahead and switch over to the Defaults node, and you can see we are allowed to supply a default value. (In Figure 14-29, I've chosen the value of 7 that we have been working with thus far.)

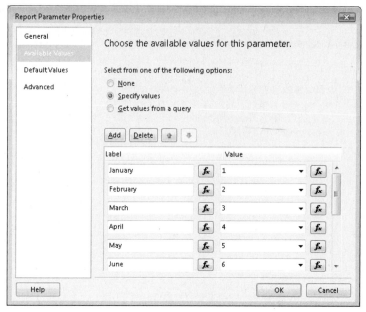

Figure 14-28

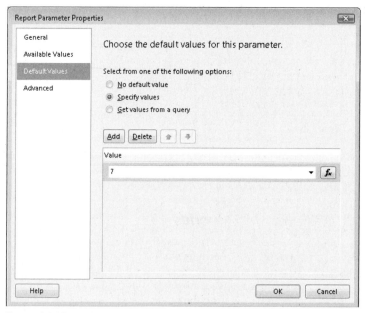

Figure 14-29

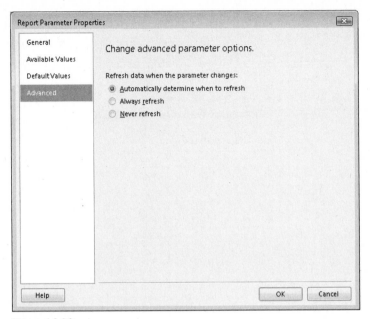

Figure 14-30

Finally, switch over to the Advanced node (shown in Figure 14-30), and we are given the option of selecting when our report data will change if the user changes the parameter value. We can force a refresh every time, require the user to explicitly call for the refresh, or allow SQL Server to decide when it is the right time.

Go ahead and try this out on your own by setting the data type for the @Year parameter to Integer and the default value to 2003. Then we're ready to preview or run the report again to check out the effects of our changes as shown in Figure 14-31.

While you can't see any significant difference in the BusinessEntityID and Year parameters, you should quickly notice that Month is now a drop-down list that supplies the name of each month even though the parameter will really use the integer value for the month. You can also test out entering text into the year field. SQL Server will indicate the type mismatch relatively gracefully. (It isn't the prettiest thing ever, but it's better than a full blown error.)

Creating Parameter Lists from Queries

Supplying a pre-populated list for our @BusinessEntityID parameter is a bit trickier than the other two parameters. We could create a fixed list much as we did with @Month, but that would mean we would have to edit the report every time the list of salespersons changed. While months are likely to remain very stable (unless Einstein comes back from the dead with a new theory on time), salespeople have a tendency to come and go with high frequency. Editing the report each time is very impractical, particularly when we already have salesperson information entered elsewhere in the system.

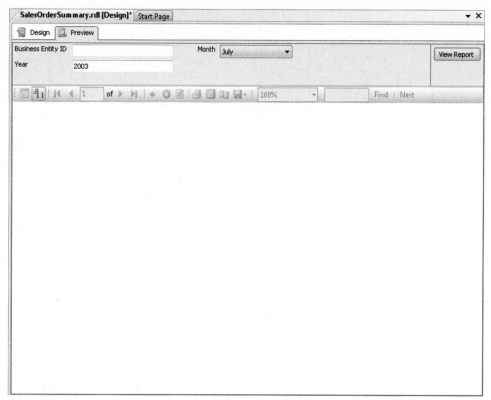

Figure 14-31

To get this started, we need to create a new data set. Start by right-clicking the data source in the Report Data tab, and select Add Dataset as shown in Figure 14-32.

Which, in turn, brings us up the dialog shown in Figure 14-33.

I've already supplied a query that lists all of the salespeople. It is entirely visible in the dialog, but just to make it clear, it looks like this:

```
SELECT p.BusinessEntityID, p.LastName + ', ' + p.FirstName
FROM Person.Person p
JOIN Sales.SalesPerson sp
  ON p.BusinessEntityID = sp.BusinessEntityID;
```

Now continue to the Fields node as shown in Figure 14-34. This allows us to select what the returned fields are going to be named (so you can access them) in any reports that use this data set. I am sticking with the defaults here, but we could have altered the names on the results if we had so chosen. Click OK and our data set is created. We're now ready to use it to populate our parameter list.

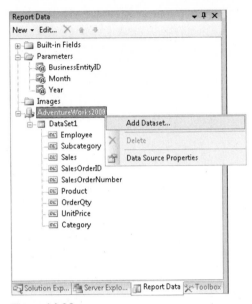

Figure 14-32

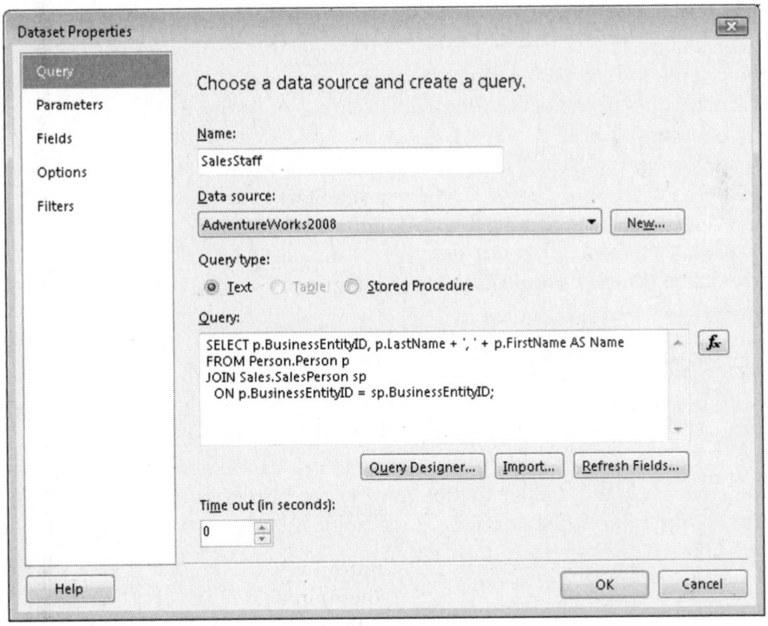

Figure 14-33

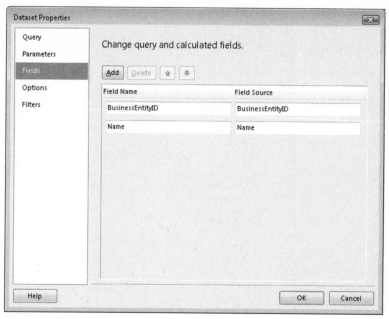

Figure 14-34

Double-click the BusinessEntityID parameter again to open it back up for editing, then move to the Available Values node shown in Figure 14-35. I have again pre-filled-in suitable values. I have, as you might expect, chosen the Get values from a query option. I have likewise chosen what data set to use as a source and which fields from the data set relate to the value and label fields (which function just as they did when we manually supplied values for them). I am also going to go to the Default Values node and set a default of 283 (our old friend, David Campbell) before previewing or executing the report as shown in Figure 14-36.

So, just that quickly we have all of our parameters defaulted and data typed as appropriate. All that leaves us is to deal with the fixed header.

Getting Headings and Other Fields from Parameters

Editing a text box to use parameter values is relatively easy. Start by selecting the text box that holds our current fixed value and get it into an edit mode. To make it dynamic, I need to combine several items. First, I'll start off with a prefix to my dynamic values. I'll use the phrase "Summary for:" I then need to again right-click and choose Create Placeholder bringing up the dialog in Figure 14-37. The placeholder will allow Reporting Services to distinguish between my literal text and my functional code. Note that the value field has a drop-down box, and that by expanding it you can choose between a wide array of dynamic values. In our case, I've supplied a reference to one of the parameters the user selected. Go ahead and click OK, and then preview or run the report to see the effect (shown in Figure 14-38).

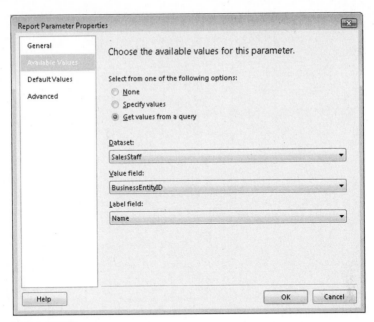

Figure 14-35

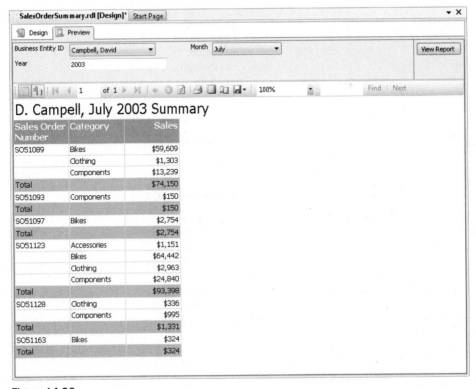

Figure 14-36

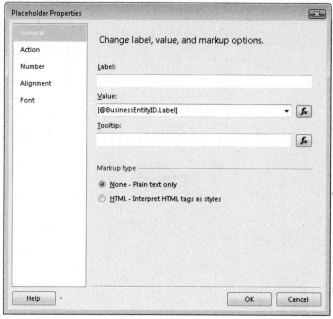

Figure 14-37

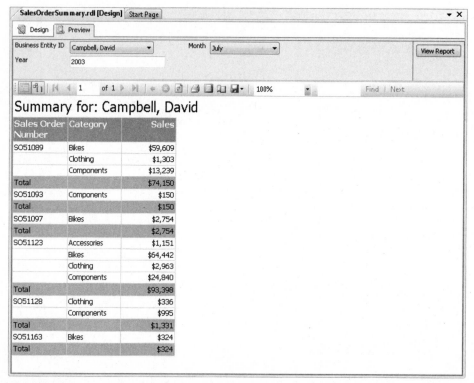

Figure 14-38

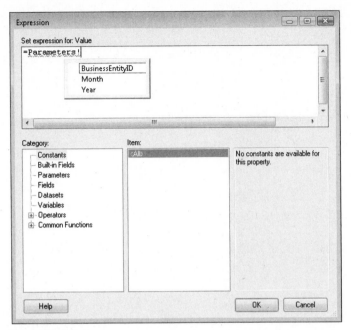

Figure 14-39

To finish out this section, let's add another placeholder or two, but this time let's use the expression editor. Add a comma and a space after the placeholder we just created, and then right-click and again choose Add Placeholder. This time, however, click the Fx button to the right of the Value field to bring up the dialog shown in Figure 14-39. In this figure, I'm in the middle of adding a reference to the Month parameter that the user selected when they ran the report, but notice that Visual Studio is providing me with IntelliSense while I edit. Go ahead and add placeholders for both Month and Year, and your report should now come out looking something like Figure 14-40.

Adding Charts

Reporting Services also supports chart objects. This is relatively powerful stuff, as it does a lot to allow our reports to become more than just a source for reporting, but also a venue for more genuine analysis. We're going to add one chart to our report to provide a visual representation of the sales this month between categories.

Start by opening the Visual Studio toolbox and dragging a Chart object onto your report. (I'm placing mine to the right of our tablix.) This brings up the dialog shown in Figure 14-41, and allows us to choose between a wide array of chart types.

Given that we don't have that many categories to choose from, I've decided to go with a pie chart in a 3D representation (shown in Figure 14-41). To get this working, I can just drag fields from data sets in my Report Data tab right into special receiver areas on the chart (shown in Figure 14-42). I've dragged the sales field from Dataset1 into the Drop Data Fields Here area, and the categories field into the Drop Category Fields Here area.

Also change the (caption) field in the chart properties to **Sales by Category**, and we're again ready to run or preview the report as shown in Figure 14-43.

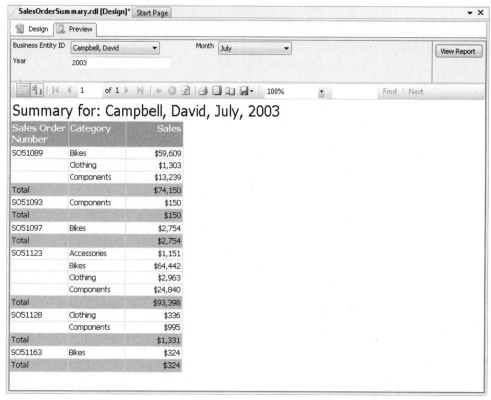

Figure 14-40

Just that quickly, we have a basic chart available to provide a visual representation of the numbers in our tablix.

> *Note that there is no interdependence between the two objects. They happen to make use of the same data set, but there is no requirement that they do so. Indeed, we did most of this report building without the chart, and we could, if we so desired, delete the tablix and work only with the chart.*

Linking Reports

Reporting Services also allows you to link multiple reports, either drilling down into finer levels of detail, or drilling across into a totally different report.

The linking process is supported through what are termed "Actions." Actions support both internal (other reports) and external (such as a website) links.

Let's add one last element to the report we've been working on in this chapter. To make use of this link, you'll want to download (if you haven't already) the code for this book, and look for the SalesOrderDetail.rdl file that I've pre-created for you. You can add it to your project by right-clicking Reports in the Solution Explorer, and choosing Add➤Existing Item.

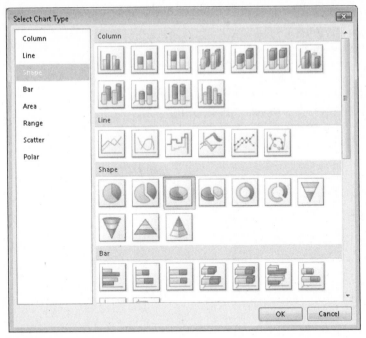

Figure 14-41

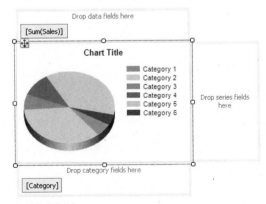

Figure 14-42

To make use of this new Sales Order Detail report, you need to edit the properties for the text box that has the Sales Order Number on your report, then access the Actions settings as shown in Figure 14-44.

Once you have the `SalesOrderDetail.rdl` file properly added to the project and have configured the SalesOrderNumber action as shown in Figure 14-44, go ahead and run or preview your summary report one last time. Now click the first Sales Order Number for David Campbell in July of 2003, and you should get the Sales Order Detail report shown in Figure 14-45.

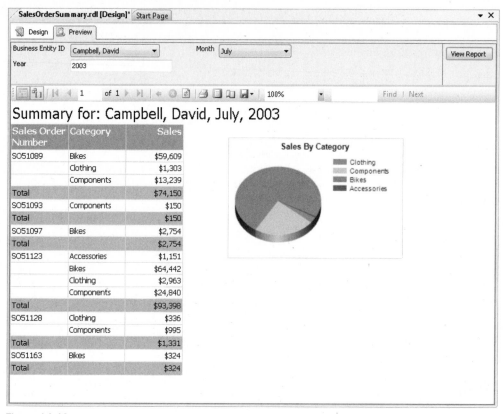

Figure 14-43

Deploying the Report

The thing left to do is deploy the report. To deploy, you right-click the report in the Solution Explorer and choose Deploy. There is, however, a minor catch — you need to define the target to deploy to in the project definition.

1. Right-click the Report Server Project and choose Properties.

2. In the TargetReportFolder field, put whatever folder you want it to reside in when you log into the Report Manager.

3. In the TargetServerURL field, enter the URL to your ReportServer. In my case, this may be as simple as `http://localhost/ReportServer`, but the server name could be any server to whom you have appropriate rights to deploy. (The Virtual Directory may also be something other than ReportServer if you defined it that way at install.)

After you've deployed (by right-clicking the project and selecting Deploy), you'll want to view the report. Navigate to your report server. (If it is on the local host and uses the default directory, it would be `http://localhost/Reports`.) Click your report folder, and choose your SalesOrderSummary report.

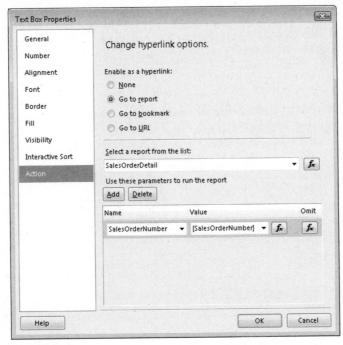

Figure 14-44

It may take a bit to come up the first time you load it but you should see your report just as we defined it in our project. (If you navigate back to it again, the report definition will be cached and thus come up fairly quickly.)

A Brief Note on RDL

RDL stands for Report Definition Language — an XML–based language that defines reports. All the changes we made to our report over the course of this chapter were translated into RDL by Visual Studio. If you want see what the RDL for your report project looks like, right-click your report and choose View Code. The following is an excerpt from the report I produced as an example for this chapter. It defines the data set that supplied the values for our sales staff to the appropriate parameter:

```
<DataSet Name="SalesStaff">
  <Fields>
    <Field Name="BusinessEntityID">
      <DataField>BusinessEntityID</DataField>
      <rd:TypeName>System.Int32</rd:TypeName>
    </Field>
    <Field Name="Name">
      <DataField>Name</DataField>
      <rd:TypeName>System.String</rd:TypeName>
    </Field>
  </Fields>
  <Query>
    <DataSourceName>AdventureWorks2008</DataSourceName>
```

```
        <CommandText>SELECT p.BusinessEntityID, p.LastName + ', ' +
p.FirstName AS Name
FROM Person.Person p
JOIN Sales.SalesPerson sp
  ON p.BusinessEntityID = sp.BusinessEntityID;</CommandText>
        <rd:UseGenericDesigner>true</rd:UseGenericDesigner>
      </Query>
    </DataSet>
```

You *can* modify the RDL directly if you wish. (But be careful. It can be a hassle to figure out what exactly you did wrong if you introduced an error through direct editing.)

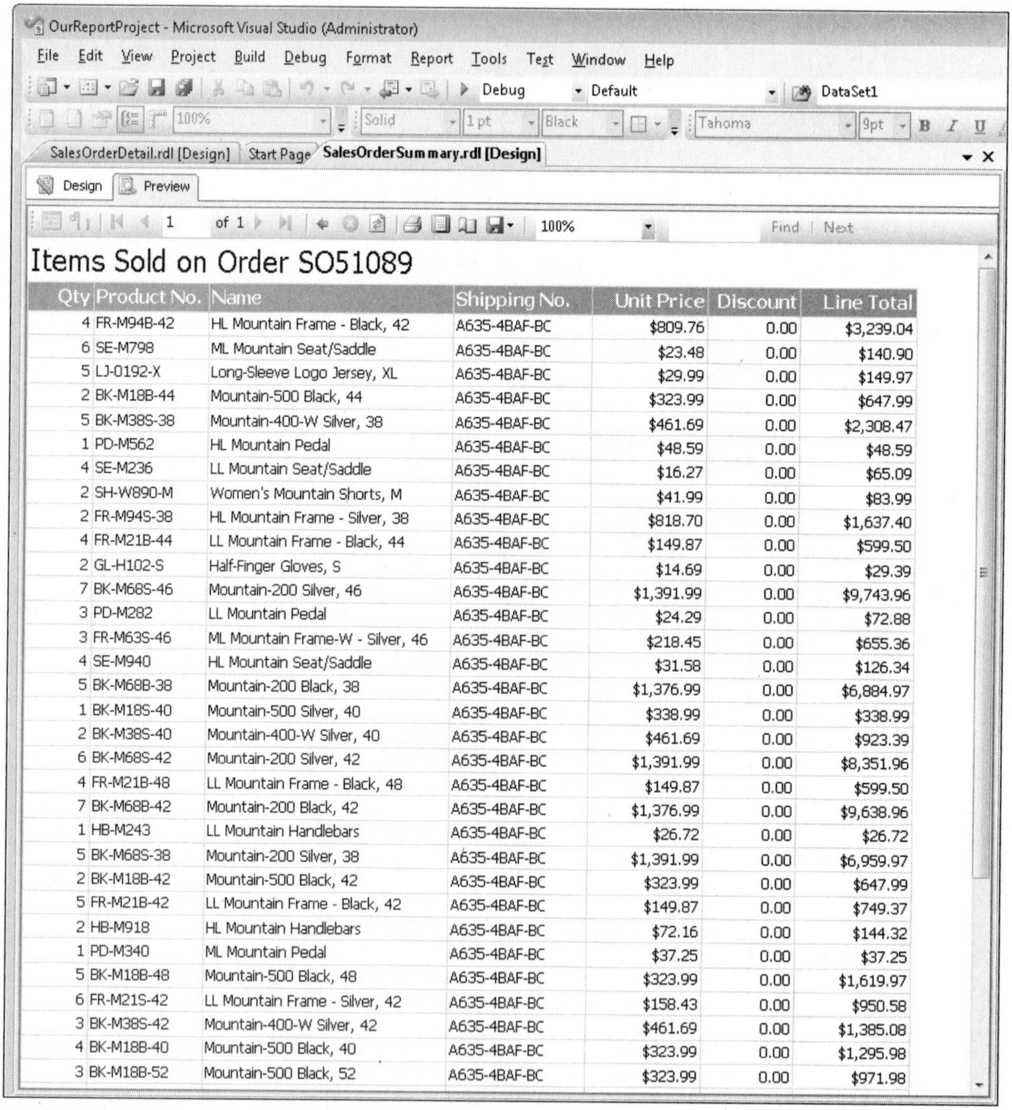

Qty	Product No.	Name	Shipping No.	Unit Price	Discount	Line Total
4	FR-M94B-42	HL Mountain Frame - Black, 42	A635-4BAF-BC	$809.76	0.00	$3,239.04
6	SE-M798	ML Mountain Seat/Saddle	A635-4BAF-BC	$23.48	0.00	$140.90
5	LJ-0192-X	Long-Sleeve Logo Jersey, XL	A635-4BAF-BC	$29.99	0.00	$149.97
2	BK-M18B-44	Mountain-500 Black, 44	A635-4BAF-BC	$323.99	0.00	$647.99
5	BK-M38S-38	Mountain-400-W Silver, 38	A635-4BAF-BC	$461.69	0.00	$2,308.47
1	PD-M562	HL Mountain Pedal	A635-4BAF-BC	$48.59	0.00	$48.59
4	SE-M236	LL Mountain Seat/Saddle	A635-4BAF-BC	$16.27	0.00	$65.09
2	SH-W890-M	Women's Mountain Shorts, M	A635-4BAF-BC	$41.99	0.00	$83.99
2	FR-M94S-38	HL Mountain Frame - Silver, 38	A635-4BAF-BC	$818.70	0.00	$1,637.40
4	FR-M21B-44	LL Mountain Frame - Black, 44	A635-4BAF-BC	$149.87	0.00	$599.50
2	GL-H102-S	Half-Finger Gloves, S	A635-4BAF-BC	$14.69	0.00	$29.39
7	BK-M68S-46	Mountain-200 Silver, 46	A635-4BAF-BC	$1,391.99	0.00	$9,743.96
3	PD-M282	LL Mountain Pedal	A635-4BAF-BC	$24.29	0.00	$72.88
3	FR-M63S-46	ML Mountain Frame-W - Silver, 46	A635-4BAF-BC	$218.45	0.00	$655.36
4	SE-M940	HL Mountain Seat/Saddle	A635-4BAF-BC	$31.58	0.00	$126.34
5	BK-M68B-38	Mountain-200 Black, 38	A635-4BAF-BC	$1,376.99	0.00	$6,884.97
1	BK-M18S-40	Mountain-500 Silver, 40	A635-4BAF-BC	$338.99	0.00	$338.99
2	BK-M38S-40	Mountain-400-W Silver, 40	A635-4BAF-BC	$461.69	0.00	$923.39
6	BK-M68S-42	Mountain-200 Silver, 42	A635-4BAF-BC	$1,391.99	0.00	$8,351.96
4	FR-M21B-48	LL Mountain Frame - Black, 48	A635-4BAF-BC	$149.87	0.00	$599.50
7	BK-M68B-42	Mountain-200 Black, 42	A635-4BAF-BC	$1,376.99	0.00	$9,638.96
1	HB-M243	LL Mountain Handlebars	A635-4BAF-BC	$26.72	0.00	$26.72
5	BK-M68S-38	Mountain-200 Silver, 38	A635-4BAF-BC	$1,391.99	0.00	$6,959.97
2	BK-M18B-42	Mountain-500 Black, 42	A635-4BAF-BC	$323.99	0.00	$647.99
5	FR-M21B-42	LL Mountain Frame - Black, 42	A635-4BAF-BC	$149.87	0.00	$749.37
2	HB-M918	HL Mountain Handlebars	A635-4BAF-BC	$72.16	0.00	$144.32
1	PD-M340	ML Mountain Pedal	A635-4BAF-BC	$37.25	0.00	$37.25
5	BK-M18B-48	Mountain-500 Black, 48	A635-4BAF-BC	$323.99	0.00	$1,619.97
6	FR-M21S-42	LL Mountain Frame - Silver, 42	A635-4BAF-BC	$158.43	0.00	$950.58
3	BK-M38S-42	Mountain-400-W Silver, 42	A635-4BAF-BC	$461.69	0.00	$1,385.08
4	BK-M18B-40	Mountain-500 Black, 40	A635-4BAF-BC	$323.99	0.00	$1,295.98
3	BK-M18B-52	Mountain-500 Black, 52	A635-4BAF-BC	$323.99	0.00	$971.98

Figure 14-45

Summary

Reporting Services has had a major impact on many SQL Server installations. For many companies, having a relatively robust reporting server built right into their central data store has been liberating by making it much easier to disseminate information to data consumers. For other organizations, Reporting Services has provided an adequate solution to replace long-standing reporting packages such as Crystal Reports. SQL Server 2008 adds several new features and controls to allow for more elegant and powerful reports, plus the engine has been redesigned to allow for much higher scalability.

Even with the relatively robust report used in this chapter, we've really only just begun to taste the possibilities. Reports can be parameterized, you can embed charts, integrate with other products (such as Microsoft Sharepoint Services or Microsoft Office Sharepoint Services), drill through from one report to another, and even embed reports inside of other reports.

For more information on reporting, I'd suggest a book specific to Reporting Services.

15

Buying in Bulk: The Bulk Copy Program (BCP) and Other Basic Bulk Operations

If your system is going to be operating in something of a bubble, then you can probably skip this chapter and move on. Unfortunately, the real world doesn't work that way, so you probably ought to hang around for a while.

For most systems, there will eventually come a time (often, it's many times) when you need to move around large blocks of data. Sometimes you need to bring in data that's in the wrong format or that's sitting in another application's data files. Sometimes, you need to extract data directly from another system. The good thing is SQL Server has two tools to help you move data fast — the *Bulk Copy Program (bcp)* and *SQL Server Integration Services (SSIS)*. In this chapter, we'll be looking primarily at the first of these. In addition, we'll take a look at bcp's close cousins — the BULK INSERT command and OPENROWSET (BULK).

We will examine SSIS in the next chapter.

bcp is something of an old friend. You know the one — where you hardly ever see them anymore, but, when you do, you reminisce on all the crazy things you used to do together. It was, for a very long time, *the* way we moved around large blocks of data; and it did so (still does as far as that goes) amazingly fast. What, however, it lacks is sex appeal — well, frankly, since SQL Server 7.0, it has lacked appeal in a whole lot of areas.

So, why then am I even spending a chapter on it? Well, because bcp still definitely has its uses. Among its advantages are:

❑   It's very compact.

❑   It can move a lot of data very quickly.

❑ It is legacy — that is, there may be code already running that is making effective use of it, so why change it?

❑ It uses a cryptic, yet very traditional scripting style (which will probably appeal to some).

❑ It is very consistent.

bcp is used for transferring text and SQL Server native format data to and from SQL Server tables. It has changed very little in the last several versions, and other bulk features have continued to erode the usefulness of bcp, but it still holds its own. You can think of bcp as a data pump, with little function-ality other than moving data from one place to the other as efficiently as possible. The various other bulk operations we'll look at in this chapter are often easier to use, but usually come at the price of less flexibility.

In this chapter, we will look at some of the ins and outs of bcp and then use what we learn about bcp to form the foundations of many of the other features that serve a similar purpose — to get data in and out of your system as quickly as possible.

bcp Utility

bcp runs from an operating system command prompt to import or export native data (specific to SQL Server), ASCII text, or Unicode text. This means that you can execute bcp from an operating system batch file or user-defined stored procedure, as well as from other places. bcp can also be run as part of a scheduled job, or executed from a .NET object through the use of a shell command.

Like most command-line utilities, options can be specified using a hyphen (-) or forward slash (/); however, unlike most DOS or Windows family utilities, option switches are case sensitive.

bcp Syntax

```
bcp {[[<database name>.][<owner>].]{<table name>|<view name>}|"<query>"}
    {in | out | queryout | format} <data file>
    [-m <maximum no. of errors>] [-f <format file>] [-x] [-e <error file>]
    [-F <first row>] [-L <last row>] [-b <batch size>]
    [-n] [-c] [-w] [-N] [-V (60 | 65 | 70 | 80 | 90)] [-6]
    [-q] [-C <code page> ] [-t <field term>] [-r <row term>]
    [-i <input file>] [-o <output file>] [-a <packet size>]
    [-S <server name>[\<instance name>]] [-U <login id>] [-P <password>]
    [-T] [-v] [-R] [-k] [-E] [-h "<hint> [,...n]"]
```

Geez — that's a lot to take in, so let's go through these switches one by one. (Thankfully, most of them are optional, so you will usually only include just a fraction of them.)

> Note that many of the switches for the bcp utility are case sensitive; often, a given letter has an entirely different meaning between cases.

Parameter	Description
Database name	Exactly what it sounds like. Basically, this is a standard part of the four-part naming scheme. If not specified, the user's default database is assumed.
owner	More of the four-part naming scheme stuff. Again, exactly what it sounds like.
Table or View name "query"	Can only be one — table, view, or query. This is the input destination or output source table or view. A SQL Server query can be used only as a bcp output destination, and only when queryout is specified. If the query returns multiple result sets, only the first result set is used by bcp.
in *data file* out *data file* queryout *data file* format *data file*	Again, can only be one. If using any of these, you must also supply a source or destination file. Establishes the direction of the bcp action. in indicates that you are importing data from a source file into a table or view. out indicates that you are exporting data from a table or view into the destination file. Use queryout only for output to the destination file using a query as its source. Use format to create a format file based on the format option you've selected. You must also specify -f, as well as format options (-n, -c, -w, -6, -C, or -N) or answer prompts from interactive bcp. The source or destination path and filename is specified as <data file> and cannot include more than 255 characters.
-m *<maximum errors>*	You can specify a maximum number of errors that you will allow before SQL Server cancels the bulk copy operation, defaulting to 10 errors. Each row that cannot be copied by bcp is counted as one error.
-f *<format file>*	A format file contains responses saved from a previous bcp operation on the same table or view. This parameter should include the full path and filename to the format file. This option is used primarily with the in and format options to specify the path and filename when making use of or creating a format file.
-x	Generates a XML-based format file instead of the straight text version that is default. (The non-XML version is legacy support, but remains default for now.) It *must* be used with both the format and -f options.
-e *<error file>*	You can specify the full path and filename for an error file to store any rows that bcp is not able to transfer. Otherwise, no error file is created. Any error messages will be displayed at the client station.
-F *first row*	Use this option if you want to specify the first row to be copied by the bulk copy operation. If not specified, bcp defaults to a value of 1 and begins copying with the first row in the source data file. This option can be handy if you want to handle your loading in chunks, and can be used to pick back up where you left off in a previous loading run.

Continued

Parameter	Description
-L *last row*	This option is the complement of -F. It provides a method for determining the last row you want loaded as part of this bcp execution. If not specified, bcp defaults to a value of 0, the last row in the source file. When used in conjunction with -F, this option can allow you to load your data one chunk at a time, loading small blocks of data and then picking up next time where the previous load left off.
-b *batch size*	You can specify the number of rows copied as a batch. A batch is copied as a single transaction. Like all transactions, the rows of the batch are committed in an "all or nothing" fashion — either every row is committed or the transaction is rolled back and it is as if the batch never happened. The -h (hint) switch has a similar option (ROWS_PER_BATCH), which should be considered to be mutually exclusive with -b (use neither or one of them, but not both).
-n	Native data types (SQL Server data types) are used for the copy operation. Using this option prevents the need to answer the questions regarding the data types to be used in the transfer (it just picks up the native type and goes with it).
-c	This specifies that the operation uses character data (text) for all fields, and, as such, does not require a separate data type question for each field. A tab character is assumed as field delimiter unless you use the -t option and a newline character as row separator unless you specify different terminator using -r.
-w	The -w option is similar to -c but specifies Unicode data type instead of ASCII for all fields. Again, unless you override with -t and -r, the tab character and row separator are assumed to be the field delimiter and newline character, respectively. This option cannot be used with SQL Server version 6.5 or earlier.
-N	This is basically the same as -w, using Unicode for character data but uses native data types (database data types) for non-character data. This option offers higher performance when going from SQL Server to SQL Server. As with -w, this option cannot be used with SQL Server version 6.5 or earlier.
-V (60|65|70|80|90)	Causes bcp to utilize data type formats that were available only in previous versions of SQL Server. 60 uses 6.0 data types, 65 uses 6.5 data types, 70 uses 7.0 data types, 80 uses 2000 data types, and 90 uses 2005 data types. This replaces the -6 option.
-6	Use this option to force bcp to use SQL Server 6.0 or 6.5 data types. This option is used in conjunction with the -c or -n format options for backward-compatibility reasons only. Use -V whenever possible (when working with SQL Server 7.0 or newer, which should be pretty much always at this point).
-q	Use -q to specify that a table or view name includes non-ANSI characters. This effectively executes a SET QUOTED_IDENTIFIERS ON statement for the connection

Parameter	Description
	used by bcp. The fully qualified name, database, owner, and table or view must be enclosed in double quotation marks, in the format *"database name.owner.table"*.
-c *<code page>*	This option is used to specify the code page for the data file data. It is only necessary to use this option with char, varchar, or text data having ASCII character values of less than 32 or greater than 127. A code page value of ACP specifies ANSI/Microsoft Windows (ISO 1252). OEM specifies the default client code page. If RAW is specified, there will be no code page conversion. You also have the option of providing a specific code page value. Avoid this option where possible; instead, use a specific collation in the format file or when asked by bcp.
-t *<field terminator>*	This option allows you to override the default field terminator. The default terminator is the tab character. You can specify the terminator as tab (\t), newline (\n), carriage return (\r), backslash (\\), null terminator (\0), any printable character, or a string of up to 10 printable characters. For example, you would use "-t," for a comma-delimited text file.
-r *<row terminator>*	This option works just like -t except that it allows you to override the default row terminator (as opposed to the field terminator). The default terminator is \n, the newline character. The rules are otherwise the same as -t.
-i *<input file>*	You have the option of specifying a response file, as the *input file*, containing the responses to be used when running bcp in interactive mode. (This can save answering a ton of questions!)
-o *<output file>*	You can redirect bcp output from the command prompt to an output file. This gives you a way to capture command output and results when executing bcp from an unattended batch or stored procedure.
-a *<packet size>*	You have the option of overriding the default packet size for data transfers across the network. Larger packet sizes tend to be more efficient when you have good line quality (few CRC errors). The specified value must be between 4096 and 65535, inclusive, and overrides whatever default has been set up for the server. At installation, the default packet size is 4096 bytes. This can be overridden using the SQL Server Management Studio or the sp_configure system stored procedure.
-S *<server name>*	If running bcp from a server, the default is the local SQL Server. This option lets you specify a different server and is required in a network environment when running bcp from a remote system.
-U *<login name>*	Unless connecting to SQL Server through a trusted connection, you must provide a valid username for login.
-P *password*	When you supply a username, you must also supply a password. Otherwise, you will be prompted for a password. Include -P as your last option with no password to specify a null password.

Continued

Parameter	Description
-T	You have the option of connecting to the server using network user credentials through a trusted connection. If a trusted connection is specified, there is no need to provide a *login name* or *password* for the connection.
-v	When this option is used, bcp returns version number and copyright information.
-R	Use this option to specify that the regional format for clients' local settings is used when copying currency, date, and time data. The default is that regional settings are ignored.
-k	Use this option to override the use of column default values during bulk copy, ignoring any default constraints. Empty columns will retain a null value rather than the column default.
-E	This option is used during import when the import source file contains identity column values and is essentially equivalent to SET IDENTITY_INSERT ON. If not specified, SQL Server will ignore the values supplied in the source file and automatically generate identity column values. You can use the format file to skip the identity column when importing data from a source that does not include identity values and have SQL Server generate the values.
-h "*hint*[, ...]"	The hint option lets you specify one or more hints to be used by the bulk copy operation. Option -h is not supported for SQL Server version 6.5 or earlier.
ORDER *column* [ASC|DESC]	You can use this hint to improve performance when the sort order of the source data file matches the clustered index in the destination table. If the destination table does not have a clustered index or if the data is sorted in a different order the ORDER hint is ignored.
ROWS_PER_ BATCH=*nn*	This can be used in place of the -b option to specify the number of rows to be transferred as a batch. Do not use this hint with the -b option.
KILOBYTES_PER_ BATCH=*nn*	You can optionally specify batch size as the approximate number of kilobytes of data to be transferred in a batch.
TABLOCK	This will cause a table-level lock to be acquired for the duration of the operation. Default locking behavior is set by the table lock on bulk load table option.
CHECK_ CONSTRAINTS	By default, check constraints are ignored during an import operation. This hint forces check constraints to be checked during import.
FIRE_TRIGGERS	Similar to CHECK_CONSTRAINTS, this option causes any triggers on the destination table to fire for the transaction. By default, triggers are not fired on bulk operations. This option is not supported in versions of SQL Server prior to 2000.

bcp runs in interactive mode, prompting for format information, unless -f, -c, -n, -w, -6, or -N is specified when the command is executed. When running in interactive mode, bcp will also prompt to create a format file after receiving the format information.

bcp Import

Okay, so up to this point we've been stuck in the preliminaries. Well, it's time to get down to the business of what bcp is all about.

Probably the most common use of bcp is to import bulk data into existing SQL Server tables and views. To import data, you must have access permissions to the server, either through a login ID or a trusted connection, and you must have INSERT and SELECT permissions on the destination table or view.

The source file can contain native code, ASCII characters, Unicode, or mixed native and Unicode data. Remember to use the appropriate option to describe the source data. Also, for the data file to be usable, you must be able to describe the field and row terminators (using -t and -r) or the fields and rows must be terminated with the default tab and newline characters, respectively.

Be sure you know your destination before you start. bcp has a few quirks that can affect data import. Values supplied for timestamp or computed columns are ignored. If you have values for those columns in the source file, they'll be ignored. If the source file doesn't have values for these columns, you'll need a format file (which we'll see later in this chapter), so you can skip over them.

> *This is one of those really bizarre behaviors that you run across from time to time in about any piece of software you might use. In this case, if your destination table contains them, you're required to have columns to represent timestamp or computed data even though SQL Server will just ignore that data — silly, isn't it? Again, the way around this is to use a format file that explicitly says to skip the columns in question.*

For bcp operations, rules are ignored. Any triggers and constraints are ignored unless the FIRE_TRIGGERS and/or CHECK_CONSTRAINTS hints are specified. Unique constraints, indexes, and primary/foreign key constraints are enforced. Default constraints are enforced unless the -k option is specified.

Data Import Example

The easiest way to see how bcp import works is to look at an example. Let's start with a simple example, a tab-delimited file containing department information for the AdventureWorks2008 database. Here's how the data looks:

```
1 Smart Guys     Research and Development    2006-04-01 00:00:00.000
2 Product Test   Research and Development    2006-04-01 00:00:00.000
```

To import this into the Department table using a trusted connection at the local server, you run:

```
BCP AdventureWorks2008.HumanResources.Department in c:\DepartmentIn.txt -c -T
```

> *Two things are important here: First, up to this point, everything we've run has been done in Management Studio. For bcp, however, you type your command into a command-prompt box. Second, you'll need to change the preceding command line to match wherever you've downloaded the sample files/data for this book.*

Because the first column in the `Department` table is an identity column and the `-E` option wasn't specified, SQL Server will ignore the identity values in the file and generate new values. The `-c` option identifies the source data as character data, and `-T` specifies to use a trusted connection.

Note that, if you have not been using Windows authentication and haven't set up your network login with appropriate rights in SQL Server, then you may need to modify the preceding example to utilize the `-S` and `-P` options.

When we execute it, SQL Server quickly tells us some basic information about how our bulk copy operation went:

```
2 rows copied.
Network packet size (bytes): 4096
Clock Time (ms.) Total      : 109    Average : (18.35 rows per sec.)
```

We can go back into Management Studio and verify that the data went into the `Department` table as expected:

```
USE AdventureWorks2008;

SELECT * FROM HumanResources.Department;
```

which gets us back several rows — most importantly, the two we expect from our bcp operation:

DepartmentID	Name	GroupName	ModifiedDate
1	Engineering	Research and Development	1998-06-01...
2	Tool Design	Research and Development	1998-06-01...
...			
...			
16	Executive	Executive General and Administration	1998-06-01...
17	Smart Guys	Research and Development	2006-04-01...
18	Product Test	Research and Development	2006-04-01...

As always, note that, other than the two rows we just imported, your data may look a bit different depending on what parts of this book you've run the examples on, and which you haven't, and how much playing around of your own you've done. For this example, you just want to see that Smart Guys and Product Test made it into the table with the appropriate information. The identity values will have been reassigned to whatever was next for your particular server.

Now let's look at a more involved example. Let's say we have a table called `CustomerList`. A `CREATE` statement to make our `CustomerList` table looks like this:

```
CREATE TABLE dbo.CustomerList
(
    CustomerID      nchar(5)      NOT NULL
        PRIMARY KEY,
    CompanyName     nvarchar(40)  NOT NULL,
    ContactName     nvarchar(30)  NULL,
    ContactTitle    nvarchar(30)  NULL,
    Address         nvarchar(60)  NULL,
    City            nvarchar(15)  NULL,
```

```
    Region          nvarchar(15) NULL,
    PostalCode      nvarchar(10) NULL,
    Country         nvarchar(15) NULL,
    Phone           nvarchar(24) NULL,
    Fax             nvarchar(24) NULL
);
```

We have a comma-delimited file (in the same format as a .csv file) with new customer information. This time, the file looks like:

```
XWALL,Wally's World,Wally Smith,Owner,,,,,,(503)555-8448,,
XGENE,Generic Sales and Services,Al Smith,,,,,,,(503)555-9339,,
XMORE,More for You,Paul Johnston,President,,,,,,(573)555-3227,,
```

> What's with all the commas in the source file? Those are placeholders for columns in the **CustomerList** table. The source file doesn't provide values for all of the columns, so commas are used to skip over those columns. This isn't the only way to handle a source file that doesn't provide values for all of the columns. You can use a format file to map the source data to the destination. We'll be covering format files a little later in the chapter.

Imagine for a moment that we are going to run bcp to import the data to a remote system. The command is:

```
BCP AdventureWorks2008.dbo.CustomerList in c:\newcust.txt -c -t, -r\n -Ssocrates -
Usa -Pbubbagump
```

The line wrapping shown here was added to make the command string easier to read. Do not press Enter to wrap if you try this example yourself. Type the command as a single string and allow it to wrap itself inside the command prompt.

Once again, the data is being identified as character data. The -t, option identifies the file as comma-delimited (terminated) data, and -r\n identifies the newline character as the row delimiter. Server connection information was also provided for a little variety this time, using sa as your login and bubbagump as the password.

Again, bcp confirms the transfer along with basic statistics:

```
Starting copy...

3 rows copied.
Network packet size (bytes): 4096
Clock Time (ms.) Total     : 15     Average : (200.00 rows per sec.)
```

And again we'll also go verify that the data got there as expected:

```
USE AdventureWorks2008;

SELECT CustomerID, CompanyName, ContactName
```

```
FROM dbo.CustomerList
WHERE CustomerID LIKE 'X%';
```

And, sure enough, all our data is there . . .

```
CustomerID CompanyName                        ContactName
---------- ---------------------------------- -------------------------
XGENE      Generic Sales and Services         Al Smith
XMORE      More for You                       Paul Johnston
XWALL      Wally's World                      Wally Smith
```

Logged vs. Non-logged

bcp can run in either fast mode (not logged) or slow mode (logged operation). Each has its advantages. Fast mode gives you the best performance, but slow mode provides maximum recoverability. Since slow mode is logged, you can run a quick transaction log backup immediately after the import and be able to recover the database should there be a failure.

Fast mode is usually your best option when you need to transfer large amounts of data. Not only does the transfer run faster, but since the operation isn't logged you don't have to worry about running out of space in the transaction log. What's the catch? There are several conditions that must be met for bcp to run as non-logged:

❑   The target table cannot be replicated.

❑   If the target table is indexed, it must not currently have any rows.

❑   If the target table already has rows, it must not have any indexes.

❑   The TABLOCK hint is specified.

❑   The target table must have no triggers.

❑   For versions prior to SQL Server 2000, the select into/bulkcopy option must be set to true.

Obviously, if you want to do a fast mode copy into an indexed table with data, you will need to:

❑   Drop the indexes

❑   Drop any triggers

❑   Run bcp

❑   Reindex the target table

❑   Re-create any triggers

You need to immediately back up the destination database after a non-logged bcp operation.

If the target table doesn't meet the requirements for fast bcp, then the operation will be logged. This means that you can run the risk of filling the transaction log when transferring large amounts of data. You can run BACKUP LOG using the WITH TRUNCATE_ONLY option to clear the transaction log. The TRUNCATE_ONLY option truncates the inactive portion of the log without backing up any data.

I can't stress enough how deadly bcp operations can be to the size of your log. If you can't achieve a minimally logged operation, then consider adjusting your batch size down and turning TRUNCATE ON

CHECKPOINT *on for the duration of the operation. Another solution is to use the* -F *and* -L *options to pull things in a block at a time and truncate the log in between each block of data. Recognize, however, that an important part of your backup strategy — the transaction log — is now missing part of the information it needs to properly restore the database. It is, therefore, critical that you create a fresh backup as soon as your bulk load activity is complete.*

bcp Export

If you're going to be accepting data in via bulk operations, then it follows that you probably want to be able to pump data out, too.

bcp allows you to export data from a table, view, or query. You must specify a destination filename. If the file already exists, it will be overwritten. Unlike import operations, you are not allowed to skip columns during export. Timestamp, rowguid, and computed columns are exported in the same manner (just like they were "real" data) as any other SQL Server columns. To run an export, you must have appropriate SELECT authority to the source table or tables.

Look at a couple of quick examples using the HumanResources.Department table in the Adventure-Works2008 database.

To export to a data file using the default format, you could run:

```
BCP AdventureWorks2008.HumanResources.Department out c:\somedir\
DepartmentOut.txt -c -T
```

Note that if you're running Vista or a later version of the Windows operating system (including Windows Server 2008), new security controls will likely prevent you from doing a bulk extra to the root directory (C:\ on most systems) — thus my use of somedir *in the preceding code.*

This would create a file that looks like:

```
1    Engineering    Research and Development    1998-06-01 00:00:00.000
2    Tool Design    Research and Development    1998-06-01 00:00:00.000
...
...
17   Smart Guys     Research and Development    2006-04-01 00:00:00.000
18   Product Test   Research and Development    2006-04-01 00:00:00.000
```

In this case, we didn't have to use a format file, nor were we prompted for any field lengths or similar information. The use of the -c *option indicated that we just wanted everything, regardless of type, exported as basic ASCII text in a default format. The default calls for tabs as field separators and the newline character to separate rows.*

Keep in mind that the destination file will be overwritten if it already exists. This will happen without any kind of prompt or warning.

To modify the separator to something custom, we could run something like:

```
BCP AdventureWorks2008.HumanResources.Department out DepartmentOut.txt -c -T -t,
```

Notice the comma at the end. That is not a typo. The next character after the t *is the field separator — in this case, a comma.*

This would give us:

```
1,Engineering,Research and Development,1998-06-01 00:00:00.000
2,Tool Design,Research and Development,1998-06-01 00:00:00.000
...
...
17,Smart Guys,Research and Development,2006-04-01 00:00:00.000
18,Product Test,Research and Development,2006-04-01 00:00:00.000
```

We used a comma separator instead of a tab, and got what amounts to a `.csv` file.

Format Files

If you have any previous experience dealing with the kinds of files we typically have handed to us with the dreaded "load this data into our database" order, then you have probably looked at my previous import examples and said "Heh — I wish my data actually came in that cleanly formatted . . . ." Yes indeed, data rarely looks as perfect as we would like it to, and that brings us to the concept of format files.

Format files were first mentioned in the previous section, and provide something of an import template. Among other things, they make it easier to support recurring import operations when:

❑   Source file and target table structures or collations do not match.

❑   You want to skip columns in the target table.

❑   Your file contains data that makes the default data typing and collation difficult or unworkable.

Format files come in two varieties: non-XML and XML. We will start off by looking at the "old" way of doing things (the non-XML version) and then take a look at the newer XML format files.

To get a better idea of how each type of format file works, let's look at some specific examples. First you'll see how the file is structured when the source and destination match. Next, you can compare this to situations where the number of source file fields doesn't match the number of table columns or where source fields are ordered differently than the table columns.

You can create a default format file (which is non-XML for backward-compatibility reasons) to use as your source when you run bcp in interactive mode. After prompting for column value information, you're given the option of saving the file. The default filename is `BCP.fmt`, but you can give the format file any valid filename.

To create a default format like this for the AdventureWorks2008 database `HumanResources.Department` table, you could run:

```
BCP AdventureWorks2008.HumanResources.Department out c:\somedir\department.txt -T
```

This is a handy way of creating a quick format file that you can then edit as needed. You can do this with any table, so you can use bcp to get a jump-start on your format file needs.

Accept the default prefix and data length information for each file, and, in this case, a comma as the field terminator. SQL Server will prompt you to save the format file after you've entered all of the format information; in my case I'm going to save it off as `Department.fmt`. You can then edit the format file to meet your particular needs with any text editor, such as Windows Notepad.

Let's take a look at the format file we just produced:

```
10.0
4
1       SQLSMALLINT    0       2       ","     1       DepartmentID                    ""
2       SQLNCHAR       2       100     ","     2       Name
SQL_Latin1_General_CP1_CI_AS
3       SQLNCHAR       2       100     ","     3       GroupName
SQL_Latin1_General_CP1_CI_AS
4       SQLDATETIME    0       8       ","     4       ModifiedDate                    ""
```

The first two lines in the file identify the bcp version number (10.0 for SQL Server 2008, 9.0 for SQL Server 2005, and so on) and the number of fields in the host file. The remaining lines describe the host data file and how the fields match up with target columns and collations.

The first column is the host file field number. Numbering starts with 1 through the total number of fields. Next is the host file data type. The example file has a mix of a few data types. All text is in Unicode format, so the data type of all fields is SQLNCHAR. Given that there are no special characters in this data, we could have just as easily gone with a SQLCHAR (ASCII) format.

The next two columns describe the prefix and data length for the data fields. The prefix is the number of prefix characters in the field. The prefix describes the length of the data in the actual bcp file and allows the data file to be compacted to a smaller size. The data field is the maximum length of the data stored in the field. Next is the field terminator (delimiter). In this case, a comma is used as the field terminator and newline as the row terminator. The next two columns describe the target table columns by providing the server column order and server column name. Since there is a direct match between the server columns and host fields in this example, the column and field numbers are the same, but it didn't necessarily have to work that way. Last, but not least, comes the collation for each column. (Remember that, with SQL Server 2000 and newer, we can have a different collation for every column in a table.)

Now, let's check the XML version. To create this, we run almost the same command, but add the -x switch:

```
BCP AdventureWorks2008.HumanResources.Department out c:\somedir\department.txt -T -x
```

The format file we wind up with looks radically different:

```
<?xml version="1.0"?>
<BCPFORMAT xmlns="http://schemas.microsoft.com/sqlserver/2004/bulkload/format"
xmlns:xsi="http://www.w3.org/2001/XMLSchema-instance">
 <RECORD>
  <FIELD ID="1" xsi:type="NativeFixed" LENGTH="2"/>
  <FIELD ID="2" xsi:type="NCharPrefix" PREFIX_LENGTH="2" MAX_LENGTH="100"
COLLATION="SQL_Latin1_General_CP1_CI_AS"/>
  <FIELD ID="3" xsi:type="NCharPrefix" PREFIX_LENGTH="2" MAX_LENGTH="100"
COLLATION="SQL_Latin1_General_CP1_CI_AS"/>
  <FIELD ID="4" xsi:type="NativeFixed" LENGTH="8"/>
 </RECORD>
 <ROW>
  <COLUMN SOURCE="1" NAME="DepartmentID" xsi:type="SQLSMALLINT"/>
```

```
    <COLUMN SOURCE="2" NAME="Name" xsi:type="SQLNVARCHAR"/>
    <COLUMN SOURCE="3" NAME="GroupName" xsi:type="SQLNVARCHAR"/>
    <COLUMN SOURCE="4" NAME="ModifiedDate" xsi:type="SQLDATETIME"/>
  </ROW>
</BCPFORMAT>
```

Notice that everything is explicitly called out. What's more, there is an XML schema document associated with XML format files, which means you can validate the XML in your XML editor of choice.

I'm not going to pick any bones about this. I LOVE the new XML-formatted version. If you don't need to worry about compatibility with versions prior to SQL Server 2005, this one seems a no-brainer to me.

The old format files work, but, every time I work with them extensively, I consider purchasing stock in a pain reliever company. They are that much of a headache if you have to do anything beyond the defaults. Everything about them has to be "just so," and in larger tables, it's easy to miss a typo since fields are not clearly separated. XML tagging fixes all that and makes clear what every little entry is there for — debugging is much, much easier.

When Your Columns Don't Match

If only the world was perfect and the data files we received always looked just like our tables.

Okay, time to come out of dreamland. I'm reasonably happy with the world I live in, but it's hardly a perfect place and the kinds of data files I need to do bulk operations on rarely look like their destination. So, what then are we to do when the source file and destination table do not match up the way we want? Or what about going the other way — from a table to an expected data file format that isn't quite the same?

Fortunately, format files allow us to deal with several different kinds of variations we may have between source and destination data. Let's take a look.

Files with Fewer Columns Than the Table

Let's start with the situation where the data file has fewer fields than the destination table. We need to modify the format file we've already been using to identify which columns do not exist in the data file and, accordingly, which columns in our table should be ignored. This is done by setting the prefix and data length to 0 for each missing field and the table column number to 0 for each column we are going to skip.

For example, if, as one might expect, the data file has only DepartmentID, Name, and GroupName, you would modify the file to:

```
10.0
4
1       SQLSMALLINT    0       2       ","     1       DepartmentID             ""
2       SQLNCHAR       2       100     ","     2       Name
SQL_Latin1_General_CP1_CI_AS
3       SQLNCHAR       2       100     ","     3       GroupName
SQL_Latin1_General_CP1_CI_AS
4       SQLDATETIME    0       0       ","     0       ModifiedDate             ""
```

As you can see, the `ModifiedDate` field and column has been zeroed out. Because `ModifiedDate` is not supplied and the column has a default value (`Getdate()`), that default value will be used for our inserted rows.

The XML version doesn't look all that different, but instead of zeroing out elements of the definition, we simply don't define it:

```xml
<?xml version="1.0"?>
<BCPFORMAT xmlns="http://schemas.microsoft.com/sqlserver/2004/bulkload/format"
xmlns:xsi="http://www.w3.org/2001/XMLSchema-instance">
 <RECORD>
   <FIELD ID="1" xsi:type="NativeFixed" LENGTH="2"/>
   <FIELD ID="2" xsi:type="NCharPrefix" PREFIX_LENGTH="2" MAX_LENGTH="100"
COLLATION="SQL_Latin1_General_CP1_CI_AS"/>
   <FIELD ID="3" xsi:type="NCharPrefix" PREFIX_LENGTH="2" MAX_LENGTH="100"
COLLATION="SQL_Latin1_General_CP1_CI_AS"/>
 </RECORD>
  <ROW>
   <COLUMN SOURCE="1" NAME="DepartmentID" xsi:type="SQLSMALLINT"/>
   <COLUMN SOURCE="2" NAME="Name" xsi:type="SQLNVARCHAR"/>
   <COLUMN SOURCE="3" NAME="GroupName" xsi:type="SQLNVARCHAR"/>
 </ROW>
 </BCPFORMAT>
```

There was no column in the file to define, so we didn't. We aren't sticking anything in the `ModifiedDate` column, so we skipped that, too (counting on the default in its case).

More Columns in the File Than in the Table

The scenario for a data file that has more columns than the table does is actually amazingly similar to the short data file scenario we just looked at. The only trick here is that you must add column information for the additional fields, but the prefix length, data length, and column number fields are all set to 0:

```
10.0
4
1         SQLSMALLINT    0      2        ","    1        DepartmentID              ""
2         SQLNCHAR       2      100      ","    2        Name
SQL_Latin1_General_CP1_CI_AS
3         SQLNCHAR       2      100      ","    3        GroupName
SQL_Latin1_General_CP1_CI_AS
4         SQLDATETIME    0      8        ","    4        ModifiedDate              ""
5         SQLDATETIME    0      0        ","    0        CreatededDate             ""
```

This time, the host file includes fields for a date the department was created. The target table doesn't have a column to receive this information. The fields are added to the original format file, as well as two dummy columns with a column number of 0. This will force bcp to ignore the fields.

For this one, the XML version does have to deal with the fact that the file has a column that needs to be addressed. The destination, however, we can continue to ignore:

```xml
<?xml version="1.0"?>
<BCPFORMAT xmlns="http://schemas.microsoft.com/sqlserver/2004/bulkload/format"
xmlns:xsi="http://www.w3.org/2001/XMLSchema-instance">
```

```
<RECORD>
 <FIELD ID="1" xsi:type="NativeFixed" LENGTH="2"/>
 <FIELD ID="2" xsi:type="NCharPrefix" PREFIX_LENGTH="2" MAX_LENGTH="100"
COLLATION="SQL_Latin1_General_CP1_CI_AS"/>
 <FIELD ID="3" xsi:type="NCharPrefix" PREFIX_LENGTH="2" MAX_LENGTH="100"
COLLATION="SQL_Latin1_General_CP1_CI_AS"/>
 <FIELD ID="4" xsi:type="NativeFixed" LENGTH="8"/>
 <FIELD ID="5" xsi:type="NativeFixed" LENGTH="8"/>

</RECORD>
 <ROW>
 <COLUMN SOURCE="1" NAME="DepartmentID" xsi:type="SQLSMALLINT"/>
 <COLUMN SOURCE="2" NAME="Name" xsi:type="SQLNVARCHAR"/>
 <COLUMN SOURCE="3" NAME="GroupName" xsi:type="SQLNVARCHAR"/>
 <COLUMN SOURCE="4" NAME="ModifiedDate" xsi:type="SQLDATETIME"/>
 </ROW>
</BCPFORMAT>
```

Mismatched Field Order

Another possibility is that the host and target have the same fields, but the field orders don't match. This is corrected by changing the server column order to match the host file order:

```
10.0
4
1        SQLSMALLINT    0      2        ","    1      DepartmentID              ""
2        SQLNCHAR       2      100      ","    3      GroupName
SQL_Latin1_General_CP1_CI_AS
3        SQLNCHAR       2      100      ","    2      Name
SQL_Latin1_General_CP1_CI_AS

4        SQLDATETIME    0      8        ","    4      ModifiedDate              ""
```

In this case, the group name is listed before the department name in the source file. The server column order has been changed to reflect this. Notice, the order in which the server columns are listed has not changed, but the server column numbers have been swapped.

So, to translate this to XML, we just need to change a field or two versus our original XML file:

```
<?xml version="1.0"?>
<BCPFORMAT xmlns="http://schemas.microsoft.com/sqlserver/2004/bulkload/format"
xmlns:xsi="http://www.w3.org/2001/XMLSchema-instance">
 <RECORD>
 <FIELD ID="1" xsi:type="NativeFixed" LENGTH="2"/>
 <FIELD ID="2" xsi:type="NCharPrefix" PREFIX_LENGTH="2" MAX_LENGTH="100"
COLLATION="SQL_Latin1_General_CP1_CI_AS"/>
 <FIELD ID="3" xsi:type="NCharPrefix" PREFIX_LENGTH="2" MAX_LENGTH="100"
COLLATION="SQL_Latin1_General_CP1_CI_AS"/>
 <FIELD ID="4" xsi:type="NativeFixed" LENGTH="8"/>
 </RECORD>
 <ROW>
 <COLUMN SOURCE="1" NAME="DepartmentID" xsi:type="SQLSMALLINT"/>
```

```
<COLUMN SOURCE="3" NAME="Name" xsi:type="SQLNVARCHAR"/>
<COLUMN SOURCE="2" NAME="GroupName" xsi:type="SQLNVARCHAR"/>

<COLUMN SOURCE="4" NAME="ModifiedDate" xsi:type="SQLDATETIME"/>
</ROW>
</BCPFORMAT>
```

Using Format Files

As an example, let's use a format file for an import. This command will copy records into the Department table based on a file named shortdept.txt. We'll use ShortDept.fmt as our non-XML format file example, and ShortDeptX.fmt as our XML-based format file.

```
BCP AdventureWorks2008.HumanResources.Department in c:\shortdept.txt -
fc:\shortdept.fmt -Usa -Pbubbagump
```

Just for a change of flavor, the preceding example command line uses SQL Server authentication instead of Windows authentication. If you prefer Windows authentication, just replace the –U and –P parameters with the –T we've used frequently.

The sample files used in this example, ShortDept.txt, ShortDept.fmt, and ShortDeptx.fmt, are available for download from the Wrox website or from ProfessionalSQL.com.

Maximizing Import Performance

One obvious way of maximizing bcp performance is to make sure that the target table meets all the requirements for running bcp as a non-logged operation. This may mean you need to:

❑ Drop any existing indexes on the target table. While this is actually required only if you want a minimally logged operation, the fact is that leaving indexes off during bulk operation is greatly beneficial performance-wise regardless of the logging status. Be sure, however, to rebuild your indexes after the bulk operation is complete.

❑ Attempt to have your source data files created in the same order that your clustered index (if there is one) is in. During your index rebuild, this will allow you to make use of the SORTED_DATA_REORG option, which greatly speeds index creation (and thus the overall time of your bcp operation). Even if you have to leave a clustered index in place, performing the bcp with sorted data will allow the use of the ORDER column option (within the -HINT option).

❑ Make sure your maintenance properties are set to simple or non-logged. If they are set to Full Recovery, then bcp will not be allowed a minimally logged operation.

If you're looking for additional improvement when importing data into a table, you can run *parallel data loads* from multiple clients. To do this, you must:

❑ Use the TABLOCK hint.

❑ Remove all indexes (you can rebuild them after the operation is complete).

❑ Set the server recovery option to Bulk-Logged.

How would this work? Rather than importing one very large file, break it up into smaller files. Then you launch bcp from multiple client systems, each client importing one of the smaller files. Obviously, you will be interested in doing this only if the expected performance increase saves more time on the import than you'll spend preparing the source files and copying them to the clients.

Parallel loads were not supported for SQL Server 6.5 or earlier.

> **With either of these operations, it will be necessary to re-create any indexes on the target table after completing the operation. Re-create the target table clustered index (if any) before any non-clustered indexes.**

You can get additional performance improvement by letting SQL Server ignore check constraints and triggers, the default option. Keep in mind that this can result in loading data that violates the table's check constraints and any data integrity rules that are enforced by your triggers.

BULK INSERT

One of the "cousins" that I mentioned at the beginning of the chapter was the BULK INSERT command. In order to make use of this command, you must be a member of either the sysadmin or bulkadminserver role.

BULK INSERT essentially operates like a limited version of bcp that is available directly within T-SQL. The syntax looks like this:

```
BULK INSERT [['<database name>'.]['<schema name>'].]'<table name>' FROM '<data file>'
    [WITH
        (
            [BATCHSIZE [ = <batch size>]]
            [, CHECK_CONSTRAINTS]
            [, CODEPAGE [={'ACP'|'OEM'|'RAW'|'<code page>'}]]
            [, DATAFILETYPE [={'char'|'native'|'widechar'|'widenative'}]]
            [, FIELDTERMINATOR [= '<field terminator>' ]]
            [, FIRSTROW [= <first row>]]
            [, FIRE_TRIGGERS]
            [, FORMATFILE = '<format file path>' ]
            [, KEEPIDENTITY]
            [, KEEPNULLS]
            [, KILOBYTES_PER_BATCH [= <no. of kilobytes>]]
            [, LASTROW [ = <last row no.>]]
            [, MAXERRORS [ = <max errors>]]
            [, ORDER ({column [ASC|DESC]} [ ,...n ] )]
            [, ROWS_PER_BATCH [= <rows per batch>]]
            [, ROWTERMINATOR [ = '<row terminator>']]
            [, TABLOCK]
            [, ERRORFILE = '<file name>']
        )
    ]
```

Now, if you are getting a sense of déjà vu, then you're on top of things for sure. These switches pretty much all have equivalents in the basic bcp import syntax with which we started off the chapter.

The special permission requirements of BULK INSERT are something of a hassle (not everyone belongs to sysadmin or bulkinsert), but BULK INSERT does carry with it a couple of distinct advantages:

❏   It can be enlisted as part of a user-defined transaction using BEGIN TRAN and its associated statements.

❏   It runs in-process to SQL Server, so it should pick up some performance benefits there as it avoids marshalling.

❏   It's slightly (very slightly) less cryptic than the command-line syntax used by bcp.

The big issue with BULK INSERT is just that. It's bulk *insert*. BULK INSERT will not help you build format files. It will not export data for you. It's just a simple and well-performing way to get bcp functionality for moving data into your database from within SQL Server.

OPENROWSET (BULK)

Yet another cousin to bcp, but this one is a far more distant one. You can think of this cousin as being from the side of the family that got most of the money and power. (In case you can't tell, I like this one!) OPENROWSET (BULK) marries the bulk rowset provider with the OPENROWSET's ability to be used within queries for fast and relatively flexible access to external files without necessarily needing to load them into an intermediate table.

One of the more common uses for bcp is to load external data files for use by some periodic process. For example, you may receive files that contain things like credit reports, vendor catalogs, and other data that is placed in a generic format by a vendor. This is vital information to you, but you're more interested in a one-time interaction with the data than in truly importing it. OPENROWSET (BULK) allows the possibility of treating that file — or just one portion of that file — as a table. What's more, it can utilize a format file to provide a better translation of the file layout than a simple linked table might provide. The syntax looks like this:

```
OPENROWSET
( BULK '<data file>' ,
        { [ FORMATFILE = '<format file>' ] [
          [, CODEPAGE [={'ACP'|'OEM'|'RAW'|'<code page>'}]]
          [, FIRSTROW [= <first row>]]
          [, LASTROW [ = <last row no.>]]
          [, MAXERRORS [ = <max errors>]]
          [, ROWS_PER_BATCH [= <rows per batch>]]
          [, ERRORFILE = '<file name>']
    ]
        | SINGLE_BLOB | SINGLE_CLOB | SINGLE_NCLOB }
  } )
```

Keep in mind that OPENROWSET is more of a bulk access method than an insert method. You can most certainly do an INSERT INTO where the source of your data is an OPENROWSET (indeed, that's often how it's used), but OPENROWSET has more flexibility than that. Now, with that in mind, let's look at a couple of important bulk option issues when dealing with OPENROWSET.

ROWS_PER_BATCH

This is misleading. The big thing to remember is that, if you use this, you are essentially providing a hint to the Query Optimizer. SQL Server will always process the entire file, but whatever you put in this value is going to be a hint to the Optimizer about how many rows are in your file. Try to make it accurate or leave it alone.

SINGLE_BLOB, SINGLE_CLOB, SINGLE_NCLOB

These say to treat the entire file as one thing — one row with just one column. The type will come through as varbinary(max). Windows encoding conventions will be applied if you use SINGLE_BLOB. SINGLE_CLOB will assume that your data is ASCII, and SINGLE_NCLOB will assume it is Unicode.

Summary

In this chapter, we looked at the first of our two major data import/export utilities. bcp is used primarily for importing and exporting data stored as text files to and from our SQL Server. We also took a look at some of bcp's brethren.

As a legacy utility, bcp will be familiar to most people who have worked with SQL Server for any length of time. Microsoft continues to enhance the core technology behind bcp, so I think it's safe to say that bcp is here to stay.

That said, bcp is quite often not your best option. Be sure to check your options with BULK INSERT (and the benefits of running in-process to SQL Server) as well as OPENROWSET (BULK).

In our next chapter, we will take a look at bcp's major competition — SQL Server Integration Services (SSIS). SSIS has the glamour and glitz that bcp is missing, but it also has its own quirks that can occasionally make the simplicity of bcp seem downright appealing.

16

Getting Integrated

SQL Server Integration Services — or SSIS — is a tool that is a descendant of another tool called Data Transformation Services — or DTS. Remembering DTS is important particularly because of how revolutionary it was at the time it was released (in early 1999 as part of SQL Server 7.0). Never before was a significant tool for moving and transforming large blocks of data included in one of the major Relational Database Management Systems (RDBMSs). All sorts of things that were either very difficult or required very expensive third-party tools were suddenly a relative piece of cake. As we fast forward to the SQL Server 2008 era, what is now called SSIS (the name was changed when the service was totally rewritten as part of SQL Server 2005) is still relatively unique in terms of making such an important tool so accessible.

In this chapter, we'll be looking at how to perform basic import and export of data, and we'll discuss some of the other things possible with tools like Integration Services. We will place our primary focus on the basics of SSIS packages, setting us up for a more advanced discussion of SSIS programmability in the Web-based chapter, Chapter 25.

Understanding the Problem

The problems being addressed by Integration Services exist in at least some form in a large percentage of systems — how to get data into or out of our system from or to foreign data sources. It can be things like importing data from the old system into the new, or a list of available items from a vendor — or who knows what. The common thread in all of it, however, is that we need to take data that doesn't necessarily match our table definitions and get that data into those tables anyway.

What we need is a tool that will let us *Extract*, *Transform*, and *Load* data into our database — a tool that does this is usually referred to simply as an "ETL" tool. Just how complex of a problem this kind of tool can handle varies, but SQL Server Integration Services — or SSIS — can handle nearly every kind of situation you may have.

This may bring about the question "Well, why doesn't everybody use it, then, since it's built in?" The answer is one of how intuitive it is in a cross-platform environment. There are third-party packages out there that are much more seamless and have fancier UI environments. These are really meant to allow unsophisticated users to move data around relatively easily — they are also outrageously expensive. Under the old DTS product, I actually had customers that were Oracle or other DBMS oriented, but purchased a full license for SQL Server just to make use of DTS. While the price of competing packages has come down, and SQL Server licensing prices have gone up, I'm sure that there are still SQL Server licenses out there that exist largely because of the need for SSIS.

An Overview of Packages

SSIS utilizes the notion of a "package" to contain a set of things to do. Each individual action is referred to as a "task." You can bundle up a series of tasks and even provide control of flow choices to conditionally run different tasks in an order of your choosing (for example, if one task were to fail, then run a different task). Packages can be created programmatically (using a rather robust object model that we will take an introductory look at in Chapter 25), but most initial package design is done in a designer that is provided in SQL Server.

Let's go ahead and create a simple package just to get a feel for the environment. To get to SSIS, you need to start the SQL Server Business Intelligence Development Studio from the Programs➤Microsoft SQL Server 2008 menu on your system — then select Integration Services Project as your project type as shown in Figure 16-1.

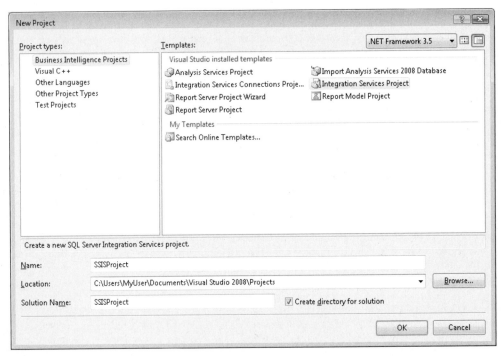

Figure 16-1

To be honest, I'm still not a fan of the Integration Services modeler being in the Intelligence Studio rather than the Management Studio. Nonetheless, Microsoft has this nasty habit of not consulting me before they move their tools around, so I guess we'll have to live with it!

So, to reiterate, the SSIS tool is in Business Intelligence Studio (much like the Reporting Services–related items) — not in Management Studio as most items we've looked at have been.

> **The exact look of the dialog in Figure 16-1 will vary depending on whether you also have Visual Studio installed and, if so, what parts of Visual Studio you included in your installation.**

In this case, I've named my project an ever-so-descriptive "SSISProject" — from there, I simply click OK and SQL Server creates the project and brings up the default project window, shown in Figure 16-2, for SSIS-related projects.

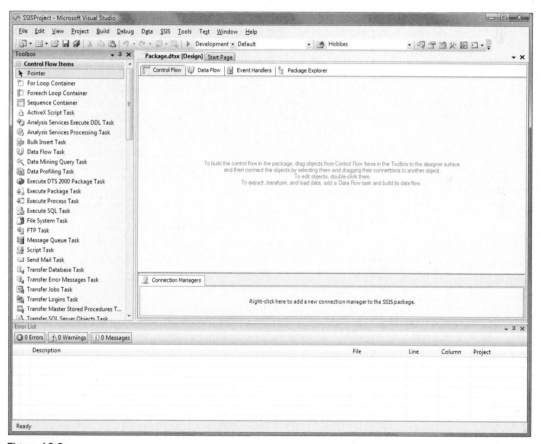

Figure 16-2

For those of you used to the Visual Studio environment, you should feel relatively at home. The only significant difference versus most Dev Studio projects is that, as we build the project, the design tab will be graphical in nature rather than in code.

There are four key windows in our project, so let's start by looking at these. We will then do a walk-through example later in the chapter.

Tasks

On the left side of our project (depending on your settings, you may have to click a tab to expand it), we have the toolbox window. The Control Flow Items list is at the top and thus what you first see, but you should also be able to find a section on Maintenance Plan tasks by scrolling down (these are more in the realm of the administrator, but you should take note of them — they underline my earlier notion that Integration Services is not just about ETL activities but also for a wide array of other actions, including many that you might have expected to find in Management Studio). You'll notice that many of these Control Flow Items entries are labeled as "tasks."

A task, much as the word implies, is generally about an action that you want to take. They range from migration tasks (such as moving objects between servers) to data migration and transformation to tasks that manage the execution of other programs or packages. Though most are called tasks, you will also find some container objects that help organize or wrap the other objects in your package.

> *It's worth noting that you can reorganize the tasks. You can, for example, drag and drop tasks in the task list to reorder them (perhaps to move those you use the most often up to the top where they are more visible), or create your own tabs to contain those tasks you use the most often. In addition, you can add new tasks to the list much as you can add new controls to other Dev Studio projects. In short, the environment is very customizable.*

There are a ton of tasks here, so let's take a quick overview at what the base tasks do.

Task	Description
Pointer	Okay, it's silly to even have to describe this, but just in case: This puts things into a generic drag-and-drop mode. When pointer is selected, clicking in the designer pane implies that you merely want to select an object that is already there as opposed to adding a new one.
For Loop Container	This is nothing more than a glorified FOR (or FOR/NEXT depending on your language of choice) statement. The FOR loop container allows you to initialize a control counter and set the conditions by which that counter is adjusted as well as under what conditions you exit the loop. Use this task to allow for controlled repetition of other tasks.
For Each Container	Again, this is your run-of-the-mill FOR/EACH statement. Like the FOR loop, it allows for controlled repetition, but this time, rather than using a counter, the loop is based on iterating through a collection of some sort (perhaps a collection of tables or other objects). The object list can come from a wide variety of sources ranging from such things as ADO and ADO.NET rowsets to SMO object lists.

Task	Description
Sequence Container	I think of this one as something of a "sub-package." The sequence container allows you to group up tasks and treat them as a single unit. This is useful for things like wrapping several tasks into a single transaction (thus allowing your overall package to contain several separate transactions — each potentially having many tasks to perform). Individual sequence containers can be made active or inactive conditionally, so you could, for example, turn off an entire set of tasks by disabling that sequence container (you could even do that programmatically, based on conditions found in previous tasks!).
Script Tasks	One of those "what it sounds like" things — these let you run your own custom code using either any ActiveX scripting language (JavaScript or VBScript for example) or any .NET-based language. Use the ActiveX Script task for ActiveX languages, and use the Script task for .NET code.
Analysis Services Tasks	These allow you to construct or alter Analysis Services objects as well as execute them.
Bulk Insert Task	As you might guess, this allows for the bulk importing of data. It uses the same Bulk Insert facilities that you touched on in the bcp chapter, but allows the bulk operation to be part of a larger control flow. The Bulk Insert task is easily the fastest way for an SSIS package to get data into your system. Note, however, that any package containing a Bulk Insert task can be run only by a login that is a member of the sysadmins server role.
Data Flow Task	The Data Flow task wraps the connection between data sources along with any transformations you want to make in moving data between those data sources. The Data Flow task is among the most complex tasks in SSIS in that it operates as both a task and a container. The Data Flow task is a container in the sense that you associate several parts of a given data flow with it. The Data Flow tasks define sources as well as destinations of data as well as the transformations to take place between the source and destination. Editing Data Flow tasks will automatically take you to a different tab within the main editing window.
Data Mining Query Task	This task requires that you have already defined Data Mining Models in Analysis Services. You can utilize this task to run predictive queries and output the results into tables (you could then define additional tasks to make use of those tables).
Execute Tasks	These are somewhat specific to what you want to execute. They can range from running other packages (there are separate tasks for running old DTS packages versus the newer SSIS packages) to executing external programs to running SQL scripts.
File System Tasks	These allow you to create, move, and delete files and directories. In a wide variety of SSIS environments, the ability to transfer files is key to both performance and execution of your package. For example, you may need to copy a file from a remote location to local storage for performance reasons as

Continued

Task	Description
	you perform operations against that file. Likewise, you may only have network access that allows you to read or to create a file, but not to change it — File System Tasks allow you to get just the right thing done.
FTP Tasks	This is something of a different slant on the File System Tasks notion. Instead, however, this allows you to use the FTP protocol to retrieve files (very handy for doing things like transferring files to or from vendors, customers, or other partners).
Message Queue Task	This allows you to send and receive messages via Microsoft Message Queue. This is actually a very powerful tool that allows for the delivery and/or receipt of files and other messages even when the remote host is not currently online. Instead, you can "queue" the file, and that host can be notified that the file is available the next time it is online. Likewise, files can be left in queue for your process to pick up when you execute the package.
Send Mail	Yup — yet another of those "what it sounds like" things. This allows you to specify a mail including attachments that may have been created earlier in your package execution. The only real trick on this one is that you must specify an SMTP connection (basically the outbound mail server) to use to send the mail. SSL and Windows-based authentication is also supported.
Transfer Tasks	These range from server migration tasks, such as transferring logins, error messages, and master database stored procedures, to more straightforward transfers such as transferring a table.
Web Service Task	This allows you to execute a Web service method and retrieve the result into a variable. You can then make use of that result in the remaining tasks in your package.
WMI Tasks	Windows Management Instrumentation (WMI) is an API that allows for system monitoring and control. It is a Windows-specific implementation of Web-Based Enterprise Management (WBEM), which is an industry standard for accessing system information. SSIS includes tasks for monitoring WMI events (so you can tell when certain things have happened on your system) and for requesting data from WMI in the form of a WMI query. You could, for example, ask WMI what the total system memory is on your server.
XML Tasks	XML Tasks allows for a wide variety of XML manipulation. You can apply XSLT transformations, merge documents, filter the XML document using XPath, and the list goes on.
Maintenance Tasks	Much of this is outside the scope of this book, but this set of tasks allows you to perform a wide variety of maintenance tasks on your server. From a developer perspective, a key use here would be things like a backup prior to a major import or another similar activity that is part of your package. Similarly, you may want to do index rebuilds or other maintenance after performing tasks that do major operations against a particular table.

The Main Window

This window makes up the center of your default SSIS package window arrangement in Dev Studio. The thing to note is that it has four tabs available, and each is something of its own realm — take a look at each of them.

It's worth noting that you can change from the default tab style interface to a window-based interface if you so choose. (It's in the options for Visual Studio.)

Control Flow

This is actually where the meat of your package comes together. No, a package isn't just made up of flow alone, but this is where you initially drag all your tasks in and establish the order in which they will execute.

Data Flow

As you place data flow objects into the Control Flow pane, they become available for further definition in the Data Flow pane. Data flow tasks require additional objects to define such things as data connections, sources, and destinations of data as well as actual transformations.

Event Handlers

SSIS packages create a ton of events as they execute, and this tab allows you to trap certain events and act upon them. Some of the more key events worth trapping include:

Event	Description
OnError	This is a glorious new feature with SSIS. DTS had a quasi–error handler, but it was weak at best. This gives you something far more robust.
OnExecStatus Changed	This event is triggered any time the task is going into a different status. The possible statuses are idle, executing, abend (abnormal ending), completed, suspended, and validating. You can set traps for each of these conditions and have code run accordingly.
OnPostExecute	This one fires immediately after execution of the task is complete. In theory, this is the same as OnExecStatusChanged firing and having a status of completed, but I have to be honest and say I haven't tested this enough to swear to it.
OnProgress	This event is called regularly when any reasonably measurable progress happens in the package. This one is probably more useful when you're controlling a package programmatically than through one of the other execution methods, but it is nice from the standpoint of providing a progress bar for your end users if you need one.

There are several other event methods available, but the preceding gives you a flavor of things.

Package Explorer

I find the location of this one to be a little odd. In a nutshell, this one presents a tree control of your package, complete with all the event handlers, connections, and executables (which include any tasks you have defined in the package). The reason I find this one a little odd is because I would have expected something like this to be part of or at least similar to Solution Explorer. Nonetheless, it does give you a way of looking over your project at an overall package level.

Solution Explorer

This is pretty much just like any other explorer window for Dev Studio. You get a listing of all the files that belong to your solution broken down by their nature (packages and data source views, for example).

The Properties Window

This one is pretty much the same as any other property window you've seen throughout SQL Server and Dev Studio. The only real trick here is paying attention to what exactly is selected so you know what you're setting properties for. If you've selected an object within the package, then it should be that particular task or event object. If you have nothing selected, then it should be the properties for the entire package.

Building a Simple Package

Okay, it's time for us to put some application to all this. This is going to be something of a quick-and-dirty example run, but, in the end, we will have shown off several of the key features of SSIS.

Let's start with a little prep work. For this sample, we're going to be making use of a vbScript file that will generate some data for us to import. You can think of this script as simulating any kind of preprocess script you need to run before a major import or export.

Create a text file called `CreateImportText.vbs` with the following code:

```
Dim iCounter
Dim oFS
Dim oMyTextFile

Set oFS = CreateObject("Scripting.FileSystemObject")
Set oMyTextFile = oFS.CreateTextFile("C:\TextImport.txt", True)

For iCounter = 1 to 10
    oMyTextFile.WriteLine(cstr(iCounter) & vbTab & """TestCol" &
cstr(iCounter) & """")
Next

oMyTextFile.Close
```

This script, when executed, will create a new text file (or replace the existing file if it's there). It will add 10 rows of text to the file containing two tab-separated columns with a newline row terminator. We will use this in conjunction with a few other tasks to create and populate a table in SQL Server.

> In its default form, the `CreateImportText.vbs` file will try and write the text file it creates to the root directory of the C drive. If your system has User Access Control enabled, you may be prevented from running the script; if so, just move it to a directory below the root and adjust the later paths in this example.

This is a pretty simplistic sample, so please bear with me here. What, in the end, I hope you see from this is the concept of running a preprocess of some sort (that's our script that generates the file in this case, but it could have been any kind of script or external process), followed by SQL Server scripting and data pump activities.

With our sample vbScript created, we're ready to start building a package.

Let's start with the SSISProject project file we created in the previous section. At this point, our Control Flow should be empty. In order to get the proverbial ball rolling on this, we need to make a call to our vbScript to generate the text file we will be importing. Drag an Execute Process Task from the Toolbox into the main Control Flow window. Very little will happen other than SSIS adding the Execute Process Task to the Control Flow window, as shown in Figure 16-3.

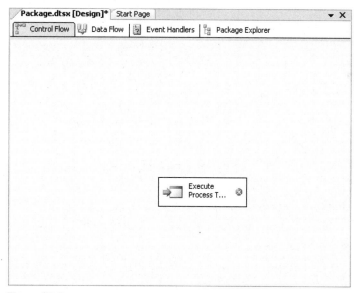

Figure 16-3

To do much with our new task, we need to double-click the task to bring up the Execute Process Task Editor shown in Figure 16-4.

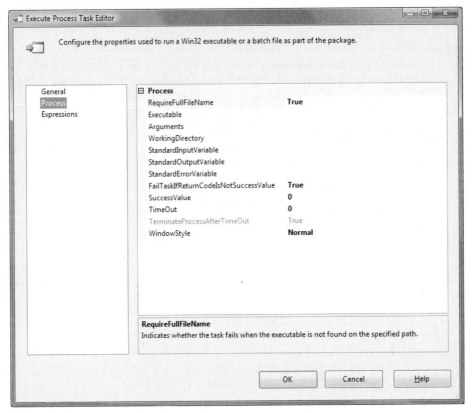

Figure 16-4

Note that I've switched to the Process options because they are a bit meatier to show in a screenshot than the General options are, but here's an overview of how we want to set things up:

Option	Setting
General≻Name	GenerateImportFile
General≻Description	Generates the text file for import
Process≻Executable	CreateImportText.vbs (prefix it with the full path to your script file)
Process≻Working Directory	C:\ (or other directory of your choosing — just make sure you're consistent)

When you're done making these changes, click OK, and very little will have changed in your Control Flow window, except that the name of the task will have been updated to GenerateImportFile.

Next, drag an Execute SQL Task object into your Control Flow. Now, select the GenerateImportFile task, and it should have an arrow hanging from the bottom of the task box, as shown in Figure 16-5.

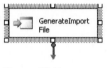

Figure 16-5

Now comes the tricky part: Click the "output" of our `GenerateImportFile` task — that is, click the end of the little arrow. Drag the arrow into the top of the Execute SQL Task, and the builder should connect the two tasks (as shown in Figure 16-6) — notice how the arrow indicates the control flow.

Figure 16-6

For the moment, let's look at what this arrow represents. Double-click it, and you'll get a Precedence Constraint Editor, as shown in Figure 16-7.

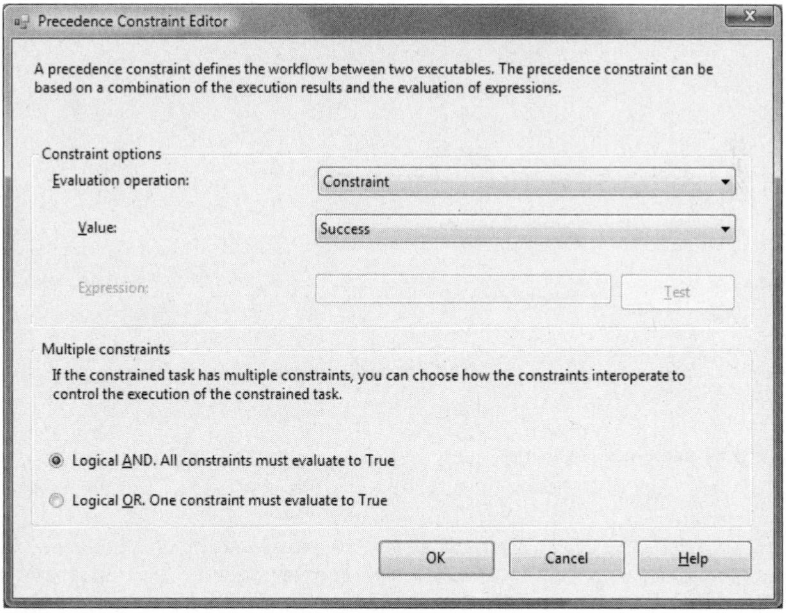

![Precedence Constraint Editor dialog box]

Precedence Constraint Editor

A precedence constraint defines the workflow between two executables. The precedence constraint can be based on a combination of the execution results and the evaluation of expressions.

Constraint options

Evaluation operation: Constraint

Value: Success

Expression: Test

Multiple constraints

If the constrained task has multiple constraints, you can choose how the constraints interoperate to control the execution of the constrained task.

◉ Logical AND. All constraints must evaluate to True

○ Logical OR. One constraint must evaluate to True

OK   Cancel   Help

Figure 16-7

Notice how it defines under what conditions this flow will be allowed to happen. In our case, it will move on to the Execute SQL Task only if our `GenerateImportFile` task completes successfully. We could define additional flows to deal with such things as the task failing or to allow for our second task to run on completion of the first task regardless of whether the first task succeeds or fails (any completion, regardless of success).

Cancel back out of this dialog, and double-click Execute SQL Task to bring up the Execute SQL Task Editor, as shown in Figure 16-8.

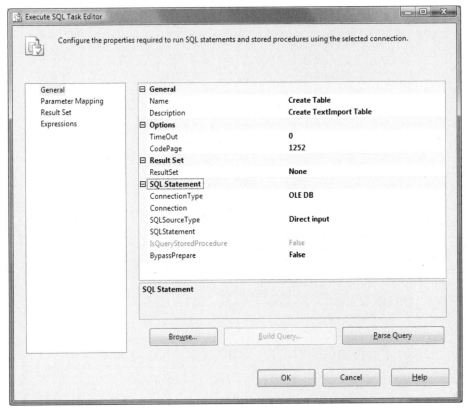

Figure 16-8

Again, I've edited the name a bit. Next, click the SQLStatement option to bring up the Enter SQL Query dialog shown in Figure 16-9.

We're checking to see whether the table already exists, and, if it does, drop it. Then, knowing that the table cannot already exist (if it did, we just dropped it), we go ahead and create our destination table.

One last thing we need is to have a connection to work with. Start by clicking in the Connection option and selecting New Connection. This will bring up a connection manager dialog (if you were paying attention, you may have noticed a connection manager pane below the main pane for our package — this is essentially the same functional area). Our package doesn't have any connections yet, so we need to click New again to get a somewhat run-of-the-mill OLE DB connection manager dialog. How I've filled out mine is shown in Figure 16-10, but adjust yours to match your database server name (the simple period "." in mine implies that I mean my local server) and security model.

Figure 16-9

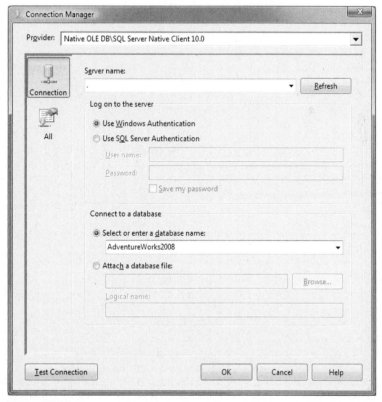

Figure 16-10

We're now able to connect to our database to create the destination table. And, with source data created and a destination table in place, we're ready to start working on actually transferring the data from our source to our destination. For that, we're going to utilize a Bulk Insert task, so go ahead and drag one of those into our model and connect the CreateTable task to the new BulkImport task, as shown in Figure 16-11.

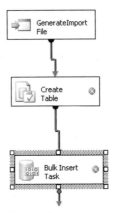

Figure 16-11

Again, double-click our task (the Bulk Insert Task in this case) to bring up a relevant editor box. Of particular interest is the Connection tab shown in Figure 16-12.

We have several things to change here. For example, I've already changed the Row Delimiter to be the line feed that is written by our vbScript's WriteLine command. We do, however, need to do even more. Start by selecting the same connection you created to run the CREATE TABLE statement against. Then enter in our destination table name ([AdventureWorks].[dbo].[TextImportTable]).

> Note that the table must already exist for you to reference it in this dialog. I just manually run the CREATE statement once to prime the database and make sure anything that needs to reference the table at compile time can do so. This should create no harm since the process will drop the table and create a new one each time anyway.

Finally, click in the File connection box and select New Connection to bring up the File Connection Management Editor for text files shown in Figure 16-13.

> Notice the error that the file doesn't exist. This is the same issue that we had with the TextImportTable table. Either create an empty dummy file or run the CreateImportText.vbs file once to get an initial file out there, and then refresh and this error should go away.

Click OK all the way back out to our Control Flow, and we're ready to rock.

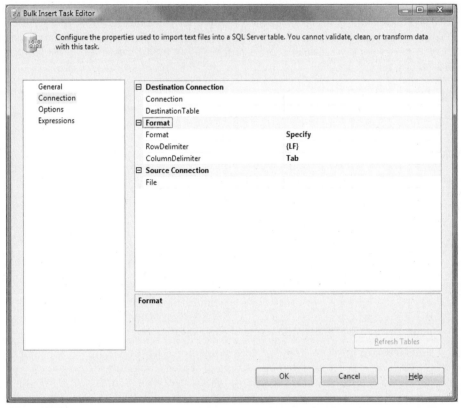

Figure 16-12

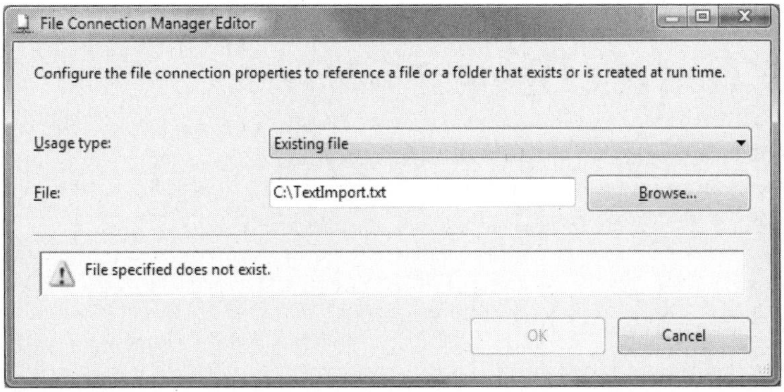

Figure 16-13

To execute our package immediately, click the run icon (the green arrow on the toolbar). Watch how Dev Studio indicates progress by changing the color of different tasks as they run.

A few more items of note: SSIS is capable of running multiple tasks at one time for you. For example, I made this project entirely linear (one piece at a time) based on the idea that we didn't want to drop the destination data until the last minute (when we are sure there's new data available). We could, however, have placed the link from the file generation directly to the build import just the same as the CREATE TABLE *dependency is linked directly to the import. If we had, SQL Server would have run both the table* DROP/CREATE *and the file creation at the same time but waited for "both" to complete before allowing the build import to execute.*

Go ahead and build your package (choose the Build option in the Build menu), as we will be utilizing it in the next section!

Executing Packages

There are a few different ways to execute an SSIS package. We utilized one of these in something of test mode within the Dev Studio, but this is hardly how you are likely to run your packages on a day-to-day basis. The more typical methods of executing a package include:

❑ **The Execute Package Utility:** This is essentially an executable in which you can specify the package you want to execute, set up any required parameters, and have the utility run it for you on demand.

❑ **As a scheduled task using the SQL Server Agent:** I'll talk more about the SQL Server Agent in Chapter 22, but for now, realize that executing an SSIS package is one of the many types of jobs that the agent understands. You can specify a package name and time and frequency with which to run it, and the SQL Server Agent will take care of it.

❑ **From within a program:** There is an entire object model supporting the notion of instantiating SSIS objects within your programs, setting properties for the packages, and executing them. This is fairly detailed stuff — so much so that Wrox has an entire book on the subject: *Professional SQL Server 2008 Integrations Services* by Knight, et. al (Wiley, 2009). We take a fast and dirty look at this in Chapter 25 (downloadable as special web content from either p2p.wrox.com or professionalsql.com), but if SSIS programmability is what you need, I recommend taking a look at Brian's work.

Using the Execute Package Utility

The Execute Package Utility is a little program by the name of DTExecUI.exe. You can fire it up to specify settings and parameters for existing packages and then execute them. You can also navigate using Windows Explorer and find a package in the file system (they end in .DTSX) and then double-click it to execute it. Do that to our text import package, and you should get the execute dialog shown in Figure 16-14.

As you can see, there are a number of different dialogs that you can select by clicking the various options to the left. Coverage of this could take up a book all to itself, but let's look at a few of the important things on several key dialogs within this utility.

General

Many fields on this first dialog are fairly self-explanatory, but let's pay particular attention to the Package Source field. We can store SSIS packages in one of three places:

❑ **The File System:** This is what you did on your Import/Export Wizard package. This option is really nice for mobility — you can easily save the package off and move it to another system.

❏ **SQL Server:** This one stores the package in SQL Server. Under this approach, your package will be backed up whenever you back up your MSDB database (which is a system database in every SQL Server installation).

❏ **SSIS Package Store:** This storage model provides the idea of an organized set of "folders" where you can store your package along with other packages of the same general type or purpose. The folders can be stored in either MSDB or the file system.

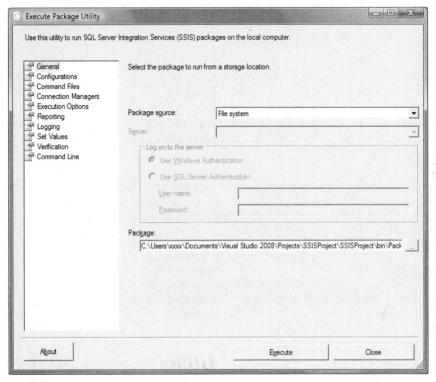

Figure 16-14

Configurations

SSIS allows you to define configurations for your packages. These are essentially a collection of settings to be used, and you can actually combine more than one of them into a suite of settings.

Command Files

These are batch files that you wish to run as part of your package. You can use these to do system-level things such as copying files around to places you need them (they will run under whatever account the Integration Services service is running under, so any required access on your network will need to be created to that account).

Connection Managers

This is a bit of misnomer — this isn't so much a list of connection managers as it is a list of connections. By taking a look at the Description column, you'll see many of the key properties for each connection your package uses. Notice that in our example package, we have two connections, and if you look closely, you'll see how one relates to file information (for our connection to the flat file we're using), and there is another that specifically relates to SQL Server (the export source connection).

Execution Options

Do not underestimate the importance of this one. Not only does it allow you to specify how, at a high level, you want things to happen if something goes wrong (if there's an error), but it also allows you to establish checkpoint tracking — making it easy to see when and where your package is getting to different execution points. This can be critical in performance tuning and debugging.

Reporting

This one is all about letting you know what is happening. You can set up for feedback: exactly how much feedback is based on which events you decide to track and the level of information you establish.

Logging

This one is fairly complex to set up and get going but has a very high "coolness" factor in terms of giving you a very flexible architecture for tracking even the most complex of packages.

Using this area, you can configure your package to write log information to a number of preconfigured "providers" (essentially, well-understood destinations for your log data). In addition to the preinstalled providers such as text files and even a SQL Server table, you can even create your own custom providers (not for the faint of heart). You can log at the package level, or you can get very detailed levels of granularity and write to different locations for different tasks within your package.

Set Values

This establishes the starting value of any runtime properties your package uses (there are none in our simple package).

Verification

Totally different packages can have the same filename (just be in a different spot in the file system, for example). In addition, packages have the ability to retain different versions of themselves within the same file or package store. The Verification dialog is all about filtering or verifying what package/version you want to execute.

Command Line

You can execute SSIS packages from the command line (handy when, for example, you're trying to run DTS packages out of a batch file). This option within the SSIS Package Execution Utility is about specifying parameters you would have used if you had run the package from the command line.

The utility will establish most of this for you — the option here is just to allow you to perform something of an override on the options used when you tell the utility to Execute.

Executing the Package

If you simply click Execute in the Package Execution Utility, your package will be off and running. After it runs, you should find a text file in whatever location you told your package to store it — open it up, take a look, and verify that it was what you expected.

Executing within Management Studio

While Management Studio doesn't give you a package editor, it does give you the ability to run your packages.

In the Object Explorer pane of Management Studio, clicking the Connect icon can choose Integration Services. Fill out the connection dialog. This should create a connection to Integration Services on that server, and add an Integration Services node in your Object Explorer.

To execute a package in this fashion (using Management Studio), the package must be local to that server (not in the file system). Fortunately, if you right-click the File System node under Stored Packages, SQL Server gives you the ability to import your package. Simply navigate the file system to the package we created, give it a name in the package store, and import it. You can then right-click and execute the package at any time. (It will bring up the execution utility we saw in a previous section, so you should be in familiar territory from here.)

Summary

SQL Server Integration Services is a robust Extract, Transform, and Load tool. You can utilize Integration Services to provide one-off or repeated import and export of data to and from your databases — mixing a variety of data sources while you're at it.

In this chapter, we actually went just slightly beyond the basics — touching on external access and multi-stage control of flow. While becoming expert in all that Integration Services has to offer is a positively huge undertaking, getting basic imports and exports up and running is a relative piece of cake. I encourage you to start out simple and then add to it as you go. As you push yourself further and further with what SSIS can do, take a look at other books that are specific to what SSIS has to offer.

17

Replication

Coming off the heels of significant change in 2005, replication is one of a few quiet areas in terms of version differences in SQL Server 2008. Indeed, virtually nothing has changed that isn't directly tied to a non-replication feature. (They had to allow for replication of the new data types, didn't they?)

Replication is one of those things that everyone loves to ignore — until they need it. Then, it seems, there is a sudden crisis about learning and implementing it instantly (and not necessarily in that order, I'm sorry to say).

So, what then, exactly, is replication? I'll shy entirely away from the Webster's definition of it and go to my own definition:

> *Replication is the process of taking one or more databases and systematically providing a rule-based copy mechanism for that data to and potentially from a different database.*

Replication is often a topology and administration question. As such, many developers have a habit of ignoring it — bad idea. Replication has importance to software architects in a rather big way, as it can be a solution to many complex load and data distribution issues such as:

- ❑ Making data available to clients that are generally not connected to your main network
- ❑ Distributing the load associated with heavy reporting demands
- ❑ Addressing latency issues with geographically dispersed database needs
- ❑ Supporting geographic redundancy

And those are just a few of the biggies.

So, with that in mind, we're going to take a long look at replication. I'm going to warn you in advance that this isn't going to have quite as many walkthroughs as I usually do, but patience, my young *padawan* — there is a reason. In simple terms, once you've built one or two of the styles of replication, you have most of the "constructing" part of the learning out of the way. What's more, the actual building up of the replication instance is indeed mostly an administrator's role. Instead, we're going to focus on understanding what's happened, and, from there, save most of the space in this chapter for understanding how different replication methods both create and solve problems for us and how we might use the different replication models to solve different problems.

In this chapter we will look at things like:

- ❑ General replication concepts
- ❑ What replication models are available (we will see an example or two here)
- ❑ Security considerations
- ❑ Replication Management Objects (RMO) — the programmatic way of managing replication

In the end, while I can't promise to make you a replication expert (to be honest, I'm not really one myself), you will hopefully have a solid understanding of the fundamentals and have a reasonable understanding of the possibilities.

Replication Basics

Replication is like a big puzzle — made up of many pieces in order to form a complete unit. We have topology considerations (publisher, subscriber, and distributor) as well as publication models (merge, transactional, snapshot). Before you get to deciding on those, there are several things to take into account.

Considerations When Planning for Replication

There are a number of things to take into account when thinking about the topology and replication methods available. These should be part of an assessment you make at design time to determine what forms of replication should even be considered for your application. Among these are:

- ❑ Autonomy
- ❑ Latency
- ❑ Data consistency

Let's take a quick look at each of these.

Autonomy

Autonomy is all about how much a replication instance is able to run as its own thing. What data needs to be replicated and at what frequency? For example, you could be supporting a sales application where each site keeps separate customer records. You would want to have these replicated to a central database for reporting and, perhaps, such other things as automatic stock replacement. Each site is highly autonomous (they really don't care whether the central database gets its data or not; they can still continue to make sales based on the data they have on-site). Indeed, even the central database, while dependent, is probably not in a catastrophic situation if it misses data from a site for a day (depends how you're using the reports that come off it or how much lag you can have before you restock).

Latency

Latency refers to the time delay between updates; in other words, the time taken for a change at the publishing server to be made available at the subscribing server. The higher the autonomy between sites, the greater the latency between updates can be.

Determining an acceptable delay can be tricky and will likely be tied into the aforementioned autonomy question. If our site information is only transmitted to the central server for periodic rollup reporting, then we can probably get away with only daily — or even longer — updates. If, however, the sites are drawing from a central shipping facility for some of the sales, then we need to update the central database in a timelier manner, so a product is not oversold (two sites trying to sell the one remaining piece of stock).

Data Consistency

Data consistency is obviously going to be a key concern of virtually any distributed system. This is, of course, all about making sure that your various replication instances contain the same values from end to end, and this can be accomplished in two ways:

❑ **Data convergence**: All sites eventually end up with the same values; however, the values aren't necessarily the same as they would be if all of the changes had taken place on one server. An example might be our overstock situation. Had our two sales happened on the same server, then the second sale would have known about the out of stock situation and perhaps not been completed. Instead, each database thought one item was available, and, depending on the way the inventory adjustment is handled, you may wind up with a negative inventory level. In the same vein, your data may wind up with exactly the same end value, but may have taken a different set of steps to arrive at that value (the actual ordering of the updates may not be the same depending on how many replication clients were involved and at what time they synchronized).

❑ **Transactional consistency**: The results at any server are the same as if all transactions were executed on a single server. This is implemented by the mechanism implied in the name — transactions. I'm sure, if you ponder this for a bit, you can recognize the latency impact (both good and bad) of this — before your transaction can complete, it has to complete on every server that is participating in that particular replication set.

Schema Consistency

Many developers who are used to developing in non-replicated environments take the ability to easily change the database schema for granted. Need to add or drop a new column? No problem. Need to add a new table? No big deal. Well, beyond the basic problems of being so cavalier with your database in any environment, you'll quickly find that life gets a bit more complicated in a replicated world.

Replication or not, remember that any time you alter the schema of your table you are essentially altering the foundation of your entire system (or at least the part that the schema object in question serves). Schema changes should always be treated as fairly serious alterations and be carefully considered as well as methodically planned. Some changes (additions in particular) can usually be made with relatively minor collateral impact. Things that change or remove existing objects, however, can be deadly when dealing with backward-compatibility issues. Also, keep in mind that others may have built "extensions" to your system that are relying on your existing schema; this can mean impacts that are hard to plan for when you change your existing schema.

The good news is that SQL Server continues to increase its support for schema changes during replication. Fields that are added or dropped on the publisher may be propagated to all subscribers during future replication operations. The bad news is that your change procedures need to be much stricter. The bottom line is that, if you need to make frequent schema changes, you'll want to fully plan what your change strategy is going to be before implementing replication at all.

When the concept of replicating schema changes was first added to SQL Server, it was done through the use of special stored procedures called sp_repladdcolumn *and* sp_repldropcolumn *rather than the more familiar* ALTER TABLE *command. This was changed back in SQL Server 2005, and* sp_repladdcolumn *and* sp_repldropcolumn *should be considered deprecated (avoid using them).*

Other Considerations

Some other things to think about include:

❑ How reliable is the connection between your servers? If it is a local connection, then you can probably count on it, but what if it is in a different geographic location? What if it's a different country?

❑ What kind of connection latency do you have? This falls somewhat into the reliability question, but is really its own issue. Do you really want to enforce transactional replication if it takes even a second or two for a simple ping to return (imagine that with a block of data now)?

❑ In the same vein as connection latency, how much bandwidth do you have? How much traffic are you going to be flushing over the wire, and what other processes are going to be using that same wire? Do you need to compress your replication related data?

❑ Is the replication method wired at all? That is, what if you don't have connectivity at all with the servers you want to replicate to? SQL Server supports a disconnected model, but what does that do to you between long updates?

Replication Roles

The process of replication is based on three basic roles: The publisher, distributor, and subscriber. Any one server can potentially be serving any one (or any subset) of these roles. Just to paint a picture of how flexible this can be, take a look at Figure 17-1.

As you can see, multiple publishers can be utilizing the same distributor, and any given publication can have multiple subscribers. Let's take a little bit closer look at these roles.

The Publisher

The publisher can be considered to be the source database. Even in situations where the publisher and its various subscribers are sharing data equally, there is one database that can be thought of as something of the control database.

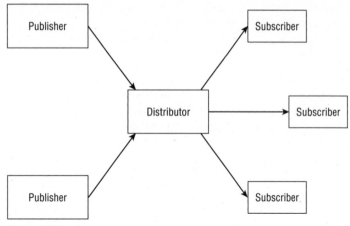

Figure 17-1

The Distributor

The distributor serves as something of the clearinghouse for changes. It has a special distribution database that keeps track of changes, as well as which subscribers have already received those changes. In addition, it will keep track of the results of any synchronization process and will know what happened in the case of any conflicts that had to be resolved (we'll look more into conflict resolution later).

The Subscriber

Any database that is participating in the replication publication, but is not the actual publisher, can be considered a subscriber. This does not, however, mean that the subscriber only receives data — indeed, depending on the specific model chosen (again, more on those later), the subscriber may well be both receiving and disseminating data.

Subscriptions

The subscriptions that a subscriber receives are called *publications*. A publication will contain one or more *articles*. An article is usually a table or some subsection of the data from a table, but it can be a stored procedure or a group of stored procedures. By subscribing to a publication, the subscriber is subscribing to all of the articles in the publication. The subscriber cannot subscribe to individual articles alone.

Subscriptions can be set up as *push* subscriptions or *pull* subscriptions:

- ❑ With **push** subscriptions, the publisher determines when updates go out to the subscriber. This is used most frequently when you want to keep latency to a minimum (since the publisher is often the only copy of the database receiving changes, it makes sense that it would be the one to know about changes as they happen and take appropriate action) or you want to keep full control at the publisher for some other reason.

- ❑ With **pull** subscriptions, the subscriber requests updates. This allows for a higher level of autonomy since the subscriber decides when updates should occur.

A publication can simultaneously support both push and pull subscriptions; however, any given subscriber is restricted to either a push or pull subscription — it cannot have both push and pull to the same publication.

Types of Subscribers

SQL Server supports three types of subscribers:

❑ The default is a **local** subscriber. The publisher is the only server that knows about the subscriber. Local subscribers are often used as a security mechanism or when you want to maximize autonomy between servers.

❑ **Global** subscribers occur where all servers participating in the publication (be they the publisher or a subscriber) know about all the other subscribers. Global subscribers are commonly used in a multiserver environment where you want to be able to combine data from different publishers at the subscriber.

❑ **Anonymous** subscribers are visible only to the publisher while the subscriber is connected. This is useful when setting up Internet-based applications.

Filtering Data

SQL Server provides for the idea of horizontally or vertically filtering tables. *Horizontal filtering* (you may come across the term *horizontal partitioning* for this as well) identifies rows within the table (by way of a WHERE clause) for publication. For example, you could divide inventory information by warehouse as a way of maintaining separate warehouse totals. *Vertical filtering* (also known as *vertical partitioning*) identifies the columns to be replicated. For example, you might want to publish quantity on hand information from an inventory table, but not quantity on order.

Replication Models

We have three different models available to us in replication. They trade off between the notions of latency, autonomy, and some of the other considerations we discussed earlier in the chapter. Deciding which to choose is something of a balancing act between:

❑ **Degree of autonomy**: Is there a constant connection available between the servers? If so, what kind of bandwidth is available? How many transactions will be replicating?

❑ **Conflict management**: What is the risk that the same data will be edited in multiple locations either at the same time or in between replicated updates? What is the tolerance for data on one or more of the replicated servers disagreeing?

Some replication scenarios don't allow for connectivity except on a sporadic basis — others may never have connectivity at all (save, perhaps, through what is sarcastically referred to as "sneaker net" — where you run, mail, fly, or the like, a disk or other portable storage medium from one site to another). Other replication scenarios have an absolute demand for perfectly consistent data at all sites with zero data loss.

From highest to lowest in autonomy, the three models are:

- ❑ **Snapshot** replication
- ❑ **Merge** replication
- ❑ **Transactional** replication

Let's look at the pros and cons of each replication model, outlining situations where it would be an appropriate solution and any data integrity concerns.

It's important to note that you can mix and match the replication types as necessary to meet your implementation requirements. There are going to be some publications where you want to allow greater autonomy between sites. There will be other publications where minimizing latency is critical.

Let me take a moment here to point out that a publication is just that — a publication. It does not necessarily map out that one publication equals one database. You may have one publication where the articles included in it make up only part of your subscribing database. Other objects in the subscribing database may be served by a different publication — potentially from a completely different publishing server.

Snapshot Replication

With *snapshot replication*, a "picture" is taken at the source of all of the data to be replicated (as shown in Figure 17-2). This is used to replace the data at the destination server.

Snapshot replication, in its simplest form, is the easiest type of replication to set up and manage. Complete tables or table segments (for partitioned tables) are written to the subscribers during replication. Since updates occur on a periodic basis only, most of the time, there is minimal server or network overhead required to support replication.

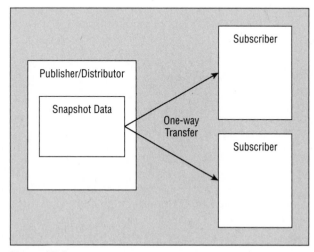

Figure 17-2

Snapshot replication is frequently used to update read-only tables on subscriber systems. It allows for a high level of autonomy at the subscriber, but at the cost of relatively high latency. You are able to keep tight control on when periodic updates occur when using snapshot replication. This means that you can schedule updates to occur when network and server activity is at a lull (or you can even carry the snapshot via disk or other hard medium). There is a potential concern about the time and resources to complete replication during the periodic updates. As source tables grow, the amount of data that has to be transferred during each update increases. Over time, it may become necessary to either change the replication type or partition the table to reduce the amount of data replicated to keep traffic to manageable levels.

> **A variation of snapshot replication is snapshot replication with immediate-updating subscribers. With this, changes can be made to the data at the subscriber. Those changes are sent to the publishing server on a periodic basis unless immediate updating has been implemented, in which case distributed transactions are executed in real time.**

How Snapshot Replication Works

Replication is implemented through *replication agents*. Each agent is essentially its own, small, independent program that takes care of the tasks of monitoring transactions and distributing data as required for that particular type of agent.

Snapshot Agent

The *Snapshot Agent* supports snapshot replication and initial synchronization of data tables for other types of replication (which all also rely on a snapshot for synchronizing data for the first time). All types of replication require that the source and destination tables must be synchronized, either by the replication agents or through manual synchronization, before replication can begin. In either case, the Snapshot Agent has the same responsibility. It takes the "picture" of the published data and stores the files on the distributor.

Distribution Agent

The *Distribution Agent* is used for moving data for initial synchronization and snapshot replication (and, as we'll see later, for transactional replication) from the publisher to the subscriber(s). For push subscriptions, the Distribution Agent typically runs on the distributor. For pull subscriptions, the Distribution Agent typically runs on the subscriber. The actual location of the Distribution Agent is an option that can be configured within Management Studio or via RMO.

The Process of Snapshot Replication

Snapshot replication uses periodic updates (the frequency is up to you, but, in general, you'll schedule a job in the job manager to run your snapshot on a regular basis). During the updates, schemas and data files are created and sent to the subscribers. Let's step through the basic procedure (see Figure 17-3):

1. The Snapshot Agent places a shared lock on all articles in the publication to be replicated, ensuring data consistency.

2. A copy of each article's table schema is written to the distribution working folder on the distributor.

3. A snapshot copy of table data is written to the snapshot folder.

4. The Snapshot Agent releases the shared locks from the publication articles.

5. The Distribution Agent creates the destination tables and database objects, such as indexes, on the subscriber and copies in the snapshot data, overwriting the existing tables, if any.

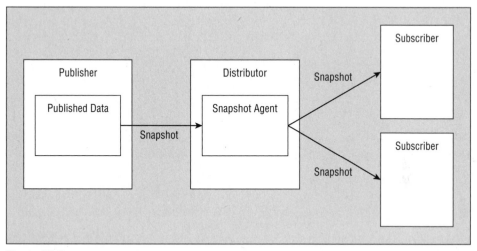

Figure 17-3

Snapshot data is stored as a native bcp (we explored these back in Chapter 15) file if all of the subscribers are Microsoft SQL Servers. Character mode files, instead of SQL Server bcp files, will be created if you are supporting heterogeneous (non-SQL Server) data sources.

> SQL Server supports heterogeneous data sources for replication. Currently, transactional and snapshot replication are supported on all O/S platforms for Oracle as well as most O/S platforms for DB2.

When to Use Snapshot Replication

Use snapshot replication to update lookup data or read-only copies of data on remote servers. You can use snapshot replication when you want (or need) to connect to the publisher only intermittently.

As an example, think of how servers might be managed for a chain of garden supply stores. You have stores in several cities. Some larger cities have multiple stores. What are some good candidates for snapshot replication?

Customer records are an obvious choice. A customer, such as a landscape gardener, may turn up at different locations. In most cases, it won't matter if there's a delay updating customer information. This would also give you a way to make sure that only users who have access to the publishing server can change customer records.

Inventory records could be a little more of a problem. The items you keep in inventory are somewhat constant with most changes taking place by season. Even then, you would probably keep the items in file, but with a zero quantity on hand. The problem is, you may want to replicate more up-to-date inventory records between stores. This would let you search for items you might not have on hand without having to call each of the stores. Timely updates would most likely mean transactional replication (which we will discuss shortly).

Special Planning Requirements

An important issue when setting up snapshot replication is timing. You need to make sure that users are not going to need write access to any published tables when the Snapshot Agent is generating its snapshot (remember that share lock that gets set on every article in the publication? Well, that's going to prevent inserts, updates, and deletes to that data for the duration of that lock — which is to say for the duration of the publishing of the distribution). You also want to be sure that the traffic generated by replication does not interfere with other network operations.

Storage space can also become an issue as published tables grow. You have to verify that you have enough physical disk space available on the destination folder (CD-ROM, DVD, jump drive, tape, and so on) to support the snapshot folder.

Merge Replication

Snapshot is great, but we do not always live in a "read-only" world. Among the choices for dealing with data changes taking place at multiple servers is through the use of *merge replication*. The changes from all of the sites are merged when they are received by the publisher (see Figure 17-4). Updates can take place either periodically (via schedule — this is the typical way of doing things) or on demand.

Merge replication has a high level of autonomy, but also has high latency and runs a risk of lower transactional consistency. Unlike transactional and snapshot replication, which guarantee consistency, merge replication does not. This is one of the more critical design considerations that you need to make when implementing merge replication — how important is consistency?

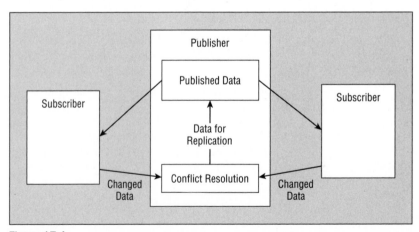

Figure 17-4

In a way, roles tend to get somewhat blurred in merge replication. The publisher is the initial source for the merge data, but changes can be made at the publisher or the subscribers. Changes can be tracked by row or by column. Transactional consistency is not guaranteed because conflicts can occur when different systems make updates to the same row. Data consistency is maintained through conflict resolution based on criteria you establish (you can even write custom resolution algorithms). You can determine whether conflicts are recognized by row or by column.

As with transactional replication, the Snapshot Agent prepares the initial snapshot for synchronization. The synchronization process is different, however, in that the Merge Agent performs synchronization. It will also apply any changes made since the initial snapshot.

Merge Agent

Just as we saw with snapshot replication, merge replication uses an agent — the *Merge Agent*. As shown in Figure 17-5, the agent copies the changes from all subscribers and applies them to the publisher. It then copies all changes at the publisher (including those made by the Merge Agent itself during the resolution process) to the subscribers. The Merge Agent typically runs on the distributor for push subscriptions and on the subscriber for pull subscriptions, but as with the snapshot and transactional replication, this can be configured to run remotely.

The Process of Merge Replication

Assuming that the initial synchronization has already taken place (remember, that will be based on a snapshot), the steps to merge replication are:

1. Triggers installed by SQL Server track changes to published data.

2. Changes from the publisher are applied to subscribers.

3. Changes from subscribers are applied to the publisher, and any conflicts resolved.

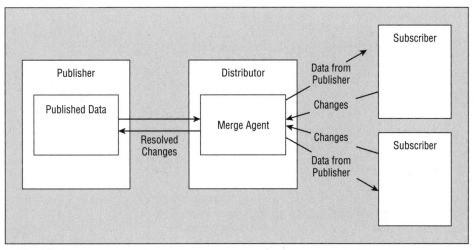

Figure 17-5

> **Merge triggers do not interfere with the placement or use of user-defined triggers.**

Changes, whether occurring at the publisher or subscriber, are applied by the Merge Agent. Conflicts are resolved automatically through the Merge Agent, using a conflict resolver (you can select one and can even build your own). The Merge Agent tracks every row update for conflicts at the row or column level, depending on how you have configured conflict resolution. You will define the priority scheme to be used when conflicts occur between new (arriving) and current data values.

When to Use Merge Replication

One way of using merge replication is to support partitioned tables. Going back to the garden supply business, you could set up filtering (partitioning) so that each store can view inventory information for any store but would only be able to directly update its own inventory. Changes would be propagated through merge replication. Data can be filtered horizontally or vertically. You can exclude rows to be replicated from a table, and you can exclude any table columns. Merge replication watches for changes to any column in a replicated row. In this particular scenario, there is little risk of conflict in inventory since each store can only update its own inventory, but what if you were allowing all stores to update customer data (such as a new address for the customer)? The right answer is situational, but this illustrates how different needs can place a different burden on your replication design.

Special Planning Requirements

When implementing merge replication, there are checks that you need to make to ensure that your data is ready for replication. While setting up merge replication, some changes may be made automatically by SQL Server to your database objects. Use care when selecting the tables to be published. Any tables required for data validation (such as lookup tables and other foreign key situations) must be included in the publication if you want that validation to apply on the subscribers.

SQL Server will identify a column as a globally unique identifier for each row in a published table. If the table already has a `uniqueidentifier` column, SQL Server will automatically use that column. Otherwise, it will add a `rowguid` column (which will, as it happens, also be called `rowguid`) to the table and create an index based on the column.

There will be triggers created on the published tables at both the publisher and the subscribers. These are used to track data changes for Merge Agent use based on row or column changes.

There will also be several tables added for tracking purposes. These tables are used by the server to manage:

- ❏ Conflict detection and resolution
- ❏ Data tracking
- ❏ Synchronization
- ❏ Reporting

For example, conflicts are detected through a column in the `MSmerge_contents` table, one of the tables created when you set up merge replication.

Transactional Replication

The difference between *transactional replication* and snapshot replication is that incremental changes, rather than full tables, are replicated to the subscribers. Any changes logged to published articles, such as `INSERT`, `UPDATE`, and `DELETE` statements, are tracked and replicated to subscribers. In transactional replication, only changed table data is distributed, maintaining the transaction sequence. In other words, all transactions are applied to the subscriber in the same order that they were applied to the publisher.

> Note that only logged actions are properly replicated. Unlogged bulk operations (such as a bcp that has logging turned off) or Binary Large Object (BLOB) operations that do not generate full log entries will not be properly replicated.

In its simplest form, as shown in Figure 17-6, changes can only be made at the publisher. Changes can be replicated to subscribers at set intervals or as near real-time updates. While you may have less control over when replication occurs, you are typically moving less data with each replication. Updates are occurring much more often and latency is kept to a minimum. Reliable and consistent near real-time subscriber updates (immediate transactional consistency) require a reliable network connection between the publisher and subscriber (make sure you have the bandwidth on your connection to handle the chatter between the publisher and the subscriber if it is a very high update frequency and/or volume).

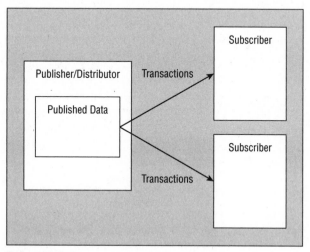

Figure 17-6

Just as with merge replication, the published articles must be initially synchronized between the publisher and the subscriber before transactional replication can take place. This is typically managed through automatic synchronization, using snapshot replication. In situations where automatic synchronization is neither practical nor efficient, manual synchronization can be used to prepare the subscriber. This is a relatively simple process:

1. Run BACKUP DATABASE to back up the Publisher database.

2. Deliver the tape backup to the subscriber system.

3. Run RESTORE DATABASE to create the database and database objects, and to load the data.

The publisher and subscriber are synchronized as of the point when the backup was run.

Transactional replication can also be used to replicate stored procedures. In its simplest implementation, changes can only be made at the publishing server. This means that you don't have to worry about conflicts.

> You can also implement transactional replication as transactional replication with immediate-updating subscribers. This means that changes can be made at the publisher or at the subscriber. Transactions occurring at the subscriber are treated as distributed transactions. Microsoft Distributed Transaction Coordinator (MS DTC) is used to ensure that both the local data and data on the publisher are updated at the same time to avoid update conflicts. Queued updating — where updates are placed in an ordered "to be done" list — can be used as a fallback in the event that there is a network connectivity issue such as a disconnection or if the network is physically offline.
>
> Another option would be to implement distributed transactions directly rather than using transactional replication. This will get you a lower latency than that provided with transactional replication, but you will still have the distribution delay in getting changes posted at the publisher out to all of the subscribers. Assuming a solid connection between the servers involved, distributed transactions could provide near immediate updates to all servers when data is changed at any server. However, depending on the connection speed and reliability between servers, this could result in performance problems, including locking conflicts.

Log Reader Agent

The *Log Reader Agent* is used in transactional replication. After a database is set up for transactional replication, the associated transaction log is monitored by the Log Reader Agent for changes to published tables. The agent then has responsibility for copying those transactions marked for replication from the publisher to the distributor as shown in Figure 17-7. The *Distribution Agent* is also used in transactional replication and is responsible for moving transactions from the distributor to the subscriber(s).

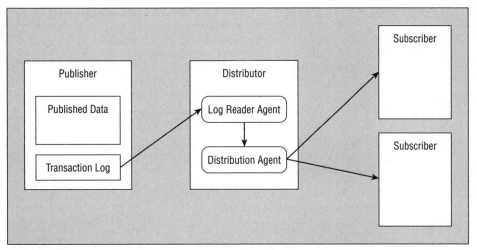

Figure 17-7

The Process of Transactional Replication

Assuming that initial synchronization has already taken place, transactional replication follows these basic steps:

1. Modifications are posted to the publisher database and recorded in the associated transaction log.

2. The Log Reader Agent reads the transaction log and identifies changes marked for replication.

3. Changes taken from the transaction log are written to the distribution database on the distributor.

4. The Distribution Agent applies the changes to the appropriate database tables.

You can set up the Log Reader Agent to read the transaction log continuously or on a schedule that you specify. As before, the Distribution Agent typically runs at the publisher for push subscriptions and at the subscriber for pull subscriptions, but this can be changed through Management Studio or RMO to run remotely.

When to Use Transactional Replication

Use transactional replication when you need or just want to reduce latency and provide subscribers with relatively up-to-date information. Near real-time updates usually require a local area network connection, but scheduled replication can often be managed through scheduled updates. If you choose to use scheduled updates, latency increases, but you gain control over when replication occurs.

Let's go back to our garden supply store and the inventory problem discussed earlier. You want each of the stores to have up-to-date, or at the very least, relatively up-to-date, inventory information. You would probably use scheduled replication to pass data to the subscribers.

Now let's see if we can make things a little more difficult. Not only do you have a chain of stores; you also have traveling salespeople who visit and take orders from your largest customers. They need to have at least relatively up-to-date inventory information but can spend their days sitting around and waiting for updates from the publisher. For systems of this type, you may want to use pull subscriptions, letting the salespeople decide when they connect to the server and download recent transactions.

You've probably noticed a potential problem in both of these scenarios. The remote servers can receive data, but they are not able to make any changes to the data. We'll cover that problem a little later. Transactional replication, when implemented in this manner, is used to support read-only copies of the data at subscriber systems.

Special Planning Requirements

Space is an important issue when planning for transactional replication. You have to make sure that you allow adequate space for the transaction log on the publisher and for the distribution database on the distributor.

Check each of the tables that you are planning to publish. For a table to be published under transactional replication, it must have a primary key. There are also potential concerns if you are supporting text or image data types in any of the tables. INSERT, UPDATE, and DELETE are supported as for any data type, but you must be sure to use an option that utilizes the transaction log when performing BLOB or bulk operations.

> You may encounter problems with the `max text repl size` parameter, which sets the maximum size of text or image data that can be replicated. Make sure that this server-level parameter is set to a high enough value to support your replication requirements.

Immediate-Update Subscribers

As indicated earlier in the chapter, you have the option of setting up subscribers to snapshot or transactional publications as immediate-update subscribers. Immediate-updating subscribers have the ability to update subscribed data, as long as the updates can be immediately reflected at the publisher. This is accomplished using the two-phase commit protocol managed by MS DTC. There is effectively no latency in updating the publisher. Updates to other subscribers are made normally (as if the change was initiated at the publisher), so latency when going to other subscribers will depend on the rate at which those subscribers are updated.

You should consider immediate-updating subscribers when you need to post changes to replicated data at one or more subscribers and propagate near-immediate updates. You might be using multiple servers to support an Online Transaction Processing (OLTP) application as a way of improving performance and providing near real-time redundancy. When a transaction is posted to any server, it will be sent to the publisher, and through the publisher, to the remaining servers.

> Much as with any form of merge replication, conflicts can arise when using immediate-updating subscribers. In order to assist with conflict identification and management, a `uniqueidentifier` column will be added to any published tables

that do not already have one (if your table has one, the column in question will have a column level property of `IsRowGUID` of true — you can only have one `RowGUID` column per table).

A high-speed, *reliable* connection is required between the publisher and any immediate-updating subscribers, such as a local area network connection, unless queued updates are used. If queued updates are configured, then the replication process can tolerate an unreliable connection and will just process any queued transactions as soon as connectivity is restored.

Keep in mind that queued updates increase the opportunities for you to have a conflict. Since the subscriber is making changes that the publisher does not know about, there is the increased prospect for the publisher to be making changes to the same rows that the subscriber is. In such a case, the conflict resolver will identify the existence of the conflict when replication occurs and resolve it according to whatever rules you have established.

Mixing Replication Types

You can mix and match replication types as needed. Indeed, not only can you have different replication types on the same server; you can even have different replication types for the same table.

As an example of why you might want to do this, imagine that a heavy equipment warehouse wants to have up-to-date inventory information and reference copies of invoices available at each of its locations. Each location has its own local SQL Server. Invoices are posted to a central location using an Internet-based application. These are replicated to all local servers through transactional replication so that inventory records are updated. You also want to have invoice and inventory information replication updated to yet another server weekly. This information on this last server is used for business analysis and running weekly reports. This server is updated weekly through a separate snapshot publication referencing the same tables used by the distributed inventory servers that were getting immediate updates.

Replication Topology

Over the years, Microsoft has outlined a number of replication topology models to describe how replication can be physically implemented. Let's look at some of these here as examples of how things are commonly implemented. It's worth noting that it is not only possible to mix and modify these models but actually rather common to do so.

Your decisions about the type of replication you need to use and your replication model topology can be made somewhat independent of each other. That said, there is a chance that restrictions imposed by your physical topology, such as transmission bandwidth, will influence your decisions.

Simple Models

Let's start with a look at the more simple models. Once you've got the basic idea, we can move on to some variations and ways these models are mixed.

Central Publisher/Distributor

This is the default SQL Server model. As shown in Figure 17-8, you have one system acting as publisher and as its own distributor. This publisher/distributor supports any number of subscribers. The publisher owns all replicated data and is the sole data source for replication. The most basic model assumes that all data is being published to the subscribers as read-only data. Read-only access can be enforced at the subscriber by giving users SELECT permission only on the replicated tables.

Since this is the easiest model to set up and manage, you should consider its use in any situation where it fits. If you have a single publisher, one or more subscribers, and read-only access to data at the subscriber, this is your best choice.

Central Publisher/Remote Distributor

You may find that the volume of replicated data and/or the amount of activity at the publisher may create the need to implement the publisher and distributor as separate systems. As shown in Figure 17-9, this is effectively, from an operational point of view, the same as the publisher/distributor model. The publisher is still the owner of — and only source for — replicated data. Once again, the simple model assumes that the data will be treated as read-only at the subscriber.

Obviously, you usually only use this model when a single publisher/distributor cannot handle both production activity and replication to subscribers.

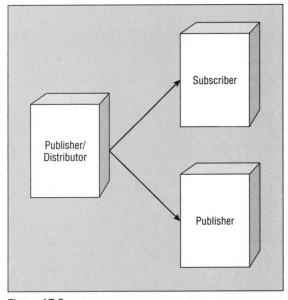

Figure 17-8

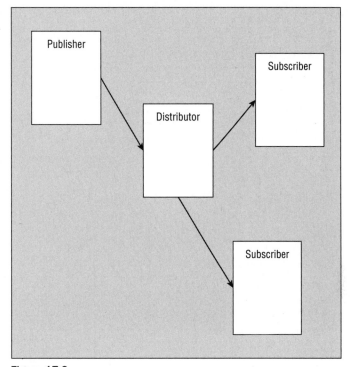

Figure 17-9

Central Subscriber

In this model, as shown in Figure 17-10, you have only one subscriber receiving data, but there are multiple publishers. The publishers can be configured as publisher/distributor systems. This model provides a way to keep just local data at the local server but still have a way of consolidating the data at one central location. Horizontal filtering may be necessary to keep publishers from overwriting each other's data at the subscriber.

This is the model to use when you have data consolidation requirements such as gathering distributed data up for use in a data warehouse.

Mixed Models

Now let's look at a few variations based on the idea that we will frequently want to mix and match the basic models. Consider these as just a taste of the possibilities — something of ''just the beginning.'' The possibilities are almost endless.

Publishing Subscriber

> Publishing subscribers (that is subscribers that are also configured as publishers) can be added to any of the basic models. This model has two publishers publishing

the same data. The original publisher replicates data to its subscribers, one of which is a publishing subscriber. The publishing subscriber can then pass the same data along to its subscribers.

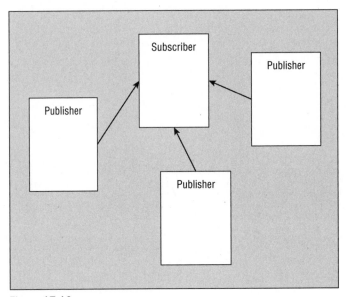

Figure 17-10

This model, shown in Figure 17-11, is useful when you have pockets of servers or when you have an especially slow or expensive link between servers. Another possibility is that you don't have a direct link between the initial publisher and all of the potential subscribers. The publisher only needs to pass data to one system on the far side of the link, and the publisher subscriber can then pass the data along to the other subscribers.

Publisher/Subscriber

This is another case where you have SQL Servers acting as both publishers and subscribers (Figure 17-12). Each server has its own set of data for which it is responsible. This model can be used when you have data changes taking place at both locations and you want to keep both servers updated. This is different from publishing subscribers in that each server is generating its own data, not just passing along updates received from another server.

Multiple Subscribers/Multiple Publishers

Figure 17-13 shows one of the more complicated scenarios. Under this scenario, you have multiple publishers and multiple subscribers. Systems may or may not act as a publisher/subscriber or publishing subscriber. This model requires very careful planning to provide optimum communications and to ensure data consistency.

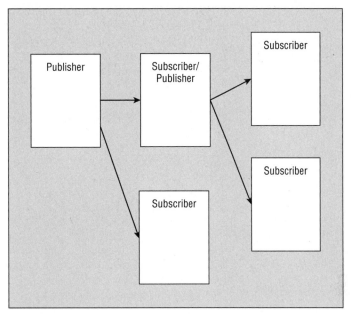

Figure 17-11

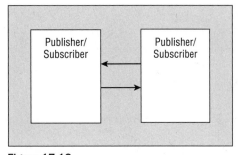

Figure 17-12

Self-Publishing

It is worth specifically calling out that you can have a server subscribe to its own published articles. This is actually fairly common in small installations, where there is a diverse need, but not necessarily enough load to justify more than one physical server. For example, you may want to segregate the data used for online transaction processing from the data used for decision making. You can use replication to make separate read-only copies of your data (updated on any schedule you consider appropriate) to be used as a reference.

Whether to locate your other databases — such as a data warehouse — on the same physical server as your core system is a matter of taste and your particular scenario. An example of where this can be very valid is the scenario where you have relatively low transactional volume but complex analysis needs. In my experience, companies that have enough need for a separate data warehouse usually have a physical or operational need for that to be on a separate server, but that is far from an "always" scenario. Consider your particular situation: does your server have room to share the load? Can you risk both databases being offline at the same time in the event of a catastrophe?

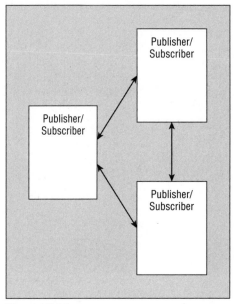

Figure 17-13

Planning for Replication

Replication is one of those things where it can be easy to "just toss something together." It's also one of those things where it is easy to create a huge mess if you take such a cavalier approach. Keep in mind that SQL Server may automatically make some alterations to your schema to implement replication — do you really want SQL Server adding columns and objects to your database without fully thinking about that first? Of course not.

Any replication installation worth doing is worth taking the time to plan out. Some planning considerations include:

❑ What data is to be replicated

❑ Replication type

❑ Replication model

Along with these are other factors that will influence your decision, such as current network topologies, current server configurations, server growth potential, activity levels, and so forth. Each replication method has its advantages and disadvantages, and there is not a one-size-fits-all approach to replicating data. For instance, if you have a slow network or unreliable connection, then you may not want to implement transactional replication. Instead, you may opt to use merge replication that runs during a scheduled connection time. As has been pointed out repeatedly in this chapter, however, you also need to balance that against consistency needs.

Data Concerns

First, you have to consider what you are going to publish and to whom. You need to identify your articles (tables and specific columns to be published) and how you plan to organize them into publications. In addition, there are some other data issues of which you need to be aware. Some of these have already been mentioned, but it's worth our time to review them here.

timestamp

Include a `timestamp` column for transaction publications. That gives you a way of detecting conflicts on updates. By having a `timestamp` column already in place, you've already met part of the requirements for adding immediate-updating subscribers.

uniqueidentifier

A unique index and globally unique identifier is required for merge replication. Remember, if a published table doesn't have a `uniqueidentifier` column, a globally unique identifier column will be added.

User-Defined Data Types

User-defined data types are not supported unless they exist on the subscriber destination database. Alternatively, you can have user-defined data types converted to base data types during synchronization.

NOT FOR REPLICATION

The `NOT FOR REPLICATION` clause lets you disable table actions on subscribers. You can disable:

❑   The `IDENTITY` property
❑   `CHECK` constraints
❑   Triggers

These actions are essentially ignored when and only when the replication process changes data on the subscriber. Any other processes would still use them normally. So, for example, an insert into the original receiving database would have an identity value assigned, but as the row was subsequently published (in the form of an `INSERT`) to subscribers, the existing identity value would be used rather than generating a new value.

Mobile Devices

SQL Server also comes in a "Mobile" version. This is an extremely small footprint version of SQL Server designed to run on Windows Mobile Edition. The Mobile edition supports replication from a subscriber point of view. Snapshot and merge replication are supported — transactional replication is not.

Many of the considerations for mobile devices are just variants of the same theme that we've seen already in replication — bandwidth and space, for example. Just keep in mind that the constraints for mobile devices may be much more extreme than with a full server class system (or even your salesmen's laptops for that matter).

Setting Up Replication in Management Studio

Setting up replication takes a few steps. In particular, you need to:

❑   Configure your publication and distribution server(s) to be ready to perform those tasks

❑   Configure your actual publications

❑   Configure subscribers

Let's take a look at how to do each of these within the Management Studio.

Configuring the Server for Replication

Before you can set up any publication or distribution on your server, your server must be configured for replication.

To get at this in Management Studio, navigate to the Replication node, right-click, and select Configure Distribution.

> **Note that, in order to configure replication, you must have connected to the Object Explorer using the actual name of the server (local, a period (.), localhost, or an ip address are not supported). If you connected using anything other than the server's DNS name, you'll get an error and be required to reconnect.**

SQL Server greets you with the standard splash screen that we've seen in other wizards, and then moves on to an intro dialog — in this case, it points out some of the options you will have as you go through this wizard. Click Next, and you are moved on to a dialog (shown in Figure 17-14) that decides if this publisher is to serve as its own distributor or if it should utilize an existing distributor.

If we select the option to use a different server as the distributor and choose Add, then we would get a standard connection dialog box (asking for login security information for the distribution server). For our example run, keep the default option (that this box will act as its own distributor) and click Next.

> **Note that which dialog comes after the Distributor dialog will change depending on whether or not you have the SQL Server Agent configured to start automatically on system startup.**

If you do not have the SQL Server Agent configured to start automatically (although you almost certainly want it to be on a production server), SQL Server will pop up a dialog, shown in Figure 17-15, to ask you about this. (It will skip this next dialog if your agent is already configured to start automatically when you start your system.)

Feel free to leave your system configured however you already have it (SQL Server will, however, default this dialog to changing your SQL Server Agent service to start automatically), but keep in mind that the agent will need to be running for some forms of replication to work.

Figure 17-14

Figure 17-15

Click Next. We move on to configuring a snapshot folder as shown in Figure 17-16. This will default to a directory in your main SQL Server folder, which for many installations may not be large enough to hold snapshots of large databases. This can be configured as a local volume or as a UNC path. Since I'm not going to assume you have a full server farm to try this stuff out on, we're going to take a "one server does everything" approach for this example, so accepting the default should be fine.

Figure 17-16

From there, it's on to configuring the actual distribution database. SQL Server gives a dialog to get some typical database creation information (what do you want to call it and where to store it), as shown in Figure 17-17.

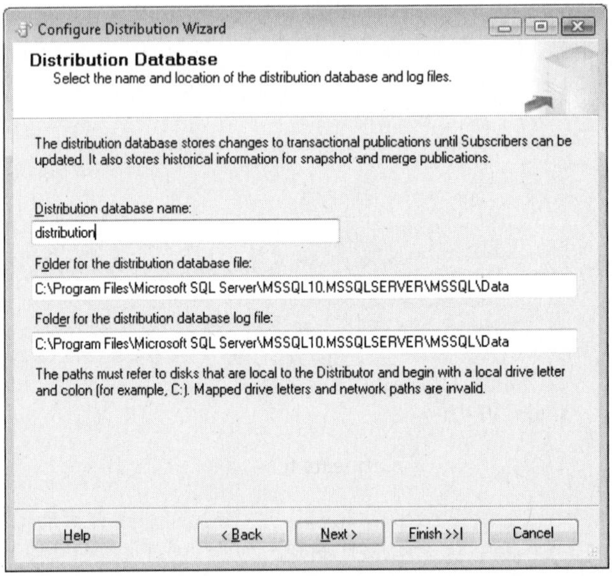

Figure 17-17

Figure 17-18

Figure 17-19

From here, we move on to what, at first, appears to be a rather boring dialog (shown in Figure 17-18) with seemingly nothing new.

Looks can, however, be deceiving. If we click on the little ellipsis (. . .) on the right, we get yet another dialog (shown in Figure 17-19) — one that does have a key item of note.

Figure 17-20

As Figure 17-19 shows, we have the ability to specifically set the connection mode we're going to use when connecting the agent to the publisher. In most cases, the default of impersonating the Agent process will be fine, but keep in mind that we can use specific SQL Server security credentials if need be.

Cancel out of this properties dialog, and click Next back in the publishers dialog (the one in Figure 17-18). Figure 17-20 shows the confirmation dialog, with what we want to do, at the end of the wizard. Note how it provides not only the option of immediately configuring the distribution, but also the concept of scripting the configuration for later or potentially remote use.

Go ahead and click Finish (the next dialog is just a summary, so there is no need to dwell there). SQL Server begins processing the configuration request. When the process is complete, go ahead and close the dialog.

And, just that quick, you have a server configured for publication and distribution of replicated data. Obviously, were this a production environment, we might have some other choices to make in terms of specific locations or even whether we wanted the publisher and distributor to be on the same system, but the basic foundations of what we are doing remains the same regardless.

If you wonder about the distribution database, you should now be able to find it under the "System Databases" subfolder of the Databases folder.

Configuring a Publication

With our server all nice and configured, we're ready to get down to creating an actual publication.

To do this, navigate to the Replication node in Management Studio, right-click the Local Publications sub-node, and choose New Publication.

Figure 17-21

After the usual intro dialog, we come to the Publication Database dialog shown in Figure 17-21. This allows us to choose what database we want to utilize for our publication. As you can see, I've selected our old friend, AdventureWorks2008.

Click Next, and you're ready to move on to the Publication Type dialog shown in Figure 17-22.

This allows us to select between the replication types that we looked at earlier in the chapter. I've chosen Transactional publication with updatable subscriptions.

Click Next, and you move on to the Articles dialog.

In Figure 17-23, I've expanded the Tables node and selected the `Person.Person` table. I'm taking most of that table, but I'm going to skip the `AdditionalContactInfo` and `Demographics` columns since they are schema-bound XML columns, and SQL Server does not allow for the replication of XML columns that are bound to an XML schema collection. I also could have taken other schema objects such as stored procedures (I'm sticking to just the one object for simplicity's sake).

Click Next to be taken to the Article Issues dialog, as shown in Figure 17-24.

Notice that SQL Server detected several issues it wants to let us know about. This is one where I say ''kudos to the SQL Server team'' for attempting to let a user know about some fundamental things *before* they become a problem.

Click Next to move on to the Filter Table Rows dialog shown in Figure 17-25.

This one allows us to do horizontal partitioning — essentially just applying a WHERE clause so that only rows that meet a specific condition will go across in our publication.

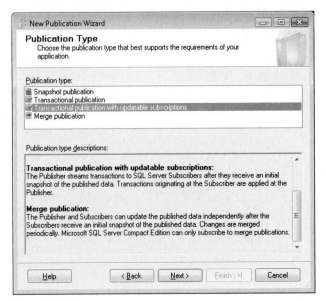

Figure 17-22

Figure 17-23

Figure 17-24

Figure 17-25

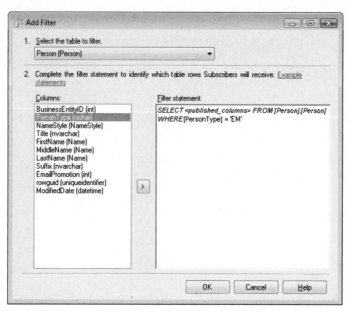

Figure 17-26

Click Add to get the dialog shown in Figure 17-26.

In our example here, we've restricted the rows being replicated to those where the persons in question have been flagged as employees (EmployeeType = 'EM').

Click OK to return to the Filter Table Rows dialog, and then click Next to move on to the Snapshot Agent dialog shown in Figure 17-27.

> **Remember that any subscription, regardless of whether it is to a snapshot, merge, or transactional replication model, must start by synchronizing based on a snapshot. Subsequent changes are begun relative to that snapshot.**

I've configured mine to run the snapshot immediately, but I could have just as easily scheduled it to be generated at a later time (remember that snapshots place share locks on every table the snapshot utilizes — do not run them at a time where such lock issues are going to block writes to your database that you need done in a timely fashion). If, for example, you are getting frequent new subscribers, you may want to schedule a periodic update to the snapshot to give them a more up-to-date time to synchronize to.

Click Next, and you're ready to define the Agent Security, as shown in Figure 17-28.

I've used the Security Settings dialogs to set the agents to use the SQL Server Agent account. This is not, however, good practice in a production environment for security reasons. Give the agents their own account to impersonate to both limit agent access and increase your ability to audit.

Figure 17-27

Figure 17-28

Figure 17-29

Click Next, and you'll find an Action dialog (just like the one back in Figure 17-20) where you can indicate whether you want the publication created immediately or scheduled for later execution.

One more click of the Next button, and you're ready for a summary and to define a publication name as shown in Figure 17-29 (I've chosen Employees).

Go ahead and click Finish to create your publication, and, just like that, you're ready to have subscribers!

Setting Up Subscribers (via Management Studio)

Setting up subscribers utilizes the same basic notions we've already leveraged with publications. Before we get started with an example, however, let's set up a dummy database to play the part of our subscriber:

```
CREATE DATABASE AWSubscriber;
```

And, with that created, we're ready to subscribe to some data.

Start by right-clicking the Local Subscriptions sub-node below the Replication node in Management Studio, and selecting New Subscription. After the usual intro dialog, we move on to identifying our publication, as shown in Figure 17-30. Since we have only one publication, there really isn't a lot to choose from, but the list could have easily been many, many publications.

Click Next to move on to the Agent location, as shown in Figure 17-31. Remember that we can run our replication agent on either the subscriber or the distributor. In our case, it doesn't matter much since these are the same box, but you may make different choices depending on server loading issues.

Figure 17-30

Figure 17-31

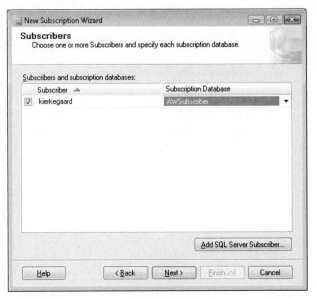

Figure 17-32

Click Next to move on to the Subscribers dialog shown in Figure 17-32. I've already chosen our AWSubscriber database, but notice how we could choose Add SQL Server Subscriber and configure multiple subscribers at one time.

From there it's on to the Distribution Agent Security dialog. Here we define what security context we want to run under for both the distributor and subscriber (in this case, it's the same system, but it could have easily been remote). In Figure 17-33 I've chosen to impersonate the SQL Server Agent security context, but, again, on a production server you would generally want a more specific security context for your replication agent for security reasons.

We can move quickly through the remaining dialogs by setting the agent to "Run continuously" and leaving the default "Commit at publisher" setting of "Simultaneously commit changes." That takes us to the Login For Updatable Subscriptions dialog shown in Figure 17-34.

Since this is all (distribution and subscription) happening on the same server, a linked server is implied (a server is always available to itself as a linked server). Were we using a remote distributor, we could have either used a regular SQL Server login or again went with a linked server (though, in the latter case, we would need to configure the linked server separately).

> *A linked server is another SQL Server or ODBC data source that has had an alias established for it on your server. When you refer to a linked server by name, you are essentially grabbing a reference to connection information to that linked server.*

Figure 17-35 allows us to choose when to initialize our subscription (I've stayed with the default of immediately). The initialization involves pulling down the snapshot from the distributor and applying it. Subsequent synchronizations will be done using the snapshot as a baseline to apply changes to.

Figure 17-33

Figure 17-34

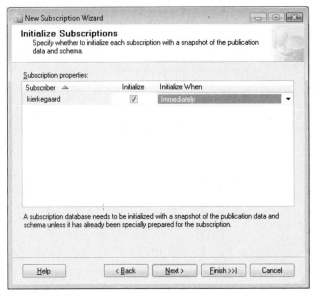

Figure 17-35

Click Next to get the same finishing dialogs that we've seen in prior examples (when to run things and a summary page), and then click Finish.

Using Our Replicated Database

Once the replicated database is in place, the problem largely becomes one of administration. If things are running smoothly, there is very little to see. Users can access our AWSubscriber database and the `Person.Person` table within it. Since we configured for updating subscribers, changes made to the `AWSubscriber` version of the `Person.Person` table will be immediately reflected in the source AdventureWorks2008 database. Likewise, changes made to our AdventureWorks2008 database will be reflected in our subscriber database.

You can start by taking a look in the `AWSubscriber` table list, a quick look at the list of tables in the database (using Management Studio, `sp_help`, or `sys.tables`) — you should find the `Person.Person` table that we replicated. Then go ahead and take a look in our AdventureWorks2008 database. You should find a table called `Person.conflict_Employees_Person`. This new table is for conflict tracking — it should receive data only in the event that changes we make in our subscriber run into a conflict with those on the publisher.

> In the event of a conflict, the default publishing agent chooses the publisher's data over the client's. You can change this to prefer things based on such things as which is the most recent change and other ready-made criteria. You can also write custom resolution algorithms to encompass any unusual rules you may have for resolving conflicts.

Now let's test out our transaction-based replication by making a change to our data. We'll start by taking a look at the starting value of the row we're going to change:

```
SELECT aw.FirstName AS PubFirst,
    aw.LastName AS PubLast,
    aws.FirstName AS SubFirst,
    aws.LastName AS SubLast
FROM AdventureWorks2008.Person.Person aw
JOIN AWSubscriber.Person.Person aws
    ON aw.BusinessEntityID = aws. BusinessEntityID
WHERE aw. BusinessEntityID = 38;
```

What I've done here is join across the databases so that we can see both the publisher and subscriber at the same time. This way, we can, in one query, compare the source and the destination. The first time we run this script (before we make any changes), we can see our starting values, and that they are indeed the same:

```
PubFirst    PubLast       SubFirst    SubLast
----------  ----------    ----------  -----------
Kim         Abercrombie   Kim         Abercrombie

(1 row(s) affected)
```

Okay, now let's make a change. We'll say that Kim has gotten married and decided to change her name to Abercrombie-Smith.

```
USE AdventureWorks2008;

UPDATE Person.Person
SET LastName = 'Abercrombie-Smith'
WHERE BusinessEntityID = 38;
```

Now, we run our original SELECT statement again to check the results:

```
PubFirst         PubLast           SubFirst          SubLast
---------------  ---------------   ---------------   ---------------
Kim              Abercrombie-Smith Kim               Abercrombie-Smith

(1 row(s) affected)
```

As you can see, both the publisher and subscriber received the update.

Now, let's change the script just slightly to run inside the subscriber database, and see what happens on the publisher's side. This time, we'll change Kim's name back (perhaps she changed her mind ...):

```
USE AWSubscriber;


UPDATE Person.Person
SET LastName = 'Abercrombie'

WHERE BusinessEntityID = 38;
```

And now we're ready to run our original select statement one more time:

```
PubFirst        PubLast          SubFirst        SubLast
--------------  ----------------  --------------  --------------------
Kim             Abercrombie       Kim             Abercrombie

(1 row(s) affected)
```

Again, our change was seen in both databases.

> **The change was seen going both directions and was replicated immediately because we had selected transactional replication with immediately updating subscribers. Other replication choices would have introduced latency in the change, or potentially not replicated the change at all without some form of manual intervention. Be sure to review all of the replication types (discussed earlier in the chapter) to understand the behavior of each.**

Replication Management Objects (RMO)

Replication Management Objects, or RMO, is a .NET object model that was first seen in SQL Server 2005 and replaced the replication portion of the COM-based Distributed Management Objects (DMO) object model that was used in SQL Server 2000 and earlier. You can think of RMO as being something of a companion to SQL Management Objects (SMO), which we discuss extensively in Chapter 23.

RMO gives you programmatic access to any portion of your replication creation and configuration using any .NET language. Examples of RMO use would be automating operations such as:

❑ **Creating and configuring a publication**: You can make use of the ReplicationDatabase as well as the TransPublication or MergePublication objects to define publications.

❑ **Adding and removing articles**: The TransArticle object supports the addition and removal of articles within your publication. In addition, you can add column filters or add a FilterClause property to limit what rows are replicated.

❑ Republishing your snapshot.

These are just some more everyday use kinds of examples. RMO is, however, capable of creating, modifying, or deleting any part of the replication process.

RMO can be utilized in Visual Studio by adding a reference to the *Microsoft.SqlServer.Replication .NET Programming Interface* library. You then point your include, imports, or using directives to Microsoft.SqlServer.RMO. As with any of the management libraries that support SQL Server, you will also need to have a reference to the Microsoft.SqlServer.ConnectionInfo library.

An example application that utilizes RMO to create the same publication we created earlier in the chapter using the GUI can be downloaded from the Wrox Web site (wrox.com) or professionalsql.com.

Summary

As much as there was to take in this chapter, this really was something of an introduction to replication. We covered a lot of the considerations for architects reasonably well, but the scope of replication is such that entire books are written on just that topic. Indeed, there is much to consider in order to build just the right model for complex scenarios. The good news is that, if you really grasped this chapter, then you are prepared for perhaps 90 percent of what you are likely to ever face. Time and the proverbial "school of hard knocks" will teach you the rest.

If you've taken anything from this chapter, I hope that it's an understanding of some of the general problems that replication can solve and how replication works best when you plan ahead both in terms of topology planning and in your application's general architecture (making sure it understands the special needs of replication).

In our next chapter, we'll take a look at yet another "extension" area for SQL Server — full-text indexing.

18

Looking at Things in Full: Full-Text Search

Full-Text Search is an area of significant architectural change in SQL Server 2008. While the core use and functionality hasn't changed all that much, the full-text features are far more integrated into the core of SQL Server as of this release. If you feel you are already familiar with full-text and are ready to skip this chapter, I would encourage you to at least browse the architectural changes and consider their ramifications on things like backup and recovery as well as expanded query result support.

Using plain old T-SQL (without full-text functionality), our options for querying text information are somewhat limited. Indeed, we have only a couple of options:

❑　Use a LIKE clause. This is generally woefully inefficient, and is not able to utilize any kind of index structure unless your search pattern starts with an explicit value. If the search starts with a wildcard (say "%" or "_"), then SQL Server wouldn't know which spot in the index to begin with — any indexes become worthless.

❑　Use some other form of pattern matching, such as PATINDEX or CHARINDEX. These are generally even more inefficient, but can allow us to do things that LIKE will not.

With Full-Text Search, however, we gain the ability to index the contents of the text — essentially keeping a word list that lets us know what words we can find and in what rows. In addition, we are not limited to just pattern-matching algorithms. We can search for the inflected forms of words. For example, we might use the word *university* but have SQL Server still find the word *universities*, or, even better, SQL Server can find a word like *drunk* when the word we asked for was *drink*. It's up to us to decide how precise we want to be, but even if the word we are searching for is located deep in the middle of a large text block, SQL Server can quickly find the rows that contain the word in question.

Full-Text Search, or FTS, supports any document type that has a filter registered on the system that supports the iFilter interface. This means that you can store things like Word, Excel,

Acrobat, and other supported files in an image data type, but still perform full-text searches against that data! Indeed, you could even write your own extensions to support other document types if necessary.

> *Personally, I find this later point to be extremely cool. Implementation of the* iFilter *interface allows you to separate what is text information versus what is formatting information, so you could, for example, write a custom* iFilter *that knows how to string XML tags out of an XML file to allow full-text searching for a custom XML document type.*

In this chapter, we'll take a look at these Full-Text Search features and more.

Among the sections we'll look at are:

❑   Full-Text Search architecture

❑   Setting up full-text indexes and catalogs

❑   Full-text query syntax

❑   Full-text quirks

❑   Noise words

In addition, we'll see how there are now two ways of completing most full-text-related operations. By the time we're done, you should be prepared for the hassles that FTS creates for you, but you should also be ready to utilize what can be some wonderful functionality in return.

Full-Text Search Architecture

The architecture of FTS got a major overhaul with this release. While some of the fundamental concepts (such as word-breakers, filters, catalogs, and indexes) still apply, the way these items are utilized has changed somewhat. A map of the new (and rather complex) architecture is shown in Figure 18-1.

In prior versions of SQL Server, the core of Full-Text Search wasn't really part of SQL Server at all. It was a shared technology item that originally came from Microsoft Index Server. You would see the separate process installed with SQL Server under the service name of MSFTESQL. With SQL Server 2008, Full-Text is now a fundamental part of the main SQL Server process. The full-text engine is excellent at examining raw text data and aggregating word lists. It maintains an association between the individual words and phrases and the places that the FTS has encountered them.

> **Full-Text is now part of the core SQL Server process. Individual filters are, however, instantiated in their own process for security reasons.**

To perform full-text queries against any SQL Server table, you must build a full-text index for that table. The construction and maintenance of this full-text index — or the population of the index — is done through a process of SQL Server instantiating an instance of a filter daemon, which is passed a text stream, the words in the stream are cataloged, and an association is made between the catalog entry and the row the word was sourced from.

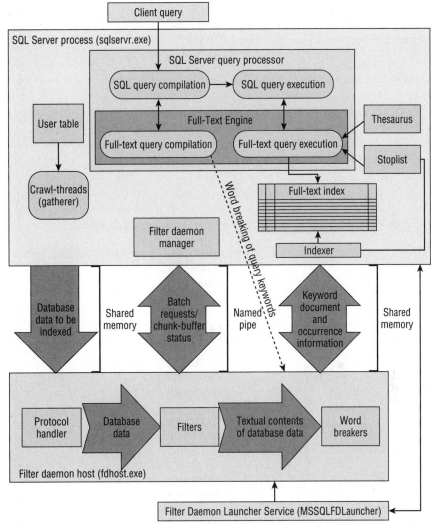

Figure 18-1

By default, tables have no full-text functionality at all. The fact that there is a table and that it has text data types is no guarantee that there is a full-text index on the table. If you want it, you need to create it. Even after you create the full-text index, the index will have nothing in it. To make the index fully functional, you need to *populate* the index.

The population process looks over the columns specified by the index and builds the word list that is going to be used. Much like standard indexes in SQL Server, only the columns you specify to include in the index will become part of the index. Unlike normal indexes in SQL Server, however, you are allowed only one full-text index per table — so every column you want to have participate in full-text queries needs to be part of the index.

The differences don't stop there though. Actually there are several. The major differences include:

❑ **Internal structure**: Typical SQL Server indexes are stored as a balanced tree structure. Full-text indexes, however, utilize a token-based structure that is inverted (essentially storing things backwards) and compressed.

❑ **Method of creation**: SQL Server indexes are created using the CREATE INDEX command in T-SQL, SQL Management Objects (SMO), or Windows Management Instrumentation (you can use the Management Studio, but it just uses SMO). Full-text indexes are created either through the use of special system stored procedures or through the use of the CREATE FULLTEXT INDEX command.

❑ **Method of update**: SQL Server indexes are automatically updated in the normal course of changes to the underlying SQL Server data. Full-text indexes can either be populated on demand or through a "change tracking" mechanism with an on-demand cleanup.

So that's the quick lesson in Full-Text Architecture 101. As we move through the rest of the chapter, the impact of the differences should become apparent versus the more "normal" way things are implemented in SQL Server.

Setting Up Full-Text Indexes and Catalogs

As we saw in the last section, each table in a SQL Server database can have zero or one full-text indexes. For SQL Server 2008, these full-text indexes are stored in with the rest of the database (you can, if you wish, specific a specific filegroup if you want the full-text items to be on separate storage). A catalog can store multiple full-text indexes. The indexes must be from the same database; you may, however, want to store indexes from one database in multiple catalogs, so you can manage the population of those indexes on separate schedules or store them in separate filegroups.

Enabling Full-Text for Your Database

Prior to SQL Server 2008, there was the concept of Full-Text being "enabled" for a database. In SQL Server 2008, all databases are always full-text enabled.

Creating, Altering, Dropping, and Manipulating a Full-Text Catalog

The CREATE syntax for Full-Text looks much like other CREATE syntaxes, but with a few additional twists:

```
CREATE FULLTEXT CATALOG <catalog name>
    [ON FILEGROUP <filegroup> ]
```

```
[IN PATH <'root path'>]
[WITH ACCENT_SENSITIVITY = {ON|OFF}]
[AS DEFAULT]
[AUTHORIZATION <owner name> ]
```

Most of this should be fairly self-explanatory, but let's take a look anyway:

ON FILEGROUP	This is here for backward compatibility with SQL Server 2005 only (the CREATE FULLTEXT CATALOG command didn't exist in SQL Server 2000). It has no effect under SQL Server 2008.
IN PATH	Again, this is a backward compatibility only thing. In prior releases, the actual full-text catalogs were not created inside the database but rather as a separate file on disk. This option told SQL Server what path you wanted that file created in. In SQL Server 2008, this option has no effect.
WITH ACCENT_ SENSITIVITY	Pretty much what it sounds like. This determines whether searches will take into account accents or not (for example, is "e" the same as "é"). Keep in mind that, if you change this setting after the catalog is created, the entire catalog will need to be repopulated. The full-text catalog will use whatever accent sensitivity the database is set to.
AS DEFAULT	Another one that is what it sounds like; this one sets the full-text catalog you're creating to be the default catalog for any new full-text indexes you create.
AUTHORIZATION	Mildly more complex. As you might imagine, this one is about security and rights. It changes the ownership of the full-text catalog to be the user or role specified instead of the default (which would be the user that actually creates the catalog). This one has gotten muddled quite a bit by SQL Server's change from ownership to schemas. Ownership has largely morphed into schemas, but the nature of this particular setting more closely fits with the older ownership notion. The key thing to realize here is that a role can be the owner of a full-text catalog — not just a user. If you're changing the ownership to a specific role, then the user creating the full-text catalog must be a member of that role at the time that he or she creates the catalog.

So, let's create a full-text catalog for AdventureWorks2008. We'll simply call it:

```
USE AdventureWorks2008;

CREATE FULLTEXT CATALOG MainCatalog;
```

This is another one of those commands you issue where you don't get much feedback. As long as you don't see an error, the catalog should be created just fine.

And just that quick we have a full-text catalog available for AdventureWorks2008. I did not specify this full-text catalog as the default, so any full-text indexes that want to make use of this catalog will need to explicitly state this catalog as their destination.

Altering Full-Text Catalogs

Altering full-text catalogs works pretty much the same as creating them, save for the fact that you are really limited in what can be altered. The syntax is:

```
ALTER FULLTEXT CATALOG <catalog name>
  { REBUILD [WITH ACCENT_SENSITIVITY = {ON|OFF} ]
      | REORGANIZE
      | AS DEFAULT
  }
```

There are three top-level options you can set with this ALTER. Let's take a look at them.

REBUILD

Does what it says it does — completely rebuilds the full-text catalog in question. By default, it will be created with exactly the same settings the catalog had before (Owner and whether it is the default or not).

Keep in mind that your full-text catalog, and every index that catalog contains, will be offline while the rebuild is in progress.

In addition to the simple rebuild that you would typically do just to compact the file (for deleted rows and such), you can also rebuild to change the accent sensitivity. If you want to reset the accent sensitivity, just specify whether you want it on or off as you issue the REBUILD command.

Any rebuild implies that all indexes in the catalog will be repopulated.

REORGANIZE

This is similar to REBUILD, but with some pros and cons.

REORGANIZE cleans up your catalog for you, but in an online fashion. The result is like most situations where you rearrange things instead of moving things all the way out and starting over. It looks pretty good, but perhaps not as good as if you had started from scratch.

You can think of REORGANIZE as being like a defragmentation process. It merges what may well be several different index structures internal to the catalog. (For performance reasons at the time the full-text was analyzed, some items may have been kept in their own substructure in the index rather than merged into the master index for the catalog.) This command attempts to rectify that. Unlike REBUILD, REORGANIZE *does* also reorganize the internal structures for your full-text catalog (the ones that store metadata).

AS DEFAULT

This works just like it did under CREATE. It establishes this particular catalog as being the default full-text catalog for new full-text indexes you create for this database.

Dropping Full-Text Catalogs

I know you can see this one coming — after all, it's that same core DROP syntax we've been using all along:

```
DROP FULLTEXT CATALOG <catalog name>
```

And, of course, it's gone.

Creating, Altering, Dropping, and Manipulating Full-Text Indexes

Okay, so what we had with a full-text catalog was largely just a container. A full-text catalog, by itself, is nothing at all — think of it like a gas can with no gas in it. What we need are the actual full-text indexes. Whereas a full-text catalog is the place to store full-text indexes, the indexes themselves are what provide the actual reference information that allows your full-text queries to operate quickly and efficiently.

Creating Full-Text Indexes

When you go to create a full-text index, the core items of the command are not all that different from regular indexes; however, much as regular indexes have properties such as whether they are clustered or non-clustered, full-text indexes also have their own properties.

The syntax for creating a full-text index looks like this:

```
CREATE FULLTEXT INDEX ON <table name>
     [( <column name> [TYPE COLUMN <type column name> ]
          [LANGUAGE <language term>] [,...n])]
     KEY INDEX <index name>
          [ON <fulltext catalog name> ]
     [WITH
          { CHANGE_TRACKING [=]{ MANUAL | AUTO | OFF }
          [, NO POPULATION] }
     ]  | [STOPLIST [=] {OFF | SYSTEM | <stop list name>}
```

Note that what is optional is a bit atypical here. Most of the time, required items are listed first, but the quirks of this syntax give us an optional parameter (a column list) before a required parameter (the key index). Let's start with a quick example and then take a look at the parts:

```
CREATE FULLTEXT INDEX ON Production.ProductModel
   ( Name LANGUAGE English)
   KEY INDEX PK_ProductModel_ProductModelID
     ON MainCatalog
   WITH CHANGE_TRACKING OFF, NO POPULATION;
```

So, what we've created here is a full-text index for the Production.ProductModel table. We've explicitly stated that the language used in that column is U.S. English. If we had wanted, we could have added a comma followed by another column name and potentially a TYPE COLUMN or another LANGUAGE identifier. After the language, we specifically stated what full-text catalog we wanted this index stored in as well as that we wanted change tracking turned off and no initial population of the index.

That's a lot to think about, so let's take a look at those parts a bit closer.

> Notice that I did not supply a name for my full-text index. There can only be one full-text index for any given table, so there is no need to name it. (It is essentially identified by the table it's built on.) Be sure what you define includes *all* the columns you want to perform full-text searches on.

Column List

This is probably the trickiest part of the whole thing. Even though it says "column name" in the preceding syntax, you're really working on a column *list*. The issue is that for each column you list you need to include everything about that column before you move on to the next column. That is, you need to include the TYPE COLUMN and LANGUAGE parameters (if you're going to) *before* you name the next column.

So, for example, if we had also wanted to include the catalog description, we could have done that, too, by adding it at the end of the first column definition:

```
CREATE FULLTEXT INDEX ON Production.ProductModel

( Name LANGUAGE English,
  CatalogDescription)

KEY INDEX PK_ProductModel_ProductModelID
  ON MainCatalog
WITH CHANGE_TRACKING OFF, NO POPULATION;
```

This example is purely for reference. It will not run since we already created a full-text index on the Production.ProductModel *table.*

LANGUAGE

This specifies what language the column we've just identified is in. This is important for determination of noise words (words that occur frequently but add little to your search — we'll see more about these later in this chapter), as well as things like collation. Any language that SQL Server has localization support for (33 localizations as of this writing) is valid. To get a list of the aliases you would use, you can query the sys.syslanguages metadata view in the master database:

```
SELECT name, alias FROM master.sys.syslanguages;
```

TYPE COLUMN

This option is for use when you want to do full-text indexing against documents stored in an image or a varbinary column. AdventureWorks2008 has a full-text index established that makes use of this. (It is on the Production.Documents table.) We'll check it out a bit later in the chapter. For now though, imagine that you're doing document management using SQL Server (not at all an uncommon use for SQL Server). If you are storing documents written in a mix of one or more applications, such as Microsoft Word (.doc), Acrobat (.PDF), Excel (.XLS), or a text editor (.TXT), then Full-Text Search will need to know what kind of document is stored for each row it analyzes, so it knows what analysis plug-in to use.

In this case, you need to add another column to your table (in addition to the image or varbinary column) that contains the extension (.DOC, .PDF, and so on) of the document stored in the binary column. This column becomes the parameter value for the TYPE COLUMN property in the CREATE FULLTEXT INDEX command.

KEY INDEX

Unlike all the other options in the CREATE FULLTEXT INDEX command, this one is required.

Any table that Full-Text is indexing *must* have a column that uniquely identifies each row. This can be a primary key or a unique constraint. The thing to remember on this point is that you are supplying the name of the *index* associated with the unique identifier, *not* the column or constraint name. Since this is used repeatedly to associate data in the full-text index, I would suggest you use the smallest primary key or unique index available.

ON

This is simply the name of the full-text catalog you want this index stored in. This is optional if your database has a default full-text catalog, and required if no default catalog has been established.

WITH

This supplies instructions regarding how your index is populated with data and how it copes with changes to the table that the index is built over.

CHANGE_TRACKING

Change tracking is all about how your full-text index deals with changes to the underlying table.

The dilemma here is how you want to balance the accuracy of your full-text searches versus the amount of overhead you incur by keeping a higher overhead system (as compares to maintaining standard B-Tree indexes) up to date.

Change tracking gives us three levels of support for changes:

OFF	The full-text index is updated only when you perform a full population of the index. Essentially, you need to rebuild from scratch each time you populate. This means there is no ongoing maintenance overhead, but it also means that there may be rows in the table that will not be returned in your full-text queries or, perhaps worse, that rows may come back as containing the word you are interested in when, due to changes, they no longer do. This option is great when your data is slow moving (doesn't change often) and/or you don't require perfect accuracy in your results. In return for giving up that accuracy, it means you have no ongoing overhead and that your indexes are always as compact as they can be because they have no issues with fragmentation. It does mean, however, that when you do repopulate, you have a period of downtime and the overall process takes longer.
AUTO	Under this model, SQL Server is constantly updating the index for things happening in the table. While there still may be a lag between when the change is made and when it is reflected in full text, that lag is minimal and you are getting something approximating real-time updates. This is the way to go when you have fast-moving data or your need for accuracy is very high. You are enduring a high degree of overhead since SQL Server will use smaller, intermediate structures to keep track of the changes. These can become inefficient over time and may hurt search performance but are not that big of a deal in the short run. If you use this option, consider still performing a reorganization or full repopulation regularly.

Continued

MANUAL	This is something of a middle ground. It does tracking to be able to identify changes but does not update the full-text index until explicitly told to do so. You can then manually perform updates that apply the changes to the existing index without a full repopulation.

NO POPULATION

This applies only if you have chosen OFF for change tracking.

By default, when you create a full-text index, SQL Server starts a background process to populate that index. If you turn off change tracking and specify NO POPULATION, then you are limiting yourself solely to *defining* the full-text index but not actually putting any data in it to start. You can then schedule your own index population job to run later (presumably in low-demand hours of the day).

STOPLIST

A stoplist replaces what was known in previous versions as a *noise word* list. Noise words are now called *stop words*. They are words that are explicitly exempt from being included in the index. In general, these equate to words that are so common (in English, these might include "the," "and," "or," and other words that occur at abnormally high frequencies, but rarely add any real value to the content. While noise words were kept in a separate file in previous releases, SQL Server 2008 stores stop words in a *stoplist*. For each language you can define for full-text indexing, there is an associated system stoplist, but you can also create your own custom stoplist. You can also turn off stoplist utilization if you want all words included regardless.

Altering Full-Text Indexes

Okay, so now you have an index, and you want to make changes to it. As you might expect, the new full-text syntax supports the notion of an ALTER statement. It is in the form of:

```
ALTER FULLTEXT INDEX ON <table name>
{       ENABLE
        | DISABLE
        | SET CHANGE_TRACKING { MANUAL | AUTO | OFF }
        | ADD (<column name>
      [TYPE COLUMN <type column name> ]
      [LANGUAGE <language alias>] [,...n] )
        | DROP (<column name> [,...n] )
        | START { FULL | INCREMENTAL | UPDATE } POPULATION
        | {STOP | PAUSE | RESUME} POPULATION
        | SET STOPLIST { OFF| SYSTEM | <stoplist name> }
      [WITH NO POPULATION]
}
```

This ALTER has some substantial differences from previous ALTER statements we've dealt with! See how verbs like START and STOP are in there? This ALTER not only changes the definition of our full-text index but also can be used to manage the index somewhat. Keep this difference in mind, as it is not very intuitive when you compare it to the other ALTER statements we use in SQL Server.

Several elements of these work exactly as they did for the CREATE statement. We are merely changing a chosen option from one thing to another. However, some of this is totally new. Let's start with the more traditional ALTER statement items and then move on to the portions of this statement that are more management-oriented.

ENABLE/DISABLE

These do what they say. If you disable a full-text index, the index is kept in place and all data remains intact. What changes is that the index is not available for full-text queries, and the index data is not updated (any updates that were in process when the DISABLE was issued will be stopped immediately).

When you ENABLE, it picks up where the index left off. (It likely has catching up to do, but any data already there is kept intact, and you do not need to do a full repopulation.)

ADD

This works just like the initial definition of columns. For example, if we wanted to add the Instructions column to our full-text index on Production.ProductModel, it would look like:

```
ALTER FULLTEXT INDEX ON Production.ProductModel
    ADD ( Instructions )
```

The LANGUAGE and TYPE COLUMN properties also work just as they did in our early CREATE.

DROP

Again, this works much as you would expect. If we were dropping the Instructions column we just added, that would look like:

```
ALTER FULLTEXT INDEX ON Production.ProductModel

    DROP ( Instructions )
```

START ... POPULATION

START gives us three options as to what kind of populations we want to use.

FULL

The nice simple one — think of this as the command to "start over!" Every row will be reexamined, and the index will be rebuilt from scratch.

INCREMENTAL

This one is valid only if you have a timestamp column in your table (otherwise it will default back to a FULL population) and will start a population of rows changes since the last time a population was performed for the table. Think of this one as the "catch up on your work please!" version of populating. Incremental population does *not* require that change tracking be turned on.

UPDATE

This one addresses the scenario where you have turned the AUTO populate off for the index, but want all updates, inserts, or deletes updated in the index. It *does* require that change tracking be turned on.

STOP, PAUSE, RESUME

These perform the specific action on any population that is currently running against this full-text index. The STOP option does *not* stop automatic change tracking — only full or incremental updates. PAUSE and RESUME operate exactly as one would expect.

Dropping Full-Text Indexes

I'm sure by this point that you could figure this one out for yourself, but for the sake of completeness, here we go:

```
DROP FULLTEXT INDEX ON <table name>
```

So, were we to run the command (don't actually run this, as we'll be using this index in our next example!):

```
DROP FULLTEXT INDEX ON Production.ProductModel
```

the full-text index would be gone!

A Note Regarding the Older Syntax

Prior to SQL Server 2005, we used a special system stored procedure called sp_fulltext_catalog. We likewise used other system stored procs to address other full-text functionality.

These have now been deprecated for two releases, and are significantly out of touch with the next full-text architecture. I will not cover them in depth there, but I do want you to be aware of them in case you bump into them in production settings. If you do, I recommend migrating them to the new syntax as fast as reasonably possible (basically, as long as SQL Server 2000 support is no longer required).

More on Index Population

Unlike "normal" SQL Server indexes, which are naturally kept up to date by the very nature of SQL Server and the way it stores data, full-text indexes operate with a different storage structure and require substantially more overhead to populate. As such, they require a certain degree of intervention before the index will be up to date with the actual data it is supposed to represent.

Population comes in three — well, more like two and a half — flavors. Let's look at each:

❑ **Full**: Is what it sounds like. With this kind of population, SQL Server basically forgets anything that it knew about the data previously and starts over. Every row is rescanned, and the index is rebuilt from scratch.

❑ **Incremental**: Under this option, SQL Server utilizes a column of type timestamp in order to keep track of what columns have changed since the last population. In this scenario, SQL Server only needs to record the changes for those rows that have changed in some manner. This option requires that the table in question have a timestamp column. Any updates that do not cause a change in the timestamp (nonlogged operations — usually BLOB activity) will not be detected unless something else in the same row changed.

❑ **Change tracking**: Tracks the actual changes since the last population. This option can help you keep your full-text indexes up to date at near real time; however, keep in mind that full-text population is very CPU and memory intensive, and can bog down your server. Weigh the notion of immediate updates against the notion that you may be able to hold your updates to off-peak hours for your server.

Unless you're using change tracking, population of your full-text indexes will occur only when you specifically start the process or according to a population schedule that you establish.

Obviously, whenever you first create a full-text index or change the list of columns participating in the index, you need to completely repopulate the index (an incremental change of a previously empty index would mean that every row would have to be scanned in — right?). SQL Server will now do this automatically unless you explicitly tell it not to. We can manually perform this repopulation at either the catalog or the table level. Typically, you'll perform repopulation at the table level for newly added or changed indexes, and repopulate at the catalog level when you are performing routine maintenance.

So, with this in mind, we should be ready to populate the full-text index we have created on our `Production.ProductModel` table. Had we not specifically stated NO POPULATION, then SQL Server would have populated the index automatically; however, since we did tell it not to populate, we have to order up our population. Since this is the first population, we probably want a full population (frankly, an incremental would have the same result, so it doesn't really matter, but it reads more logically this way). Using the new syntax, this would look like:

```
ALTER FULLTEXT INDEX ON Production.ProductModel
    START FULL POPULATION;
```

> **Full-text population runs as a background process. As such, your command will return a "completed successfully" message as soon as the population job is *started*. Do not take this message to mean that your index is done populating, which, if the index is against a large table, could potentially take hours to complete.**

> **If you need to know the status of your full-text population process, right-click the name of your full-text index under the Storage➤Full Text Catalogs node of your database, and then check the property called "Population Status."**

Since this table is relatively small, you shouldn't have to wait terribly long before you can run a query against it and get results:

```
SELECT ProductModelID, Name
FROM Production.ProductModel
WHERE CONTAINS(Name, 'Frame');
```

This should get back something on the order of 10 rows:

```
ProductModelID Name
-------------- ---------------------------------------------------
5              HL Mountain Frame
6              HL Road Frame
7              HL Touring Frame
8              LL Mountain Frame
9              LL Road Frame
10             LL Touring Frame
14             ML Mountain Frame
15             ML Mountain Frame-W
16             ML Road Frame
17             ML Road Frame-W(10 row(s) affected)
```

We have a full-text index, and it works! Time to move on to what that query we just ran is supposed to do and what other options we have available.

Full-Text Query Syntax

Full-Text Search has its own brand of query syntax. It adds special commands to extend T-SQL and to clearly indicate that we want the full-text engine to support our query rather than the regular SQL Server engine.

Fortunately, the basics of full-text queries are just that — basic. There are only four base statements to work with the full-text engine. They actually fall into two overlapping categories of two statements each:

	Exact or Inflectional Term	**Meaning**
Conditional	CONTAINS	FREETEXT
Ranked Table	CONTAINSTABLE	FREETEXTTABLE

The conditional predicates both work an awful lot like an EXISTS operator. Essentially they, for each row, provide a simple yes or no as to whether the row qualifies against the search condition provided. You use both of these in the WHERE clause of your queries. On the other hand, the two ranked queries do not provide conditions at all. Instead, they return a tabular result set (which you can join to) that includes the key value of all the rows that found matches (that's what you join to) as well as a ranking to indicate the strength of the match.

Let's look more closely at each of the four keywords.

CONTAINS

This term looks for a match based on a particular word or phrase. By default, it's looking for an exact match (that is, *swim* must be *swim* — not *swam*), but it can also use modifiers to look for what are called inflectional matches (words that have the same root — such as *swim* and *swam*). CONTAINS recognizes certain keywords.

For now, we're going to stick with the simple form of CONTAINS. We will look at the advanced features after we have the basics of our four statements down (since they share certain modifiers, we'll look at those all at once).

The basic syntax, then, looks like this:

```
CONTAINS({<column>|*} , '<search condition>')
```

You can name a specific column to check, or use *, in which case the condition will be compared for matches against any of the indexed columns. In its simplest form, the search condition should contain only a word or phrase.

> *There are two things worth pointing out here. First, remember that you will only get back results against columns that were included in the full-text index. In the final index we created on the ProductModel table. That means the search includes only the Name and CatalogDescription columns. Columns like Introduction are not included in the search because they are not included in the index. (You may recall that we dropped that column in a test of our ALTER syntax.) Second, the search condition can be far more complex than the simple condition that we've shown here, but we'll get to that after you have the basic operations down.*

For an example, let's go back to the query we used to prove that our population exercise had worked:

```
SELECT ProductModelID, Name
FROM Production.ProductModel
WHERE CONTAINS(Name, 'Frame');
```

What we've said we want here is the ProductModelID and Name columns for all the rows where the Name column in the index includes the word Frame.

If you check out the Name column for the results, you'll see that every row has an exact match.

Let's quickly look at another example. This time, we're going to run pretty much the same query, but we're going to look for the word *Sport*:

```
SELECT ProductModelID, Name
FROM Production.ProductModel

WHERE CONTAINS(Name, 'Sport');
```

This time we get back just one row:

```
ProductModelID Name
-------------- -------------------------------------------------
33             Sport-100

(1 row(s) affected)
```

Again, we got back all the rows where the `Name` column had an exact match with the word *Sport*. Were you to look through the other rows in the table, however, you would find that there were other variations of the word *Sport* (a plural in this case), but they were not returned.

Again — the default behavior of `CONTAINS` is an exact match behavior.

FREETEXT

`FREETEXT` is an incredibly close cousin to `CONTAINS`. Indeed, their syntax is nearly identical:

```
FREETEXT({<column>|*} , '<search condition>')[;]
```

So, the only real difference is in the results you get back. You see, `FREETEXT` is a lot more forgiving in just how exact of a match it looks for. It is more interested in the meaning of the word than it is the exact letter-for-letter spelling.

To illustrate my point rather quickly here, let's look at our *Sport* query from the previous section, but modify it to use `FREETEXT` instead of `CONTAINS`:

```
SELECT ProductModelID, Name
FROM Production.ProductModel
WHERE FREETEXT(Name, 'Sport');
```

When we execute this, we get back slightly different results than we did with `CONTAINS`:

```
ProductModelID Name
-------------- --------------------------------------------------
13             Men's Sports Shorts
33             Sport-100

(2 row(s) affected)
```

The difference in this case comes in interpretation of the plurals — our `FREETEXT` query has picked up the row that contains the word *Sports* — not just those with the word *Sport*. `FREETEXT` can also handle things like swim versus swam and other word variations.

CONTAINSTABLE

`CONTAINSTABLE`, in terms of figuring out which rows would be a match, works identically to `CONTAINS`. The difference is how the results are dealt with.

The syntax is similar, but with the twist of identifying which table the `CONTAINSTABLE` is going to operate against plus an optional limitation to just a top set of matches:

```
CONTAINSTABLE (<table>, {<column>|*}, '<contains search condition>' [, <top 'n'>])
```

Where `CONTAINS` returns a simple Boolean response suitable for use in a `WHERE` clause, `CONTAINSTABLE` returns a table — complete with rankings of how well the search phrase matched the row being returned.

Let's see what I mean here by running our original query, but with a CONTAINSTABLE this time:

```
SELECT *
FROM CONTAINSTABLE(Production.ProductModel,Name, 'Sport');
```

This gets us back one row — just like with CONTAINS — but the information provided by the returned values is somewhat different:

```
KEY         RANK
----------- -----------
33          128

(1 row(s) affected)
```

We are provided with two columns:

❑   **KEY**: Remember when we said that our full-text index had to be able to relate to a single column key in the indexed table? Well, the KEY returned by CONTAINSTABLE relates exactly to that key column. That is, the value output in the column called KEY matches with a single unique row, as identified by the key, in the index table.

❑   **RANK**: A value from 0 to 1000 that indicates just how well the search result matched the row being returned — the higher the value, the better the match.

To make use of CONTAINSTABLE, we simply join our original table back to the CONTAINSTABLE result. For example:

```
SELECT Rank, ProductModelID, Name
FROM Production.ProductModel p
JOIN CONTAINSTABLE(Production.ProductModel,Name, 'Sport') ct
  ON p.ProductModelID = ct.[KEY];
```

Notice the use of brackets around the KEY column name. The reason why is that KEY is also a keyword. Remember from our rules of naming that, if we use a keyword for a column or table name (which you shouldn't do), you need to enclose them in square brackets.

This gets us back our original row, but this time we have the extra information from the underlying table:

```
Rank        ProductModelID Name
----------- -------------- -------------------------------------------------
128         33             Sport-100

(1 row(s) affected)
```

In this case, the values in the Rank are the same, but, given more diverse values, we could have done things like:

❑   Filter based on some arbitrary Rank value. For example, we could want to return only the best matches based on score.

❑   Order by the rank (sort the rankings — most likely highest to lowest).

FREETEXTTABLE

Much as FREETEXT was the close cousin to CONTAINS, so too is FREETEXTTABLE the close cousin to CONTAINSTABLE. FREETEXTTABLE simply combines the more inexact word matching of FREETEXT with the tabular presentation found in CONTAINSTABLE.

We can then combine some of our previous examples to see how FREETEXTTABLE changes things:

```
SELECT Rank, ProductModelID, Name
FROM Production.ProductModel p
JOIN FREETEXTTABLE(Production.ProductModel,Name, 'Sport') ct
  ON p.ProductModelID = ct.[KEY];
```

This gets us the same two rows we had with our original FREETEXT query, but with the kind of rankings we had with our CONTAINSTABLE:

```
Rank        ProductModelID Name
----------- -------------- ----------------------------------------------------
102         13             Men's Sports Shorts
102         33             Sport-100(2 row(s) affected)
```

Experiment with this some in your full-text efforts, and you'll see how rankings can give you a lot to work with.

Dealing with Phrases

All of our various full-text keywords can deal with the concept of phrases. How the phrases are parsed and handled, however, is somewhat different.

Let's start off with the most simple of examples — a simple two-word phrase. This time we'll say that the phrase we want to look for is *damaged seats*. To add a twist to things, we want it no matter what column it is in (as long as the column is part of our full-text index).

```
SELECT DocumentNode, DocumentSummary, Document
FROM Production.Document
WHERE CONTAINS(*, '"damaged seats"');
```

Notice that the phrase was included in double quotation marks. We need to do this any time we want a set of words to be considered as a single unit. This does, however, get us back one row. The result is a little large (due to the size of the Document and DocumentSummary columns) to put in this text, but the relevant section is:

```
DocumentNode DocumentSummary      Document
------------ -------------------- --------------------------------
0x7C20       Worn or damaged se ...   0xD0CF11E0A1B11AE100000000000000...

(1 row(s) affected)
```

Our CONTAINS will check for rows that exactly match the phrase, as long as we enclose that phrase in double quotation marks. (Within the single quotes we always need on our search phrase.) FREETEXT works in the same way.

Booleans

SQL Server also supports the use of Booleans in your searches. The Boolean keywords apply:

- ❑ AND
- ❑ OR
- ❑ AND NOT

There really isn't a whole lot of rocket science to these, so I'll launch right into a simple example and point out one caveat. Let's go with a variation on an example we used earlier:

```
SELECT DocumentNode, DocumentSummary, Document
FROM Production.Document
WHERE CONTAINS(*, '"damaged" OR "seats"');
```

What we've done here is change from where we were searching for the exact phrase *damaged seats* to a search that is looking for *either* word without worrying about whether the words are used together or not. Execute this, and you'll see we get back two rows instead of just one.

The caveat that I mentioned earlier is that NOT cannot be used on its own. NOT is relevant only to full-text searches when used in conjunction with AND.

Proximity

Full-Text Search also allows us to make use of proximity terms. Currently, the list of supported proximity terms is a whopping one term long — NEAR. NEAR works a lot like it sounds. It says that the terms on either side of the NEAR keyword must be close to each other. Microsoft hasn't told us how close the words have to be to be considered NEAR, but figure around eight to ten words for most situations.

> *Technically, there is one more "word" on the proximity keyword list, but it isn't a "word" at all — rather a symbol. You can, if you choose, use a tilde (~) instead of the NEAR keyword. It works just the same. Personally, I recommend against this for readability reasons. Not too many readers of your code are going to recognize what ~ means, but most of them will at least make a guess at NEAR.*

For examples on how NEAR works, we're going to stick with CONTAINSTABLE. NEAR works much the same in the other full-text query operators, so we're just going to focus on what happens to the rankings in a NEAR query as well as what does and doesn't get included in the query.

For this example, we'll look at the words *repair* and *instructions*:

```
SELECT Rank, DocumentNode, DocumentSummary
FROM Production.Document pd
JOIN CONTAINSTABLE(Production.Document, *, 'repair near instructions') ct
  ON pd.DocumentNode = ct.[KEY];
```

I include only the first two columns here for brevity, but notice that we have different rankings on the two rows returned.

```
Rank         DocumentNode
-----------  ------------------------
3            0x5B40
2            0x7B40
```

(2 row(s) affected)

If you look carefully at the DocumentSummary column in your results (again, for brevity's sake, I haven't included all of the column here), you'll see that both rows do indeed have both words but that the word *repair* occurs twice in the DocumentNode 0x5B40 row, thus it receives a higher ranking.

Don't be surprised to see situations where a record that has your search criteria closer together gets ranked lower than one where the search criteria are not as close. Remember that, even when you use the NEAR keyword, nearness is only one of several criteria that SQL Server uses to rank the rows. Other considerations such as percentage of words that match, case values, and more can play with the numbers on you.

Weighting

So, these rankings are all cool and whatnot, but what would we do if one of the words in our search criteria was more important than another?

To deal with situations where you need to give precedence to one or more words, Full-Text provides us with the ISABOUT() function and WEIGHT keyword. This syntax looks like this:

```
ISABOUT(<weighted term> WEIGHT (<weight value>), <weighted term> WEIGHT (<weighted
term>),...n)
```

Let's say that you want to allow customers to select among several kinds of bikes, but to further allow for selecting "preferred" options. For our example, let's say our customer is most interested in mountain bikes but is also interested in touring and road bikes — in that order. You could get a ranked listing using the following:

```
SELECT Rank, ProductModelID, Name
FROM Production.ProductModel pm
JOIN CONTAINSTABLE(
    Production.ProductModel,
    Name,
    'ISABOUT (Road WEIGHT (.2), Touring WEIGHT (.4), Mountain WEIGHT (.8) )'
    ) ct
  ON pm.ProductModelID = ct.[KEY]
ORDER BY Rank DESC;
```

Now take a look at the results:

```
Rank         ProductModelID Name
-----------  -------------- ----------------------------------------------------
31           5              HL Mountain Frame
31           7              HL Touring Frame
31           8              LL Mountain Frame
...
```

```
  . . .
  . . .
  31           123              LL Mountain Rear Wheel
  31           124              ML Mountain Rear Wheel
  31           125              HL Mountain Rear Wheel
  7            126              LL Road Rear Wheel
  7            113              Road Bottle Cage
  7            93               Road Tire Tube
  . . .
  . . .
  . . .
  7            16               ML Road Frame
  7            17               ML Road Frame-W
  7            9                LL Road Frame
  7            6                HL Road Frame

(89 row(s) affected)
```

Note that not everything is perfect in our world — some touring entries come before our more heavily weighted mountain options, but if you look the list over, you will see we have indeed created a very heavy bias toward mountain bikes in our rankings.

Inflectional

This one doesn't really apply to FREETEXT, as FREETEXT is inherently inflectional. What is INFLECTIONAL you ask? Well, it's basically telling SQL Server that different forms of the word have the same general meaning. The syntax looks like this:

```
FORMSOF(INFLECTIONAL, <term>[, <term>[, ...n]] )
```

An inflectional form of a word is one that has the same general meaning. For example, *swam* is just the past tense of *swim*. The underlying meaning is the same.

Stop Words

As we discussed earlier, there are tons and tons of words in use in different languages (Full-Text supports more than just U.S. English!). Most languages have certain words that appear over and over again with little intrinsic meaning to them. In the English language, for example, prepositions (you, she, he, and so on), articles (the, a, an), and conjunctions (and, but, or) are just few examples of words that appear in many, many sentences but are not integral to the meaning of that sentence. If SQL Server paid attention to those words, and we did searches based on them, then we would drown in the results that SQL Server gave us in our queries. Quite often, every single row in the table would be returned! The solution comes in the form of what is called a *stoplist* (called a noise word list in previous releases). This is a list of words (individual words are referred to as *stop words*) that SQL Server ignores when considering matches.

SQL Server includes a default stoplist for each language it supports. You can either use this system-supplied stoplist (usually referred to as SYSTEM if you need to explicitly reference it in a command), or you can create your own using the CREATE FULLTEXT STOPLIST command. The full syntax looks like this:

```
CREATE FULLTEXT STOPLIST <stoplist name>
  [FROM { [<database name>.] <source stoplist name> } | SYSTEM STOPLIST ]
```

```
    [AUTHORIZATION <owner name> ]
[;]
```

In general, you'll want a well-populated stoplist, and thus will want to prepopulate your list from some existing stoplist. So, for example, I could create a stoplist for AdventureWorks2008 that starts with the same stop words in the SYSTEM stoplist:

```
CREATE FULLTEXT STOPLIST ADStopList
    FROM SYSTEM STOPLIST;
```

> Stoplists you create are not automatically associated with any full-text index — you need to manually attach the new stoplist to the full-text index via the ALTER FULLTEXT INDEX command.

You can add and delete words from this list as suits the particular needs of your application. For example, if you are in the business of selling tractor-trailer rigs, then you might want to add words like *hauling* to your noise word list. More than likely, a huge percentage of your customers have that word in their name, so it is relatively unhelpful in searches. To make additions or subtractions from a stoplist, you use the ALTER FULLTEXT STOPLIST command. The full syntax looks like this:

```
ALTER FULLTEXT STOPLIST stoplist_name
{
      ADD '<stop word>' LANGUAGE <language number or moniker>
    | DROP
      {
                '<stop word>' LANGUAGE <language number or moniker>
        | ALL LANGUAGE <language number or moniker>
        | ALL       }
[;]
```

Let's try this out by adding a stop word to the AWStopList we just created:

```
ALTER FULLTEXT STOPLIST ADStopList
  ADD 'bicycle' LANGUAGE 1033;
```

Were we to repopulate our full-text index, the word bicycle (which may be a worthless search term in a business where every document is going to discuss bicycles), would be ignored.

Adding and removing words from a stoplist is something of a double-edged sword. When you add a word to the list, it means that searches involving that word are no longer going to return the results that users are more than likely going to expect. By the same token, it also, depending on the frequency with which the word is used, can dramatically shrink the processing time and size of your catalogs.

Summary

Full-Text is now core to the SQL Server engine (it was a separate service in prior releases), but a separate process is spawned by the Full-Text daemon manager each time a search is issued.

When you implement Full-Text, also consider the load the population process is going to place on your server, and balance that against how quickly you need changes reflected in search results. If possible, delay repopulation of full-text indexes until the non-peak hours on your system

Full-Text Search is a powerful and fast way of referencing the contents of most any character-based columns. It is substantially more efficient and powerful than a LIKE clause but comes with additional overhead in terms of both space and processing time.

19

Feeling Secure

There are probably as many ideas on security as there are programmers. It's one of those things where there isn't necessarily a right way to do it, but there are definitely plenty of wrong ones.

The first thing to understand about security is that there is no such thing as a totally secure application. If you can make it secure, rest assured that someone, somewhere, can defeat your efforts and "hack" into the system. Even with this knowledge, the goal still needs to be to keep unwanted intruders out of your system. The good news about security is that, for most instances, you can fairly easily make it such a hassle that 99.999 percent of people out there won't want to bother with it. For the other .001 percent, I can only encourage you to make sure that all your employees have a life so they fall into the 99.999 percent. The .001 percent will hopefully find someplace else to go.

SQL Server 2005 marked the start of a very concerted effort by Microsoft to raise the level of security in SQL Server. For those who have been around long enough, you may remember the hubbub surrounding the "slammer" virus that happened during the SQL Server 2000 lifespan. Microsoft radically altered the security profile of SQL Server in a service pack that followed the slammer scare, but SQL Server 2005 marked the first full release after the advent of the slammer virus, and it was just the beginning of a series of features not so much focused just around deterring hackers as a more far reaching protection of the safety and privacy of data in SQL Server. A ton of new features were added in SQL Server 2005, some more are added in SQL Server 2008, and there are more to come in the next version of SQL Server. Needless to say, all this leaves us with a lot to cover in the security realm.

In this chapter, we're going to cover:

- ❑ Security basics
- ❑ SQL Server security options
- ❑ Database and server roles
- ❑ Application roles

❑ Credentials

❑ Certificates

❑ Schema management

❑ XML integration security issues

❑ More advanced security

What we'll discover is that there are a lot of different ways to approach the security problem. Security goes way beyond giving someone a user ID and a password — we'll see many of the things that you need to think about.

Before beginning any of the examples in this chapter, you'll need to load and execute the script called NorthwindSecure.sql. This builds a special database we'll use throughout this chapter. You can download what you need for this at the book's Web site at www.wrox.com or at www.professionalsql.com.

> *Okay, so this is a chapter where I have to make you create a working database in order for the examples to work — my apologies for that. What we're going to utilize is the old Northwind database but with any changes to permissions removed. The NorthwindSecure database that we'll use throughout this chapter is a more typical database scenario — that is, it has absolutely no permissions added to it beyond what comes naturally with creating tables and objects (which means NONE). We'll learn how to deal with this and explicitly add what permissions we want as the chapter progresses.*

Security Basics

I'm sure that a fair amount of what we're going to look into in this section is going to seem exceedingly stupid — I mean, won't everyone know this stuff? Judging by how often I see violations of even the most simple of these rules, I would say, "No, apparently they don't." All I can ask is that you bear with me, and don't skip ahead. As seemingly obvious as some of this stuff is, you'd be amazed how often it gets forgotten or just plain ignored.

Among the different basics that we'll look at here are:

❑ One person, one login ID, one password

❑ Password expirations

❑ Password length and makeup

❑ Number of attempts to log in

❑ Storage of user ID and password information

One Person, One Login, One Password

It never ceases to shock me how, everywhere I go, I almost never fail to find that the establishment has at least one "global" user — some login into the network or particular applications that is usually known by nearly everyone in the department or even the whole company. Often, this "global" user has *carte blanche* (in other words, complete) access. For SQL Server, it used to be common that installations hadn't even bothered to set the sa password to something other than a blank password. This is a very bad scenario indeed.

> *Prior to SQL Server 2000, the default password for the sa account was null — that is, it didn't have one. Thankfully, SQL Server 2000 not only changed this default, SQL Server will now, by default, not allow you to use a weak password (depends on your Windows policy settings), and, assuming your Windows policy settings allow a blank password, SQL Server will proactively tell you that you are effectively being an idiot if you insist on making it blank. The thing to watch out for is that, while you're developing, it's really common to still set it to something "easy." You still need to remember to change it before you go into production or to make it something hard from the beginning if your development server is going to be exposed directly to the Internet or some other non-trustworthy access.*

Even now, when most installations do have something other than a null password, it is very common for lots of people to know what that password is.

The first basic, then, is that if everyone has access to a user ID that is essentially anonymous (if everyone knows it, it could be that anyone has used it) and has access to everything, then you've defeated your security model entirely. Likewise, if you give every user a login that has full access to everything, you've again severely damaged your security prospects. The only real benefit that's left is being able to tell who's who as far as who is connected at any point in time (assuming that they are really using their individual login rather than the global login).

Users that have *carte blanche* access should be limited to just one or two people. Ideally, if you need passwords for such *carte blanche* access, then you would want separate logins that each have the access, but only one person would know the password for each login.

> *You'll find that users will often share their passwords with someone else in order to let someone temporarily gain some level of access (usually because the owner of the login ID is either out of the office or doesn't have time to bother with doing it themselves at the time.) You should make this nothing short of a hanging offense if possible.*

> *The problem created by password sharing is multifold. First, some users are getting access to something that you previously decided not to give them (otherwise, why don't they have the necessary rights for themselves?). If you didn't want them to have that access before, why do you want them to have it now? Second, a user that's not supposed to have access probably will now have that access semi-permanently. Since users almost never change their passwords (unless forced to), the person they gave the password to will probably be able to use that login ID indefinitely and, I assure you, they will! Third, you again lose auditing. You may have something that tracks which user did what based on the login ID. If more than one person has the password for that login ID, how can you be sure which person was logged in to that login ID at the time?*

> *This means that if someone is going to be out of the office for some time, perhaps because he is sick or on vacation, and someone else is temporarily going to be doing his job, a new login ID and password should be created specifically for that replacement person (or a modification to the access rights of his existing login ID should be made), and it should be deleted as soon as the original person has returned.*

To summarize, stay away from global user accounts whenever possible. If you must have them, keep their use limited to as few people as at all possible. Usually this should be kept to just two (one to be a main user, and one person as a backup if the first person isn't available). If you really must have more than one person with significant access, then consider creating multiple accounts (one per user) that have the necessary level of access. By following these simple steps, you'll find you'll do a lot for both the security and auditability of the system.

Password Expiration

Using expiration of passwords tends to be either abused or ignored. That's because it's a good idea that often goes bad.

The principle behind password expiration is to set up your system to have passwords that automatically expire after a certain period of time. After that time, the user must change the password to continue to have access to the account. The concept has been around many years, and if you work in a larger corporation, there's a good chance that the auditors from your accounting firm are already insisting that you implement some form of password expiration (no, it's not just your IT department being controlling — they may well have been forced to a given policy by the same people who audit your financial statements).

With SQL Server 2005 and later, you can enforce Windows authentication rights even for your SQL Server–specific passwords. Alternatively, you can just use Windows-based security (more on that in the next section).

What Do You Get for Your Effort?

So, what does password expiration get you? Well, remember that, in the final part of a previous section, I said that once a password is shared, the user would have that access forever? Well, this is the exception. If you expire passwords, then you refresh the level of your security — at least temporarily. The password would have to be shared a second time in order for the user to regain access. While this is far from foolproof (often, the owner of the login ID will be more than happy to share it again), it does deal with the situation where the sharing of the password was really just intended for one-time use. Often, users who share their passwords don't even realize that months later the other user still has the password and may be using it on occasion to gain access to something they would not have, based on their own security.

Now the Bad News

It is very possible to get too much of a good thing. I mentioned earlier how many audit firms will expect their clients to implement a model where a user's password regularly expires, say, every 30 days. This is a very bad idea indeed.

Every installation that I've seen that does this — without exception — has *worse* security after implementing a 30-day expiration policy. The problem is, as you might expect, multifold in nature.

❑ First, technical support calls go way up. When users change passwords that often, they simply can't memorize them all. They can't remember which month's password they are supposed to use, so they are constantly calling for support to reset the password because they forgot what it is.

❑ Second, and much more important, the users get tired of both thinking of new passwords and remembering them. Experience has shown me that, for more than 90 percent of the users I've worked with in installations that use a 30-day expiration, users change their passwords to incredibly predictable (and therefore hackable) words or word/number combinations. Indeed, this often gets to a level where perhaps 50 percent or more of your users will have the same password — they are all using things like MMMYY where MMM is the month and YY is the year. For example, for January 1996 they might have used JAN96 for their password. Pretty soon, everyone in the place is doing something like that.

I've seen some companies try and deal with this by implementing something of a password sniffer; it checks the password when you go to change it. The sniffing process looks for passwords that incorporate your name or start with a month prefix. These mechanisms are weak at best.

Users are far smarter than you often give them credit for. It took about a week for most users to circumvent the first one of these password sniffers I saw; they simply changed their passwords to have an "X" prefix on them, and otherwise stayed with the same MMMYY format they had been using before. In short, the sniffer wound up doing next to nothing. It doesn't stop there though: they share their newfound algorithm with coworkers so they can get around the "problem" too.

The bottom line here is to not get carried away with your expiration policy. Make it short enough to get reasonable turnover and deal with shared or stolen passwords but don't make it so often that users rebel and start using weak passwords. Personally, I suggest nothing more frequent than 90 days and nothing longer than 180 days.

Password Length and Makeup

Ah, an era of rejoicing for SQL Server in this area. In previous versions, you really didn't have much control over this if you were using SQL Server security. You can now have SQL Server enforce your Windows password policy (which you can adjust using utilities in Windows).

Password Length

Realize that, for each possible alphanumeric digit the user includes in the password, they are increasing the number of possible passwords by a factor of at least 36 (really a few more given special characters, but even 36 is enough to make the point here). That means there are only 36 possible single character passwords, but 1,296 possible two-character passwords. Go up to three characters, and you increase the possibilities to 46,656. By the time you add a fourth character, you're well over a million possibilities. The permutations just keep going up as you require more and more characters. The downside, though, is that it becomes more and more difficult for your users to remember what their password was and to actually think up passwords. Indeed, I suspect that you'll find that requiring anything more than 5 or 6 characters will generate a full-scale revolt from your end users.

Password Makeup

All right, so I've pointed out that, if you make it a requirement to use at least four alphanumeric characters, you've created a situation where there are over a million possible password combinations. The problem comes when you realize that people aren't really going to use all those combinations; they are going to use words or names that they are familiar with. Considering that the average person only uses about 5,000 words on a regular basis, that doesn't leave you with very many words to try out if you're a hacker.

If you're implementing something other than the default Windows password policy, then consider requiring that at least one character be alphabetic in nature (no numbers, just letters) and that at least one character be numeric. This rules out simple numbers that are easy to guess (people really like to use their Social Security number, telephone number, or birthdays) and all words. The users can still create things that are easy to remember for them — say "77pizzas" — but the password can't be pulled out of a dictionary. Any hacker is forced to truly try each permutation in order to try and break in.

Number of Tries to Log In

Regardless of how you're physically storing the user and password information, your login screen should have logic to it that limits the number of tries that someone gets to log in. The response if they go over the limit can range in strength, but you want to make sure you throw in some sort of device that makes it difficult to set up a routine to try out all the passwords programmatically.

How many tries to allow isn't really that important as long as it's a reasonably small number. I usually use three times, but I've seen four and five in some places and that's fine too.

If you're utilizing the Windows password policy enforcement, then SQL Server will check the login attempts versus a bad password limit and enforce that policy.

Storage of User and Password Information

This obviously applies only if you are cooking your own security system rather than using the built-in Windows and/or SQL Server security systems (but many Web applications will do that), and, for the most part, there's no rocket science in how to store user profile and password information. There are, however, a few things to think about:

❑ Since you need to be able to get at the information initially, you will have to do one of the following three things:

    ❑ Compile a password right into the client application or component (and then make sure that the proper login and password are created on any server that you install your application on).

    ❑ Utilize SQL Server's encryption technologies to encrypt and decrypt the data in the database.

    ❑ Require something of a double password situation — one to get the user as far as the regular password information, and one to get them to the real application. Forcing a user into two logins is generally unacceptable, which pushes you back to one of the other two options in most cases.

❑ If you go with a double password scenario, you'll want the access for the first login to be limited to just a stored procedure execution if possible. By doing this, you can allow the first login to obtain the validation that it needs while not revealing anything to anyone that tries to login through Management Studio. Have your stored procedure (sproc) accept a user ID and password, and simply pass back either a Boolean (true/false that they can log in) or pass back a recordset that lists what screens and functions the user can see at the client end. If you use a raw SELECT statement, then you won't be able to restrict what they can see.

    One solution I've implemented close to this scenario was to have a view that mapped the current SQL Server login to other login information. In this case, an application role was used that gave the application complete access to everything. The application had to know what the user could and couldn't do. All the user's login had a right to do was execute a stored procedure to request a listing of their rights. The sproc looked something like this (this is just pseudo-code, so don't try and actually execute this):

```
CREATE PROC GetUserRights
AS

DECLARE @User varchar(128)
SELECT @User = USER_NAME()
SELECT * FROM UserPermissions WHERE LoginID = @User
```

❑ If you're going to store password information in the system — encrypt it!!! I can't say enough about the importance of this. Most users will use their passwords for more than one thing; it just makes life a lot easier when you have less to remember. By encrypting the data before you put it in the database, you ensure that no one is going to stumble across a user's password information — even accidentally. They may see it, but what they see is not usable unless they have the key to decrypt it.

What form of encryption to use is up to you. You can utilize the built-in encryption methods (we'll discuss some of these later in the chapter), or you can implement your own encryption at the application level. One way or the other, there is little excuse for not properly protecting password information.

Personally, I am a big believer in one-way encryption. That is, once it's encrypted, there really isn't any reasonable way to decrypt it. If a user loses their password, then they need to go through some form of reset mechanism and choose a new password. Why do I feel this way? Well, realize that most users will reuse the same password for many applications, so the password they use to get into your system may very well be the same password they use to get into their personal online banking system. Creating a one-way encryption system minimizes the risk that an administrator of your system is able to get at users' passwords for nefarious use.

Security Options

As far as built-in options go, you have two choices in how to set up security under SQL Server.

❑ **Windows integrated security**: The user logs in to Windows not SQL Server. Authentication is done via Windows with trusted connections.

❑ **Standard security**: The user logs in to SQL Server separately from logging in to Windows. Authentication is done using SQL Server.

Let's take a look at both.

SQL Server Security

We'll start with SQL Server's built-in login model. This was a security black hole for a very long time, but got substantially more robust in SQL Server 2005. The relatively simplistic model is still available, but there is now tons more you can do to add extra touches to just how secure your server and databases are.

With SQL Server security, you create a *login ID* that is completely separate from your network login information. Some of the pros for using SQL Server security include:

❑ The user doesn't necessarily have to be a domain user in order to gain access to the system.

❑ It's easier to gain programmatic control over the user information.

Some of the cons are:

❑ Your users may have to log in twice or more — once into whatever network access they have, and once into the SQL Server for each connection they create from a separate application.

❑ Two logins mean more maintenance for your DBA.

❑ If multiple passwords are required, they can easily get out of synch, and that leads to an awful lot of failed logins or forgotten passwords. (Does this sound familiar, "Let's see now, which one was it for this login?")

An example of logging in using SQL Server security would be the use of the sa account that you've probably been using for much of this book. It doesn't matter how you've logged in to your network, you log in to the SQL Server using a login ID of sa and a separate password (which you've hopefully set to something very secure).

> On an ongoing basis, you really don't want to be doing things day-to-day logged in as **sa**. Why? Well, it will probably only take you a minute or two of thought to figure out many of the terrible things you can do by sheer accident when you're using the **sa** account (or any other account with system administrator access for that matter). Using **sa** means you have complete access to everything; that means the DROP TABLE statement you execute when you are in the wrong database will actually do what you told it — drop that table!!! About all you'll be left to say is "oops!" Your boss will probably be saying something completely different.

> Even if you do want to always have *carte blanche* access, just use the **sa** account to make your regular user account a member of the sysadmins server role. That gives you the power of **sa**, but gains you the extra security of separate passwords and the audit trail (in Profiler or when looking at system activity) of who is currently logged in to the system.

Creating and Managing Logins

There are currently four major ways to create logins on a SQL Server:

❑ By using CREATE LOGIN

❑ By using the Management Studio

❑ SQL Management Objects (SMO)

❑ By using one of the several other options that remain solely for backward compatibility

CREATE LOGIN

CREATE LOGIN was added in SQL Server 2005 as part of a general effort by Microsoft to standardize the syntax used to create database and server objects. It deprecated the older sp_addlogin, which was the procedural way of adding logins in prior versions, and looks like the CREATE <object> <object type> syntax that we've seen repeatedly in SQL but with some of the extra option requirements that we've seen with things like stored procedures.

The most basic syntax is straightforward, but how the options can be mixed can become something of a pain to understand. The overall syntax looks like this:

```
CREATE LOGIN <login name>
    [ { WITH
            PASSWORD = '<password>' [ HASHED ] [ MUST_CHANGE ]
            [, SID = <sid>
            | DEFAULT_DATABASE = <database>
            | DEFAULT_LANGUAGE = <language>
            | CHECK_EXPIRATION = { ON | OFF}
            | CHECK_POLICY = { ON | OFF}
            [ CREDENTIAL = <credential name>
            [, ... <next option>] ]
    } |
    { FROM
        WINDOWS
            [ WITH DEFAULT_DATABASE = <database>
                    | DEFAULT_LANGUAGE = <language> ]
        | CERTIFICATE <certificate name>
        | ASYMMETRIC KEY <asymmetric key name>
    }
    ]
```

The key part that sets the tone for things is the choice of a FROM versus a WITH clause immediately following the login name, so let's look at those along with the options as they are relevant to either the FROM or WITH clause they belong to.

CREATE LOGIN ... WITH

The WITH clause immediately puts you into defining options that go with SQL Server authentication–based logins as opposed to any other authentication method. It is only relevant if you have SQL Server security enabled (as opposed to just Windows authentication). The number of options here can seem daunting, so let's break them down.

Option	Description
PASSWORD	This is, of course, just what it sounds like. The tricky part of this is the question of whether the password is in clear text (in which case SQL Server will encrypt it as it adds it) or whether it is already hashed (in which case you need to supply the HASHED keyword that is covered next).
HASHED	This follows your password, and is used only if the password you supplied was already hashed (encrypted). In that case, SQL Server adds the password without re-encrypting it.

Continued

Option	Description
MUST_CHANGE	This is another one of those "is what it sounds like" things. In short, if you supply this option, then the users will be prompted to change their password the first time they login.
SID	Allows you to manually specify what GUID SQL Server will use to identify this login. If you don't supply this (and doing so is something I would consider to be an extreme case), then SQL Server will generate one for you.
DEFAULT_DATABASE	This is the database that will be made current each time the user logs in.
DEFAULT_LANGUAGE	This is the language that things like errors and other system messages will be delivered in for the user.
CHECK_EXPIRATION	Sets whether SQL Server will enforce the password expiration policy. By default, the password will *not* expire. Setting this to ON will enforce policy.
CHECK_POLICY	Sets whether SQL Server will enforce the password policy (length, character requirements, and so on). By default, the password must meet the Windows password policy. Setting this to OFF will allow virtually any password to be used.
CREDENTIAL	This names a credential (and we'll cover what these are later) for this login to be mapped to. In short, this maps this login to a set of permissions that may allow them to perform actions outside of SQL Server (such as network access and such).

Any of these can be mixed together, and the order in which you provide them matters only in the case of HASHED and MUST_CHANGE (which must follow the PASSWORD option if you're going to utilize them at all).

CREATE LOGIN ... FROM

The FROM clause implies that this login isn't SQL Server–specific. The FROM clause specifies the source of that login. The source falls into a few different categories:

❑ **WINDOWS**: In this case, we are mapping to an existing Windows login or group. This is basically saying "Take this existing Windows user or group, and give them rights to my SQL Server." Notice that I say "or group." You can map SQL Server to a Windows group, and that implies that any member of that group will be granted that level of access to your SQL Server. This is really handy for managing users in your network. For example, if you want everyone in accounting to have a certain set of rights in SQL Server, you could create a Windows group called Accounting and map that to a SQL Server login. If you hire someone new, then as soon as you add them to the Accounting group they will have access not only to whatever Windows resources the Accounting group has, but also all the SQL Server permissions that the Accounting group has.

If you use Windows as your FROM sources, then you can also supply a WITH clause similar to a SQL Server–based login, but limited to just the default database and language.

❑ **CERTIFICATE:** This kind of login is based off of an X.509 certificate that you've already associated with your server by using the CREATE CERTIFICATE command. Certificates can be used in several different ways, but in the end, they essentially serve as a recognized secure encryption key. SQL Server has its own "certificate authority" or can import those generated from other sources. Essentially, presentation of this certificate serves as authorization to log in to the SQL Server.

❑ **ASYMMETRIC KEY:** Asymmetric keys are a different flavor of the same general notion that certificates work under. Essentially, it is a key that is presented that SQL Server trusts, and therefore it grants access. Asymmetric keys are merely a different method of presenting a secure key.

To prepare for the examples we'll use the rest of this chapter, you'll need to set up a user in Windows that we'll supply and remove access to and from over the course of the chapter. I've named my test user TestAccount, but you can substitute another name as you see fit (just make sure you remember to also substitute it in the chapter examples). Once you have an account to test with set up in Windows, try adding it to SQL Server (again, you'll need to change "HOBBES" to the name of your system):

```
CREATE LOGIN [HOBBES\TestAccount] FROM WINDOWS
    WITH DEFAULT_DATABASE = NorthwindSecure;
```

And our test account now has login rights to the SQL Server. Note, however, that even though we've defaulted our TestAccount to the NorthwindSecure database, the account still does not have access to that database (we'll get to that shortly).

ALTER LOGIN

As with most CREATE statements we've seen in SQL, CREATE LOGIN has a complementing statement in the form of ALTER LOGIN. As with most ALTER statements, the syntax is primarily a subset of the options found in the related CREATE statement:

```
ALTER LOGIN <login name>
    [ { ENABLE | DISABLE } ]
    [ { WITH
          PASSWORD = '<password>'
          [ { OLD_PASSWORD = '<old password>'
            | [ UNLOCK ] [ MUST_CHANGE ] }
            | DEFAULT_DATABASE = <database>
            | DEFAULT_LANGUAGE = <language>
            | NAME = <new login name>
            | CHECK_EXPIRATION = { ON | OFF}
            | CHECK_POLICY = { ON | OFF}
            [ CREDENTIAL = <credential name>
            | NO CREDENTIAL
```

Most of these are exactly the same as they were with the CREATE statement, but let's look at the few differences.

Option	Description
ENABLE | DISABLE	Enables or disables the login. This is something of an indicator of whether or not the login is considered active in the system, and ENABLE should not be confused with UNLOCK (they are different things). Disabling a login leaves it in place but disallows use of the login. Enabling reactivates the login.
OLD PASSWORD	This one applies only if a given login is utilizing ALTER LOGIN to change its own password. Security administrators with the rights to change the password at all are unlikely to know the old password and have the right to set a new password without knowing the old one.
UNLOCK	This allows a user to attempt to log in again after the login has been locked out due to exceeding the bad password count.
NAME	This allows you to change the login name, while otherwise retaining all of the old rights and other properties of the login.
NO CREDENTIAL	This disassociates the login with whatever credential it may have previously been mapped to.

DROP LOGIN

This works just like any other DROP statement in SQL Server.

```
DROP LOGIN <login name>
```

And it's gone.

Creating a Login Using the Management Studio

Creating a login using Management Studio is fairly straightforward and is much the same as it is for most other objects in SQL Server. Just navigate to the appropriate mode in the Object Explorer (in this case, Security@@Logins), right-click, and choose New Login. This gets us the typical CREATE dialog that we've seen repeatedly in this book, but adjusted for the properties that are appropriate for a login (all the same things we reviewed in the "CREATE LOGIN" section earlier in the chapter, plus a number of additional areas we have yet to take a look at), as shown in Figure 19-1.

Figure 19-1

Only this first set of properties (the General properties) maps to the CREATE LOGIN syntax. The additional tabs map to other objects we will be creating as we continue through the chapter.

We will be reviewing several other kinds of objects that get associated with logins in some fashion. For now, the thing to notice is how the user interface in Management Studio lets you do everything at once. As we'll see as we continue the chapter, when creating these objects using code, we have to do each step separately rather than all at once as Management Studio offers. (As you might imagine, it's really just collecting all the necessary information in advance and then issuing all those individual programmatic steps for us.)

SQL Management Objects

This is largely out of scope for this chapter (we cover SMO in its own chapter later on), but I did want to specifically point out that SMO can create logins for you using a straightforward object model as opposed to the CREATE statement approach. See Chapter 23 for more information.

Legacy Options

There are three older options of significance when considering the way that logins have been created in past versions of SQL Server.

❑ **sp_addlogin and related sprocs**: This was a stored procedure that essentially maps to CREATE LOGIN except that several parts of the CREATE LOGIN statement implement things that were not supported prior to SQL Server 2005. The basics (creating the typical login as opposed to the certificate or asymmetric key approach) are all there though. We'll take a more detailed look at sp_addlogin shortly.

❑ **WMI**: Windows Management Instrumentation is an implementation of an industry-standard Web management protocol. When SQL Server 2000 first came out, the thinking was that a WMI-based model was going to take over as the primary way of automating SQL Server management. In the end, there was no WMI-based model implemented that came anywhere close to being up to the task of exposing all the things we need in SQL Server, and that effort would seem to have been largely junked. WMI is now outside the scope of this book, but realize that it's out there and remains an option if you need to manage older versions of SQL Server or are familiar with WMI for other purposes and want to add SQL Server scripting into your larger WMI plan.

A Quick Look at sp_addlogin

This sproc does exactly what it says, and it was the old way of implementing the things that CREATE LOGIN does for us today. While I highly recommend avoiding sp_addlogin for new development, it is still in wide use in legacy code. It requires only one parameter, but most of the time you'll use two or three. There are a couple of additional parameters, but you'll find that you use those far more rarely. The syntax looks like this:

```
EXEC sp_addlogin [@loginame =] <'login'>
    [,[@passwd =] <'password'>]
    [,[@defdb =] <'database'>]
    [,[@deflanguage =] <'language'>]
```

```
[,[@sid =] 'sid']
[,[@encryptopt =] <'encryption_option'>]
```

Parameter	Description
@loginame	Just what it sounds like — this is the login ID that will be used.
@passwd	Even more what it sounds like — the password that is used to log in using the aforementioned login ID.
@defdb	The default database. This defines what is the first "current" database when the user logs in. Normally, this will be the main database your application uses. If left unspecified, the default will be the master database (you usually don't want that, so be sure to provide this parameter).
@deflanguage	The default language for this user. You can use this to override the system default if you are supporting localization.
@sid	A binary number that becomes the *security identifier (SID)* for your login ID. If you don't supply an SID, SQL Server generates one for you. Since SIDs must be unique, any SID you supply must not already exist in the system. Using a specific SID can be handy when you are restoring your database to a different server or are otherwise migrating login information.
@encryptopt	The user's login ID and password information is stored in the sysusers table in the master database. The @encryptopt determines whether or not the password stored in the master database is encrypted. By default (or if you provide a NULL in this parameter), the password is indeed encrypted. The other options are skip_encryption, which does just what it says — the password is not encrypted, and skip_encryption_old, which is there only for backward compatibility, and should not be used.

As you can see, most of the items here map directly to CREATE LOGIN, and that is the way I recommend doing things unless you need to utilize sp_addlogin for backward-compatibility reasons.

sp_password

Since we've looked at sp_addlogin, we ought to look at sp_password. While ALTER LOGIN gives you the ability to address password maintenance on a login (and it is what you should be using), sp_addlogin had no such functionality — sp_password takes care of that. The syntax is pretty straightforward:

```
sp_password [[@old =] <'old password'>,]
    [@new =] <'new password'>
    [,[@loginame =] <'login'>]
```

The new and old password parameters work, of course, just exactly as you would expect. You need to accept those from the user and pass them into the sproc. Note, however, that the login is an optional parameter. If you don't supply it, then it will assume that you want to change the password on the login used for the current connection. Note that sp_password cannot be executed as part of a transaction.

You might be thinking something like, "Don't most systems require you to enter the new password twice?" Indeed they do. So the follow up question is, "How come sp_password doesn't do that?" The answer is a simple one — because SQL Server leaves that up to you. You would include the logic to check for a double entry of the new password in your client application before you ever got as far as using sp_password. *This same issue exists for* ALTER LOGIN.

sp_grantlogin

This simulates the CREATE LOGIN...FROM functionality as relates to Windows logins (prior to SQL Server 2005, mapping from certificates and asymmetric keys did not exist as they do now). The syntax is straightforward:

```
sp_grantlogin [@loginname = ]'<Domain Name>\<Windows User Name>'
```

Again, this is for backward compatibility only. Use the CREATE LOGIN ... FROM syntax for 2005 and later installations (which should be the vast majority of new code at this point).

Windows Authentication

Windows authentication gives us the capability to map logins from trusted Windows domains into our SQL Server.

It is simply a model where you take existing Windows domain user accounts or groups and provide SQL Server rights to them directly rather than forcing users to keep separate passwords and make separate logins.

Windows authentication allows:

❑ Maintenance of a user's access from just one place

❑ Granting of SQL Server rights simply by adding a user to a Windows group (this means that you often don't have to even go into SQL Server in order to grant access to a user)

❑ Your users need to remember only one password and login

That being said, let's take a look at how to grant specific rights to specific users.

User Permissions

The simplest definition of what a *user permission* is would be something like, "what a user can and can't do." In this case, the simple definition is a pretty good one.

User permissions fall into three categories:

❑ Permission to log in

❑ Permission to access a specific database

❑ Permission to perform specific actions on particular objects within that database

Since we've already looked at creating logins, we'll focus here on the specific permission that a login can have.

Granting Access to a Specific Database

The first thing that you need to do if you want a user to have access to a database is to grant the user permission to access that database. This can be done in Management Studio by adding the user to the Users member of the Databases node of your server. To add a user using T-SQL, you should use CREATE USER. Similar to sp_addlogin there is also, for backward compatibility, the sp_grantdbaccess stored procedure.

> Note that as you CREATE a user in the database, those permissions are actually stored in the database and mapped to the server's identifier for that user. As you restore a database, you may have to remap user rights to the server identifiers where you restored the database.

CREATE USER

The CREATE USER command adds a new user to the database. That user can be sourced from an existing login, certificate, or asymmetric key, or can be local to just the current database. The syntax looks like this:

```
CREATE USER <user name>
    [ { { FOR | FROM }
      {
        LOGIN <login name>
        | CERTIFICATE <certificate name>
        | ASYMMETRIC KEY <key name>
      }
      | WITHOUT LOGIN ]
    [ WITH DEFAULT_SCHEMA = <schema name> ]
```

Let's take a quick look at what some of these elements mean:

Option	Description
LOGIN	The name of the login you want to grant access to for the current database.
CERTIFICATE	Logical name of the certificate to be associated with this user. Note that the certificate must have already been created using the CREATE CERTIFICATE command.
ASYMMETRIC KEY	Logical name of the asymmetric key to be associated with this user. Note that the key must have already been created using the CREATE ASYMMETRIC KEY command.
WITHOUT LOGIN	Creates a user that is local to the current database. It can be used to set up a specific security context but cannot be mapped to a login outside of the current database nor can it access any other database.
WITH DEFAULT_SCHEMA	Establishes a schema other than the default "dbo" as being the default schema for the current user.

So, to grant access to our NorthwindSecure database for our TestAccount, we would issue a command such as:

```
CREATE USER [HOBBES\TestAccount]
   FOR LOGIN [HOBBES\TestAccount]
   WITH DEFAULT_SCHEMA = dbo;
```

This grants our login access to the specified database (NorthwindSecure in this case) and sets that login's default schema to the database owner.

sp_grantdbaccess

This is the legacy method for granting a login access to a specific database. The syntax looks like this:

```
sp_grantdbaccess [@loginame =] <'login'>[, [@name_in_db =] <'name in this db'>
```

Note that the access granted will be to the current database — that is, you need to make sure that the database you want the user to have access to is the current database when you issue the command. The login name is the actual login ID that was used to log in to SQL Server. The name_in_db parameter allows you to alias this user to another identification. The alias serves for this database only — all other databases will still use the default of the login ID or whatever alias you defined when you granted the user access to that database. The aliasing will affect identification functions such as USER_NAME(). Functions that look at things at the system level, such as SYSTEM_USER, will still return the base login ID.

Granting Object Permissions within the Database

Okay, so the user has a login and access to the database you want him or her to have access to, so now everything's done — right? Ah, if only it were that simple! We are, of course, not done yet.

SQL Server gives us a pretty fine degree of control over what our users can access. Most of the time, you have some information that you want your users to be able to get to, but you also have other information in the database to which you don't want them to have access. For example, you might have a customer service person who has to be able to look at and maintain order information — but you probably don't want them messing around with the salary information. The opposite is also probably true — you need your human resource people to be able to edit employee records, but you probably don't want them giving somebody a major discount on a sale.

SQL Server allows you to assign a separate set of rights to some of the different objects within SQL Server. The objects you can assign rights to include tables, views, and stored procedures. Triggers are implied to have the rights of the person that created them.

User rights on objects fall into six different types:

User Right	Description
SELECT	Allows a user to "see" the data. If a user has this permission, the user has the right to run a SELECT statement against the table or view on which the permission is granted.

Continued

User Right	Description
INSERT	Allows a user to create new data. Users with this permission can run an INSERT statement. Note that, unlike many systems, having INSERT capability does not necessarily mean that you have SELECT rights.
UPDATE	Allows a user to modify existing data. Users with this permission can run an UPDATE statement. Like the INSERT statement, having UPDATE capability does not necessarily mean that you have SELECT rights.
DELETE	Allows a user to delete data. Users with this permission can run a DELETE statement. Again, having DELETE capability does not necessarily mean that you have SELECT rights.
REFERENCES	Allows a user to insert rows, where the table that is being inserted into has a foreign key constraint, which references another table to which that user doesn't have SELECT rights.
EXECUTE	Allows a user to EXECUTE a specified stored procedure.

You can mix and match these rights as needed on the particular table, view, or sproc to which you're assigning rights.

You can assign these rights in the Management Studio simply by navigating to the Logins option of the Security node of your server. Just right-click the user and choose Properties. You'll be presented with a different dialog depending on whether you're in the database or security node, but, in either case, you'll have the option of setting permissions. Assigning rights using T-SQL uses three commands that are good to know even if you're only going to assign rights through Management Studio (the terminology is the same).

GRANT

GRANT gives the specified user or role the access specified for the object that is the subject of the GRANT statement.

The syntax for a GRANT statement looks like this:

```
GRANT
    ALL [PRIVILEGES] | <permission>[,...n]
    ON
    <table or view name>[(<column name>[,...n])]
        |<stored or extended stored procedure name>
    TO <login or role name>[,...n]
    [WITH GRANT OPTION]
    [AS <role name>]
```

The ALL keyword indicates that you want to grant all the rights that are applicable for that object type (EXECUTE *never* applies to a table). If you don't use the ALL keyword, then you need to supply one or more specific permissions that you want granted for that object.

PRIVILEGES is a keyword that has no real function other than to provide ANSI/ISO compatibility.

The ON keyword serves as a placeholder to say that what comes next is the object for which you want the permissions granted. Note that, if you are granting rights on a table, you can specify permissions down to the column level by specifying a column list to be affected — if you don't supply specific columns, then it's assumed to affect all columns.

> *Microsoft appears to have done something of an about face in their opinion of column-level permissions. Being able to say that a user can do a SELECT on a particular table but only on certain columns seems like a cool idea, but it really convolutes the security process both in its use and in the work it takes Microsoft to implement it. As such, literature on the subject over the last several years has sometimes said little, and sometimes seemed to indicate that Microsoft wishes that column-level security would go away. They have occasionally recommended against its use (and other times seemed to offer no opinion) — if you need to restrict a user to seeing particular columns, consider using a view instead.*

The TO statement does what you would expect: it specifies those to whom you want this access granted. It can be a login ID or a role name.

WITH GRANT OPTION allows the user that you're granting access to, in turn, also grant access to other users.

> *I recommend against the use of this option since it can quickly become a pain to keep track of who has got access to what. Sure, you can always go into Management Studio and look at the permissions for that object, but then you're in a reactive mode rather than a proactive one — you're looking for what's wrong with the current access levels rather than stopping unwanted access up front.*

Last, but not least, is the AS keyword. This one deals with the issue of a login belonging to multiple roles.

Now, we can go ahead and move on to an example or two. We'll see later that the TestAccount that we created already has some access based on being a member of the Public role — something that every database user belongs to, and from which you can't remove them. There are, however, a large number of items to which TestAccount doesn't have access (because Public is the only role it belongs to, and Public doesn't have rights either).

Start by logging in with the TestAccount user. Then try a SELECT statement against the Region table:

```
SELECT * FROM Region;
```

You'll quickly get a message from SQL Server telling you that you are a scoundrel, and you are attempting to go to places that you shouldn't be going:

```
Server: Msg 229, Level 14, State 5, Line 1
SELECT permission denied on object 'Region', database 'NorthwindSecure', owner 'dbo'.
```

Log in separately as sa — you can do this in the same instance of QA if you like by choosing the File@@Connect menu choice. Then select SQL Server security for the new connection and log in as sa with the appropriate password. Now execute a GRANT statement:

```
USE NorthwindSecure;

GRANT SELECT ON Region TO [HOBBES\TestAccount];
```

Note that you'll need to replace the "HOBBES" with the name of your computer or domain as appropriate.

Now switch back to the `TestAccount` connection (remember, the information for what user you're connected in as is in the title bar of the connection window), and try that `SELECT` statement again: This time, you get better results:

```
RegionID          RegionDescription
---------------   -------------------------
1                 Eastern
2                 Western
3                 Northern
4                 Southern

(4 row(s) affected)
```

Let's go ahead and try another one. This time, let's run the same tests and commands against the `EmployeeTerritories` table:

```
SELECT * FROM EmployeeTerritories;
```

This one fails — again, you don't have rights to it, so let's grant the rights to this table:

```
USE NorthwindSecure;

GRANT SELECT ON EmployeeTerritories TO [HOBBES\TestAccount];
```

Now, if you re-run the select statement, things work just fine:

```
EmployeeID        TerritoryID
---------------   --------------
1                 06897
1                 19713
...
...
...
9                 48304
9                 55113
9                 55439

(49 row(s) affected)
```

To add an additional twist, however, let's try an `INSERT` into this table:

```
INSERT INTO EmployeeTerritories
VALUES
     (1, '01581');
```

SQL Server wastes no time in telling us to get lost. We don't have the required permissions, so let's grant them (using the `sa` connection):

```
USE NorthwindSecure;

GRANT INSERT ON EmployeeTerritories TO [HOBBES\TestAccount];
```

Now try that INSERT statement again:

```
INSERT INTO EmployeeTerritories
VALUES
    (1, '01581');
```

Everything works great.

DENY

DENY explicitly prevents the user from the access specified on the targeted object. The key to DENY is that it overrides any GRANT statements. Since a user can belong to multiple roles (discussed shortly), it's possible for a user to be part of a role that's granted access but also have a DENY in effect. If a DENY and a GRANT both exist in a user's mix of individual and role-based rights, then the DENY wins every time. In short, if the user or any role the user belongs to has a DENY for the right in question, then the user will not be able to make use of that access on that object.

The syntax looks an awful lot like the GRANT statement:

```
DENY
    [ALL] [PRIVILEGES]|<permission>[,...n]
    ON
    <table or view name>[(column[,...n])]
        |<stored or extended stored procedure name>
    TO <login ID or roll name>[,...n]
    [CASCADE]
```

Again, the ALL keyword indicates that you want to deny all the rights that are applicable for that object type (EXECUTE *never* applies to a table). If you don't use the ALL keyword, then you need to supply one or more specific permissions that you want to be denied for that object.

> Note that the **ALL** keyword is now included solely for backward compatibility. It's also important to understand that **ALL** no longer truly affects "all" privileges. While it does affect most mainstream privileges (such as a **SELECT**), there is, as **ALL** becomes more out of date, an ever increasing list of privileges not affected by **ALL**.

PRIVILEGES is still a new keyword and has no real function other than to provide ISO compatibility.

The ON keyword serves as a placeholder to say that what comes next is the object on which you want the permissions denied.

Everything has worked pretty much the same as with a GRANT statement until now. The CASCADE keyword matches up with the WITH GRANT OPTION that was in the GRANT statement. CASCADE tells SQL Server that you want to also deny access to anyone that this user has granted access to under the rules of the WITH GRANT OPTION.

To run an example on DENY, let's try a simple SELECT statement using the TestAccount login:

```
USE NorthwindSecure;

SELECT * FROM Employees;
```

This should get you nine records or so. How did you get access when we haven't granted it to TestAccount? TestAccount belongs to Public, and Public has been granted access to Employees.

Let's say that we don't want TestAccount to have access. For whatever reason, TestAccount is the exception, and we don't want that user snooping in that data — we just issue our DENY statement (remember to issue the DENY using the sa login):

```
USE NorthwindSecure;

DENY ALL ON Employees TO [HOBBES\TestAccount];
```

When you run the SELECT statement again using TestAccount, you'll get an error. You no longer have access. Note also that, since we used the ALL keyword, the INSERT, DELETE, and UPDATE access that Public has is now also denied from TestAccount.

Again, note that ALL is deprecated, so you will receive a warning when running the previous example code. I have kept this example so you understand the breadth of the ALL keyword, which you may still find in your legacy code.

REVOKE

REVOKE eliminates the effects of a previously issued GRANT or DENY statement. Think of this one as like a targeted "Undo" statement.

The syntax is a mix of the GRANT and DENY statements:

```
REVOKE [GRANT OPTION FOR]
    [ALL] [PRIVILEGES] | <permission>[,...n]
    ON
    <table or view name>[(<column name> [,...n])]
      |<stored or extended stored procedure name>
    TO | FROM <login ID or roll name>[,...n]
    [CASCADE]
    [AS <role name>]
```

The explanations here are virtually identical to those of the GRANT and DENY statements. I put them here again in case you're pulling the book back off the shelf for a quick lookup on REVOKE.

Once again, the ALL keyword indicates that you want to revoke all the rights that are applicable for that object type. If you don't use the ALL keyword, then you need to supply one or more specific permissions that you want to be revoked for that object.

PRIVILEGES still has no real function other than to provide ANSI/ISO compatibility.

The ON keyword serves as a placeholder to say that what comes next is the object on which you want the permissions revoked.

The CASCADE keyword matches up with the WITH GRANT OPTION that was in the GRANT statement. CASCADE tells SQL Server that you want to also revoke access from anyone that this user granted access to under the rules of the WITH GRANT OPTION.

The AS keyword again just specifies which role you want to issue this command based on.

Using the sa connection, let's undo the access that we granted to the Region table in Northwind-Secure:

```
REVOKE ALL ON Region FROM [HOBBES\TestAccount];
```

After executing this, our TestAccount can no longer run a SELECT statement against the Region table.

In order to remove a DENY, we also issue a REVOKE statement. This time, we'll regain access to the Employees table:

```
USE NorthwindSecure;

REVOKE ALL ON Employees TO [HOBBES\TestAccount]
```

Now that we've seen how all the commands to control access work for individual users, let's take a look at the way we can greatly simplify management of these rights by managing in groupings.

User Rights and Statement-Level Permissions

User permissions don't just stop with the objects in your database — they also extend to certain statements that aren't immediately tied to any particular object. SQL Server gives you control over permissions to run several different statements, including:

- ❑ CREATE DATABASE
- ❑ CREATE DEFAULT
- ❑ CREATE PROCEDURE
- ❑ CREATE RULE
- ❑ CREATE TABLE
- ❑ CREATE VIEW
- ❑ BACKUP DATABASE
- ❑ BACKUP LOG

At this point, we've already seen all of these commands at work except for the two backup commands — what those are about is pretty self-explanatory, so I'm not going to spend any time on them here (we'll look at them in Chapter 22) — just keep in mind that they are something you can control at the statement level.

Okay, so how do we assign these permissions? Actually, now that you've already seen GRANT, REVOKE, and DENY in action for objects, you're pretty much already schooled on statement-level permissions, too. Syntactically speaking, they work just the same as object-level permissions, except that they are even simpler (you don't have to fill in as much). The syntax looks like this:

```
GRANT {ALL | <statement[,...n]>} TO <login ID>[,...n]
```

Easy, hey? To do a quick test, let's start by verifying that our test user doesn't already have authority to CREATE. Make sure you are logged in as your TestAccount, and then run the following command. Don't forget to switch your domain name for HOBBES in the following:

```
USE NorthwindSecure;

CREATE TABLE TestCreate
(
    Col1 int Primary Key
);
```

This gets us nowhere fast:

```
Server: Msg 262, Level 14, State 1, Line 2
CREATE TABLE permission denied, database 'NorthwindSecure', owner 'dbo'.
```

Now log in to SQL Server using the sa account (or another account with dbo authority for Northwind-Secure). Then run our command to grant permissions:

```
GRANT CREATE TABLE TO [HOBBES\TestAccount];
```

You should get confirmation that your command completed successfully. Then just try running the CREATE statement again. Remember to log back in using the TestAccount:

```
USE NorthwindSecure;

CREATE TABLE TestCreate
(
    Col1 int Primary Key
);
```

This time everything works.

DENY and REVOKE also work the same way as they did for object-level permissions.

Server and Database Roles

A role is, in the most general sense, the same thing as a group in Windows, that is, it is a collection of access rights (or denials) that are automatically associated with a user when they are assigned that role.

> A role is a collection of access rights that can be assigned to a user en masse simply by assigning a user to that role.

A user can belong to as little as one or potentially several roles at one time. This can be incredibly handy since you can group access rights into smaller and more logical groups and then mix and match them into the formula that best fits a user.

Roles fall into two categories:

❑   Server roles

❑   Database roles

We'll soon see a third thing that's also called role — though I wish that Microsoft had chosen another name — application roles. These are a special way to alias a user into a different set of permissions. An application role isn't something you assign a user to; it's a way of letting an application have a different set of rights from the user. For this reason, I don't usually think of application roles as a "role" in the true sense of the word.

Server roles are limited to those that are already built into SQL Server when it ships and are primarily there for the maintenance of the system as well as granting the capability to do non-database-specific things like creating login accounts and creating linked servers.

Much like server roles, there are a number of built-in (or "fixed") database roles, but you can also define your own database roles to meet your particular needs. Database roles are for setting up and grouping specific user rights within a single given database.

Let's look at both of these types of roles individually.

Server Roles

All server roles available are "fixed" roles and are there right from the beginning. All the server roles that you're ever going to have existed from the moment your SQL Server was installed.

Role	Nature
sysadmin	This role can perform any activity on your SQL Server. Anyone with this role is essentially the sa for that server. The creation of this server role provides Microsoft with the capability to one day eliminate the sa login — indeed, the Books Online refers to sa as being legacy in nature. It's worth noting that the Windows Administrators group on the SQL Server is automatically mapped into the sysadmin role. This means that anyone who is a member of your server's Administrators group also has sa-level access to your SQL data. You can, if you need to, remove the Windows administrators group from the sysadmin role to tighten that security loophole.
serveradmin	This one can set server-wide configuration options or shut down the server. It's rather limited in scope, yet the functions controlled by members of this role can have a very significant impact on the performance of your server.
setupadmin	This one is limited to managing linked servers and startup procedures.
securityadmin	This one is very handy for logins that you create specifically to manage logins, read error logs, and CREATE DATABASE permissions. In many ways, this one is the classic system operator role — it can handle most of the day-to-day stuff, but doesn't have the kind of global access that a true omnipotent superuser would have.

Continued

Role	Nature
processadmin	Has the capability to manage processes running in SQL Server — this one can kill long-running processes if necessary.
dbcreator	Is limited to creating and altering databases.
diskadmin	Manages disk files (what file group things are assigned to, attaching and detaching databases, and so on).
bulkadmin	This one is something of an oddity. It is created explicitly to give rights to execute the BULK INSERT statement, which otherwise is executable only by someone with sysadmin rights. Frankly, I don't understand why this statement isn't granted with the GRANT command like everything else, but it isn't. Keep in mind that, even if a user has been added to the bulkadmin group, that just gives them access to the statement, not the table that they want to run it against. This means that you need, in addition to adding the user to the bulkadmin task, to GRANT them INSERT permissions to any table you want them to be able to perform the BULK INSERT against. In addition, you'll need to make sure they have proper SELECT access to any tables that they will be referencing in their BULK INSERT statement.

You can mix and match these roles to individual users that are responsible for administrative roles on your server. In general, I suspect that only the very largest of database shops will use more than the sysadmin and securityadmin roles, but they're still handy to have around.

Earlier in this chapter, I got into a lengthy soapbox diatribe on the evils of global users. It probably comes as no surprise to you to learn that I was positively ecstatic when the new sysadmin role was added back in version 7.0. The existence of this role means that, on an ongoing basis, you should not need to have anyone have the sa login. Just let the users that need that level of access become members of the sysadmin role, and they shouldn't ever need to log in as sa. Be careful though; having a user always have that level of access can lead to accidents (it won't, on the basis of security, stop you from dropping objects and the like). I've known many IT shops that give their administrators more than one login: one for full sysadmin access, and another "day to day" login that has the privileges they need to get most things done, but limits privileges that have a high risk of being destructive. The admin can still do what they need to do, but they need to make the conscious effort to log in with the special high access account to do the more risky activities (which means they are much more likely to be thinking about it as they do it).

Database Roles

Database roles are limited in scope to just one database — just because a user belongs to the db_datareader role in one database doesn't mean that it belongs to that role in another database. Database roles fall into two subcategories: fixed and user defined.

Fixed Database Roles

Much as there are several fixed server roles, there are also a number of fixed database roles. Some of them have a special predefined purpose, which cannot be duplicated using normal statements (that is you cannot create a user-defined database role that had the same functionality). However, most exist to deal with the more common situations and make things easier for you.

Role	Nature
db_owner	This role performs as if it were a member of all the other database roles. Using this role, you can create a situation where multiple users can perform the same functions and tasks as if they were the database owner.
db_accessadmin	Performs a portion of the functions similar to the securityadmin server role, except this role is limited to the individual database where it is assigned and the creation of users (not individual rights). It cannot create new SQL Server logins, but members of this role can add Windows users and groups as well as existing SQL Server logins into the database.
db_datareader	Can issue a SELECT statement on all user tables in the database.
db_datawriter	Can issue INSERT, UPDATE, and DELETE statements on all user tables in the database.
db_ddladmin	Can add, modify, or drop objects in the database.
db_securityadmin	The other part of the database-level equivalent of the securityadmin server role. This database role cannot create new users in the database, but does manage roles and members of database roles as well as manage statement and object permissions in the database.
db_backupoperator	Backs up the database (gee, bet you wouldn't have guessed that one!).
db_denydatareader	Provides the equivalent of a DENY SELECT on every table and view in the database.
db_denydatawriter	Similar to db_denydatareader, only affects INSERT, UPDATE, and DELETE statements.

Much as with the fixed server roles, you're probably not going to see all of these used in anything but the largest of database shops. Some of the roles are not replaceable with your own database roles, and others are just very handy to deal with the quick-and-dirty situations that seem to frequently come up.

User-Defined Database Roles

The fixed roles that are available are really only meant to be there to help you get started. The real mainstay of your security is going to be the creation and assignment of user-defined database roles. For these roles, you decide what permissions they include.

With user-defined roles, you can GRANT, DENY, and REVOKE in exactly the same way as we did for individual users. The nice thing about using roles is that users tend to fall into categories of access needs. By using roles you can make a change in one place and have it propagate to all the similar users (at least the ones that you have assigned to that role).

We have two means of creating a user-defined role:

- ❑ CREATE ROLE (the preferred choice)
- ❑ sp_addrole (for backward compatibility)

Let's take a look at each.

Creating a User-Defined Role Using CREATE ROLE

To create our own role, the preferred option is to use the CREATE ROLE command. Much like many of the other commands we've looked at in this chapter, the functionality of this command has been migrated to a more ANSI/ISO-compliant syntax, but was previously supported by a system stored procedure — in this case, the sp_addrole system sproc. As with the others, the syntax is pretty straightforward:

```
CREATE ROLE <role name> [AUTHORIZATION <owner name>][;]
```

The role name is simply what you want to call that role. Examples of common naming schemas would include by department (Accounting, Sales, Marketing, and so on) or by specific job (CustomerService, Salesperson, President, and so on). Using roles like this can make it really easy to add new users to the system. If your accounting department hires someone new, you can just add him or her to the Accounting role (or, if you're being more specific, it might even be the AccountsPayable role) and forget it — no researching "What should this person have for rights?"

The AUTHORIZATION parameter is optional, and allows you to override what database user or role owns this new role. (By default, it will be owned by whoever ran the CREATE command, usually someone in the db_owner role).

Let's go ahead and create ourselves a role:

```
USE NorthwindSecure;

CREATE ROLE OurTestRole;
```

When you execute this, you should get back a nice friendly message telling you that the new role has been added.

Now what we need is to add some value to this role in the form of it actually having some rights assigned to it. To do this, we just use our GRANT, DENY, or REVOKE statements just as we did for actual users earlier in the chapter:

```
USE NorthwindSecure;

GRANT SELECT ON Territories TO OurTestRole;
```

Anyone who belongs to our role now has SELECT access to the Territories table (unless they have a DENY somewhere else in their security information).

Using sp_addrole

As I mentioned earlier, there is an older, system stored procedure–based command that remains for backward compatibility.

The syntax is again pretty simple:

```
sp_addrole [@rolename =] <'role name'>
    [,[@ownername =] <'owner'>]
```

The `owner` is the same thing as it is for all other objects in the system. The default is the database owner, and I strongly suggest leaving it that way (in other words, just ignore this optional parameter). If we were going to add our special test role using the older syntax, it would look something like:

```
USE NorthwindSecure;

EXEC sp_addrole 'OurTestRole';
```

Regardless of which syntax you use, you should, at this point, be ready to start adding users.

Adding Users to a Role

Having all these roles around is great, but they are of no use if they don't have anyone assigned to them. Surprisingly, there isn't, as yet anyway, a new command that addresses this. Instead, we go back to the older system stored procedure model, calling the `sp_addrolemember` system sproc and providing the database name and login ID:

```
sp_addrolemember [@rolename =] <role name>,
    [@membername =] <Login ID>[;]
```

Everything is pretty self-explanatory on the parameters for this one, so let's move right into an example.

Let's start off by verifying that our `TestAccount` doesn't have access to the `Territories` table:

```
SELECT * FROM Territories;
```

Sure enough, we are rejected (no access yet):

```
Server: Msg 229, Level 14, State 5, Line 1
SELECT permission denied on object 'Territories', database 'Northwind', owner 'dbo'.
```

Now we'll go ahead and add our `TestAccount` Windows user to our `OurTestRole` role:

```
USE NorthwindSecure;

EXEC sp_addrolemember OurTestRole, [HOBBES\TestAccount];
```

It's time to try and run the SELECT statement again — this time with much more success (you should get about 53 rows back).

Removing a User from a Role

What goes up must come down, and users that are added to a role will also inevitably be removed from roles.

Removing a user from a role works almost exactly as adding them does, except we use a different system sproc called `sp_droprolemember` in the form of:

```
sp_droprolemember [@rolename =] <role name>,
    [@membername =] <security account>[;]
```

So, let's go right back to our example and remove the `TestAccount` from the `OurTestRole` database role:

```
USE NorthwindSecure;

EXEC sp_droprolemember OurTestRole, [HOBBES\TestAccount];
```

You should receive another friendly confirmation that things have gone well. Now try our `SELECT` statement again:

```
SELECT * FROM Territories;
```

And, sure enough, we are again given the error that we don't have access.

You can add and drop users from any role this way. It doesn't matter whether the role is user-defined or fixed, or whether it's a system or database role. In any case, they work pretty much the same.

Note also that you can do all of this through the Management Studio. To change the rights associated with a role, just click the Roles member of the Security node (under your specific database), and assign permissions by using the checkboxes. When you want to add a user to the role, go to the users node (again, under the specific database) and right-click to select Properties. Then select either the server or database roles by putting a check mark in all the roles you want that user to have.

Dropping Roles

Dropping a role is as easy as adding one. The syntax is simply:

```
EXEC sp_droprole <'role name'>[;]
```

And it's gone.

Application Roles

Application roles are something of a different animal than are database and server roles. Indeed, the fact that the term *role* is used would make you think that they are closely related. They aren't.

Application roles are really much more like a security alias for the user. Application roles allow you to define an access list (made up of individual rights or groupings of databases). They are also similar to a user in that they have their own password. They are, however, different from a user login because they cannot "log in" as such. A user account must first log in, then he or she can activate the application role.

So what do we need application roles for? For applications — what else? Time and time again, you'll run into the situation where you would like a user to have a separate set of rights depending on under what context he or she is accessing the database. With an application role, you can do things like grant users no more than read-only access to the database (SELECT statements only), but still allow them to modify data when they do so within the confines of your application.

The process works like this:

1. The user logs in (presumably using a login screen provided by your application).

2. The login is validated, and the user receives his or her access rights.

3. The application executes a system sproc called sp_setapprole and provides a role name and password.

4. The application role is validated, and the connection is switched to the context of that application role (all the rights the user had are gone — he or she now has the rights of the application role).

5. The user continues with access based on the application role rather than his or her personal login throughout the duration of the connection; the user cannot go back to his or her own access information.

You would only want to use application roles as part of a true application situation, and you would build the code to set the application role right into the application. You would also compile the required password into the application or store the information in some local file to be accessed when it is needed.

Creating Application Roles

To create an application role, we use a variation on the CREATE ROLE theme — CREATE APPLICATION ROLE. This is another pretty easy one to use; its syntax looks like this:

```
CREATE APPLICATION ROLE <role name>
    WITH PASSWORD = <'password'> [, DEFAULT_SCHEMA = <schema name>][;]
```

Much like the other flavors of CREATE in this chapter, the parameters are pretty self-explanatory; so let's move right on to using it by creating ourselves an application role:

```
CREATE APPLICATION ROLE OurAppRole WITH PASSWORD = 'P@ssw0rd';
```

Just that quick, our application role is created. Like most of the security items thus far, there is a system stored procedure that used to serve this functionality that is still supported, but, again, only for backward compatibility. It is very similar to the CREATE syntax, but looks like this:

```
sp_addapprole [@rolename =] <role name>,
    [@password =] <'password'>[;]
```

So creating the previous example using the system stored procedure instead would look like:

```
EXEC sp_addapprole OurAppRole, 'P@ssw0rd';
```

Adding Permissions to the Application Role

Adding permissions to application roles works just like adding permissions to anything else. Just substitute the application role name anywhere that you would use a login ID or regular server or database role.

Again, we'll move to the quick example:

```
GRANT SELECT ON Region TO OurAppRole;
```

Our application role now has SELECT rights on the Region table — it doesn't, as yet, have access to anything else.

Using the Application Role

Using the application role is a matter of calling a system sproc (sp_setapprole) and providing both the application role name and the password for that application role. The syntax looks like this:

```
sp_setapprole [@rolename =] <role name>,
    [@password =] {Encrypt N<'password'>}|<'password'>
    [,[@encrypt =] {'none' | 'odbc']
    [, [@fCreateCookie = ] {true | false} ]
    [, [@cookie = ] <variable holding cookie> OUTPUT][;]
```

The role name is simply the name of whatever application role you want to activate.

The password can be either supplied as is or encrypted using the ODBC encrypt function. If you're going to encrypt the password, then you need to enclose the password in quotes after the Encrypt keyword and precede the password with a capital N — this indicates to SQL Server that you're dealing with a Unicode string (which the password must be in if you're going to encrypt it), and it will be treated accordingly. If you don't want encryption, then just supply the password without using the Encrypt keyword.

> It's worth noting that encryption is only an option with ODBC and OLE DB clients. Thus you cannot test it inside the Query window (which uses SqlClient). Furthermore, if you're not using encryption, realize that the password you supply is going to be plainly viewable to anyone sniffing packets on your network. In short, if you're not using ODBC encryption for sending your password, then you'll want to use SSL or IPSec (two secure transport methods) for the connection.

This takes us to the cookie side of things. Setting a cookie (and storing the value you get back in the @cookie output variable) provides a bookmark of sorts for the permission set that was active before you activated the application role. You can then use the sp_unsetapprole stored procedure to revert back to the previous security context (the one indicated by the cookie). The syntax for sp_unsetapprole looks like this:

```
sp_unsetapprole <cookie variable>
```

Execute this, and your security context should return to the previous state.

Moving right into a simple example, let's start by verifying a couple of things about the status of our TestAccount user. At this point in the chapter (assuming you've been following along with all the examples), your TestAccount user should not be able to access the Region table but should be able to access the EmployeeTerritories table. You can verify this to be the case by running a couple of SELECT statements:

```
SELECT * FROM Region;

SELECT * FROM EmployeeTerritories;
```

The first SELECT should give you an error, and the second should return around 50 rows or so.

Now let's activate the application role that we created a short time ago; type this in using TestAccount user:

```
EXEC sp_setapprole OurAppRole, 'P@ssw0rd';
```

When you execute this, you should get back a confirmation that your application role is now "active."

Try it out by running our two SELECT statements. You'll find that what does and doesn't work has been exactly reversed. That is, TestAccount had access to EmployeeTerritories, but that was lost when we went to the application role. TestAccount did not have access to the Regions table, but the application role now provides that access.

Since we didn't store a cookie (I'm deliberately making a point here . . .), there is no way to terminate the application role for the current connection. We're stuck with few options other than, perhaps, switching to yet another application role. We have no way of returning to our original security context without the cookie.

Go ahead and terminate your TestAccount connection. Then, create a new connection with Windows authentication for your TestAccount. Try running those SELECT statements again, and you'll find that your original set of rights has been restored.

Getting Rid of Application Roles

When you no longer need the application role on your server, you can use the same DROP command that you should, by now, be very familiar with:

```
DROP APPLICATION ROLE <role name>
```

There is, of course, also a system stored procedure version of this (again, backward compatibility only please!) called sp_dropapprole. The syntax is as follows:

```
sp_dropapprole [@rolename =] <role name>
```

To eliminate our application role from the system using the DROP syntax, we would just issue the command (from sa):

```
DROP APPLICATION ROLE OurAppRole;
```

More Advanced Security

This section is really nothing more than an "extra things to think about" section. All of these fall outside the realm of the basic rules we defined at the beginning of the chapter, but they address ways around some problems and also how to close some common loopholes in your system.

What to Do About the Guest Account

The guest account provides a way of having default access. When you have the guest account active, several things happen:

❑   Logins gain guest-level access to any database to which they are not explicitly given access.

❑   Outside users can log in through the guest account to gain access. This requires that they know the password for guest, but they'll already know the user exists (although, they probably also know that the sa account exists).

Personally, one of the first things I do with my SQL Server is to eliminate every ounce of access the guest account has (by default, it has zero, so there should be little to do). It's a loophole, and it winds up providing access in a way you don't intuitively think of. (You probably think that when you assign rights to someone — that's all the rights they have. With guest active, that isn't necessarily so.)

There is, however, one use that I'm aware of where the guest account actually serves a fairly slick purpose — when it is used with application roles. In this scenario, you leave the guest account with access to a database but without any rights beyond simply logging in to that database — that is, the guest account only makes the logged-on database "current." You can then use sp_setapprole to activate an application role, and, boom, you now have a way for otherwise anonymous users to log in to your server with appropriate rights. They can, however, only perform any *useful* login if they are using your application.

> This is definitely a scenario where you want to be protecting that application role password as if your job depended on it (it probably does). Use the ODBC encryption option and I would not allow this kind of access via the Internet!

TCP/IP Port Settings

By default when using TCP/IP, SQL Server uses port number 1433. A port can be thought of as something like a radio channel; it doesn't matter what channel you're broadcasting on, it won't do you any good if no one is listening to that channel.

Leaving things with the default value of 1433 can be very convenient. All of your clients will automatically use port 1433 unless you specify otherwise, so this means that you have one less thing to worry about being set right if you just leave well enough alone.

The problem, however, is that just about any potential SQL Server hacker also knows that port 1433 is the one to which 99 percent of all SQL Servers are listening. If your SQL Server has a direct connection to the Internet, I strongly recommend changing to a non-standard port number. Check with your network administrator for what he or she recommends as an available port. Just remember that, when you change what the server is "listening" to, you'll also need to change what all the IP-based clients are using. For example, if we were going to change to using port 1402, we would go into the Client Network Utility and set up a specific entry for our server with 1402 as the IP port to use.

We also have the option of telling the client to dynamically determine the port, by checking the "Dynamically determine port" box.

Note that this isn't really that huge of a security gain. The reality is that a hacker is probably going to use a port scanner or other tool to determine what every open port is on your firewall and, based on responses it seems, to make a fairly accurate guess as to what kind of software is utilizing that port. That said, every little thing you do can make it just a little more difficult for the would-be hacker.

Don't Use the sa Account

Everyone who's studied SQL Server for more than about 10 minutes knows about the system administrator account. SQL Server has the sysadmin fixed server role to simulate the sa user's level of access, so I strongly suggest adding true logins to that role, then changing the sa password to something very long and very incomprehensible — something not worth spending the time to hack into. If you only need Windows authentication, then turn SQL Server security off, and that will deal with the sa account issue once and for all.

Keep xp_cmdshell under Wraps

Remember to be careful about who you grant access to use xp_cmdshell. It will run any Windows command prompt command. The amount of authority that it grants to your users depends on what account SQL Server is running under. If it is a system or administrator account (as the majority are), then the users of xp_cmdshell will have very significant access to your server. (They could, for example, copy files onto the server from elsewhere on the network, then execute those files.) Let's raise the stakes a bit though — there are also a fair number of servers running out there under the context of a Windows *domain* administrator account — anyone using xp_cmdshell now has fairly open access to your entire network!!!

The short rendition here is not to give anyone access to xp_cmdshell that you wouldn't give administrative rights to for your server or possibly even your domain.

Don't Forget Views, Stored Procedures, and UDFs as Security Tools

Remember that views, sprocs, and UDFs all have a lot to offer in terms of hiding data. Views can usually take the place of column-level security. They can do wonders to make a user think they have access to an entire table, when they, in reality, have access to only a subset of the entire data (remember our example of filtering out sensitive employee information, such as salary?). Sprocs and UDFs can do much the same. You can grant execute rights to a sproc or UDF, but that doesn't mean users get all the data from a table (they only get what the sproc or UDF gives them) — the end user may not even know what underlying table is supplying the data. In addition, views, sprocs, and UDFs have their own implied authority — that is, just because views and sprocs use a table, it doesn't mean that the user has access rights for that table.

Certificates and Asymmetric Keys

We have, at a few different points in the book (including earlier in this chapter), mentioned the notion of encryption. Certificates and asymmetric keys are the primary mechanism for defining the encryption keys for the different levels of your server architecture. Both of these are different methods of doing the same basic thing, and they are largely interchangeable. Whether you use certificates or asynchronous keys, you need to keep in mind that these are much like the keys to your house — if you let everyone have them, then they quickly lose their value (now anyone can get in, so why bother locking anyone out?).

SQL Server supports the notion of keys at several different levels based on the notion that you may want to separate several different silos of control under different encryption keys. SQL Server maintains a *Service Master Key* that goes with each server installation. It is encrypted by the Windows-level Service Master Key. Likewise, each database contains a *Database Master Key*, which can, if you choose, itself be encrypted based on the Service Master Key. Then, within each database, you can define certificates and/or asymmetric keys (both of which are a form of key). Overall, the hierarchy looks something like Figure 19-2.

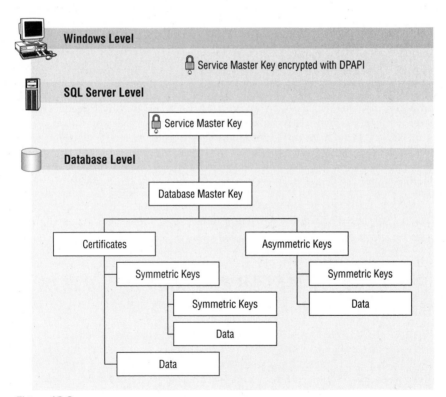

Figure 19-2

Certificates

Since SQL Server 2000, SQL Server has included its own *certificate authority*, or CA. Third-party CAs are also supported. A CA issues a certificate, which includes an encryption key along with some basic information to go with the certificate such as what date range the certificate is valid for (a starting and expiration date), the name of the holder, and information on the authority that issued the certificate. A certificate is added to a server using the CREATE CERTIFICATE command.

Asymmetric Keys

An asymmetric key works much as a certificate does but is specified directly and is not validated by any issuing authority. Like a certificate, the encryption key is specified and then utilized to encrypt sensitive information. Asymmetric keys are added using the CREATE ASYMMETRIC KEY command.

Database Encryption

Most of the encryption functions that were added in SQL Server 2005 are oriented around the idea of encrypting a particular piece of data. They require you to utilize special functions (which specific functions depend on the type of encryption being used) to encrypt the data, and then another set of functions to decrypt the data.

Beginning with SQL Server 2008, we also have the option of encrypting the entire database. Note that the idea here is not to password protect the data in the database, but rather to protect the wholesale theft of the entire database. Using database-level encryption, the database file and any backups made of it are effectively keyed to the server the database is on (unless you copy the server's certificate, so make sure you have a backup of that or your backups of the database will become effectively useless in the event of total server failure).

Summary

Security is one of those areas that tend to be ignored by developers. Unfortunately, the security of your system is going to be determined by how your client application handles things, so there's only so much a DBA can do after you've shipped your application.

Treat security as if it is the lifeblood for the success or failure of your system at your customer site (which, if you're building internal projects, may be your site) — it probably is a critical factor.

A Grand Performance: Designing a Database That Performs Well

This, and the chapter that follows, are probably the toughest chapters in the book from my perspective as the author, but not for the normal reasons. Usually, the issue is how to relate complex information in a manner that's easy to understand. As we're getting near the end of the book, I hope that I've succeeded there — even if there is still more to come. At this point, you should, from prior experience and the topics covered in this book, have a solid foundation in everything we're going to discuss in this chapter. That means I'm relatively free to get to the nitty-gritty and not worry quite as much about confusion.

Why then would this be a tough chapter for me to write? Well, because deciding exactly what to put into this and the sibling chapter that follows is difficult. You see, this isn't a book on performance tuning — that can easily be a book unto itself. It is, however, a book about making you successful in your experience developing with SQL Server. Having a well-performing system is critical to that success. The problem lies in a line from Bob Seger: "What to leave in, what to leave out." What can we focus on here that's going to get you the most bang for your buck?

Perhaps the most important thing to understand about performance tuning is that you are never going to know everything there is to know about it. If you're the average SQL developer, you're going to be lucky if you know 20 percent of what there is to know. Fortunately, performance tuning is one of those areas where the old 80-20 rule (80 percent of the benefit comes from the right 20 percent of the work) definitely applies.

For this edition of the book, I've decided to expand this topic a bit, maintaining coverage of the structural decisions, and adding additional content on "how to figure out where performance opportunities exist." This chapter will largely be on topics that have been around for a while including such things as:

❑ Index choices

❑ Client vs. server-side processing

❑ Strategic de-normalization

❑ Organizing your sprocs

❑ Uses for temporary tables

❑ Small gains in repetitive processes vs. big gains in long-running processes

The focus for this chapter is really going to be about things you should be thinking about in the area of design, those that are somewhat structural in nature. In many cases, it will be a subject we've already covered, but with a particular eye on performance. In our next chapter, we'll take a look at what to do once the system is already in place (maintenance, locating problems, and planning future changes).

There is, however, a common theme that one should get out of both chapters: This is only the beginning. The biggest thing in performance is really just to stop and think about it. There is, for some strange reason, a tendency when working with SQL to use the first thing that comes to mind that will work. You need to give the same kind of thought to your queries, sprocs, database designs — whatever — that you would give to any other development work that you're doing. Also, keep in mind that your T-SQL code is only one part of the picture — hardware, client code, SQL Server configuration, and network issues are examples of things that are "outside the code" that can have a dramatic impact on your system.

> **Performance means a lot of different things to a lot of different people. For example, many will think in terms of simple response time (how fast does my query finish). There is also the notion of *perceived* performance (many users will think in terms of how fast they receive enough to start working on, rather than how fast it actually finishes). Yet another perspective might focus on scalability (for example, how much load can I put on the system before my response time suffers or until users start colliding with each other?).**

> **Many of the examples and suggestions in the two performance chapters are about raw speed — how fast do I return results — we do, however, touch on perceived performance and scalability issues where appropriate. Make sure that all facets of performance are considered in your designs — not just time to completion.**

When to Tune

Okay, so this is probably going to seem a little obvious, but performance starts much earlier in the process than when you are writing your code. Indeed, it really should start in the requirements-gathering process and then never end.

What's the big deal about performance tuning in the requirements-gathering stage? Well, while you obviously can't do anything yet to *physically* tune your system, you can do a lot to *logically* tune your system. For example, is the concern of the customer more toward the side of *perceived* performance or actual completion of the job? For interactive processes, users will generally be more satisfied and *think* the system is faster if you do something to show them that something is happening (even if it's just a progress bar). In addition, sometimes it's worth having a process that completes a little more slowly as long as the "first response" — that is, when it starts outputting something — is faster. Which of these is preferable is something you should know in the requirements-gathering stage. Finally, you should, in the requirements-gathering process, determine what your performance requirements are for the system.

> *Many is the time that I have seen the system that the developer thought was "fast enough" only to find out that the performance was unacceptable to the user. This can happen for a lot of reasons, though the most common is certainly the developer having his or her head buried in the sand.*

> *Find out what's expected! Also, remember to test whether you've met expectations under a realistic load on something resembling the real live hardware — not a load based on one or two developers sitting at their development system.*

Performance obviously also continues into design. If you design for performance, then you will generally greatly reduce the effort required to tune at completion. What's more, you'll find that you've greatly enhanced what are the "best" numbers you can achieve.

I'm starting to drone on here, but performance never stops — when you're actually coding, get it working, but then STOP! Stop and take a look at your code. Once an entire system is together, the actual code will almost never be looked at again unless:

❑ Something breaks (there's a bug).

❑ You need to upgrade that part of the system.

❑ There is an overt performance problem (usually, a *very* bad one).

In the first two of these instances, you probably won't be looking at the performance issues, just how to get things fixed or the additional functionality added. The point here is that an extra few minutes of looking at your code and asking yourself "Could I have done it better?" or "Hey, have I done anything stupid here?" can shave a little bit here and a little bit there and, occasionally, a whole lot in some other place.

> *Simply put: I make stupid mistakes, and so will you. It is, however, amazing how often you can step back from your code for a minute or two, then look at it again with a critical eye and say, "Geez, I can't believe I did that!" Hopefully, those moments will be rare, but, if you take the time to be critical of your own code, you'll find most of those critical gaffes that could really bog your system down. As for the ones you don't find, well, that's what the next chapter is for!*

The next big testing milestone time is in the quality assurance process. At this juncture you should be establishing general system benchmarks and comparing those against the performance requirements established during the requirements phase.

Last, but not least — never stop. Ask end users where their pain is from a performance perspective. Is there something they say is slow? Don't wait for them to tell you (often, they think "that's just the way it is" and say nothing — except to your boss, of course); go ask.

Index Choices

Again, this is something that was covered in extreme depth previously, but the topic still deserves something more than a mention here because of its sheer importance to query performance.

People tend to go to extremes with indexes — I'm encouraging you not to follow any one rule but to instead think about the full range of items that your index choices impact.

Any table that has a primary key (and with very rare exception, all tables should have a primary key) has at least one index. This doesn't mean, however, that it is a very useful index from a performance perspective. Indexes should be considered for any column that you're going to be frequently using as a target in a WHERE or JOIN, and, to a lesser extent, an ORDER BY clause.

Remember though, that the more indexes you have, the slower your inserts, updates, and deletes are going to be. When you modify a record, one or more entries may (depending on what's going on in the non-leaf levels of the B-Tree) have to be modified for that index (certainly true in the case of an insert or delete, and true for updates on any column participating in the index). That means more indexes and also more for SQL Server to do on modification statements. In an Online Transaction Processing (OLTP) environment (where you tend to have a lot of inserts, updates, and deletes), this can be a killer. In an Online Analytical Processing (OLAP) environment, this is probably no big deal since your OLAP data is usually relatively stable (few inserts), and what inserts are made are usually done through a highly repetitive batch process (doesn't have quite the lack of predictability that users have).

> Technically speaking, the problem is smaller on updates and deletes. For updates, your indexes need to be updated only if the column that was changed is part of the key for that index. If you do indeed need to update the index though, think about it as a delete and an insert — that means that you're exposed to page splits again.

> So, what, then, about deletes? Well, again, when you delete a record you're going to need to delete all the entries from your indexes too, so you do add some additional overhead, but you don't have to worry about page splits and having to physically move data around.

The bottom line here is that if you're doing a lot more querying than modifying, then more indexes are okay. However, if you're doing lots of modifications to your data, keep your indexes limited to high use columns.

If you're treating this book as more of a reference than a full "learn how" book and haven't taken the time to read the index chapters (Chapters 6 and 7) yet — do it!

Check the Index Tuning Tool in the Database Engine Tuning Advisor

The *Database Engine Tuning Advisor* is a descendant of the Index Tuning Wizard that made its first appearance back in version 7.0. While the Database Tuning Advisor has grown to include much more than just index tuning, it still has this key feature.

Be very careful when using automated tuning tools with indexes. In particular, watch out about what indexes you let it delete. It makes its recommendations based on the workload it has been exposed to — that workload may not include all of the queries that make up your system. Take a look at the recommendations and ask yourself why those recommendations might help. Particularly with deletions, ask yourself what that index might be used for — does deleting it make sense? Is there some long-running report that didn't run when you were capturing the workload file that might make use of that index?

Client vs. Server-Side Processing

Where you decide to "do the work" can have a very serious impact — for better or worse — on overall system performance.

When client/server computing first came along, the assumption was that you would get more/faster/cheaper by "distributing" the computing. For some tasks, this is true. For others though, you lose more than you gain.

Here's a quick review of some preferences and how they perform on client-side versus server side:

Static cursors	Usually much better on the client. Since the data isn't going to change, you want to package it up and send it all to the client in one pass — thus limiting roundtrips and network impact. The obvious exception is if the cursor is generated for the sole purpose of modifying other records. In such a case, you should try and do the entire process at the server-side (most likely in the form of a stored procedure) — again eliminating round-trips.
Forward-only, read-only cursors	Client-side again. ODBC and other libraries can take special advantage of the FAST_FORWARD cursor type to gain maximum performance. Just let the server spew the records into the client cursor, and then move on with life.
HOLDLOCK situations	Most transactioning works much better on the server than on the client.
Processes that require working tables	This is another of those situations where you want to try to have the finished product created before you attempt to move records to the client. If you keep all of the data server-side until it is really ready to be used, you minimize round-trips to the server and speed up performance.
Minimizing client installations	Okay, so this isn't "performance" as such, but it can be a significant cost factor. If you want to minimize the number of client installations you have to do, then keep as much of the business logic out of the client as possible. Either perform that logic in sprocs, or look at using component-based development with .NET. In an ideal world, you'll have what I like to call "data logic" (logic that exists only for the purpose of figuring out how to get the final data) in sprocs and "business logic" in components.

Continued

Significant filtering and/or resorting	Use ADO.NET or LINQ. They have a great set of tools for receiving the data from the server just once (fewer round-trips!), then applying filters and sorts locally. If you wanted the data filtered or sorted differently by SQL Server, it would run an entirely new query using the new criteria. It doesn't take a rocket scientist to figure out that the overhead on that can get rather expensive. Both ADO.NET and LINQ also have some cool things built-in to allow you to join different data sets (including homogeneous data sets) right at the client.
	Note, however, that with very large result sets, your client computer may not have the wherewithal to deal with the filters and sorts effectively — you may be forced to go back to the server.

These really just scratch the surface. The big thing to remember is that round-trips are a killer even in this age of gigabit Ethernet (keep in mind that connection overhead is often more of the issue than raw bandwidth). What you need to do is move the smallest amount of data back and forth — and only move it once. Usually, this means that you'll preprocess the data as much as possible on the server side, and then move the entire result to the client if possible.

Keep in mind, though, that you need to be sure that your client is going to be able to handle what you give it. Servers are usually much better equipped to handle the resource demands of larger queries. By the same token, you also have to remember that the server is going to be doing this for multiple users — that means the server needs to have adequate resources to store all of the server-side activity for that number of users. If you take a process that was too big for the client to handle and move it server-side for resource reasons, just remember that you may also run out of resources on the server, if more than one client uses that process at one time. The best thing is to try to keep result sets and processes in the smallest size possible.

> Realize that the term "client" has more than one possible meaning. The client, from a data connection perspective, may not be where the end user sits. If it is a browser-based application, then the client that is truly handling the data is more likely the Web server. While a Web server is likely on some very solid hardware, it may be dealing with multiple such queries at the same time (multiple large data sets), so plan accordingly.

Strategic De-Normalization

This could also be called, "When following the rules can kill you." Normalized data tends to work for both data integrity and performance in an OLTP environment. The problem is that not everything that goes on in an OLTP database is necessarily transaction-processing related. Even OLTP systems have to do a little bit of reporting (a summary of transactions entered that day, for example).

Often, adding just one extra column to a table can prevent a large join, or worse, a join involving several tables. I've seen situations where adding one column made the difference between a two-table join and a nine-table join. We're talking the difference between 100,000 records being involved and several million.

This one change made the difference in a query dropping from a runtime of several minutes down to just seconds.

Like most things, however, this isn't something with which you should get carried away. Normalization is the way that most things are implemented for a reason. It adds a lot to data integrity and can make a big positive difference performance-wise in many situations. Don't de-normalize just for the sake of it. Know exactly what you're trying to accomplish, and test to make sure that it had the expected impact. If it didn't, then look at going back to the original way of doing things.

Organizing Your Sprocs Well

I'm not talking from the outside (naming conventions and such are important, but that's not what I'm getting at here) but rather from a "how they operate" standpoint. The next few sections discuss this.

Keeping Transactions Short

Long transactions cannot only cause deadlock situations but also basic blocking (where someone else's process has to wait for yours because you haven't finished with the locks yet). Anytime you have a process that is blocked — even if it will eventually be able to continue after the blocking transaction is complete — you are delaying, and therefore hurting the performance of, that blocked procedure. There is nothing that has a more immediate effect on performance than that a process has to simply stop and wait.

Using the Least Restrictive Transaction Isolation Level Possible

The tighter you hold those locks, the more likely that you're going to wind up blocking another process. You need to be sure that you take the number of locks that you really need to ensure data integrity — but try not to take any more than that.

If you need more information on isolation levels, check out transactions and locks in Chapter 11.

Implementing Multiple Solutions if Necessary

An example here is a search query that accepts multiple parameters but doesn't require all of them. It's quite possible to write your sproc so that it just uses one query, regardless of how many parameters were actually supplied — a "one-size-fits-all" kind of approach. This can be a real timesaver from a development perspective, but it is really deadly from a performance point of view. More than likely, it means that you are joining several unnecessary tables for every run of the sproc!

The thing to do here is to add a few IF...ELSE statements to check things out. This is more of a "look before you leap" kind of approach. It means that you will have to write multiple queries to deal with each possible mix of supplied parameters, but once you have the first one written, the others can often be cloned and then altered from the first one.

This is a real problem area in lots of code out there. Developers are a fickle bunch. We generally only like doing things as long as they are interesting. If you take the preceding example, you can probably see that it would get very boring very quickly to be writing what amounts to a very similar query over and over to deal with the nuances of what parameters were supplied.

All I can say about this is — well, not everything can be fun, or everyone would want to be a software developer! Sometimes you just have to grin and bear it for the sake of the finished product.

Avoiding Cursors if Possible

If you're a programmer who has come from an ISAM or VSAM environment (these were older database storage methods), doing things by cursor is probably going to be something toward which you'll naturally gravitate. After all, the cursor process works an awful lot more like what you're used to in those environments (such looping structures are also common in many non-database data handling constructs).

Don't go there!

Almost all things that are first thought of as something you can do by cursors can actually be done as a set operation. Sometimes it takes some pretty careful thought, but it usually can be done.

By way of illustration, I was asked several years ago for a way to take a multiline cursor-based operation and make it into a single statement if possible. The existing process ran something like 20 minutes. The runtime was definitely problematic, but the customer wasn't really looking to do this for performance reasons (they had accepted that the process was going to take that long). Instead, they were just trying to simplify the code.

They had a large product database, and they were trying to set things up to automatically price their available products based on cost. If the markup had been a flat percentage (say 10 percent), then the UPDATE statement would have been easy — say something like:

```
UPDATE Products
SET UnitPrice = UnitCost * 1.1
```

The problem was that it wasn't a straight markup — there was a logic pattern to it. The logic went something like this:

❑ If the pennies on the product after the markup are greater than or equal to .50, then price it at .95.

❑ If the pennies are below .50, then mark it at .49.

The pseudocode to do this by cursor would look something like:

```
Declare and open the cursor
Fetch the first record
Begin Loop Until the end of the result set
Multiply cost * 1.1
If result has cents of < .50
   Change cents to .49
Else
   Change cents to .95
Loop
```

This is, of course, an extremely simplified version of things. There would actually be about 30–40 lines of code to get this done. Instead, we changed it around to work with one single correlated subquery (which had a CASE statement embedded in it). The runtime dropped down to something like 12 seconds.

The point here, of course, is that, by eliminating cursors wherever reasonably possible, we can really give a boost to not only reduce complexity (as was the original goal here) but also performance.

Uses for Temporary Tables

The use of temporary tables can sometimes help performance — usually by allowing the elimination of cursors or by allowing working data to be indexed while it is needed.

Using Temp Tables to Break Apart Complex Problems

As we've seen before, cursors can be the very bane of our existence. Using temporary tables, we can sometimes eliminate the cursor by processing the operation as a series of two or more set operations. An initial query creates a working data set. Then another process comes along and operates on that working data.

We can actually make use of the pricing example we laid out in the last section to illustrate the temporary table concept, too. This solution wouldn't be quite as good as the correlated subquery, but it is still quite workable and much faster than the cursor option. The steps would look something like:

```
SELECT ProductID, FLOOR(UnitCost * 1.1) + .49 AS TempUnitPrice
    INTO #WorkingData
    FROM Products
    WHERE (UnitCost * 1.1) - FLOOR(UnitCost * 1.1) < .50
INSERT INTO #WorkingData
SELECT ProductID, FLOOR(UnitCost * 1.1) + .95 AS TempUnitPrice
    FROM Products
    WHERE (UnitCost * 1.1) - FLOOR(UnitCost * 1.1) >= .50
UPDATE p
    SET p.UnitPrice = t.TempUnitPrice
    FROM Product p
    JOIN #WorkingData t
      ON p.ProductID = t.ProductID
```

With this, we wind up with three steps instead of thirty or forty. This won't operate quite as fast as the correlated subquery would, but it still positively screams in comparison to the cursor solution.

Keep this little interim step using temporary tables in mind when you run into complex problems that you think are going to require cursors. Try to avoid the temptation of just automatically taking this route — look for the single statement query before choosing this option — but if all else fails, this can really save you a lot of time versus using a cursor option.

Using Temp Tables to Allow Indexing on Working Data

Often we will run into a process in which we are performing many different operations on what is fundamentally the same data. This is characterized by a situation in which you are running different kinds of updates (perhaps to totally different tables), but utilizing the same source data to figure out what to change or what values to change things to. I've seen many scenarios where the same fundamental data is reused — in the same procedure — hundreds or even thousands of times.

Under such "reuse" situations, consider querying the data once and placing it into a temp table. Also consider applying indexes to this data as warranted by the queries you're going to be performing against it.

> *Even for data you're only going to be hitting twice, I've seen a temp table solution make a huge difference if the original query for the source data was, for whatever reason, inefficient. Sometimes this is due to a lack of suitable indexing on the source data, but, more often, it is a scenario with a multi-table join against a large data set. Sucking it into a temp table often allows you to explicitly filter down a large data set early in the overall process. Again, try and avoid the temptation of automatically taking this approach, but keep it in mind as an option.*

Update Your Code In a Timely Fashion

Are you still supporting SQL Server 2000? How about 7.0? OK, so you most definitely shouldn't be supporting 7.0 by now, and even 2000 support should be gone (or at least in the late stages of sunsetting it). So, if you're no longer supporting those older editions, why does your system code and design look like you still are?

OK, OK, I understand it isn't as simple as all that, but with each release of your application, make sure that you have time set aside (I recommend 10%–25%) that is oriented around improving existing performance and features. If you only need to support SQL Server 2008, look for special code you may have to address situations now addressed natively by SQL Server 2008, such as:

❑ Procedures or code streams that handle INSERT, UPDATE, and DELETE scenarios into a specific table; these can use the new MERGE command to make all three modifications, as indicated, in a single pass over the data. It also has the advantage of being a single statement, which means you may be able to avoid explicitly defining transactions around the three separate statements.

❑ Special hierarchy handling: SQL Server now has native constructs for something that is actually very common. The functionality includes not only hierarchy-specific functions (such as pruning or grafting), but both vertical and horizontal index functionality (very cool stuff!).

❑ Date and Time data type handling.

Sometimes, It's the Little Things

A common mistake in all programming for performance efforts is to ignore the small things. Whenever you're trying to squeeze performance, the natural line of thinking is that you want to work on the long-running stuff.

It's true that the long-running processes are the ones for which you stand the biggest chance of getting big one-time performance gains. It's too bad that this often leads people to forget that it's the total time saved that they're interested in — that is, how much time when the process is really live.

While it's definitely true that a single change in a query can often turn a several-minute query into seconds (I've actually seen a few that took literally days trimmed to just seconds by index and query tuning), the biggest gains for your application often lie in getting just a little bit more out of what already seems like a fast query. These are usually tied to often-repeated functions or items that are often executed within a loop.

Think about this for a bit. Say you have a query that currently takes three seconds to run, and this query is used every time an order taker looks up a part for possible sale — say 5,000 items looked up a day. Now imagine that you are able to squeeze one second off the query time. That's 5,000 seconds, or over an hour and 20 minutes!

Hardware Considerations

Forgive me if I get too bland here — I'll try to keep it interesting, but if you're like the average developer, you'll probably already know enough about this to make it very boring, yet not enough about it to save yourself a degree of grief.

Hardware prices have been falling like a rock over the years — unfortunately, so has what your manager or customer is probably budgeting for your hardware purchases. When deciding on a budget for your hardware, remember:

- ❏ Once you've deployed, the hardware is what's keeping your data safe — just how much is that data worth?

- ❏ Once you've deployed, you're likely to have many users — if you're creating a public website, it's possible that you'll have tens of thousands of users active on your system 24 hours per day. What is it going to cost you in terms of productivity loss, lost sales, loss of face, and just general credibility loss if that server is unavailable or — worse — you lose some of your data?

- ❏ Maintaining your system will quickly cost more than the system itself. Dollars spent early on a mainstream system that is going to have fewer quirks may save you a ton of money in the long run.

There's a lot to think about when deciding from whom to purchase and what specific equipment to buy. Forgetting the budget for a moment, some of the questions to ask yourself include:

- ❏ Will the box be used exclusively as a database server?

- ❏ Will the activity on the system be processor or I/O intensive? (For databases, it's almost always the latter, but there are exceptions.)

- ❏ Am I going to be running more than one production database? If so, is the other database of a different type (OLTP versus OLAP)?

- ❏ Will the server be on-site at my location, or do I have to travel to do maintenance on it?

- ❏ What are my risks if the system goes down?

- ❏ What are my risks if I lose data?

- ❏ Is performance "everything"?

- ❏ What kind of long-term driver support can I expect as my O/S and supporting systems are upgraded?

Again, we're just scratching the surface of things — but we've got a good start. Let's look at what these issues mean to us.

Exclusive Use of the Server

I suppose it doesn't take a rocket scientist to figure out that, in most cases, having your SQL Server hardware dedicated to just SQL Server and having other applications reside on totally separate system(s) is the best way to go. Note, however, that this isn't always the case.

If you're running a relatively small and simple application that works with other sub-systems (say IIS as a Web server, for example), then you may actually be better off, performance-wise, to stay with one box. Why? Well, if there are large amounts of data going back and forth between the two sub-systems (your database in SQL Server and your Web pages or whatever in a separate process), then memory space to memory space communications are going to be much faster than the bottleneck that the network can create — even in a relatively dedicated network backbone environment.

Remember that this is the exception, though, not the rule. The instance where this works best usually meets the following criteria:

❑　The systems have a very high level of interaction.

❑　The systems have little to do beyond their interactions (the activity that's causing all the interaction is the main thing that the systems do).

❑　Only one of the two processes is CPU intensive and only one is I/O intensive.

If in doubt, go with conventional thinking on this and separate the processing into two or more systems.

I/O vs. CPU Intensive

I can just hear a bunch of you out there yelling "Both!" If that's the case, then I hope you have a very large budget — but we'll talk about that scenario, too. Assuming you haven't installed yet, it's guesswork. While almost anything you do in SQL Server is data-based and will, therefore, certainly require a degree of I/O, how much of a burden your CPU is under varies widely depending on the types of queries you're running:

Low CPU Load	High CPU Load
Simple, single-table queries and updates	Large joins
Joined queries over relatively small tables	Aggregations (SUM, AVG, etc.) Sorting of large result sets

With this in mind, let's focus in a little closer on each situation.

I/O Intensive

I/O-intensive tasks should cause you to focus your budget more on the drive array than on the CPU(s). Notice that I said the drive "array" — I'm not laying that out as an option. In my not-so-humble opinion on this matter, if you don't have some sort of redundancy arrangement on your database storage mechanism, then you have certainly lost your mind. Any data worth saving at all is worth protecting — we'll talk about the options there in just a moment.

Before we get into talking about the options on I/O, let's look briefly into what I mean by I/O intensive. In short, I mean that a lot of data retrieval is going on, but the processes being run on the system are almost exclusively queries (not complex business processes), and those do not include updates that require wild calculations. Remember — your hard drives are, more than likely, the slowest thing in your system (short of a CD-ROM) in terms of moving data around.

A Brief Look at RAID

RAID; it brings images of barbarian tribes raining terror down on the masses. Actually, most of the RAID levels are there for creating something of a fail-safe mechanism against the attack of the barbarian called "lost data." If you're not a RAID aficionado, then it might surprise you to learn that not all RAID levels provide protection against lost data.

RAID originally stood for *Redundant Array of Inexpensive Disks*. The notion was fairly simple — at the time, using a lot of little disks was cheaper than using one great big one. In addition, an array of disks meant that you had multiple drive heads at work and could also build in (if desired) redundancy.

Since drive prices have come down so much (I'd be guessing, but I'd bet that drive prices are, dollar per meg, far less than 1 percent of what they were when the term RAID was coined), I've heard other renditions of what RAID stands for. The most common are Random Array of Independent Disks (this one seems like a contradiction in terms to me) and Random Array of Individual Disks (this one's not that bad). The thing to remember, no matter what you think it's an acronym for, is that you have two or more drives working together — usually for the goal of some balance between performance and safety.

There are lots of places you can get information on RAID, but let's take a look at the three (well, four if you consider the one that combines two of the others) levels that are most commonly considered:

RAID Level	Description
RAID 0	a.k.a. Disk Striping without Parity. Out of the three that you are examining here, this is the one you are least likely to know. This requires at least three drives to work just as RAID 5 does. Unlike RAID 5, however, you get no safety net from lost data. (Parity is a special checksum value that allows reconstruction of lost data in some circumstances — as indicated by the time, RAID 0 doesn't have parity.) RAID 0's big claim to fame is giving you maximum performance without losing any drive space. With RAID zero, the data you store is spread across all the drives in the array (at least 3). While this may seem odd, it has the advantage of meaning that you always have three or more disk drives reading or writing your data for you at once. Under mirroring, the data is all on one drive (with a copy stored on a separate drive). This means you'll just have to wait for that one head to do the work for you.
RAID 1	a.k.a. Mirroring. For each active drive in the system, there is a second drive that "mirrors" (keeps an exact copy of) the information. The two drives are usually identical in size and type, and store all the information to each drive at the same time. (Windows NT has software-based RAID that can mirror any two volumes as long as they are the same size.) Mirroring provides no performance increase when writing data (you still have to write to both drives) but can, depending on your controller arrangement, double your read

Continued

RAID Level	Description
	performance since it will use both drives for the read. What's nice about mirroring is that as long as only one of the two mirrored drives fails, the other will go on running with no loss of data or performance (well, reads may be slower if you have a controller that does parallel reads). The biggest knock on mirroring is that you have to buy two drives to every one in order to have the disk space you need.
RAID 5	The most commonly used. Although, technically speaking, mirroring is a RAID (RAID 1), when people refer to using RAID, they usually mean RAID 5. RAID 5 works exactly as RAID 0 does with one very significant exception — parity information is kept for all the data in the array. Say, for example, that you have a five-drive array. For any given write, data is stored across all five of the drives, but a percentage of each drive (the sum of which adds up to the space of one drive) is set aside to store parity information. Contrary to popular belief, no one drive is the parity drive. Instead, some of the parity information is written to all the drives — it's just that the parity information for a given byte of data is not stored on the same drive as the actual data is. If any one drive is lost, then the parity information from the other drives can be used to reconstruct the data that was lost. The great thing about RAID 5 is that you get the multi-drive read performance. The downside is that you lose one drive's worth of space (if you have a three-drive array, you'll see the space of two; if it's a seven-drive array, you'll see the space of six). It's not as bad as mirroring in the price per megabyte category, but you still see great performance.
RAID 6	Raid can be considered to be something of an extension of RAID 5 and is generally only used in very large arrays (where the overhead of algorithm required to provide the extra redundancy can be spread out and therefore provides less waste on a per disk basis). RAID 6 provides extra parity encoding versus RAID 5, and the extra information can be utilized to recover from multiple drive loss. RAID 5 is generally less expensive at lower array sizes, but RAID 6 maintains a level of redundancy even while rebuilding a single failed drive.
RAID 10, (a.k.a. RAID 1 + 0) or RAID 0 + 1	RAID 10 offers the best of both RAID 0 and RAID 1 in terms of performance and data protection. It is, however, far and away the most expensive of the options discussed here. RAID 10 is implemented in a coupling of both RAID 1 (Mirroring) and RAID 0 (striping without parity). The end result is mirrored sets of striped data. You will also hear of RAID 0 + 1. These are striped sets of mirrored data. The end result in total drive count is the same, but RAID 10 performs better in recovery scenarios and is therefore what is typically implemented.
RAID 50	This is implemented by mirroring two RAID 5 arrays. While it is arguably the most redundant, it is still at risk of failure if two drives happen to fail in the same array. It is the most expensive of the options provided here, and generally only implemented in the most extreme of environments.

The long and the short of it is that RAID 5 is the de facto minimum for database installations. That being said, if you have a loose budget, then I'd actually suggest mixing things up a bit.

RAID 10 has become the standard in larger installations. For the average shop, however, RAID 5 will likely continue to rule the day for a while yet — perhaps that will change as we get into the era where even server level drives are measured in multi-tera-, peta-, and even exabytes. We certainly are getting there fast.

What you'd like to have is at least a RAID 5 setup for your main databases but a completely separate mirrored set for your logs. People who manage to do both usually put both Windows and the logs on the mirror set and the physical databases on the RAID 5 array, but those with a little more cash to spend often put the O/S on a separate mirror set from the logs (with the data files still on their own RAID 5 array). Since I'm sure inquiring minds want to know why you would want to do this, let's make a brief digression into how log data is read and written.

Unlike database information, which can be read in parallel (thus why RAID 5 or 10 works so well performance-wise), the transaction log is chronology dependent — that is, it needs to be written and read serially to be certain of integrity. I'm not necessarily saying that physically ordering the data in a constant stream is required; rather, I'm saying that everything needs to be logically done in a stream. As such, it actually works quite well if you can get the logs into their own drive situation where the head of the drive will only seldom have to move from the stream from which it is currently reading and writing. The upshot of this is that you really want your logs to be in a different physical device than your data, so the reading and writing of data won't upset the reading and writing of the log.

Note that this sequential read/write performance of the mirror set disappears if you are keeping logs for multiple databases on the same mirror set (it has to jump around between the separate logs!).

Logs, however, don't usually take up nearly as much space as the read data does. With mirroring, we can just buy two drives and have our redundancy. With RAID 5, we would have to buy three, but we don't see any real benefit from the parallel read nature of RAID 5. When you look at these facts together, it doesn't make much sense to go with RAID 5 for the logs or O/S.

> **You can have all the RAID arrays in the world, and they still wouldn't surpass a good backup in terms of long-term safety of your data. Backups are easy to take off-site, and are not subject to mechanical failure. RAID units, while redundant and very reliable, can also become worthless if two (instead of just one) drives fail. Another issue — what if there's a fire? Probably all the drives will burn up — again, without a backup, you're in serious trouble. We'll look into how to back up your databases in Chapter 22.**

CPU Intensive

On a SQL Server box, you'll almost always want to make sure that you go multiprocessor (yes, even in these days of multi-core processors), even for a relatively low-utilization machine. This goes a long way to preventing little "pauses" in the system that will drive your users positively nuts, so consider this part of things to be a given — particularly in this day of dual core processors. Keep in mind that the Workgroup version of SQL Server supports only up to two processors — if you need to go higher than that, you'll need to go up to either Standard (four processors) or the Enterprise edition (which is limited only by your hardware and budget).

> *Even if you're only running SQL Server Express — which supports only one processor — you'll want to stick with the dual-proc box if at all possible. Remember, there is more going on in your system than SQL Server, so having that other proc available to perform external operations cuts down on lag on your SQL Server.*

Perhaps the biggest issue of all, though, is memory. This is definitely one area that you don't want to short change. In addition, remember that if you are in a multiprocessor environment (and you should be), then you are going to have more things going on at once in memory. In these days of cheap memory, no SQL Server worth installing should ever be configured with less than 512MB of RAM — even in a development environment. Production servers should be equipped with no less than 2GB of RAM — quite likely more.

Things to think about when deciding how much RAM to use include:

❑ How many user connections will there be at one time (each one takes up space)? Each connection takes up about 24K of memory (it used to be even higher). This isn't really a killer since 1,000 users would only take up 24MB, but it's still something to think about.

❑ Will you be doing a lot of aggregations and/or sorts? These can be killers depending on the size of the data set you're working with in your query.

❑ How large is your largest database? If you have only one database, and it is only 1GB (and, actually, most databases are much smaller than people think), then having 4GB of RAM probably doesn't make much sense depending on how many queries you're running simultaneously and exactly what actions they are taking.

❑ The Workgroup edition of SQL Server 2008 only supports addressing of memory up to 3GB. If you need more than this, you'll need to go with at least the Standard edition.

In addition, once you're in operation — or when you get a fully populated test system up and running — you may want to take a look at your cache-hit ratio in perfmon. We'll talk about how this number is calculated a little bit in Chapter 21. For now, it's sufficient to say that this can serve as something of a measurement for how often we are succeeding at getting things out of memory rather than off disk (memory is going to run much, much faster than disk). A low cache-hit ratio is usually a certain indication that more memory is needed. Keep in mind though, that a high ratio does not necessarily mean that you shouldn't add more memory. The read-ahead feature of SQL Server may create what is an artificially high cache-hit ratio and may disguise the need for additional memory.

OLTP vs. OLAP

The needs between these two systems are often at odds with each other. We discuss some of the design differences in Chapter 24, so I hope you will come to have a concept of just how different the design considerations can be.

In any case, I'm going to keep my "from a hardware perspective" recommendation short here:

> **If you are running databases to support both of these kinds of needs, run them on different servers — it's just that simple.**

I can't stress enough the need to separate these two. A large data warehouse import, export, or even a large report run can cause significant turnover in your OLTP procedure and/or data caches and simply decimate the performance of your system for what can be many users (and, therefore, a whole lot of cost).

On-Site vs. Off-Site

It used to be that anything that would be SQL Server–based would be running on-site with those who were responsible for its care and upkeep. If the system went down, people were right there to worry about reloads and to troubleshoot.

In the Internet era, many installations are co-located with an Internet service provider (ISP). The ISP is responsible for making sure that the entire system is backed up — they will even restore according to your directions — but they do not take responsibility for your code. This can be very problematic when you run into a catastrophic bug in your system. While you can always connect remotely to work on it, you're going to run into several configuration and performance issues, including:

❑ **Security** — Remote access being open to you means that you're also making it somewhat more open to others who you may not be interested in having access. My two bits' worth on this is to make sure that you have very tight routing and port restrictions in place. For those of you not all that network savvy (which includes me), this means that you restrict what IP addresses are allowed to be routed to the remote server, what ports they have available, and even what protocols (SSL vs. non-SSL) are allowed through.

❑ **Performance** — You're probably going to be used to the 100 Mbps to 1 Gbps network speeds that you have around the home office. Now you're communicating via virtual private network (VPN) over the Internet or, worse, dialup, and you are starting to hate life (things are SLOW!).

❑ **Responsiveness** — It's a bit upsetting when you're running some e-commerce site or whatever and you can't get someone at your ISP to answer the phone, or they say that they will get on it right away and hours later you're still down. Make sure you investigate your remote hosting company very closely — don't assume that they'll still think you're important after the sale.

❑ **Hardware maintenance** — Many co-hosting facilities will not do hardware work for you. If you have a failure that requires more than a reloading, you may have to travel to the site yourself or call yet another party to do the maintenance — that means that your application will be offline for hours or possibly days.

If you're a small shop doing this with an Internet site, then off-site can actually be something of a saving grace. It's expensive, but you'll usually get lots of bandwidth plus someone to make sure that the backups actually get done — just make sure that you really check out your ISP. Many of them don't know anything about SQL Server, so make sure that expertise is there.

One recent trend in major ISPs has been to locate major hosting facilities in far more remote locations than you might, at first, expect. This is usually done for accessibility to water (for cooling), cheap power, or both (near hydroelectric facilities seems to be popular). In many ways, this shouldn't matter, but think about it if you're using a third-party hardware support company — does that support company have appropriate staff located near the facility where you will be hosted?

If you were thinking of your hosting company as being located in a major metropolitan area, then you would reasonably assume that your hosting company had a large number of support staff within 30–60 minutes' response time of your ISP location. If, however, your ISP is, let's say, "outside Portland, Oregon," you may want to make sure that "outside" doesn't mean 60 or 80 miles away. If it is, check with your support company about just how many people they keep on staff truly close to your ISP location.

The Risks of Being Down

How long and how often can I afford to be down? This may seem like a silly question. When I ask it, I often get this incredulous look. For some installations, the answer is obvious — they can't afford to be down, period. This number is not, however, as high as it might seem. You see, the only true life-and-death kinds of applications are the ones that are in acute medical applications or are immediately tied to safety operations. Other installations may lose money — they may even cause bankruptcy if they go down — but that's not life and death either.

That being said, it's really not as black and white as all that. There is really something of a continuum in how critical downtime is. It ranges from the aforementioned medical applications at the high end to data-mining operations on old legacy systems at the low end (usually — for some companies, it may be all they have). The thing that pretty much everyone can agree on for every system is that downtime is highly undesirable.

So, the question becomes one of just how undesirable is it? How do we quantify that?

If you have a bunch of bean counters (I can get away with saying that since I was one) working for you, it shouldn't take you all that long to figure out that there are a lot of measurable costs to downtime. For example, if you have a bunch of employees sitting around saying that they can't do anything until the system comes back up, then the number of affected employees times their hourly cost (remember, the cost of an employee is more than just his or her wages) equals the cost of the system being down from a productivity standpoint. But wait, there's more. If you're running something that has online sales — how many sales did you lose because you couldn't be properly responsive to your customers? Oops — more cost. If you're running a plant with your system, then how many goods couldn't be produced because the system was down — or, even if you could still build them, did you lose quality assurance or other information that might cost you down the line?

I think by now you should be able to both see and sell to your boss the notion that downtime is very expensive — how expensive depends on your specific situation. Now the thing to do is to determine just how much you're willing to spend to make sure that it doesn't happen.

Lost Data

There's probably no measuring this one. In some cases, you can quantify this by the amount of cost you're going to incur reconstructing the data. Sometimes you simply can't reconstruct it, in which case you'll probably never know for sure just how much it cost you.

Again, how much you want to prevent this should affect your budget for redundant systems as well as things like backup tape drives and off-site archival services.

Is Performance Everything?

More often than not, the answer is no. It's important, but just how important has something of diminishing returns to it. For example, if buying those extra 10 percent of CPU power is going to save you two seconds per transaction — that may be a big deal if you have 50 data entry clerks trying to enter as much as they can a day. Over the course of a day, seemingly small amounts of time saved can add up. If each of those 50 clerks is performing 500 transactions a day, then saving two seconds per transaction adds up to over 13 man hours (that's over one person working all day!). Saving that time may allow you to delay a little longer in adding staff. The savings in wages will probably easily pay for the extra computing power.

The company next door may look at the situation a little differently, though — they may only have one or two employees; furthermore, the process that they are working in might be one where they spend a lengthy period of time just filing out the form — the actual transaction that stores it isn't that big of deal. In such a case, their extra dollars for the additional speed may not be worth it.

Driver Support

Let's start off by cutting to the chase — I don't at all recommend that you save a few dollars (or even a lot of dollars) when buying your server by purchasing it from some company like "Bob's Pretty Fine Computers." Remember all those risks? Now, try introducing a strange mix of hardware and driver sets. Now imagine when you have a problem — you're quickly going to find all those companies pointing the finger at each other saying, "It's their fault!" Do you really want to be stuck in the middle?

What you want is the tried and true — the tested — the known. Servers — particularly data servers — are an area to stick with well-known, trusted names. I'm not advocating anyone in particular (no ads in this book!), but I'm talking very mainstream people like Dell, IBM, HP, and so on. Note that, when I say well-known, trusted names, I mean names that are known in servers. Just because someone sells a billion desktops a year doesn't mean they know anything about servers — it's almost like apples and oranges. They are terribly different.

By staying with well-known equipment, in addition to making sure that you have proper support when something fails, it also means that you're more likely to have that equipment survive upgrades well into the future. Each new version of the O/S only explicitly supports just so many pieces of equipment — you want to be sure that yours is one of them.

The Ideal System

Let me preface this by saying that there is no one ideal system. That being said, there is a general configuration (size excluded) that I and a very large number of other so-called "experts" seem to almost universally push as where you'd like to be if you had the budget for it. What we're talking about is drive arrangements here (the CPU and memory tends to be relative chicken feed budget- and setup-wise).

What you'd like to have is a mix of mirroring and RAID 5 or 10. You place the O/S and the logs on the mirrored drives (ideally on separate mirror sets). You place the data on the RAID 5/10 array. That way, the O/S and logs — which both tend to do a lot of serial operations — have a drive setup all of their own without being interfered with by the reads and writes of the actual data. The data has a multi-head read/write arrangement for maximum performance, while maintaining a level of redundancy.

Summary

Performance could be, and should be, in a book by itself (indeed, there is a Wrox title around the very subject). There's simply just too much to cover and get acquainted with to do it all in one or even several chapters. The way I've tried to address this is by pointing out performance issues throughout the book, so you could take them on a piece at a time. This chapter is all about the first of two different slants I'm taking on it — design (addressing performance *before* it is a problem). In our next chapter, we'll look at how we can identify and address performance issues when our system is already live. It's important to note that the techniques discussed there are ones you may want to also utilize while you're still in test so you can tweak your design accordingly.

21

What Comes After: Forensic Performance Tuning

Well, wouldn't it be nice if we could just develop the software, get paid for it, and forget it ... ? Yeah, well .... You can stop dreaming now — it just doesn't work that way.

At some point, any software we consider to be part of a successful development project is going to get rolled out in front of some user base. Even if it's just a prototype, we're going to be analyzing how the prototype matched our original goals. Part of assessing whether we met our goals is taking a look at performance and asking ourselves what we could be doing better.

In the previous chapter, I suggested that the most important thing to understand about performance tuning is that you are never going to know everything there is to know about it. If I were to come up with a competing idea for "most important thing to understand," it would be that you are never really done with performance tuning. The content of your system will change, the state of your server will change, the use of your system will change. In short, the overall system will change, and that will affect performance. The trick is to understand what's working poorly, what's working well, and what's working "well enough."

Just as we did the previous chapter, we're going to be roaming around quite a bit in terms of the topics covered. Everything we talk about is going to be performance related in some fashion, but this time we'll be more focused on figuring out what is hurting performance. If you did your job in design and development, you should already have a great design in place, but the reality of software is that the design requirements rarely exactly match the reality of a live system. So, this chapter will be all about figuring out what's already occurring in our system and deciding what we can do better. Topics we'll cover in this chapter include:

❏   Routine maintenance

❏   Hardware configuration issues

❑   The SQL Server Profiler

❑   Data Collector

When to Tune (Mark Two)

So, I had a section in the previous chapter named this very thing — When to Tune. If you paid attention at all, you know the process should have started well before the "in test or production" mode that we're in with this chapter. That said, the new answer for this chapter is simply "regularly." Don't wait until users are screaming at you about something — instead plan on a regular optimization process.

Much of the post-release maintenance is thought of as in the realm of the DBA, and I'm not necessarily going to dispute that, save for a few problems with that philosophy:

❑   You are producing a product that is used by many (are you going to expect every customer's DBA to individually deal with the problem you handed them?).

❑   What if there isn't a DBA (depending on your install, there may not be a DBA on staff, so what is your system and/or recommendations doing to prevent trouble for your end users?)?

❑   What if *you* are the DBA?

This is all oversimplified, but the real key here is that you should be thinking about performance even after the product has been released and gone live. Whether it's how to build it better for the next release or simply trying to keep your paying customers happy, you should always be looking for problems (best if you know about them before your customer does) or simple ways of making your system a bit better.

Routine Maintenance

I hate it when good systems go bad. It happens on a regular basis though. It usually happens when people buy or build systems, put them into operation, and then forget about them.

Maintenance is as much about performance as it is about system integrity. Query plans get out of date, index pages get full (so you have a lot of page splits), fragmentation happens, the best indexes need to be changed as usage and the amount of data in various tables changes.

Watch the newsgroups. Talk to a few people who have older systems running. Visit some of the many SQL Server support sites on the Web. You'll hear the same story over and over again. "My system used to run great, but it just keeps getting slower and slower — I haven't changed anything, so what happened?" Well, systems will naturally become slower as the amount of data they have to search through increases; however, the change doesn't have to be all that remarkable and usually it shouldn't be. Instead, the cause is usually that the performance enhancements you put in place when you first installed the system don't really apply anymore; as the way your users use the system and the amount of data has changed, so has the mix of things that will give you the best performance.

We'll be looking at maintenance quite a bit in the next chapter; however, we've discussed it here for two reasons. First, it will help if you are checking out this chapter because you have a specific perfor-mance problem; second, and perhaps more importantly, because there is a tendency to just think about maintenance as being something you do to prevent the system from going down and to ensure back-ups are available should the worst happen. This simply isn't the case. Maintenance is also a key from a performance perspective.

Troubleshooting

SQL Server offers a number of options to help with the prevention, detection, and measurement of long-running queries. The options range from a passive approach of measuring actual performance, so you know what's doing what, to a more active approach of employing a query "governor" to automatically kill queries that run over a length of time you choose. These tools are very often ignored or used only sparingly — which is something of a tragedy — they can save hours of troubleshooting by often lead-ing you right to the problem query and even to the specific portion of your query that is creating the performance issues.

Tools to take a look at include:

- ❑ The Data Collector
- ❑ SHOWPLAN TEXT | ALL and Graphical showplan
- ❑ STATISTICS IO
- ❑ Database Console Commands (DBCC)
- ❑ The sys.processes system view
- ❑ The Activity Monitor
- ❑ The SQL Server Profiler
- ❑ PerfMon

Many people are caught up in just using one of these, but the reality is that there is little to no (depending on which two you're comparing) overlap between them. This means that developers and DBAs who try to rely on just one of them are actually missing out on a lot of potentially important information.

Also, keep in mind that many of these are still useful in some form even if you are writing in a client-side language and sending the queries to the server (no sprocs). You can either watch the query come through to your server using the SQL Server Profiler, or you could even test the query in QA before moving it back to your client code.

The Data Collector

The Data Collector is new with SQL Server 2008 and provides a framework that pulls together the col-lection of data about your system's data and activity and performs analysis, troubleshooting (yes, SQL Server can use data to actually troubleshoot some of its own problems!), as well as persistence of the results for further analysis and diagnostics.

Things included in the Data Collector include:

❏ The actual data collection engine

❏ Active performance monitoring, troubleshooting, and tuning

❏ Reporting

This is a quantum leap in diagnostic possibilities over what we had in previous releases. Data collection can be aggregated on an enterprise-wide basis and reporting and analysis can span multiple servers.

Setup and configuration of the Data Collector requires significant thought and analysis in its own right, and is largely deemed beyond the scope of this book (very much an administrator sort of thing), but some of the key elements include:

❏ Setting up logins to have appropriate rights to collect data and monitor collected data

❏ Creation of *collection sets* (groups of objects that collect data using one or more *collection providers*)

❏ Scheduling of data collection

This is obviously far from comprehensive, but it gives a taste of the idea that setting up the data collection is non-trivial. Still, it can provide a wealth of information and is very worthwhile for test systems when doing scalability analysis and for larger production environments.

> **The Data Collector and its associated framework of tools are domain aware, and can collect and warehouse data from multiple servers for comparison and overall enterprise analysis. Setup of enterprise-wide data collection is in the realm of the DBA and is considered outside the scope of this book (but it's a great thing to be aware is available!).**

The Various Showplans and STATISTICS

SQL Server gives you a few different options for showing the specific plan being used by any given query. The information that they provide varies a bit depending on what option you choose, but this is one area where there is a fair amount of overlap between your options; however, each one definitely has its own unique thing that it brings to the picture. In addition, there are a number of options available to show query statistics.

Let's take a look at the options and what they do.

SHOWPLAN TEXT/ALL

When either of these two SHOWPLAN options (they are mutually exclusive) is executed, SQL Server changes what results you get for your query. Indeed, the NOEXEC option (which says, "Figure out the query plan but don't actually perform the query") is put in place, and you receive no results other than those put out by the SHOWPLAN.

The syntax for turning the SHOWPLAN on and off is pretty straightforward:

```
SET SHOWPLAN TEXT|ALL ON|OFF
```

When you use the TEXT option, you get back the query plan along with the estimated costs of running that plan. Since the NOEXEC option automatically goes with SHOWPLAN, you won't see any query results.

When you use the ALL option, you receive everything you received with the TEXT option, plus a slew of additional statistical information, including such things as:

❑ The actual physical and logical operations planned

❑ Estimated row counts

❑ Estimated CPU usage

❑ Estimated I/O

❑ Average row size

❑ Whether or not the query will be run in parallel

Let's run a very brief query utilizing (one at a time) both of these options:

```
USE AdventureWorks2008;
GO


SET SHOWPLAN_TEXT ON;
GO


SELECT *
FROM Sales.SalesOrderHeader;
GO


SET SHOWPLAN_TEXT OFF;
GO


SET SHOWPLAN_ALL ON;
GO


SELECT *
FROM Sales.SalesOrderHeader;
GO


SET SHOWPLAN_ALL OFF;
GO
```

Notice that every statement is followed by a GO — thus making it part of its own batch. The batches that contain the actual query could have had an unlimited number of statements, but the batches setting the SHOWPLAN option have to be in a batch by themselves.

The SHOWPLAN_TEXT portion of the results should look something like this:

```
StmtText
-----------------------------------------

SELECT *
FROM Sales.SalesOrderHeader

(1 row(s) affected)
```

```
StmtText
----------------------------------------------------------------------------
|--Compute Scalar(DEFINE:([AdventureWorks2008]....
        |--Compute Scalar(DEFINE:([AdventureWorks2008]...
            |--Clustered Index Scan(OBJECT:([AdventureWorks2008]...

(3 row(s) affected)
```

Unfortunately, the results are far too wide to fit all of it gracefully in the pages of this book, but there are a couple of key things I want you to notice about what was produced:

❑ There are multiple steps displayed.

❑ At each step, what object is being addressed and what kind of operation is being supplied.

If we had been running a larger query — say something with several joins — then even more sub-processes would have been listed with indentations to indicate hierarchy.

I'm not going to include the ALL results here since they simply will not fit in a book format (it's about 800 characters wide and won't fit in any readable form in a book — even if we flipped things sideways), but it includes a host of other information. Which one of these to use is essentially dependent on just how much information you want to be flooded with. If you just want to know the basic plan — such as is it using a merge or hash join, you probably just want to use the TEXT option. If you really want to know where the costs are and such, then you want the ALL option.

> Since the **SHOWPLAN** options imply the **NOEXEC**, that means nothing in your query is actually being executed. Before you do anything else, you need to set the option back to off; that even includes switching from one showplan option to the other (for example, **SET SHOWPLAN_ALL ON** wouldn't have any effect if you had already run **SET SHOWPLAN_TEXT ON** and hadn't yet turned it off).

> I like to make sure that every script I run that has a **SET SHOWPLAN** statement in it has both the on and off within that same script. It goes a long way toward keeping me from forgetting that I have it turned on and being confused when things aren't working the way I expect.

Graphical Showplan

The graphical showplan tool combines bits and pieces of the SHOWPLAN_ALL and wraps them up into a single graphical format. Graphical showplan is a Management Studio–only tool. It is selected through options in Management Studio rather than through T-SQL syntax — this means that it is only available when using Management Studio.

The graphical showplan comes in two versions: estimated and actual. The estimated version is more like the SHOWPLAN in T-SQL. It implies that the query plan is just developed but not actually executed. This essentially waits until the query is done and shows you the way the query was actually done in the end.

Why are these different? Well, SQL Server is smart enough to recognize when it starts down a given query plan based on an estimated cost and then finds the reality to be something other than what its estimates were based on. SQL Server uses statistics it keeps on tables and indexes to estimate cost. Those statistics can sometimes become skewed or downright out of date. The Query Optimizer will adjust on the fly if it starts down one path and finds something other than what it expected.

For most things we do, the estimated execution plan is just fine. We have three options to activate the graphical showplan option:

❑   Select the Display Estimated Execution Plan option from the Query menu

❑   Press Control+L on your keyboard

❑   Click the Display Estimated Execution Plan button on the toolbar and in the Query menu (this option just shows us the plan with the NOEXEC option active)

Personally, I like the option of having the graphical showplan in addition to my normal query run. While it means that I have to put the actual hit of the query on my system, it also means that the numbers I get are no longer just estimates but are based on the actual cost numbers. Indeed, if you run the showplan both ways and wind up with wildly different results, then you may want to take a look at the last time your statistics were updated on the tables on which the query is based. If necessary, you can then update them manually and try the process again.

The hierarchy of the different subprocesses is then shown graphically. In order to see the costs and other specifics about any subprocess, just hover your mouse over that part of the graphical showplan and a tooltip will come up with the information:

This arrangement, as shown in Figure 21-1, can often make it much easier to sort out the different pieces of the plan. The downside is that you can't print it out for reporting the way that you can with the text versions.

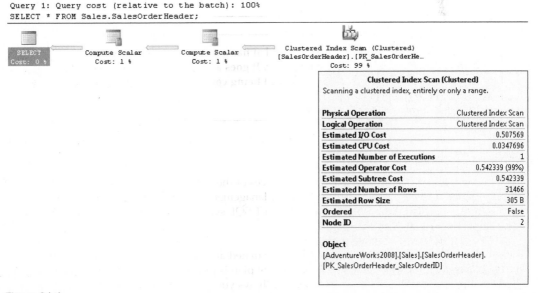

Figure 21-1

STATISTICS

In addition to using the graphical showplan with actual execution of the query, you have a couple of other options for retrieving the "real" information on the statistics of your query: using SQL Server Profiler (discussed later in this chapter) and turning on STATISTICS PROFILE.

STATISTICS actually has a couple of options that can be very handy in troubleshooting query performance, including those discussed in the following sections.

SET STATISTICS IO ON|OFF

This one is a very commonly used tool to figure out where and how the query is performing. STATISTICS IO provides several key pieces of information regarding the actual work necessary to perform your query. Information provided includes:

❑ **Physical Reads:** This represents the actual physical pages read from disk. It is never any more than, and is usually smaller than, the number for logical reads. This one can be very misleading in the sense that it will usually change (be less than the first run) the second time that you run your query. Any page that is already in the buffer cache will not have a physical read done on it, so, the second time you run the query in a reasonably short succession, the pages involved will, more than likely, still be in cache. In addition, this number will not be incremented if the page has already been read due to the read-ahead mechanism that is part of SQL Server. This means that your query may be responsible for loading the page physically into cache, but it still may not show up as part of the physical reads.

❑ **Logical Reads:** This is the number of times that the page was actually looked at — regardless of where it came from. That is, any page already in the memory cache will still create a logical read if the query makes use of it. Note that I said it is how many times the page was looked at. That means that you may have several logical reads for a single page if the page is needed several times (say for a nested loop that affects a page that has several rows on it).

❑ **Read-Ahead Reads:** This is the number of pages that SQL Server reads into the cache as a result of the read-ahead mechanism anticipating that the pages will be needed. The page may actually be used — or it may not. In either case, the read still counts as a read ahead. Read aheads are very similar to physical reads in the sense that they represent data being physically read from disk. The problem is that the number you get is based on the optimistic nature of the read-ahead mechanism and does not necessarily mean that all that work was actually put to use.

❑ **Scan Count:** The scan count represents the number of times that a table was accessed. This is somewhat different from logical reads, which was focused on page access. This is another situation where a nested loop is a good example. The outer table that is forming the basis for the condition on the query that is on the inside may only have a scan count of 1, where the inner loop table would have a scan count added for every time through the loop — that is, every record in the outer table.

Some of the same information that forms the basis for STATISTICS IO is the information that feeds your cache-hit ratio if you look in PerfMon. The cache-hit ratio is based on the number of logical reads, less the physical reads, divided into the total actual reads (logical reads).

The thing to look for with STATISTICS IO is for any one table that seems disproportionately high in either physical or logical reads.

A very high physical read count could indicate that the data from the table is being pushed out of the buffer cache by other processes. If this is a table that you are going to be accessing with some regularity, then you may want to look at purchasing (or, if you're an ISV developing a SQL Server product, recommending) more memory for your system.

If the logical reads are very high, then the issue may be more one of proper indexing. I'll give an example here from a client I had some time back. A query was taking approximately 15 seconds to run on an otherwise unloaded system. Since the system was to be a true OLTP system, this was an unacceptable time for the user to have to wait for information. (The query was actually a fairly simple lookup that happened to require a four-table join.) In order to find the problem, I used what amounted to STATISTICS IO. It happened to be the old graphical version that came with 6.5, but the data was much the same. After running the query just once, I could see that the process was requiring less than 20 logical reads from three of the tables, but it was performing over 45,000 logical reads from the fourth table. This is what I liked about the old graphical version; it took about a half a second to see that the bar on one table stretched all the way across the screen when the others were just a few pixels! From there, I knew right where to focus — in about two minutes, I had an index built to support a foreign key (remember, they aren't built by default), and the response time dropped to less than a second. The entire troubleshooting process on this one took literally minutes. Not every performance troubleshooting effort is that easy (indeed, most aren't), but using the right tools can often help a lot.

SET STATISTICS TIME ON | OFF

This one is amazingly little known. It shows the actual CPU time required to execute the query. Personally, I often use a simple SELECT GETDATE() before and after the query I'm testing — as we've done throughout most of the book — but this one can be handy because it separates out the time to parse and plan the query versus the time required to actually execute the query. It's also nice to not have to figure things out for yourself. (It will calculate the time in milliseconds; using GETDATE() you have to do that yourself.)

Include Client Statistics

You also have the ability to show statistical information about your connection as part of your query run. To make use of this, just select Include Client Statistics from the Query menu. As long as that option is set, every execution you make will produce a Client Statistics tab in the results pane of the Query window, as shown in Figure 21-2.

Database Console Commands (DBCC)

The Database Console Commands (or DBCC) has a number of different options available to allow you to check the integrity and structural makeup of your database. This is far more the realm of the DBA than the developer, so I am, for the most part, considering the DBCC to be out of scope for this book.

> *You may also hear of DBCC referred to as the Database Consistency Checker. This is what DBCC used to stand for. To be honest, I have no idea when what DBCC stood for changed, but, if you hear the other term, now you know why.*

Dynamic Management Views

Over the last edition or two of SQL Server, Microsoft has been adding an increasing number of what are called *dynamic management views* — or DMVs. There is description and use information on these provided in Appendix B. They can provide a wide range of information on the current state of your server and/or database in a very code readable fashion (they can be wonderful for automating administrative tasks). To get a quick example, however, of how powerful these can be, let's take a quick look at one DMV that might be of interest.

	Trial 1		Average
Client Execution Time	14:29:56		
Query Profile Statistics			
Number of INSERT, DELETE and UPDATE statements	0	→	0.0000
Rows affected by INSERT, DELETE, or UPDATE statem...	0	→	0.0000
Number of SELECT statements	1	→	1.0000
Rows returned by SELECT statements	31466	→	31466.0000
Number of transactions	0	→	0.0000
Network Statistics			
Number of server roundtrips	1	→	1.0000
TDS packets sent from client	1	→	1.0000
TDS packets received from server	1445	→	1445.0000
Bytes sent from client	108	→	108.0000
Bytes received from server	5917780	→	5917780.0000
Time Statistics			
Client processing time	591	→	591.0000
Total execution time	744	→	744.0000
Wait time on server replies	153	→	153.0000

Figure 21-2

I can't stress enough that what I'm showing you in this section is really just a very small taste of what is possible with the various metadata and dynamic management views now available in SQL Server. You can get a solid start on learning them by checking out Appendix B in this book, but if you're looking to build a robust support tool, you may want to look for a book that is highly focused on this growing toolset in SQL Server.

We will start by reviewing one that we first visited back in Chapter 13. We'll make a variation on a query we used in a cursor example:

```
SELECT SCHEMA_NAME(CAST(OBJECTPROPERTYEX(i.object_id, 'SchemaId') AS int))
        + '.' +
        OBJECT_NAME(i.object_id)
        + '.' +
        i.name AS Name,
        ps.avg_fragmentation_in_percent
   FROM sys.dm_db_index_physical_stats (DB_ID(), NULL, NULL, NULL, NULL) AS ps
   JOIN sys.indexes AS i
     ON ps.object_id = i.object_id
    AND ps.index_id = i.index_id
   WHERE SCHEMA_NAME(CAST(OBJECTPROPERTYEX(i.object_id, 'SchemaId') AS int)) =
'Purchasing'
     AND avg_fragmentation_in_percent > 30;
```

This gives us all the indexes — regardless of what specific table they belong to — that are associated with a table in the Purchasing schema, but, more importantly, have index fragmentation in excess of 30%.

What's powerful here is that we can easily script maintenance tasks based on the condition of our table. This is a major advance versus the older Database Console Commands options we previously used to view fragmentation.

This is, as I suggested earlier, a relatively simple example. As is the case with many SQL Server topics, I'm sure there will be entire books written purely around the dynamic management views now available in SQL Server. Again, check out Appendix B for more information.

The Activity Monitor

The Activity Monitor has received a major face lift and some extra muscle with SQL Server 2008. All the old process information is there, but there is now a host of other information collected from a variety of other sources, such as PerfMon (a Windows tool for monitoring your system) and the Data Collector.

The Activity Monitor can be found by right-clicking the server node of the Management Studio. Open it up and you get five major subject areas:

- ❑ Overview
- ❑ Processes
- ❑ Resource Waits
- ❑ Data File I/O
- ❑ Recent Expensive Queries

Let's take a quick look at each of these.

Overview

This section is the one that will most remind you of PerfMon. It provides a relatively straightforward graph (as shown in Figure 21-3) of system activity as sampled on a adjustable interval (the default is every 10 seconds). Note that the values presented here are information on what *SQL Server* is utilizing — not your entire system.

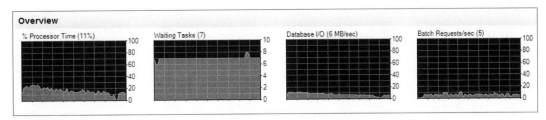

Figure 21-3

Processes

This largely maps, as shown in Figure 21-4, to the Activity Monitor as you would have seen it in SQL Server 2005. It provides information about what processes are running, the command they are currently executing, and metrics on resource and blocking used or incurred by that process.

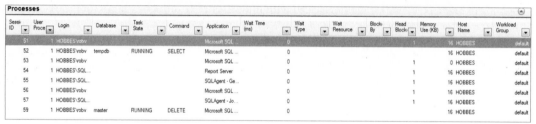

Session ID	User Proce	Login	Database	Task State	Command	Application	Wait Time (ms)	Wait Type	Wait Resource	Block By	Head Block	Memory Use (KB)	Host Name	Workload Group
51	1	HOBBES\robv				Microsoft SQL...	0				1	16	HOBBES	default
52	1	HOBBES\robv	tempdb	RUNNING	SELECT	Microsoft SQL...	0					16	HOBBES	default
53	1	HOBBES\robv				Microsoft SQL...	0				1	0	HOBBES	default
54	1	HOBBES\SQL...				Report Server	0				1	16	HOBBES	default
55	1	HOBBES\SQL...				SQLAgent - Ge...	0				1	16	HOBBES	default
56	1	HOBBES\robv				Microsoft SQL...	0				1	16	HOBBES	default
57	1	HOBBES\SQL...				SQLAgent - Jo...	0				1	16	HOBBES	default
59	1	HOBBES\robv	master	RUNNING	DELETE	Microsoft SQL...	0					16	HOBBES	default

Figure 21-4

Resource Waits

Much like the Overview, this should remind you of PerfMon, providing metrics on wait times for a number of different counters (as shown in Figure 21-5).

Wait Category	Wait Time (ms/sec)	Recent Wait Time (ms/sec)	Average Waiter Count	Cumulative Wait Time (sec)
Other	4990	4957	5.0	1211760
SQLCLR	1996	1996	2.0	484687
Network I/O	535	553	0.5	54
Logging	13	30	0.0	4
Buffer I/O	2	11	0.0	18
Latch	0	10	0.0	1
Lock	0	0	0.0	13
Buffer Latch	0	0	0.0	0
CPU	0	0	0.0	1
Memory	0	0	0.0	0

Figure 21-5

Data File I/O

Still providing largely PerfMon-based numbers here, this one provides information on the physical files being utilized by SQL Server. Prior to this information being gathered in one place (as shown in Figure 21-6), you would have had to set each file up individually in PerfMon. SQL Server now pulls that kind of metric up for you automatically.

Database	File Name	MB/sec Read	MB/sec Written	Response Time (ms)
tempdb	C:\Program Files\Microsoft SQL Server\MSSQ...	0.0		5.5
AdventureWorks2008	C:\Program Files\Microsoft SQL Server\MSSQ...	0.0	0.0	0
AdventureWorks2008	C:\Program Files\Microsoft SQL Server\MSSQ...	0.0	0.0	0
DataCollector	C:\Program Files\Microsoft SQL Server\MSSQ...	0.0	0.0	0
DataCollector	C:\Program Files\Microsoft SQL Server\MSSQ...	0.0	0.0	0
master	C:\Program Files\Microsoft SQL Server\MSSQ...	0.0	0.0	0
master	C:\Program Files\Microsoft SQL Server\MSSQ...	0.0	0.0	0
model	C:\Program Files\Microsoft SQL Server\MSSQ...	0.0	0.0	0
model	C:\Program Files\Microsoft SQL Server\MSSQ...	0.0	0.0	0
modb	C:\Program Files\Microsoft SQL Server\MSSQ...	0.0	0.0	0

Figure 21-6

Recent Expensive Queries

This section, as shown in Figure 21-7, provides information we didn't really have prior to SQL Server 2008. We could map out some of this by using the SQL Server Profiler (discussed shortly), but it was tedious at best and very likely to be flooded with information we didn't really want or need (thus masking the information we were really after).

It's definitely worth noting that the expensive query information is among the information that can be logged to the Performance Data Warehouse, which means that you can use the warehouse to gather metrics not only for the last few minutes, but days or even weeks depending on the retention rules you've set up for your warehouse.

Recent Expensive Queries

Query	Executions/min	CPU (ms/sec)	Physical Reads/sec	Logical Writes/sec	Logical Reads/sec	Average Duration (ms)	Plan Count
SELECT [Session ID] = s.session_id, [Us...	17	20	0	0	0	100	1
SELECT @current_request_count = cntr_value...	51	3	0	0	0	5	1
INSERT INTO #am_wait_stats_snapshots SEL...	55	1	0	0	221	1	1
SELECT @current_total_io_mb = SUM(num_of...	55	0	0	0	0	0	1
DELETE FROM #am_wait_stats_snapshots W...	55	0	0	0	24	0	1
DELETE FROM #am_dbfilestats WHERE colle...	17	0	0	0	4	0	1
SELECT TOP 1 @previous_collection_time = c...	51	0	0	0	1	0	1
SELECT TOP 1 @previous_collection_time = l...	55	0	0	0	1	0	1
SELECTdtb.collation_name AS [Collation],dtb.n...	0	0	0	0	0	0	1

Figure 21-7

The SQL Server Profiler

The true lifesaver among the tools provided with SQL Server, this one is about letting you "sniff out" what's really going on with the server.

Profiler can be started from the Start menu in Windows. You can also run it by selecting the Tools menu in Management Studio. When you first start it up, you can either load an existing profile template or create a new one.

Let's take a look at some of the key points of the main Profiler by walking through a brief example.

Start by choosing New➤Trace from the File menu. Log in to the server you've been working with, and you should be presented with the dialog box in Figure 21-8.

The trace name is probably obvious enough, but the template information might not be. A template is a set of pre-established events, data columns, and filters that you want to see in a trace, and the templates provided with SQL Server are named for the kind of situation that you might want to use them in. Any templates that are stored in the default profiler template directory (which is under the tools subdirectory of wherever you installed SQL Server) are included in the Use the Template drop-down box.

> **Pay particular attention to what template you choose. It determines exactly how much is available to you on the next tab. If you choose too restrictive of a template, you can select Show All Events and Show All Columns to expose all possible choices.**

Next up, you can choose whether to capture the trace to a file on disk or a table in the database. If you save to a file, then that file will be available only to the system that you store it on (or anyone who has access to a network share if that's where you save it). If you save it to a table, then everyone who can connect to the server and has appropriate permissions will be able to examine the trace.

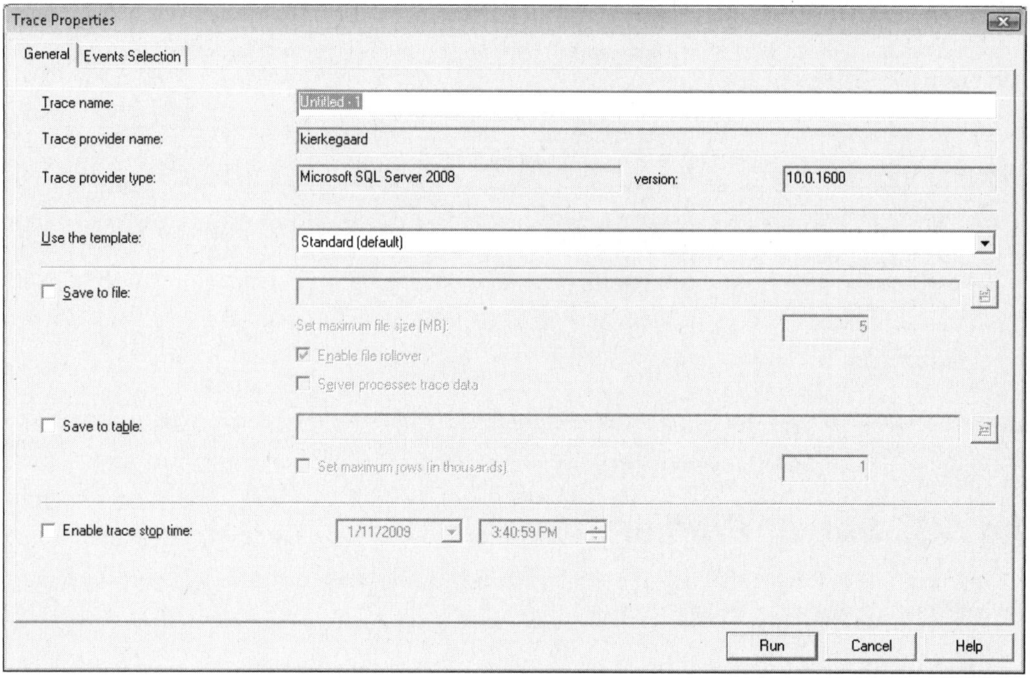

Figure 21-8

Last, but not least, on this dialog is the stop time feature. This allows you to leave a trace running (for example, for a workload file or some other long-running trace need) and have it shut down automatically at a later time.

Things get somewhat more interesting on the tab that comes next (Events Selection), as shown in Figure 21-9.

I've chosen the "blank" template here, and have scrolled down to the Performance area and expanded it. This tab is all about what events you are going to track, and, as you can see, there's quite a range. If, for example, you chose the Tuning trace template, then the initial setup is one that tracks what's needed for the Database Engine Tuning Advisor plus a bit more. In addition, you use the table to select what information you want collected for each class of event.

The temptation here is just to select everything under the sun, so you'll be sure to have all the information. There are a couple of reasons not to do this. First, it means that a lot of additional text has to come back down the pipe to your server. Remember that SQL Server Profiler has to place some audits in the system, and this means that your system is having an additional burden placed on it whenever the

Profiler is running. The bigger the trace, the bigger the burden. Second, it often means lower productivity for you since you have to wade through a huge morass of data — much of which you probably won't need.

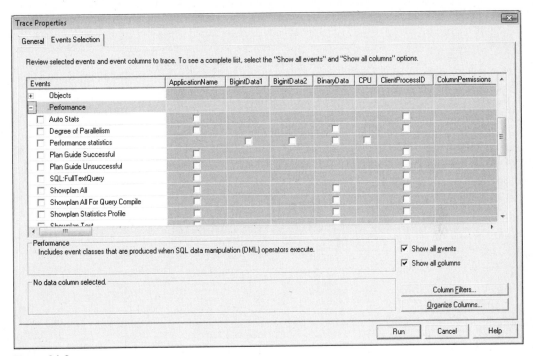

Figure 21-9

I want to point out a couple of key fields here before we move on:

❑ **TextData:** This is the actual text of the statement that the Profiler happens to have added to the trace at that moment in time.

❑ **Application Name:** Another of those highly underutilized features. The application name is something you can set when you create the connection from the client. If you're using ADO.NET or some other data object model and underlying connection method, you can pass the application name as a parameter in your connection string. It can be quite handy for your DBAs when they are trying to troubleshoot problems in the system.

❑ **NT User Name:** This one is what it sounds like. What's great about this is that it can provide a level of accountability.

❑ **Login Name:** Same as NT User Name, only used when operating under SQL Server Security rather than Windows Security.

❑ **CPU:** The actual CPU cycles used.

❑ **Duration:** How long the query ran — includes time waiting for locks and such (where the CPU may not have been doing anything, so doesn't reference that load).

❑ **SPID (SQL Process ID):** This one can be nice if your trace reveals something where you want to kill a process. This is the number you would use with your KILL statement.

Moving right along, let's take a look at what I consider to be one of the most important options — Column Filters.

This is the one that makes sure that, on a production or load test server, you don't get buried in several thousand pages of garbage just by opening a trace up for a few minutes.

With Column Filters, you can select from a number of different options to use to filter out data and limit the size of your result set. By default, Profiler automatically sets up to exclude its own activity in order to try to reduce the Profiler's impact on the end numbers. For the example in Figure 21-10, I'm adding in a Duration value where I've set the minimum to 3,000 milliseconds with no maximum.

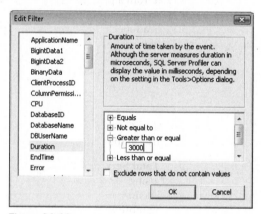

Figure 21-10

Odds are that, if you run this with a query against the Sales.SalesOrderHeaders table, you're not going to see it appear in the trace. Why is that? Because that query will probably run very fast and not meet the criteria for being included in our trace — this is an example of how you might set up a trace to capture the query text and username of someone who has been running very long-running queries on the system. Now try running something a little longer — such as a query that joins many large tables. There's a good chance that you'll now exceed the duration threshold, and your query will show up in the Profiler (if not, then try adjusting down the duration expectation that you set in Profiler).

I can't say enough about how important this tool is in solving performance and other problems. There have been too many times to count in which I've thought that my sproc was running down one logic path only to find that a totally different branch was being executed. How did I originally find out? I watched it execute in Profiler.

The Performance Monitor (PerfMon)

When you install SQL Server on Windows, SQL Server adds several counters to the *Reliability and Performance Monitor* (which is sometimes called *PerfMon* because of the executable's filename — perfmon.msc).

This can be an excellent tool for finding where problems are happening and even determining the nature of some problems.

> Prior to Windows Vista and Windows Server 2008, the *Reliability and Performance Monitor* was known simply as *Performance Monitor*.

While many of the relevant counters are now in the Activity Monitor within the Management Studio, the Reliability and Performance Monitor can be accessed through the Administrative Tools menu in Windows. SQL Server has a number of different Performance Objects, and, within each of these, you will find a series of counters related to that object. Historically, some of the important ones have included:

❑ **SQLServer Cache Manager: Buffer Hit Cache Ratio:** This is the number of pages that were read from the buffer cache rather than from a physical read from disk. The thing to watch out for here is that this number can be thrown off depending on how effective the read-ahead mechanism was — anything that the read-ahead mechanism got to and put in cache before the query actually needed it is counted as a buffer-cache hit — even though there really was a physical read related to the query. Still, this one is going to give you a decent idea of how efficient your memory usage is. You want to see really high numbers here (in the 90+ percent range) for maximum performance. Generally speaking, a low buffer hit cache ratio is indicative of needing more memory.

❑ **SQLServer General Statistics: User Connections:** Pretty much as it sounds, this is the number of user connections currently active in the system.

❑ **SQLServer Memory Manager: Total Server Memory:** The total amount of dynamic memory that the SQL Server is currently using. As you might expect, when this number is high relative to the amount of memory available in your system (remember to leave some for the O/S!), you need to seriously consider adding more RAM.

❑ **SQLServer SQL Statistics: SQL Compilations/sec:** This is telling you how often SQL Server needs to compile things (sprocs, triggers). Keep in mind that this number will also include recompiles (due to changes in index statistics or because a recompile was explicitly requested). When your server is first getting started, this number may spike for a bit, but it should become stable after your server has been running for a while at a constant set and rate of activities.

❑ **SQLServer Buffer Manager: Page Reads/sec:** The number of physical reads from disk for your server. You'd like to see a relatively low number here. Unfortunately, because the requirements and activities of each system are different, I can't give you a benchmark to work from here.

❑ **SQLServer Buffer Manager: Page Writes/sec:** The number of physical writes performed to disk for your server. Again, you'd like a low number here.

If you want to add or change any of these, just click the plus (+) sign up on the toolbar. You'll be presented with a dialog, as shown in Figure 21-11, that lets you choose between all the different objects and counters available on your system (not just those related to SQL Server):

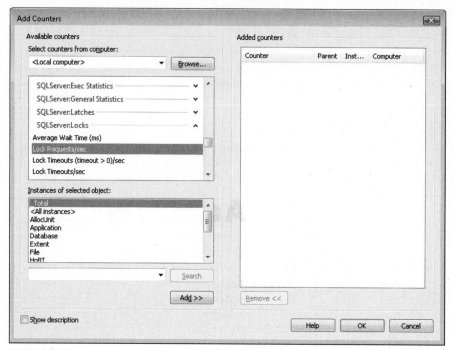

Figure 21-11

The big thing here is to realize that you can mix and match a wide variety of counters to be able to reach a better understanding of what's going on with your server and make the appropriate adjustments. Much of the time, this kind of task is going to have more to do with the DBA than the developer, but many of these stats can be helpful to you when you are doing load testing for your application.

Summary

Performance could be, and should be, in a book by itself. There's simply just too much to cover and get acquainted with to do it all in one or even several chapters. The way I've tried to address this is by pointing out performance issues throughout the book, so you could take them on a piece at a time.

The biggest thing is to have a plan — a performance plan. Make performance an issue from the first stages of your project. Set benchmarks early on, and continually measure your system against those benchmarks to know where you are improving and what problems you might need to address.

In this chapter, we've reviewed a number of the performance considerations touched on throughout the book, plus added several new tools and ideas to consider.

In the next chapter, we'll be taking a look at administration issues. As you've seen through some of the portions of this chapter, proper administration can also be a key ingredient to performance.

22

Administration

So, at this point we've covered all of the core database topics and then some. We still have a chapter or two to clean up the edges around our development effort, but we've mostly covered everything — heh, NOT!!! For the developer, we like to think our job is done, but for the application we're building, it's just beginning. And so, it's time to talk a bit about maintenance and administration of the databases you develop.

If there is anything I hope to instill in you in your database development efforts, it's to avoid the "hey, I just build 'em — now it's your problem" attitude that is all too common in the world of database-driven applications. Far too many developers are guilty of attempting to build relatively bug-free code, and calling it good. Well, just because it runs, doesn't mean your end user is going to be successful with your software over the long haul. It is, therefore, important for you to look at how your system is going to be used, and what will be necessary to keep it functioning properly.

In this chapter, we're going to take a look at some of the tasks that are necessary to make sure that your end users can not only recover from problems and disasters but also perform some basic maintenance that will help things keep running smoothly.

Among the things we'll touch on are:

- ❑ Scheduling jobs
- ❑ Backing up and recovering
- ❑ Basic defragmenting and index rebuilding
- ❑ Setting alerts
- ❑ Archiving
- ❑ Using PowerShell
- ❑ Considering Policy-Based Management

While these are far from the only administration tasks available, these do represent something of "the minimum" you should expect to address in the deployment plans for your app. We'll also take a further look at monitoring (several items in that area were discussed as part of the performance tuning coverage in the preceding chapter) through the use of the Policy-Based Management framework that was added with SQL Server 2008.

This is one of those chapters where I feel that overlap with some of the coverage in my Beginning *title is an unfortunate necessity. The reality is that most developers I know — even relative experts in SQL Server — know precious little about the job scheduling, index fragmentation, and even backup and recovery. Be careful, however, assuming that you've seen everything this chapter has to offer just because you may have read the* Beginning *title. I've added more advanced coverage of several of these topics, and I also include code-driven handling of many administrative tasks.*

Scheduling Jobs

Many of the tasks that we'll go over in the remainder of the chapter can be *scheduled*. Scheduling jobs allows you to run tasks that place a load on the system at off-peak hours. It also ensures that you don't forget to take care of things. From index rebuilds to backups, you'll hear of horror stories over and over about shops that "forgot" to do that, or thought they had set up a scheduled job but never checked on it.

If your background is in Windows Server, and you have scheduled other jobs using the Windows Scheduler service, you could utilize that scheduling engine to support SQL Server. Doing things all in the Windows Scheduler allows you to have everything in one place, but SQL Server has some more robust branching options.

There are basically two terms to think about: jobs and tasks.

❑ **Tasks:** These are single processes that are to be executed, or batches of commands that are to be run. Tasks are not independent — they exist only as members of jobs.

❑ **Jobs:** These are a grouping of one or more tasks that should be run together. You can, however, set up dependencies and branching depending on the success or failure of individual tasks (for example, task A runs if the previous task succeeds, but task B runs if the previous task fails).

Jobs can be scheduled based on:

❑ A daily, weekly, or monthly basis

❑ A specific time of the day

❑ A specific frequency (say, every 10 minutes, or every hour)

❑ When the CPU becomes idle for a period of time

❑ When the SQL Server Agent starts

❑ In response to an alert

Tasks are run by virtue of being part of a job and based on the branching rules you define for your job. Just because a job runs doesn't mean that all the tasks that are part of that job will run. Some may be executed and others not depending on the success or failure of previous tasks in the job and what *branching rules* you have established. SQL Server not only allows one task to automatically fire when another finishes, but it also allows for doing something entirely different (such as running some sort of recovery task) if the current task fails.

In addition to branching you can, depending on what happens, also tell SQL Server to:

❑ Provide notification of the success or failure of a job to an operator. You're allowed to send a separate notification for a network message (which would pop up on a user's screen as long as they are logged in), a pager, and an e-mail address to one operator each.

❑ Write the information to the event log.

❑ Automatically delete the job (to prevent executing it later and generally "clean up").

Let's take a quick look at how to create operators in Management Studio, and then we'll move on to creating the other objects needed to get jobs scheduled.

Creating an Operator

If you're going to make use of the notification features of the SQL Agent, then you must have an operator set up to define the specifics for who is notified. This side of things — the creation of operators — isn't typically done through any kind of automated process or as part of the developed code. These are usually created manually by the DBA. We'll go ahead and take a rather brief look at creating operators here just to understand how it works in relation to the scheduling of tasks.

Creating an Operator Using Management Studio

To create an operator using Management Studio, you need to navigate to the SQL Server Agent node of the server for which you're creating the operator. Expand the SQL Server Agent node, right-click the Operators member, and choose New Operator.

Be aware that, depending on your particular installation, the SQL Server Agent Service may not start automatically by default. If you run into any issues or if you notice the SQL Server Agent icon in the Management Studio has a little red square in it, then the service is probably set to manual or even disabled — you will probably want to change the service to start automatically. Regardless, make sure that it is running for the examples found in this chapter. You can do this by right-clicking the Agent node and selecting Start.

You should be presented with the dialog box shown in Figure 22-1 (mine is partially filled in).

You can then fill out a schedule for what times this operator is to receive e-mail notifications for certain kinds of errors that we'll see on the Notifications tab.

Speaking of that Notifications tab, go ahead and click over to that tab. It should appear as in Figure 22-2.

Until you have more alerts in your system (we'll get to those later in this chapter), this page may not make a lot of sense. What it is about is setting up what notifications you want this operator to receive depending on what defined alerts get triggered. Again, hard to understand this concept before we've gotten to alerts, but suffice to say that alerts are triggered when certain things happen in your database, and this page defines which alerts this particular operator receives.

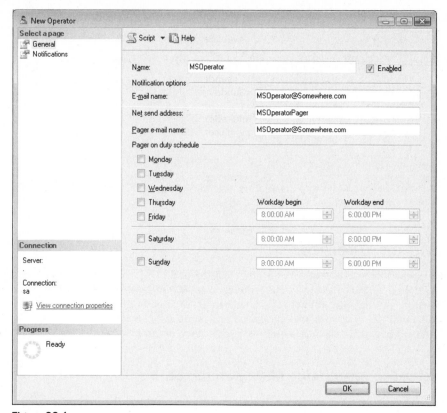

Figure 22-1

Creating an Operator Using T-SQL

If you do decide to create operators programmatically, you can make use of the sp_add_operator sproc found in msdb.

> Note that **sp_add_operator** and most other SQL Server Agent–related stored procedures are managed through the msdb database rather than being true system stored procedures. As such, you need to either have msdb current when you call them or use three-part naming.

After seeing all the different things you need to choose in Management Studio, it probably won't surprise you to find out that this sproc has a ton of different parameters. Fortunately, a number of them are optional, so you need to supply them only if you're going to make use of them. The syntax looks like this:

```
sp_add_operator [@name =] '<operator name>'
    [, [@enabled =] <0 for no, 1 for yes>]
    [, [@email_address =] '<email alias or address>']
```

```
[, [@pager_address =] '<pager address>']
[, [@weekday_pager_start_time =] <weekday pager start time>]
[, [@weekday_pager_end_time =] <weekday pager end time>]
[, [@saturday_pager_start_time =] <Saturday pager start time>]
[, [@saturday_pager_end_time =] <Saturday pager end time>]
[, [@sunday_pager_start_time =] <Sunday pager start time>]
[, [@sunday_pager_end_time =] <Sunday pager end time>]
[, [@pager_days =] <pager days>]
[, [@netsend_address =] '<netsend address>']
[, [@category_name =] '<category name>']
```

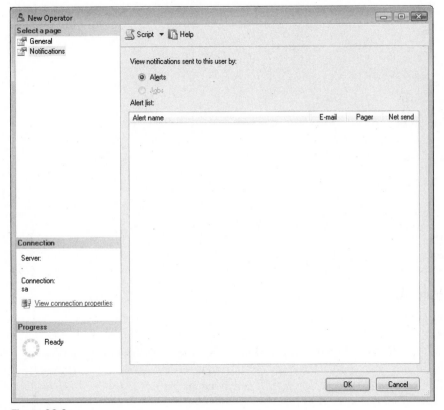

Figure 22-2

Most of the parameters in this sproc are self-explanatory, but there are a few we need to take a closer look at:

❑ **@enabled:** This is a Boolean value and works just the way you would typically use a bit flag — 0 means disable this operator and 1 means enable the operator.

❑ **@email_address:** This one is just a little tricky. In order to use e-mail with your SQL Server, you need to configure Database Mail to be operational using a specific mail server. This parameter assumes that whatever value you supply is an alias on that mail server. If you are providing the more classic e-mail address type (somebody@SomeDomain.com), then you need to enclose it in square brackets — like [somebody@SomeDomain.com]. Note that the entire address — including the brackets — must still be enclosed in quotation marks.

❑ **@pager_days:** This is a number that indicates the days that the operator is available for pages. This is probably the toughest of all the parameters. This uses a single-byte bit-flag approach similar to what we saw with the @@OPTIONS global variable described in the system functions appendix at the back of the book). You simply add the values together for all the values that you want to set as active days for this operator. The options are:

Value	Day of Week
Sunday	1
Monday	2
Tuesday	4
Wednesday	8
Thursday	16
Friday	32
Saturday	64

Okay, so let's go ahead and create our operator using sp_add_operator. We'll keep our use of parameters down, since many of them are redundant:

```
USE msdb;
DECLARE @PageDays int;

SELECT @PageDays = 2 + 8 + 32 -- Monday, Wednesday, and Friday;

EXEC sp_add_operator @name = 'TSQLOperator',
        @enabled = 1,
        @pager_address = 'YourEmail@YourDomain.com',
        @weekday_pager_start_time = 080000,
        @weekday_pager_end_time = 170000,
        @pager_days = @PageDays;
```

If you go back into Management Studio and refresh your Operators list, you should see your new operator there.

There are three other sprocs (plus one to retrieve information) that you need to make use of in order to have power over your operator from T-SQL:

❑ **sp_help_operator:** Provides information on the current settings for the operator.

❑ **sp_update_operator:** Accepts all the same information as sp_add_operator; the new information completely replaces the old information.

❑ **sp_delete_operator:** Removes the specified operator from the system.

❏ **sp_add_notification:** Accepts an alert name, an operator name, and a method of notification (e-mail, pager, netsend). Adds a notification such that, if the alert is triggered, then the specified operator will be notified via the specified method.

Now that you've seen how to create operators, let's take a look at creating actual jobs and tasks.

Creating Jobs and Tasks

As I mentioned earlier, jobs are a collection of one or more tasks. A task is a logical unit of work, such as backing up one database or running a T-SQL script to meet a specific need, such as rebuilding all your indexes.

Even though a job can contain several tasks, this is no guarantee that every task in a job will run. They will either run or not run depending on the success or failure of other tasks in the job and what you've defined as the response for each case of success or failure. For example, you might cancel the remainder of the job if one of the tasks fails.

Like operators, jobs can be created in Management Studio as well as programmatic constructs.

Creating Jobs and Tasks Using Management Studio

The SQL Server Management Studio makes it very easy to create scheduled jobs. Just navigate to the SQL Server Agent node of your server. Then right-click the Jobs member and select New Job. You should get a multinode dialog box, shown in Figure 22-3, that will help you build the job one step at a time.

The name can be whatever you like as long as it adheres to the SQL Server rules for naming, as discussed early in this book.

Most of the rest of the information is, again, self-explanatory with the exception of Category — which is just one way of grouping together jobs. Many of your jobs that are specific to your application are going to be Uncategorized, although you will probably on occasion run into instances where you want to create Web Assistant, Database Maintenance, Full Text, or Replication Jobs. Those each go into their own category for easy identification.

We can then move on to Steps, as shown in Figure 22-4. This is the place where we tell SQL Server to start creating our new tasks that will be part of this job.

To add a new step to our job, we just click the New button and fill in the new dialog box, shown in Figure 22-5. We'll use a T-SQL statement to raise a bogus error just so we can see that things are really happening when we schedule this job. Note, however, that there is an Open button to the left of the command box — you can use this to import SQL Scripts that you have saved in files.

Let's go ahead and move on to the Advanced tab for this dialog, shown in Figure 22-6 — it's here that we really start to see some of the cool functionality that our job scheduler offers.

Notice several things in this dialog:

❏ You can automatically set the job to retry at a specific interval if the task fails.

❑ You can choose what to do if the job succeeds or fails. For each result (success or failure), you can:

  ❑ Quit reporting success

  ❑ Quit reporting failure

  ❑ Move on to the next step

❑ You can output results to a file. (This is very nice for auditing.)

❑ You can impersonate another user (for rights purposes). Note that you have to have the rights for that user. Because we're logged in as a sysadmin, we can run the job as the dbo or just about anyone. The average user would probably only have, at most, the guest account available (unless they were the database owner) — but, hey, in most cases a general user shouldn't be scheduling his or her own jobs this way anyway (let your client application provide that functionality).

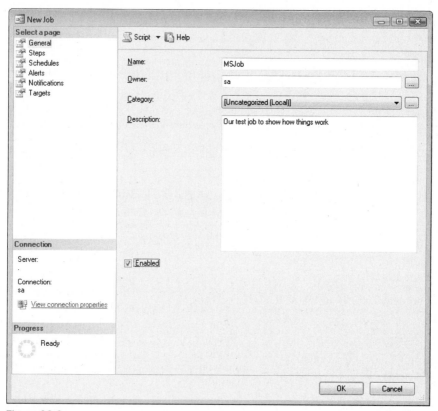

Figure 22-3

Okay, so there's little chance that our RAISERROR statement is going to fail, so we'll just take the default of "Quit the job reporting failure" on this one (we'll see other possibilities later in the chapter when we come to backups).

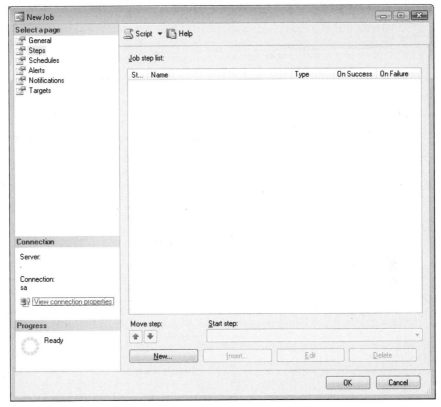

Figure 22-4

That moves us back to the main New Job dialog, and we're now ready to move on to the Schedules node, shown in Figure 22-7.

In this dialog, we can manage one or more scheduled times for this job to run. To actually create a new scheduled time for the job to run, we need to click the New button. That brings up yet another dialog, shown in Figure 22-8.

I've largely filled this one out already (lest you get buried in a sea of screenshots), but it is from this dialog that we create a new schedule for this job. Recurrence and frequency are set here.

The frequency side of things can be a bit confusing because of the funny way that they've worded things. If you want something to run at multiple times every day, then you need to set the job to Occur Daily — every 1 day. This seems like it would run only once a day, but then you also have the option of setting whether it runs once or on an interval. In our case, we want to set our job to run every 5 minutes.

Now we're ready to move on to the next node of our job properties — Alerts, shown in Figure 22-9.

From here, we can select which alerts we want to make depending on what happens. Choose Add and we get yet another rich dialog, shown in Figure 22-10.

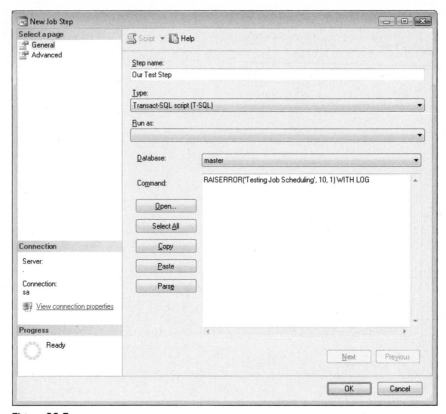

Figure 22-5

Our first node — General — is going to let us fill out some of the basics. We can, for example, limit this notification to one particular database. We also define just how severe the condition needs to be before the alert will fire (in terms of severity of the error).

From there, it is on to the Response node (see Figure 22-11).

Notice that I was able to choose either of the operators that we created earlier in the chapter. (I've just stuck with the one we created using the Management Studio.) It is through the definitions of these operators that the SQL Server Agent knows what e-mail address or netsend address to make the notification to. Also notice that we have control, on the right-hand side, over how our operator is notified.

Last, but not least, we have the Options node (see Figure 22-12), to complete the creation of our new alert.

With the new alert created, we can go back to the Notifications node of the main New Job dialog (see Figure 22-13).

This window lets you bypass the older alerts model and define a response that is specific to this one job — we'll just stick with what we already have for now, but you could define specific additional notifications in this dialog.

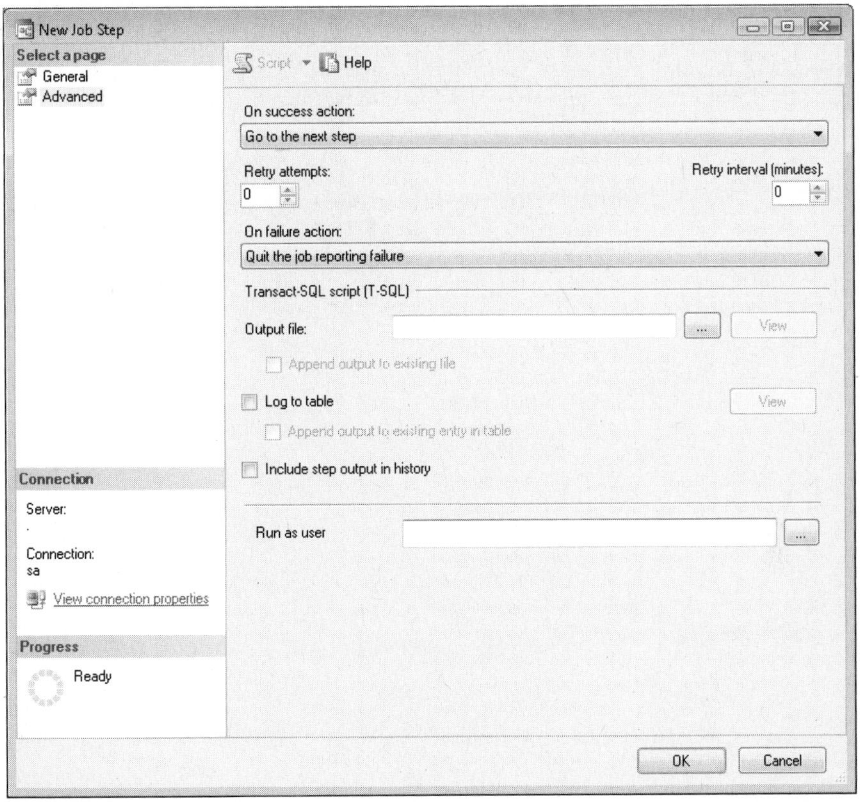

Figure 22-6

At this point, you are ready to say OK and exit the dialog. You'll need to wait a few minutes before the task will fire, but you should start to see log entries appear every five minutes in the Windows event log. You can look at this by navigating to the Event Viewer in the Computer Management utility for your system (where to find this varies a bit depending on what version and edition of Windows you are running). You'll need to switch the view to use the Application log (under Windows logs).

> Don't forget that, if you're going to be running scheduled tasks like this one, you need to have the SQL Server Agent running in order for them to be executed. You can check the status of the SQL Server Agent by running the SQL Server Configuration Manager and selecting the SQL Server Agent service, or by navigating to the SQL Server Agent node of the Object Explorer in Management Studio.

> Also, don't forget to disable this job (right-click the job in Management Studio after you've seen that it's working the way you expect). Otherwise, it will just continue to sit there and create entries in your Application log. Eventually, the Application log will fill up and you can have problems with your system.

Creating Jobs and Tasks Using T-SQL

Before we get started, I want to point out that using T-SQL for this kind of stuff (creating scheduled jobs and tasks) is not usually the way things are done on a day-to-day basis. Most jobs wind up being scheduled by the DBA based on a specific need and a specific schedule that is required. If you're not in a situation where you need to script the installation of tasks, then you may want to just skip this section (it's a lot to learn if you aren't going to use it!). That being said, there can be times where your end users won't have a DBA handy (small shops, for example, often don't have anything even remotely resembling a DBA), so you'll want to script some jobs to help out unsophisticated users.

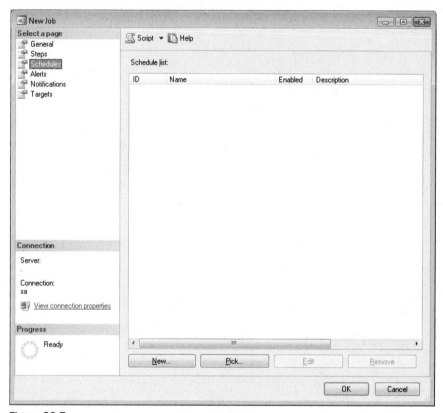

Figure 22-7

Automating the creation of certain jobs is very frequently overlooked in installation procedures — particularly for shrink-wrap software. If you're working in some form of consulting or private IS shop environment, then there's a good chance that you are going to need to take care of scheduling all the needed tasks when you do the install. With shrink-wrap software, however, you often aren't at all in control of the installation process — indeed, you may be hundreds or thousands of miles away from the install and may not even know that it's happening.

How then do you make sure that basic tasks (like backups, for example) get done? You can make it part of your installation process.

Jobs can be added to SQL Server using T-SQL by using three different stored procedures:

- ❑ **sp_add_job:** This creates the actual job.
- ❑ **sp_add_job_step:** This creates a task within the job.
- ❑ **sp_add_jobschedule:** This determines when the job will run.

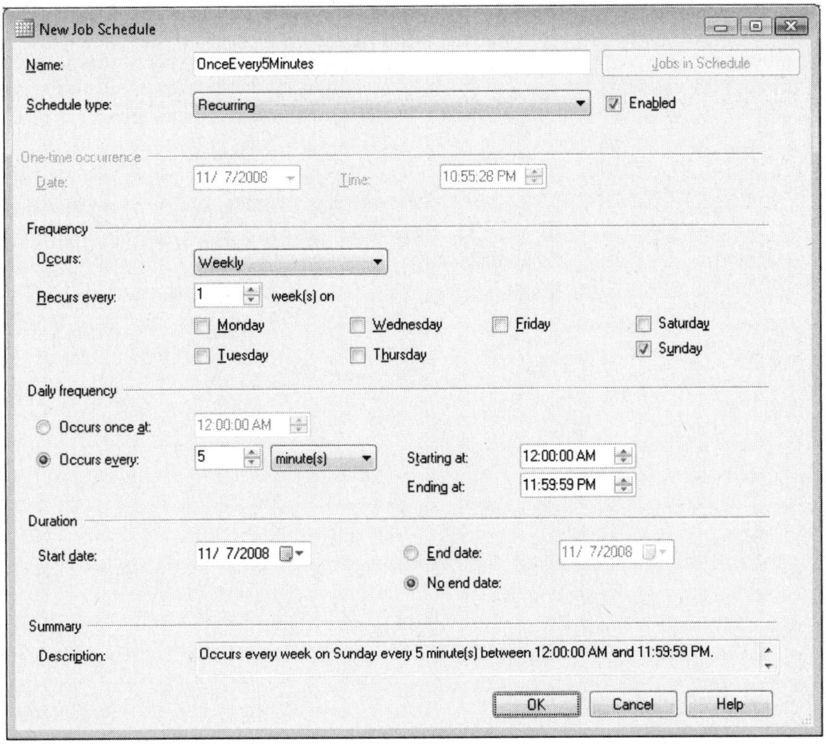

Figure 22-8

Each of these builds a piece of the overall execution of the scheduled task much as the different tabs in Management Studio did. The next sections take a look at each individually.

> All jobs and tasks are stored in the msdb database. As such, you'll need to make sure that msdb is the current database (utilizing the USE command) when calling any of these sprocs.

sp_add_job

This one creates the top-level of a hierarchy and establishes who owns the job and how notifications should be handled. There are quite a few parameters, but most of them are fairly easy to figure out:

```
sp_add_job [@job_name =] '<job name>'
    [,[@enabled =] <0 for no, 1 for yes>]
    [,[@description =] '<description of the job>']
    [,[@start_step_id =] <ID of the step you want to start at>]
    [,[@category_name =] '<category>']
    [,[@category_id =] <category ID>]
    [,[@owner_login_name =] '<login>']
    [,[@notify_level_eventlog =] <eventlog level>]
    [,[@notify_level_email =] <email level>]
```

```
[,[@notify_level_netsend =] <netsend level>]
[,[@notify_level_page =] <page level>]
[,[@notify_email_operator_name =] '<name of operator to email>']
[,[@notify_netsend_operator_name =] '<name of operator for network message>']
[,[@notify_page_operator_name =] '<name of operator to page>']
[,[@delete_level =] <delete level>]
[,[@job_id =] <job id> OUTPUT]
```

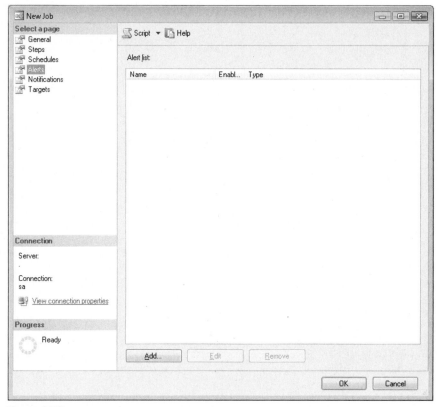

Figure 22-9

Again, most of the parameters here are self-explanatory, but let's again touch on some of the more sticky ones.

❑ **@start_step_id:** This one is going to default to 1, and that's almost always going to be the place to leave it. We'll be adding steps shortly, but those steps will have identifiers to them, and this just lets the SQL Server Agent know where to begin the job.

❑ **@category_name:** This one equates directly with the category we saw in Management Studio. It will often be none (in which case, see @category_ID) but could be a Database Maintenance (another common choice), Full Text, Web Assistant, Replication, or a category that you add yourself using sp_add_category.

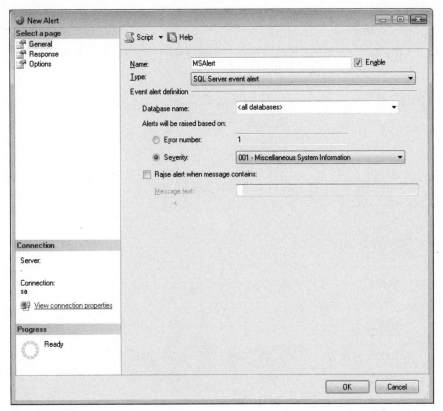

Figure 22-10

❑ **@category_id:** This is just a way of providing a category without being dependent on a particular language. If you don't want to assign any particular category, then I recommend using this option instead of the name and supplying a value of either 0 (Uncategorized, but runs local) or 1 (Uncategorized Multi-Server).

❑ **@notify_level_eventlog:** For each type of notification, this determines under what condition the notification occurs. To use this sproc, though, we need to supply some constant values to indicate when we want the notification to happen. The constants are:

Constant Value	When the Notification Occurs
0	Never
1	When the task succeeds
2	When the task fails (this is the default)
3	Every time the task runs

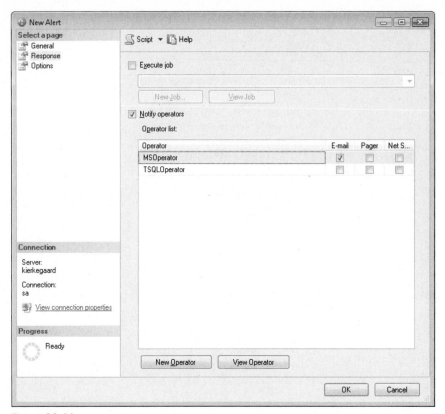

Figure 22-11

❑ **@job_id:** This is just a way of finding out what job ID was assigned to your newly created job. You'll need this value when you go to create job steps and the job schedule(s). The big things on this one are:

> ❑ Remember to receive the value into a variable so you can reuse it.
>
> ❑ The variable needs to be of type uniqueidentifier rather than the types you might be more familiar with at this point.

Note that all the non-level "notify" parameters are expecting an operator name. You should create your operators before running this sproc.

So, let's create a job to test this process out. What we're going to do here is create a job that's nearly identical to the job we created in Management Studio.

First, we need to create our top-level job. All we're going to do for notifications is to send a message on failure to the Windows event log. If you have Database Mail set up, then feel free to add in notification parameters for your operator.

```
USE msdb;

DECLARE @JobID  uniqueidentifier;

EXEC sp_add_job
    @job_name = 'TSQLCreatedTestJob',
    @enabled = 1,
    @notify_level_eventlog = 3,
    @job_id = @JobID OUTPUT;

SELECT 'JobID is ' + CONVERT(varchar(128),@JobID);
```

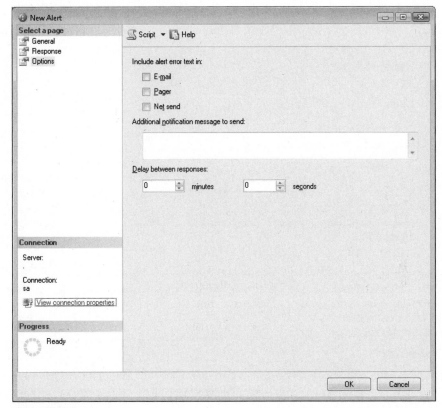

Figure 22-12

Now, execute this, and you should wind up with something like this:

```
----------------------------------------------------------------------
JobID is 83369994-6C5B-45FA-A702-3511214A2F8A

(1 row(s) affected)
```

671

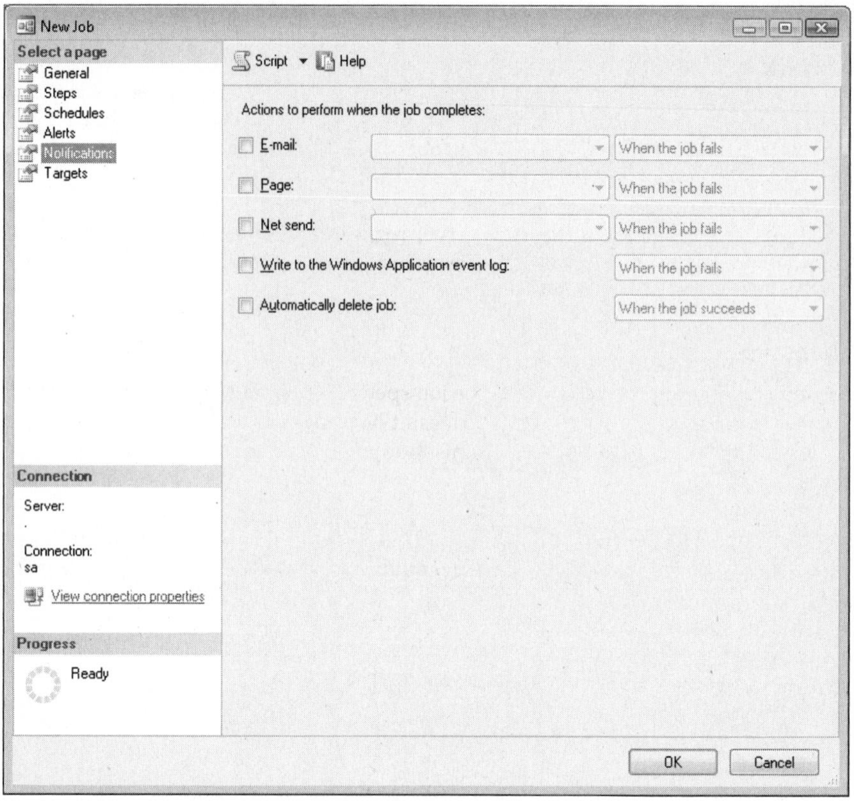

Figure 22-13

Note that your particular GUID will be different from the one I got here. (Remember that GUIDs are effectively guaranteed to be unique across time and space.) You can either use this value or you can use the job name to refer to the job later. (I happen to find this a lot easier, but it can create problems when dealing with multiple servers.)

sp_add_jobserver

This is a quick-and-dirty one. We've now got ourselves a job, but we don't have anything assigned for it to run against. You see, you can create a job on one server but still run it against a completely different server if you choose.

In order to target a particular server, we'll use a sproc (in msdb still) called `sp_add_jobserver`. The syntax is the easiest by far of any we'll be looking at in this section, and looks like this:

```
sp_add_jobserver [@job_id =] <job id>|[@job_name =] '<job name>',
[@server_name =] '<server>'
```

Note that you supply either the job ID or the job name — not both.

So, to assign a target server for our job, we need to run a quick command:

```
USE msdb;

EXEC sp_add_jobserver
    @job_name = 'TSQLCreatedTestJob',
    @server_name = "(local)";
```

Note that this will just point at the local server regardless of what that server is named. We could have also put the name of another valid SQL Server in to be targeted.

sp_add_jobstep

The second step in the process is to tell the job specifically what it is going to do. At the moment, all we have in our example is the shell. The job doesn't have any tasks to perform, and that makes it a very useless job indeed. There is a flip side to this though — a step can't even be created without some job to assign it to.

The next step then is to run sp_add_jobstep. This is essentially adding a task to the job. If we had multiple steps we wanted the job to do, then we would run this particular sproc several times.

The syntax looks like this:

```
sp_add_jobstep [@job_id =] <job ID> | [@job_name =] '<job name>']
    [, [@step_id =] <step ID>]
    [, [@step_name =] '<step name>']
    [, [@subsystem =] '<subsystem>']
    [, [@command =] '<command>']
    [, [@additional_parameters =] '<parameters>']
    [, [@cmdexec_success_code =] <code>]
    [, [@on_success_action =] <success action>]
    [, [@on_success_step_id =] <success step ID>]
    [, [@on_fail_action =] <fail action>]
    [, [@on_fail_step_id =] <fail step ID>]
    [, [@server =] '<server>']
    [, [@database_name =] '<database>']
    [, [@database_user_name =] '<user>']
    [, [@retry_attempts =] <retry attempts>]
    [, [@retry_interval =] <retry interval>]
    [, [@os_run_priority =] <run priority>]
    [, [@output_file_name =] '<file name>']
    [, [@flags =] <flags>]
```

Not as many of the parameters are self-explanatory here, so let's look at the more confusing ones in the list:

❑ **@job_id vs. @job_name:** This is actually a rather odd sproc in the sense that it expects you to enter one of the first two parameters, but not both. You can either attach this step to a job by its GUID (as you saved from the last sproc run) or by the job name.

❑ **@step_id:** All the steps in any job have an ID. SQL Server assigns these IDs automatically as you insert the steps. So why, if it does it automatically, do we have a parameter for it? That's in case we want to insert a step in the middle of a job. If there are already numbers 1–5 in the job, and we insert a new step and provide a step ID of 3, then our new step will be assigned to position number 3. The previous step 3 will be moved to position 4 with each succeeding step being incremented by 1 to make room for the previous step.

❑ **@step_name:** Is what it says — the name of that particular task. Just be aware that there is no default here. You must provide a step name.

❑ **@subsystem:** This ties in very closely to job categories and determines which subsystem within SQL Server (such as the replication engine, or the command line — the command prompt — or Integration Services) is responsible for executing the script. The default is that you're running a set of T-SQL statements. The possible subsystems are:

SubSystem	Description
ACTIVESCRIPTING	The scripting engine (VB Script). Note that this one is considered deprecated, and Microsoft will remove it from the product at some point.
ANALYSISQUERY	Analysis Services query (MDX, DMX).
ANALYSISCOMMAND	Analysis Services command (XMLA).
CMDEXEC	Gives you the capability to execute compiled programs or batch files from a command (DOS) prompt.
DISTRIBUTION	The Replication Distribution Agent.
'Dts'	Integration Services package execution.
LOGREADER	Replication Log Reader Agent.
MERGE	The Replication Merge Agent.
'PowerShell'	PowerShell script.
'QueueReader'	Replication Queue Reader Agent job.
SNAPSHOT	The Replication Snapshot Agent.
TSQL	A T-SQL batch. This is the default.

❑ **@command:** This is the actual command you're issuing to a specific subsystem. In our example, this is going to be the RAISERROR command just like we issued when using Management Studio, but it could be almost any T-SQL command. What's cool here is that there are some system-supplied values you can use in your commands. You place these in the middle of your scripts as needed, and they are replaced at runtime (we'll make use of this in our example). The possible system-supplied values are:

Tag	Description
A-DBN	Substitutes in the database name.
A-SVR	Substitutes the server name in the place of the tag.
A-ERR	Error number.
A-SEV	Error severity.
A-MSG	The message text from the error.
DATE	Supplies the current date (in YYYYMMDD format).
INST	Provides the name of the current instance of SQL Server (it's blank if it is the default instance).
JOBID	Supplies the current Job ID.
MACH	The current computer name.
MSSA	Master SQL Server Agent name.
OSCMD	The program that runs CmdExec steps.
SQLDIR	The directory in which SQL Server is installed (usually `C:\Program Files\Microsoft SQL Server\MSSQL10.MSSQLSERVER\MSSQL`).
STEPCT	A count of the number of times this step has executed (excluding retries). You could use this one to keep count of the number of executions and force the termination of a multistep loop.
STEPID	Step ID.
SVR	The name of the computer the job is running on, including the SQL Server instance name if applicable.
TIME	The current time in HHMMSS format.
STRTTM	The start time for the job in HHMMSS format.
STRTDT	The start date for the job in YYYYMMDD format.

Note that all of these tokens must be wrapped in parentheses. This is a somewhat different requirement than was required through SQL Server 2005 RTM (which, like SQL Server 2000, required a square bracket instead). Beginning with SQL Server 2005 SP1, parentheses replaced the earlier square bracket requirement, and an escape sequence is required (we'll look at that in a bit).

Beginning with SQL Server 2005 SP1, you must wrap any of the previous tokens used in the @COMMAND parameter in an escape clause. Value escape functions include:

$(ESCAPE_SQUOTE (*token name*))	Replaces any single quotation mark with two single quotation marks in the token replacement string.
$(ESCAPE_DQUOTE (*token name*))	Replaces any single instance of a double quotation mark with two double quotation marks in the token replacement string.
$(ESCAPE_RBRACKET (*token name*))	Replaces any single instance of a right bracket in the token replacement string with two right brackets.
$(ESCAPE_NONE (*token name*))	Provided solely for backward compatibility, this performs the token replacement without escaping any characters in the string.

❑ **@cmdexec_success_code:** This is the value you expect to be returned by whatever command interpreter ran your job if the job ran successfully (applies only to command prompt subsystem). The default is zero.

❑ **@on_success_action and @on_fail_action:** This is where you say what to actually do at the success or failure of your step. Remember that at the job level we define what notifications we want to happen, but, at the step level, we can define how we want processing to continue (or end). For this parameter, you need to supply one of the following constant values:

Value	Description
1	Quit with success. This is the default for successful task executions.
2	Quit with failure. This is the default for failed tasks.
3	Go to the next step.
4	Go to a specific step as defined in on_success_step_id or on_fail_step_id.

❑ **@on_success_step_id and @on_fail_step_id:** What step you want to run next if you've selected option 4 in the preceding table.

❑ **@server:** The server the task is to be run against (you can run tasks on multiple target servers from a single master server).

❑ **@database_name:** The database to be set as current when the task runs.

❑ **@retry_interval:** This is set in minutes.

❑ **@os_run_priority:** Ah, an undocumented feature. The default here is normal, but you can adjust how important Windows is going to think that your cmdExec (command line) scheduled task is. The possible values are:

Value	Priority
–15	Run at idle only
–1 thru –14	Increasingly below normal
0	Normal (this is the default)
1 thru 14	Increasingly above normal
15	Time critical

I just can't help but think of the old *Lost in Space* TV show here and think of the robot saying "DANGER Will Robinson — DANGER!" Don't take messing with these values lightly. If you're not familiar with the issues surrounding Windows thread priorities, I'd suggest staying as far away from this one as possible. Going with the higher values, in particular, can have a very detrimental impact on your system — including creating significant instabilities. When you say that this is the most important thing, remember that you are taking away some of the importance of things like operating system functions — not something that's smart to do. Stay clear of this unless you really know what you're doing.

❑ **@flags:** This one relates to the Output File parameter, and indicates whether to overwrite or append your output information to the existing file. The options are:

Value	Description
0	No option specified (currently, this means your file will be overwritten every time).
2	Append information to the existing file (if one exists).
4	Explicitly overwrite the file.

Okay, now that we've looked at the parameters, let's add a step to the job we created a short time ago:

```
EXEC sp_add_jobstep
    @job_name = 'TSQLCreatedTestJob',
    @step_name = 'This Is The Step',
    @command = 'RAISERROR
        (''RAISERROR ('''''TSQL Task is Job ID
$(ESCAPE_SQUOTE(JOBID)).'''',10,1) WITH LOG'',10,1)
        WITH LOG',
    @database_name = 'AdventureWorks2008',
    @retry_attempts = 3 ,
    @retry_interval = 5;
```

Note the requirement for the escape function. Without the escape function (in this case, any one of the four would have worked), the JOBID would not be treated as a substitution token, and would have been left as the literal string of `"JOBID"`.

Technically speaking, our job should be able to be run at this point. The reason I say "technically speaking" is because we haven't scheduled the job, so the only way to run it is to manually tell the job to run. Let's take care of the scheduling issue, and then we'll be done.

sp_add_jobschedule

This is the last piece of the puzzle. We need to tell our job when to run. To do this, we'll make use of `sp_add_jobschedule`, which, like all the other sprocs we've worked on in this section, can only be found in the msdb database. Note that we could submit an entry from this sproc multiple times to create multiple schedules for our job. Keep in mind though that getting too many jobs scheduled can lead to a great deal of confusion, so schedule jobs wisely. (For example, don't schedule one job for every day of the week when you can schedule a single job to run daily.)

The syntax has some similarities to what we've already been working with, but adds some new pieces to the puzzle:

```
sp_add_jobschedule
    [@job_id =] <job ID>, | [@job_name =] '<job name>', [@name =] '<name>'
    [,[@enabled =] <0 for no, 1 for yes>]
    [,[@freq_type =] <frequency type>]
    [,[@freq_interval =] <frequency interval>]
    [,[@freq_subday_type =] <frequency subday type>]
    [,[@freq_subday_interval =] <frequency subday interval>]
    [,[@freq_relative_interval =] <frequency relative interval>]
    [,[@freq_recurrence_factor =] <frequency recurrence factor>]
    [,[@active_start_date =] <active start date>]
    [,[@active_end_date =] <active end date>]
    [,[@active_start_time =] <active start time>]
    [,[@active_end_time =] <active end time>]
```

Again, let's look at some of these parameters:

❑ **@freq_type:** Defines the nature of the intervals that are set up in the following parameters. This is another of those parameters that uses bit flags (although you should only use one at a time). Some of the choices are clear, but some aren't until you get to @freq_interval (which is next). Your choices are:

Value	Frequency
1	Once
4	Daily
8	Weekly
16	Monthly (fixed day)
32	Monthly (relative to @freq_interval)
64	Run at start of SQL Server Agent
128	Run when CPU is idle

❑ **@freq_interval:** Decides the exact days that the job is executed, but the nature of this value depends entirely on @freq_type (see the preceding point). This one can get kind of confusing; just keep in mind that it works with both @freq_type and @frequency_relative_interval. The interpretation works like this:

freq_type Value	Matching freq_interval Values
1 (once)	Not Used
4 (daily)	Runs every x days where x is the value in the frequency interval
8 (weekly)	The frequency interval is one or more of the following: 1 (Sunday) 2 (Monday) 4 (Tuesday) 8 (Wednesday) 16 (Thursday) 32 (Friday) 64 (Saturday)
16 (monthly - fixed)	Runs on the exact day of the month specified in the frequency interval
32 (monthly - relative)	Runs on exactly one of the following: 1 (Sunday) 2 (Monday) 3 (Tuesday) 4 (Wednesday) 5 (Thursday) 6 (Friday) 7 (Saturday) 8 (Specific Day) 9 (Every Weekday) 10 (Every Weekend Day)
64 (Run at Agent startup)	Not Used
128 (Run at CPU idle)	Not Used

❑ **@freq_subday_type:** Specifies the units for @freq_subday_interval. If you're running daily, then you can set a frequency to run within a given day. The possible values here are:

Value	Description
1	At the specified time
4	Every x *minutes* where x is the value of the frequency sub-day interval
8	Every x *hours* where x is the value of the frequency sub-day interval

❑ **@freq_subday_interval:** This is the number of @freq_subday_type periods to occur between each execution of the job (x in the preceding table).

❑ **@freq_relative_interval:** This is used only if the frequency type is monthly (relative) (32). If this is the case, then this value determines in which week a specific day of week job is run or flags things to be run on the last day of the month. The possible values are:

Value	Description
1	First Week
2	Second Week
4	Third Week
8	Fourth Week
16	Last Week or Day

❑ **@freq_recurrence_factor:** How many weeks or months between execution. The exact treatment depends on the frequency type and is applicable only if the type was weekly or monthly (fixed or relative). This is an integer value, and, for example, if your frequency type is 8 (weekly) and the frequency recurrence factor is 3, then the job would run on the specified day of the week every third week.

The default for each of these parameters is 0.

Okay, so let's move on to getting that job scheduled to run every five minutes as we did when using Management Studio:

```
EXEC sp_add_jobschedule
    @job_name = 'TSQLCreatedTestJob',
    @name = 'Every 5 Minutes',
    @freq_type = 4,
    @freq_interval = 1,
    @freq_subday_type = 4,
    @freq_subday_interval = 5,
    @active_start_date = 20080731;
```

Now, if you go and take a look at the job in Management Studio, you'll find that you have a job that is (other than the name) identical to the job we created directly in Management Studio. Our job has been fully implemented using T-SQL this time.

Maintaining and Deleting Jobs and Tasks

Maintaining jobs in Management Studio is pretty simple. Just double-click the job and edit it just as if you were creating a new job. Deleting jobs and tasks in Management Studio is simpler. Just highlight the job and press the Delete button. After one confirmation, your job is gone.

Checking out what you have, editing it, and deleting it are all slightly trickier in T-SQL. The good news, however, is that maintaining jobs, tasks, and schedules works pretty much as creating did, and that deleting any of them is a snap.

Editing and Deleting Jobs with T-SQL

To edit or delete each of the four steps we just covered for T-SQL, you just use (with one exception) the corresponding update sproc — the information provided to the update sproc completely replaces that of the original add (or prior updates) — or delete sproc. The parameters are the same as the add sproc for each:

If the Add Was	Then Update With	And Delete With
sp_add_job	sp_update_job	sp_delete_job
sp_add_jobserver	None (drop and add)	sp_delete_jobserver
sp_add_jobstep	sp_update_jobstep	sp_delete_jobstep
sp_add_jobschedule	sp_update_jobschedule	sp_delete_jobschedule

Backup and Recovery

No database-driven app should ever be deployed or sold to a customer without a mechanism for dealing with backup and recovery. As I've probably told people at least 1,000 times: You would truly be amazed at the percentage of database operations that I've gone into that do not have any kind of reliable backup. In a word: EEEeeeeeek!

There is one simple rule to follow regarding backups — do them early and often. The follow up to this is to not just back up to a file on the same disk and forget it — you need to make sure that a copy moves to a completely separate place (ideally off-site) to be sure that it's safe. I've personally seen servers catch fire (the stench was terrible, as were all the freaked out staff). You don't want to find out that your backups went up in the same smoke that your original data did.

For apps being done by the relative beginner, then, you're probably going to stick with referring the customer or on-site administrator to SQL Server's own backup and recovery tools, but, even if you do, you should be prepared to support them as they come up to speed in its use. In addition, there is no excuse for not understanding what it is the customer needs to do.

Creating a Backup — a.k.a. "A Dump"

Creating a backup file of a given database in the Management Studio is actually pretty easy. Simply navigate in the Object Explorer to the database you're interested in, and right-click.

Now choose Tasks and Back Up, as shown in Figure 22-14.

And you'll get a dialog that lets you define pretty much all of the backup process, as in Figure 22-15.

The first setting here is pretty self-explanatory. Here you indicate which database you want to back up. From there, however, things get a bit trickier.

Getting into the items that may not yet make sense, first up is the Recovery Model. The Recovery Model field here is just notifying you of what the database you've selected for backup is set to. It is actually a database-level setting. We're going to defer discussion of what this is for a bit — we'll get to it in the next section when we talk about backing up transaction logs.

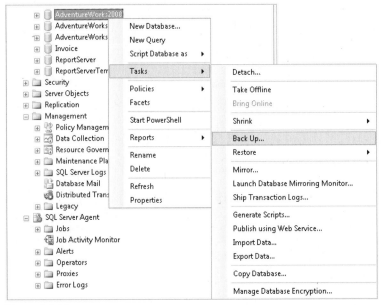

Figure 22-14

Now, those are the simple parts, but let's break down some of the rest of the options that are available.

Backup Type

First of the choices to be made is the Backup Type. Depending on the recovery model for your database (again, be patient with me, we'll get there on what this is!), you'll have either two or three types of backups available:

❏ **Full:** This is just what it sounds like — a full backup of your actual database file as it is as of the last transaction that was committed prior to you issuing the Backup command.

❏ **Differential:** This might be referred to as a "backup *since*" backup. When you take a differential backup, it only writes out a copy of the extents (see Chapter 6 if you've forgotten!) that have changed since you did the last full backup. These typically run much faster than a Full backup and will take up less space. How much less? Well, that depends on how much your data actually changes. For very large databases where backups can take a very long time to run, it is very common to have a strategy where you take a full backup only once a week or even only once a month, and then take differential backups in between to save both space and time.

❏ **Transaction Log:** This is again just what it sounds like — a copy of the transaction log. This option will only show up if your database is set to Full or Bulk logging (this option is hidden if you are using simple logging). Again, a full discussion of what these are is coming up shortly.

A subtopic of the Backup Type is the Backup Component, which applies only to Full and Differential backups.

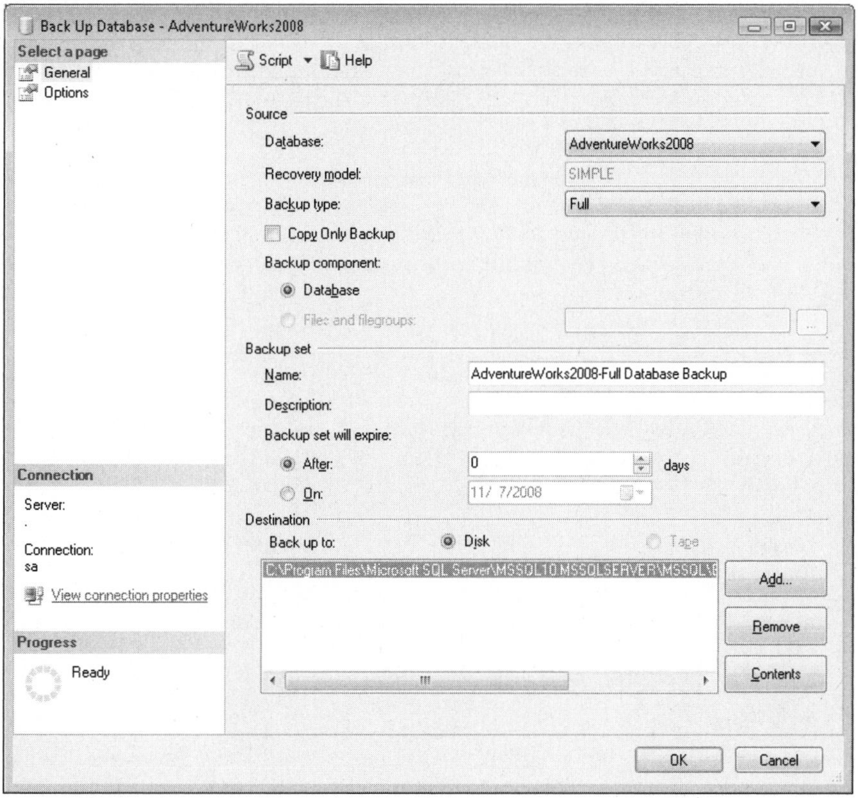

Figure 22-15

For purposes of this book, we should pretty much just be focused on backing up the whole database. That said, you'll notice another option titled "Files and Filegroups." Back in Chapter 1, we touched briefly on the idea of filegroups and individual files for data to be stored in. This option lets you select just one file or filegroup to participate in for this backup. I highly recommend avoiding this option until you have graduated to the "expert" class of SQL Server user.

Again, I want to stress avoiding this particular option until you've got yourself something just short of a doctorate in SQL Server backups. These are special use — designed to help with very large database installations (figure terabytes) that are in high-availability scenarios. There are major consistency issues to be considered when taking and restoring from this style of backup, and they are not for the faint of heart.

Backup Set

A *backup set* is basically a single name used to refer to one or more destinations for your backup.

SQL Server allows for the idea that your backup may be particularly large or that you may otherwise have reason to back up across multiple devices — be it drives or tapes. When you do this, however, you need to have all of the devices you used as a destination available in order to recover from any of them — that is, they are a "set." The backup set essentially holds the definition of what destinations were involved in your particular backup. In addition, a backup set contains some property information for your backup. You can, for example, identify an expiration date for the backup. Creating a backup set is as easy as naming multiple file or tape destinations at the time you define your backup.

Destination

This is where your data is going to be backed up to. Here is where you define potentially several destinations to be utilized for one backup set. For most installations this will be a file location, but it can also be any valid UNC path (which may wind up being something other than a disk. SQL Server doesn't care as long as it's valid storage).

Options

In addition to those items we just covered from the General node of the dialog, you also have a node that lets you set other miscellaneous options. Most of these are fairly self-explanatory. Of particular note, however, is the Transaction Log area.

Schedule

With all this set up, wouldn't it be nice to set up a job to run this backup on a regular basis? Well, the Schedule button up at the top of the dialog is meant to facilitate your doing just that. Click it, and it will bring up the Job Schedule dialog you saw earlier in the chapter. You can then define a regular schedule to run the backup you just defined.

Backing Up Using T-SQL

To back up the database or the log in T-SQL, we make use of the BACKUP command. The syntax for BACKUP works almost, but not quite, the same, depending on whether you're backing up the database or the log. The syntax looks like this.

```
BACKUP DATABASE|LOG <database name>
     {WITH
          NO_LOG|TRUNCATE_ONLY}
   | TO {DISK|TAPE} <backup device(s)> [,...n]
     [MIRROR TO <backup device(s)> [, ... n]]
     [WITH
     [BLOCKSIZE = <block size>]
     [[,] CHECKSUM | NO CHECKSUM ]
     [[,] COMPRESSION | NO COMPRESSION]
     [[,] STOP_ON_ERROR | CONTINUE_AFTER_ERROR]
     [[,] DESCRIPTION = <description of backup>]
     [[,] DIFFERENTIAL]
     [[,] EXPIREDATE = <expiration date> | RETAINDAYS = <days>]
     [[,] PASSWORD = <password>]
     [[,] FORMAT|NOFORMAT]
     [[,] INIT|NOINIT]
     [[,] MEDIADESCRIPTION = <description>]
     [[,] MEDIANAME = <media name>]
     [[,] MEDIAPASSWORD = <media password>]
     [[,] NAME = <backup set name>]
     [[,] REWIND|NOREWIND]
     [[,] NOSKIP|SKIP]
```

```
[[,] NOUNLOAD|UNLOAD]
[[,] RESTART]
[[,] STATS [= <percentage>]]
[[,] COPY_ONLY]
```

Let's look at some of the parameters:

❏   **<backup device>:** That's right; you can back up to more than one device. This creates what's called a *media set*. These can really speed up your backups if the media are spread over several disks, as it creates a parallel load situation. You're not bound by the I/O limitations of any of the individual devices. However, beware — you must have the entire media set intact to restore from this kind of backup.

Also note that the TAPE option is only provided for backward compatibility — all backups should now appear to SQL Server as being to DISK (even if the actual device does happen to be a tape).

❏   **BLOCKSIZE:** This is automatically determined in a hard drive backup, but, for tape, you need to provide the correct block size. Contact your vendor for help on this one.

❏   **COMPRESSION:** This is what it sounds like: an indication of whether or not you want compression used in the backup. The default is no compression, but this can be changed at a server-wide level.

❏   **DIFFERENTIAL:** This is to perform a *differential backup*. A differential backup only backs up the data that is changed since your last full backup. Any log or other differential backup is ignored. Any row/column changed, added, or deleted since the last full backup is included in the new backup. Differential backups have the advantage of being much faster to create than a full backup and much faster to restore than applying each individual log when restoring.

❏   **EXPIREDATE/RETAINDAYS:** You can have your backup media expire after a certain time. Doing so lets SQL Server know when it can overwrite the older media.

❏   **FORMAT/NOFORMAT:** Determines whether or not the media header (required for tapes) should be rewritten. Be aware that formatting affects the entire device — this means that formatting for one backup on a device destroys all the other backups on that device as well.

❏   **INIT/NOINIT:** Overwrites the device data but leaves the header intact.

❏   **MEDIADESCRIPTION and MEDIANAME:** Just describes and names the media — maximum of 255 characters for a description and 128 for a name.

❏   **SKIP/NOSKIP:** Decides whether or not to pay attention to the expiration information from previous backups on the tape. If SKIP is active, then the expiration is ignored so the tape can be overwritten.

❏   **UNLOAD/NOUNLOAD:** Used for tape only. This determines whether to rewind and eject the tape (UNLOAD) or leave it in its current position (NOUNLOAD) after the backup is complete.

❏   **RESTART:** Picks up where a previously interrupted backup left off.

❏   **STATS:** Displays a progress bar indicating progress as the backup runs.

❏   **COPY_ONLY:** Creates a backup but does not affect any other backup sequence you have in any way. For example, logs that are differential backups will continue as if the copy backup had never occurred.

Now let's try one out for a true backup:

```
BACKUP DATABASE AdventureWorks2008
TO DISK = 'C:\Program Files\Microsoft SQL
Server\MSSQL10.MSSQLSERVER\MSSQL\Backup\TSQLDataBackup.bck'

    WITH
        DESCRIPTION = 'My what a nice backup!',
        STATS;
```

The highlighted code should appear on one line.

Note that you may need to change the path to a different location depending on the specifics of your particular installation.

We now have a backup of our AdventureWorks2008 database.

SQL Server is even nice enough to provide progress messages as it processes the backup:

```
10 percent processed.
20 percent processed.
30 percent processed.
40 percent processed.
50 percent processed.
60 percent processed.
70 percent processed.
80 percent processed.
90 percent processed.
Processed 25448 pages for database 'AdventureWorks2008', file
'AdventureWorks2008_Data' on file 1.
Processed 36 pages for database 'AdventureWorks2008', file 'FileStreamDocuments'
on file 1.
Processed 1 pages for database 'AdventureWorks2008', file 'AdventureWorks2008_Log'
 on file 1.
100 percent processed.
BACKUP DATABASE successfully processed 25484 pages in 10.825 seconds (18.391 MB/sec).
```

It's that simple, so let's follow it up with a simple backup of the log:

```
BACKUP LOG AdventureWorks2008
TO DISK = 'C:\Program Files\Microsoft SQL
Server\MSSQL10.MSSQLSERVER\MSSQL\Backup\TSQLLogBackup.bck'

    WITH
        DESCRIPTION = 'My what a nice backup of a log!',
        STATS;
```

The highlighted code should appear on one line.

> It's worth noting that you can't do a backup of a log while the database recovery model is set to Simple. To change this to a different recovery model, right-click the

> AdventureWorks2008 database, select Properties and the Options tab — in T-SQL, use the **sp_dboption** system sproc. If you think about it, this makes sense given that your log is always going to be essentially free of any committed transactions.
>
> It's also worth noting that backups work just fine while there are users in your database. SQL Server is able to reconcile the changes that are being made by knowing the exact point in the log that the backup was begun, and using that as a reference point for the rest of the backup.

Recovery Models

Well, I spent most of the last section promising that we would discuss them, so it's time to ask: What is a *recovery model*?

Well, back in Chapter 11, we talked about the transaction log. In addition to keeping track of transactions to deal with transaction rollback and atomicity of data, transaction logs are also critical to being able to recover data right up to the point of system failure.

Imagine for a moment that you're running a bank. Let's say you've been taking deposits and withdrawals for the last six hours — the time since your last full backup was done. Now, if your system went down, I'm guessing you're not going to like the idea of going to last night's backup and losing all track of what money went out the door or came in during the interim. See where I'm going here? You really need every moment's worth of data.

Keeping the transaction log around gives us the ability to "roll forward" any transactions that happened since the last full or differential backup was done. Assuming both the data backup *and* the transaction logs are available, you should be able to recover right up to the point of failure.

The recovery model determines how long and what types of log records are kept. There are three options:

❑ **Full:** This is what it says. Everything is logged. Under this model, you should have no data loss in the event of system failure, assuming you had a backup of the data available and have all transaction logs since that backup. If you are missing a log or have one that is damaged, then you'll be able to recover all data up through the last intact log you have available. Keep in mind, however, that as keeping everything suggests, this can take up a fair amount of space in a system that receives a lot of changes or new data.

❑ **Bulk-Logged:** This is like "Full recovery light." Under this option, regular transactions are logged just as they are with the Full recovery method, but bulk operations are not. The result is that, in the event of system failure, a restored backup will contain any changes to data pages that did not participate in bulk operations (bulk import of data or index creation, for example), but any bulk operations must be redone. The good news on this one is that bulk operations perform *much* better. This performance comes with risk attached, so your mileage may vary . . . .

❑ **Simple:** Under this model, the transaction log essentially exists to support transactions as they happen. The transaction log is regularly truncated, with any completed or rolled back transactions essentially being removed from the log (not quite that simple, but that is the effect). This gives us a nice tight log that is smaller and often performs a bit better, but the log is of zero use for recovery from system failure.

For most installations, Full recovery is going to be what you want to have for a production-level database — end of story.

Recovery

This is something of the reverse of the backup side of things. You've done your backups religiously, and now you want to restore one — either for recovery purposes or merely to make a copy of a database somewhere.

Once you have a backup of your database, it's fairly easy to restore it to the original location. To get started — it works much as it did for backup: navigate to the database you want to restore to and right-click — then select Tasks≯Restore, and up comes your Restore dialog, as in Figure 22-16.

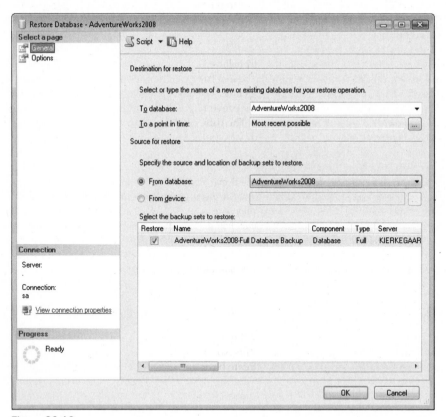

Figure 22-16

As long as what you're after is to take your old backup and slam it over the top of the database you made the backup of, this is pretty straightforward. Simply say OK, and it should restore for you without issue.

Restoring to a Different Location

When things get tricky is when you want to change something about where you're restoring to. As part of the backup process, the backup knows the name of the database that was backed up, and, perhaps more important, it knows the path(s) to the physical files that it was supposed to be using.

Changing the destination database name is right there — no biggie — the problem is that changing the destination database name does nothing to change what physical files (the .MDF and .LDF files) it's going to try to store to. To deal with this, go to the Options node of the Restore dialog.

Again, most of the options here are self-explanatory, but, in particular, notice the "Restore As" column. In this part of the dialog, you can replace every original file's destination, location, and name, which provides you with a way to deal with restoring multiple copies of a database to the same server (perhaps for test purposes) or installing your database to a new volume or even a new system.

Recovery Status

This one is merely about the state you want to have the database in when you are done with this restore. This has particular relevance when you are restoring a database and still have logs to apply to the database later.

If you go with the default option (which translates to using the WITH RECOVERY option if you were using T-SQL), then the database will immediately be in a full online status when the restore operation is complete. If, for example, you wanted to restore logs after your initial restore was done, you would want to select one of the two other options. Both of these prevent updates happening to the database and leave it in a state where more recovery can be done. The difference is merely one of whether users are allowed to access the database in a "read-only" mode or whether the database should appear as still being offline.

> *The issue of availability is a larger one than you probably think it is. As big of a deal as I'm sure it already seems, it's really amazing how quickly users will find their way into your system when the restore operation suddenly marks the database as available. Quite often, even if you know that you will be "done" after the current restore is done, you'd like a chance to look over the database prior to actual users being in there. If this is the case, then be sure to use the NO RECOVERY method of restoring. You can later run a restore that is purely for a WITH RECOVERY option, and get the database fully back online once you're certain you have things just as you want them.*

Restoring Data Using T-SQL

We use the RESTORE command to recover the data that we have in our backups. The basic syntax looks like this (there are a ton of variations on this, so, if you need every nuance, I'd suggest a book oriented toward administration, which will investigate backup and recovery as a chapter unto itself):

```
RESTORE DATABASE|LOG <database name>
    [FROM <backup_device> [,...n]]
    [WITH
    [DBO_ONLY]
    [[,] FILE = <file number>]
    [[,] MEDIANAME = <media name>]
    [[,] MOVE '<logical file name>' TO '<operating system file name>'][,...n]
    [[,] {NORECOVERY|RECOVERY|STANDBY = <undo file name>}]
```

```
[[,] {NOUNLOAD|UNLOAD}]
[[,] REPLACE]
[[,] RESTART]
[[,] STATS [= percentage]]
[[,] { STOPAT = { <date and time> }
    | STOPATMARK = { '<name of mark>' }
         [ AFTER <date and time> ]
    | STOPBEFOREMARK = { '<name of mark>' }
         [ AFTER <date and time> ]
```

Let's look at some of these options:

❑ **DBO_ONLY:** When the restore is done, the database will be set with the dbo_only database option turned on. This gives the dbo a chance to look around and test things out before allowing users back onto the system.

> This is a biggie, and I very strongly recommend that you always use it. You would be amazed at how quickly users will be back on the system once it's backed up for even a moment. When a system is down, you'll find users very impatient to get back to work. They'll constantly be trying to log in, and they won't bother to ask if it's okay or not. They'll assume that when it's up, it's okay to go into it.

❑ **FILE:** You can back up multiple times to the same media. This option lets you select a specific version to restore. If this one isn't supplied, SQL Server will assume that you want to restore from the most recent backup.

❑ **MOVE:** Allows you to restore the database to a different physical file that the database was using when it was originally backed up.

❑ **NORECOVERY/RECOVERY/STANDBY:** RECOVERY and NORECOVERY are mutually exclusive. STANDBY works in conjunction with NORECOVERY. They work as follows:

Option	Description
NORECOVERY	Restores the database but keeps it marked as offline. Uncommitted transactions are left intact. This allows you to continue with the recovery process — for example, if you still have additional logs to apply.
RECOVERY	As soon as the restore command is done successfully, the database is marked as active again. Data can again be changed. Any uncommitted transactions are rolled back. This is the default if none of the options are specified.
STANDBY	STANDBY allows you to create an undo file so that the effects of a recovery can be undone. STANDBY allows you to bring the database up for read-only access before you have issued a RECOVERY (which means at least part of your data's been restored, but you aren't considering the restoration process complete yet). This allows users to make use of the system in a read-only mode while you verify the restoration process.

- ❑ **REPLACE:** Overrides the safety feature that prevents you from restoring over the top of an existing database.

- ❑ **RESTART:** Tells SQL Server to continue a previously interrupted restoration process.

Let's go ahead and look at an example run of restoring the AdventureWorks2008 database. Do not run this statement unless you are absolutely certain that your backup was successful and is intact.

First, we drop the existing AdventureWorks2008 database:

```
USE master;

DROP DATABASE AdventureWorks2008;
```

Once that's done, we'll try to restore it using my RESTORE command:

```
RESTORE DATABASE AdventureWorks2008
    FROM DISK = 'C:\Program Files\Microsoft SQL
Server\MSSQL10.MSSQLSERVER\MSSQL\Backup\TSQLDataBackup.bck'

    WITH
        DBO_ONLY,
        NORECOVERY,
        STATS;
```

The highlighted code should appear on one line.

We restored with NORECOVERY because we want to add another piece to the puzzle. Our log will contain any transactions that happened between when our database or log was last backed up and when this log was backed up. "Apply" this log, and that should bring the database as up to date as we can make it:

```
RESTORE LOG AdventureWorks2008
    FROM DISK = 'C:\Program Files\Microsoft SQL
Server\MSSQL10.MSSQLSERVER\MSSQL\Backup\TSQLLogBackup.bck'
    WITH
        DBO_ONLY,
        NORECOVERY,
        STATS;
```

Note that if we had several logs to apply from this one device, then we would have to name them as we wanted to apply them. They would also need to be applied in the order in which they were backed up.

Now, we could have turned everything on there, but we want to hold off for a bit before making the database active again. Even though we don't have any more logs to apply, we still need to re-run the RESTORE statement to make the database active again:

```
RESTORE LOG AdventureWorks2008 WITH RECOVERY;
```

We should now be able to test our database:

```
USE AdventureWorks2008;

SELECT * FROM Region;
```

And, sure enough, we get the results we're looking for. Run a few SELECT statements to see that, indeed, our database was restored properly.

After you've checked things out, remember that we chose the DBO_ONLY option for all this. If we run sp_dboption, we'll see that no one else is able to get in:

```
EXEC sp_dboption;
```

Look for the dbo use only:

```
Settable database options:
-----------------------------------
ANSI null default
ANSI nulls
ANSI padding
ANSI warnings
arithabort
auto create statistics
auto update statistics
autoclose
autoshrink
concat null yields null
cursor close on commit
db chaining
dbo use only
default to local cursor
merge publish
numeric roundabort
offline
published
quoted identifier
read only
recursive triggers
select into/bulkcopy
single user
subscribed
torn page detection
trunc. log on chkpt.
```

Remember to turn that option off or your users won't be able to get into the system:

```
EXEC sp_dboption AdventureWorks2008, 'dbo use only', 'false';
```

We now have a restored and active database.

Index Maintenance

Back in Chapter 6, we talked about how indexes can become fragmented. This can become a major impediment to the performance of your database over time, and it's something that you need to have a strategy in place to deal with. Fortunately, SQL Server has commands that will reorganize your data and indexes to clean things up. Couple that with the job scheduling that we've already learned about, and you can automate routine defragmentation.

ALTER INDEX is the workhorse of database maintenance. It is simultaneously much easier and slightly harder than the previous maintenance mainstay — DBCC — used to be. Let's take a look at this one real quick, and then at how to get it scheduled.

ALTER INDEX

The command ALTER INDEX is somewhat deceptive in what it does. Up until now, ALTER commands have always been about changing the definition of our object. We ALTER tables to add or disable constraints and columns, for example. ALTER INDEX is different; it is all about maintenance and zero about structure. If you need to change the make-up of your index, you still need to either DROP and CREATE it, or you need to CREATE and use the DROP_EXISTING=ON option.

The ALTER INDEX syntax looks like this:

```
ALTER INDEX { <name of index> | ALL }
    ON <table or view name>
    { REBUILD
        [ [ WITH ( <rebuild index option> [ ,...n ] ) ]
          | [ PARTITION = <partition number>
                [ WITH ( <partition rebuild index option>
                        [ ,...n ] ) ] ] ]
    | DISABLE
    | REORGANIZE
        [ PARTITION = <partition number> ]
        [ WITH ( LOB_COMPACTION = { ON | OFF } ) ]
    | SET ( <set_index_option> [ ,...n ] )
    }
[ ; ]
```

A decent amount of this is fairly detailed "Realm of the advanced DBA" stuff — usually used on an ad hoc basis to deal with very specific problems. But there are some core elements here that should be part of our regular maintenance planning. We'll start by looking at a couple of top parameters, and then look at the options that are part of our larger maintenance planning needs.

Index Name

You can name a specific index if you want to maintain one specific index, or use ALL to indicate that you want to perform this maintenance on every index associated with the named table.

Table or View Name

Pretty much just what it sounds like — the name of the specific object (table or view) that you want to perform the maintenance on. Note that it needs to be one specific table. (You can't feed it a list and say "do all of these please!")

REBUILD

This is the "industrial strength" approach to fixing an index. If you run ALTER INDEX with this option, the old index is completely thrown away and reconstructed from scratch. The result is a truly optimized index, where every page in both the leaf and non-leaf levels of the index have been reconstructed as you have defined them (either the defaults, or using switches to change things like the fill factor).

> *Careful on this one. As soon as you kick off a* REBUILD, *the index you are working on is essentially gone until the rebuild is complete. Any queries that relied on that index may become exceptionally slow (potentially by orders of magnitude). This is the sort of thing you want to test on an offline system first to have an idea how long it's going to take, and then schedule to run in off hours (preferably with someone monitoring it to be sure it's back online when peak hours come along).*

This one can have major side effects while it runs, and thus it falls squarely in the domain of the database administrator in my not-so-humble opinion.

DISABLE

This one does what it says, only in somewhat drastic fashion. It would be nice if all this command did was take your index offline until you decided further what you want to do, but instead it essentially marks the index as unusable. Once an index has been disabled, it must be rebuilt (not reorganized, but rebuilt) before it will be active again.

This is one you're very, very rarely going to do yourself. (You would more likely just drop the index.) It is far more likely to happen during a SQL Server upgrade or some other oddball situation.

> *Yet another BE CAREFUL!!! warning on this one. If you disable the clustered index for your table, it has the effect of disabling the table. The data will remain but will be inaccessible by all indexes (since they all depend on the clustered index) until you rebuild the clustered index.*

REORGANIZE

BINGO!!! from the developer perspective. With REORGANIZE we hit much more of a happy medium in life. When you reorganize your index, you get a slightly less complete optimization than you get with a full rebuild, but one that occurs online (users can still utilize the index).

This should, if you're paying attention, bring about the question "What exactly do you mean by '*slightly less complete*'?" Well, REORGANIZE only works on the leaf level of your index — non-leaf levels of the index go untouched. This means that we're not quite getting a full optimization, but, for the lion's share of indexes, that is not where your real cost of fragmentation is (though it can happen and your mileage may vary).

Given its much lower impact on users, this is usually the tool you'll want to use as part of your regular maintenance plan. Let's take a look at running an index reorganization command.

To run this through its paces, we're going to do a reorg on a table in the AdventureWorks2008 database. The Production.TransactionHistory table is an excellent example of a table that is likely to have many rows inserted over time and then have rows purged back out of it as the transactions become old enough to delete. In this case, we'll reorganize all the indexes on the table in one simple command:

```
USE AdventureWorks2008;

ALTER INDEX ALL
```

```
ON Production.TransactionHistory
REORGANIZE;
```

The ALTER INDEX command sees that ALL was supplied instead of a specific index name, and looks up what indexes are available for our Production.TransactionHistory table (leaving out any that are disabled since a reorganization will do nothing for them). It then enumerates each index behind the scenes and performs the reorganization on each — reorganizing just the leaf level of each index (including reorganizing the actual data since the clustered index on this table will also be reorganized).

You should get back essentially nothing from the database — just a simple "Command(s) completed successfully."

Archiving of Data

Ooh — here's a tricky one. There are as many ways of archiving data as there are database engineers. If you're building an OLAP database — for example, to utilize with Analysis Services — then that will often address your archiving for long-term reporting needs. Regardless of how you're making sure the data you need long-term is available, there will likely come a day when you need to deal with the issue of your data becoming too voluminous for your system to perform well.

As I said, there are just too many ways to go about archiving because every database is a little bit different. The key is to think about archiving needs at the time that you create your database. Realize that, as you start to delete records, you're going to be hitting referential integrity constraints and/or orphaning records — design in a logical path to delete or move records at archive time. Here are some things to think about as you write your archive scripts:

❑   If you already have the data in an OLAP database, then you probably don't need to worry about saving it anywhere else. Talk to your boss and your attorney on that one.

❑   How often is the data really used? Is it worth keeping? Human beings are natural born pack rats in a larger size. Simply put, we hate giving things up — that includes our data. If you're only worried about legal requirements, think about just saving a copy of never or rarely used data to tape (I'd suggest multiple backups for archive data) and reducing the amount of data you have online — your users will love you for it when they see improved performance.

❑   Don't leave orphans. As you start deleting data, your referential integrity constraints should keep you from leaving that many orphans, but you'll wind up with some where referential integrity didn't apply. This situation can lead to serious system errors.

❑   Realize that your archive program will probably need a long time to run. The length of time it runs and the number of rows affected may create concurrency issues with the data your online users are trying to get at — plan on running it at a time when your system will not be used.

❑   TEST! TEST! TEST!

PowerShell

SQL Server now has support for a command environment known as PowerShell. For those who haven't heard of PowerShell before, it's worth a look well beyond what we'll go into here, so I recommend a good search on the Web.

What is PowerShell? At its most basic level, PowerShell is a classic command-line environment — and is not, on the surface, much different than a Windows Command window. PowerShell, however, is extensible through .NET integration and can be hosted within other applications (much as it is for SQL Server 2008). Examples of applications and operating systems that include special functionality for PowerShell include:

❑   SQL Server 2008 (why else would we be talking about it, eh?) and above

❑   Exchange 2007 and above

❑   Microsoft Office SharePoint Services (MOSS) 2007 and above

❑   Vista, Widows XP, Windows Server 2003 (through downloaded functionality add ons)

❑   Windows Server 2008 and later include it natively or as an option (depending on edition and version)

The extensibility of PowerShell is implemented via what are called cmdlets (pronounced commandlets). These are specialized .NET assemblies that implement functionality for a given application within the PowerShell environment. The real power here is that, through the mix of different cmdlets available to PowerShell, we can create powerful scripts utilizing a mix of operating system commands and functionality that is specific to one or more applications (for example, waiting for confirmation on a load script to the database before kicking off an application hosted in another environment).

PowerShell cmdlets have a standardized command structure based on a verb-noun combination such as Get-Help, or Get-Children. It also includes a robust help mechanism that is updated regularly (via TechNet).

Trying Out PowerShell

To get a feel for how it works, we're going to take a fairly quick test drive of PowerShell. Start by opening a command prompt window (Start➤Run and type **cmd** before hitting Enter). At the command line, simply type **PowerShell**.

```
C:\Users\Administrator.Kierkegaard>sqlps
```

There is relatively little indication that you've left the standard command prompt and entered the world of PowerShell. Indeed, the only significant indication (besides the PowerShell header) is the PS prefix on a line that otherwise looks just like your command prompt:

```
Microsoft SQL Server PowerShell
Version 10.0.1600.22
Microsoft Corp. All rights reserved.

PS SQLSERVER:\>
```

Let's go ahead and issue our first PowerShell command. We'll simply ask for the help page:

```
PS SQLSERVER:\> Get-Help
```

This spews forth a page or so worth of information:

```
TOPIC
    Get-Help


SHORT DESCRIPTION
    Displays help about PowerShell cmdlets and concepts.


LONG DESCRIPTION


SYNTAX
    get-help {<CmdletName> | <TopicName>}
    help {<CmdletName> | <TopicName>}
    <CmdletName> -?


    "Get-help" and "-?" display help on one page.
    "Help" displays help on multiple pages.

    Examples:
      get-help get-process  : Displays help about the get-process cmdlet.
      get-help about-signing : Displays help about the signing concept.
      help where-object     : Displays help about the where-object cmdlet.
      help about_foreach    : Displays help about foreach loops in PowerShell.
      match-string -?       : Displays help about the match-string cmdlet.


    You can use wildcard characters in the help commands (not with -?).
    If multiple help topics match, PowerShell displays a list of matching
    topics. If only one help topic matches, PowerShell displays the topic.


    Examples:
      get-help *        : Displays all help topics.
      get-help get-*    : Displays topics that begin with get-.
      help *object*     : Displays topics with "object" in the name.
      get-help about*   : Displays all conceptual topics.



    For information about wildcards, type:
      get-help about_wildcard



REMARKS
    To learn about PowerShell, read the following help topics:
      get-command : Displays a list of cmdlets.
```

```
                about_object : Explains the use of objects in PowerShell.
                get-member   : Displays the properties of an object.


           Conceptual help files are named "about_<topic>", such as:
             about_regular_expression.

           The help commands also display the aliases on the system.
           For information about aliases, type:

             get-help about_alias


       PS SQLSERVER:\>
```

This is just basic information about getting help in PowerShell. Little if anything provided in this particular help window is SQL Server specific. We can, however, get help on a cmdlet that runs generic T-SQL commands:

```
       PS SQLSERVER:\> Get-Help Invoke-Sqlcmd
```

This gets us helpful information about the SQL Server–specific cmdlet called Invoke-Sqlcmd:

```
    NAME
        Invoke-Sqlcmd

    SYNOPSIS
        Runs a script containing statements from the languages
    (Transact-SQL and XQuery) and commands supported by the SQL Server sqlcmd utility.


    SYNTAX
        Invoke-Sqlcmd [-ServerInstance <PSObject>] [-Database <String>] [-EncryptCo
        nnection] [-Username <String>] [-Password <String>] [[-Query] <String>] [-Q
        ueryTimeout <Int32>] [-ConnectionTimeout <Int32>] [-ErrorLevel <Int32>] [-S
        everityLevel <Int32>] [-MaxCharLength <Int32>] [-MaxBinaryLength <Int32>] [
        -AbortOnError] [-DedicatedAdministratorConnection] [-DisableVariables] [-Di
        sableCommands] [-HostName <String>] [-NewPassword <String>] [-Variable <Str
        ing[]>] [-InputFile <String>] [-OutputSqlErrors] [-SuppressProviderContextW
        arning] [-IgnoreProviderContext] [<CommonParameters>]


    DETAILED DESCRIPTION
        Runs a script containing the languages and commands supported by the SQL Se
        rver sqlcmd utility. The languages supported are Transact-SQL and the XQuer
        y syntax supported by the Database Engine. Invoke-Sqlcmd also accepts many
        of the  commands supported by sqlcmd, such as GO and QUIT. Invoke-Sqlcmd ac
        cepts the sqlcmd scripting variables, such as SQLCMDUSER. Invoke-Sqlcmd doe
        s not set sqlcmd scripting variables by default.
        Invoke-Sqlcmd does not support the sqlcmd commands primarily related to int
        eractive script editing. The commands not supported include :!!, :connect,
        :error, :out, :ed, :list, :listvar, :reset, :perftrace, and :serverlist.
        The first result set the script returns is displayed as a formatted table.
```

```
Result sets after the first are not displayed if their column list is diffe
rent from the column list of the first result set. If result sets after the
 first set have the same column list, their rows are appended to the format
ted table that contains the rows that were returned by the first result set
.

Invoke-Sqlcmd does not return message output, such as the output of PRINT s
tatements, unless you use the PowerShell -Verbose parameter.


RELATED LINKS
    SQL Server Books Online: Transact-SQL Reference
    SQL Server Books Online: sqlcmd Utility
    SQL Server Books Online: XQuery Reference

REMARKS
    For more information, type: "get-help Invoke-Sqlcmd -detailed".
    For technical information, type: "get-help Invoke-Sqlcmd -full".



PS SQLSERVER:\>
```

Let's take a quick look at this using a relatively simple system stored procedure (sp_help):

```
PS SQLSERVER:\> Invoke-Sqlcmd -Query "EXEC sp_helpdb"
```

sp_helpdb provides a listing of all databases in the system. Normally we would see a column-oriented result set, but PowerShell has reoriented the output in a manner that is much more suitable to the limited number of characters a command window can display:

```
name                  : AdventureWorks2008
db_size               :     245.81 MB
owner                 : sa
dbid                  : 7
created               : Dec  6 2008
status                : Status=ONLINE, Updateability=READ_WRITE, UserAccess=MULTI
                        _USER, Recovery=SIMPLE, Version=655,
 Collation=SQL_Latin1
                        _General_CP1_CI_AS, SQLSortOrder=52, IsAnsiNullsEnabled,
                        IsAnsiPaddingEnabled, IsAnsiWarningsEnabled, IsArithmetic
                        AbortEnabled, IsAutoCreateStatistics,
IsAutoUpdateStatist
                        ics, IsFullTextEnabled, IsNullConcat,
IsQuotedIdentifiers
                        Enabled, IsPublished
compatibility_level : 100

name                  : AdventureWorksDW2008
db_size               :     71.06 MB
owner                 : sa
dbid                  : 8
created               : Dec  6 2008
status                : Status=ONLINE, Updateability=READ_WRITE,
UserAccess=MULTI
```

```
                                  _USER, Recovery=SIMPLE, Version=655,
        Collation=SQL_Latin1
                                  _General_CP1_CI_AS, SQLSortOrder=52, IsAnsiNullsEnabled,
                                  IsAnsiPaddingEnabled, IsAnsiWarningsEnabled,
        IsArithmetic
                                  AbortEnabled, IsAutoCreateStatistics,
        IsAutoUpdateStatist
                                  ics, IsFullTextEnabled, IsNullConcat,
        IsQuotedIdentifiers
                                  Enabled
        compatibility_level : 100


        name                : AdventureWorksLT2008
        db_size             :        7.13 MB
        owner               : sa
        dbid                : 9
        created             : Dec  6 2008
        status              : Status=ONLINE, Updateability=READ_WRITE,
        UserAccess=MULTI
                                  _USER, Recovery=SIMPLE, Version=655,
        Collation=SQL_Latin1
                                  _General_CP1_CI_AS, SQLSortOrder=52, IsAnsiNullsEnabled,
                                  IsAnsiPaddingEnabled, IsAnsiWarningsEnabled, IsArithmetic
                                  AbortEnabled, IsAutoCreateStatistics,
        IsAutoUpdateStatist
                                  ics, IsFullTextEnabled, IsNullConcat,
        IsQuotedIdentifiers
                                  Enabled
        compatibility_level : 100


        name                : tempdb
        db_size             :        8.75 MB
        owner               : sa
        dbid                : 2
        created             : Dec 31 2008
        status              : Status=ONLINE, Updateability=READ_WRITE,
        UserAccess=MULTI
                                  _USER, Recovery=SIMPLE, Version=655,
        Collation=SQL_Latin1
                                  _General_CP1_CI_AS, SQLSortOrder=52,
        IsAutoCreateStatisti
                                  cs, IsAutoUpdateStatistics
        compatibility_level : 100


        PS SQLSERVER:\>
```

I have, for the sake of brevity, snipped a few databases out of the middle of the result sets here, but you can see how we were able to execute virtually any command from within PowerShell. Many commands will, over time, have specific cmdlets supporting them — supporting stronger typing and parameterization. For now, most implemented cmdlets support four major object models:

❑ **The Database Engine:** This allows you to navigate a given server.

❑ **Policy-Based Management:** The rules-based management tool that is new with SQL Server 2008 (we will discuss this in brief in our next major section).

❑ **Database Collection:** This contains the meat of manipulating a given database or set of databases.

❑ **Server Registration:** This is all about identifying servers and registering them locally to make them somewhat easier to access.

Through the use of these object models, PowerShell can provide scripted access to almost any administrative task. Watch for more specific support and help to be added via download over the life cycle of SQL Server 2008.

Navigating in PowerShell

PowerShell also provides the ability to navigate in a more directory-like fashion than we have previously experienced with SQL Server. Indeed, you can think of the SQL Server world as one large hierarchy (much as a domain/directory structure is). You can navigate from a collection of registered servers to specific servers, and, from there, to roles and users on that server, or perhaps to databases and objects within the database.

Let's check this out real quick by issuing a simple `dir` command, much as you would in a command window for the operating system:

```
PS SQLSERVER:\> dir
```

This may surprise you by providing a listing of the four object model areas I mentioned at the end of the previous section:

```
Name            Root                      Description
----            ----                      -----------
SQL             SQLSERVER:\SQL            SQL Server Database Engine
SQLPolicy       SQLSERVER:\SQLPolicy      SQL Server Policy Management
SQLRegistration SQLSERVER:\SQLRegistration SQL Server Registrations
DataCollection  SQLSERVER:\DataCollection SQL Server Data Collection


PS SQLSERVER:\>
```

We can actually navigate these just as we would a directory structure in Windows — for example:

```
PS SQLSERVER:\> cd SQL
```

You should quickly notice that we are climbing down a directory structure:

```
PS SQLSERVER:\SQL>
```

Let's jump forward a bit, and navigate much deeper into the tree. We'll need to navigate through our specific server (mine is KIERKEGAARD; you should replace it with the name of your SQL Server system), for instance (mine is the default, so I'll refer to it as DEFAULT), and on into the DATABASES node (we could also do other server-level objects, such as LOGINS):

```
PS SQLSERVER:\SQL> cd KIERKEGAARD\DEFAULT\DATABASES
```

We cut straight down to our databases node of the hierarchy just as if we were navigating a directory structure:

```
PS SQLSERVER:\SQL\KIERKEGAARD\DEFAULT\DATABASES>
```

But it gets better. We can issue a directory listing (in the form of the `dir` command) and get a list of databases, much like the one we created using `sp_help` earlier in the chapter (albeit not quite as verbose):

```
PS SQLSERVER:\SQL\KIERKEGAARD\DEFAULT\DATABASES> dir
```

This gets us:

```
WARNING: column "Owner" does not fit into the display and was removed.

Name                    Status    Recovery Model CompatLvl Collation
----                    ------    -------------- --------- ---------
AdventureWorks2008      Normal    Simple               100 SQL_Latin1_Genera
                                                           l_CP1_CI_AS
AdventureWorksDW2008 Normal       Simple               100 SQL_Latin1_Genera
                                                           l_CP1_CI_AS
AdventureWorksLT2008 Normal       Simple               100 SQL_Latin1_Genera
                                                           l_CP1_CI_AS
AWSubscriber            Normal    Full                 100 SQL_Latin1_Genera
                                                           l_CP1_CI_AS
OurInsteadOfTest        Normal    Full                 100 SQL_Latin1_Genera
                                                           l_CP1_CI_AS
ReportServer            Normal    Full                 100 Latin1_General_CI
                                                           _AS_KS_WS
ReportServerTempDB      Normal    Simple               100 Latin1_General_CI
                                                           _AS_KS_WS
Test                    Normal    Full                 100 SQL_Latin1_Genera
                                                           l_CP1_CI_AS


PS SQLSERVER:\SQL\KIERKEGAARD\DEFAULT\DATABASES>
```

This is, of course, a pretty simplistic example, but it can be taken much further. For example, PowerShell will allow you to enumerate a list such as the directory list we just created. You can then script different behaviors depending on the contents of the script.

A Final Word on PowerShell

As I write this, PowerShell is, from a SQL Server point of view, just getting started. The documentation on the cmdlets available is still rather sparse, but new items are being published regularly, and the nature of the PowerShell model is such that they will be able to continue extending the functionality within PowerShell even before Kilimanjaro (code name for the next release of SQL Server) is released.

I highly recommend watching the SQL Server community on the Internet (or just Google SQL Server PowerShell from time to time) to keep an eye on what's new and where this new scripting tool is going. I can say, for example, that it is quickly becoming my preferred installation and upgrade scripting environment!

Policy-Based Management

Policy-Based Management — known during much of the beta phase of SQL Server 2008 as the Distributed Management Framework — is a rules-based management infrastructure primarily aimed at the management of SQL Server farms in larger enterprises. The concept is pretty simple. There are too many SQL Servers out there managed by too many different people (often completely different IT departments or DBAs that don't even know anything about the other servers and DBAs out there), so why not allow for all your SQL Servers to police themselves according to a set of "policies." What is enforced by the policies can vary ranging from things as simple as object naming guidelines to blocking specific changes to server settings. The management engine can just note violations of policy (simply be able to report on it), or it can actually block or reverse the change.

The full effect of Policy-Based Management on the developer community is yet to be seen. I suspect that there are going to be some good scripting applications for it, but how exactly Policy-Based Management is going to be rolled out and just how enforcement policies are going to be implemented is something still being explored in many companies. For now, all I can say is that all of the Policy-Based Management features are exposed through SMO (in the Microsoft.SqlServer.Management.Dmf library) and through PowerShell. There is much left to be desired for documentation of the object model outside of the Management Studio, but a number of individual functions are documented in Books Online and I suspect updates to Books Online over the life of SQL Server 2008 will help fill in the picture of the Policy-Based Management object model.

Summary

Well, that gives you a few things to think about. It's really easy as a developer to think about many administrative tasks and establish what the inaccurately named *Hitchhiker's Guide to the Galaxy* trilogy called an "SEP" field. That's something that makes things like administration seem invisible because it's "somebody else's problem." Don't go there!

A project I'm familiar with from several years ago is a wonderful example of taking responsibility for what can happen. A wonderful system was developed for a nonprofit group that operates in the north-western United States. After about eight months of operation, an emergency call was placed to the company that developed the software (it was a custom job). After some discussion, it was determined that the database had somehow become corrupted, and it was recommended to the customer that the database be restored from a backup. The response? "Backup?" The development company in question missed something very important — they knew they had an inexperienced customer that would have no administration staff, and who was going to tell the customer to do backups and help set it up if the development company didn't? I'm happy to say that the development company in question learned from that experience — and so should you.

Think about administration issues as you're doing your design and especially in your deployment plan. If you plan ahead to simplify the administration of your system, you'll find that your system is much more successful — that usually translates into rewards for the developer (that is, you!).

SMO: SQL Management Objects

It's been a long road, and we're getting closer and closer to the end of our walk through SQL Server. It is, of course, no coincidence that the chapter about how to manage your SQL Server programmatically has been held until very close to the end. Among other things, we needed to have a solid idea as to what objects we were managing and what administrative needs we had before we were ready to understand the SMO object model and talk about some of the reasons we might want to use SMO.

So, what exactly is SMO? Well, as the title of this chapter implies, SMO is an object model for managing SQL Server. Whereas connectivity models like ADO and LINQ are all about accessing data, SMO is all about access to the structure and health of your system.

In this chapter, we'll look at:

❑ The convoluted history of SQL Server management object models

❑ The basics of the SQL SMO object model

❑ A simple SMO example project

As with many of the SQL Server topics we cover in this book, SQL SMO is a book unto itself, so please do not expect to come out of this chapter as an expert. That said, hopefully, you will have the fundamentals down to at least the point to where you know what's possible and how much work is likely to be involved. From there, you can look for sources of more information as necessary.

The History of SQL Server Management Object Models

This is, to me — even as someone who genuinely loves the product — not an area where SQL Server shines. This is not to say that SMO is a bad thing but rather that the history of SQL Server management object models is a rather sordid history indeed. The team has had a tough time picking a horse and sticking with it.

As I write this, I've been working with SQL Server for just under 15 years. In that time, the methods of managing SQL Server have changed several different times. "A new release? A new management method!" could be the motto for SQL Server.

The good news is that SMO, at least so far, seems to be here to stay. It's on its second version as the primary object model for managing SQL Server (I know it's sad that two releases worth seems like an accomplishment). Still, there are other models that remain out there, so let's look at the highlights from the last couple of releases. These are some of the different models and technologies you may bump into as you work on legacy code out there.

SQL Distributed Management Objects

Distributed Management Objects, or DMO, is the relative "old dog" of the management models. When you think of the old Enterprise Manager from SQL Server 2000 and earlier, most of its underlying functionality ended up in a DMO call. The DMO model supported COM, and could perform all the basic tasks you might want management-wise, such as:

- ❑ Start a backup
- ❑ Restore from backup
- ❑ Create a database
- ❑ Create jobs and other agent-related tasks
- ❑ Reverse engineer tables into SQL code

The list goes on.

So, what went wrong with DMO? Well, the object model was often deemed "clunky" at best. Indeed, parts of DMO often did not work well together, and the scripting engine was buggy. In short, most developers I know only used DMO after going through an electroshock therapy program to desensitize them to the pain of it (okay, it wasn't that bad, but not far from there).

SQL Namespaces

SQL Namespaces (SQL NS) is actually largely about providing UI-level functionality. SQL NS encapsulates all of the functionality that you would find in the old Enterprise Manager — complete with the UI elements. You instantiate the UI objects, and those objects already utilizing SQL DMO underneath, and remove that layer of programming from the equation. In short, if you needed to build a tool that already had the UI to do management tasks, then SQL NS was your tool. The problem? Well, put it this way — EM? They decided they needed to replace it. DMO? They decided they need to replace it, too. As you can guess, apparently not even Microsoft was all that impressed.

Now, lest I sound like all I am is a Microsoft basher or that I think EM was a bad product, I'll put it this way: EM was a fairly good "first shot at it." None of the RDBMS systems out there had anything remotely as powerful and useful as Enterprise Manager was when it first came out — it was a huge part of why SQL Server has been perceived as so much more usable than, say, Oracle (although Oracle has certainly made inroads in the management area). That usability, coupled with what used to be a very cheap price tag, is a big part of Microsoft's success with SQL Server.

EM did, however, have a number of flaws that became more and more obvious as the Windows era taught us what a Windows application should look and act like.

Windows Management Instrumentation

Windows Management Instrumentation (WMI) is very different from the other management objects we've talked about this far in the sense that it is not SQL Server specific, but, rather, an implementation of a management scripting model that was already taking hold to manage servers across Windows and beyond.

WMI is an implementation of the industry open standard Web-Based Enterprise Management (WBEM) initiative. WBEM goes well beyond Microsoft products, and the idea was that server administrators would be able to learn one core scripting model and manage all of their servers with it. Exchange, SQL Server, Windows O/S features, and more — it was all going to be managed using WMI (and, indeed, most of it can be).

Going into SQL Server 2000, the message was clear: WMI was the future. Many of the SQL Server stalwarts (like me) were told over and over again — DMO would be going away (well, that much turned out to be true), and we should do any new management in WMI (that much turned out to be not so true).

The reality is that WMI was never fully implemented for SQL Server, but what there is of it will also not go away any time soon. WMI is, as I've said, an industry standard, and many other Windows servers use WMI for configuration management. Having WMI available for the configuration fundamentals makes a lot of sense, and, for that space, it's likely here to stay (with no complaints from me).

It's worth noting that WMI is now implemented as a layer over SMO — go figure.

SMO

It's unclear to me exactly when Microsoft decided to make the move to SMO. What I can say is that they knew they had a problem: DMO was clearly at the end its useful life, and a complete rewrite of Enterprise Manager was already planned for SQL Server 2005. At the same time, WMI was clearly not going to address everything that needed to be done. (WMI is configuration oriented, but SQL Server needs more administrative love than WMI was likely to give in any kind of usable way.)

So, as SQL Server 2000 was coming to market, .NET was already clearly on the horizon. What has become Visual Studio 2005 was already in heavy design. C# was already being sold as the programming language of the future. The decision was made to use Visual Studio plug-ins as the management center (indeed, you still see that very clearly for Reporting, Integration, and somewhat for Analysis Services).

In the end, what we have in SMO is a very useful set of .NET assemblies. Management Studio has gone back to being its own thing (being too tied in to Visual Studio apparently didn't work out so well, but I like the decision to keep them separate), but it is based on Visual Studio, and leverages several Visual Studio notions right down to the IntelliSense that became part of the product in SQL Server 2008. The services that require the notion of a designer-use Business Intelligence Development Studio, which is still basically a set of projects, controls, and templates for Visual Studio (indeed, it says Visual Studio as you start it up).

My guess? Well, depending on how long it is before SQL Server goes to a new version again, I think it's safe to say you can count on SMO as being the object model for no less than another 1–2 releases. There is no replacement on the horizon, and SMO looks very viable (no reason to replace it in the foreseeable future). In short, you should be able to count on it for at least 5–10 years, which is about as much as anyone can hope for anything in the software business.

> **Even though it's safe to assume SMO will be around for at least a few more releases, it's worth noting that SMO is not 100% code compatible from release to release. For example, certain classes that were part of the core `Microsoft.SqlServer.Smo.dll` have been moved to a new file called `Microsoft.SqlServer.SmoExtended.dll`. If you don't have the new reference as part of your project, then things will break when you compile using the SQL Server 2008 libraries.**

The SMO Object Model

Server Management Objects, or SMO, replaces DMO. That said, SMO goes well beyond anything DMO was conceived to do. Beyond basic configuration or even statement execution, SMO has some truly advanced features such as:

❑   Event handling: SMO supports the notion of trapping events that are happening on the server and injecting code to handle the event situation.

❑   The ability to address types of objects in your server as collections (making it easy to enumerate them and provide consistent and complete treatment for all objects of that type).

❑   The ability to address all of the various server objects that are part of SQL Server in a relatively consistent manner.

Like all object models, SMO establishes something of a hierarchy among objects. Because SQL Server is such a complex product, there are many, many objects to consider. Figure 23-1 includes an example of the hierarchy of what I would consider to be "core" objects in SQL Server.

Note that this is not at all a comprehensive list! If you want a diagram with everything, check Books Online (they have one that isn't bad, though it's not great either — at least it's complete). This is my attempt at giving you something that is more readable and has all the core objects plus a few.

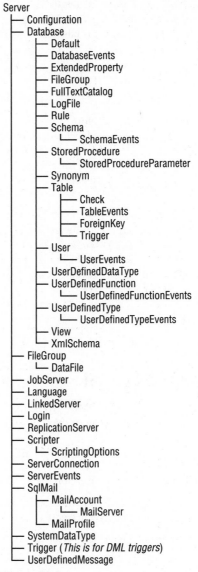

```
Server
  ├─ Configuration
  ├─ Database
  │     ├─ Default
  │     ├─ DatabaseEvents
  │     ├─ ExtendedProperty
  │     ├─ FileGroup
  │     ├─ FullTextCatalog
  │     ├─ LogFile
  │     ├─ Rule
  │     ├─ Schema
  │     │     └─ SchemaEvents
  │     ├─ StoredProcedure
  │     │     └─ StoredProcedureParameter
  │     ├─ Synonym
  │     ├─ Table
  │     │     ├─ Check
  │     │     ├─ TableEvents
  │     │     ├─ ForeignKey
  │     │     └─ Trigger
  │     ├─ User
  │     │     └─ UserEvents
  │     ├─ UserDefinedDataType
  │     ├─ UserDefinedFunction
  │     │     └─ UserDefinedFunctionEvents
  │     ├─ UserDefinedType
  │     │     └─ UserDefinedTypeEvents
  │     ├─ View
  │     └─ XmlSchema
  ├─ FileGroup
  │     └─ DataFile
  ├─ JobServer
  ├─ Language
  ├─ LinkedServer
  ├─ Login
  ├─ ReplicationServer
  ├─ Scripter
  │     └─ ScriptingOptions
  ├─ ServerConnection
  ├─ ServerEvents
  ├─ SqlMail
  │     ├─ MailAccount
  │     │     └─ MailServer
  │     └─ MailProfile
  ├─ SystemDataType
  ├─ Trigger (This is for DML triggers)
  └─ UserDefinedMessage
```

Figure 23-1

Walking through Some Examples

This may well be the messiest section in the entire book in terms of hearing me "talk" about things, as it includes a ton of Visual Studio stuff that goes well beyond what is built into the base SQL Server Business Intelligence Studio.

You must have some version of Visual Studio .NET in order to actually build these examples yourself. Not to fear, however, if you don't — I do show all the lines of code here, so you can at least look them over.

Also, the following examples are done in C#, but the basic object references and method calls are the same — conversion to VB or C++ should be simple for those more comfortable in those languages.

What we're going to be doing in this section is building up a little application that does a number of different "basics" that you might be interested in. Among the things that will happen at least once among all these various actions are:

❑ Creating a reference to a specific server, including a connection to a server using a trusted connection

❑ Creating an entirely new database

❑ Creating tables in a database

❑ Creating primary key constraints for those tables

❑ Creating a foreign key referencing from one table to another

❑ Dropping a database

❑ Backing up a database

❑ Scripting a database object

Each of these is a hyper-simplified version of what is required. Keep in mind that each of the objects I reference here has many more possible properties and methods to be set. For example, in the scripting example, we could play around with scripting options to change what general property commands do and do not appear in the script.

Getting Started

Start by creating a new Windows Application project in Visual Studio. I called mine SQLSMOExample. In order to make use of the SMO assemblies, you'll need to set references in your project to at least five assemblies:

❑ Microsoft.SqlServer.ConnectionInfo

❑ Microsoft.SqlServer.Management.Sdk.Sfc

❑ Microsoft.SqlServer.Smo

❑ Microsoft.SqlServer.SmoExtended

❑ Microsoft.SqlServer.SqlEnum

Setting a reference is as easy as right-clicking References in the Solution Explorer (or in the Project menu) and choosing Add Reference. Select the five assemblies in the preceding list, and click OK.

For my example, all of my code is, for simplicity's sake, done in a Form called frmMain. In most cases, you would want to set up separate component files for your methods and just call them from a form as needed.

Declarations

We need to add declarations to a couple of the management libraries to make it simple to utilize those objects in our code:

```
using Microsoft.SqlServer.Management.Smo;
using Microsoft.SqlServer.Management.Common;
using Microsoft.SqlServer.Management.Smo.SqlEnum;
```

This will allow us to reference several objects within these libraries without having to fully qualify them.

Basic Connection and Server References

There is a block of code you will see me reuse in every one of the methods we'll create in this chapter. The purpose of the code is to establish a connection and a server reference — everything we do will need these.

In practice, we would likely establish one or more connections that would be global to the application rather than a specific method, but, again, I am trying to keep the code blocks somewhat independent, so that you can look at them individually.

The connection and server reference code looks like this:

```
// Create the server and connect to it.
ServerConnection cn = new ServerConnection();
cn.LoginSecure = true;

Server svr = new Server(cn);
svr.ConnectionContext.Connect();
```

Creating a Database

Creating a database is pretty straightforward. In the implementation that follows, I create a Database object and immediately initialize with a reference to our svr Server object. Note, however, that all I am creating is a database definition object. The database itself is not actually created on the server until we call the Create() method of the database object. So, in short, we define the object, modify the various properties that define it, and then, and only then, do we call the Create() method to actually create the database on the server that is referenced in our Server object.

Drop a button onto the main form — I've called mine btnCreateDB — and you're ready to add some code. A simple method to create the database this might include:

```
private void btnCreateDB_Click(object sender, EventArgs e)
{

    // Create the server and connect to it.
    ServerConnection cn = new ServerConnection();
    cn.LoginSecure = true;

    Server svr = new Server(cn);
    svr.ConnectionContext.Connect();
```

```
        Database db = new Database();

        db.Parent = svr;
        db.Name = "SMODatabase";
        db.Create();

        txtResult.Text = "Database Created";

        cn.Disconnect();

    }
```

I've established a generic database object. I then associated it with a specific server, gave the logic name for the database, and then created it.

The result is really nothing different than if we had connected to our database and issued the command:

```
CREATE DATABASE SMODatabase
```

We wind up with an empty database that is created completely with defaults. We could, however, have set things like the physical file location (including creating it with multiple filegroups), default collation, growth and size properties — basically anything you normally think of as a property of the database. More importantly, however, we are operating in a native .NET environment, so any errors, success messages, or other notifications can be handled easily within our client language.

Creating Tables

In this example, I'm going to add a pair of tables to our empty SMODatabase. We'll add ParentTable and ChildTable. ChildTable will have a foreign key to ParentTable. Both will have primary keys.

First, we'll need to set a reference to what database we want to create our tables in:

```
        private void btnCreateTables_Click(object sender, EventArgs e)
        {

            // Create the server and connect to it.
            ServerConnection cn = new ServerConnection();
            cn.LoginSecure = true;

            Server svr = new Server(cn);
            svr.ConnectionContext.Connect();

            // Get a reference to our test SMO Database
            Database db = svr.Databases["SMODatabase"];
```

Notice that this time I did not create the Database object as "new." Instead, I associated it with an existing database object from our referenced Server object.

From there, I create a new table object. Much as when we created the Database object, all we are doing is creating an object definition in our application. No table will be created in the database until after we've fully defined our Table object and called its Create() method.

```
// Create Table object, and begin defining said table
Table ParentTable = new Table(db, "ParentTable");
```

Now we're ready to start adding some meat to the definition of our table. Unlike a database, which has enough defaults that you really only need to specify a name to create one (the rest it will just be copied from the model database), tables require a lot of specification — specifically, it needs at least one column.

Let's add a column that will eventually serve as our primary key:

```
// Build up the table definition
Column ParentKey = new Column(ParentTable, "ParentKey");
ParentKey.DataType = DataType.Int;
ParentKey.Nullable = false;
ParentKey.Identity = true;
```

We've created a new column object. It has been templated from the ParentTable and named ParentKey. I've given it a data type of int, made it non-nullable, and defined it as an IDENTITY column.

> Even though we've templated the column from the **ParentTable**, it is not yet associated directly with that table! The templating reference just helps establish what the initial property values are for the column (such as collation).

Now let's add another column called ParentDescription:

```
Column ParentDescription = new Column(ParentTable, "ParentDescription");
ParentDescription.DataType = DataType.NVarCharMax;
ParentDescription.Nullable = false;
```

Again, the column is created, but not directly associated with the Table object yet — let's take care of that now:

```
// Now actually add them to the table definition
ParentTable.Columns.Add(ParentKey);
ParentTable.Columns.Add(ParentDescription);
```

It is not until we add them to the Columns collection of the Table object that they become directly associated with that table.

So, we have a table object defined, and it has two columns associated with it. What we need now is a primary key.

```
// Add a Primary Key
Index PKParentKey = new Index(ParentTable, "PKParentKey");
PKParentKey.IndexKeyType = IndexKeyType.DriPrimaryKey;


PKParentKey.IndexedColumns.Add(new IndexedColumn(PKParentKey,
"ParentKey"));

ParentTable.Indexes.Add(PKParentKey);
```

Notice that we're defining the primary key as an index rather than as anything explicitly called a constraint. Instead, we define the index, and then tell the index (via its IndexKeyType) that it is a primary key. When the index is created, the constraint definition will also be added.

> **Primary and Unique constraints are not added specifically as constraints. They are, instead, added as indexes with an IndexKeyType that implies that they are to be added as a constraint rather than a raw index.**

Much like our columns, the primary key is not directly associated with the table until we explicitly add it to the Indexes collection of our table.

With all that done, we're ready to create our table:

```
ParentTable.Create();
```

It is at this point that the table is physically created in the database.

Okay, with our parent table created, we're ready to add our child table. The code up through the creation of the primary key looks pretty much just as the ParentTable object did:

```
// Create Table object for child, and begin defining said table
Table ChildTable = new Table(db, "ChildTable");

// Build up the Child table definition
Column ChildParentKey = new Column(ChildTable, "ParentKey");
ChildParentKey.DataType = DataType.Int;
ChildParentKey.Nullable = false;

Column ChildKey = new Column(ChildTable, "ChildKey");
ChildKey.DataType = DataType.Int;
ChildKey.Nullable = false;

Column ChildDescription = new Column(ChildTable, "ChildDescription");
ChildDescription.DataType = DataType.NVarCharMax;
ChildDescription.Nullable = false;

// Now actually add them to the table definition
ChildTable.Columns.Add(ChildParentKey);
ChildTable.Columns.Add(ChildKey);
ChildTable.Columns.Add(ChildDescription);

// Add a Primary Key that is a composite key
Index PKChildKey = new Index(ChildTable, "PKChildKey");
PKChildKey.IndexKeyType = IndexKeyType.DriPrimaryKey;

PKChildKey.IndexedColumns.Add(new IndexedColumn(PKChildKey,
"ParentKey"));
PKChildKey.IndexedColumns.Add(new IndexedColumn(PKChildKey,
"ChildKey"));

ChildTable.Indexes.Add(PKChildKey);
```

But with `ChildTable`, we want to add a twist in the form of a foreign key. To do this, we create a `ForeignKey` object:

```
// Add a Foreign Key
ForeignKey FKParent = new ForeignKey(ChildTable, "FKParent");
```

And then create `ForeignKeyColumn` objects to add to the `ForeignKey` object.

```
// The first "Parent Key" in the definition below is the name in the
// current table
// The second is the name (of just the column) in the referenced table.
ForeignKeyColumn FKParentParentKey = new ForeignKeyColumn(FKParent,
// "ParentKey", "ParentKey");

FKParent.Columns.Add(FKParentParentKey);
```

Next, set a reference to a specific table:

```
FKParent.ReferencedTable = "ParentTable";

// I could have also set a specific schema, but since the table was created
// using just a
// default schema, I'm leaving the table reference to it default also. They
// would be
// created using whatever the user's default schema is

/*
** Note that there are several other properties we could define here
** such as CASCADE actions. We're going to keep it simple for now.
*/
```

Then actually add the foreign key to and create the table:

```
ChildTable.ForeignKeys.Add(FKParent);

ChildTable.Create();

cn.Disconnect();

txtResult.Text = "Tables Created";


}
```

I recognize that this probably seems convoluted compared to just connecting and issuing a CREATE TABLE statement, but there are several advantages:

❑ If you are dynamically building a table, you can encapsulate the various parts of the table construction more easily than trying to do string manipulation.

❑ Changes to the properties of the various objects involved are far less sensitive to specific order of execution than trying to build a string would be.

❑ All the properties remain discrete, so they are easily addressed and edited without significant string manipulation.

❑ It is the SMO way of doing things — if the other actions you're taking are already in SMO, then doing things consistently in SMO is probably going to yield less confusion than if you mix string-based commands with SMO commands.

Dropping a Database

As with most drop situations, this one is pretty straightforward. We start with our now-familiar server and connection info and then set a reference to what database we're interested in:

```
private void btnDropDB_Click(object sender, EventArgs e)
{
    // Create the server and connect to it.
    ServerConnection cn = new ServerConnection();
    cn.LoginSecure = true;

    Server svr = new Server(cn);
    svr.ConnectionContext.Connect();

    Database db = svr.Databases["SMODatabase"];
```

Then just call the `Drop()` method and we're done:

```
    db.Drop();

    txtResult.Text = "Database Dropped";

    cn.Disconnect();

}
```

> Note that we do not have any error trapping added here (there really isn't anything different than other error-trapping issues in your language of choice). You may run into some issues dropping the database if you still have connections open to that database elsewhere in this or other applications (such as Management Studio). I encourage you to experiment with this and what you might do in your error handler (remember, we have robust error handling in most .NET languages), such as identifying and killing all connections that have locks on the database we want to drop.

Backing Up a Database

For this one, we're actually going to switch over and use the AdventureWorks database just to give us something in which to make a meatier backup.

As you might suspect from how many different objects we've seen so far, the `Backup` object is its own thing. It is considered a child of the `Server` object but has its own set of properties and methods.

To create a backup, you do the same server connection code that we've seen several times now:

```
private void btnBackupDB_Click(object sender, EventArgs e)
{
    // Create the server and connect to it.
    ServerConnection cn = new ServerConnection();
    cn.LoginSecure = true;

    Server svr = new Server(cn);
    svr.ConnectionContext.Connect();
```

We're then ready to create a new Backup object. Note that, unlike the Database object, which we associated with a server early on, we don't need to reference a specific server for our Backup object until we actually go to execute the backup.

```
    // Create and define backup object
    Backup bkp = new Backup();
    bkp.Action = BackupActionType.Database;
    bkp.Database = "AdventureWorks2008";
    bkp.Devices.AddDevice(@"c:\SMOSMOSample.bak", DeviceType.File);
```

I've created the Backup object and told it what kind of a backup it should expect to do (A Database backup as opposed to, say, a Log backup). I've also set what database it's going to be backing up and defined a device for it to use.

Note that, while here I defined a file device and path on the fly, you could just as easily connect to the server and query what devices are already defined on the server and then select one of those for your backup. Similarly, the device could be of a different type — such as a tape.

Now we're ready to execute the backup. We have two different methods available for this:

❑ **SqlBackup**: This is a synchronous backup — your code will not gain control again until the backup is either complete or errors out.

❑ **SqlBackupAsync**: This tells the server to start the backup and then returns control to your application as soon as the server accepts the backup request as being valid (the backup will then run in the background). It's important to note that you do have the ability to receive notifications as the backup reaches completion points (you can define the granularity of those completion points).

I've chosen the asynchronous backup method in my example.

```
    // Actually start the backup. Note that I've said to do this Asynchronously
    // I could easily have make it synchronous by choosing SqlBackup instead
    // Also note that I'm telling it to initialize (overwrite the old if it's
    // there).
    // Without the initialize, it would append onto the existing file if found.
    bkp.Initialize = true;
    bkp.SqlBackupAsync(svr);
    cn.Disconnect();

}
```

After you've run this, go take a look for the `SQLSMOSample.bak` file in the root of your C: drive and it should be there! Also try running the backup multiple times and notice that it is overwritten each time. If we removed the `bkp.Initialize` command, then each new backup would append to the existing file.

Scripting

Perhaps one of the most compelling abilities that SMO offers the true developer crown is the ability to script out objects that are already in the database. Indeed, SMO can script out backups, reverse engineer tables, and even record the statements being sent to the server.

For our example, we're going to reverse engineer a script for the `HumanResources.Employee` table in the AdventureWorks database. We'll see just how easily even a relatively complex table definition can be scripted out for other use.

We start with the same server, connection, and database reference code we've used several times in this chapter:

```csharp
private void btnScript_Click(object sender, EventArgs e)
{
        // Create the server and connect to it.
        ServerConnection cn = new ServerConnection();
        cn.LoginSecure = true;

        Server svr = new Server(cn);
        svr.ConnectionContext.Connect();

        // Now define the database we want to reference the table from.
        Database db = svr.Databases["AdventureWorks2008"];
```

Next, we set a reference to the table that we want to script out — we could just as easily be scripting out a different type of SQL Server object such as a stored procedure, a view, or even a database. Indeed, it can even be a server-level object such as a device or login.

```csharp
        // Get a reference to the table. Notice that schema is actually the *2nd*
        // parameter
        // not the first.
        Table Employee = db.Tables["Employee", "HumanResources"];
```

We're then ready to call the `Script()` method. The only real trick here is to realize that it returns not just a single string but rather a collection of strings. In order to receive this, we'll need to set up a variable of the proper `StringCollection` type, which is not defined in any of our `using` declarations; we will, therefore, need to fully qualify that variable declaration.

```csharp
        // Call the Script method. The issue with this is that it returns a string
        // *collection* rather than a string. We'll enumerate it into a string
        // shortly.
```

```
        System.Collections.Specialized.StringCollection script =
Employee.Script();
```

Okay, so we've received our script, but now we want to take a look. I'll define a holding variable and copy all of the separate strings into just one string to use in a `MessageBox`:

```
string MyScript = "";

foreach (string s in script)
{
    MyScript = MyScript + s + "\r\n";
}

// Now show what we got out of it - very cool stuff.
MessageBox.Show(MyScript);

cn.Disconnect();

}
```

Execute this, and you get a very usable script returned, as shown in Figure 23-2.

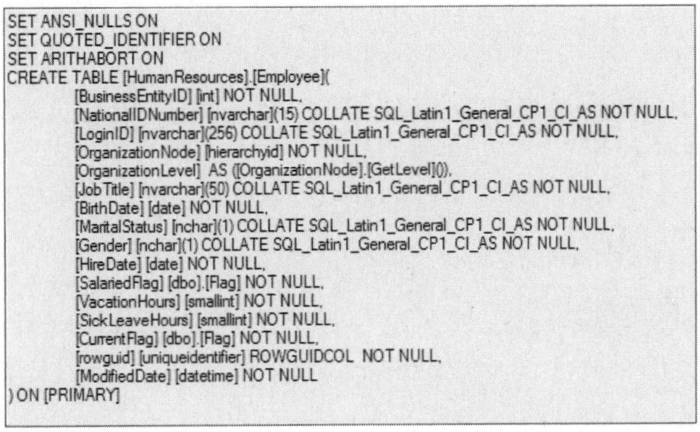

```
SET ANSI_NULLS ON
SET QUOTED_IDENTIFIER ON
SET ARITHABORT ON
CREATE TABLE [HumanResources].[Employee](
    [BusinessEntityID] [int] NOT NULL,
    [NationalIDNumber] [nvarchar](15) COLLATE SQL_Latin1_General_CP1_CI_AS NOT NULL,
    [LoginID] [nvarchar](256) COLLATE SQL_Latin1_General_CP1_CI_AS NOT NULL,
    [OrganizationNode] [hierarchyid] NOT NULL,
    [OrganizationLevel]  AS ([OrganizationNode].[GetLevel]()),
    [JobTitle] [nvarchar](50) COLLATE SQL_Latin1_General_CP1_CI_AS NOT NULL,
    [BirthDate] [date] NOT NULL,
    [MaritalStatus] [nchar](1) COLLATE SQL_Latin1_General_CP1_CI_AS NOT NULL,
    [Gender] [nchar](1) COLLATE SQL_Latin1_General_CP1_CI_AS NOT NULL,
    [HireDate] [date] NOT NULL,
    [SalariedFlag] [dbo].[Flag] NOT NULL,
    [VacationHours] [smallint] NOT NULL,
    [SickLeaveHours] [smallint] NOT NULL,
    [CurrentFlag] [dbo].[Flag] NOT NULL,
    [rowguid] [uniqueidentifier] ROWGUIDCOL  NOT NULL,
    [ModifiedDate] [datetime] NOT NULL
) ON [PRIMARY]
```

Figure 23-2

Pulling It All Together

Okay, we looked at the code in fragments, so I wanted to provide something of a reference section to show what all my code looked like when pulled together. How you choose to do your form is up to you, but mine looks like Figure 23-3. Which buttons are which in the code should be self-descriptive based on the button names you'll see in the code. The very bottom box is a text box that I called `txtReturn` in the code.

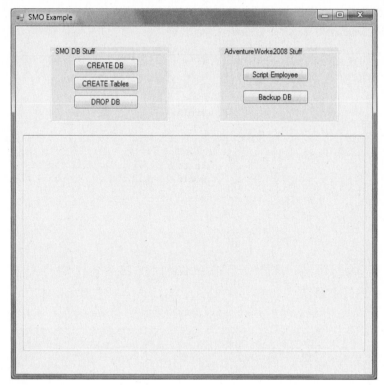

Figure 23-3

Following is my entire form code:

```
using System;
using System.Text;
using System.Windows.Forms;
using Microsoft.SqlServer.Management.Smo;
using Microsoft.SqlServer.Management.Common;
using Microsoft.SqlServer.Management.Smo.SqlEnum;

namespace SQLSMOSample
{
    public partial class frmMain : Form
    {
        public frmMain()
        {
            InitializeComponent();
        }

        private void btnBackupDB_Click(object sender, EventArgs e)
        {
            // Create the server and connect to it.
            ServerConnection cn = new ServerConnection();
            cn.LoginSecure = true;
```

```csharp
    Server svr = new Server(cn);
    svr.ConnectionContext.Connect();

    // Create and define backup object
    Backup bkp = new Backup();
    bkp.Action = BackupActionType.Database;
    bkp.Database = "AdventureWorks2008";
    bkp.Devices.AddDevice(@"c:\SMOSample.bak", DeviceType.File);

    // Actually start the backup. Note that I've said to do this Asynchronously
    // I could easily have make it synchronous by choosing SqlBackup instead
    // Also note that I'm telling it to initialize (overwrite the old if it's there).
    // Without the initialize, it would append onto the existing file if found.
    bkp.Initialize = true;
    bkp.SqlBackupAsync(svr);
    cn.Disconnect();

}


private void btnCreateDB_Click(object sender, EventArgs e)
{
    // Create the server and connect to it.
    ServerConnection cn = new ServerConnection();
    cn.LoginSecure = true;

    Server svr = new Server(cn);
    svr.ConnectionContext.Connect();

    Database db = new Database();

    db.Parent = svr;
    db.Name = "SMODatabase";
    db.Create();

    txtResult.Text = "Database Created";

    cn.Disconnect();

}

private void btnScript_Click(object sender, EventArgs e)
{
    // Create the server and connect to it.
    ServerConnection cn = new ServerConnection();
    cn.LoginSecure = true;

    Server svr = new Server(cn);
    svr.ConnectionContext.Connect();

    // Now define the database we want to reference the table from.
    Database db = svr.Databases["AdventureWorks2008"];

    // Get a reference to the table. Notice that schema is actually the *2nd* parameter
    // not the first.
```

```
        Table Employee = db.Tables["Employee", "HumanResources"];

        // Call the Script method. The issue with this is that it returns a string
        // *collection* rather than a string. We'll enumerate it into a string shortly.
        System.Collections.Specialized.StringCollection script = Employee.Script();
        string MyScript = "";

        foreach (string s in script)
        {
            MyScript = MyScript + s + "\r\n";
        }

        // Now show what we got out of it - very cool stuff.
        //MessageBox.Show(MyScript);
        this.txtResult.Text = MyScript;

        cn.Disconnect();

    }

    private void btnDropDB_Click(object sender, EventArgs e)
    {
        // Create the server and connect to it.
        ServerConnection cn = new ServerConnection();
        cn.LoginSecure = true;

        Server svr = new Server(cn);
        svr.ConnectionContext.Connect();

        Database db = svr.Databases["SMODatabase"];

        db.Drop();

        txtResult.Text = "Database Dropped";

        cn.Disconnect();

    }

    private void btnCreateTables_Click(object sender, EventArgs e)
    {
        // Create the server and connect to it.
        ServerConnection cn = new ServerConnection();
        cn.LoginSecure = true;

        Server svr = new Server(cn);
        svr.ConnectionContext.Connect();

        // Get a reference to our test SMO Database
        Database db = svr.Databases["SMODatabase"];

        // Create Table object, and begin defining said table
        Table ParentTable = new Table(db, "ParentTable");

        // Build up the table definition
```

```
Column ParentKey = new Column(ParentTable, "ParentKey");
ParentKey.DataType = DataType.Int;
ParentKey.Nullable = false;
ParentKey.Identity = true;

Column ParentDescription = new Column(ParentTable, "ParentDescription");
ParentDescription.DataType = DataType.NVarCharMax;
ParentDescription.Nullable = false;

// Now actually add them to the table definition
ParentTable.Columns.Add(ParentKey);
ParentTable.Columns.Add(ParentDescription);

// Add a Primary Key
Index PKParentKey = new Index(ParentTable, "PKParentKey");
PKParentKey.IndexKeyType = IndexKeyType.DriPrimaryKey;


PKParentKey.IndexedColumns.Add(new IndexedColumn(PKParentKey, "ParentKey"));

ParentTable.Indexes.Add(PKParentKey);

ParentTable.Create();

// Create Table object for child, and begin defining said table
Table ChildTable = new Table(db, "ChildTable");

// Build up the Child table definition
Column ChildParentKey = new Column(ChildTable, "ParentKey");
ChildParentKey.DataType = DataType.Int;
ChildParentKey.Nullable = false;

Column ChildKey = new Column(ChildTable, "ChildKey");
ChildKey.DataType = DataType.Int;
ChildKey.Nullable = false;

Column ChildDescription = new Column(ChildTable, "ChildDescription");
ChildDescription.DataType = DataType.NVarCharMax;
ChildDescription.Nullable = false;

// Now actually add them to the table definition
ChildTable.Columns.Add(ChildParentKey);
ChildTable.Columns.Add(ChildKey);
ChildTable.Columns.Add(ChildDescription);

// Add a Primary Key that is a composite key
Index PKChildKey = new Index(ChildTable, "PKChildKey");
PKChildKey.IndexKeyType = IndexKeyType.DriPrimaryKey;

PKChildKey.IndexedColumns.Add(new IndexedColumn(PKChildKey, "ParentKey"));
PKChildKey.IndexedColumns.Add(new IndexedColumn(PKChildKey, "ChildKey"));

ChildTable.Indexes.Add(PKChildKey);

// Add a Foreign Key
```

```
        ForeignKey FKParent = new ForeignKey(ChildTable, "FKParent");

        // The first "Parent Key" in the definition below is the name in the current table
        // The second is the name (of just the column) in the referenced table.
        ForeignKeyColumn FKParentParentKey = new ForeignKeyColumn(FKParent,
"ParentKey", "ParentKey");

        FKParent.Columns.Add(FKParentParentKey);

        FKParent.ReferencedTable = "ParentTable";

        // I could have also set a specific schema, but since the table was created
        // using just a
        // default schema, I'm leaving the table reference to it default also. They would be
        // created using whatever the user's default schema is

        /*
        ** Note that there are several other properties we could define here
        ** such as CASCADE actions. We're going to keep it simple for now.
        */

        ChildTable.ForeignKeys.Add(FKParent);

        ChildTable.Create();

        cn.Disconnect();

        txtResult.Text = "Tables Created";


    }

    private void frmMain_Load(object sender, EventArgs e)
    {

    }

    }
}
```

Summary

Well, all I can say is "Wow!" Okay, so, in a way, this is nothing all that new — after all, DMO used to do a lot of this stuff (indeed, most everything we've looked at with actual code). SMO has, however, made things simpler. The "Wow!" is about thinking of the possibilities:

❑ Imagine issuing commands asynchronously.

❑ Imagine still being able to monitor the progress of those commands by receiving events as progress continues.

❑ Imagine being able to generate script code to support most anything you might want to do.

❑   Imagine being able to register event handlers on your SQL Server and being notified when custom events occur on the server.

The list goes on and on.

Most of the concepts in this chapter are nothing new. We've already looked at ways to create tables, as well as create, back up, and drop databases. The power, then, is in how discretely you can manage those tasks using SMO. We have the prospect for very robust event and error handling. We can far more easily receive configuration information about objects already in the server in a form that yields separate properties as opposed to trying to parse those values out of system-stored procedures.

This chapter truly just scratches the surface of what you can do. If I've piqued your interest at all, I encourage you to consider the use of SMO in your design work, and, of course, go get a book specific to SMO if you need one (you probably will!).

24

Data Warehousing

Well, while it may seem that we've already roamed all over the realm of SQL Server, we have, up to this point, been working safely within the type of databases that are the most common, and that most database developers are the most comfortable with: The Online Transaction Processing — or OLTP — database.

This chapter, however, will turn things somewhat upside down (in terms of the traditional "rules" that determine how we do things). When, for example, we talked about design earlier in this book or in my *Beginning* title, we were talking mostly in terms of a *normalized* database. In this chapter, we'll be largely tossing that out the window. Instead of the transaction-oriented databases we've focused on up to this point, we're going to focus on databases and models that are oriented around the notion of data *analysis*. We will, for now, focus primarily on data warehousing and the special needs relating to its storage ramifications and reporting in data warehousing situations. We'll explore a new sea of terms that you may not have heard before — the lingo of data warehousing and analytics — the language of Business Intelligence (often referred to simply as BI). We'll also explore the world of multidimensional modeling by taking a quick look at yet another service included with SQL Server — Analysis Services.

In this chapter we will:

❑   Discuss the differences between the needs of transaction processing versus analysis processing

❑   Discuss how these differences necessarily lead to substantially different solutions

❑   Explore the problems with the idea of using your OLTP solution as your OLAP solution

❑   Define the concept of a data cube, and indicate how they can help provide a solution to the special requirements of an analytics environment

❑   Look at some other aspects of Analysis Services that come as part of SQL Server 2008

Considering Differing Requirements

As corporations build increasingly complex applications and store their daily data in the databases that support those applications, the databases grow in size. As the size of each database increases, there are typically negative impacts on the system performance of the applications that utilize it. Left unchecked, databases can grow to sizes that seriously impact response times, increase contention (conflict between users trying to get at the same data), or even causing the entire system to go offline.

End users may use data sources differently from one another. From a "how they use it" perspective, users fall into four significant categories:

❑ Those who want to access the data sources on a daily basis, retrieving certain records, adding new records, updating, or deleting existing records

❑ Those who want to make sense of the enormous amounts of data piling in the database, generating reports that will help them come up with the right decisions for the corporation and give it the competitive edge that will make it succeed in the marketplace

❑ Those who want to take the knowledge they gained from their analytical or transactional systems a step further by predicting business performance and analyzing trends for the future

❑ Those who want to make use of highly focused "at a glance" information to obtain fast indications of where they should focus their time

The separate OLTP and OLAP systems help satisfy the different requirements of the first two categories of users. Data mining and cube analysis (through pivot tables and other "What if?" analysis) help satisfy the requirements of the third category. The final item listed tends to be served by targeted screens — or "Dashboards" — that are typically presented when someone first logs in to their system. The following sections present the characteristics of these systems and technologies, and how and when each of them can be used.

Online Transaction Processing (OLTP)

As previously mentioned, the OLTP systems we have focused on until now are designed to allow for high concurrency, making it possible for many users to access the same data source and conduct the processing they need. They also tend to be the "system of authority" for most data, so they place an exceptionally high value on data integrity. In addition, they tend to store data at the detail level, so they implement strategies that minimize the amount of space required to store the data.

As the "transaction processing" in the name implies, OLTP systems are oriented around the idea of transaction processing against the database. Transactions further imply controlled changes to the data in the tables, due to inserts, updates, and deletes during the operation of your business. Typically, an OLTP system will have numerous client applications accessing the database to address small pieces of information in a variety of ways (inserts, updates, deletes — virtually anything).

Examples of OLTP systems include data-entry programs such as banking, ticket reservation, online sales, and inventory management systems (such as AdventureWorks2008), but, no matter what the application is, OLTP systems are usually built with the following objectives in mind:

❑ Process data generated by transactions

❑ Maintain a high degree of accuracy by eliminating data redundancy

❑ Ensure data and information integrity

❑ Produce timely (generally "real time") documents and reports, such as receipts and invoices

❑ Increase work efficiency

In focusing on these particular objectives, the design of the database is usually in the third normal form we discussed back in Chapter 5, eliminating redundancy and maximizing the power of relationships between tables.

Online Analytical Processing (OLAP)

The Online Analytical Processing (or OLAP) systems fall under the broader scope of Decision Support Systems (DSS), or, as is becoming more popular these days, Business Intelligence (BI). The goal of BI systems is to analyze huge amounts of data, generating summaries and aggregations in many different ways ranging from daily, weekly, quarterly, and annual reports to highly focused scorecards and dashboards typically aimed at very specific users who are prepared to act on that data to gain a competitive edge.

With OLAP and BI, we generally forget about keeping our data normalized. Instead, we deliberately *de*-normalize the database (or flatten it) to some extent, allowing some redundancy to avoid joins and focus performance specifically on data retrieval rather than modification. Why is this okay in a data warehouse? Well, once the data arrives in the data warehouse, it is rarely changed. The data is kept there for query purposes; to generate reports that would help decision makers plan the future of their enterprise, but, since it is usually viewed as history by the time it arrives in a data warehouse environment, it doesn't need to concern itself with inserts, updates, or deletes. Instead of a highly normalized, transactional database, we wind up with what is usually called a dimensional database that follows a specific structure or schema. Dimensional databases can be used to build data cubes, which are multidimensional representations of the data that facilitates online business analysis and query performance. The *dimensions* of a cube represent distinct categories for analyzing business data. The dimensions found in a typical cube will almost always include time, and will usually also include geography and something akin to a product line. From there, the possibilities are endless, depending on the specific characteristics of your organization.

> Just because it is called a "cube," don't allow yourself to fall into the trap of considering it limited to three dimensions. Cubes allow for queries that are of n-dimensions. The "cube" representation is merely meant to get across that we are beyond the typical tabular representation seen in OLTP systems.

A Brief Word on Data Mining

Traditional querying techniques such as the queries we've largely focused on in this book and queries into a data warehouse help you find information from your data that is based on relationships you likely already know. (Heck, they are probably declared in your transactional system.) For instance, you can use queries or even a cube to find the number of customers who bought a certain product in a certain period of time per state or city. The information you are seeking is already in your database and the query to retrieve it is usually based on a question you know intuitively.

Data mining, on the other hand, shows its power by helping you discover hidden relationships in your data. You might use it for discovering new trends, speculating on causes for certain events, or even forecasting the performance or direction of certain aspects of your data. For example, data mining might help you find out why a certain product is selling more than another product in a certain region. Data mining makes use of algorithms that bring non-intuitive relationships to our attention. For example, data mining done many years ago discovered that people who bought beer were more inclined to also purchase cheese. Retailers picked up on this, and, for a time, it wasn't uncommon to see cheese located very near the beer aisle to facilitate and encourage the sales of those products as a pair rather than just a single sale at a time.

SQL Server 2008 continues SQL Server's strong support for data mining. The complexities of data mining are, however, well beyond the scope of this book. I did, however, want to make sure you were aware of its availability should you get comfortable enough with analytics to explore data mining.

OLTP or OLAP?

Now that you have seen the general ideas behind the two systems of OLAP and OLTP, let's consider the banking business, for example. During the bank's working hours, bank tellers help customers perform transactions, like depositing funds into their accounts, transferring funds between accounts, and withdrawing funds from these accounts. The customers may also conduct their own transactions using an ATM (Automatic Teller Machine), or a phone-based and/or computer-based banking service. In other words, such transactions are not limited to a particular part of the day but can take place around the clock. All of these operations lead to changes in the data stored in the database. These changes could be inserting new records, or updating or deleting existing records.

OLTP is built to allow these transactions to be made by a large number of users accessing the database concurrently. Databases serving OLTP systems are usually highly normalized relational databases, and their table indexes need to be selected carefully for the right fields. OLTP databases should be built to balance performance away from reporting and toward high frequency of transactions. Queries executed in OLTP systems include a significant mix of inserts, updates, deletes, and selects.

Let's now look at a different scenario with the banking example. Suppose that the bank managers are conducting future planning. They need to look at both current and historical performance data of the bank. If they were to query the database that is used for the OLTP system, they will likely run into significant contention issues with employees who are conducting the day-to-day business of the bank. The variety of reporting and analysis that bank management is likely to be looking for are often long running, and it can put a significant load on the transactional system as many tables are joined to relate a wide range of information and are formatted in a way that is meant to summarize and aggregate the data. For example, they might want to know the total amount of transactions conducted by all customers in a certain region. Such a query would have to sift through large amounts of data that is fragmented and scattered over many joined tables. For example, an accounting general ledger transaction could be stored in a dozen different tables. The queries will have to pull fields from these joined tables to build the views needed by the management, grouping and performing aggregations as it does so. Now imagine this process being repeated over and over again as multiple managers all ask the same general questions and look at the same data.

To face these challenges, it is necessary to isolate the managers who use existing bank data to build their future outlook and planning, and have them use a different system based on OLAP principles. This means creating two different systems: an OLTP system for transaction processing by bank staff and customers, and an OLAP system to help with the decision making.

Now we have two different systems; should these systems use the same database with separate tables for each system, or should they use two completely different databases? The answer to this question depends on how much effect one of the systems will have on the performance of the other, and on how the management and administration plans of these systems work. It is very likely that the two systems will be used at the same time. This causes performance problems even if the tables are separate. This is because the two systems still share many resources on the database server, and these resources may be depleted quickly with the two systems in use. These two systems are usually optimized differently. If we optimize for OLAP, we may adversely affect the performance of the OLTP system, and vice versa. Also, the two systems may have to be administered differently, with different user accounts, backup and maintenance strategies, and so on. Therefore, even though it is theoretically possible to tap into the same database, it is a good idea to keep separate databases on separate database servers for the two systems. With this, each system will have its own resources, and optimizing it will not affect the other system.

Dimensional Databases

The solution to the problems inherent with requesting complex queries from OLTP systems is to build a separate database that would represent the business *facts* more concisely. The structure of this database will not be relational; instead, it will be *dimensional*.

The Fact Table

The central table of a dimensional database is called the *fact* table. Its rows are known as facts and the central theme of a fact table will be *measures* of some kind of distinct instance of an activity or event.

For example, the AdventureWorksDW2008 data warehouse sample includes a table called `FactInternetSales` and several related tables (shown in Figure 24-1). It focuses on individual sales, but on the key metrics for the sale at a line item level. It holds a set of measures (usually numeric) — in this case Order Quantity, Unit Price, and Extended Amount among other measures — and relates them to a set of appropriate dimensions. (In this case, product information, relevant dates, customer information, and other dimensions on which we may want to base our analysis.)

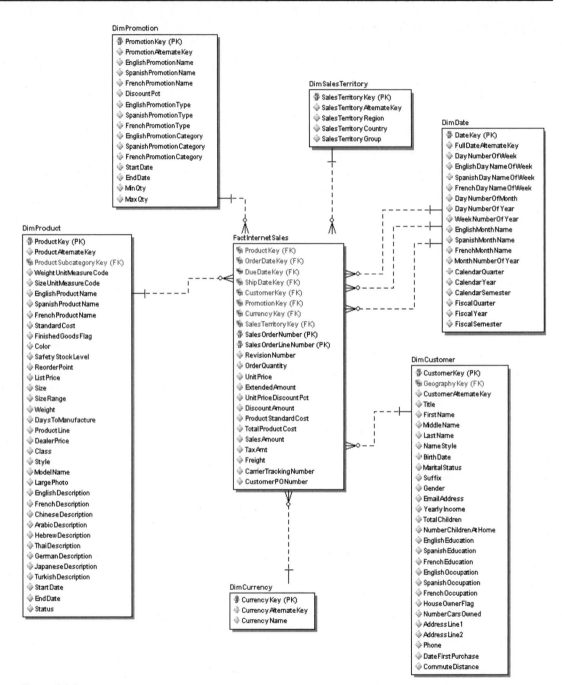

DimPromotion
- 🔑 Promotion Key (PK)
- ⬦ Promotion Alternate Key
- ⬦ English Promotion Name
- ⬦ Spanish Promotion Name
- ⬦ French Promotion Name
- ⬦ Discount Pct
- ⬦ English Promotion Type
- ⬦ Spanish Promotion Type
- ⬦ French Promotion Type
- ⬦ English Promotion Category
- ⬦ Spanish Promotion Category
- ⬦ French Promotion Category
- ⬦ Start Date
- ⬦ End Date
- ⬦ Min Qty
- ⬦ Max Qty

DimSalesTerritory
- 🔑 Sales Territory Key (PK)
- ⬦ Sales Territory Alternate Key
- ⬦ Sales Territory Region
- ⬦ Sales Territory Country
- ⬦ Sales Territory Group

DimDate
- 🔑 Date Key (PK)
- ⬦ Full Date Alternate Key
- ⬦ Day Number Of Week
- ⬦ English Day Name Of Week
- ⬦ Spanish Day Name Of Week
- ⬦ French Day Name Of Week
- ⬦ Day Number Of Month
- ⬦ Day Number Of Year
- ⬦ Week Number Of Year
- ⬦ English Month Name
- ⬦ Spanish Month Name
- ⬦ French Month Name
- ⬦ Month Number Of Year
- ⬦ Calendar Quarter
- ⬦ Calendar Year
- ⬦ Calendar Semester
- ⬦ Fiscal Quarter
- ⬦ Fiscal Year
- ⬦ Fiscal Semester

DimProduct
- 🔑 Product Key (PK)
- ⬦ Product Alternate Key
- 🔑 Product Subcategory Key (FK)
- ⬦ Weight Unit Measure Code
- ⬦ Size Unit Measure Code
- ⬦ English Product Name
- ⬦ Spanish Product Name
- ⬦ French Product Name
- ⬦ Standard Cost
- ⬦ Finished Goods Flag
- ⬦ Color
- ⬦ Safety Stock Level
- ⬦ Reorder Point
- ⬦ List Price
- ⬦ Size
- ⬦ Size Range
- ⬦ Weight
- ⬦ Days To Manufacture
- ⬦ Product Line
- ⬦ Dealer Price
- ⬦ Class
- ⬦ Style
- ⬦ Model Name
- ⬦ Large Photo
- ⬦ English Description
- ⬦ French Description
- ⬦ Chinese Description
- ⬦ Arabic Description
- ⬦ Hebrew Description
- ⬦ Thai Description
- ⬦ German Description
- ⬦ Japanese Description
- ⬦ Turkish Description
- ⬦ Start Date
- ⬦ End Date
- ⬦ Status

FactInternetSales
- 🔑 Product Key (FK)
- 🔑 Order Date Key (FK)
- 🔑 Due Date Key (FK)
- 🔑 Ship Date Key (FK)
- 🔑 Customer Key (FK)
- 🔑 Promotion Key (FK)
- 🔑 Currency Key (FK)
- 🔑 Sales Territory Key (FK)
- 🔑 Sales Order Number (PK)
- 🔑 Sales Order Line Number (PK)
- ⬦ Revision Number
- ⬦ Order Quantity
- ⬦ Unit Price
- ⬦ Extended Amount
- ⬦ Unit Price Discount Pct
- ⬦ Discount Amount
- ⬦ Product Standard Cost
- ⬦ Total Product Cost
- ⬦ Sales Amount
- ⬦ Tax Amt
- ⬦ Freight
- ⬦ Carrier Tracking Number
- ⬦ Customer PO Number

DimCustomer
- 🔑 Customer Key (PK)
- 🔑 Geography Key (FK)
- ⬦ Customer Alternate Key
- ⬦ Title
- ⬦ First Name
- ⬦ Middle Name
- ⬦ Last Name
- ⬦ Name Style
- ⬦ Birth Date
- ⬦ Marital Status
- ⬦ Suffix
- ⬦ Gender
- ⬦ Email Address
- ⬦ Yearly Income
- ⬦ Total Children
- ⬦ Number Children At Home
- ⬦ English Education
- ⬦ Spanish Education
- ⬦ French Education
- ⬦ English Occupation
- ⬦ Spanish Occupation
- ⬦ French Occupation
- ⬦ House Owner Flag
- ⬦ Number Cars Owned
- ⬦ Address Line 1
- ⬦ Address Line 2
- ⬦ Phone
- ⬦ Date First Purchase
- ⬦ Commute Distance

DimCurrency
- 🔑 Currency Key (PK)
- ⬦ Currency Alternate Key
- ⬦ Currency Name

Figure 24-1

The Dimension Tables

Dimensions help put the facts in context and represent such things as time, product, customer, and location. The dimensions describe the data in the fact table. Continuing with our AdventureWorksDW2008 example, it would make sense to have date, customer, and product dimensions, among other things.

The fact table, `FactInternetSales`, captures transactions on a daily level for all customers and all products. Since it has a row for every line of detail, this table will likely grow to be very large (or, at least, we hope so since that means we made many sales!). Since storing every piece of customer data for every sale would take up a prohibitive amount of space, we go ahead and break out the items that don't change with every instance of a measure. These tables we link to the fact table are called dimension tables. They are used to create something of a group by which to determine the level of aggregations from the fact table. For instance, we could find the total monthly sales of all products in all sales territories if we were to query the `FactInternetSales` table grouping by month of the year. Alternatively, we could find the total sales by sales territory at all times, for all customers, and for all products if we queried the `FactInternetSales` table grouping on state. We can also have aggregations on a combination of the dimensions in `FactInternetSales`. For example, we could find the total sales for a particular product model by sales territory on a monthly basis for a specific type of customer by grouping on state and month and adding the appropriate criteria in the `WHERE` clause for the customer and product.

The Star and Snowflake Schemas

The database schema in Figure 24-1, where there is a single fact table with a number of dimension tables linked directly to it, is an example of a *star schema*. In a star schema, all objects likely to be involved in a query are no more than one join away from the fact table. You may also hear of a *snowflake schema*. In a snowflake schema, multiple tables may relate to a dimension that, in turn, is the one to relate directly to the fact table. A snowflake schema can be considered an extension of the star schema, providing a bit more normalization, but also requiring additional tables be joined to relate all the data.

Data Cubes

Until now, we have seen that data is moved from the transactional system into a data warehouse — most likely in the form of a star or snowflake schema. In a dimensional model such as we've described here, the database is frequently used as the basis for constructing what are known as *cubes*. To understand what cubes are, think of the data in the dimensional database as the transformed raw data for your analysis. In other words, if you look at the example in the previous section, you notice that the fact table includes the transaction information and pointers (foreign keys) to the dimensions we wish to analyze. The reports we generate based on the schema in Figure 24-1 are usually something like total sales for customers in a particular territory over a particular period of time for a specific product or category of products. To obtain such a result, you have to aggregate the values in the fact table based on the dimensions you are using to construct the needed report. SQL Server's Analysis Services allows you to pre-calculate such results and store them in a cube. Hence, the cube is a structure that stores the data aggregations from the dimensional database by combining all possible dimension values with the Internet sales facts in the fact table. With this, retrieving the final reports becomes much more efficient, since no complex queries are evaluated at runtime.

To visualize what a cube looks like, look at Figure 24-2. The dimensions of the cube represent the dimensions of the fact table. Each cell in the cube represents a fact corresponding to a level of detail for the different dimensions of the cube. Although the graphical representation of the cube can only show three dimensions, a data cube can have many more dimensions when using Analysis Services. The following figure shows a representation of a data cube for the `FactInternetSales` table, with the territory, product category, and time dimensions shown.

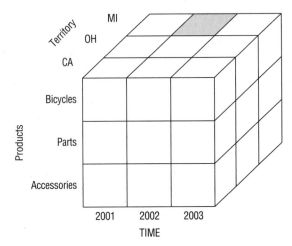

Figure 24-2

If you want to use this cube to find the total sales in the Michigan territory during 2002 for the bicycles category, you need to look at the shaded cell in the figure, which is the resulting cell from the intersection of those three dimensions.

Analysis Services allows you to build your cube from any source of data that has an OLE DB provider. This source can be a relational database in any database management system that has an ODBC driver (such as Oracle, DB2, or even MySQL) or a native OLE DB provider (such as SQL Server, Oracle, or MS Access). The data source for the cube can also be a dimensional database, text files, or even a lightweight directory access protocol (LDAP) data source.

Data Warehouse Concepts

Now that we have seen what cubes and dimensional databases are, let's define the larger concept of what a data warehouse is and how it might be built in SQL Server 2008.

A data warehouse is a data store that holds the data collected during the company's conduct of business over a long period of time. The data warehouse may be made up of one or more *data marts* (smaller collections of summary or dimensional data that is generally focused on a subset of the data warehouse as a whole). The data warehouse typically uses the OLTP systems that collect the data from everyday activities and transactions as its source. The data warehouse concept also includes the processes that extract, scrub (see "Data Scrubbing" later in the chapter), and transform the data, making it ready for the data warehouse. Finally, it also includes the tools needed by the business analysts to present and use the data. These tools include BI tools (such as pivot tables in Excel, or Performance Point Server), as well as data mining and reporting tools. Figure 14-3 depicts the conceptual structure and components of a data warehouse solution.

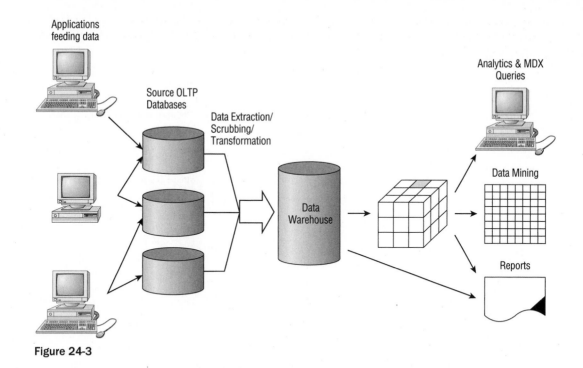

Figure 24-3

Data Warehouse Characteristics

A data warehouse is usually built to support decision making and analytics because it is designed with the following unique characteristics:

❑ **Consolidated and consistent data:** In a data warehouse, data is collected from different sources and consolidated and made consistent in many ways, including the use of naming conventions, measurements, physical attributes, and semantics. This is important because business analysts accessing the data warehouse and using its data for their decision-making processes have to use consistent standards. For example, date formats may all follow one standard, showing day, month, quarter, and year. Data should be stored in the data warehouse in a single, acceptable format. This allows for the referencing, consolidating, and cross-referencing of data from numerous heterogeneous sources, such as legacy data on mainframes, data in spreadsheets, or even data from the Internet, giving the analysts a better understanding of the business.

I can't stress enough the need to treat your data consistently, including the name you use to refer to it. Make sure that you don't use the same name to refer to different things in your database. If, for example, you have more than one type of sales you're going to refer to, then require *every* instance of sales to be name qualified — for example, "bicycle sales" versus "apparel sales" with a separate name for "aggregate sales." I strongly suggest keeping a data "dictionary" that defines the meaning of each name you use and the source of that data.

❑ **Subject-oriented data:** The data warehouse organizes key business information from OLTP sources so that it is available for business analysis. In the process, it weeds out irrelevant data that might exist in the source data store. The organization takes place based on the subject of the data, separating customer information from product information, which may have been inter-mingled in the source data store.

❑ **Historical data:** Unlike OLTP systems, the data warehouse represents historical data. In other words, when you query the data warehouse, you use data that was collected using the OLTP system in the past. The historical data could cover a long period of time compared to the OLTP system, which contains current data that accurately describes the system, for the most part.

❑ **Read-only data:** After data has been moved to the data warehouse, you may not be able to change it unless the data was incorrect in the first place. The data in the data warehouse cannot be updated because it represents historical data, which cannot be changed. Deletes, inserts, and updates (other than those involved in the data-loading process) are not applicable in a data warehouse. The only operations that occur in a data warehouse once it has been set up are loading of additional data and querying.

Data Marts

You may find out, after building your data warehouse, that many people in your organization access only certain portions of the data in the data warehouse. For instance, the sales managers may access only data relevant to their departments. Alternatively, they may access only data for the last year. In this case, it would be inefficient to have these people query the whole data warehouse to get their reports. Instead, it would be wise to partition the data warehouse in smaller units, called data marts, which are based on their business needs.

In addition, some people in your organization may want to be able to access the data in the data warehouse in remote areas far from the company buildings. For instance, a sales manager may want to access data about products and sales particular to his or her market area while on a sales venture. People such as this would benefit from a data mart, as they would be able to carry a section of the data warehouse on their laptop computers, allowing them to access the data they need at any time.

> As often as not, this process actually works backwards, with a smaller data mart serving as the beginning of a larger data warehouse. Indeed, many enterprise data warehouses in use today were created through a process of unifying multiple disparate data marts under one data dictionary and consistent definition before providing additional data aggregation and rollup that takes data from all the various data marts.

Of course, with data marts, the data should be kept in synch with the data warehouse at all times. This can be done in a variety of ways, such as using SQL Server Integration Services, scripting (of T-SQL or other languages), or full-blown data management

SQL Server Integration Services

We already looked at Integration Services extensively back in Chapter 16, but given its consistent use in association with data warehousing, it's worth mentioning again here.

Many organizations need to centralize data to improve decision making. The data being centralized is often stored in a large variety of formats and comes from a number of different sources. The row data that exists in these sources has to be reconciled and transformed in many cases before it can be stored in the data warehouse. SSIS is a fabulous tool for performing this task by providing a means to move data from the source to the destination data warehouse while validating, cleaning up, consolidating, and transforming the data when needed.

Data Validation

Conducting data validation before the data is transferred to the destination data warehouse is extremely important. If the data is not valid, the integrity of the business analysis conducted with it will be in question. For example, if one of the fields is a currency field, and the OLTP data sources exist in multiple countries around the globe, the data in this currency field must always be transferred in the currency of the destination data warehouse and the values must always be properly adjusted for exchange rates at the time the transaction took place (not just the value that was current when the transfer took place).

Data Scrubbing

Often the degree or nature of "clean up" required is such that it can't be performed directly during the transformation process. You may, for example, need to reconcile data between multiple sources feeding the same data warehouse. The process of reconciling multiple data sources and applying other consistency rules to your data is referred to as data scrubbing. For example, if a bicycle is classified in one source as the mountain bike category, and in another source as the recreational category, aggregations in the data warehouse involving this category will yield inaccurate results unless the two data sources have been reconciled during the data transformation process.

Data scrubbing can be achieved in different ways. These methods are beyond the scope of this book, but are mentioned briefly here:

❑   Using SSIS to modify data as it is copied from the source to the destination data store

❑   Use of T-SQL scripts applied to a temporary "scrubbing" database or set of tables

Creating an Analysis Services Solution

In this section, we're going to take a quick look at what cubes are all about, and how to create them. Then we move on to a quick example of how to use them. This is going to be a simple walk-through meant to let you get a quick taste of what's possible. If, after you get done with this taste of Analysis Services, you want more, I would suggest picking up an Analysis Services book and books on data warehousing, business intelligence, and dimensional modeling.

It really is important to realize that, just because you're a great database developer, you are not automatically a great developer of data warehouses or business intelligence systems. The way of thinking required to create a great decision support system is very different from that required to build a great transactional processing system. History is littered with dead projects created when a seemingly experienced database developer assured management that he or she knew all about data warehousing and analytics. Make sure you know what you're getting into before you make such a commitment.

> The example shown in the remainder of this chapter requires the
> AdventureWorksDW2008 database.

Start by firing up the Business Intelligence Development Studio (aka, BIDS). It's been discussed in earlier chapters that used BIDS, but, again, this is just a special version of Visual Studio 2008 that is included with SQL Server. Go ahead and select New Project. What you see will vary somewhat depending on whether you have Visual Studio 2008 installed separately from SQL Server and, if so, what edition of Visual Studio you have.

In any case, you should wind up with a dialog that looks something like Figure 24-4. The exact set of project types may vary from mine somewhat (again, depending on what edition of Visual Studio you're working with). I have already selected Business Intelligence Projects and, more specifically, the Analysis Services template.

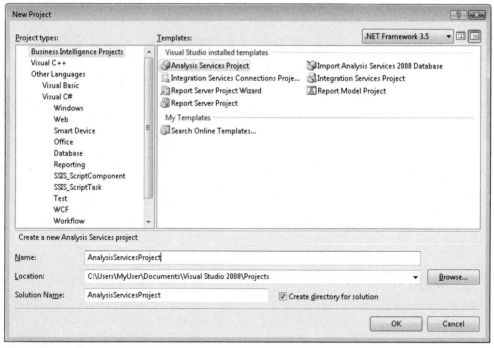

Figure 24-4

After you select a name for your project (I've chosen the oh-so-descriptive "AnalysisServicesProject"), click OK to create the project. Visual Studio will give you an empty Analysis Services project, but notice the various folders created for you. While we won't work with every one of these in this book, it does give you a feel for how broad the work on an Analysis Services project can be.

Let's move right along and create a new data source. To do this, simply right-click the Data Sources folder and select New Data Source, as shown in Figure 24-5.

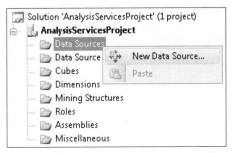

Figure 24-5

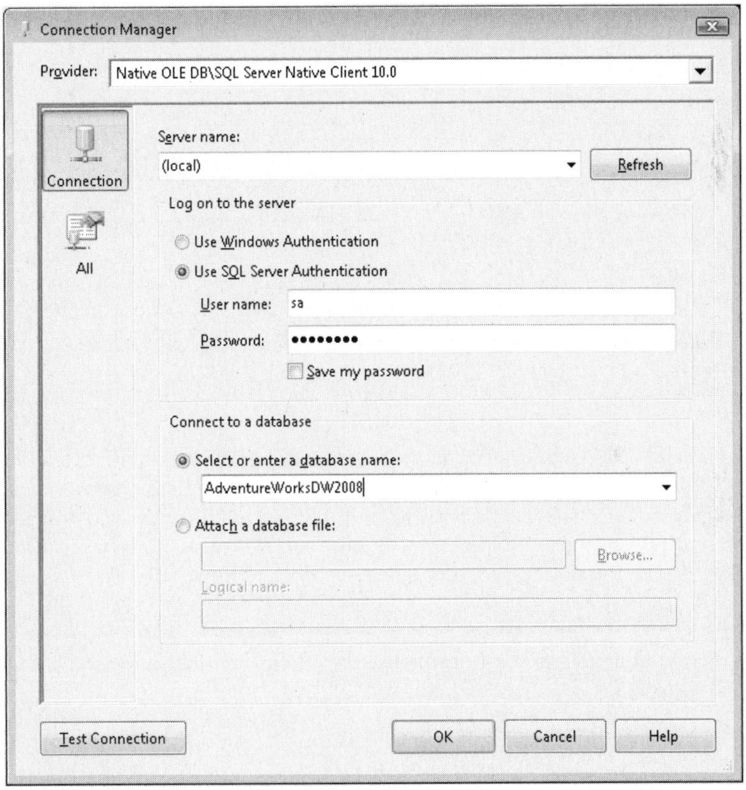

Figure 24-6

This should give you a Welcome dialog (unless you've had it up before and selected the "Don't show this page again" option). Click Next to get to a dialog that allows you to choose a method for defining the data source. Stick with the default of "Create a data source based on an existing or new connection" and then click New to bring up the dialog shown in Figure 24-6.

I have already filled in several key fields to fit my particular need. (You may want to choose a remote server or to use Windows Authentication.) Click OK to create the data source and go back to the previous

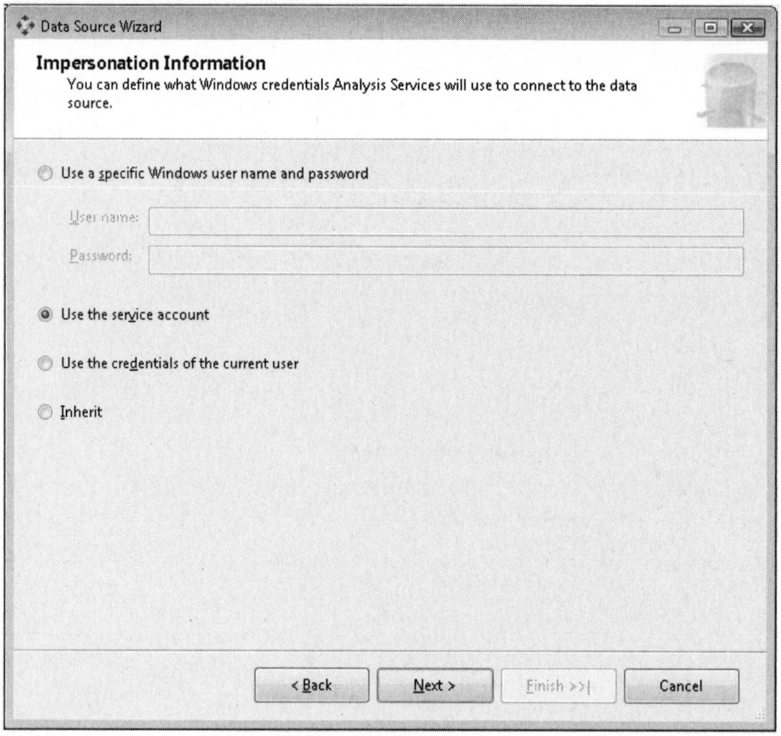

Figure 24-7

dialog. (The new data source should now show in the Data Connections list). Click Next to move on to the Impersonation Information dialog shown in Figure 24-7. We can utilize one of four security options here to determine what credentials Analysis Services will pass when it needs to connect to the data source we're defining. I've told it to use the service account, which equates to whatever Windows account Analysis Services is running under. (So, if you use this option, make sure that accounts has rights to your source data.)

Clicking Next should take you to the Completing the Wizard dialog, where you can name your data source and click Finish.

Next, right-click the Data Source Views folder and choose New Data Source View. This should bring up the dialog shown in Figure 24-8. As you can see, the data source we created a few moments ago is listed and chosen by default. (It also gives us a shortcut to create a new data source if we so choose.) Click Next to select the tables and views you want to work with. I've selected all the tables we saw in our star schema example earlier in the chapter as shown in Figure 24-9.

Again click Next to get the Completing the Wizard dialog. Choose a name (I'm going with the default of Adventure Works 2008) and click Finish. This time we get a more dramatic result, as our main project window (as shown in Figure 24-10) opens up with a view designer for our new data source view.

Notice that it has figured out that our tables are related, and even mapped the visual into a decent representation of the "star" idea.

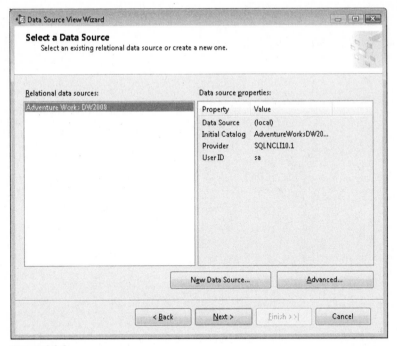

Figure 24-8

Figure 24-9

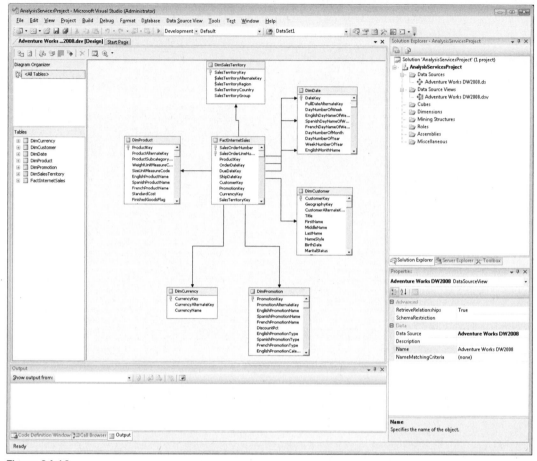

Figure 24-10

We're going to briefly skip down to the Dimensions folder. Again, right-click and select New Dimension. Click Next to go past the Welcome dialog and get to the Select Creation Method dialog shown in Figure 24-11.

Notice that there are utilities here for producing a time dimension table if we needed one (Adventure-WorksDW2008 comes with one already). Keep the default and again click Next to see the Specify Source Information dialog shown in Figure 24-12. I've left it at the default table of DimCurrency (this was chosen alphabetically). It has chosen the correct column as the key, so we'll again click Next to get to the Dimension Attributes dialog shown in Figure 24-13. Note that I've added Currency Name as an attribute.

Again click Next for the Completing the Wizard dialog. Change the name to be Currency, and click Finish to finish the wizard and create the dimension.

Now repeat the New Dimension process for the rest of the dimension tables in our data source view (all of the tables that start with Dim), selecting all attributes for each dimension. You should wind up with a Dimensions node in the Solution Explorer that looks like Figure 24-14.

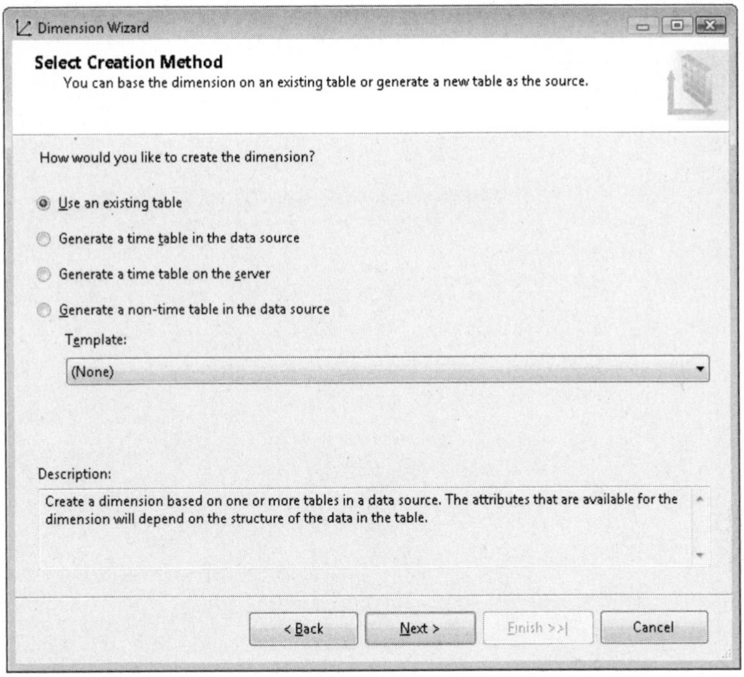

Figure 24-11

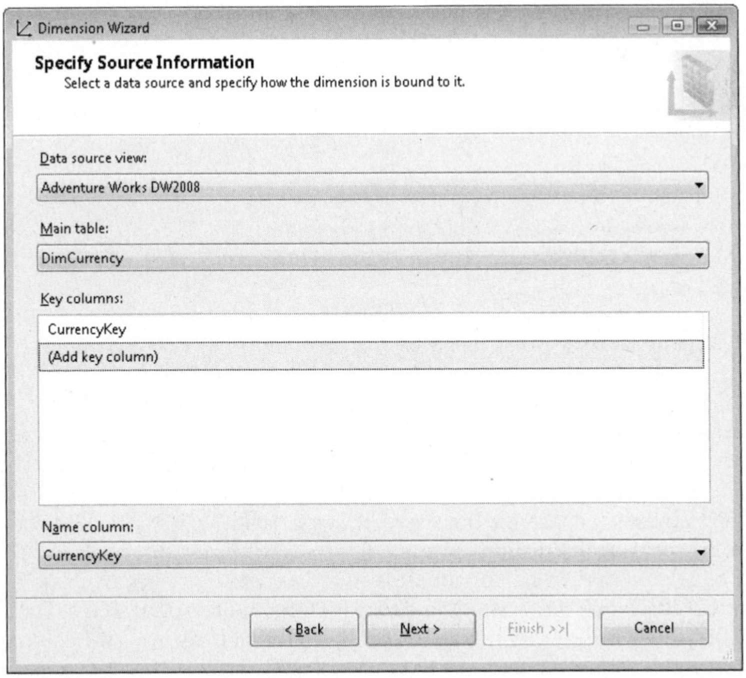

Figure 24-12

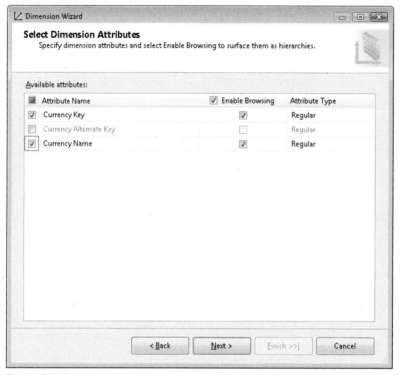

Figure 24-13

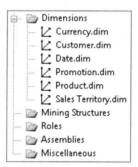

Figure 24-14

Okay, so our dimensions are created, but we're not quite ready to build a cube yet. The issue we need to take care of first is the construction of a time dimension. "But wait!" you say, "We already have a time dimension." If you said that, you would be correct. There is, however, a small problem. SQL Server doesn't know that it's a time dimension. To fix this, select the Date.dim entry (if you didn't rename it as you created it, it would still be called DimDate.dim) under Dimensions, then look at the Attributes list on the left as shown in Figure 24-15.

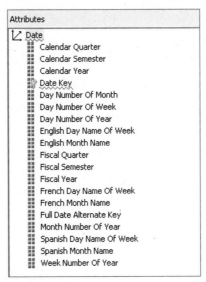

Figure 24-15

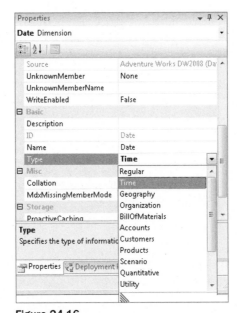

Figure 24-16

Right-click the Date node and select Properties. In the Properties pane, scroll down to the Basic section and notice the entry for Type. We need to change that to Time as shown in Figure 24-16.

With all this created, we're ready to build our cube. Simply right-click the project and select Deploy (you could also choose to limit things to a build), as shown in Figure 24-17.

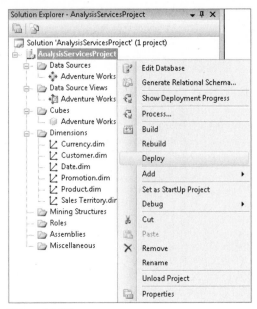

Figure 24-17

This should get us a fully realized cube. What we need from there is to take a quick look at what exactly a cube gives us.

Accessing a Cube

So, given the example we just created, we're ready to actually make use of our cube. We can do this in several ways:

❑ Microsoft Excel (if you connect, as we will momentarily, you'll automatically get a pivot table)

❑ Direct connection and query using Multi-Dimensional Expressions or MDX (the Analysis Services equivalent of T-SQL)

❑ Other tools that are analytics centric, such as Performance Point Server

As a quick example, we're going to connect to the cube we just built using a pivot table in Excel 2007. Excel has a rich set of functionalities for asking "What if?" questions, and the pivot table and pivot chart features integrate fairly easily with Analysis Services cubes.

Let's check this out by firing up Excel 2007 and navigating to the Data ribbon as show in Figure 24-18. Note that I've clicked the From Other Sources tab and selected the From Analysis Services option. (This is built in, and requires no special configuration!) This will bring up the Data Connection Wizard dialog that is very similar to many other connection dialogs we've seen throughout this book. Enter the name of your server (or simply (local) if the cube is on the same server on which you are running Excel) and click Next to move on to the Select Database and Table dialog shown in Figure 24-19. Now go ahead and click Finish to bring up the Import Data dialog shown in Figure 24-20. This allows us to position where the data goes on our sheet and to confirm what we want to do with the data (in this case, create a pivot table). Go ahead and click OK here to accept the defaults.

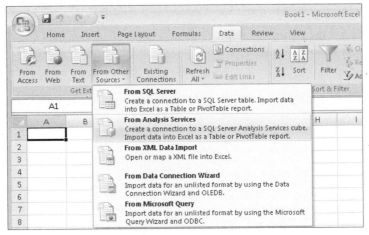

Figure 24-18

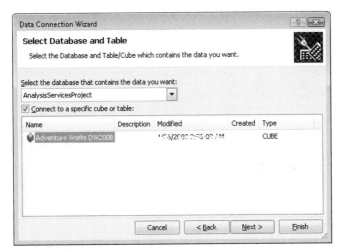

Figure 24-19

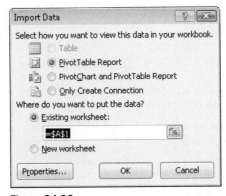

Figure 24-20

If you're new to pivot tables, the sheet that appears (shown in Figure 24-21) may seem a bit anticlimactic. After all, there are no numbers and no real report. Looks, however, are deceiving. The secret to the horsepower in Excel pivot tables is found in the panes along the right-hand side of the workbook as we see in Figure 24-21.

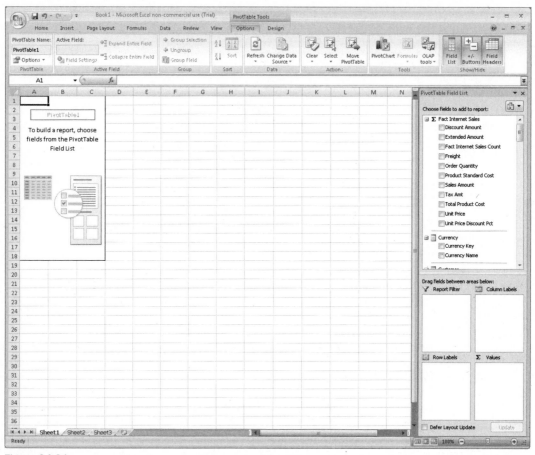

Figure 24-21

At first it appears you have no report. However, a template makes it easy for you to manipulate the kind of information you want on your report and, more importantly, explore the results. To check this out, let's manipulate the data a bit. You can do this by dragging fields you are interested in from the PivotTable Field List into the areas listed below (as shown in Figure 24-22). As you do this, notice the effect that dropping a field in each box has on the main PivotTable area.

> **Be careful as you click around in the main sheet area. If you click outside of the PivotTable, all the PivotTable fields will vanish. If this happens, just click in the area of the PivotTable and they should all re-appear.**

Figure 24-22

I'm going to leave full exploration of what PivotTables can do to a book on Excel, but hopefully you've got a taste of just how easily an Analysis Services cube can enable you to explore your data. Keep in mind that this was just an example of one easy way to connect to your data. You can also issue complex queries against the cube using MDX. Such queries can compare multiple dimensions and allow for special functions for such things as comparing year over year results. What's more, the data coming out of the cube is highly optimized for just this kind of comparison.

Summary

What we covered in this chapter was not really meant to make you an expert in data warehousing, Analysis Services, or business intelligence. Instead, the idea is to give you a concept of what is involved in creating cubes and perhaps a little taste of what they might do for you. I can't stress enough just how surface our coverage of the product was. Analysis Services is a full book to itself. Hopefully the information covered here has given you enough of a feel for Analysis Services to know whether you want to pursue it further.

25

Being Well Connected

Having a SQL Server but not allowing programs to connect to it is almost the same as not having a SQL Server at all. Sure, we may log in to Management Studio and write queries, but the reality is that the vast majority of our users out there never actually see the database directly. They are just using input and reporting screens in some system we've written. (Ok, it is today's massively multiplayer online world and with other large applications out there, they could be on some other highly scalable system too, but not too many of us are going to work on one of those.)

With this in mind, it probably makes sense to figure out how your application is actually going to talk to the database. There are tons of books out there that cover this topic directly (and, outside of a basic connection, it really is a huge topic unto itself), so I'm not even going to attempt to discuss every fine point of every access model in every language. Instead, we're going to explore basic concepts and some fundamental issues of performance, memory use, and general best practices. As I've done with some of the other broad topics we spend time with in this book, the idea is to get you some fundamentals in a quick but useful way and give you something of a taste of what's involved and what kinds of questions you should be asking.

So, having tempted you with a teaser, it's time for what may seem like bad news (but it's not and we'll get to why in a moment). This particular chapter is a "Web release only" chapter, which is a long-winded way of saying, "You need to go download it off the Web." You can fetch it from either the p2p.wrox.com support site or my personal site at www.professionalsql.com. Why did we do that? Well, it's a multifold thing. Some of it was, I'll admit, time constraints on the book. There is, however, another reason — timeliness. Connectivity has been one of the most changing areas of database work over the last decade or slightly more. As we'll discuss to some extent in the downloaded copy of this chapter, history is littered with various access models that have come and gone. (Heck, there are quite a few still in use.) As I write this, the .NET world is largely using ADO.NET and LINQ. Up and coming, however, is Microsoft's whole Entity Frameworks initiative — who knows what else by the time Kilimanjaro (the code name for the next version of SQL Server) is out and we publish another book. Going to a Web release makes it far more realistic that we can update this chapter if there are enough changes to warrant it. (While we still need to go through all the editing, we don't have to typeset or deal with page numbers.)

Once downloaded, you'll find information such as:

❑   Various data access object models past and present (a little history)

❑   Some basic best practices for data access

❑   Some *brief* examples of connecting to your database in .NET

System Functions

SQL Server includes a number of "System Functions" as well as more typical functions with the product. Some of these are used often and are fairly clear right from the beginning in terms of how to use them. Others, though, are both rarer in use and more cryptic in nature.

In this appendix, we'll try to clarify the use of most of these functions in a short, concise manner.

> *Just as an FYI, in prior releases, many system functions were often referred to as "Global Variables." This was a misnomer, and Microsoft has striven to fix it over the last few releases — changing the documentation to refer to them by the more proper "System Function" name. Just keep the old terminology in mind in case any old fogies (such as myself) find themselves referring to them as Globals.*

The T-SQL functions available in SQL Server 2008 fall into 14 categories:

- ❏ Legacy "system" functions
- ❏ Aggregate functions
- ❏ Configuration functions
- ❏ Cryptographic functions
- ❏ Cursor functions
- ❏ Date and time functions
- ❏ Mathematical functions
- ❏ Metadata functions
- ❏ Ranking functions
- ❏ Rowset functions

- ❏ Security functions
- ❏ String functions
- ❏ System functions
- ❏ Text and image functions

In addition, we have the OVER operator, which largely works as a ranking tool, and can be applied to other forms of T-SQL functions (most notably aggregates). While I only discuss it as part of the ranking functions, you may see it referenced several other places in this appendix.

Legacy System Functions (a.k.a. Global Variables)

@@CONNECTIONS

Returns the number of connections attempted since the last time your SQL Server was started.

This one is the total of all connection *attempts* made since the last time your SQL Server was started. The key thing to remember here is that we are talking about attempts, not actual connections, and that we are talking about connections as opposed to users.

Every attempt made to create a connection increments this counter regardless of whether or not that connection was successful. The only catch with this is that the connection attempt has to have made it as far as the server. If the connection failed because of NetLib differences or some other network issue, then your SQL Server wouldn't even know that it needed to increase the count; it only counts if the server saw the connection attempt. Whether the attempt succeeded or failed does not matter.

It's also important to understand that we're talking about connections instead of login attempts. Depending on your application, you may create several connections to your server, but you'll probably only ask the user for information once. Indeed, even Query Analyzer does this. When you click for a new window, it automatically creates another connection based on the same login information.

This, like a number of other system functions, is often better served by a system stored procedure, sp_monitor. This procedure, in one command, produces the information from the number of connections, CPU busy, through to the total number of writes by SQL Server. So, if basic information is what you're after, sp_monitor may be better. If you need discrete data that you can manipulate, then @@CONNECTIONS provides a nice, neat, scalar piece of data.

@@CPU_BUSY

Returns the time in milliseconds that the CPU has been actively doing work since SQL Server last started. This number is based on the resolution of the system timer, which can vary, and can therefore vary in accuracy.

This is another of the "since the server started" kind of functions. This means that you can't always count on the number going up as your application runs. It's possible, based on this number, to figure out a percentage of the CPU that your SQL Server is taking up. Realistically though, I'd rather tap right into the Performance Monitor for that if I had some dire need for it. The bottom line is that this is one of those really cool things from a "gee, isn't it swell to know that" point of view, but doesn't have all that many practical uses in most applications.

@@IDLE

Returns the time in milliseconds (based on the resolution of the system timer) that SQL Server has been idle since it was last started.

You can think of this one as being something of the inverse of @@CPU_BUSY. Essentially, it tells you how much time your SQL Server has spent doing nothing. If anyone finds a programmatic use for this one, send me an e-mail (robv@professionalsql.com). I'd love to hear about it (I can't think of one).

@@IO_BUSY

Returns the time in milliseconds (based on the resolution of the system timer) that SQL Server has spent doing input and output operations since it was last started. This value is reset every time SQL Server is started.

This one doesn't really have any rocket science to it, and it is another one of those that I find falls into the "no real programmatic use" category.

@@PACK_RECEIVED and @@PACK_SENT

Respectively return the number of input packets read to and written from the network by SQL Server since it was last started.

Primarily, these are network troubleshooting tools.

@@PACKET_ERRORS

Returns the number of network packet errors that have occurred on connections to your SQL Server since the last time the SQL Server was started.

Primarily a network troubleshooting tool.

@@TIMETICKS

Returns the number of microseconds per tick. This varies by machines and is another of those that falls under the category of "no real programmatic use."

@@TOTAL_ERRORS

Returns the number of disk read/write errors encountered by the SQL Server since it was last started.

Don't confuse this with runtime errors or as having any relation to @@ERROR. This is about problems with physical I/O. This one is another of those of the "no real programmatic use" variety. The primary use here would be more along the lines of system diagnostic scripts. Generally speaking, I would use the Windows Reliability and Performance Monitor for this instead.

@@TOTAL_READ and @@TOTAL_WRITE

Respectively return the total number of disk reads/writes by SQL Server since it was last started.

The names here are a little misleading, as these do not include any reads from cache. They are only physical I/O.

@@TRANCOUNT

Returns the number of active transactions — essentially the transaction nesting level — for the current connection.

This is a very big one when you are doing transactioning. I'm not normally a big fan of nested transactions, but there are times where they are difficult to avoid. As such, it can be important to know just where you are in the transaction-nesting side of things. (For example, you may have logic that only starts a transaction if you're not already in one.)

If you're not in a transaction, then @@TRANCOUNT is 0. From there, let's look at a brief example:

```
SELECT @@TRANCOUNT As TransactionNestLevel      --This will be zero at this
  point

BEGIN TRAN
SELECT @@TRANCOUNT As TransactionNestLevel      --This will be one at this
  point
  BEGIN TRAN
    SELECT @@TRANCOUNT As TransactionNestLevel  --This will be two at this
  point
  COMMIT TRAN
SELECT @@TRANCOUNT As TransactionNestLevel      --This will be back to one
                                                --at this point
ROLLBACK TRAN
SELECT @@TRANCOUNT As TransactionNestLevel      --This will be back to zero
                                                --at this point
```

Note that, in this example, the @@TRANCOUNT at the end would also have reached zero if we had a COMMIT as our last statement.

Aggregate Functions

Aggregate functions are applied to sets of records rather than to a single record. The information in the multiple records is processed in a particular manner and then is displayed in a single record answer. Aggregate functions are often used in conjunction with the GROUP BY clause.

The aggregate functions are:

- AVG
- CHECKSUM
- CHECKSUM_AGG
- COUNT
- COUNT_BIG
- GROUPING
- MAX
- MIN
- STDEV
- STDEVP
- SUM
- VAR
- VARP

In most aggregate functions, the ALL or DISTINCT keywords can be used. The ALL argument is the default and will apply the function to all the values in the expression, even if a value appears numerous times. The DISTINCT argument means that a value will only be included in the function once, even if it occurs several times.

Aggregate functions cannot be nested. The expression cannot be a subquery.

AVG

AVG returns the average of the values in expression. The syntax is as follows:

```
AVG([ALL | DISTINCT] <expression>)
```

The expression must contain numeric values. NULL values are ignored. This function supports the OVER operator described in the ranking functions section of this appendix.

CHECKSUM

This is a basic hash algorithm usually used to detect changes or consistency in data. This particular function accepts either an expression as an argument or a * (which implies that you want all columns in all the joined tables to be included). The basic syntax is:

```
CHECKSUM(<expression>, [ ... n] | * )
```

Note that the order of your expression, or in the case of a *, the join order, will affect the checksum value, so, for example:

```
CHECKSUM(SalesOrderID, OrderDate)
```

would not give the same result as:

```
CHECKSUM(OrderDate, SalesOrderID )
```

This function is *not* compatible with the OVER operator.

CHECKSUM_AGG

Like CHECKSUM, this is a basic hash algorithm usually used to detect changes or consistency in data. The primary difference is that CHECKSUM is oriented around rows, whereas CHECKSUM_AGG is oriented around columns. The basic syntax is:

```
CHECKSUM_AGG( [ALL | DISTINCT] <expression>)
```

The expression value can be virtually anything, including, if you wish, concatenation of columns (just remember to cast as necessary); however, remember that expression order does matter, so if you're concatenating, Col1 + Col2 does not equal Col2 + Col1.

COUNT

COUNT returns the number of items in expression. The data type returned is of type int. The syntax is as follows:

```
COUNT
(
    [ALL | DISTINCT] <expression> | *
)
```

The expression cannot be of the uniqueidentifier, text, image, or ntext data types. The * argument returns the number of rows in the table; it does not eliminate duplicate or NULL values.

This function supports the OVER operator described in the ranking functions section of this appendix.

COUNT_BIG

COUNT_BIG returns the number of items in a group. This is very similar to the COUNT function, with the exception that the return value has a data type of bigint. The syntax is as follows:

```
COUNT_BIG
(
    [ALL | DISTINCT ] <expression> | *
)
```

Like COUNT, this function supports the OVER operator described in the ranking functions section of this appendix.

GROUPING

GROUPING adds an extra column to the output of a SELECT statement. The GROUPING function is used in conjunction with CUBE or ROLLUP to distinguish between normal NULL values and those added as a result of CUBE and ROLLUP operations. Its syntax is:

```
GROUPING (<column_name>)
```

GROUPING is used only in the SELECT list. Its argument is a column that is used in the GROUP BY clause and that is to be checked for NULL values.

This function supports the OVER operator described in the ranking functions section of this appendix.

MAX

The MAX function returns the maximum value from expression. The syntax is as follows:

```
MAX([ALL | DISTINCT] <expression>)
```

MAX ignores any NULL values.

This function supports the OVER operator described in the ranking functions section of this appendix.

MIN

The MIN function returns the smallest value from expression. The syntax is as follows:

```
MIN([ALL | DISTINCT] <expression>)
```

MIN ignores NULL values.

This function supports the OVER operator described in the ranking functions section of this appendix.

STDEV

The STDEV function returns the standard deviation of all values in expression. The syntax is as follows:

```
STDEV(<expression>)
```

STDEV ignores NULL values.

This function supports the OVER operator described in the ranking functions section of this appendix.

STDEVP

The STDEVP function returns the standard deviation for the population of all values in expression. The syntax is as follows:

```
STDEVP(<expression>)
```

STDEVP ignores NULL values.

This function supports the OVER operator described in the ranking functions section of this appendix.

SUM

The SUM function will return the total of all values in expression. The syntax is as follows:

```
SUM([ALL | DISTINCT] <expression>)
```

SUM ignores NULL values.

This function supports the OVER operator described in the ranking functions section of this appendix.

VAR

The VAR function returns the variance of all values in expression. The syntax is as follows:

```
VAR(<expression>)
```

VAR ignores NULL values.

This function supports the OVER operator described in the ranking functions section of this appendix.

VARP

The VARP function returns the variance for the population of all values in expression. The syntax is as follows:

```
VARP(<expression>)
```

VARP ignores NULL values.

This function supports the OVER operator described in the ranking functions section of this appendix.

Configuration Functions

Well, I'm sure it will come as a complete surprise (ok, not really ...), but configuration functions are those functions that tell us about options as they are set for the current server or database (as appropriate).

@@DATEFIRST

Returns the numeric value that corresponds to the day of the week that the system considers the first day of the week.

The default in the United States is 7, which equates to Sunday. The values convert as follows:

- ❑ 1 — Monday (the first day for most of the world)
- ❑ 2 — Tuesday
- ❑ 3 — Wednesday
- ❑ 4 — Thursday
- ❑ 5 — Friday
- ❑ 6 — Saturday
- ❑ 7 — Sunday

This can be really handy when dealing with localization issues, so you can properly layout any calendar or other day-of-week-dependent information you have.

Use the SET DATEFIRST *function to alter this setting.*

@@DBTS

Returns the last used timestamp for the current database.

At first look, this one seems to act an awful lot like @@IDENTITY in that it gives you the chance to get back the last value set by the system (this time, it's the last timestamp instead of the last identity value). The things to watch out for on this one include:

- ❑ The value changes based on any change in the database, not just the table you're working on.
- ❑ *Any* timestamp change in the database is reflected, not just those for the current connection.

Because you can't count on this value truly being the last one that you used (someone else may have done something that would change it), I personally find very little practical use for this one.

@@LANGID and @@LANGUAGE

Respectively return the ID and the name of the language currently in use.

These can be handy for figuring out if your product has been installed in a localization situation or not, and if so what language is the default.

For a full listing of the languages currently supported by SQL Server, use the system stored procedure, sp_helplanguage.

@@LOCK_TIMEOUT

Returns the current amount of time in milliseconds before the system will time out waiting for a blocked resource.

If a resource (a page, a row, a table, whatever) is blocked, your process will stop and wait for the block to clear. This determines just how long your process will wait before the statement is canceled.

The default time to wait is 0 (which equates to indefinitely) unless someone has changed it at the system level (using sp_configure). Regardless of how the system default is set, you will get a value of −1 from this global unless you have manually set the value for the current connection using SET LOCK_TIMEOUT.

@@MAX_CONNECTIONS

Returns the maximum number of simultaneous user connections allowed on your SQL Server.

Don't mistake this one to mean the same thing as you would see under the Maximum Connections property in the Management Console. This one is based on licensing and will show a very high number if you have selected "per seat" licensing.

> Note that the actual number of user connections allowed also depends on the version of SQL Server you are using and the limits of your application(s) and hardware.

@@MAX_PRECISION

Returns the level of precision currently set for decimal and numeric data types.

The default is 38 places, but the value can be changed by using the /p option when you start your SQL Server. The /p can be added by starting SQL Server from a command line or by adding it to the Startup parameters for the MSSQLServer service in the Windows Services applet.

@@NESTLEVEL

Returns the current nesting level for nested stored procedures.

The first stored procedure (sproc) to run has an nTLEVEL of 0. If that sproc calls another, then the second sproc is said to be nested in the first sproc (and nTLEVEL is incremented to a value of 1). Likewise, the second sproc may call a third, and so on up to maximum of 32 levels deep. If you go past the level of 32 levels deep, not only will the transaction be terminated, but you should revisit the design of your application.

@@OPTIONS

Returns information about options that have been applied using the SET command.

Since you get back only one value, but can have many options set, SQL Server uses binary flags to indicate what values are set. In order to test whether the option you are interested in is set, you must use the option value together with a bitwise operator. For example:

```
IF (@@OPTIONS & 2)
```

If this evaluates to `True`, then you would know that `IMPLICIT_TRANSACTIONS` had been turned on for the current connection. The values are:

Bit	SET Option	Description
1	DISABLE_ DEF_CNST_CHK	Interim vs. deferred constraint checking.
2	IMPLICIT_ TRANSACTIONS	A transaction is started implicitly when a statement is executed.
4	CURSOR_CLOSE ON_COMMIT	Controls behavior of cursors after a COMMIT operation has been performed.
8	ANSI_WARNINGS	Warns of truncation and NULL in aggregates.
16	ANSI_PADDING	Controls padding of fixed-length variables.
32	ANSI_NULLS	Determines handling of nulls when using equality operators.
64	ARITHABORT	Terminates a query when an overflow or divide-by-zero error occurs during query execution.
128	ARITHIGNORE	Returns NULL when an overflow or divide-by-zero error occurs during a query.
256	QUOTED_ IDENTIFIER	Differentiates between single and double quotation marks when evaluating an expression.
512	NOCOUNT	Turns off the row(s) affected message returned at the end of each statement.
1024	ANSI_NULL_ DFLT_ON	Alters the session's behavior to use ANSI compatibility for nullability. Columns created with new tables or added to old tables without explicit null option settings are defined to allow nulls. Mutually exclusive with ANSI_NULL_DFLT_OFF.
2048	ANSI_NULL_ DFLT_OFF	Alters the session's behavior not to use ANSI compatibility for nullability. New columns defined without explicit nullability are defined not to allow nulls. Mutually exclusive with ANSI_NULL_DFLT_ON.
4096	CONCAT_NULL_ YIELDS_NULL	Returns a NULL when concatenating a NULL with a string.
8192	NUMERIC_ ROUNDABORT	Generates an error when a loss of precision occurs in an expression.

@@REMSERVER

Returns the value of the server (as it appears in the login record) that called the stored procedure.

Used only in stored procedures. This one is handy when you want the sproc to behave differently depending on what remote server (often a geographic location) the sproc was called from.

@@SERVERNAME

Returns the name of the local server that the script is running from.

If you have multiple instances of SQL Server installed (a good example would be a Web hosting service that uses a separate SQL Server installation for each client), then @@SERVERNAME returns the following local server name information if the local server name has not been changed since setup:

Instance	Server Information
Default instance	*<servername>*
Named instance	*<servername\instancename>*
Virtual server — default instance	*<virtualservername>*
Virtual server — named instance	*<virtualservername\instancename>*

@@SERVICENAME

Returns the name of the registry key under which SQL Server is running.

Only returns something under Windows 2000/2003/XP, and (under either of these) should always return MSSQLService unless you've been playing games in the registry.

@@SPID

Returns the server process ID (SPID) of the current user process.

This equates to the same process ID that you see if you run sp_who. What's nice is that you can tell the SPID for your current connection, which can be used by the DBA to monitor, and if necessary terminate, that task.

@@TEXTSIZE

Returns the current value of the TEXTSIZE option of the SET statement, which specifies the maximum length, in bytes, returned by a SELECT statement when dealing with text or image data.

The default is 4096 bytes (4KB). You can change this value by using the SET TEXTSIZE statement.

@@VERSION

Returns the current version of SQL Server as well as the processor type and OS architecture.

For example, a run on an old SQL Server 2005 box might look like this:

```
SELECT @@VERSION
```

and gives:

```
---------------------------------------------------------------------------
Microsoft SQL Server 2008 (RTM) - 10.0.1600.22 (X64)
   Jul  9 2008 14:17:44
   Copyright (c) 1988-2008 Microsoft Corporation
   Developer Edition (64-bit) on Windows NT 6.0 <X64> (Build 6001: Service Pack 1)


(1 row(s) affected)
```

Unfortunately, this doesn't return the information into any kind of structured field arrangement, so you have to parse it if you want to use it to test for specific information.

Consider using the xp_msver system sproc instead. It returns information in such a way that you can more easily retrieve specific information from the results.

Cryptographic Functions

These are functions that help support the encryption, decryption, digital signing, and digital signature validation. Some of these are new with SQL Server 2008, and some came with SQL Server 2005. Notice that there are duplicates of most functions from a general use point of view, but that they are different in that one supports a symmetric key and the duplicate (usually with an "Asym" in the name) supports an asymmetrical key.

Now, you may ask "why would I need these?" The answer is as varied as the possible applications for SQL Server. The quick answer though is this: Anytime you're sending or accepting data that you want to protect during transport. For example, since SQL Server supports HTTP endpoints, and, from that, hosting of its own Web services, you may want to accept or return encrypted information with a client of your Web service. Perhaps a more basic example is simply that you've chosen to encrypt the data in your database, and now you need to get it back out in a useful manner.

AsymKey_ID

Given the name of an asymmetric key, this function returns an int that corresponds to the related ID from the database. The syntax is simple:

```
AsymKey_ID('<Asymmetric Key Name>')
```

You must have permissions to the key in question to use this function.

Cert_ID

Similar to AsymKey_ID, this returns an ID that relates to the name of a certificate name. The syntax is simple:

```
Cert_ID('<Certificate Name>')
```

You must have permissions to the certificate in question to use this function.

CertProperty

Allows you to fetch various properties of a given certificate (as identified by the certificate's ID). Valid properties include the start date, expiration date, certificate issuer's name, serial number, security ID (The 'SID', which can also be returned as a string), and the subject of the certificate (who or what is being certified). The syntax looks like this:

```
CertProperty ( Cert_ID ,
    'Expiry_Date'|'Start_Date'|'Issuer_Name'|'Cert_Serial_Number'|'Subject'
    |'SID'|'String_SID' )
```

The data type returned will vary depending on the specific property you're looking for (datetime, nvarchar, or varbinary as appropriate).

DecryptByAsmKey

As you can imagine by the name, this one decrypts a chunk of data utilizing an asymmetric key. It requires the key (by ID), the encrypted data (either as a literal string or a string coercible variable), and the password used to encrypt the asymmetric key in the database. The syntax is straightforward enough:

```
DecryptByAsymKey(<Asymmetric Key ID>, {'<encrypted string>'|<string variable>}
    [, '<password>'])
```

DecryptByCert

This is basically the same as DecryptByAsmKey, except that it expects a certificate rather than an asymmetric key. Like DecryptByAsmKey, this one decrypts a chunk of data utilizing a key. It requires the certificate (by ID), the encrypted data (either as a literal string or a string coercible variable), and the password used to encrypt the private key of the certificate (if one was used). The syntax looks almost just like DecryptByAsmKey:

```
DecryptByCert(<Certificate ID>, {'<encrypted string>'|<string variable>}
    [, '<password>'])
```

Again, any password utilized when encrypting the private key of the certificate will be needed to properly decrypt it.

DecryptByKey

Like its asymmetric and certificate-based brethren, this one decrypts a chunk of data utilizing a key. What's different is that this one not only expects a symmetric key (instead of the other types of key), but it also expects that key to already be "open" (using the OPEN SYMMETRIC KEY command). Other than that, it is fairly similar in use, with the encrypted data (either as a literal string or a string coercible variable) fed in as a parameter and, in this case, a hash key optionally accepted as an authenticator:

```
DecryptByKey({'<encrypted string>'|<string variable>},
    [<add authenticator value>, '<authentication hash>'|<string variable>])
```

Note that if you provide an add authenticator value (in the form of an int), that value must match the value supplied when the string was encrypted, and you must also supply a hash value that matches the hash supplied at encryption time.

DecryptByPassPhrase

Like the name says, this one decrypts data that was encrypted not by a formal key, but by a passphrase. Other than accepting a passphrase parameter instead of assuming an open key, DecryptByPassPhrase works almost exactly like DecryptByKey:

```
DecryptByPassPhrase({'<passphrase>'|<string variable>},
    {'<encrypted string>'|<string variable>},
    [<add authenticator value>, '<authentication hash>'|<string variable>])
```

As with DecryptByKey, if you provide an add authenticator value (in the form of an int), that value must match the value supplied when the string was encrypted, and you must also supply a hash value that matches the hash supplied at encryption time.

EncryptByAsmKey

Encrypts a chunk of data utilizing an asymmetric key. It requires the key (by ID) and the data to be encrypted (either as a literal string or a string coercible variable). The syntax is straightforward enough:

```
EncryptByAsymKey(<Asymmetric Key ID>, {'<string to encrypt>'|<string variable>})
```

EncryptByCert

This is basically the same as EncryptByAsmKey, except that it expects a certificate rather than an asymmetric key. Like EncryptByAsmKey, this one encrypts a chunk of data utilizing the provided key. It requires the certificate (by ID) and the data to be encrypted (either as a literal string or a string coercible variable). The syntax looks almost just like EncryptByAsymKey:

```
EncryptByCert(<Certificate ID>, {'<string to be encrypted>'|<string
variable>})
```

EncryptByKey

This one not only expects a symmetric key (instead of the other types of key), but it also expects that key to already be "open" (using the OPEN SYMMETRIC KEY command) and a GUID to be available to reference that key by. Other than that, it is fairly similar in use, with the data to be encrypted (either as a literal string or a string coercible variable) fed in as a parameter and, in this case, a hash key optionally accepted as an authenticator:

```
EncryptByKey({<Key GUID>, '<string to be encrypted>'|<string variable>},
    [<add authenticator value>, '<authentication hash>'|<string variable>])
```

Note that if you provide an add authenticator value (in the form of an int), that value must be supplied when the string is decrypted, and you must also supply a hash value (which again will be needed at decryption time).

EncryptByPassPhrase

This one encrypts data not by using a formal key, but by a passphrase. Other than accepting a passphrase parameter instead of assuming an open key, EncryptByPassPhrase works almost exactly like EncryptByKey:

```
EncryptByPassPhrase({'<passphrase>'|<string variable>},
    {'<string to be encrypted>'|<string variable>},
    [<add authenticator value>, '<authentication hash>'|<string variable>])
```

As with EncryptByKey, if you provide an add authenticator value (in the form of an int), that value must be supplied when the string is decrypted, and you must also supply a hash value.

Key_GUID

Fetches the GUID for a given symmetric key in the current database:

```
Key_GUID('<Key Name>')
```

Key_ID

Fetches the GUID for a given symmetric key in the current database:

```
Key_ID('<Key Name>')
```

SignByAsymKey

Adds an asymmetric key signature to a given plain text value:

```
SignByAsymKey(<Asymmetric Key ID>, <string variable> [, '<password>'])
```

SignByCert

Returns a varbinary(8000) containing the resulting signature provided a given certificate and plain text value:

```
SignByCert(<Certificate ID>, <string variable> [, '<password>'])
```

VerifySignedByAsymKey

Returns an int (though, personally I think this odd since it is functionally a bit) indicating successful or failed validation of a signature against a given asymmetric key and plain text value:

```
VerifySignedByAsymKey(<Asymmetric Key ID>, <plain text> , <signature>)
```

VerifySignedByCert

Returns an int (though, personally I think this odd since it is functionally a bit) indicating successful or failed validation of a signature against a given asymmetric key and plain text value:

```
VerifySignedByCert(<Certificate ID>, <signed plain text> , <signature>)
```

Cursor Functions

These provide various information on the status or nature of a given cursor.

@@CURSOR_ROWS

How many rows are currently in the last cursor set opened on the current connection. Note that this is for cursors, not temporary tables.

Keep in mind that this number is reset every time you open a new cursor. If you need to open more than one cursor at a time, and you need to know the number of rows in the first cursor, then you'll need to move this value into a holding variable before opening subsequent cursors.

It's possible to use this to set up a counter to control your WHILE loop when dealing with cursors, but I strongly recommend against this practice. The value contained in @@CURSOR_ROWS can change depending on the cursor type and whether or not SQL Server is populating the cursor asynchronously. Using @@FETCH_STATUS is going to be far more reliable and at least as easy to use.

If the value returned is a negative number larger than −1, then you must be working with an asynchronous cursor, and the negative number is the number of records so far created in the cursor. If, however, the value is −1, then the cursor is a dynamic cursor, in that the number of rows is constantly changing. A returned value of 0 informs you that either no cursor has been opened or the last cursor opened is no longer open. Finally, any positive number indicates the number of rows within the cursor.

To create an asynchronous cursor, set `sp_configure cursor threshold` *to a value greater than* 0. *Then, when the cursor exceeds this setting, the cursor is returned, while the remaining records are placed into the cursor asynchronously.*

@@FETCH_STATUS

Returns an indicator of the status of the last cursor FETCH operation.

If you're using cursors, you're going to be using @@FETCH_STATUS. This one is how you know the success or failure of your attempt to navigate to a record in your cursor. It will return a constant depending on whether or not SQL Server succeeded in your last FETCH operation, and, if the FETCH failed, why. The constants are:

❑   0 — Success

❑   −1 — Failed. Usually because you are beyond either the beginning or end of the cursorset.

❑   −2 — Failed. The row you were fetching wasn't found, usually because it was deleted between the time when the cursorset was created and when you navigated to the current row. Should only occur in scrollable, non-dynamic cursors.

For purposes of readability, I often will set up some constants prior to using @@FETCH_STATUS.

For example:

```
DECLARE @NOTFOUND int
DECLARE @BEGINEND int

SELECT @NOTFOUND = −2
SELECT @BEGINEND = −1
```

I can then use these in my conditional in the WHILE statement of my cursor loop instead of just the row integer. This can make the code quite a bit more readable.

CURSOR_STATUS

The CURSOR_STATUS function allows the caller of a stored procedure to determine if that procedure has returned a cursor and result set. The syntax is as follows:

```
CURSOR_STATUS
    (
        {'<local>', '<cursor name>'}
        | {'<global>', '<cursor name>'}
        | {'<variable>', '<cursor variable>'}
    )
```

local, global, and variable all specify constants that indicate the source of the cursor. Local equates to a local cursor name, global to a global cursor name, and variable to a local variable.

If you are using the `cursor name` form, then there are four possible return values:

❑   1 — The cursor is open. If the cursor is dynamic, its result set has zero or more rows. If the cursor is not dynamic, it has one or more rows.

❑   0 — The result set of the cursor is empty.

❑   −1 — The cursor is closed.

❑   −3 — A cursor of `cursor name` does not exist.

If you are using the `cursor variable` form, there are five possible return values:

❑   1 — The cursor is open. If the cursor is dynamic, its result set has zero or more rows. If the cursor is not dynamic, it has one or more rows.

❑   0 — The result set is empty.

❑   −1 — The cursor is closed.

❑   −2 — There is no cursor assigned to the `cursor variable`.

❑   −3 — The variable with name `cursor variable` does not exist, or if it does exist, has not had a cursor allocated to it yet.

Date and Time Functions

This is an area with several new items in SQL Server 2008. In addition to working with timestamp data (which is actually more oriented toward versioning than anything to do with a clock or calendar), date and time functions perform operations on values that have any of the various date and time data types supported by SQL Server.

When working with many of these functions, SQL Server recognizes eleven "dateparts" and their abbreviations, as shown in the following table:

Datepart	Abbreviations
year	yy, yyyy
quarter	qq, q
month	mm, m
dayofyear	dy, y
day	dd, d
week	wk, ww
weekday	dw
hour	hh

Continued

Datepart	Abbreviations
minute	mi, n
second	ss, s
millisecond	ms

CURRENT_TIMESTAMP

The CURRENT_TIMESTAMP function simply returns the current date and time as a datetime type. It is equivalent to GETDATE(). The syntax is as follows:

```
CURRENT_TIMESTAMP
```

DATEADD

The DATEADD function adds an interval to a date and returns a new date. The syntax is as follows:

```
DATEADD(<datepart>, <number>, <date>)
```

The datepart argument specifies the time scale of the interval (day, week, month, and so on) and may be any of the dateparts recognized by SQL Server. The number argument is the number of dateparts that should be added to the date.

DATEDIFF

The DATEDIFF function returns the difference between two specified dates in a specified unit of time (for example: hours, days, weeks). The syntax is as follows:

```
DATEDIFF(<datepart>, <startdate>, <enddate>)
```

The datepart argument may be any of the dateparts recognized by SQL Server and specifies the unit of time to be used.

DATENAME

The DATENAME function returns a string representing the name of the specified datepart (for example: 1999, Thursday, July) of the specified date. The syntax is as follows:

```
DATENAME(<datepart>, <date>)
```

DATEPART

The DATEPART function returns an integer that represents the specified datepart of the specified date. The syntax is as follows:

```
DATEPART(<datepart>, <date>)
```

The DAY function is equivalent to DATEPART(dd, <date>); MONTH is equivalent to DATEPART(mm, <date>); YEAR is equivalent to DATEPART(yy, <date>).

DAY

The DAY function returns an integer representing the day part of the specified date. The syntax is as follows:

```
DAY(<date>)
```

The DAY function is equivalent to DATEPART(dd, <date>).

GETDATE

The GETDATE function returns the current system date and time. The syntax is as follows:

```
GETDATE()
```

GETUTCDATE

The GETUTCDATE function returns the current UTC (Universal Time Coordinate) time. In other words, this returns Greenwich Mean Time. The value is derived by taking the local time from the server, and the local time zone, and calculating GMT from this. Daylight saving is included. GETUTCDATE cannot be called from a user-defined function. The syntax is as follows:

```
GETUTCDATE()
```

ISDATE

The ISDATE function determines whether an input expression is a valid date. The syntax is as follows:

```
ISDATE(<expression>)
```

MONTH

The MONTH function returns an integer that represents the month part of the specified date. The syntax is as follows:

```
MONTH(<date>)
```

The MONTH function is equivalent to DATEPART(mm, <date>).

SYSDATETIME

Much like the more venerable GETDATE function, SYSDATETIME returns the current system date and time. The differences are twofold: First, SYSDATETIME returns a higher level of precision. Second, the newer function returns the newer `datetime2` data type (to support the higher precision — a precision of 7 in this case). The syntax is as follows:

```
SYSDATETIME()
```

SYSDATETIMEOFFSET

Similar to `SYSDATETIME`, this returns the current system date and time. Instead of the simple `datetime2` data type, however, `SYSDATETIMEOFFSET` returns the time in the new `datetimeoffset` data type (with a precision of 7), thus providing offset information versus universal time. The syntax is as follows:

```
SYSDATETIMEOFFSET()
```

SYSUTCDATETIME

Much like the more venerable `GETUTCDATE` function, `SYSDATETIME` returns the current UTC date and time. `SYSDATETIME`, however, returns the newer function returns the newer `datetime2` data type (to a precision of7). The syntax is as follows:

```
SYSUTCDATETIME()
```

SWITCHOFFSET

This one accepts two arguments — an input value of type `datetimeoffset()`, and a new offset to represent the time as. The syntax looks like this:

```
SWITCHOFFSET(<datetimeoffset data instance>, <newoffset>)
```

So, if we run a quick test:

```
CREATE TABLE TimeTest
(
  MyTime   datetimeoffset
);

INSERT TimeTest
  VALUES ('2008-12-31 6:00:00 -5:00');

SELECT SWITCHOFFSET(MyTime, '-08:00') AS Pacific
FROM TimeTest;

DROP TABLE TimeTest;
```

we would get back:

```
(1 row(s) affected)
Pacific
---------------------------------
2008-12-31 03:00:00.0000000 -08:00

(1 row(s) affected)
```

TODATETIMEOFFSET

Accepts a given piece of date/time information and adds a provided time offset to produce a `datetimeoffset` data type. The syntax is:

```
TODATETIMEOFFSET(<data that resolves to datetime>, <time zone>)
```

So, for example:

```
DECLARE @OurDateTimeTest datetime;
SELECT @OurDateTimeTest = '2008-01-01 12:54';
SELECT TODATETIMEOFFSET(@OurDateTimeTest, '-07:00');
```

yields:

```
----------------------------------
1/1/2008 12:54:00 PM -07:00

(local)(sa): (1 row(s) affected)
```

YEAR

The YEAR function returns an integer that represents the year part of the specified date. The syntax is as follows:

```
YEAR(<date>)
```

The YEAR function is equivalent to DATEPART(yy, <date>).

Mathematical Functions

The mathematical functions perform calculations. They are:

- ABS
- ACOS
- ASIN
- ATAN
- ATN2
- CEILING
- COS
- COT
- DEGREES
- EXP
- FLOOR
- LOG

❑   LOG10

❑   PI

❑   POWER

❑   RADIANS

❑   RAND

❑   ROUND

❑   SIGN

❑   SIN

❑   SQRT

❑   SQUARE

❑   TAN

ABS

The ABS function returns the positive, absolute value of numeric expression. The syntax is as follows:

```
ABS(<numeric expression>)
```

ACOS

The ACOS function returns the angle in radians for which the cosine is the expression (in other words, it returns the arccosine of expression). The syntax is as follows:

```
ACOS(<expression>)
```

The value of expression must be between −1 and 1 and be of the float data type.

ASIN

The ASIN function returns the angle in radians for which the sine is the expression (in other words, it returns the arcsine of expression). The syntax is as follows:

```
ASIN(<expression>)
```

The value of expression must be between −1 and 1 and be of the float data type.

ATAN

The ATAN function returns the angle in radians for which the tangent is expression. (In other words, it returns the arctangent of expression.) The syntax is as follows:

```
ATAN(<expression>)
```

The expression must be of the float data type.

ATN2

The ATN2 function returns the angle in radians for which the tangent is between the two expressions provided. (In other words, it returns the arctangent of the two expressions.) The syntax is as follows:

```
ATN2(<expression1>, <expression2>)
```

Both expression1 and expression2 must be of the float data type.

CEILING

The CEILING function returns the smallest integer that is equal to or greater than the specified expression. The syntax is as follows:

```
CEILING(<expression>)
```

COS

The COS function returns the cosine of the angle specified in expression. The syntax is as follows:

```
COS(<expression>)
```

The angle given should be in radians and expression must be of the float data type.

COT

The COT function returns the cotangent of the angle specified in expression. The syntax is as follows:

```
COT(<expression>)
```

The angle given should be in radians and expression must be of the float data type.

DEGREES

The DEGREES function takes an angle given in radians (expression) and returns the angle in degrees. The syntax is as follows:

```
DEGREES(<expression>)
```

EXP

The EXP function returns the exponential value of the value given in expression. The syntax is as follows:

```
EXP(<expression>)
```

The expression must be of the float data type.

FLOOR

The FLOOR function returns the largest integer that is equal to or less than the value specified in expression. The syntax is as follows:

```
FLOOR(<expression>)
```

LOG

The LOG function returns the natural logarithm of the value specified in expression. The syntax is as follows:

```
LOG(<expression>)
```

The expression must be of the float data type.

LOG10

The LOG10 function returns the base10 logarithm of the value specified in expression. The syntax is as follows:

```
LOG10(<expression>)
```

The expression must be of the float data type.

PI

The PI function returns the value of the constant. The syntax is as follows:

```
PI()
```

POWER

The POWER function raises the value of the specified expression to the specified power. The syntax is as follows:

```
POWER(<expression>, <power>)
```

RADIANS

The RADIANS function returns an angle in radians corresponding to the angle in degrees specified in expression. The syntax is as follows:

```
RADIANS(<expression>)
```

RAND

The RAND function returns a random value between 0 and 1. The syntax is as follows:

```
RAND([<seed>])
```

The seed value is an integer expression, which specifies the start value. Once a seed is specified, all subsequent calls to RAND() on the current connection will choose the next value based on the original seed. If no seed is supplied, then SQL Server will use a random value as the initial seed.

Be careful if you use explicit seed values. For a given seed, you will always get the same sequence of numbers so if, for instance, you start every connection to your server with a RAND(10), then every connection's first three calls to RAND() will yield 0.713759689954247, 0.182458908613686, and 0.586642279446948 — not very random if you ask me. You can use your own randomized value, such as something based on the current time, but that still has you in a relatively finite set of starting points, so I personally recommend just starting with the SQL Server randomized value.

ROUND

The ROUND function takes a number specified in expression and rounds it to the specified length:

```
ROUND(<expression>, <length> [, <function>])
```

The length parameter specifies the precision to which expression should be rounded. The length parameter should be of the tinyint, smallint, or int data type. The optional function parameter can be used to specify whether the number should be rounded or truncated. If a function value is omitted or is equal to 0 (the default), the value in expression will be rounded. If any value other than 0 is provided, the value in expression will be truncated.

SIGN

The SIGN function returns the sign of the expression. The possible return values are +1 for a positive number, 0 for zero, and −1 for a negative number. The syntax is as follows:

```
SIGN(<expression>)
```

SIN

The SIN function returns the sine of an angle. The syntax is as follows:

```
SIN(<angle>)
```

The angle should be in radians and must be of the float data type. The return value will also be of the float data type.

SQRT

The SQRT function returns the square root of the value given in expression. The syntax is as follows:

```
SQRT(<expression>)
```

The expression must be of the float data type.

SQUARE

The SQUARE function returns the square of the value given in expression. The syntax is as follows:

```
SQUARE(<expression>)
```

The expression must be of the float data type.

TAN

The TAN function returns the tangent of the value specified in expression. The syntax is as follows:

```
TAN(<expression>)
```

The expression parameter specifies the number of radians and must be of the float or real data type.

Basic Metadata Functions

The metadata functions provide information about the database and database objects. They are:

- ❑ COL_LENGTH
- ❑ COL_NAME
- ❑ COLUMNPROPERTY
- ❑ DATABASEPROPERTY
- ❑ DATABASEPROPERTYEX
- ❑ DB_ID
- ❑ DB_NAME
- ❑ FILE_ID
- ❑ FILE_NAME
- ❑ FILEGROUP_ID
- ❑ FILEGROUP_NAME
- ❑ FILEGROUPPROPERTY
- ❑ FILEPROPERTY
- ❑ FULLTEXTCATALOGPROPERTY
- ❑ FULLTEXTSERVICEPROPERTY
- ❑ INDEX_COL
- ❑ INDEXKEY_PROPERTY
- ❑ INDEXPROPERTY
- ❑ OBJECT_ID
- ❑ OBJECT_NAME

- ❏ OBJECTPROPERTY
- ❏ OBJECTPROPERTYEX
- ❏ @@PROCID
- ❏ SCHEMA_ID
- ❏ SCHEMA_NAME
- ❏ SQL_VARIANT_PROPERTY
- ❏ TYPE_ID
- ❏ TYPE_NAME
- ❏ TYPEPROPERTY

COL_LENGTH

The COL_LENGTH function returns the defined length of a column. The syntax is as follows:

```
COL_LENGTH('<table>', '<column>')
```

The column parameter specifies the name of the column for which the length is to be determined. The table parameter specifies the name of the table that contains that column.

COL_NAME

The COL_NAME function takes a table ID number and a column ID number and returns the name of the database column. The syntax is as follows:

```
COL_NAME(<table_id>, <column_id>)
```

The column_id parameter specifies the ID number of the column. The table_id parameter specifies the ID number of the table that contains that column.

COLUMNPROPERTY

The COLUMNPROPERTY function returns data about a column or procedure parameter. The syntax is as follows:

```
COLUMNPROPERTY(<id>, <column>, <property>)
```

The id parameter specifies the ID of the table/procedure. The column parameter specifies the name of the column/parameter. The property parameter specifies the data that should be returned for the column or procedure parameter. The property parameter can be one of the following values:

- ❏ AllowsNull — Allows NULL values.
- ❏ IsComputed — The column is a computed column.
- ❏ IsCursorType — The procedure is of type CURSOR.
- ❏ IsFullTextIndexed — The column has been full-text indexed.

❏ IsIdentity — The column is an IDENTITY column.

❏ IsIdNotForRepl — The column checks for IDENTITY NOT FOR REPLICATION.

❏ IsOutParam — The procedure parameter is an output parameter.

❏ IsRowGuidCol — The column is a ROWGUIDCOL column.

❏ Precision — The precision for the data type of the column or parameter.

❏ Scale — The scale for the data type of the column or parameter.

❏ UseAnsiTrim — The ANSI padding setting was ON when the table was created.

The return value from this function will be 1 for True, 0 for False, and NULL if the input was not valid — except for Precision (where the precision for the data type will be returned) and Scale (where the scale will be returned).

DATABASEPROPERTY

The DATABASEPROPERTY function returns the setting for the specified database and property name. The syntax is as follows:

```
DATABASEPROPERTY('<database>', '<property>')
```

The database parameter specifies the name of the database for which data on the named property will be returned. The property parameter contains the name of a database property and can be one of the following values:

❏ IsAnsiNullDefault — The database follows the ANSI-92 standard for NULL values.

❏ IsAnsiNullsEnabled — All comparisons made with a NULL cannot be evaluated.

❏ IsAnsiWarningsEnabled — Warning messages are issued when standard error conditions occur.

❏ IsAutoClose — The database frees resources after the last user has exited.

❏ IsAutoShrink — Database files can be shrunk automatically and periodically.

❏ IsAutoUpdateStatistics — The autoupdate statistics option has been enabled.

❏ IsBulkCopy — The database allows nonlogged operations (such as those performed with the Bulk Copy Program).

❏ IsCloseCursorsOnCommitEnabled — Any cursors that are open when a transaction is committed will be closed.

❏ IsDboOnly — The database is only accessible to the dbo.

❏ IsDetached — The database was detached by a detach operation.

❏ IsEmergencyMode — The database is in emergency mode.

❏ IsFulltextEnabled — The database has been full-text enabled.

❏ IsInLoad — The database is loading.

❏ IsInRecovery — The database is recovering.

- ❑   `IsInStandby` — The database is read-only and restore log is allowed.

- ❑   `IsLocalCursorsDefault` — Cursor declarations default to `LOCAL`.

- ❑   `IsNotRecovered` — The database failed to recover.

- ❑   `IsNullConcat` — Concatenating to a `NULL` results in a `NULL`.

- ❑   `IsOffline` — The database is offline.

- ❑   `IsQuotedIdentifiersEnabled` — Identifiers can be delimited by double quotation marks.

- ❑   `IsReadOnly` — The database is in a read-only mode.

- ❑   `IsRecursiveTriggersEnabled` — The recursive firing of triggers is enabled.

- ❑   `IsShutDown` — The database encountered a problem during startup.

- ❑   `IsSingleUser` — The database is in single-user mode.

- ❑   `IsSuspect` — The database is suspect.

- ❑   `IsTruncLog` — The database truncates its logon checkpoints.

- ❑   `Version` — The internal version number of the SQL Server code with which the database was created.

The return value from this function will be 1 for true, 0 for false, and `NULL` if the input was not valid, except for `Version` (where the function will return the version number if the database is open and `NULL` if the database is closed).

DATABASEPROPERTYEX

The `DATABASEPROPERTYEX` function is basically a superset of `DATABASEPROPERTY`, and also returns the setting for the specified database and property name. The syntax is pretty much just the same as `DATABASEPROPERTY` and is as follows:

```
DATABASEPROPERTYEX('<database>', '<property>')
```

`DATABASEPROPERTYEX` just has a few more properties available, including:

- ❑   `Collation` — Returns the default collation for the database (remember, collations can also be overridden at the column level).

- ❑   `ComparisonStyle` — Indicates the Windows comparison style (for example, case sensitivity) of the particular collation.

- ❑   `IsAnsiPaddingEnabled` — Whether strings are padded to the same length before comparison or insert.

- ❑   `IsArithmaticAbortEnabled` — Whether queries are terminated when a major arithmetic error (such as a data overflow) occurs.

The `database` parameter specifies the name of the database for which data on the named property will be returned. The `property` parameter contains the name of a database property and can be one of the following values.

DB_ID

The DB_ID function returns the database ID number. The syntax is as follows:

```
DB_ID(['<database_name>'])
```

The optional database_name parameter specifies which database's ID number is required. If the database_name is not given, the current database will be used instead.

DB_NAME

The DB_NAME function returns the name of the database that has the specified ID number. The syntax is as follows:

```
DB_NAME([<database_id>])
```

The optional database_id parameter specifies which database's name is to be returned. If no database_id is given, the name of the current database will be returned.

FILE_ID

The FILE_ID function returns the file ID number for the specified file name in the current database. The syntax is as follows:

```
FILE_ID('<file_name>')
```

The file_name parameter specifies the name of the file for which the ID is required.

FILE_NAME

The FILE_NAME function returns the file name for the file with the specified file ID number. The syntax is as follows:

```
FILE_NAME(<file_id>)
```

The file_id parameter specifies the ID number of the file for which the name is required.

FILEGROUP_ID

The FILEGROUP_ID function returns the filegroup ID number for the specified filegroup name. The syntax is as follows:

```
FILEGROUP_ID('<filegroup_name>')
```

The filegroup_name parameter specifies the filegroup name of the required filegroup ID.

FILEGROUP_NAME

The FILEGROUP_NAME function returns the filegroup name for the specified filegroup ID number. The syntax is as follows:

```
FILEGROUP_NAME(<filegroup_id>)
```

The filegroup_id parameter specifies the filegroup ID of the required filegroup name.

FILEGROUPPROPERTY

The FILEGROUPPROPERTY returns the setting of a specified filegroup property, given the filegroup and property name. The syntax is as follows:

```
FILEGROUPPROPERTY(<filegroup_name>, <property>)
```

The filegroup_name parameter specifies the name of the filegroup that contains the property being queried. The property parameter specifies the property being queried and can be one of the following values:

❏   IsReadOnly — The filegroup name is read-only.

❏   IsUserDefinedFG — The filegroup name is a user-defined filegroup.

❏   IsDefault — The filegroup name is the default filegroup.

The return value from this function will be 1 for True, 0 for False, and NULL if the input was not valid.

FILEPROPERTY

The FILEPROPERTY function returns the setting of a specified file name property, given the file name and property name. The syntax is as follows:

```
FILEPROPERTY(<file_name>, <property>)
```

The file_name parameter specifies the name of the filegroup that contains the property being queried. The property parameter specifies the property being queried and can be one of the following values:

❏   IsReadOnly — The file is read-only.

❏   IsPrimaryFile — The file is the primary file.

❏   IsLogFile — The file is a log file.

❏   SpaceUsed — The amount of space used by the specified file.

The return value from this function will be 1 for True, 0 for False, and NULL if the input was not valid, except for SpaceUsed (which will return the number of pages allocated in the file).

FULLTEXTCATALOGPROPERTY

The FULLTEXTCATALOGPROPERTY function returns data about the full-text catalog properties. The syntax is as follows:

```
FULLTEXTCATALOGPROPERTY(<catalog_name>, <property>)
```

The catalog_name parameter specifies the name of the full-text catalog. The property parameter specifies the property that is being queried. The properties that can be queried are:

- ❏ PopulateStatus — For which the possible return values are: 0 (idle), 1 (population in progress), 2 (paused), 3 (throttled), 4 (recovering), 5 (shutdown), 6 (incremental population in progress), 7 (updating index).

- ❏ ItemCount — Returns the number of full-text indexed items currently in the full-text catalog.

- ❏ IndexSize — Returns the size of the full-text index in megabytes.

- ❏ UniqueKeyCount — Returns the number of unique words that make up the full-text index in this catalog.

- ❏ LogSize — Returns the size (in bytes) of the combined set of error logs associated with a full-text catalog.

- ❏ PopulateCompletionAge — Returns the difference (in seconds) between the completion of the last full-text index population and 01/01/1990 00:00:00.

FULLTEXTSERVICEPROPERTY

The FULLTEXTSERVICEPROPERTY function returns data about the full-text service-level properties. The syntax is as follows:

```
FULLTEXTSERVICEPROPERTY(<property>)
```

The property parameter specifies the name of the service-level property that is to be queried. The property parameter may be one of the following values:

- ❏ ResourceUsage — Returns a value from 1 (background) to 5 (dedicated).

- ❏ ConnectTimeOut — Returns the number of seconds that the Search Service will wait for all connections to SQL Server for full-text index population before timing out.

- ❏ IsFulltextInstalled — Returns 1 if Full-Text Service is installed on the computer and a 0 otherwise.

INDEX_COL

The INDEX_COL function returns the indexed column name. The syntax is as follows:

```
INDEX_COL('<table>', <index_id>, <key_id>)
```

The table parameter specifies the name of the table, index_id specifies the ID of the index, and key_id specifies the ID of the key.

INDEXKEY_PROPERTY

This function returns information about the index key.

```
INDEXKEY_PROPERTY(<table_id>, <index_id>, <key_id>, <property>)
```

The table_id parameter is the numerical ID of data type int, which defines the table you wish to inspect. Use OBJECT_ID to find the numerical table_id. index_id specifies the ID of the index, and is also of data type int. key_id specifies the index column position of the key; for example, with a key of three columns, setting this value to 2 will determine that you are wishing to inspect the middle column. Finally, the property is the character string identifier of one of two properties you wish to find the setting of. The two possible values are ColumnId, which will return the physical column ID, and IsDescending, which returns the order that the column is sorted (1 is for descending and 0 is ascending).

INDEXPROPERTY

The INDEXPROPERTY function returns the setting of a specified index property, given the table ID, index name, and property name. The syntax is as follows:

```
INDEXPROPERTY(<table_ID>, <index>, <property>)
```

The property parameter specifies the property of the index that is to be queried. The property parameter can be one of these possible values:

- ❑ IndexDepth — The depth of the index.
- ❑ IsAutoStatistic — The index was created by the autocreate statistics option of sp_dboption.
- ❑ IsClustered — The index is clustered.
- ❑ IsStatistics — The index was created by the CREATE STATISTICS statement or by the autocreate statistics option of sp_dboption.
- ❑ IsUnique — The index is unique.
- ❑ IndexFillFactor — The index specifies its own fill factor.
- ❑ IsPadIndex — The index specifies space to leave open on each interior node.
- ❑ IsFulltextKey — The index is the full-text key for a table.
- ❑ IsHypothetical — The index is hypothetical and cannot be used directly as a data access path.

The return value from this function will be 1 for True, 0 for False, and NULL if the input was not valid, except for IndexDepth (which will return the number of levels the index has) and IndexFillFactor (which will return the fill factor used when the index was created or last rebuilt).

OBJECT_ID

The OBJECT_ID function returns the specified database object's ID number. The syntax is as follows:

```
OBJECT_ID('<object>')
```

OBJECT_NAME

The OBJECT_NAME function returns the name of the specified database object. The syntax is as follows:

```
OBJECT_NAME(<object_id>)
```

OBJECTPROPERTY

The OBJECTPROPERTY function returns data about objects in the current database. The syntax is as follows:

```
OBJECTPROPERTY(<id>, <property>)
```

The id parameter specifies the ID of the object required. The property parameter specifies the information required on the object. The following property values are allowed:

CnstIsClustKey	ExecIsTriggerDisabled
CnstIsColumn	ExecIsTriggerNotForRepl
CnstIsDeleteCascade	ExecIsUpdateTrigger
CnstIsDisabled	HasAfterTrigger
CnstIsNonclustKey	HasDeleteTrigger
CnstIsNotRepl	HasInsertTrigger
CnstIsNotTrusted	HasInsteadOfTrigger
CnstIsUpdateCascade	HasUpdateTrigger
ExecIsAfterTrigger	IsAnsiNullsOn
ExecIsAnsiNullsOn	IsCheckCnst
ExecIsDeleteTrigger	IsConstraint
ExecIsFirstDeleteTrigger	IsDefault
ExecIsFirstInsertTrigger	IsDefaultCnst
ExecIsFirstUpdateTrigger	IsDeterministic
ExecIsInsertTrigger	IsExecuted
ExecIsInsteadOfTrigger	IsExtendedProc
ExecIsLastDeleteTrigger	IsForeignKey
ExecIsLastInsertTrigger	IsIndexed
ExecIsLastUpdateTrigger	IsIndexable
ExecIsQuotedIdentOn	IsInlineFunction
ExecIsStartup	IsMSShipped

IsPrimaryKey	TableFulltextPopulateStatus
IsProcedure	TableHasActiveFulltextIndex
IsQuotedIdentOn	TableHasCheckCnst
IsQueue	TableHasClustIndex
IsReplProc	TableHasDefaultCnst
IsRule	TableHasDeleteTrigger
IsScalarFunction	TableHasForeignKey
IsSchemaBound	TableHasForeignRef
IsSystemTable	TableHasIdentity
IsTable	TableHasIndex
IsTableFunction	TableHasInsertTrigger
IsTrigger	TableHasNonclustIndex
IsUniqueCnst	TableHasPrimaryKey
IsUserTable	TableHasRowGuidCol
IsView	TableHasTextImage
OwnerId	TableHasTimestamp
TableDeleteTrigger	TableHasUniqueCnst
TableDeleteTriggerCount	TableHasUpdateTrigger
TableFullTextBackgroundUpdateIndexOn	TableInsertTrigger
TableFulltextCatalogId	TableInsertTriggerCount
TableFullTextChangeTrackingOn	TableIsFake
TableFulltextDocsProcessed	TableIsLockedOnBulkLoad
TableFulltextFailCount	TableIsPinned
TableFulltextItemCount	TableTextInRowLimit
TableFulltextKeyColumn	TableUpdateTrigger
TableFulltextPendingChanges	TableUpdateTriggerCount

The return value from this function will be 1 for True, 0 for False, and NULL if the input was not valid, except for:

❑ OwnerId — Returns the database user ID of the owner of that object — note that this is different from the SchemaID of the object and will likely not be that useful in SQL Server 2005 and beyond.

- ❑ `TableDeleteTrigger`, `TableInsertTrigger`, `TableUpdateTrigger` — Return the ID of the first trigger with the specified type. Zero is returned if no trigger of that type exists.

- ❑ `TableDeleteTriggerCount`, `TableInsertTriggerCount`, `TableUpdateTriggerCount` — Return the number of the specified type of trigger that exists for the table in question.

- ❑ `TableFulltextCatalogId` — Returns the ID of the full-text catalog if there is one, and zero if no full-text catalog exists for that table.

- ❑ `TableFulltextKeyColumn` — Returns the ColumnID of the column being utilized as the unique index for that full-text index.

- ❑ `TableFulltextPendingChanges` — The number of entries that have changed since the last full-text analysis was run for this table. Change tracking must be enabled for this function to return useful results.

- ❑ `TableFulltextPopulateStatus` — This one has multiple possible return values:

  - ❑ `0` — Indicates that the full-text process is currently idle.

  - ❑ `1` — A full population run is currently in progress.

  - ❑ `2` — An incremental population is currently running.

  - ❑ `3` — Changes are currently being analyzed and added to the full-text catalog.

  - ❑ `4` — Some form of background update (such as that done by the automatic change tracking mechanism) is currently running.

  - ❑ `5` — A full-text operation is in progress, but has either been throttled (to allow other system requests to perform as needed) or has been paused.

- ❑ You can use the feedback from this option to make decisions about what other full-text-related options are appropriate (to check whether a population is in progress so you know whether other functions, such as `TableFulltextDocsProcessed`, are valid).

- ❑ `TableFulltextDocsProcessed` — Valid only while full-text indexing is actually running, this returns the number of rows processed since the full-text index processing task started. A zero result indicates that full-text indexing is not currently running (a null result means full-text indexing is not configured for this table).

- ❑ `TableFulltextFailCount` — Valid only while full-text indexing is actually running, this returns the number of rows that full-text indexing has, for some reason, skipped (no indication of reason). As with `TableFulltextDocsProcessed`, a zero result indicates the table is not currently being analyzed for full text, and a null indicates that full text is not configured for this table.

- ❑ `TableIsPinned` — This is left in for backward compatibility only and will always return "0" in SQL Server 2005 and beyond.

OBJECTPROPERTYEX

OBJECTPROPERTYEX is an extended version of the OBJECTPROPERTY function.

```
OBJECTPROPERTYEX(<id>, <property>)
```

Like OBJECTPROPERTY, the id parameter specifies the ID of the object required. The property parameter specifies the information required on the object. OBJECTPROPERTYEX supports all the same property values as OBJECTPROPERTY but adds the following property values as additional options:

❑ BaseType — Returns the base data type of an object.

❑ IsPrecise — Indicates that your object does not contain any imprecise computations. For example an int or decimal is precise, but a float is not. Computations that utilize imprecise data types must be assumed to return imprecise results. Note that you can specifically mark any .NET assemblies you produce as being precise or not.

❑ IsSystemVerified — Indicates whether the IsPrecise and IsDeterministic properties can be verified by SQL Server itself (as opposed to just having been set by the user).

❑ SchemaId — Just what it sounds like. Returns the internal system ID for a given object. You can then use SCHEMA_NAME to put a more user-friendly name on the schema ID.

❑ SystemDataAccess — Indicates whether the object in question relies on any system table data.

❑ UserDataAccess — Indicates whether the object in question utilizes any of the user tables or system user data.

@@PROCID

Returns the stored procedure ID of the currently running procedure.

Primarily a troubleshooting tool when a process is running and using up a large amount of resources. Is used mainly as a DBA function.

SCHEMA_ID

Given a schema name, returns the internal system ID for that schema. Utilizes the syntax:

```
SCHEMA_ID( <schema name> )
```

SCHEMA_NAME

Given an internal schema system ID, returns the user-friendly name for that schema. The syntax is:

```
SCHEMA_NAME( <schema id> )
```

SQL_VARIANT_PROPERTY

SQL_VARIANT_PROPERTY is a powerful function and returns information about a sql_variant. This information could be from BaseType, Precision, Scale, TotalBytes, Collation, MaxLength. The syntax is:

```
SQL_VARIANT_PROPERTY (expression, property)
```

Expression is an expression of type sql_variant. Property can be any one of the following values:

Value	Description	Base Type of sql_variant Returned
BaseType	Data types include: char, int, money, nchar, ntext, numeric, nvarchar, real, smalldatetime, smallint, smallmoney, text, timestamp, tinyint, uniqueidentifier, varbinary, varchar	sysname
Precision	The precision of the numeric base data type: datetime = 23 smalldatetime = 16 float = 53 real = 24 decimal (p,s) and numeric (p,s) = p money = 19 smallmoney = 10 int = 10 smallint = 5 tinyint = 3 bit = 1 All other types = 0	int
Scale	The number of digits to the right of the decimal point of the numeric base data type: decimal (p,s) and numeric (p,s) = s money and smallmoney = 4 datetime = 3 All other types = 0	int
TotalBytes	The number of bytes required to hold both the metadata and data of the value. If the value is greater than 900, index creation will fail.	int
Collation	The collation of the particular sql_variant value.	sysname
MaxLength	The maximum data type length, in bytes.	int

TYPEPROPERTY

The TYPEPROPERTY function returns information about a data type. The syntax is as follows:

```
TYPEPROPERTY(<type>, <property>)
```

The type parameter specifies the name of the data type. The property parameter specifies the property of the data type that is to be queried; it can be one of the following values:

- ❑ Precision — Returns the number of digits/characters.
- ❑ Scale — Returns the number of decimal places.

❑ AllowsNull — Returns 1 for True and 0 for False.

❑ UsesAnsiTrim — Returns 1 for True and 0 for False.

Rowset Functions

The rowset functions return an object that can be used in place of a table reference in a T-SQL statement. The rowset functions are:

❑ CHANGETABLE

❑ CONTAINSTABLE

❑ FREETEXTTABLE

❑ OPENDATASOURCE

❑ OPENQUERY

❑ OPENROWSET

❑ OPENXML

CHANGETABLE

```
CHANGETABLE (
      {    CHANGES <table> , <last sync version>
        | VERSION <table> , <primary key values> } )
[AS] <table alias> [ ( <column alias> [ ,...n ] )
```

Returns all rows in the specified table since the point specified in the "last sync version" argument.

CONTAINSTABLE

The CONTAINSTABLE function is used in full-text queries. Please refer to Chapter 18 for an example of its usage. The syntax is as follows:

```
CONTAINSTABLE (<table>, {<column> | *}, '<contains_search_condition>')
```

FREETEXTTABLE

The FREETEXTTABLE function is used in full-text queries. Please refer to Chapter 18 for an example of its usage. The syntax is as follows:

```
FREETEXTTABLE (<table>, {<column> | *}, '<freetext_string>')
```

OPENDATASOURCE

The OPENDATASOURCE function provides ad hoc connection information. The syntax is as follows:

```
OPENDATASOURCE (<provider_name>, <init_string>)
```

The `provider_name` is the name registered as the ProgID of the OLE DB provider used to access the data source. The `init_string` should be familiar to VB programmers, as this is the initialization string to the OLE DB provider. For example, the `init_string` could look like:

```
"User Id=wonderison;Password=JuniorBlues;DataSource=MyServerName"
```

OPENQUERY

The `OPENQUERY` function executes the specified pass-through `query` on the specified `linked_server`. The syntax is as follows:

```
OPENQUERY(<linked_server>, '<query>')
```

OPENROWSET

The `OPENROWSET` function accesses remote data from an OLE DB data source. The syntax is as follows:

```
OPENROWSET('<provider_name>'
    {
     '<datasource>';'<user_id>';'<password>'
     | '<provider_string>'
    },
    {
        [<catalog.>][<schema.>]<object>
        | '<query>'
    })
```

The `provider_name` parameter is a string representing the friendly name of the OLE DB provided as specified in the registry. The `data_source` parameter is a string corresponding to the required OLE DB data source. The `user_id` parameter is a relevant username to be passed to the OLE DB provider. The `password` parameter is the password associated with the `user_id`.

The `provider_string` parameter is a provider-specific connection string and is used in place of the `datasource`, `user_id`, and `password` combination.

The `catalog` parameter is the name of the catalog/database that contains the required object. The `schema` parameter is the name of the schema or object owner of the required object. The `object` parameter is the object name.

The `query` parameter is a string that is executed by the provider and is used instead of a combination of `catalog`, `schema`, and `object`.

OPENXML

By passing in an XML document as a parameter, or by retrieving an XML document and defining the document within a variable, `OPENXML` allows you to inspect the structure and return data, as if the XML document were a table. The syntax is as follows:

```
OPENXML(<idoc_int> [in],<rowpattern> nvarchar[in],[<flags> byte[in]])
[WITH (<SchemaDeclaration> | <TableName>)]
```

The `idoc_int` parameter is the variable defined using the `sp_xml_prepareddocument` system sproc. `Rowpattern` is the node definition. The `flags` parameter specifies the mapping between the XML document and the rowset to return within the `SELECT` statement. `SchemaDeclaration` defines the XML schema for the XML document; if there is a table defined within the database that follows the XML schema, then `TableName` can be used instead.

Before being able to use the XML document, it must be prepared by using the `sp_xml_prepareddocument` system procedure.

Security Functions

The security functions return information about users and roles. They are:

- ❏   HAS_DBACCESS
- ❏   IS_MEMBER
- ❏   IS_SRVROLEMEMBER
- ❏   SUSER_ID
- ❏   SUSER_NAME
- ❏   SUSER_SID
- ❏   USER
- ❏   USER_ID
- ❏   USER_NAME

HAS_DBACCESS

The `HAS_DBACCESS` function is used to determine whether the user that is logged in has access to the database being used. A return value of 1 means the user does have access, and a return value of 0 means that he or she does not. A `NULL` return value means the `database_name` supplied was invalid. The syntax is as follows:

```
HAS_DBACCESS ('<database_name>')
```

IS_MEMBER

The `IS_MEMBER` function returns whether the current user is a member of the specified Windows NT group/SQL Server role. The syntax is as follows:

```
IS_MEMBER ({'<group>' | '<role>'})
```

The `group` parameter specifies the name of the NT group and must be in the form `domain\group`. The `role` parameter specifies the name of the SQL Server role. The role can be a database fixed role or a user-defined role but cannot be a server role.

This function will return a 1 if the current user is a member of the specified group or role, a 0 if the current user is not a member of the specified group or role, and `NULL` if the specified group or role is invalid.

IS_SRVROLEMEMBER

The IS_SRVROLEMEMBER function returns whether a user is a member of the specified server role. The syntax is as follows:

```
IS_SRVROLEMEMBER ('<role>' [,'<login>'])
```

The optional login parameter is the name of the login account to check. The default is the current user. The role parameter specifies the server role and must be one of the following possible values:

- sysadmin
- dbcreator
- diskadmin
- processadmin
- serveradmin
- setupadmin
- securityadmin

This function returns a 1 if the specified login account is a member of the specified role, a 0 if the login is not a member of the role, and a NULL if the role or login is invalid.

SUSER_ID

The SUSER_ID function returns the specified user's login ID number. The syntax is as follows:

```
SUSER_ID(['<login>'])
```

The login parameter is the specified user's login ID name. If no value for login is provided, the default of the current user will be used instead.

The SUSER_ID system function is included in SQL Server 2000 for backward compatibility, so if possible you should use SUSER_SID, which is inherently more secure, instead.

SUSER_NAME

The SUSER_NAME function returns the specified user's login ID name. The syntax is as follows:

```
SUSER_NAME([<server_user_id>])
```

The server_user_id parameter is the specified user's login ID number. If no value for server_user_id is provided, the default of the current user will be used instead.

The SUSER_NAME system function is included in SQL Server 2000 for backward compatibility only, so if possible you should use SUSER_SNAME instead.

SUSER_SID

The SUSER_SID function returns the security identification number (SID) for the specified user. The syntax is as follows:

```
SUSER_SID(['<login>'])
```

The login parameter is the user's login name. If no value for login is provided, the current user will be used instead.

SUSER_SNAME

The SUSER_SNAME function returns the login ID name for the specified security identification number (SID). The syntax is as follows:

```
SUSER_SNAME([<server_user_sid>])
```

The server_user_sid parameter is the user's SID. If no value for the server_user_sid is provided, the current user's will be used instead.

USER

The USER function allows a system-supplied value for the current user's database username to be inserted into a table if no default has been supplied. The syntax is as follows:

```
USER
```

USER_ID

The USER_ID function returns the specified user's database ID number. The syntax is as follows:

```
USER_ID(['<user>'])
```

The user parameter is the username to be used. If no value for user is provided, the current user is used.

USER_NAME

The USER_NAME function is the functional reverse of USER_ID, and returns the specified user's username in the database given a database ID number. The syntax is as follows:

```
USER_NAME(['<user id>'])
```

The user id parameter is the id of the user you want the name for. If no value for user id is provided, the current user is assumed.

String Functions

The string functions perform actions on string values and return strings or numeric values. The string functions are:

- ❑ ASCII
- ❑ CHAR
- ❑ CHARINDEX
- ❑ DIFFERENCE
- ❑ LEFT
- ❑ LEN
- ❑ LOWER
- ❑ LTRIM
- ❑ NCHAR
- ❑ PATINDEX
- ❑ QUOTENAME
- ❑ REPLACE
- ❑ REPLICATE
- ❑ REVERSE
- ❑ RIGHT
- ❑ RTRIM
- ❑ SOUNDEX
- ❑ SPACE
- ❑ STR
- ❑ STUFF
- ❑ SUBSTRING
- ❑ UNICODE
- ❑ UPPER

ASCII

The ASCII function returns the ASCII code value of the leftmost character in character_expression. The syntax is as follows:

```
ASCII(<character_expression>)
```

CHAR

The CHAR function converts an ASCII code (specified in expression) into a string. The syntax is as follows:

```
CHAR(<expression>)
```

The expression can be any integer between 0 and 255.

CHARINDEX

The CHARINDEX function returns the starting position of an expression in a character_string. The syntax is as follows:

```
CHARINDEX(<expression>, <character_string> [, <start_location>])
```

The expression parameter is the string to be found. The character_string is the string to be searched, usually a column. The start_location is the character position to begin the search; if this is anything other than a positive number, the search will begin at the start of character_string.

DIFFERENCE

The DIFFERENCE function returns the difference between the SOUNDEX values of two expressions as an integer. The syntax is as follows:

```
DIFFERENCE(<expression1>, <expression2>)
```

This function returns an integer value between 0 and 4. If the two expressions sound identical (for example, blue and blew) a value of 4 will be returned. If there is no similarity, a value of 0 is returned.

LEFT

The LEFT function returns the leftmost part of an expression, starting a specified number of characters from the left. The syntax is as follows:

```
LEFT(<expression>, <integer>)
```

The expression parameter contains the character data from which the leftmost section will be extracted. The integer parameter specifies the number of characters from the left to begin; it must be a positive integer.

LEN

The LEN function returns the number of characters in the specified expression. The syntax is as follows:

```
LEN(<expression>)
```

LOWER

The LOWER function converts any uppercase characters in the expression into lowercase characters. The syntax is as follows:

```
LOWER(<expression>)
```

LTRIM

The LTRIM function removes any leading blanks from a character_expression. The syntax is as follows:

```
LTRIM(<character expression>)
```

NCHAR

The NCHAR function returns the Unicode character that has the specified integer_code. The syntax is as follows:

```
NCHAR(<integer code>)
```

The integer_code parameter must be a positive whole number from 0 to 65,535.

PATINDEX

The PATINDEX function returns the starting position of the first occurrence of a pattern in a specified expression or zero if the pattern was not found. The syntax is as follows:

```
PATINDEX('<%pattern%>', <expression>)
```

The pattern parameter is a string that will be searched for. Wildcard characters can be used, but the % characters must surround the pattern. The expression parameter is character data in which the pattern is being searched for — usually a column.

QUOTENAME

The QUOTENAME function returns a Unicode string with delimiters added to make the specified string a valid SQL Server delimited identifier. The syntax is as follows:

```
QUOTENAME('<character string>'[, '<quote character>'])
```

The character_string parameter is Unicode string. The quote_character parameter is a one-character string that will be used as a delimiter. The quote_character parameter can be a single quotation mark ('), a left or a right bracket ([]), or a double quotation mark ("). The default is for brackets to be used.

REPLACE

The REPLACE function replaces all instances of the second specified string in the first specified string with a third specified string. The syntax is as follows:

```
REPLACE('<string expression1>', '<string expression2>', '<string expression3>')
```

The string_expression1 parameter is the expression in which to search. The string_expression2 parameter is the expression to search for in string_expression1. The string_expression3 parameter is the expression with which to replace all instances of string _expression2.

REPLICATE

The REPLICATE function repeats a character_expression a specified number of times. The syntax is as follows:

```
REPLICATE(<character expression>, <integer>)
```

REVERSE

The REVERSE function returns the reverse of the specified character_expression. The syntax is as follows:

```
REVERSE(<character expression>)
```

RIGHT

The RIGHT function returns the rightmost part of the specified character_expression, starting a specified number of characters (given by integer) from the right. The syntax is as follows:

```
RIGHT(<character expression>, <integer>)
```

The integer parameter must be a positive whole number.

RTRIM

The RTRIM function removes all the trailing blanks from a specified character_expression. The syntax is as follows:

```
RTRIM(<character expression>)
```

SOUNDEX

The SOUNDEX function returns a four-character (SOUNDEX) code, which can be used to evaluate the similarity of two strings. The syntax is as follows:

```
SOUNDEX(<character expression>)
```

SPACE

The SPACE function returns a string of repeated spaces, the length of which is indicated by integer. The syntax is as follows:

```
SPACE(<integer>)
```

STR

The STR function converts numeric data into character data. The syntax is as follows:

```
STR(<numeric expression>[, <length>[, <decimal>]])
```

The numeric_expression parameter is a numeric expression with a decimal point. The length parameter is the total length including decimal point, digits, and spaces. The decimal parameter is the number of places to the right of the decimal point.

STUFF

The STUFF function deletes a specified length of characters and inserts another set of characters in their place. The syntax is as follows:

```
STUFF(<expression>, <start>, <length>, <characters>)
```

The expression parameter is the string of characters in which some will be deleted and new ones added. The start parameter specifies where to begin deletion and insertion of characters. The length parameter specifies the number of characters to delete. The characters parameter specifies the new set of characters to be inserted into the expression.

SUBSTRING

The SUBSTRING function returns part of an expression. The syntax is as follows:

```
SUBSTRING(<expression>, <start>, <length>)
```

The expression parameter specifies the data from which the substring will be taken, and can be a character string, binary string, text, or an expression that includes a table. The start parameter is an integer that specifies where to begin the substring. The length parameter specifies how long the substring is.

UNICODE

The UNICODE function returns the Unicode number that represents the first character in character_expression. The syntax is as follows:

```
UNICODE('<character expression>')
```

UPPER

The UPPER function converts all the lowercase characters in character_expression into uppercase characters. The syntax is as follows:

```
UPPER(<character expression>)
```

System Functions

The system functions can be used to return information about values, objects, and settings with SQL Server. The functions are as follows:

- APP_NAME
- CASE
- CAST and CONVERT
- COALESCE
- COLLATIONPROPERTY
- CURRENT_TIMESTAMP
- CURRENT_USER
- DATALENGTH
- FORMATMESSAGE
- GETANSINULL
- HOST_ID
- HOST_NAME
- IDENT_CURRENT
- IDENT_INCR
- IDENT_SEED
- IDENTITY
- ISDATE
- ISNULL
- ISNUMERIC

- ❑ NEWID
- ❑ NULLIF
- ❑ PARSENAME
- ❑ PERMISSIONS
- ❑ ROWCOUNT_BIG
- ❑ SCOPE_IDENTITY
- ❑ SERVERPROPERTY
- ❑ SESSION_USER
- ❑ SESSIONPROPERTY
- ❑ STATS_DATE
- ❑ SYSTEM_USER
- ❑ USER_NAME

APP_NAME

The APP_NAME function returns the application name for the current session if one has been set by the application as an nvarchar type. It has the following syntax:

```
APP_NAME()
```

CASE

The CASE function evaluates a list of conditions and returns one of multiple possible results. It also has two formats:

- ❑ The simple CASE function compares an expression to a set of simple expressions to determine the result.
- ❑ The searched CASE function evaluates a set of Boolean expressions to determine the result.

Both formats support an optional ELSE argument.

Simple CASE function:

```
CASE <input_expression>
    WHEN <when_expression> THEN <result_expression>
    ELSE <else_result_expression>
END
```

Searched CASE function:

```
CASE
    WHEN <Boolean_expression> THEN <result_expression>
```

```
        ELSE <else_result_expression>
    END
```

CAST and CONVERT

These two functions provide similar functionality in that they both convert one data type into another type.

Using CAST:

```
CAST(<expression> AS <data_type>)
```

Using CONVERT:

```
CONVERT (<data_type>[(<length>)], <expression> [, <style>])
```

where style refers to the style of date format when converting to a character data type.

COALESCE

The COALESCE function is passed an undefined number of arguments and it tests for the first non-null expression among them. The syntax is as follows:

```
COALESCE(<expression> [,...n])
```

If all arguments are NULL then COALESCE returns NULL.

COLLATIONPROPERTY

The COLLATIONPROPERTY function returns the property of a given collation. The syntax is as follows:

```
COLLATIONPROPERTY(<collation_name>, <property>)
```

The collation_name parameter is the name of the collation you wish to use, and property is the property of the collation you wish to determine. This can be one of three values:

Property Name	Description
CodePage	The non-Unicode code page of the collation.
LCID	The Windows LCID of the collation. Returns NULL for SQL collations.
ComparisonStyle	The Windows comparison style of the collation. Returns NULL for binary or SQL collations.

CURRENT_USER

The CURRENT_USER function simply returns the current user as a sysname type. It is equivalent to USER_NAME(). The syntax is as follows:

```
CURRENT_USER
```

DATALENGTH

The DATALENGTH function returns the number of bytes used to represent expression as an integer. It is especially useful with varchar, varbinary, text, image, nvarchar, and ntext data types because these data types can store variable-length data. The syntax is as follows:

```
DATALENGTH(<expression>)
```

@@ERROR

Returns the error code for the last T-SQL statement that ran on the current connection. If there is no error, then the value will be zero.

If you're going to be writing stored procedures or triggers, this is a bread-and-butter kind of system function. You pretty much can't live without it.

The thing to remember with @@ERROR is that its lifespan is just one statement. This means that, if you want to use it to check for an error after a given statement, then you either need to make your test the very next statement, or you need to move it into a holding variable. In general, I recommend using ERROR_NUMBER() in a TRY ... CATCH block unless you need to support pre SQL Server 2005 code.

A listing of all the system errors can be viewed by using the sys.messages system table in the master database.

To create your own custom errors, use sp_addmessage.

FORMATMESSAGE

The FORMATMESSAGE function uses existing messages in sysmessages to construct a message. The syntax is as follows:

```
FORMATMESSAGE(<msg_number>, <param_value>[,...n])
```

where msg_number is the ID of the message in sysmessages.

FORMATMESSAGE looks up the message in the current language of the user. If there is no localized version of the message, the U.S. English version is used.

GETANSINULL

The GETANSINULL function returns the default nullability for a database as an integer. The syntax is as follows:

```
GETANSINULL(['<database>'])
```

The database parameter is the name of the database for which to return nullability information.

When the nullability of the given database allows NULL values and the column or data type nullability is not explicitly defined, GETANSINULL returns 1. This is the ANSI NULL default.

HOST_ID

The HOST_ID function returns the ID of the workstation. The syntax is as follows:

```
HOST_ID()
```

HOST_NAME

The HOST_NAME function returns the name of the workstation. The syntax is as follows:

```
HOST_NAME()
```

IDENT_CURRENT

The IDENT_CURRENT function returns the last identity value created for a table, within any session or scope of that table. This is exactly like @@IDENTITY and SCOPE_IDENTITY; however, this has no limit to the scope of its search to return the value.

The syntax is as follows:

```
IDENT_CURRENT('<table name>')
```

The table_name is the table for which you wish to find the current identity.

IDENT_INCR

The IDENT_INCR function returns the increment value specified during the creation of an identity column in a table or view that has an identity column. The syntax is as follows:

```
IDENT_INCR('<table or view>')
```

The table_or_view parameter is an expression specifying the table or view to check for a valid identity increment value.

IDENT_SEED

The IDENT_SEED function returns the seed value specified during the creation of an identity column in a table or a view that has an identity column. The syntax is as follows:

```
IDENT_SEED('<table or view>')
```

The table_or_view parameter is an expression specifying the table or view to check for a valid identity increment value.

@@IDENTITY

Returns the last identity value created by the current connection.

If you're using identity columns and then referencing them as a foreign key in another table, you'll find yourself using this one all the time. You can create the parent record (usually the one with the identity you need to retrieve), then select @@IDENTITY to know what value you need to relate child records to.

If you perform inserts into multiple tables with identity values, remember that the value in @@IDENTITY will only be for the *last* identity value inserted; anything before that will have been lost, unless you move the value into a holding variable after each insert. Also, if the last column you inserted into didn't have an identity column, then @@IDENTITY will be set to NULL.

IDENTITY

The IDENTITY function is used to insert an identity column into a new table. It is used only with a SELECT statement with an INTO table clause. The syntax is as follows:

```
IDENTITY(<data type>[, <seed>, <increment>]) AS <column name>
```

Where:

- ❑ data_type is the data type of the identity column.
- ❑ seed is the value to be assigned to the first row in the table. Each subsequent row is assigned the next identity value, which is equal to the last IDENTITY value plus the increment value. If neither seed nor increment is specified, both default to 1.
- ❑ increment is the increment to add to the seed value for successive rows in the table.
- ❑ column_name is the name of the column that is to be inserted into the new table.

ISNULL

The ISNULL function checks an expression for a NULL value and replaces it with a specified replacement value. The syntax is as follows:

```
ISNULL(<check expression>, <replacement value>)
```

ISNUMERIC

The ISNUMERIC function determines whether an expression is a valid numeric type. The syntax is as follows:

```
ISNUMERIC(<expression>)
```

NEWID

The NEWID function creates a unique value of type uniqueidentifier. The syntax is as follows:

```
NEWID()
```

NULLIF

The NULLIF function compares two expressions and returns a NULL value. The syntax is as follows:

```
NULLIF(<expression1>, <expression2>)
```

PARSENAME

The PARSENAME function returns the specified part of an object name. The syntax is as follows:

```
PARSENAME('<object name>', <object_piece>)
```

The object_name parameter specifies the object name from the part that is to be retrieved. The object_piece parameter specifies the part of the object to return. The object_piece parameter takes one of these possible values:

- ❏ 1 — Object name
- ❏ 2 — Owner name
- ❏ 3 — Database name
- ❏ 4 — Server name

PERMISSIONS

The PERMISSIONS function returns a value containing a bitmap, which indicates the statement, object, or column permissions for the current user. The syntax is as follows:

```
PERMISSIONS([<objectid> [, '<column>']])
```

The object_id parameter specifies the ID of an object. The optional column parameter specifies the name of the column for which permission information is being returned.

@@ROWCOUNT

Returns the number of rows affected by the last statement.

One of the most used globals. My most common use for this one is to check for nonruntime errors — that is, items that are logically errors to your program but that SQL Server isn't going to see any problem with. An example is a situation where you are performing an update based on a condition, but you find that it affects zero rows. Odds are that, if your client submitted a modification for a particular row, then it was expecting that row to match the criteria given; zero rows affected is indicative of something being wrong.

However, if you test this system function on any statement that does not return rows, then you will also return a value of 0.

ROWCOUNT_BIG

The ROWCOUNT_BIG function is very similar to @@ROWCOUNT in that it returns the number of rows from the last statement. However, the value returned is of a data type of bigint. The syntax is as follows:

```
ROWCOUNT_BIG()
```

SCOPE_IDENTITY

The SCOPE_IDENTITY function returns the last value inserted into an identity column in the same scope (that is, within the same sproc, trigger, function, or batch). This is similar to IDENT_CURRENT, discussed previously, although that was not limited to identity insertions made in the same scope.

This function returns a sql_variant data type, and the syntax is as follows:

```
SCOPE_IDENTITY()
```

SERVERPROPERTY

The SERVERPROPERTY function returns information about the server you are running on. The syntax is as follows:

```
SERVERPROPERTY('<propertyname>')
```

The possible values for propertyname are:

Property Name	Values Returned
Collation	The name of the default collation for the server.
Edition	The edition of the SQL Server instance installed on the server. Returns one of the following nvarchar results: 'Desktop Engine' 'Developer Edition' 'Enterprise Edition' 'Enterprise Evaluation Edition' 'Personal Edition' 'Standard Edition'

Property Name	Values Returned
Engine Edition	The engine edition of the SQL Server instance installed on the server: 1 — Personal or Desktop Engine 2 — Standard 3 — Enterprise (returned for Enterprise, Enterprise Evaluation, and Developer)
InstanceName	The name of the instance to which the user is connected.
IsClustered	Will determine if the server instance is configured in a failover cluster: 1 — Clustered 0 — Not clustered NULL — Invalid input or error
IsFullText Installed	To determine if the full-text component is installed with the current instance of SQL Server: 1 — Full-text is installed. 0 — Full-text is not installed. NULL — Invalid input or error
IsIntegrated SecurityOnly	To determine if the server is in integrated security mode: 1 — Integrated security 0 — Not integrated security NULL — Invalid input or error
IsSingleUser	To determine if the server is a single-user installation: 1 — Single user 0 — Not single user NULL — Invalid input or error
IsSync WithBackup	To determine if the database is either a published database or a distribution database, and can be restored without disrupting the current transactional replication: 1 — True 0 — False
LicenseType	What type of license is installed for this instance of SQL Server: PER_SEAT — Per-seat mode PER_PROCESSOR — Per-processor mode DISABLED — Licensing is disabled
MachineName	Returns the Windows NT computer name on which the server instance is running. For a clustered instance (an instance of SQL Server running on a virtual server on Microsoft Cluster Server), it returns the name of the virtual server.
NumLicenses	Number of client licenses registered for this instance of SQL Server, if in per-seat mode. Number of processors licensed for this instance of SQL Server, if in per-processor mode.
ProcessID	Process ID of the SQL Server service. (The ProcessID is useful in identifying which sqlservr.exe belongs to this instance.)

Continued

Property Name	Values Returned
ProductVersion	Very much like Visual Basic projects, in that the version details of the instance of SQL Server are returned, in the form of `'major.minor.build'`.
ProductLevel	Returns the value of the version of the SQL Server instance currently running. Returns: `'RTM'` — Shipping version `'SPn'` — Service pack version `'Bn'` — Beta version
ServerName	Both the Windows NT server and instance information associated with a specified instance of SQL Server.

The SERVERPROPERTY *function is very useful for multi-sited corporations where developers need to find out information from a server.*

SESSION_USER

The SESSION_USER function allows a system-supplied value for the current session's username to be inserted into a table if no default value has been specified. The syntax is as follows:

```
SESSION_USER
```

SESSIONPROPERTY

The SESSIONPROPERTY function is used to return the SET options for a session. The syntax is as follows:

```
SESSIONPROPERTY (<option>)
```

This function is useful when there are stored procedures that are altering session properties in specific scenarios. This function should rarely be used as you should not alter too many of the SET options during runtime.

STATS_DATE

The STATS_DATE function returns the date that the statistics for the specified index were last updated. The syntax is as follows:

```
STATS_DATE(<table id>, <index id>)
```

SYSTEM_USER

The SYSTEM_USER function allows a system-supplied value for the current system username to be inserted into a table if no default value has been specified. The syntax is as follows:

```
SYSTEM_USER
```

USER_NAME

The USER_NAME returns a database username. The syntax is as follows:

```
USER_NAME([<id>])
```

The id parameter specifies the ID number of the required username; if no value is given the current user is assumed.

Text and Image Functions

The text and image functions perform operations on text or image data. They are:

❑   PATINDEX (This was covered in the "String Functions" section earlier in the appendix.)

❑   TEXTPTR

❑   TEXTVALID

TEXTPTR

The TEXTPTR function checks the value of the text pointer that corresponds to a text, ntext, or image column and returns a varbinary value. The text pointer should be checked to ensure that it points to the first text page before running READTEXT, WRITETEXT, and UPDATE statements. The syntax is as follows:

```
TEXTPTR(<column>)
```

TEXTVALID

The TEXTVALID function checks whether a specified text pointer is valid. The syntax is as follows:

```
TEXTVALID('<table.column>', <text ptr>)
```

The table.column parameter specifies the name of the table and column to be used. The text_ptr parameter specifies the text pointer to be checked.

This function will return 0 if the pointer is invalid and 1 if the pointer is valid.

B

Going Meta: Getting Data About Your Data

Over the last few releases, Microsoft has done an amazing job of increasing types and volume of data programmatically available about your server and database. It's reached a level where I would be remiss if I didn't give it some kind of coverage.

So, what am I talking about here? Well, SQL Server provides a set of functions — both scalar and tabular — that return targeted information about the current state of your server or database. This can range from simple things like what objects exist on your server (this information was always available, but actual access to it was "unsupported" in many cases) to fragmentation levels for specific indexes.

In this appendix, we're going to provide basic information on a number of things that are called "metadata functions" – also sometimes referred to as dm functions (which stands for database metadata) as well as system views. Much of this tends to be in the domain of the database administrator, but it's important that you have an idea of what information is available for performance tuning as well as for any system state dashboards you may want to include in the administration panels of your application (if you have any). You can also use these for programmatically handling scheduled maintenance tasks (such as only defragmenting indexes that are beyond a certain level of fragmentation or periodic space checks and warnings).

Note that I am going to be largely sticking with the table-valued functions or system views for this appendix (the more mainstream system functions were already covered in Appendix A).

System Views

"Back in the day" as the saying goes, SQL Server provided very limited metadata information in terms of "official" methods of getting that data. You could tell whether or not a transaction was open, but you could not query a list of tables in the database (or even databases on the server) except by directly accessing special "system tables" — something Microsoft would tell you was "unsupported."

The demand for this functionality is so high that the development and administrative community essentially ignored Microsoft's "unsupported" comments, and accessed them anyway (it is very difficult to run a system without some of this data!). The use of system tables was rampant when we headed into the SQL Server 7.0 era, when Microsoft first introduced information schema views (an ANSI construct) to the product. When those didn't get the kind of acceptance and use Microsoft was looking for, they added in the new system views — mapping many directly to the old system tables (for example, the sys.objects view maps column for column to the older sysobjects table). They didn't stop there though. They added a wide variety of new, queryable views, so let's take a look at some of the key views you may want to make use of in your development.

> Let me stress again that this is not a comprehensive list; instead, this is a focus on those items you are
> more likely to use programmatically. Likewise, coverage of the columns in the views and table-valued
> functions is limited to those with a higher likelihood of being used.

Several of the system views are providing what I consider to be server-level information. While some of them may point to information on a specific database, they are in the context of the server level — meaning they can provide information on any of the databases on the server.

sys.assemblies

This view and its related views (sys.assembly_files and sys.assembly_references) can provide extensive information about what assemblies are installed and registered in your SQL Server environment.

sys.assemblies acts as a header table, and returns a single row for each assembly installed on your system (using CREATE ASSEMBLY). Key pieces of information you should be interested in from the sys.assemblies catalog view include:

Column	Type	Description
name	sysname	The logical name of the assembly within the database (not the name of the file or namespace).
principal_id	int	The ID of the schema the assembly belongs to.
assembly_id	int	The unique ID of the assembly within the database.
clr_name	nvarchar (4000)	A string that contains several pieces of information including: Simple name Version number Culture Public key Architecture This is effectively the ID of the assembly to the CLR.

Column	Type	Description
permission_set permission_set_desc	tinyint nvarchar (60)	The ID/Plain text indicator of the security access for this assembly. Valid values include: 1 (SAFE_ACCESS) 2 (EXTERNAL_ACCESS) 3 (UNSAFE_ACCESS)
create_date	datetime	The date and time the assembly was created.
modify_date	datetime	The date and time the assembly was last modified.
is_user_defined	bit	True/false indicator of whether or not this assembly was created by a user. (False implies that it was a system-included assembly.)

sys.columns

You can think of this one as a child of sys.objects, but one that applies only to objects that supply some form of tabular result (tables, views, table-valued functions regardless of whether they are user or system created). It will include one row for each column the object returns and provide substantial information about that column. Important items included in this view are:

Column	Type	Description
object_id	int	The object_id of the parent object for this column. You can easily join this to the object_id in sys.objects to obtain information (such as the name) of the parent object.
name	sysname	The name of the column.
column_id	int	The ID of the column. This is unique within the table.
system_type_id	tinyint	The system identifier for the data type of this column. You can join to the sys.types catalog view to resolve the common name of the data type.
user_type_id	int	This is the data type of the column as defined by the user — again, join to the sys.types catalog view to resolve this to something more usable.
max_length	smallint	The maximum allowable length for the column defined in bytes (remember than an nchar or nvarchar takes up two bytes per character!). This value will be –1 for most blob-capable data types (varchar (max), nvarchar (max), varbinary (max), xml), but, for the text data type, will be either 16 (the size of the blob pointer) or the value of the text in row option if one has been applied.
precision	tinyint	The precision of numeric-based columns (0 for non-numerics).
scale	tinyint	The scale of numeric-based columns (0 for non-numerics).

Continued

Column	Type	Description
collation_name	sysname	The collation name for any character-based column (NULL for non-character–based data).
is_nullable is_ansi_padded is_rowguildcol is_identity is_computed is_filestream is_replicated is_non_sql_subscribed is_merge_published is_dts_replicated	bit	These are largely described by their names, but, in short, are a series of true/false indicators regarding many properties a column can have.
is_xml_document	bit	Again, largely self-describing, but with a bit of nuance, so we'll address it more specifically. In short, this indicates whether the column is not only XML, but is valid as a complete XML document rather than just a fragment. 1 = a complete document, and 0 = an XML fragment or non-XML data.
is_sparse is_column_set	bit	I call these out separately mostly because they are both related specifically to sparse columns, and, unless you're familiar with sparse columns, the is_column_set piece probably won't make sense (check out sparse columns for more info there, but I wanted to at least provide context for is_column_set).
xml_collection_id	int	Only relevant for typed XML columns, this one calls out the ID of the XML schema collection that is enforcing the type information for the XML.

sys.databases

This one maps to the old sysdatabases table, providing information such as (key columns here; this is not a complete list):

Column	Type	Description
name	sysname	The logical name of the database.
database_id	int	The ID of the database. This ID is used in a number of system functions and can be a foreign key column for many other system views or metadata functions.
create_date	datetime	The date and time the database was created. Note that this value is reset if the database is renamed.

Column	Type	Description
compatibility_level	tinyint	Indicates the version of SQL Server this database is set for compatibility with. Valid values are: 70 (SQL Server 7.0) 80 (SQL Server 2000) 90 (SQL Server 2005) 100 (SQL Server 2008) NULL (The database isn't online)
collation_name	sysname	Collation the database is using (sort order as well as sensitivity to case, accents, kana, and width).
state	tinyint	The current state of the database. Valid values include: 0 (Online) 1 (Restoring) 2 (Recovering) 3 (Recovery pending) 4 (Suspect) 5 (Emergency) 6 (Offline) The clear text versions of what these mean can be found in the state_desc column.
is_in_standby	bit	True/false indicator of whether the database is ready to have a transaction log or differential backup applied.
is_ansi_nulls_on is_ansi_padding_on is_ansi_warnings_on is_arithabort_on is_quoted_identifier_on is_fulltext_enabled is_trustworthy_on is_encrypted	Bit	These are all separate true/false columns that indicate whether or not a given database setting is active. A zero indicates that the setting is off, and a one indicates that the setting is on.

sys.database_files

This one loosely (and I do mean *very* loosely) maps to the old sysfiles system table. Consider it, however, to be sysfiles on steroids in the sense that it contains vastly more information. What information am I talking about here? Information about each and every physical file involved in your database. For the vast majority of databases, this will be two (the primary data file and the log), but if you are using filegroups (including for partitioning), then they will show here also.

> sys.database_files is focused on a specific database. You can also use
> sys.master_files to obtain a similar list for all databases on your server (all the
> same key fields are there in addition to a database_id).

You'll care about this one if you're supporting advanced database configuration within your application. Some of the key columns for this view include:

Column	Type	Description
file_id	int	The internal ID of the file within the database.
file_guid	uniqueidentifier	The GUID for the file. This may be null if you upgraded from a previous version of SQL Server.
type	tinyint	Indicates the type of file. Valid file types include: 0 (holds actual data, index, or full-text rows) 1 (Log data) 2 (FILESTREAM information) 4 (For versions prior to 2008, full-text) Note that the type_desc column pre-translates these values for you (but keep in mind that the FULLTEXT value will only be for SQL Server 2005 and earlier. 2008 full text will come back as ROWS).
data_space_id	int	The filegroup ID of the filegroup this particular file belongs to.
name	sysname	Logical name of the database.
physical_name	nvarchar (260)	The physical file name at the operating system level.
state	tinyint	The current state of the database. Valid values include: 0 (Online) 1 (Restoring) 2 (Recovering) 3 (Recovery pending) 4 (Suspect) 5 (Emergency) 6 (Offline) The clear text versions of what these mean can be found in the state_desc column.
size	int	Actual size of the file in 8KB data pages.
max_size	int	The maximum file size this file is allowed to grow to (maps to the value we use in the file section of the CREATE DATABASE statement).

Column	Type	Description
growth	int	Whether or not this file is allowed to auto grow, and by how much. If the value is zero, the file is not allowed to grow. Values greater than zero will be either the amount to grow or the percentage to grow as determined by the is_percent_growth column.

sys.identity_columns

This is one of those that falls under the heading of "subtly useful" to me. It seems rather fringe in nature, and, to be honest, it is, but when you need it, it's very nice to have.

So, what does it provide? Well, as the name suggest, it provides a list of all identity columns in the database. The need to do this is relatively unusual, but, when you need it, sys.identity_columns is like gold (it makes it easy).

So, if, for example, we wanted to know what tables had identity columns, what those identity columns were, and what their current increment values were, we could write something like:

```
USE AdventureWorks2008;

SELECT so.name AS TableName,
       sic.name AS ColumnName,
       CAST(last_value AS bigint)
     + CAST(increment_value AS bigint) AS NextValue
FROM sys.identity_columns sic
JOIN sys.objects so
    on sic.object_id = so.object_id
   AND so.type = 'U';
```

Note the need to cast the values, as those are stored in a sql_variant data type and the math I used in the example requires explicit casting. Also pay attention to the fact that I limited the results to those objects that are actual user tables. This addresses an issue where sys.identity_columns returns all columns flagged as an identity column regardless of the nature of the object, which means that views will return columns based on a table column that is an identity column, and system tables can also be returned (if they use an identity column, which some do). By limiting to user tables, I make sure I do not mess with system objects and that I only see the root source of the identity column (that is, the identity column in the table — not in any views that happen to show the base table column).

The results are very straightforward:

```
TableName                      ColumnName                     NextValue
------------------------------ ------------------------------ ---------------
SpecialOffer                   SpecialOfferID                 17
```

```
Address              AddressID              32522
AddressType          AddressTypeID          7
ProductModel         ProductModelID         129
...
...
...
ShoppingCartItem     ShoppingCartItemID     6
DatabaseLog          DatabaseLogID          1596
ErrorLog             ErrorLogID             NULL

(47 row(s) affected)
```

> If no rows have ever been inserted since the creation of the identity column, then there is no `last_value` to be shown, and it will thus return a **NULL**.

sys.indexes

As I'm sure you can imagine, this one is all about indexes. This is something of the master system catalog view dealing with indexes, and has several child or extender views associated with it. There is one entry in this table for each index in your database regardless of the type of index. No specific column information is supplied (see `sys.index_columns` for that), and extended information for special index types (xml, geospatial) is stored in special index-type–specific extensions to this table (they map one for one to rows in `sys.indexes` for the particular index type, and include all `sys.indexes` columns as well as a few columns specific to that type of index).

Key columns in `sys.indexes` include:

Column	Type	Description
object_id	int	ID of the object this index is built on or belongs to. This column ties to the `object_id` column in the `sys.objects` table.
name	sysname	The logical name of the index. A null in this column implies that the index is a heap.
index_id	int	The ID of the index. The value of this column is predictable for the heap (0) or clustered index (1) on the table (and there will only be one or the other — not both). Values equal or greater than two are non-clustered indexes built against the heap or clustered index as appropriate.
type	tinyint	Indicates the type of index. Valid index types are: 0 (Heap) 1 (Clustered) 2 (Non-clustered) 3 (XML) 4 (Spatial) Note that 0 and 1 are mutually exclusive (you must have one of these values for any table, but can only have one).

Column	Type	Description
type_desc	nvarchar (60)	A clear text (text instead of numeric values) version of the type column.
is_unique	bit	True/false value indicating whether the index values must be unique.
data_space_id	int	Identifier of the filegroup or partition scheme this index is stored in.
ignore_dup_key	bit	True/false indication of whether or not the option to ignore duplicate keys is active for this index.
is_primary_key is_unique_constraint	bit	True/false indicators of whether index is supporting a primary key or unique constraint. Note that, while neither is required, they are mutually exclusive (an index cannot be both a unique constraint and primary key).
fill_factor	tinyint	The fill factor that was used when this index was defined or last altered. A zero indicates that the default fill factor was accepted.
is_padded	bit	True/false indication of whether the PAD_INDEX option was used when this index was last created or altered.
is_disabled	bit	Just what the name implies — a true/false indication of whether the index has been disabled. Remember that disabled indexes are completely unavailable and must be rebuilt to become active again. Disabling a clustered index has the effect of taking a table entirely offline, and the clustered index will need to be rebuilt in order to access the table data.
is_hypothetical	bit	True/false indicator of whether this is really just a statistics entry rather than a true index (all the stats of an index, but without any of the sorted data storage).
allow_row_locks allow_page_locks	bit	As you might expect from the name, these are true/false indicators of whether row or page locks are allowed when accessing this index. The affect is restricted to the index (it doesn't affect the table as a whole) unless the index in question is a heap or clustered index. These columns are *not* mutually exclusive. Prohibiting both row and page locks has the effect of generating a table lock for any queries that utilize this index.
has_filter	bit	True/false indication of whether this is a filtered index (the vast majority of indexes, and all pre-2008 indexes will be unfiltered).
filter_definition	nvarchar (max)	Effectively a WHERE clause, this value indicates the expression that is applied to filter the values participating in this index.

As you can tell from the lengthy list of very useful columns, this system catalog view can be very useful in terms of determining what you have (for performance and use analysis) and many maintenance scripts you may wish to write.

Consider joining values in this table with the "missing index" set of system catalog views.

sys.index_columns

While sys.indexes is all about the header-level information for an index, this one is all about the column-by-column details of the index definition. An entry will exist in this view for each column that participates in any way in the index (there are indicators that tell whether the column participates in the actual key or is just an included column). In general, this system catalog view will have virtually no usefulness without being joined to the parent view (sys.indexes). Indeed, sys.index_columns has no information that isn't column specific.

Column	Type	Description
object_id	int	ID of the object containing the index this column participates in. This column ties to the object_id column in the sys.objects table.
index_id	int	The ID of the index this column is associated with. Note that, when joining back to the index header information, you will need both this column and the object_id.
index_column_id	int	The ID of the column as it exists within this particular index.
column_id	int	The ID of the column as it exists within the object this column of the index is based on. If the index is on a view, you may see duplicate column_id values, as this column is only unique within the context of a specific object. A zero in this column indicates that this column is an internal column (doesn't visibly appear in the original object) holding the row identifier (RID) on a non-clustered index on a heap.
key_ordinal	tinyint	1 based ordinal value indicating this column's position within the index key definition (exclusive of included columns). A 0 value indicates that his is a non-key column.
partition_ordinal	tinyint	1 based ordinal value within a set of partitioning columns (this will generally be zero, indicating it is not a partitioning column).
is_descending_key	bit	True/false indication of whether the this column is to be treated in descending order.
is_included_column	bit	True/false indicator of whether this column is just an included column (exists only at the leaf level of the index, and is not included in sort order considerations).

sys.objects

> sys.objects can be considered to be something of the parent to several other system catalog views. Much of the information about the basic existence of virtually any object can be determined from the sys.objects view, but be aware that there are views with object type specific information for several object types (views, tables, constraints, procedures, and so on).

Much as sys.database_files maps loosely to the old sysfiles system table, sys.objects maps to the old system table sysobjects (in this case, pretty much exactly).

Sys.objects can be a source for a tremendous amount of information on what objects exist in your database and what the nature of those objects is. Some of the more key columns available in sys.objects include:

> Note that sys.objects is limited in scope to those objects in the database that are scoped to a schema. While this includes most relevant objects in a database, it's worth noting that it does mean that DDL triggers will not show up in sys.objects.

Column	Type	Description
name	sysname	The logical name of the object.
object_id	int	The ID of the object database. This ID is unique within a given database.
principal_id	int	The ID of the owner of the object if it is different from the owner of the schema that contains the object (if the owner of the object and schema is the same, this column will be NULL). Note that this column does not apply (and is set to NULL) if the object is of a type that is a child object to a table (any type of constraint or trigger) or is one of the old-style DEFAULT or RULE objects (which are only supported in the product for backward compatibility).
schema_id	int	The ID of the schema that contains the object (join to sys.schemas if you need the name of that schema).
parent_object_id	int	The object_id of the object that is the parent of the current object (for example, the table that is the parent of a trigger or constraint).
type	char(2)	A one- to two-letter moniker for the type of object this is (a more plain text version is stored in the sister column — type_desc). Valid values include: AF (CLR Aggregate function) C (Check constraint) D (Constraint or stand-alone default)

Continued

Column	Type	Description
		F (Foreign key constraint)
		FN (SQL scalar function)
		FS (CLR scalar-function)
		FT (CLR table-valued function)
		IF (Inline table-valued function)
		IT (Internal table)
		P (Stored procedure)
		PC (CLR stored-procedure)
		PG (Plan guide)
		PK (Primary key)
		R (Rule)
		RF (Replication-filter)
		S (System table)
		SN (Synonym)
		SQ (Service queue)
		TA (CLR DML trigger)
		TF (Table-valued function)
		TR (Non-CLR DML trigger)
		U (Non-system table)
		UQ (Unique constraint)
		V (Non-system view)
		X (Extended stored procedure)
type_desc	nvarchar (60)	A relatively plain text version of type of object (a longer moniker than was found in the type column).
create_date	datetime	The date and time the object was created. Note that, unlike a database in the sys.databases view, the create time shown in sys.objects is *not* reset if the object is renamed.
modify_date	datetime	The date and time the object was altered. Changes to an underlying clustered index (if the object is a table or indexed view) will affect this time stamp, but changes to non-clustered indexes will not.
is_ms_shipped	bit	A flag indicating whether or not this is effectively a system object (if it is an object that shipped with SQL Server as opposed to user or application created).

sys.partitions

As you might imagine, this one is about what partitions your database has defined in it. Whether or not you realize it, every table has at least one partition; even if you do not explicitly create partition schemes, there is still one partition per table (it just has everything for that table). The key thing on this system view is to be able to figure out whether or not your table is explicitly partitioned and how many partitions are in it. The key useful things from a development point of view are:

Column	Type	Description
partition_id	bigint	The internal ID of the partition within the database (note that it's by database — not table).
object_id	int	The specific object (by object_id) that this partition is associated with.
index_id	int	The base 1 partition number indicating what partition this is within the individual table.
rows	bigint	The approximate number of rows for this partition. Note that this is maintained with statistics, so may be inexact.
data_compression	int	Why they didn't use a tinyint on this one I have no idea. This indicates how compression is being handled within this partition: 0 (no compression) 1 (compressed at row level) 2 (compressed at the page level. Like some of the indicators we've seen in other system views, there is also a column (in this case, called data_compression_desc) that contains the plain text description of this setting.

sys.partition_functions

In general, this one would only make sense when your application is supporting a very high scalability model. This system view gives you the ability to identify the number and nature of partition functions in use. Use of this view would imply that you are doing some pretty heady stuff with table partitioning.

Column	Type	Description
name	sysname	As you might expect, this is the name of the partition function. It must be unique within a given database.
function_id	int	The internal identifier for the function. Again, this is unique within a given database.
fanout	int	Indicates how many partitions are logically created by the function.
boundary_value_on_right	bit	Table partitioning in SQL Server 2008 continues to be based solely on the notion of ranges. This column is a true/false field indicating whether the hard boundary for a range is on the right (if false, then the boundary must be on the left).

sys.schemas

This one is incredibly simple. Since schemas are largely very simple containers, there really isn't all that much to identify about them. The primary purpose of this table is to resolve the name of a schema that owns an object and provide who the owner of the schema is. This view provides just three columns:

Column	Type	Description
name	sysname	The name of the schema (no surprise here).
schema_id	int	The internal identifier for the schema; this is unique within a given database.
principal_id	int	The id of the security principal (as found in sys.user_token) that owns this schema.

sys.servers

Provides a row for the local server as well as each linked and remote server registered with this server instance. For each server, this view provides information on the communication properties, as well as several other properties required to interact with that server.

Column	Type	Description
server_id	int	The internal ID of the server. The local server will have an ID of zero, and all other registered servers (linked or remote) will have a value greater than zero that is unique within this particular local server instance.
name	sysname	As you might expect, this is the name of the partition function. It must be unique within a given database.
product	sysname	Equates to the product property as it is specified in an OLE DB connection. If this is the local server or another SQL Server, this value will be SQL Server.
provider	sysname	The OLE DB provider name — for example, SQLNCLI (the SQL native client), MSDASQL (the OLE DB provider for ODBC), MSDAORA (Oracle), Microsoft.Jet.OLEDB.4.0 (Access).
data_source	nvarchar (4000)	The data source as used in OLE DB. This will vary by the provider, but, for SQL Server, it will be the name or IP address of the server you're connecting to.
location	nvarchar (4000)	The location as used in OLE DB connections. This is often null (again, depends on the provider).

Column	Type	Description
provider_string	nvarchar (4000)	The OLE DB provider-string property. While in other settings you can often just set the connection utilizing this one property, you will only see this populated in SQL Server through an ALTER (you must originally use the discrete properties described previously).
catalog	sysname	The OLE DB catalog property. For SQL Server connections, this equates to setting the default database for the connection used by this linked server connection.
connect_timeout	int	How long the connection can sit idle before it is automatically closed (the default is 0, which translates to no timeout).
query_timeout	int	How long a query is allowed to run before being terminated. Again, this default is 0, which translates to no timeout.
is_linked	bit	True/false indication of whether this is a linked server or some other form of remote server connection.
is_data_access_enabled	bit	True/false as to whether distributed queries are allowed via this connection.
is_collation_compatible	bit	True/false indication of whether the linked server utilizes a data collation that is compatible with the local server. If they are, it can have very significant performance impact on distributed queries since any collation casting is ignored.
uses_remote_collation	bit	True/false indication of whether, assuming incompatible collations, the collation on the remote server is utilized instead of the local collation.
collation_name	sysname	If not using the remote collation, then what collation to use. The default is NULL, which assumes you want to use the local collation.

sys.spatial_indexes

Much like sys.xml_indexes, this is a simple extension to the sys.indexes catalog view. It includes all columns found in sys.indexes (there is, therefore, no need to join back to the sys.indexes view), but also returns three additional spatial data specific columns (though, since all three are based on the same thing, I have no idea why you need all three) and filters the results to just those indexes that are defined as being spatial.

The extra three columns included are:

Column	Type	Description
spatial_index_type	tinyint	The type of spatial index: 1 (Geometric) 2 (Geographic)
spatial_index_type	nvarchar (60)	A clear text equivalent to the more basic type column. Valid values are: GEOMETRY (equates to type 1) GOEGRAPHY (equates to type 2)
tessellation_scheme	sysname	Name of the tessellation scheme being utilized to index the data. This will correlated to the type of spatial index being used. Valid values are: GEOMETRY_GRID GEOGRAPHY_GRID

sys.synonyms

This view is something of an extension and filter of the base sys.objects catalog view. It includes all columns found in sys.objects, but adds an additional column called base_object_name that is used as a pointer (in the form of a fully quoted name of up to 1035 characters) of the base object that this synonym is an alias for.

sys.user_token

This contains one row for every security principal with access to the database. Note that this does not necessarily equate to a token per login that has access (the access may be granted via a role, which would, instead, be what had the token here and could provide access to many logins).

The columns provided are:

Column	Type	Description
principal_id	int	The unique, internal ID of the principal within this database.
sid	varbinary (85)	The external security identifier of the principal. If this is a Windows user or group, it will be the Windows SID. If it is a SQL Server login, it will be a SID created by SQL Server when the login was generated.
name	nvarchar (128)	The name of the principal as it is to be used within this database. Note that this may not be the same as the external name for the principal. It must be unique within any given database.

Column	Type	Description
type	nvarchar (128)	A clear text indication of what type of principal this is. Valid values include: APPLICATION ROLE ASYMMETRIC KEY CERTIFICATE DATABASE ROLE ROLE SQL USER USER MAPPED TO ASYMMETRIC KEY USER MAPPED TO CERTIFICATE WINDOWS LOGIN WINDOWS GROUP
usage	nvarchar (128)	Indicates whether the principal is evaluated for GRANT/DENY permissions, or serves solely as an authenticator (which is used for context information in encryption).

sys.xml_indexes

This serves as a relatively simple extension to the sys.indexes catalog view. It includes all columns found in sys.indexes (so there is no need to join back to that view), but returns three additional XML index–specific columns and limits the rows returned to just indexes of type XML.

The extra three columns included are:

Column	Type	Description
using_xml_index_id	int	If this is NULL, then this index is the primary XML index for the table (remember that the first XML index you create on a table has to be marked as the primary, and you can only have one primary XML index per table). Any non-null value indicates that this is a secondary index, and provides a unique ID within the set of XML indexes on this table.
secondary_type	char(1)	Only relevant to non-primary indexes (it will be NULL if this is a primary index), this indicates the nature of secondary index: P (Path) V (Value) R (Property)
secondary_type_desc	nvarchar (60)	A clear text version of the secondary_type column.

Dynamic Management Views

These first started making a wide-scale appearance in SQL Server 2005, and fall under the heading of SQL Server items I would refer to as "really cool." Much like the system views, these provide information on the state of your server and/or database.

> A word of warning: Unlike system views, which are relatively stable in nature, Microsoft makes no promises that dynamic management — or dm — views will be stable between releases. Microsoft considers these views to be specific to the implementation choices made in each release of SQL Server, and, therefore, reserves the right to change them from release to release.

> Most core columns in dm views are probably relatively safe, but the more specific a column is, the more likely it is to be altered in some way from release to release.

> Dynamic management views are simply too powerful to ignore, but be aware that you may have to have some version-specific code running around them as your support moves from version to version of SQL Server.

Dynamic management views vary in what kind of data you're getting back. It may be the kind of relatively static data you expect from system views (data that stays pretty stable from day to day), and it may well be data that is always changing (such as lock states, resource governor information, and other constantly changing information).

Under the heading of "one more thing," it's probably important to note that not all objects typically referred to as dm views are really views; several of them are actually table-valued functions. Nonetheless, the entire set of objects that return dynamic management information is generally referred to as dm views.

Index-Related dm Views and Functions

I can't stress enough how much of a leap having the dm views for indexes was over the previous forms of information available about views. In SQL Server 2000 and prior, we used DBCC SHOWCONTIG or other Database Consistency Checker commands to get at our index information. While much of what we wanted was in there, it was in more of a report format, and was very difficult to use programmatically. The dm views give us a tabular result set that we can easily apply WHERE or other SQL constructs to — very powerful. The SQL Server team didn't stop there though; with SQL Server 2008 we pick up information regarding indexes we don't even have (yet)!

As I mention in Chapter 22, SQL Server now provides analysis at query optimization on what indexes it thinks may have been useful had they been available. It logs that analysis information to make it available in various metadata sources including some of the index-related dm views we will look at over the next few pages.

sys.db_db_index_physical_stats

This is something of the new "bread and butter" source of information for index state. Using this table-valued function can provide a plethora of information on such things as the fragmentation, depth of the index, and how many records are participating in the index, among other things.

This function has a standard function parameter format that includes several required parameters. The syntax looks like this:

```
sys.dm_db_index_physical_stats (
     { <database id> | NULL | 0 | DEFAULT },
     { <object id> | NULL | 0 | DEFAULT },
     { <index id> | NULL | 0 | -1 | DEFAULT },
     { <partition number> | NULL | 0 | DEFAULT },
     { <mode> | NULL | DEFAULT }
)
```

Parameter	Data Type	Description
database id	smallint	Internal identifier for the database you want index statistics on. NULL, 0, and DEFAULT all have the same functional result here, which is to return data for all databases.
object id	int	Internal identifier for the individual object you want index statistics on. Again, NULL, 0, and DEFAULT have the same functional effect here (return all objects). Utilize the OBJECT_ID() function to resolve an object by name into an id.
index id	int	Internal identifier for the individual index you want statistics on. A 0 indicates that you want statistics solely for the heap (the base data pages) and not for other indexes in the table. Likewise, any positive number will be matched up against the 1 based index ID for the particular table or view specified in the object ID parameter. NULL, -1 (notice the change from 0), and DEFAULT have the same functional effect here (return all indexes).
partition number	int	The internal partition number (1 based) you want index information for. DEFAULT, NULL, and 0 are functionally equivalent, and indicate you want information on all partitions. Any integer larger than zero will be matched against a specific partition number.
mode	sysname	Indicates the level of scan you want used to create the statistics you receive. Valid inputs are DEFAULT, NULL, LIMITED, SAMPLED, and DETAILED. DEFAULT, NULL, and LIMITED are functionally equivalent.

We looked at examples of using this table-valued function a few times over the course of the book, but, for example, we could execute:

```
USE AdventureWorks2008;

SELECT OBJECT_NAME(object_id) AS ObjectName,
       index_type_desc,
       avg_fragmentation_in_percent
FROM sys.dm_db_index_physical_stats(
       DB_ID('AdventureWorks2008'),
       DEFAULT,
       DEFAULT,
       DEFAULT,
       DEFAULT)
WHERE avg_fragmentation_in_percent > 50;
```

Notice that, like all table-valued functions, I can specify an explicit select list and grab only those columns that are meaningful to me for whatever my need happens to be. I could, of course, also join this to other tables or views to get additional information or insight into the results (for example, I could join to the sys.indexes system view to retrieve the name of the indexes).

If I run this, I get a short list of tables or views that have index fragmentation above 50%:

```
ObjectName                  index_type_desc avg_fragmentation_in_percent
--------------------------- --------------- ----------------------------
ProductListPriceHistory     CLUSTERED IND   66.6666666666667
SpecialOfferProduct         CLUSTERED IND   66.6666666666667
ProductReview               NONCLUSTERED    66.6666666666667
Employee                    NONCLUSTERED    66.6666666666667
Product                     NONCLUSTERED    66.6666666666667
ProductCostHistory          CLUSTERED IND   66.6666666666667
ProductDescription          NONCLUSTERED    66.6666666666667
DatabaseLog                 NONCLUSTERED    66.6666666666667

(8 row(s) affected)
```

This is actually a much wider view than I've shown in the previous results. Some of the more interesting columns available in this view include:

Column name	Data type	Description
database_id	smallint	The internal identifier of the table or view. You can use the DB_NAME function to retrieve the name of the database.
object_id	int	Object ID of the table or view that the index is on. Use the OBJECT_NAME function to return the name associated with this ID.

Column name	Data type	Description
index_id	int	Index identifier of the index listed. Note that this value will be unique only within a given table or view. A value of 0 indicates that this is the heap in a non-clustered table. A 1 indicates that this is the clustered index for the table.
partition_number	int	1-based partition number within the owning object; a table, view, or index. 1 = Nonpartitioned index or heap.
index_type_desc	nvarchar (60)	Description of the index type: HEAP CLUSTERED INDEX NONCLUSTERED INDEX PRIMARY XML INDEX SPATIAL INDEX XML INDEX
alloc_unit_type_desc	nvarchar (60)	Description of the allocation unit type: IN_ROW_DATA LOB_DATA ROW_OVERFLOW_DATA The LOB_DATA allocation unit contains the data that is stored in columns of type text, ntext, image, varchar (max), nvarchar (max), varbinary (max), and xml. The ROW_OVERFLOW_DATA allocation unit contains the data that is stored in columns of type varchar(n), nvarchar(n), varbinary(n), and sql_variant that have been pushed off-row.
index_depth	tinyint	Number of index levels. 1 = Heap, or LOB_DATA or ROW_OVERFLOW _DATA allocation unit.
index_level	tinyint	Current level of the index. 0 for index leaf levels, heaps, and LOB_DATA or ROW_OVERFLOW_DATA allocation units. Greater than 0 for non-leaf index levels. *index_level* will be the highest at the root level of an index. The non-leaf levels of indexes are only processed when mode = DETAILED.
avg_fragmentation_in _percent	float	Logical fragmentation for indexes, or extent fragmentation for heaps in the IN_ROW_DATA allocation unit. The value is measured as a percentage and takes into account multiple files

Continued

Column name	Data type	Description
		0 for LOB_DATA and ROW_OVERFLOW_DATA allocation units. NULL for heaps when *mode* = SAMPLED.
fragment_count	bigint	Number of fragments in the leaf level of an IN_ROW_DATA allocation unit. NULL for non-leaf levels of an index, and LOB_DATA or ROW_OVERFLOW_DATA allocation units. NULL for heaps when *mode* = SAMPLED.
avg_fragment_size_in_pages	float	Average number of pages in one fragment in the leaf level of an IN_ROW_DATA allocation unit. NULL for non-leaf levels of an index, and LOB_DATA or ROW_OVERFLOW_DATA allocation units. NULL for heaps when *mode* = SAMPLED.
page_count	bigint	Total number of index or data pages. For an index, the total number of index pages in the current level of the b-tree in the IN_ROW_DATA allocation unit. For a heap, the total number of data pages in the IN_ROW_DATA allocation unit. For LOB_DATA or ROW_OVERFLOW_DATA allocation units, total number of pages in the allocation unit.
avg_page_space_used_in _percent	float	Average percentage of available data storage space used in all pages. For an index, average applies to the current level of the b-tree in the IN_ROW_DATA allocation unit. For a heap, the average of all data pages in the IN_ROW_DATA allocation unit. For LOB_DATA or ROW_OVERFLOW_DATA allocation units, the average of all pages in the allocation unit. NULL when *mode* = LIMITED.
record_count	bigint	Total number of records. For an index, total number of records applies to the current level of the b-tree in the IN_ROW_DATA allocation unit. For a heap, the total number of records in the IN_ROW_DATA allocation unit. For a heap, the number of records returned from this function might not match the number of rows that are returned by running a SELECT COUNT(*) against the heap. This is because a row may contain multiple records. For example, under some update situations, a single heap row

Column name	Data type	Description
		may have a forwarding record and a forwarded record as a result of the update operation. Also, most large LOB rows are split into multiple records in LOB_DATA storage. For LOB_DATA or ROW_OVERFLOW_DATA allocation units, the total number of records in the complete allocation unit.NULL when *mode* = LIMITED.
ghost_record _count	bigint	Number of ghost records ready for removal by the ghost cleanup task in the allocation unit. 0 for non-leaf levels of an index in the IN_ROW_DATA allocation unit. NULL when *mode* = LIMITED.
version_ghost_record _count	bigint	Number of ghost records retained by an outstanding snapshot isolation transaction in an allocation unit. 0 for non-leaf levels of an index in the IN_ROW_DATA allocation unit. NULL when *mode* = LIMITED.
min_record_size_in _bytes	int	Minimum record size in bytes. For an index, minimum record size applies to the current level of the b-tree in the IN_ROW_DATA allocation unit. For a heap, the minimum record size in the IN_ROW_DATA allocation unit. For LOB_DATA or ROW_OVERFLOW_DATA allocation units, the minimum record size in the complete allocation unit. NULL when *mode* = LIMITED.
max_record_size_in _bytes	int	Maximum record size in bytes. For an index, the maximum record size applies to the current level of the b-tree in the IN_ROW_DATA allocation unit. For a heap, the maximum record size in the IN_ROW_DATA allocation unit. For LOB_DATA or ROW_OVERFLOW_DATA allocation units, the maximum record size in the complete allocation unit. NULL when *mode* = LIMITED.
avg_record_size_in _bytes	float	Average record size in bytes. For an index, the average record size applies to the current level of the b-tree in the IN_ROW_DATA allocation unit. For a heap, the average record size in the IN_ROW_DATA allocation unit. For LOB_DATA or ROW_OVERFLOW_DATA allocation units, the average record size in the complete allocation unit. NULL when *mode* = LIMITED.

Continued

Column name	Data type	Description
forwarded_record_count	bigint	Number of records in a heap that have forward pointers to another data location. (This state occurs during an update, when there is not enough room to store the new row in the original location.) NULL for any allocation unit other than the IN_ROW_DATA allocation units for a heap. NULL for heaps when *mode* = LIMITED.
compressed_page_count	bigint	The number of compressed pages. For heaps, newly allocated pages are not PAGE compressed. A heap is PAGE compressed under two special conditions: when data is bulk imported or when a heap is rebuilt. Typical DML operations that cause page allocations will not be PAGE compressed. Rebuild a heap when the compressed_page_count value grows larger than the threshold you want.For tables that have a clustered index, the compressed_page_count value indicates the effectiveness of PAGE compression.

sys.dm_db_index_usage_stats

This is a subtle one that probably does not get enough attention from the SQL Server pundits of the world. What is it? Well, it is the current status from a series of counters SQL Server maintains whenever an index (including a raw heap) is used in an index. You can get rather robust information regarding which indexes are and are not being utilized during the normal operation of your system and, perhaps just as important, *how* they are being used. You can get operation-specific information such as scans, seeks, and lookups as well as how often changes are occurring. You are even provided with information on the date and time the index was last used (it may have been a heavily used index at one time, but perhaps a new index or change in the makeup of your data has caused it not to be used in quite some time). This can be key in terms of knowing whether your index is really worth it.

> *Note that anything referred to as an "update" in this view can be more than just a result of an* UPDATE *statement — anything that changes the row (including inserts or deletes regardless of whether they are an explicit* INSERT *or* DELETE *statement or by a* MERGE*).*

The row counters used in sys.dm_db_index_usage_stats are reset each time the SQL Server service is restarted. Counters for any individual database are reset any time that database becomes offline for any reason (you detach it or it is closed for some other reason, such as AUTO_CLOSE, which is frequently used in SQL Server Express installations).

The usage is pretty straightforward; use it just as you would a table:

```
SELECT *
FROM sys.dm_db_index_usage_stats;
```

As you can see, there is no rocket science involved in this one. A count and date of last instance is supplied for each of four types of use with system versus user access each separated into individual buckets (aggregate them as you need for your specific application). Again, a date is included for each of these, and user access versus system access is also separated.

Column	Type	Description
database_id	smallint	Internal identifier for the database containing the object being reported on. Remember you can use the DB_NAME() function to resolve the id into the name you are used to. Likewise, you could use the DB_ID() function to resolve a name to an id you could use in a WHERE clause.
object_id	int	Internal identifier for the individual object you want index usage on. Again, utilize the OBJECT_ID() function to resolve an object by name into an id for use in a WHERE clause. Likewise, use the OBJECT_NAME() function to resolve it back to a more user-friendly name in your select list. You can also join to the sys.objects table for more information on the particular object in question.
index_id	int	Internal identifier for the individual index the usage information is on. Use a 0 if you want statistics solely for the heap (the base data pages in a non-clustered index) and a 1 for the clustered index on a clustered table. Join against the sys.indexes table if you're looking for more specific information on the nature of the index (what columns are used or included, type of index, name, and so on).
user_seeks system_seeks	bigint	Count of index seeks. This would be an instance where SQL Server followed the index to a specific row.
user_scans system_scans	bigint	This can be a full scan of the index (much like a scan of the entire table, but only of the data included in that index), or can be a ranged scan (seek to a specific point in the index, and then read every row until a specific end point is reached).
user_lookups system_lookups	bigint	The system used a row identifier (RID) or cluster key to "look up" a specific row — think of this as another form of seek.
user_updates system_updatess	bigint	Incremented when some form of change happened to the index row. Despite being called an "update," this counter is actually incremented for any change to the data regardless of insert, update, or delete.
last_user_seek last_system_seek	datetime	Date a user or the system (as indicated in the name) last caused a seek operation to be performed against this index.
last_user_scan last_system_scan	datetime	Date a user or the system (as indicated in the name) last caused an index scan operation to be performed against this index.

Continued

Column	Type	Description
last_user_lookup last_system_lookup	datetime	Date a user or the system (as indicated in the name) last caused a bookmark lookup operation to be performed against this index.
last_user_update last_system_update	datetime	Date a user or the system (as indicated in the name) last changed data associated with this index.

The sys.dm_db_missing_index_ * family of views

Full discussion of these gets complex and probably could be its own appendix.

You may recall me discussing in a few different chapters that, with 2008, SQL Server now not only recognizes the indexes that it has available, but also optionally recognizes those that do not exist but would have been useful if they had been there. In addition to the administration tools that show you much of this data, you can access missing index information programmatically through the use of four missing index views — these include:

- ❑ sys.dm_db_missing_index_groups
- ❑ sys.dm_db_missing_index_group_stats
- ❑ sys.dm_db_missing_index_details
- ❑ sys.dm_db_missing_index_columns

The key thing to understand about these system views is that they collectively provide information on such things as:

- ❑ What index would have been helpful had it been there?
- ❑ What columns are involved in the index?
- ❑ How many compilations/optimizations would have utilized the query had it been available?
- ❑ How exactly would that index have been utilized?

Information stored in these views is temporary in nature, and can be thought of as working much like the tempdb database; that is, they are completely removed and all information starts from zero each time the SQL Server service is restarted.

C

The Basics

As I mentioned back in the introduction of this book, I've gone even more towards the idea of fully separating the *Beginning* and *Professional* titles into their own pair. My hope is that, between the two, we'll be back at the full compendium we had in my first two books (before the content grew so large that it couldn't fit in a single book). That said, I recognize that many more advanced developers aren't going to be comfortable buying a book with "Beginning" in the title, but may still want to easily look up, review, or make some other kind of study of some of the more extended syntax of an otherwise basic context. If you are one of those people, then this appendix is for you. The idea is simple here: Provide syntax information and, in some cases (and not in others), see some basic examples of the statement in use. There will be no fanfare here, and anywhere from no real description to relatively minor discussion of key concepts. Several hundred pages in the *Beginning* book that is the companion of this one will be shrunk down to tens of pages here.

There are a few places where I'll provide just a little "extra" coverage (still pretty minimal). Such coverage will generally be limited to "beginning" commands that may not have existed until recent releases, or other places where changes have been such that you might make a different choice today than you've gotten used to using from having learned in "the olden days."

Everything to Do with Queries

In this section, we'll take a look at all the various themes that relate directly to DML — or "Data Manipulation Language." Everything in this section is going to be, in some form, directly tied to the execution of one of four statements:

❑ **SELECT:** The statement for reading data (though, in a rare circumstance or two, it can be utilized as part of the insertion of data too.

❑ **INSERT:** The statement for getting data into our database.

❑ **UPDATE:** Changing values in existing data.

❑ **DELETE:** Removing data from the system.

While these four will serve as the major statements in all of the discussion in this section, they are just the top level of the statement. We'll also be looking at various predicates, options, and operational concepts that are used within each of the four statements mentioned.

Most things here will be "old hat" — that is, they should be familiar already — but don't rush through too fast. There are a number of at least intermediate concepts addressed here, and many keywords that are used relatively infrequently, and thus may have been missed in your learning or be something you've simply forgotten was available.

The Basic SELECT Statement

The SELECT statement and the structures used within it form the basis for the lion's share of all the commands we will perform with SQL Server. The basic syntax rules for a SELECT statement are:

```
SELECT <column list>
[FROM <source table(s)> [[AS] <table alias>]
[[{FULL|INNER|{LEFT|RIGHT} OUTER|CROSS}] JOIN <next table>
[ON <join condition>] [<additional JOIN clause> ...]]]
[WHERE <restrictive condition>]
[GROUP BY <column name or expression using a column in the SELECT list>]
[HAVING <restrictive condition based on the GROUP BY results>]
[ORDER BY <column list>]
[[FOR XML {RAW|AUTO|EXPLICIT|PATH [(<element>)]}[, XMLDATA][, ELEMENTS][, BINARY
base 64]]
[OPTION (<query hint>, [, ...n])]
[{ UNION [ALL] | EXCEPT | INTERSECT }]
[;]
```

For anyone reading a "Professional" level book, *most* of this should be well understood. Let's look at the syntax of two quick examples (with a GROUP BY and without).

Let's start with a basic multi-table, ordered query with a WHERE clause:

```
SELECT p.Name AS ProductName, soh.AccountNumber, soh.ShipDate
FROM Production.Product p
JOIN Sales.SalesOrderDetail sod
    ON p.ProductID = sod.ProductID
JOIN Sales.SalesOrderHeader soh
    ON soh.SalesOrderID = sod.SalesOrderDetailID
WHERE soh.ShipDate >= '07/01/2001'
  AND soh.ShipDate < '08/01/2001'
ORDER BY AccountNumber, ShipDate;
```

Note that, since we omitted the optional FULL, INNER, OUTER, and CROSS keywords, this is assumed to be the default (INNER) join. We could write a similar query, but utilize a GROUP BY clause (in this case, to get a number of different accounts that ordered each product that shipped in July regardless of when it was ordered):

```
SELECT p.Name AS ProductName,
       COUNT(DISTINCT soh.AccountNumber) AS UniqueAccounts
FROM Production.Product p
JOIN Sales.SalesOrderDetail sod
```

```
    ON p.ProductID = sod.ProductID
JOIN Sales.SalesOrderHeader soh
    ON soh.SalesOrderID = sod.SalesOrderDetailID
WHERE soh.ShipDate >= '07/01/2001'
  AND soh.ShipDate < '08/01/2001'
GROUP BY p.Name
ORDER BY p.Name;
```

Note here that the ORDER BY clause still needed to be last (the GROUP BY was inserted above the ORDER BY).

The WHERE Clause

The WHERE is a basic filter condition; if a row doesn't meet all WHERE conditions, then it isn't included in the results. Let's take a look at all the operators we can use with the WHERE clause:

Operator	Example Usage	Effect
=, >, <, >=, <=, <>, !=, !>, !<	<Column Name> = <Other Column Name> <Column Name> = 'Bob'	Standard comparison operators — these work as they do in pretty much any programming language with a couple of notable points: 1. What constitutes "greater than," "less than," and "equal to" can change, depending on the collation order you have selected. For example, "ROMEY" = "romey" in places where case-insensitive sort order has been selected, but "ROMEY" < > "romey" in a case-sensitive situation. 2. != and <> both mean "not equal." !< and !> mean "not less than" and "not greater than," respectively.
AND, OR, NOT	<Column1> = <Column2> AND <Column3> >= <Column 4> <Column1> != "MyLiteral" OR <Column2> = "MyOtherLiteral"	Standard Boolean logic. You can use these to combine multiple conditions into one WHERE clause. NOT is evaluated first, then AND, then OR. If you need to change the evaluation order, you can use parentheses. Note that XOR is not supported.
BETWEEN	<Column1> BETWEEN 1 AND 5	Comparison is TRUE if the first value is between the second and third values inclusive. It is the functional equivalent of A>=B AND A<=C. Any of the specified values can be column names, variables, or literals.
LIKE	<Column1> LIKE "ROM%"	Uses the % and _ characters for wildcarding. % indicates that a value of any length can replace the % character. _ indicates that any one character can replace the _ character.

Continued

		Enclosing characters in [] symbols indicates that any single character within the [] is okay (`[a-c]` means a, b, and c are okay. `[ab]` indicates a or b is okay). ^ operates as a NOT operator — indicating that the next character is to be excluded.
`IN`	`<Column1> IN (List of Numbers)` `<Column1> IN ("A", "b", "345")`	Returns TRUE if the value to the left of the IN keyword matches any of the values in the list provided after the IN keyword. This is frequently used in subqueries, which we look at in Chapter 3.
`ALL, ANY, SOME`	`<column|expression>` (comparison operator) `<ANY|SOME> (subquery)`	These return TRUE if any or all (depending on which you choose) values in a subquery meet the comparison operator (for example, <, >, =, >=) condition. ALL indicates that the value must match all the values in the set. ANY and SOME are functional equivalents and will evaluate to TRUE if the expression matches any value in the set.
`EXISTS`	`EXISTS (subquery)`	Returns TRUE if at least one row is returned by the subquery. Again, we look into this one further in Chapter 3.

ORDER BY

This does what it says; you specify for which columns you want the results to be presented and in which order. The default is ascending order, but you can also supply the optional DESC switch if you want it to be in descending order.

So, in the earlier SELECT example, we could have changed things to be in descending account number order by simply adding the DESC keyword (note that I haven't specified anything for ShipDate, so that sub-sort would continue to be in ascending order).

```
ORDER BY AccountNumber DESC, ShipDate;
```

The GROUP BY Clause

With ORDER BY, we took things somewhat out of order compared with how the SELECT statement reads at the top of the section. The GROUP BY clause is used to aggregate information. Let's look at a simple query without a GROUP BY. In our GROUP BY example at the start of the section, we got back a count that was the aggregation of orders as grouped together by the product name. The key thing to realize with a GROUP BY is that, when using a GROUP BY, any columns specified in the select list must either be part of what you're grouping by (that is, they must appear in the GROUP BY list), or they must be the target of an aggregate function.

> While aggregates show their power when used with a GROUP BY clause, they are not limited to grouped queries — if you include an aggregate without a GROUP BY, then the aggregate will work against the entire result set (all the rows that match the WHERE clause). The catch here is that, when not working with a GROUP BY, some aggregates can only be in the SELECT list with other aggregates — that is, they can't be paired with a column name in the SELECT list unless you have a GROUP BY. For example, unless there is a GROUP BY, AVG can be paired with SUM, but not with a specific column.

Let's review a few of the most common aggregate functions (be aware that you can write your own aggregate function using a CLR-based user-defined function).

❑   **AVG:** This one is for computing averages. 'Nuff said.

❑   **MIN/MAX:** These, as you might expect, grab the minimum and maximum amounts for each grouping for a selected column.

❑   **COUNT(Expression|*):** The COUNT(*) function is about counting the rows in a query.

> All aggregate functions ignore NULLs except for COUNT(*). This can have a very significant impact on your results, so be careful. Many users expect NULL values in numeric fields to be treated as zero when performing averages, but a NULL does not equal zero, and as such, shouldn't be used as one. If you perform an AVG or other aggregate function on a column with NULLs, the NULL values will not be part of the aggregation unless you manipulate them into a non-NULL value inside the function (using COALESCE() or ISNULL(), for example).

The HAVING Clause

The HAVING clause is used only if there is also a GROUP BY in your query; whereas the WHERE clause is applied to each row before it even has a chance to become part of a group, the HAVING clause is applied to the aggregated value for that group.

To demonstrate this, we'll use the same query we used in our GROUP BY clause example, but adding a HAVING clause:

```
SELECT p.Name AS ProductName, COUNT(DISTINCT soh.AccountNumber) AS UniqueAccounts
FROM Production.Product p
JOIN Sales.SalesOrderDetail sod
    ON p.ProductID = sod.ProductID
JOIN Sales.SalesOrderHeader soh
    ON soh.SalesOrderID = sod.SalesOrderDetailID
WHERE soh.ShipDate >= '07/01/2001'
  AND soh.ShipDate < '08/01/2001'
GROUP BY p.Name
```

```
HAVING COUNT(DISTINCT soh.AccountNumber) > 1

ORDER BY p.Name;
```

Beyond Inner Joins

Perhaps 95% or more of the queries we write are going to use either no joins or an inner join. For far too many SQL developers, 100% of the queries they write will fall into one of the aforementioned categories. An inner join is based on the idea of matching rows on both sides of the join — that is, when both the "left" and "right" side of the join meet the join condition, then an inner join is satisfied and the rows from both sides of the join are matched up and returned. An inner join is, therefore, exclusive in nature; if the rows don't match, then they are excluded from the result. There are, however, other joins available, so let's take a look at outer joins, full joins, and cross joins.

OUTER Joins

Whereas an inner join is exclusive in nature, an outer join is inclusive in nature. Whichever side you choose (left or right) will have all rows returned regardless of whether or not they match. Rows from the remaining side will have to match the "outer" side or they will be excluded. A simple way to look at an outer join would be:

```
SELECT <SELECT list>
FROM <the table you want to be the "LEFT" table>
<LEFT|RIGHT> [OUTER] JOIN <table you want to be the "RIGHT" table>
                ON <join condition>
```

You choose whether you want the left or right side to be the all inclusive side of the join. An example of this in the AdventureWorks2008 database might look something like:

```
SELECT sso.SpecialOfferID, Description, DiscountPct, ProductID
FROM Sales.SpecialOffer sso
LEFT OUTER JOIN Sales.SpecialOfferProduct ssop
ON sso.SpecialOfferID = ssop.SpecialOfferID
```

This would pull all rows from the SpecialOffer table (the left side of the join) regardless of whether they meet the join condition, but would only include rows from the SpecialOfferProduct table (the right side) if the row met the join condition. If we used the RIGHT keyword instead of LEFT, the roles of each table would be reversed.

FULL Joins

Think of this one as something of a LEFT and a RIGHT join coming together. With a FULL join, you are telling SQL Server to include all rows on *both* sides of the join. AdventureWorks2008 doesn't give me any really great examples to show you this one, but since the concept is fairly easy once you already understand outer joins, we'll just toss together a pretty simple demonstration:

```
CREATE TABLE Film
(FilmID            int              PRIMARY KEY,
 FilmName          varchar(20)      NOT NULL,
 YearMade          smallint         NOT NULL
);
```

```
CREATE TABLE Actors
(FilmID           int              NOT NULL,
 FirstName        varchar(15)      NOT NULL,
 LastName         varchar(15)      NOT NULL,
   CONSTRAINT PKActors PRIMARY KEY(FilmID, FirstName, LastName)
);

INSERT INTO Film
VALUES
   (1, 'My Fair Lady', 1964);
INSERT INTO Film
VALUES
   (2, 'Unforgiven', 1992);

INSERT INTO Actors
VALUES
   (1, 'Rex', 'Harrison');
INSERT INTO Actors
VALUES
   (1, 'Audrey', 'Hepburn');
INSERT INTO Actors
VALUES
   (3, 'Anthony', 'Hopkins');
```

Okay, now let's run a FULL JOIN and see what we get:

```
SELECT *
FROM Film f
FULL JOIN Actors a
   ON f.FilmID = a.FilmID;
```

When you check the results, you'll see data that has been joined where they match, data from just the left if that's all there is (and nulls for the columns on the right), and data from just the right if that happens to be all there is (and, of course, nulls for the columns on the left).

FilmID	FilmName	YearMade	FilmID	FirstName	LastName
1	My Fair Lady	1964	1	Audrey	Hepburn
1	My Fair Lady	1964	1	Rex	Harrison
2	Unforgiven	1992	NULL	NULL	NULL
NULL	NULL	NULL	3	Anthony	Hopkins

(4 row(s) affected)

CROSS JOIN

Our last type of join, the CROSS JOIN, is a very strange critter indeed. A CROSS JOIN differs from other JOINs in that there is no ON operator and in that it joins every record on one side of the JOIN with every record on the other side of the JOIN. In short, you wind up with a Cartesian product of all the records on both sides of the JOIN. The syntax is the same as any other JOIN except that it uses the keyword CROSS (instead of INNER, OUTER, or FULL), and that it has no ON operator.

So, let's say we were just playing games and wanted to mix every film with every actor using the little sample we just built for FULL joins:

```
SELECT *
FROM Film f

CROSS JOIN Actors a;
```

We get every record in the Film table matched with *every* actor in the Actors table:

```
FilmID      FilmName            YearMade FilmID   FirstName     LastName
----------- ------------------- -------- -------- ------------- -------------
1           My Fair Lady        1964     1        Audrey        Hepburn
1           My Fair Lady        1964     1        Rex           Harrison
1           My Fair Lady        1964     3        Anthony       Hopkins
2           Unforgiven          1992     1        Audrey        Hepburn
2           Unforgiven          1992     1        Rex           Harrison
2           Unforgiven          1992     3        Anthony       Hopkins

(6 row(s) affected)
```

Now, this has to bring out the question of "Why would you ever want this?" Good question. The answer is difficult because it's very situational. To date, I've seen CROSS JOINs used in just two situations:

- ❑ **Sample Data:** CROSS JOINs are good for putting together small sets of data and then mixing the two sets of data together in every possible way so that you get a much larger sample set to work with.

- ❑ **Scientific Data:** I believe this, again, has to do with samples, but I know there are a number of scientific calculations that make use of Cartesians. I'm told that doing CROSS JOINs is a way of "preparing" data for some types of analysis. I'm not going to pretend to understand the statistics of it, but I know that it's out there.

The end story is — they are only very, very rarely used, but keep them in mind in case you need them!

The INSERT Statement

An INSERT statement is, obviously, the command we use to put data into our table. The basic syntax for an INSERT statement looks like this:

```
INSERT [INTO] <table> [(<column list>)]
    VALUES (<data values>)
        [, (<data values>) [, ... n]]
```

Let's look at the parts:

- ❑ INSERT is the action statement. It tells SQL Server what it is that we're going to be doing with this statement, and everything that comes after this keyword is merely spelling out the details of that action.

❑ The INTO keyword is pretty much just fluff. Its sole purpose in life is to make the overall statement more readable. It is completely optional, but I recommend its use for the very reason that they added it to the statement — it makes things much easier to read.

❑ Next comes the table into which you are inserting.

❑ Now comes the part that's a little more difficult: the column list. An explicit column list (where you specifically state the columns to receive values) is optional, but not supplying one means that you have to be extremely careful. If you don't provide an explicit column list, then each value in your INSERT statement will be assumed to match up with a column in the same ordinal position of the table in order (first value to first column, second value to second column, and so on). Additionally, a value must be supplied for every column, in order, until you reach the last column that both does not accept nulls and has no default. In summary, this will be a list of one or more columns that you are going to be providing data for in the next part of the statement.

❑ Finally, you'll supply the values to be inserted. There are two ways of doing this: explicitly supplied values and values derived from a SELECT statement.

❑ To supply the values, we'll start with the VALUES keyword and then follow that with a list of values, separated by commas and enclosed in parentheses. The number of items in the value list must exactly match the number of columns in the column list. The data type of each value must match or be implicitly convertible to the type of the column with which it corresponds (they are taken in order). If we want to add more than one row, we add a comma and then a new list of values again separated by commas and enclosed in parentheses.

> The ability to include multiple inserted rows as part of a single INSERT is new with SQL Server 2008. You cannot use this option if you need SQL Server 2005 compatibility.

So, for example, we might have an INSERT statement that looks something like:

```
INSERT INTO HumanResources.JobCandidate
VALUES
   (1, NULL, DEFAULT),
..(55, NULL, GETDATE());
```

As stated earlier, unless we provide a different column list (we'll cover how to provide a column list shortly), all the values have to be supplied in the same order as the columns are defined in the table. The exception to this is if you have an identity column, in which case that column is assumed to be skipped.

> If you check the definition of the HumanRescoures.JobCandidate table, you will indeed see that it starts with an identity column called JobCandidateID. Since it is an identity column, we know that the system is going to automatically generate a value for that column, so we can skip it.

Since, in theory (because you're reading this book instead of the beginning one), we already mostly know this stuff and are just reviewing, I've crammed several concepts into this.

❏   I've skipped the identity column entirely (the system will fill that in for us).

❏   I've supplied actual values (the number 1 for EmployeeID in the first inserted row, and the number 55 for EmployeeID for the second inserted row, and an explicit declaration of NULL as a value for Resume in both inserted rows).

❏   I've used the DEFAULT keyword (for ModifiedDate) in the first insert row to explicitly tell the server to use whatever the default value is for that column.

❏   I've inserted multiple rows with just one statement (again, this is new with SQL Server 2008).

Now let's try it again with modifications for inserting into specific columns:

```
INSERT INTO HumanResources.JobCandidate

    (EmployeeID, Resume, ModifiedDate)

VALUES
    (1, NULL, DEFAULT),
..(55, NULL, GETDATE());
```

Note that we are still skipping the identity column. Other than that, we are just explicitly supplying names — nothing else has changed.

The INSERT INTO . . . SELECT Statement

It is, of course, great to be able to explicitly define the data we want to go into our table, but what if we have a block of data from a queryable source and want it inserted? Examples of where you might want to do this include data sourced from:

❏   Another table in our database

❏   A totally different database on the same server

❏   A heterogeneous query from another SQL Server or other data

❏   The same table (usually, you're doing some sort of math or other adjustment in your SELECT statement in this case)

The INSERT INTO...SELECT statement can do all of these. The syntax for this statement comes from a combination of the two statements we've seen thus far — the INSERT statement and the SELECT statement. It looks something like this:

```
INSERT INTO <table name>
[<column list>]
<SELECT statement>
```

The result set created from the SELECT statement becomes the data that is added in your INSERT statement. So, a scripted example might look something like:

```
USE AdventureWorks2008;

/* This next statement declares our working table.
** This particular table is table variable we are creating on the fly.
```

```
*/
DECLARE @MyTable Table
(
    SalesOrderID      int,
    CustomerID        int
);
/* Now that we have our table variable, we're ready to populate it with data
** from our SELECT statement. Note that we could just as easily insert the
** data into a permanent table (instead of a table variable).
*/
INSERT INTO @MyTable
    SELECT SalesOrderID, CustomerID
    FROM AdventureWorks.Sales.SalesOrderHeader
    WHERE SalesOrderID BETWEEN 50222 AND 50225;

-- Finally, let's make sure that the data was inserted like we think
SELECT *
FROM @MyTable;
```

This should yield you results that look like this:

```
(4 row(s) affected)
SalesOrderID CustomerID
------------ -----------
50222        638
50223        677
50224        247
50225        175

(4 row(s) affected)
```

The UPDATE Statement

The UPDATE statement, like most SQL statements, does pretty much what it sounds like it does — it updates existing data. The structure is a little bit different from a SELECT, though you'll notice definite similarities. Let's look at the syntax:

```
UPDATE <table name>
SET <column> = <value> [,<column> = <value>]
[FROM <source table(s)>]
[WHERE <restrictive condition>]
```

An UPDATE can be created from multiple tables, but can affect only one table. Take, for a moment, the case of Jo Brown. It seems that Jo has recently gotten married, and we need to make sure that her data is accurate. Let's run a query to look at one row of data:

```
SELECT e.BusinessEntityID,
    e.MaritalStatus,
    p.FirstName,
    p.LastName
FROM HumanResources.Employee e
```

```
JOIN Person.Person p
   ON e.BusinessEntityID = p.BusinessEntityID
WHERE p.FirstName = 'Jo'
   AND p.LastName = 'Brown';
```

which returns the following:

```
EmployeeID  MaritalStatus FirstName               LastName
----------- ------------- ----------------------- ---------------------------
16          S             Jo                      Brown

(1 row(s) affected)
```

Let's update the MaritalStatus value to the more proper "M":

```
UPDATE e
SET MaritalStatus = 'M'
FROM HumanResources.Employee e
JOIN Person.Person pe
   ON e.BusinessEntityID = p.BusinessEntityID
WHERE p.FirstName = 'Jo'
   AND p.LastName = 'Brown';
```

Note that we could have changed more than one column just by adding a comma and the additional column expression. For example, the following statement would have also given Jo a promotion:

```
UPDATE e

SET MaritalStatus = 'M', JobTitle = 'Shift Manager'

FROM HumanResources.Employee e
JOIN Person.Person pe
   ON e.BusinessEntityID = p.BusinessEntityID
WHERE p.FirstName = 'Jo'
   AND p.LastName = 'Brown';
```

> While SQL Server is nice enough to let us update pretty much any column (there are a few that we can't, such as timestamps), be very careful about updating primary keys. Doing so puts you at very high risk of "orphaning" other data (data that has a reference to the data you're changing).

The DELETE Statement

The DELETE statement is perhaps the easiest statement of them all. There's no column list — just a table name and, usually, a WHERE clause. The syntax couldn't be much easier:

```
DELETE [TOP (<expression>) [PERCENT]
[FROM ] <table name>
[FROM ] <table list/JOIN conditions>
[WHERE <search condition>]
```

The tricky thing with DELETE is the two FROM clauses (nope, that is not a typo). The first is what object you want the DELETE to act on, and the second is a more traditional FROM clause (similar to in a SELECT) that is defining how to decide what rows to act on. The WHERE clause works just like all of the WHERE clauses we've seen thus far. We don't need to provide a column list because we are deleting the entire row (you can't delete half a row, for example).

So, for example, if we want to delete all rows from the Actors table (used in a few samples earlier in this appendix) where there are no matching rows in the Film table, this requires a query that is aware of both tables (so a JOIN is required). In addition, however, it requires realizing that there is no match on one side of the join (that Film does not have a record that matches a particular actor).

You may recall that an OUTER join will return a NULL on the side where there is no match. We are going to utilize that here by actually testing for NULL:

```
DELETE FROM Actors
FROM Actors a
LEFT JOIN Film f
  ON a.FilmID = f.FilmID
WHERE f.FilmID IS NULL;
```

So, if we skip ahead for a moment to our second FROM clause, you can see that we are utilizing a LEFT JOIN. That means all actors will be returned. Films will be returned if there is a matching FilmID, but the film side of the columns will be NULL if no match exists. In the DELETE statement in the example, we are leveraging this knowledge, and testing for it — if we find a FilmID that is null, then we must not have found a match there (and, therefore, our actor needs to be deleted).

Exploring Alternative Syntax for Joins

Again, most "Pro" level people should have some familiarity with this, but since it is finally getting fairly scarce, we'll go ahead and touch on what many people still consider to be the "normal" way of coding joins.

Most queries today use an ANSI/ISO-complaint SQL syntax (as they should). It is worth noting that the old syntax is actually reasonably well supported across platforms at the current time, but the ANSI/ISO syntax is now also supported by every major platform out there.

The primary reason I continue to cover the old syntax is that there is absolutely no doubt that, sooner or later, you will run into it in legacy code. I don't want you staring at that code saying, "What the heck is this?" That being said, I want to reiterate my strong recommendation that you use the ANSI/ISO syntax wherever possible. Among other reasons, it is more functional. Under old syntax, it was actually possible to create ambiguous query logic — where there was more than one way to interpret the query. The ANSI/ISO syntax eliminates this problem.

An Alternative Inner Join

Quickly, an inner join such as:

```
SELECT *
FROM HumanResources.Employee e
```

```
INNER JOIN HumanResources.Employee m
  ON e.ManagerID = m.EmployeeID;
```

can be rewritten using a WHERE clause–based join syntax. Just eliminate the words INNER JOIN and add a comma, and replace the ON operator with a WHERE clause:

```
SELECT *
FROM HumanResources.Employee e, HumanResources.Employee m
WHERE e.ManagerID = m.EmployeeID;
```

This syntax is supported by virtually all major SQL systems (Oracle, DB2, MySQL, and so on) in the world today.

An Alternative Outer Join

With SQL Server 2005 and beyond, we do not necessarily have the alternative outer join syntax available to us. Indeed, by default it is now turned off — you must set your database compatibility level to be 80 or lower (80 is SQL Server 2000). Thankfully, there is very little code left out there using this syntax, and, given the lack of default support, I suspect the amount of code of this type will be effectively zero by the end of the SQL Server 2008 life cycle.

That said, I'll provide a taste of it in case you do bump into it. The basics work pretty much the same as the inner join, except that, because we don't have the LEFT or RIGHT keywords (and no OUTER or JOIN for that matter), we need some special operators especially built for the task. These look like this:

Alternative	ANSI
*=	LEFT JOIN
=*	RIGHT JOIN

So, an outer join such as:

```
SELECT e.EmployeeID, m.EmployeeID AS ManagerID
FROM HumanResources.Employee e
LEFT OUTER JOIN HumanResources.Employee m
  ON e.ManagerID = m.EmployeeID;
```

can be translated into the old outer join syntax like this:

```
SELECT e.EmployeeID, m.EmployeeID AS ManagerID
FROM HumanResources.Employee e, HumanResources.Employee m
WHERE e.ManagerID *= m.EmployeeID;
```

> The alternative syntax for outer joins is not available by default. You must be running 80 or lower as your compatibility mode in order to use this functionality.

An Alternative CROSS JOIN

This is far and away the easiest of the bunch. To create a cross join using the old syntax, you just do nothing. That is, you don't put anything in the WHERE clause of the form: TableA.ColumnA = TableB.ColumnA.

So, an ANSI syntax cross join such as:

```
SELECT *
FROM Film f
CROSS JOIN Actors a;
```

would change to:

```
SELECT *

FROM Film f, Actors a;
```

UNION

This is again something you should already be at least somewhat familiar with, but I am often surprised to find relatively experienced SQL programmers who, although they know it exists, really do not understand a UNION statement. UNION is a special operator we can use to cause two or more queries to generate one result set.

A UNION appends of the data from one query right onto the end of another query (functionally, it works a little differently from this, but this is the easiest way to look at the concept). Where a JOIN combines information horizontally (adding more columns), a UNION combines data vertically (adding more rows), as illustrated in Figure C-1.

When dealing with queries that use a union, there are just a few key points:

❑ All the unioned queries must have the same number of columns in the SELECT list.

❑ The headings returned for the combined result set will be taken only from the first of the queries.

❑ The data types of each column in a query must be implicitly compatible with the data type in the same relative column in the other queries.

❑ Unlike non-union queries, the default return option for unions is DISTINCT rather than ALL. Unless you use the ALL keyword in your query, only one of any repeating rows will be returned.

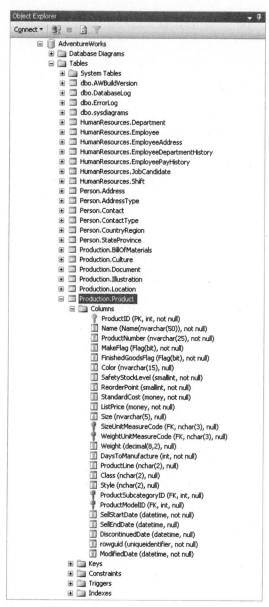

Figure C-1

In this case, we are creating two tables from which we will select. We'll then insert three rows into each table, with one row being identical between the two tables. If our query is performing an ALL, then every row (six of them) will show up. If the query is performing a DISTINCT, then it will return only five rows (tossing out one duplicate):

```
CREATE TABLE UnionTest1
(
```

```
    idcol    int        IDENTITY,
    col2     char(3),
);

CREATE TABLE UnionTest2
(
    idcol    int        IDENTITY,
    col4     char(3),
);

INSERT INTO UnionTest1
VALUES
    ('AAA');
INSERT INTO UnionTest1
VALUES
    ('BBB');
INSERT INTO UnionTest1
VALUES
    ('CCC');

SELECT *
FROM UnionTest1;

INSERT INTO UnionTest2
VALUES
    ('CCC');
INSERT INTO UnionTest2
VALUES
    ('DDD');
INSERT INTO UnionTest2
VALUES
    ('EEE');

PRINT 'Regular UNION---------------'
SELECT col2
FROM UnionTest1
   UNION
SELECT col4
FROM UnionTest2;

PRINT 'UNION ALL-------------------'

SELECT col2
FROM UnionTest1
   UNION ALL
SELECT col4
FROM UnionTest2;

DROP TABLE UnionTest1;
DROP TABLE UnionTest2;
```

Run it, and the key results look like this:

```
Regular UNION---------------
col2
```

```
----
AAA
BBB
CCC
DDD
EEE

(5 row(s) affected)

UNION ALL------------------
col2
----
AAA
BBB
CCC
CCC
DDD
EEE

(6 row(s) affected)
```

Subqueries and Derived Tables

Subqueries represent the basic concept of one query providing results that are to be used by yet another query. These utilize parentheses to embed them in the top-level query, and come in three basic forms:

❑ **Nested Subqueries:** Generally, the "inner" query provides a simple lookup to serve some need of the outer query. These can be used to provide a lookup in the select list that is, for example, not sourced for the same place as other data in the query, or in the WHERE clause to force the query to meet some lookup condition.

❑ **Correlated Subqueries:** These are similar to regular nested subqueries, but are bi-directional in nature. That is, the inner query receives information from the outer query, and then utilizes that information to know what information to supply back to the outer query.

❑ **Derived Tables (also known as in-line views):** These utilize the idea that a query returns what amounts to a table, and allows you to refer to a query as though it is a table. You can join a full table or view to the results generated from a query (the query used for the join is then referred to as a derived table).

Let's do a very simple review of syntax and example of each.

Nested Subqueries

A nested subquery is one that goes in only one direction — returning either a single value for use in the outer query, or perhaps a full list of values to be used with the IN operator.

In the loosest sense, your query syntax is going to look something like one of these two syntax templates:

```
SELECT <SELECT list>
FROM <SomeTable>
WHERE <SomeColumn> = (
        SELECT <single column>
```

```
        FROM <SomeTable>
        WHERE <condition that results in only one row returned>)
```

Or:

```
SELECT <SELECT list>
FROM <SomeTable>
WHERE <SomeColumn> IN (
        SELECT <single column>
        FROM <SomeTable>
        [WHERE <condition>)]
```

Obviously, the exact syntax will vary, not only because you will be substituting the select list and exact table names, but also because you may have a multi-table join in either the inner or outer queries — or both.

So, a simple example (in this case, utilizing the second of the two templates) of the nested select would be:

```
SELECT ProductID, Name
FROM Production.Product
WHERE ProductID IN (
    SELECT ProductID FROM Sales.SpecialOfferProduct);
```

The key thing to grasp is that we are simply embedding another query in parentheses and, whatever that query returns must fit the use (a scalar value if the situation it's being used in would expect a scalar value, or a list if a list is suitable).

Correlated Subqueries

What makes correlated subqueries different from the nested subqueries we just looked at is that the information travels in *two* directions rather than one.

Rather than just feed information out to the top query, a correlated subquery is bi-directional and works in a three-step process:

1. The outer query obtains a record, and passes it into the inner query.
2. The inner query executes based on the passed-in value(s).
3. The inner query then passes the values from its result back to the outer query, which uses that result to finish its processing.

So, an example of using a correlated subquery in the select list might look something like:

```
SELECT sc.AccountNumber,
    (SELECT Min(OrderDate)
        FROM Sales.SalesOrderHeader soh
        WHERE soh.CustomerID = sc.CustomerID)
        AS OrderDate
FROM Sales.Customer sc
```

This query would, on a customer-by-customer basis, look up the first order we have on file for them and return it along with the Account Number.

Derived Tables

This lesser-known SQL construct is made up of the columns and rows of a result set from a query. (Heck, they have columns, rows, data types, and so on just like normal tables, so why not use them as such?). Like the subqueries we looked at earlier in this appendix, you simply wrap the embedded query in parentheses; you are then ready to use it as if the results were a table. You can think of it as being a view that you wrapped in parentheses rather than named as an object. The only additional requirement is that, since you do not have a formal name for it as you would a table or view, you must use an alias.

So, the following is an example with multiple derived tables (it utilizes the AdventureWorks2008 database to show the account numbers and territories for all customers that have ordered both HL Mountain Rear Wheel and HL Mountain Front Wheel bicycles):

```
SELECT DISTINCT sc.AccountNumber, sst.Name
FROM Sales.Customer AS sc
JOIN Sales.SalesTerritory sst
 ON sc.TerritoryID = sst.TerritoryID
JOIN
  (SELECT CustomerID
 FROM Sales.SalesOrderHeader soh
 JOIN Sales.SalesOrderDetail sod
        ON soh.SalesOrderID = sod.SalesOrderID
 JOIN Production.Product pp
        ON sod.ProductID = pp.ProductID
 WHERE pp.Name = 'HL Mountain Rear Wheel') AS dt1
  ON sc.CustomerID = dt1.CustomerID
JOIN
  (SELECT CustomerID
 FROM Sales.SalesOrderHeader soh
 JOIN Sales.SalesOrderDetail sod
        ON soh.SalesOrderID = sod.SalesOrderID
 JOIN Production.Product pp
        ON sod.ProductID = pp.ProductID
 WHERE Name = 'HL Mountain Front Wheel') AS dt2
  ON sc.CustomerID = dt2.CustomerID
```

Pay particular attention to the use of parentheses to enclose the boundaries of each derived table as well as the use of aliases for both (dt1 and dt2).

Summary

This was just a quick review of some ultra basic concepts in SQL Server. The assumption as I wrote this book is that you already have fairly decent understanding of most things covered here. The idea is largely one of review. If you find that you're struggling with any of the concepts here, then you probably should consider picking up a copy of *Beginning SQL Server 2008 Programming*.

Index

G